Lecture Notes in Computer Science

AF167509

Lecture Notes in Artificial Intelligence 16045

Founding Editor

Jörg Siekmann

Series Editors

Randy Goebel, *University of Alberta, Edmonton, AB, Canada*
Wolfgang Wahlster, *DFKI, Berlin, Germany*
Zhi-Hua Zhou, *Nanjing University, Nanjing, China*

The series Lecture Notes in Artificial Intelligence (LNAI) was established in 1988 as a topical subseries of LNCS devoted to artificial intelligence.

The series publishes state-of-the-art research results at a high level. As with the LNCS mother series, the mission of the series is to serve the international R & D community by providing an invaluable service, mainly focused on the publication of conference and workshop proceedings and postproceedings.

Ana Cavalcanti · Simon Foster ·
Robert Richardson
Editors

Towards Autonomous Robotic Systems

26th Annual Conference, TAROS 2025
York, UK, August 20–22, 2025
Proceedings

 Springer

Editors
Ana Cavalcanti 🆔
University of York
York, UK

Simon Foster 🆔
University of York
York, UK

Robert Richardson 🆔
University of Leeds
Leeds, UK

ISSN 0302-9743   ISSN 1611-3349 (electronic)
Lecture Notes in Artificial Intelligence
ISBN 978-3-032-01485-6   ISBN 978-3-032-01486-3 (eBook)
https://doi.org/10.1007/978-3-032-01486-3

LNCS Sublibrary: SL7 – Artificial Intelligence

Preface

TAROS 2025 was the 26th iteration of the longest-running UK-hosted international conference on Robotics and Autonomous Systems (RAS), which is aimed at the presentation and discussion of cutting-edge results and methods in autonomous robotics research and applications. TAROS offers a friendly environment for robotics researchers and industry to take stock and plan future progress. It welcomes senior and early-career researchers alike and specifically provides opportunities for research students and young research scientists to present their groundbreaking work to the scientific community. In 2025 it took place in the historic city of York in the north of England over three days, hosted by the RoboStar Centre of Excellence in Software Engineering for Robotics and the University of York.

The 2025 edition of TAROS used a programme committee mixing renowned roboticists from all over the world at different career stages to review all submissions. Their work helped us to put together a high-quality proceedings volume, which is the book you now see before you. We received a total of 74 submissions and, after a rigorous review process involving an international group of 48 academics from 8 different countries, 36 papers were selected for publication: an acceptance rate of just under 50%. Each paper was reviewed by at least three members of the programme committee. This includes 4 short papers (6 pages + references), and 32 full papers (12 pages + references).

We welcomed papers in the area of Software Engineering for Robotics for a track on this subject. We accepted 5 submissions for this session, along with 3 invited papers. There were eight world-class keynote speakers. We were delighted to have contributions by Yiannis Demiris (Imperial College London), Sabine Hauert (University of Bristol), Thierry Lecomte (CLEARSY), and Dejanira Araiza Illan (Johnson & Johnson), for the first two days. The last day was dedicated to early-career researchers, and we were pleased to count on Jon Timmis (Aberystwyth University), Kaiqiang Zhang (University of Bristol), Rich Walker (Shadow Robotics), and Lucy Wheeler (Royal Academy of Engineering) to share their views on the future of robotics, from various perspectives: academia, industry, and funding bodies.

The papers were categorised into eight groups: Human-Robot Interaction and Teleoperation, Sensing and Perception, Locomotion and Control, Manipulation and Dexterous Interaction, Software Engineering for Robotics, Underwater Robotics and Autonomy, Aerial Robotics and Path Planning, and Challenging Environments. Due to the large number of quality submissions, it was necessary to run two sets of sessions in parallel at the conference. In addition to the main technical sessions, TAROS included poster sessions over the three days, and an exciting ARIA session on "Modularity and Interoperability for Robotics and Autonomous Systems", and further special sessions on Safety for Autonomous Systems and Robotics, Automation in Agriculture and Food Production and Security, Robotics and Artificial Intelligence for Critical Asset Monitoring, and Autonomous Robotic Systems for Laboratory Experiments.

RoboStar would like to thank the sponsors of TAROS 2025 for their generous support: AgileX, ARIA, DOBOT, D-RisQ, Haption, Mathworks, Saab UK, UniTree Robotics, Verified Systems International, RoboSavvy, and the Royal Academy of Engineering. We would also like to thank the University of York, the University of Leeds, and the Centre for Assuring Autonomy, for their support. We thank the members of the programme committee for their dedication to supporting a high-quality programme, and the authors for their excellent research papers. Finally, we thank the EasyChair team and Springer for supporting the review process and publishing of the proceedings. We hope that you enjoy reading this volume.

July 2025

Ana Cavalcanti
Simon Foster
Robert Richardson

Organization

General Chair

Ana Cavalcanti University of York, UK

Program Committee Chairs

Ana Cavalcanti University of York, UK
Simon Foster University of York, UK
Robert Richardson University of Leeds, UK

Program Committee

Manith Adikari University of Manchester, UK
Kaspar Althoefer Queen Mary University of London, UK
David A. Anisi Norwegian University of Life Sciences, Norway
Farshad Arvin Durham University, UK
Ziggy Attala University of York, UK
Philip Breedon Nottingham Trent University, UK
Giuseppe Carbone University of Calabria, Italy
Gustavo Carvalho Universidade Federal de Pernambuco, Brazil
Ana Cavalcanti University of York, UK
Xinyun Chi University of Manchester, UK
Marie Farrell University of Manchester, UK
Simon Foster University of York, UK
Mirgita Frasheri Aarhus University, Denmark
Maria Gini University of Minnesota, USA
Mario Gleirscher Currently unaffiliated
Cláudio Gomes Aarhus University, Denmark
Nick Hawes University of Oxford, UK
Holly Hendry University of York, UK
Baoru Huang University of Liverpool, UK
Kefeng Huang University of York, UK
Nazmul Huda Brunel University London, UK
James Kell Amentum, UK
Alperen Kenan University of the West of England, UK

Frederic Labrosse	Aberystwyth University, UK
James Law	University of Sheffield, UK
Hae-In Lee	Cranfield University, UK
Liying Li	University of Glasgow, UK
Cunjia Liu	Loughborough University, UK
Pengcheng Liu	University of York, UK
Matt Luckcuck	University of Nottingham, UK
Alvaro Miyazawa	University of York, UK
Mohammad Reza Mousavi	King's College London, UK
Colin O'Halloran	University of Oxford, UK
Min Pan	University of Bath, UK
Annabelle Partis	University of York, UK
Yvan Petillot	Heriot-Watt University, UK
Marija Popovic	University of Bonn, Germany
Mark Post	University of York, UK
Hamidreza Raei	Italian Institute of Technology, Italy
Pedro Ribeiro	University of York, UK
Robert Richardson	University of Leeds, UK
Thomas Roehr	Simula Research Laboratory, UK
Matteo Rossi	Politecnico di Milano, UK
Philippa Ryan	University of York, UK
Shabnam Sadeghi Esfahlani	Anglia Ruskin University, UK
Sahar Sadeghi Kordkheili	Universidad de Sevilla, Spain
Uwe Schulze	University of Bremen, Germany
Francesco Semeraro	University of Manchester, UK
Nabil Shaukat	University of Leeds, UK
Patricia Shaw	Aberystwyth University, UK
Weiyong Si	University of Essex, UK
Andrew Sogokon	Lancaster University, UK
Adriana Tapus	ENSTA Paris, France
Antonia Tzemanaki	University of Bristol, UK
Mien Van	Queen's University Belfast, UK
Mingfeng Wang	Brunel University London, UK
Ning Wang	Sheffield Hallam University, UK
Barbara Webb	University of Edinburgh, UK
Andrew Weightman	University of Manchester, UK
Fang Yan	University of York, UK
Shibao Yang	University of York, UK
Houxiang Zhang	Norwegian University of Science and Technology, Norway
Kaiqiang Zhang	United Kingdom Atomic Energy Authority, UK
Jihong Zhu	University of York, UK

CDT Track Chair

Pedro Ribeiro   University of York, UK

Software Engineering for Robotics Special Session Chair

Alvaro Miyazawa   University of York, UK

Poster Session Chairs

Holly Hendry   University of York, UK
Annabelle Partis   University of York, UK

Demonstrations Chairs

Fang Yan   University of York, UK
Pengcheng Liu   University of York, UK

Financial Chair and Conference Secretary

Emily Ellis   University of York, UK

Publicity Chairs

Kumar Acharjee   University of York, UK
James Baxter   University of York, UK
Ana McIntosh   University of York, UK
Jihong Zhu   University of York, UK

TAROS Steering Committee

Farshad Arvin   Durham University, UK
Ana Cavalcanti   University of York, UK
Maria Galvez Trigo   Cardiff University, UK
Yang Gao   King's College London, UK

Nazmul Huda	Brunel University London, UK
Fumiya Iida	University of Cambridge, UK
Barry Lennox	University of Manchester, UK
Cunjia Liu	Loughborough University, UK
Robert Richardson	University of Leeds, UK
Antonia Tzemanaki	University of Bristol, UK
Chenguang Yang	University of Liverpool, UK
Philip Guodong Zhao	University of Manchester, UK

Invited Speakers

Yiannis Demiris	Imperial College London, UK
Sabine Hauert	University of Bristol, UK
Thierry Lecomte	CLEARSY, France
Dejanira Araiza Illan	Johnson & Johnson, Belgium
Jon Timmis	Aberystwyth University, UK
Kaiqiang Zhang	University of Bristol, UK
Rich Walker	Shadow Robotics, UK
Lucy Wheeler	Royal Academy of Engineering, UK

Additional Reviewers

Adam, Mustafa	Kenan, Alperen
Adiuku, Ndidiamaka	Kongezos, Valentinos
Argin, Omer Faruk	Lacaze, Peter
Atapour-Abarghouei, Amir	Lampinen, Vilma
Azaiez, Atef	Lestingi, Livia
Bahaidarah, Mazen	Liu, Zheyu
Bjugstad, Nils	Lopez, Erwin
Chen, Kan	Louca, Joe
Chen, Shuang	Marshall, Benjamin
Coombes, Matthew	Meyer, Oliver
Fazliu, Mal	Milella, Ferdinando
Fearn, Tomos	Mondal, Sabyasachi
Garcia Cardenas, Juan José	Mou, Farzana
Han, Linyan	Mulkana, Sundas Rafat
Han, Xiaoran	Naz, Nabila
Hei, Xiaoxuan	Ozdemir, Burak
Herschmann, Sam	Pan, Honghao
Hinton, Claire	Raimondi, Luca
Imrie, Calum	Rekabi Bana, Fatemeh

Rozsypálek, Zdeněk
Russo, Matteo
Saood, Adnan
Schutz, Alex
Shangguan, Zhegong
Tagliaferro, Alberto
Taourarti, Imane
Taylor, Hazel
Tessier, Romain
Uzunoglu, Emre
Vintr, Tomas

Woolley, Robert
Wu, Kefan
Xiaoxuan, Hei
Xu, Xiangmin
Yang, Jiaming
Yang, Shibao
Ye, Kangfeng
Zahmatkesh, Mohsen
Zhao, Junjie
Zhong, Zhipeng

Keynote Speaker Abstracts

Personal Assistive Robots

Yiannis Demiris

Yiannis Demiris will present the Personal Robotics Lab's research on robots that perceive human sensorimotor and cognitive states through multimodal sensors, learn about their skills and intentions, and personalise how the robots will assist their users. He will present the algorithmic foundations of such assistive systems, from perception to deformable object manipulation, along with a number of examples from assisting users with their mobility, object handovers, and activities of daily living, including dressing, cooking, feeding and hygiene.

Nano to Macro: Building Trustworthy Swarms for People

Sabine Hauert

Building on 20 years of progress, swarm robotics is now ready to enable out-of-the-box solutions in real-world environments that adapt, scale, and are robust. To enable this, we propose a shift towards trustworthy swarms with emergent properties that are easy to design, monitor, control, and validate by humans. At the nano scale, these swarms can interface with the body, enabling applications in cancer treatment, wound healing or tissue engineering. At the macro scale, future swarms will leverage AI, integrate advanced local perception, and share information not only locally but also quasi-globally. Ultimately, we envision a future where specialised robots operate with shared situational awareness, coexisting and coordinating seamlessly in environments such as construction sites, farms, logistics hubs, and natural ecosystems. The goal is to foster an ecosystem where next-generation robots collaborate with each other–and with humans–at scale.

From Safe Rails to Autonomous Realms

Thierry Lecomte

Thierry Lecomte presents CLEARSY's journey from safety-critical railway automation to broader applications in autonomous mobility. Drawing from global deployments of automatic train systems, we show how railways function as large-scale robotic systems with embedded autonomy, localization, and fail-safe mechanisms. We then explore CLEARSY's innovations in ground, aerial, and underwater autonomy, highlighting shared challenges in navigation, sensor fusion, and environment interaction. The role of advanced sensors, robust hardware, and formal modeling is emphasized across all domains. A core theme is the integration of safety, verification, and validation into robotics design—rooted in CLEARSY's railway experience. The talk also addresses the transition from deterministic systems to complex, uncertain environments, proposing cross-domain methodologies for trustworthy autonomy. By bridging industry and research, CLEARSY supports the development of safe, deployable autonomous technologies. This keynote invites collaboration to ensure that the next generation of robotic systems is as safe as it is intelligent.

Robotics and automation from the lab to industrial deployments: challenges and opportunities

Dejanira Araiza Illan

Global supply chains across different industries are subject to emerging challenges due to the volatility, uncertainty, complexity, and ambiguity of the world we live in. Robotic and automation solutions powered by artificial intelligence and multi-faceted software stacks on one hand, and powerful hardware on the other, promise to offer increased agility and resilience in manufacturing and logistics. As smarter robots are created aiming to take over difficult tasks currently performed by human operators, the challenges to deploy these robots in industrial environments are increasing too. Hence, how do we successfully achieve the scaling up of robots from laboratory environments into industrial deployments?

This talk will start with an overview of technological trends in robotics for supply chain applications. Then, we will reflect on the most pressing challenges when deploying automation technologies in a diverse range of industries, from fast moving to highly regulated. Finally, opportunities to address these challenges will be highlighted, to open room for inspiration in the development of the next generation of robotics solutions.

Contents

Locomotion and Control

Manipulation and Dexterous Interaction

Software Engineering for Robotics

Underwater Robotics and Autonomy

Aerial Robotics and Path Planning

Challenging Environments

Invited Paper

From Safe Rails to Autonomous Realms
(Invited Paper)

Thierry Lecomte[✉]

CLEARSY, Aix en Provence, France
thierry.lecomte@clearsy.com

Abstract. This keynote presents CLEARSY's journey from safety-critical railway automation to broader applications in autonomous mobility. Drawing from global deployments of automatic train systems, we show how railways function as large-scale robotic systems with embedded autonomy, localization, and fail-safe mechanisms. We then explore CLEARSY's innovations in ground, aerial, and underwater autonomy, highlighting shared challenges in navigation, sensor fusion, and environment interaction. The role of advanced sensors, robust hardware, and formal modeling is emphasized across all domains. A core theme is the integration of safety, verification, and validation into robotics design—rooted in CLEARSY's railway experience. The talk also addresses the transition from deterministic systems to complex, uncertain environments, proposing cross-domain methodologies for trustworthy autonomy. By bridging industry and research, CLEARSY supports the development of safe, deployable autonomous technologies. This keynote invites collaboration to ensure that the next generation of robotic systems is as safe as it is intelligent.

Keywords: Safety critical · Railways · Automatic mobility · Autonomous mobility · Formal Methods

1 Introduction

Mobility has been evolving steadily over the decades, adapting to population growth and increasingly complex travel needs. This transformation is driven by technological innovations and lifestyle changes, reflecting the growing demands of a dynamic and mobile society. As a result, mobility is now a major concern for both cities and individuals, who strive to balance efficiency, sustainability, and quality of life. Expectations regarding transport safety have risen significantly, mirroring society's decreasing tolerance for accidents. People now view safe mobility—not only for daily commutes but also for leisure travel—as a fundamental right rather than a privilege associated with risk. These evolving expectations are pushing industries and governments to innovate and implement enhanced safety measures to meet the demand for near-absolute protection. Rail transport, particularly through its progressive automation, offers a partial

© The Author(s), under exclusive license to Springer Nature Switzerland AG 2026
A. Cavalcanti et al. (Eds.): TAROS 2025, LNAI 16045, pp. 3–7, 2026.
https://doi.org/10.1007/978-3-032-01486-3_1

response to this need. Future developments in autonomy aim to deliver transport solutions in less constrained environments, potentially beyond traditional rail infrastructure.

This paper examines the broader evolution of transport from a safety perspective, focusing on the transition from rail automation to general autonomous mobility, drawing on CLEARSY's experience.

The remainder of this paper is organized as follows. Section 2 introduces the concept of safe software-based systems. Section 3 reviews the development of automated railway transport since the 1990 s. Section 4 discusses the ongoing transition toward autonomous railway mobility. Section 5 explores the extension of railway technologies and methodologies to general autonomous mobility, before concluding.

2   What Safety Means

Safety is a multi-dimensional concept that extends beyond the traditional idea of "freedom from accidents or harm." It encompasses not only the prevention of physical injury or damage but also involves ensuring predictable, reliable, and fail-safe behaviour in complex environments. In rail transport, safety includes fail-safe signal systems, automatic train protection (ATP), and strict certification processes to ensure software correctness. In robotics, especially for collaborative or service robots, safety includes limiting speed and force near humans, using sensors to detect contact, and adhering to ISO standards. In autonomous vehicles, safety integrates real-time perception, decision-making under uncertainty, and compliance with traffic laws—all with verification mechanisms.

The certification of such systems takes into account not only the technical elements, hardware and software, but also the organisational elements, procedures, the operational environment in which such systems operate and possible (sometimes harmful) interactions with humans.

3   Automated Railways

Since the 1990 s, automated metro systems [1] [2] have experienced significant advancements, transitioning from manual or semi-automated operations to fully automated, driverless networks. All signalling has been digitized and the control is entirely performed by computer. However, it is necessary to ensure a human presence to supervise the system and manage degraded situations. Automatic train control (ATC), automatic train protection (ATP) and platform screen doors [4] have been integrated, improving efficiency, reducing human error, and enhancing safety by ensuring precise control over train speed, positioning, and emergency braking.

The development of diverse advanced sensors, (wireless) communication systems (beacons, 5G), and real-time data processing further allowed for more complex automation, enabling trains to operate safely with minimal human intervention. These systems have proven effective in lowering operational costs, improving punctuality, and enhancing overall passenger experience.

The integration of formal methods is playing a pivotal role in boosting the reliability and safety of automatic metro systems. Formal development and verification techniques [3], which mathematically prove the correctness of software, increase confidence in system safety [5], particularly in critical functions like collision avoidance, route setting, and emergency handling. By rigorously modeling and verifying system behavior, formal methods help addressing edge cases and reduce the likelihood of system failures.

4   Autonomous Railways

The contribution of train autonomy [6] is probably linked to availability and operating cost reduction objectives. Possible interactions between trains and their environment (level crossings, trains from other operators, loss of train integrity due to derailment, vegetation on the tracks, collisions with animals, etc.) require human intervention to deal with multiple non-nominal scenarios. The addition of remote control was the first decision made regarding autonomous train projects in France where technologies are actively developed through a combination of large-scale national programs. SNCF, in partnership with companies like Alstom, Thales, and Bosch, is testing autonomous Regio2N passenger trains, targeting full automation (GoA4) by 2026. Freight trains have also been tested in semi-autonomous modes, with SNCF aiming for commercial rollout of autonomous freight and passenger services post-2026. These projects are addressing current rolling stock and existing infrastructure with the objective of replacing drivers by computers and sensors while maintaining the same level of safety.

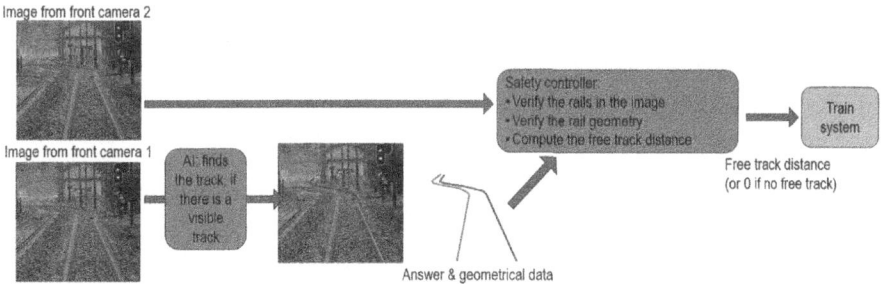

Fig. 1. Free track detection system using ML with verifiable results + safety controller.

For regional light-train, low-traffic lines, autonomous rail projects are underway—such as TELLi, DRAISY, FLEXY, Taxirail, INFRAlight and Ecotrain—focused on revitalizing rural lines with cost-efficient, small-capacity vehicles. Often there is only one train per track at any time and the signalling system can be simplified. These projects emphasize obstacle detection, low emissions, and minimal infrastructure needs. AI-based prototypes and lab trains are developed to explore automation in controlled environments. Regulatory challenges, particularly around signalling and certification, remain key barriers to wide deployment. While some demonstrations are successful, large-scale GoA4 deployment is not expected before 2030.

CLEARSY is involved in several lightweight rail projects where low traffic reduces the need for expensive signalling and where new techniques are used to lower the development and exploitation costs.

Moreover, CLEARSY is contributing to the UIC 3-year project "New Methods for Safety Demonstration" (Fig. 1) where AI-based tools are used to set-up certifiable safety controllers. The results of the projects are going to be published among all worldwide exploiting companies by the end of 2025 and could become a technical specification. The aim is to provide experts with elements for consideration to facilitate their decision-making when certifying AI-based safety systems.

5   Autonomous Mobility

In parallel with its railway activities, CLEARSY has been called upon to ensure safety for mobile, automated, and autonomous applications. Examples include:

– a civilian underwater drone capable of navigating autonomously for several weeks, equipped with a function that triggers its ballasts when a gyroscope position calculation error is detected,
– a multi-tonne land-based firefighting robot that must be continuously monitored and, for safety reasons, must be able to stop immediately if communication with its base is lost,
– an autonomous shuttle that transports passengers on both roads and forest tracks, for which driving deviations (sudden steering wheel movements, rapid acceleration or deceleration) must be monitored,
– An aerial firefighting robot, which must maintain communication with the supervision centre and have sufficient energy capacity to return to base.

These autonomous systems are unique in that they do not (yet) have established standards or any standards at all for demonstrating safety related to autonomous behaviour and possible interactions with surrounding mobile objects and humans. They do not yet have decades of experience behind them, unlike rail transport, and decisions on their use are often based on financial rather than safety considerations. Until we have truly reliable AI, the experience gained in rail automation should help improve the safety of these systems through low-level safeguards.

6   Conclusion and Perspectives

CLEARSY's trajectory from railway automation to broader autonomous mobility illustrates how decades of safety-critical expertise can inform the development of trustworthy autonomous systems across diverse domains. As we confront increasingly complex and uncertain environments, the fusion of rigorous engineering practices—such as formal modeling, sensor integration, and fail-safe design—becomes essential. However AI-based control systems, usually based on vision, remain difficult to characterize in all possible scenarios. The combination of AI systems and low-level safety controller could be a first step toward acceptance for certification.

By extending these principles beyond rail (guided systems) to aerial, ground, and underwater platforms, CLEARSY demonstrates that safety and intelligence are not opposing goals but complementary pillars of robust autonomy. Looking ahead, collaboration between industry and research will be key to creating systems that are not only technically advanced but also verifiably safe. This journey affirms that the future of autonomy depends not only on innovation, but on a foundation of discipline, trust, and cross-domain synergy.

Acknowledgements. The work and results described in this article were partly funded by UIC (International Union of Railways) as part of the project "New Methods for Safety Demonstration".

References

1. ter Beek, M.H., et al.: Formal methods in industry. Form. Asp. Comput. 37(1) (2024). https://doi.org/10.1145/3689374
2. Burdy, L., Meynadier, J.M.: Experience on the use of a formal method in a railway company. IFAC Proc. Vol. 33, 193–197 (2000)
3. Hansen, D., Schneider, D., Leuschel, M.: Using B and ProB for Data Validation Projects. In: Butler, M., Schewe, K.-D., Mashkoor, A., Biro, M. (eds.) ABZ 2016. LNCS, vol. 9675, pp. 167–182. Springer, Cham (2016). https://doi.org/10.1007/978-3-319-33600-8_10
4. Lecomte, T.: Safe and Reliable Metro Platform Screen Doors Control/Command Systems. In: Cuellar, J., Maibaum, T., Sere, K. (eds.) FM 2008. LNCS, vol. 5014, pp. 430–434. Springer, Heidelberg (2008). https://doi.org/10.1007/978-3-540-68237-0_32
5. Sabatier, D.: Using formal proof and B method at system level for industrial projects. In: Lecomte, T., Pinger, R., Romanovsky, A. (eds.) Reliability, Safety, and Security of Railway Systems. Modelling, Analysis, Verification, and Certification - 1st Int'l Conf., RSSRail 2016, Paris, France, June 28-30, 2016, Proc. LNCS, vol. 9707, pp. 20–31. Springer (2016)
6. Song, H., Li, L., Li, Y., Tan, L., Dong, H.: Functional safety and performance analysis of autonomous route management for autonomous train control system. In: IEEE Transactions on Intelligent Transportation Systems PP, 1–14 (2024)

Human-Robot Interaction
and Teleoperation

A New Semi-Automatic Strategy for Teleoperating Mobile Manipulators Using a Haptic Device

Bandar Aldhafeeri$^{(\boxtimes)}$ ⓘ, Joaquin Carrasco ⓘ, and Bruno V. Adorno ⓘ

Manchester Centre for Robotics and AI, The University of Manchester,
Manchester, UK
bandar.aldhafeeri@postgrad.manchester.ac.uk,
{joaquin.carrasco,bruno.adorno}@manchester.ac.uk

Abstract. When teleoperating wheeled mobile manipulator robots using haptic devices, users usually use rate control for navigation and position control for manipulation. Manually switching between those two modes (for example, via a push button) while relying on visual feedback is often challenging, as using a single camera significantly reduces depth perception, making contact-based tasks difficult due to reduced spatial awareness and depth cues. Adding proximity sensors or auditory cues for distance detection requires processing more data, raising both the cognitive load and associated costs. On the other hand, typical automatic hybrid switching schemes employ restoring forces in navigation mode to assist the human operator. However, performing contact-based tasks in navigation mode deteriorates transparency due to interference between environmental and restoring forces while impairing fine-manipulation capabilities. Therefore, to overcome these challenges, we propose a new hybrid scheme that detects interaction with the environment via a force sensor to facilitate the automatic transition from navigation to manipulation mode. We use constrained task-space controllers to address obstacle avoidance directly in the control law and enable safe interaction. We conducted an ethically approved study involving nine humans to assess the proposed scheme and used task completion time (TCT) and NASA Task Load Index (TLX) to assess human operator workload. Paired t-tests indicate a reduction of 23.3% ($p = 0.0058$) in TCT and mental demand by 57.1% ($p = 0.0021$), highlighting the advantages of the proposed semi-automatic switching scheme over the manual one.

Keywords: Teleoperation · Switching · Mobile Manipulator · Haptics

This work was funded by Majmaah University, Riyadh, Saudi Arabia, and by the Royal Academy of Engineering under the Research Chairs and Senior Research Fellowships programme.

1   Introduction

Wheeled mobile manipulator (WMM) robots are among the most widely used robotic systems with manipulation and mobility capabilities [1]. They offer greater stability than humanoid and aerial mobile manipulators, making them highly suitable for diverse applications in warehousing, healthcare, and industrial and domestic environments. Unlike fixed-base manipulators, which usually operate in well-defined environments [2], WMM robots may navigate vast, unstructured, and unpredictable environments. This increased complexity makes executing tasks autonomously much more difficult, requiring advanced perception, planning, and control capabilities to adapt dynamically to constantly changing conditions. Alternatively, teleoperating these robots to leverage human intelligence enables many important applications, particularly in scenarios where distance, safety concerns, or human physical limitations restrict direct interaction [3].

Teleoperating WMM robots using a single haptic device presents several challenges, including disparate workspaces, redundancy, operation in cluttered environments, and mismatched mechanical structures. A commonly adopted approach to address these issues relies on a hybrid control strategy that integrates rate control [4] and position control [5]. In navigation mode, rate control is employed to compensate for workspace differences by mapping the haptic device's displacement into desired velocities for the remote robot. Conversely, in manipulation mode, position control is used to ensure precise interaction with the environment. These two control modes are combined within a hybrid scheme that governs the switching mechanism, which can be either manual or automatic [6–9]. Despite advancements in automatic switching techniques, manual switching remains the most widely adopted method.

Two key observations have been found in the literature concerning the teleoperation of WMM robots with haptic and visual modalities. First, to tackle control challenges, the robotic system is controlled via two modes: the first facilitates commanding the base only while the robotic arm remains stationary, and the second allows for the opposite scenario [10]. This approach requires the human operator to be acquainted with teleoperating completely different systems, increasing training needs and cognitive load. The second observation notes that contemporary automatic hybrid control schemes based on partitioning the haptic device's workspace into manipulation and navigation regions (e.g., a virtual sphere) are developed without considering force reflection [9]. Consequently, the human operator relies on visual feedback to manipulate objects. Furthermore, the remote robot might interact with the environment in an incorrect operation mode without the user's knowledge, which could lead to deterioration of the bilateral system transparency [11].

1.1   Statement of Contributions

This work builds upon our previous research [11], which only addressed transparency deterioration in locally-based hybrid schemes that often overlook environmental interactions. However, in our earlier study, we did not consider full-directional navigation, safe interaction, obstacle avoidance, and visual feedback. Thus, the contributions of this work can be summarised as follows:

- A new locally-based hybrid scheme for teleoperating WMM robots using a single haptic device is proposed. This scheme enables users to navigate and manipulate with haptic and visual feedback while enhancing transparency and reducing task completion time and mental demand.
- To ensure the robot's and surroundings' safety, we implement a safe inter-action strategy that limits the end-effector's approach velocity to workspace objects by exponentially decreasing distance functions, minimising impact forces upon contact.
- Obstacle avoidance is addressed so the robot can navigate effectively in a cluttered environment without user intervention.

2   Kinematic Control

Since WMM robots can navigate and manipulate, the desired commands generated by the human operator through the haptic device must be interpreted differently. To accomplish this, different control laws are required to achieve distinct control objectives, such as the position-position (PP) strategy for manipulation and position-velocity (PV) for navigation.

In this paper, both control strategies are based on whole-body kinematics. The whole-body forward kinematics is given by $x = f(q)$, where $x \in \mathbb{R}^m$ is the task vector and $q \in \mathbb{R}^n$ is the robot configuration. The whole-body differential kinematics is given by $\dot{x} = J(q)\dot{q}$, where $J(q) = \partial f(q)/\partial q \in \mathbb{R}^{m \times n}$ is the analytical Jacobian matrix of the holonomic mobile manipulator [12].

Kinematic control laws based on the first-order robot kinematics that enforce task-space constraints can be implemented very efficiently using quadratic programming and usually have the following form:

$$u \in \arg\min_{\dot{q}} \; \mathcal{G}(q, \dot{q}) + \lambda^2 \|\dot{q}\|_2^2$$

$$\text{subject to} \quad W\dot{q} \preceq w, \tag{1}$$

where $\mathcal{G}(q, \dot{q})$ is a quadratic function that usually determines the task-space dynamics, $W \triangleq W(q) \in \mathbb{R}^{s \times n}$ and $w \triangleq w(q) \in \mathbb{R}^s$ are used to enforce s linear constraints in the control inputs, and $\lambda \in [0, \infty)$ is a damping factor penalizing solutions that generate large configuration velocities. Different control objectives use the same structure as in (1) by changing the task function $\mathcal{G}(q, \dot{q})$.

For PP control, given the task error $\tilde{x} \triangleq x - x_d$ with a constant desired task vector x_d, the desired closed-loop error dynamics aiming at an exponential convergence is given by

$$\dot{\tilde{x}} + \beta\tilde{x} = 0 \implies J(q)\dot{q} + \beta\tilde{x} = 0, \tag{2}$$

where $\beta \in (0, \infty)$ determines the convergence rate. In this case, we define the task function $\mathcal{G}_1(q, \dot{q}) \triangleq \|J(q)\dot{q} + \beta\tilde{x}\|_2^2$, so that the resulting closed-loop system under control law (1), with $\mathcal{G}(q, \dot{q}) = \mathcal{G}_1(q, \dot{q})$, is stable [13].

On the other hand, for PV control, the term $\mathcal{G}(q, \dot{q})$ in (1) is modified to address the different scales in the haptic interface's workspace and the robot's workspace. To achieve this, we make the task-space velocity $\dot{x}$ converge to the desired vector $\dot{x}_d$ by defining $\mathcal{G}(q, \dot{q}) = \mathcal{G}_2(q, \dot{q}) \triangleq \|J(q)\dot{q} - \dot{x}_d\|_2^2$, which minimises the error between the desired and current task-space velocities.

3   Vector Field Inequalities

Vector Field Inequalities (VFIs) is a technique that converts nonlinear task-space equality constraints in the robot configurations into linear inequality constraints in the control inputs [14]. It requires a differentiable signed distance function $d(q) \in \mathbb{R}$ between two collidable geometric entities and the Jacobian matrix that satisfies

$$\dot{d}(q) = J_d\dot{q}, \tag{3}$$

where $J_d = \partial d(q)/\partial q \in \mathbb{R}^{1 \times n}$.

A geometrical entity is typically represented by simple geometric shapes, such as points, lines, and planes. Using dual quaternion algebra to describe these shapes makes it straightforward to compute the distance between two entities [15], one attached to the robot and the other typically located in the environment.[1]

A typical use of VFIs is to prevent the robot from entering a restricted area [14]. Let $d_{\text{safe}} \geq 0$ be a constant safe distance that outlines the boundary of the restricted zone. The distance to the boundary is defined as

$$\tilde{d}(q) = d(q) - d_{\text{safe}}. \tag{4}$$

It is possible to show that enforcing

$$\dot{\tilde{d}}(q(t)) \geq -\eta_d\tilde{d}(q(t)), \tag{5}$$

for $t \geq 0$ and $\eta_d \in (0, \infty)$ ensures that $\tilde{d}(q(t)) \geq e^{-\eta_d t}\tilde{d}(q(0))$ for all $t \geq 0$. Since d_{safe} is constant, we use (3) to obtain

$$J_d(q)\dot{q} \geq -\eta_d\tilde{d}(q) \iff -J_d(q)\dot{q} \leq \eta_d\tilde{d}(q). \tag{6}$$

4   Bilateral Teleoperation System

This section outlines the hybrid control scheme and the haptic feedback provided to the human operator. Specifically, we describe the force rendering mechanism

---

[1] The second geometric primitive might also be attached to the robot when avoiding self-collisions.

and how the movements of the haptic device are interpreted as desired commands for the remote robot end-effector. We define an operation mode index, $\zeta \in \{0, 1\}$, where $\zeta = 0$ indicates the navigation mode whereas $\zeta = 1$ denotes the manipulation mode. We also define several coordinate systems used throughout the paper: the haptic device frame $\mathcal{F}_H$, the remote world frame $\mathcal{F}_W$, the remote robot end-effector frame $\mathcal{F}_E$, and an offset frame $\mathcal{F}_O$ with respect to $\mathcal{F}_W$.

4.1   Navigation Mode ($\zeta = 0$)

In this operation mode, the force rendering restricts the user's hand movements. This is beneficial because the haptic device's displacement translates to desired velocities, and larger forces represent large velocities. Furthermore, this force helps keeping the probe within a virtual sphere with a radius $r \in (0, \infty)$ centered at the origin of $\mathcal{F}_H$. Thus, we define the restoring force $\boldsymbol{f}_r^H(t) \in \mathbb{H}_p$, where $(\mathbb{H}_p, +) \cong (\mathbb{R}^3, +)$, to be proportional to the haptic interface's displacement in navigation mode as follows

$$\boldsymbol{f}_r^H(t) = -k_r \boldsymbol{p}_h^H(t), \tag{7}$$

where $k_r \in (0, \infty)$ is the stiffness, and $\boldsymbol{p}_h^H(t) \in \mathbb{H}_p$ is the position of the haptic device's end-effector in $\mathcal{F}_H$.

To explore the remote environment, the robot must translate and rotate. For the former, the haptic device's displacement is used as a desired linear velocity for the remote robot end-effector. For the latter, the user must rotate the stylus to activate the command. Because a camera is mounted on the robot end-effector, the commands are generated considering the visual feedback.

In this operation mode, two sub-modes $\mathcal{K} \in \{0, 1\}$ are implemented: one corresponding to translation ($\mathcal{K} = 0$) and the other corresponding to rotation ($\mathcal{K} = 1$). The automatic switching between sub-modes in the navigation mode is defined as

$$\mathcal{K} = \begin{cases} 0, & \text{if } \|\boldsymbol{p}_h^H\| > r, \\ 1, & \text{if } \|\boldsymbol{p}_h^H\| \leq r \text{ and } |\theta| > \theta_{\text{limit}}, \end{cases} \tag{8}$$

where θ denotes the stylus's joint angle controlled by the user and $\theta_{\text{limit}} \in (0, 2\pi)$ represents a predefined limit. When $\|\boldsymbol{p}_h^H\| \leq r$ and $|\theta| \leq \theta_{\text{limit}}$, the robot stops completely.

Translation Command ($\mathcal{K} = 0$): In this sub-mode, the human operator commands the robot end-effector to move forward or backward, right or left, and up or down relative to the camera's view while maintaining a fixed orientation to ensure the camera image plane remains perpendicular to the ground. Thus, the desired linear velocity of the robot end-effector with respect to the remote world frame is given as

$$\boldsymbol{\dot{t}}_d^W(t) = \text{Ad}(\boldsymbol{r}_E^W(t))\boldsymbol{p}_d^E(t), \tag{9}$$

where
$$p_d^E(t) = (\|p_h^H\| - r)\mathrm{Ad}(r_H^E)\overline{p}_h^H(t),$$

with $\overline{p}_h^H(t) = p_h^H(t)/\|p_h^H\|$, and $r_H^E \in \mathbb{S}^3 \subset \mathbb{H}$ being the constant unit quaternion that represents the orientation of $\mathcal{F}_H$ relative to $\mathcal{F}_E$, which is determined by inspection, and Ad is the adjoint operator [16]. Therefore, we let $\mathcal{G}(q,\dot{q}) = \mathcal{G}_3(q,\dot{q})$ in (1), where

$$\mathcal{G}_3(q,\dot{q}) \triangleq \|J_r(q)\dot{q} + \beta\mathrm{vec}_4(\tilde{r})\|_2^2 + \left\|J_t(q)\dot{q} - \mathrm{vec}_3\left(\dot{t}_d^W\right)\right\|_2^2, \tag{10}$$

in which $\tilde{r} = r^W(t) - r_d^W$, with $r^W, r_d^W \in \mathbb{S}^3$ being the current and desired orientation of the remote robot end-effector, respectively. The operators $\mathrm{vec}_4 : \mathbb{H} \to \mathbb{R}^4$ and $\mathrm{vec}_3 : \mathbb{H}_p \to \mathbb{R}^3$ map quaternion and pure quaternion coefficients into four and three-dimensional vectors. Lastly, $J_r(q) \in \mathbb{R}^{4\times n}$ and $J_t(q) \in \mathbb{R}^{3\times n}$ represent the rotational and translational Jacobian matrices that satisfy $\mathrm{vec}_4\,\dot{r}^W = J_r\dot{q}$ and $\mathrm{vec}_3\,\dot{t}^W = J_t\dot{q}$, respectively [12]. Note that it is essential to maintain a fixed orientation in this sub-mode, which is enforced by the first term in (10); otherwise, any drifts or disturbances in the orientation will affect the desired linear velocity of the remote robot end-effector.

Yaw Command ($\mathcal{K} = 1$): For the robot end-effector to yaw (i.e., rotate about the vertical axis), the desired rotation time derivative is

$$\dot{r}_d^W(t) = \frac{1}{2}r_E^W(t)\omega_{W,E}^E, \tag{11}$$

where $\omega_{W,E}^E = \dot{\phi}_d n_d^E$ is the desired angular velocity of the robot end-effector with respect to $\mathcal{F}_W$, expressed in $\mathcal{F}_E$, whereas $n_d^E \in \mathbb{H}_p \cap \mathbb{S}^3$ is the rotation axis, and $\dot{\phi}_d \in \mathbb{R}$ is a constant desired rate. When the robot end-effector rotates, the camera might tilt. To prevent this issue, the camera should be aligned horizontally with the ground. By attaching one plane to the bottom of the camera and another to the ground, controlling their normals ensures their alignment.

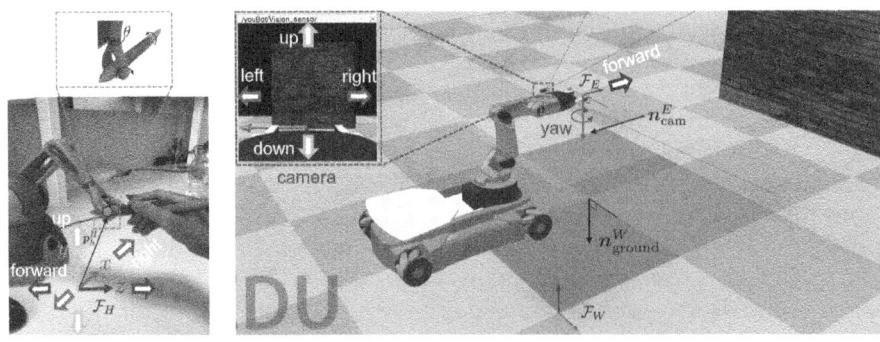

Fig. 1. On the left, desired commands are generated by manipulating the haptic device, while on the right, the remote robot end-effector is controlled either in manipulation or navigation modes.

Let $\boldsymbol{n}^W_{\text{ground}} \in \mathbb{H}_p \cap \mathbb{S}^3$ be the normal to the ground plane, expressed in $\mathcal{F}_W$, and $\boldsymbol{n}^E_{\text{cam}} \in \mathbb{H}_p \cap \mathbb{S}^3$ be the normal to the plane attached to the bottom of the camera, expressed in $\mathcal{F}_E$, see Fig. 1. By defining $\tilde{\boldsymbol{n}} = \text{Ad}(\boldsymbol{r}^W_E(t))\boldsymbol{n}^E_{\text{cam}} - \boldsymbol{n}^W_{\text{ground}}$, the term $\mathcal{G}(\boldsymbol{q}, \dot{\boldsymbol{q}})$ in the control law (1) is given by

$$\mathcal{G}_4(\boldsymbol{q}, \dot{\boldsymbol{q}}) \triangleq \|\boldsymbol{J}_{\text{cam}}(\boldsymbol{q})\dot{\boldsymbol{q}} + \beta\tilde{\boldsymbol{n}}\|^2_2 + \|\boldsymbol{J}_r(\boldsymbol{q})\dot{\boldsymbol{q}} - \dot{\boldsymbol{r}}^W_d\|^2_2, \tag{12}$$

where $\boldsymbol{J}_{\text{cam}} \in \mathbb{R}^{3 \times n}$ satisfies $\text{vec}_3 \dot{\boldsymbol{n}}^W_{\text{cam}} = \boldsymbol{J}_{\text{cam}}\dot{\boldsymbol{q}}$ [14].

4.2 Manipulation Mode ($\zeta = 1$)

In this operation mode, force rendering is implemented for two purposes. First, it restricts the hand's motion by applying a repulsive force. Second, it allows the human operator to perceive touch when the remote robot interacts with its environment, provided that a force sensor is available.

For interaction with the environment, the force rendering is implemented using a force sensor. Let $\mathcal{F}_S$ represent the force sensor frame in $\mathcal{F}_W$. Let $\boldsymbol{f}^S_e(t) \in \mathbb{H}_p$ be the force measurement obtained from the force sensor expressed in $\mathcal{F}_S$. The rendered force $\boldsymbol{f}^H_e(t) \in \mathbb{H}_p$ is

$$\boldsymbol{f}^H_e(t) = \begin{cases} \kappa\text{Ad}(\boldsymbol{r}^H_S)\boldsymbol{f}^S_e(t), & \text{if } \|\boldsymbol{f}^S_e\| > \gamma, \\ \boldsymbol{0}, & \text{otherwise,} \end{cases} \tag{13}$$

where $\kappa \in (0, \infty)$ is the force feedback constant, which is equivalent to a constant stiffness, and $\gamma \in (0, \infty)$ is a small threshold to avoid generating spurious force feedback due to sensor noise. The orientation of $\mathcal{F}_S$ relative to $\mathcal{F}_H$ is represented by $\boldsymbol{r}^H_S$ and obtained by inspection.

For free motion during manipulation mode, force rendering is designed to inform the human operator haptically about how closely the robot follows the desired command. Otherwise, rapid movements of the device can significantly reduce trajectory tracking accuracy [11]. Consider a repulsive force $\boldsymbol{f}^W_m(t) \in \mathbb{H}_p$ that is dependent upon the difference between the actual and desired positions of the remote robot end-effector, namely, $\tilde{\boldsymbol{t}}^W(t) = \boldsymbol{t}^W(t) - \boldsymbol{t}^W_d(t)$. We define the virtual force $\boldsymbol{f}^W_m(t)$ during free motion as

$$\boldsymbol{f}^W_m(t) = k_s\tilde{\boldsymbol{t}}^W(t) + k_d\dot{\tilde{\boldsymbol{t}}}^W(t), \tag{14}$$

where $k_s \in (0, \infty)$ and $k_d \in [0, \infty)$. The virtual force $\boldsymbol{f}^W_m(t)$ in $\mathcal{F}_H$ is

$$\boldsymbol{f}^H_m(t) = \text{Ad}((\boldsymbol{r}^W_E(t)\boldsymbol{r}^E_H)^*)\boldsymbol{f}^W_m(t). \tag{15}$$

To facilitate a smooth transition between the forces defined in (13) and (15) during contact and non-contact states in manipulation mode, we implement the same strategy detailed in our previous research [11].

In this manipulation mode, there is a direct mapping between the haptic device's displacement and the remote robot end-effector. The desired position is realised as

$$\boldsymbol{p}_d^E(t) = \alpha \mathrm{Ad}(\boldsymbol{r}_H^E)\boldsymbol{p}_h^H(t), \tag{16}$$

$$\boldsymbol{t}_d^W(t) = \mathrm{Ad}(\boldsymbol{r}_E^W(t))\boldsymbol{p}_d^E(t) + \boldsymbol{p}_s^W, \tag{17}$$

where $\boldsymbol{p}_s^W \in \mathbb{H}_p$ is the origin of the offset frame $\mathcal{F}_O$ in $\mathcal{F}_W$. The offset position updates when switching from navigation to manipulation mode, which is achieved by using a force sensor to detect collision. Hence, $\boldsymbol{p}_s^W \triangleq \boldsymbol{t}^W(t_c)$ where $t_c \in (0, \infty)$ is the time when the collision is detected (see [11] for the switching strategy). Furthermore, we ensure the end-effector's orientation remains perpendicular to the walls by using a predefined rotation $\boldsymbol{r}_d^W$ associated with each wall to avoid complications during the interaction, such as undesirable torques. Thus, we use control law (1) with an objective function that accounts for the full pose containing both position $\boldsymbol{t}_d^W(t)$ and desired orientation $\boldsymbol{r}_d^W$ [14].

Figure 1 illustrates the setup for haptic teleoperation of a WMM robot. The translational and rotational motions of the haptic device are decoupled by design, with the human operator observing the scene solely through the camera.

5 Simulation and Discussions

To evaluate the proposed hybrid control scheme, we have prepared a semi-physical bilateral system that comprises a human operator, a real haptic device (i.e., Geomagic Touch), a WMM robot, and a remote environment. The remote site is simulated in the CoppeliaSim 4.5.1 software. The DQ Robotics library [15] is used for the kinematic modelling and control of the remote robot and for solving the quadratic optimization problem numerically via its solver interface. The experiments were conducted in Ubuntu Linux OS with Intel Core i5 CPU 1.60 Hz and Intel UHD Graphics 620. The constrained controller runs at 20 Hz, whereas the servo loop of the haptic device operates at 1 kHz. The communication between the controller and the scene is carried through the ZeroMQ remote API with no artificial time delay.

5.1 Simulation Setup

In the simulation, the human operator remotely controls a WMM robot with eight degrees of freedom using a single haptic device. The goal is to provide an exploration and interaction experience in a cluttered environment with visual and haptic modalities while maintaining transparency, as outlined in [11], and reducing the operator's mental workload and task completion time. For this purpose, we implemented a large scene in CoppeliaSim, illustrated in Fig. 2. Two walls are located four metres from the origin of $\mathcal{F}_W$ along the x, y-axes, and five ground obstacles are represented as cylinders spread on the floor. Additionally, only the positions and velocities of the robot's joints are constrained, while the mobile base position and heading are unconstrained to facilitate exploration activities. The constraints for avoiding obstacles and safe interaction are outlined as follows.

For the robot's base, obstacle avoidance is managed by setting seven constraints: five for ground obstacles and two for the walls. For the former, the constraints are classified as a point-line type [14], where the mobile base is enclosed by a cylinder with radius $r_{base} = 0.365$ m, and the cylindrical obstacles have a radius given by $r_{cylinder} = 0.1$ m; therefore, the base's safe distance with respect to the cylinders is $d_{safe} = r_{base} + r_{cylinder}$ and $\eta_d = 1$.

For the robot end-effector, four constraints are imposed on the end-effector using a point-plane type [14]. Two planes parallel to the ground at 0.38 m (π_{top}) and 0.18 m (π_{down}), respectively, are defined to restrict the end-effector's height, with ($\eta_d = 10$). To enable safe interaction with the walls, two planes (π_1 and π_2) are set one centimetre inward to reduce the impact forces while allowing the interaction to happen. The safe distance for the four planes is set to zero.

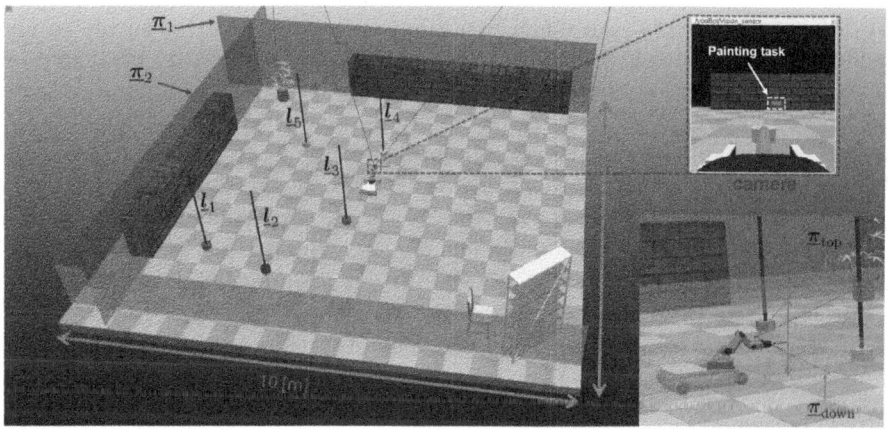

Fig. 2. Large remote site filled with coloured ground obstacles and two walls for interaction. The human operator observes the scene through the camera.

5.2   Human Workload Evaluation

This study aims to assess the potential benefits of implementing an automatic transition from navigation to manipulation in tasks requiring interaction with the environment to reduce the operator's mental workload and task completion time. We conducted a study involving nine human subjects to compare the proposed switching scheme with the manual one. We used the NASA Task Load Index (TLX), a widely recognised tool, to subjectively assess the workload of human operators [17,18]. NASA-TLX assesses six dimensions:

1. Mental Demand (MD): How mentally demanding was the task?

2. Physical Demand (PD): How physically demanding was the task?
3. Temporal Demand (TD): How hurried or rushed was the pace of the task?
4. Performance (PF): How successful were you in accomplishing what you were asked to do?
5. Effort (ET): How hard did you have to work to accomplish your level of performance?
6. Frustration (FT): How insecure, discouraged, irritated, stressed, and annoyed were you?

Participants rate their experience using a 21-point scale ranging from 0 to 100 for each dimension [19].

Hypotheses: Using a single camera during teleoperation limits depth perception, which is vital for interaction. We believe our method can reduce mental workload and shorten task completion time. Thus, our hypotheses are **H1:** The automatic transition from navigation to manipulation has the potential to reduce the task completion time and **H2:** The automatic transition from navigation to manipulation has the potential to reduce the human operator's mental workload.

Ethics and Subjects: An email invitation was sent to PhD students in our engineering department, resulting in nine participants voluntarily participating in this study. The study has been reviewed and approved by the proportionate university research ethics committee (UREC) at the University of Manchester, and all participants provided written informed consent accordingly.

Procedure: After a short training period to become comfortable with the system, all participants were instructed to perform the same bilateral teleoperation task twice, utilising the proposed and manual switching schemes. Upon completing the task, the NASA TLX questionnaire was immediately administered, resulting in each participant filling out the survey twice.

In the bilateral teleoperation task, participants teleoperate the robot to paint a marked area on the wall yellow, as shown in Fig. 2. After completion of the painting, the robot end-effector needs to be positioned at a predefined spot beyond the green plane located at -4 m from the origin of $\mathcal{F}_W$ along the y-axis. Participants were asked to perform the painting task in manipulation mode, where they relied solely on a single camera for visual feedback and received haptic feedback during the interaction with the environment. In the manual switching approach, they used a stylus with two buttons to switch between modes. In contrast, the proposed method simplifies the process by requiring only one button to switch back to navigation mode, with the transition from navigation to manipulation mode occurring automatically based on force data from the force sensor whenever the robot detects contact with the environment.

Figure 3 details the teleoperation task. Part (a) illustrates the robot's base and end-effector trajectories, including starting and ending points. Part (b) shows the painting task locations and highlights how the base avoids obstacles. Part (d) illustrates the human operator carrying out the painting task in the manipulation mode, while part (c) depicts the haptic feedback received by the operator. Additionally, part (d) highlights the challenges of visual feedback, as the user is completely unaware of the base.

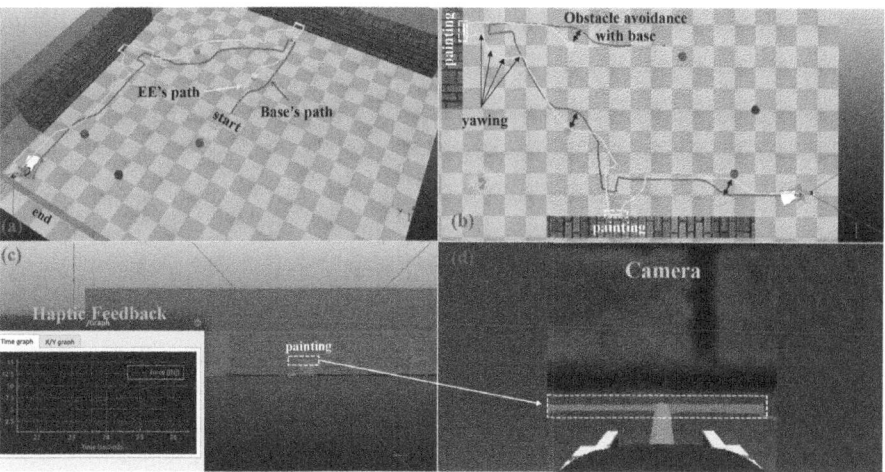

Fig. 3. A user commanding the robot to carry out painting tasks with haptic and visual modalities.

5.3   Results and Discussion

For statistical analysis, we used MATLAB. The sample size is $N = 9$. For NASA-TLX and TCT, we applied the Shapiro-Wilk test to analyse data distributions. All data passed the normality test, and paired t-tests were conducted, except for the PD data in the manual method, which did not pass the normality test; therefore, the Wilcoxon signed rank test was applied only to the PD data.

Some descriptive statistic data for NASA-TLX dimensions and TCT are presented in Fig. 4 and Table 1. It is important to note that lower ratings signify positive experiences, whereas higher ratings imply negative experiences.

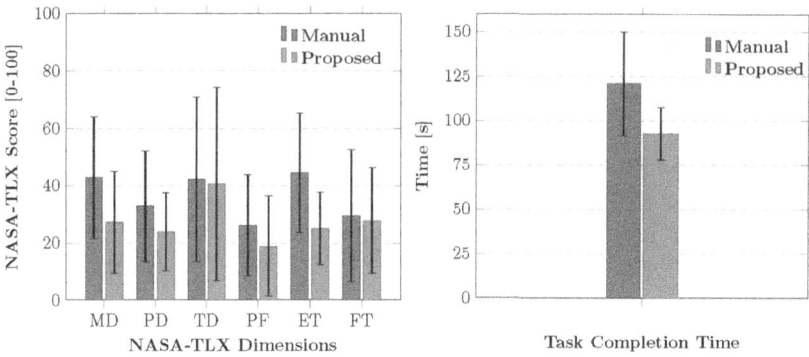

Fig. 4. Means of NASA-TLX ratings (*left*) and task completion time (*right*), where error bars denote the standard deviations.

From Table 1, the p-values for TCT and MD show a statistically significant difference (i.e., $p < 0.05$) between the proposed and manual methods. Using the means, a reduction in TCT by 23.3% and in MD by 57.1% was obtained, validating our hypotheses. Furthermore, from ET's p-value, participants found it easier to achieve their performance level using the proposed method by 43.75% compared to the manual method.

Table 1. Descriptive statistic data of NASA-TLX and TCT.

	Mean		StdDev		Max		Min		p-value	Sig
	Man.	Prop.	Man.	Prop.	Man.	Prop.	Man.	Prop.		
MD	42.8	27.2	21.4	17.7	80	60	15	5	0.0021	Yes
PD	32.8	23.9	19.2	13.6	75	45	15	5	0.0625	No
TD	42.2	40.6	28.7	33.7	100	100	5	10	0.7978	No
PF	26.1	18.9	17.6	17.5	50	50	0	0	0.3071	No
ET	44.4	25.0	21.0	12.7	70	50	15	10	0.0095	Yes
FT	29.4	27.8	23.1	18.4	65	60	0	0	0.7802	No
TCT	120.8	92.6	29.1	14.8	165.2	113.6	81.7	69.3	0.0058	Yes

On the other hand, there is no strong statistical evidence for PD, TD, PF, and FT to claim a significant difference between the proposed and manual methods. Nonetheless, it is important to note that we do not expect considerable changes in PD from removing one button, as it contributes only slightly to physical exertion. Additionally, while TCT is recorded, no time constraints are imposed on the participants. Moreover, the descriptive statistical data for TD is very similar across both methods. This may suggest that the participants felt similarly about how hurried or rushed the pace of the task was. A similar conclusion can also be drawn for FT due to the similarity in the descriptive statistical data for this dimension.

6   Conclusion

In this paper, we have proposed a new switching strategy for the teleoperation of WMM robots with haptic and visual modalities. The technique allows human operators to teleoperate a robotic system with greater degrees of freedom by using a single haptic device, facilitating exploration and interaction with remote environments while providing safe interaction and obstacle avoidance. The results indicate that participants exhibit a reduced level of mental demand when utilising the proposed scheme. Furthermore, the time taken to complete tasks is diminished compared to a manual switching scheme.

VFIs effectively prevent collision by reducing robot speed when approaching obstacles. However, conflicts may arise between the commands of the human operator and the constrained controller, which has the authority to prioritise safety. In these situations, the operator may be unaware of why the robot is not following the desired commands, potentially leading to unintended human behaviours due to these discrepancies. Rather than completely removing control from the human operator in such cases, it is more effective at least to inform or guide the user, which can be achieved through haptic cues. This problem will be explored in future work.

Future work will focus on increasing the number of scenarios to generalise the results, recruiting more participants to improve the results' statistical power, and using physiological metrics to support the TLX questionnaire data further.

References

1. Khatib, O.: Mobile manipulation: the robotic assistant. Robot. Auton. Syst. **26**(2–3), 175–183 (1999)
2. Haddadin, S., Shahriari, E.: Unified force-impedance control. Int. J. Robot. Res. **43**(13), 2112–2141 (2024)
3. Hokayem, P.F., Spong, M.W.: Bilateral teleoperation: an historical survey. Automatica **42**(12), 2035–2057 (2006)
4. Lee, D., Martinez-Palafox, O., Spong, M.W.: Bilateral teleoperation of a wheeled mobile robot over delayed communication network. In: Proceedings 2006 IEEE International Conference on Robotics and Automation, 2006, ICRA 2006, pp. 3298–3303. IEEE (2006)
5. Siciliano, B., Khatib, O., Kröger, T.: Springer Handbook of Robotics. Springer, vol. 200 (2008)
6. Pham, C.D., From, P.J.: Control allocation for mobile manipulators with on-board cameras. In: 2013 IEEE/RSJ International Conference on Intelligent Robots and Systems, pp. 5002–5008. IEEE (2013)
7. Wrock, M., Nokleby, S.B.: An automatic switching approach to teleoperation of mobile-manipulator systems using virtual fixtures. Robotica **35**(8), 1773–1792 (2017)
8. Farkhatdinov, I., Ryu, J.-H.: Switching of control signals in teleoperation systems: formalization and application. In: IEEE/ASME International Conference on Advanced Intelligent Mechatronics, vol. 2008, pp. 353–358 (2008)
9. Pepe, A., Chiaravalli, D., Melchiorri, C.: A hybrid teleoperation control scheme for a single-arm mobile manipulator with omnidirectional wheels. In: 2016 IEEE/RSJ International Conference on Intelligent Robots and Systems (IROS), pp. 1450–1455. IEEE (2016)
10. Frejek, M.C., Nokleby, S.B.: Simplified tele-operation of mobile-manipulator systems using knowledge of their singular configurations. In: International Design Engineering Technical Conferences and Computers and Information in Engineering Conference, vol. 49002, pp. 411–418 (2009)
11. Aldhafeeri, B., Carrasco, J., Adorno, B.V., Pulgarin, E.J.L.: A new hybrid teleoperation control scheme for holonomic mobile manipulator robots using a ground-based haptic device. In: Annual Conference Towards Autonomous Robotic Systems, pp. 283–295, Springer (2024)
12. Adorno, B.V.: Two-arm manipulation: from manipulators to enhanced human-robot collaboration, Ph.D. dissertation, Université Montpellier II-Sciences et Techniques du Languedoc (2011)

13. Marinho, M.M., Adorno, B.V.: Adaptive constrained kinematic control using partial or complete task-space measurements. IEEE Trans. Rob. **38**(6), 3498–3513 (2022)
14. Marinho, M.M., Adorno, B.V., Harada, K., Mitsuishi, M.: Dynamic active constraints for surgical robots using vector-field inequalities. IEEE Trans. Rob. **35**(5), 1166–1185 (2019)
15. Adorno, B.V., Marinho, M.M.: Dq robotics: a library for robot modeling and control. IEEE Robot. Autom. Mag. **28**(3), 102–116 (2020)
16. Vilhena Adorno, B.: Robot kinematic modeling and control based on dual quaternion algebra — part i: fundamentals, February 2017, working paper or preprint. https://hal.archives-ouvertes.fr/hal-01478225
17. Hart, S.G.: Nasa-task load index (nasa-tlx); 20 years later. In: Proceedings of the Human Factors and Ergonomics Society Annual Meeting, vol. 50, no. 9. Sage Publications Sage CA, Los Angeles, CA, pp. 904–908 (2006)
18. Darvish, K., et al.: Teleoperation of humanoid robots: a survey. IEEE Trans. Rob. **39**(3), 1706–1727 (2023)
19. Bolton, M.L., Biltekoff, E., Humphrey, L.: The mathematical meaninglessness of the nasa task load index: a level of measurement analysis. IEEE Trans. Hum.-Mach. Syst. **53**(3), 590–599 (2023)

Mixed Reality Visualisations for Interpretable Transparent Robot Behaviour

Omar Ali$^{(\boxtimes)}$ [iD], Paul Baxter [iD], and Helen Harman [iD]

School of Physical Sciences and Engineering, University of Lincoln, Lincoln, UK
28587497@students.lincoln.ac.uk, {pbaxter,hharman}@lincoln.ac.uk

Abstract. Human-Robot Interaction (HRI) often suffers from a lack of transparency, making it difficult for users to interpret robot behaviours, anticipate movements, and feel secure during interactions. This paper presents a technical framework that integrates Extended Reality (XR) with robotics to enhance user understanding through real-time visualisation. Our primary contribution is the development of an integration pipeline that connects XR headsets with the TIAGo robot via the Robot Operating System (ROS). Leveraging recent advancements in XR hardware, including improved spatial mapping and high-resolution passthrough, the system accurately transforms coordinate data between the XR environment and the robot's localised map. This enables real-time visualisation of critical information such as the robot's planned trajectory and pose. A pilot study was then conducted to validate this system architecture as a tool for HRI research, demonstrating that augmented visual cues can significantly improve spatial awareness, trust and user intuition. The findings support XR's role in fostering safer and more intuitive HRI. This research lays the foundation for future developments in XR-driven robotic interaction. The associated repository with the code, setup guide and pilot study data are available at: https://github.com/LCAS/XRVis_for_robots

Keywords: Human-Robot Interaction (HRI) · Mixed Reality (MR) · Extended Reality (XR) · Human-Robot Collaboration

1 Introduction

Human–Robot Interaction (HRI) presents a fundamental challenge: humans often struggle to interpret a robot's behaviours and intentions, leading to uncertainty, reduced trust, and limited usability. A lack of transparency in robotic actions can result in interactions that feel unnatural, ultimately impacting user confidence and overall system efficiency. Addressing this issue requires innovative solutions that enhance human perception and prediction of robotic behaviour.

Extended Reality (XR) technologies, encompassing Virtual Reality (VR), Augmented Reality (AR), and Mixed Reality (MR), offer a promising approach to improving HRI. By embedding contextual information directly into the user's field of view, XR provides intuitive visual cues that clarify robot intentions and

A. Cavalcanti et al. (Eds.): TAROS 2025, LNAI 16045, pp. 25–38, 2026.
https://doi.org/10.1007/978-3-032-01486-3_3

movements [21]. Prior research shows augmented cues enhance spatial awareness and improve safety perceptions [10], while visualising a robot's state and
trajectory within an XR interface enables users to engage more effectively in collaborative tasks with robots [6]. However, only in recent years have XR headsets
reached a level of fidelity suitable for MR applications, marking a technological inflection point. This advancement has been driven by the integration of
passthrough capabilities, enabling seamless blending of AR and VR within a
unified, immersive environment [5].

This paper presents a technical integration framework connecting an XR
headset with the TIAGo robot [17] via the Robot Operating System (ROS) [18].
This framework establishes a real-time communication pipeline, enabling seamless exchange of robot state information (including pose and planned trajectory)
within the XR environment, leveraging the ROS-TCP-Endpoint connector [3].
This integration of XR technologies aligns closely with Industry 5.0 principles,
emphasising a human-centric approach to manufacturing by combining advanced
technologies with human intelligence and creativity [1].

To evaluate the feasibility of this integration, a pilot study was conducted in
which participants interacted with the TIAGo robot while using the XR interface. The study assessed whether XR-based trajectory visualisations improved
spatial awareness, safety perception, comfort, and intuition in participants' interactions with the robot.

The paper is structured as follows: Sect. 2 reviews related work. Section 3
details the system architecture. Section 4 presents the pilot study methodology
and results. Finally, Sects. 5 and 6 discuss the findings and conclusions.

2   Background

The integration of XR technologies into HRI has significantly progressed, driven
by the need for safer, more intuitive, and responsive interaction methods. Recent
developments in real-time spatial mapping, gesture recognition, and multimodal feedback systems have facilitated natural interactions, enabling effective
user engagement with robots through immersive interfaces [10]. Virtual environments also provide controlled settings for evaluating robot navigation and
training, reducing physical testing risks and simulating complex real-world scenarios. Despite these advancements, effectively conveying a robot's intentions
and planned actions in real-time, particularly through XR interfaces exploring
nuanced user perceptions beyond task performance, remains an area of ongoing
research.

Advancements in XR hardware, e.g., Meta Quest 3 and Quest Pro, have significantly improved passthrough technology and spatial localisation. They enable
users to maintain physical awareness while engaging with high-resolution digital
overlays, enhancing AR/MR experiences [5]. Additionally, ergonomic improvements, advanced tracking, and controller-free interaction via hand tracking make
XR devices increasingly suitable for long-duration HRI applications [16].

Traditional HRI systems often rely on manual controllers or graphical user interfaces, limiting intuitive, fluid interactions. In contrast, XR provides embedded visual cues directly within the user's field of view. AR-based trajectory displays, for example, significantly improve spatial awareness and robot movement predictability [11, 14, 20]. Digital twins in XR environments further enhance robotic task validation by enabling realistic interaction with robot representations pre deployment [6, 13].

Communicating robot intent is critical in HRI, and XR offers a powerful modality for this. Gruenefeld et al. conducted a study on real-time AR visualisation of robot motion intent, comparing various visual cues (Path, Preview, Volume) to help users avoid robot shutdowns in shared workspaces [9]. Their work displayed how different visualisations influence user perception and head movements in collaborative tasks. Similarly, Cogurcu et al. investigated safety zone visualisations (e.g., virtual cage bars, transparent volumes) for virtual and physical robot arms, assessing their impact on depth and spatial awareness [7]. Their findings suggested that explicit visual cues like virtual cage bars could enhance spatial awareness and perceived safety. San Martin et al. explored multimodal mixed reality displays for hazard zones (audio, visual, audio-visual), evaluating user control over safety and overall user experience in a collaborative setting with a physical robot [19]. They indicated that multimodal displays could be highly preferred despite similar performance.

Despite the potential of XR in HRI, evidence quantifying its impact on user intuition, comfort, safety, and spatial awareness remains limited. Current studies predominantly offer qualitative insights, with very few systematically assessing XR's role in anticipating robot movements or behaviours. Ensuring accurate AR-based trajectory visualisation interpretation remains a significant challenge, particularly in dynamic/multi-robot scenarios where misinterpretation can lead to unintended errors [10].

User comfort is crucial for XR adoption in HRI, as extended headset use can lead to eye strain, dizziness, and cognitive fatigue in tasks requiring sustained attention to digital/physical environments [10]. Understanding these limitations is necessary in developing studies and future implementations to optimise interface designs and enhance usability by mitigating comfort issues.

Safety remains a critical consideration in XR-driven HRI, especially in high-risk contexts (e.g., industrial robotics, collaborative autonomous systems). Misinterpreting XR-presented safety indicators could lead to accidents or reduced trust. Thus, intuitive, real-time safety mechanisms aligning with natural human perception/response patterns are essential [12].

Existing studies demonstrate robust XR-robot integration and effective visualisation of robot states or safety zones. However, a comprehensive framework for enhancing robot transparency is lacking, particularly one leveraging real-time planned trajectory and current pose visualisations alongside a systematic breakdown of user experience metrics (intuition, comfort, safety, spatial awareness) in HRI. This work addresses this gap by developing and evaluating an XR framework for real-time visualisation of TIAGo's planned path and current pose, focusing on the system's abilities to understand its impact on these perception metrics and their interrelationships.

3 System Architecture and Implementation

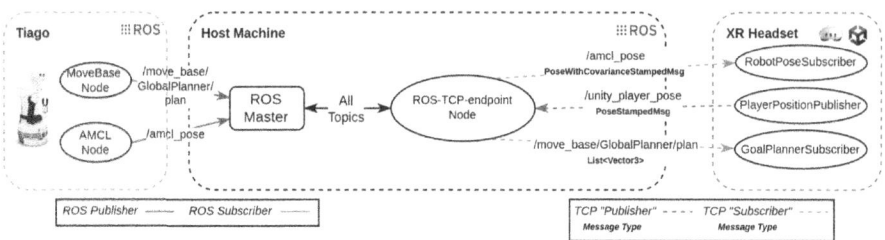

Fig. 1. Overall technical integration of the system, displaying how the ROS Master communicates with the XR Headset using the ROS-TCP connector.

System Architecture: The overall system comprises three core components: the XR headset (Quest 3), the robotic platform (TIAGo), and a host machine running the ROS Master, as illustrated in Fig. 1. The software framework employs ROS (Noetic), Unity (2022.3.41), and Unity's `ROS-TCP-Connector` package. ROS acts as the middleware for message exchange and control, while Unity provides the XR development environment. A dedicated ROS node, using the `ROS-TCP-Endpoint` package, establishes a TCP connection for bidirectional data flow between ROS and Unity. On the hardware side, the TIAGo robot was selected for its autonomous navigation capabilities (using `move_base` [15] and `amcl` [8]) and humanoid design [4,17], while the Quest 3 headset was chosen for its accurate localisation, high-quality visuals, and passthrough functionality [16].

Coordinate Transformations: Due to differing coordinate conventions (Unity uses a *left-handed* coordinate system, Fig. 2a, ROS uses a *right-handed* one, Fig. 2b) pose data must be transformed when communicating between the two

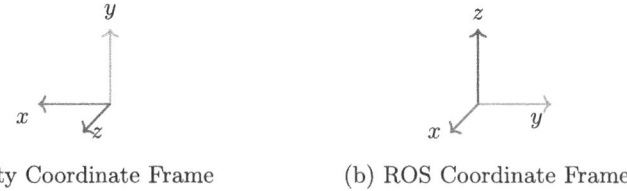

(a) Unity Coordinate Frame   (b) ROS Coordinate Frame

Fig. 2. Displaying the coordinate frames of Unity and ROS to illustrate the necessity for the transformations described below.

environments. These transformations are implemented within the Unity subscriber and publisher scripts to ensure consistency in spatial data representation.

Accurate spatial alignment between ROS and Unity environments necessitates specific coordinate transformations. For ROS to Unity, position data $(x, y, z) \mapsto (y, z, -x)$, and quaternions $(q_x, q_y, q_z, q_w) \mapsto (q_y, q_z, -q_x, -q_w)$. Conversely, for Unity to ROS, position data $(x, y, z) \mapsto (-z, x, y)$, while quaternions $(q_x, q_y, q_z, q_w) \mapsto (q_x, q_z, q_w, q_y)$. These transformations ensure consistent spatial data representation between the robot and the XR environment.

ROS Data Synchronisation: Real-time data exchange is fundamental for synchronising the virtual and physical environments, enabling accurate visual feedback. The key ROS topics enabling this, also seen in Fig. 1, facilitating the synchronisation between the XR environment and the robotic platform include:

- /amcl_pose: Pose of the TIAGo's position and orientation.
- /move_base/GlobalPlanner/: Vector list containing the robot's trajectory.
- /unity_user_pose: Pose of the XR headset's position and orientation.

Trajectory Visualisation: A visualisation was developed in Unity using a GameObject which is Unity's fundamental scene object used to represent entities such as characters, props, or markers. This visualisation was used to display TIAGo's planned path within the XR environment, allowing users to anticipate the robot's movements. For example, Fig. 4a shows the XR view of the trajectory, where each point in the path is represented bya visualised prefab, a reusable template of the GameObject that can easily be instantiated and destroyed.

System Calibration: The Quest 3 XR headset requires calibration to align its coordinate frame accurately with the ROS map frame. This involves first positioning the TIAGo robot at the ROS map origin (Fig. 3a). The user then stands directly over the robot and presses and holds the home button on the Quest 3 controller to reorient the headset (Fig. 3b). After calibration, the origin axes should be clearly visible through the headset at the robot's location, confirming correct alignment (Fig. 3c). Care must be taken to align the headset rotation precisely with the robot's centre to prevent cumulative angular errors as the robot moves away from the origin.

Deployment and Reproducibility: With calibration complete, the system is now prepared for deployment in real-time interactions, enabling users to observe TIAGo's trajectory and movements within their shared spatial environment. This calibration procedure must be performed each time the environment starts, but once done, it remains valid for the entire experiential session. To validate the system's effectiveness and gather insights for future refinements, a pilot study was conducted, serving as a crucial step in evaluating its utility as a tool for HRI research. To facilitate reproducibility and further research, the Unity project, including a guide for its requirements and setup, has been made publicly available [2]. This repository serves as a resource for researchers and developers to

  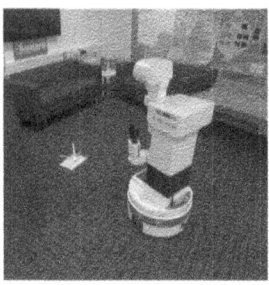

| (a) TIAGo at the ROS map origin. | (b) Headset aligned and origin. | (c) Headset view confirming origin axes. |

Fig. 3. Calibration process aligning the XR headset frame with the ROS map frame: (a) robot at origin, (b) headset alignment via controller, (c) visual confirmation of alignment.

replicate, extend, or build upon the integrated XR-robot system presented here: https://github.com/LCAS/XRVis_for_robots.

4 Pilot Study

The purpose of this pilot study is to test and validate the system proposed in Sect. 3 for HRI research. The study uses the system to evaluate the change in experience that users may have when interacting with a robot through added information, which in this case was limited to visualisation of the robot's trajectory. Metrics include safety, comfort, intuition, and spatial awareness, assessed despite identical robot behaviours apart from the XR system's added information. This study aims to refine the system and experimental design for future XR-based HRI research. The study was approved by the University of Lincoln Ethics Board (Reference: UoL2024_14564). Fourteen participants (students/academic staff) took part; 29% had little to no robotics experience, and 92% little to no prior XR experience. The following sections detail the study's experimental design and results, presenting qualitative and quantitative feedback.

4.1 Experimental Design

This section outlines the different experimental configurations participants engaged with and the specific scenarios designed to evaluate their experiences of the metrics within the pilot study.

Configurations: Participants completed all three configurations in random order to mitigate learning effects and order biases:

1. No XR: Participants **did not wear** the XR headset.

2. No Visual: Participants **wore** the XR headset **without** the robot's path visualised.
3. Path Visual: Participants **wore** the XR headset **with** robot's path visualised.

Scenarios: Two scenarios were prepared to understand the impact of these configurations on the user's experience of comfort, safety, intuition and spatial awareness:

1. **Standing Still:** Participants remain stationary as TIAGo traverses around them (see Fig. 4).

(a) Starting Movement   (b) Middle of Movement   (c) Reaching Goal

Fig. 4. First task scenario: TIAGo navigates around a stationary participant (represented by the Pepper robot). The large axes indicate the map origin (see Fig. 3). TIAGo's trajectory is visualised by a line extending from its base to the goal position (small axes). Mesh walls depict XR environment boundaries.

2. **Path Interception:** Participants deliberately stepped into TIAGo's path, enabling a more dynamic experience with the robot (see Fig. 5).

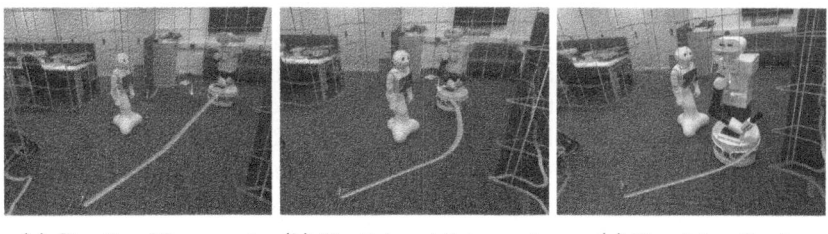

(a) Starting Movement   (b) Participant Intercepts   (c) Reaching Goal

Fig. 5. Second task scenario: the participant intercepts TIAGo's path, causing a dynamic trajectory adjustment from a straight line to a curved route. See Fig. 4 for visual context.

4.2   Results

Participants completed a questionnaire assessing metrics for `Comfort`, `Intuition`, and `Safety` using a 5-point Likert scale (1 = Very Uncomfortable/Unsafe/Unintuitive, 5 = Very Comfortable/Safe/Intuitive). Open-ended questions were also provided to obtain richer context and feedback. This facilitated the collection of both quantitative and qualitative data throughout the study.

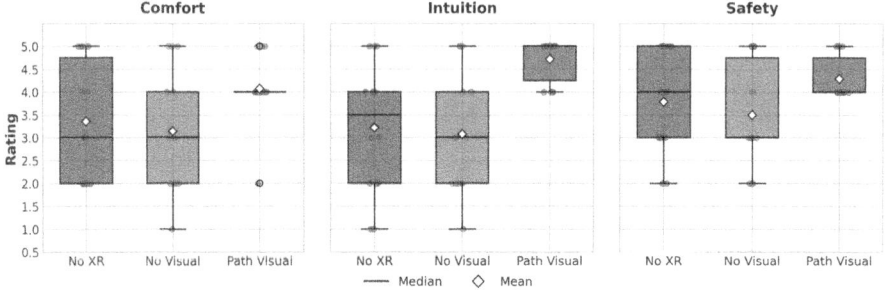

Fig. 6. Boxplots of the questionnaire ratings across the metrics and configurations ($n = 14$).

Quantitative Analysis. Figure 6 displays the median and interquartile range (IQR), as data non-normality was confirmed by the Shapiro-Wilk Test. Participants reported the highest scores across all metrics in the `Path Visual` configuration, indicating visual cues significantly enhanced user experience and confidence. Conversely, the absence of visuals in `No Visual`resulted in noticeably lower ratings, with `No XR` performing moderately better in Comfort and Safety but underperforming compared to the `Path Visual` configuration.

Due to the small sample size ($n = 14$) and non-normal data distribution, robust statistical methods were essential; therefore, bootstrap resampling, a non-parametric technique, was used. Bootstrapping repeatedly draws samples with replacement from the original data to generate new datasets, building empirical sampling distributions for statistics like means and correlations. This approach is valuable for smaller samples or if data distribution is unknown, as it does not rely on strong parametric assumptions, thus ensuring the reliability of our findings. We performed 5,000 bootstrap iterations to derive these confidence intervals used to conduct a Spearman correlation analysis with bootstrapped confidence intervals (Table 1) to examine relationships between metrics within each configuration. The resampling technique was also used to estimate confidence intervals for the differences in means between the configurations for each metric (Table 3), complementing the Wilcoxon Signed-Rank non-parametric test (Table 2).

The Spearman Correlation Analysis revealed that the `No XR` and `No Visual` configurations had significant positive correlations across all metrics, suggesting

Table 1. Spearman Correlation Coefficients across experimental configurations (Bootstrapping with 5000 resamples used to derive 95% confidence intervals of mean differences), with significance determined at the $\alpha = 0.05$ level.

Configuration	Metric Correlation	Coefficient (ρ)	95% CI	p-value	Significant
	Comfort vs. Intuition	0.81	[0.57, 0.92]	0.0004	*Yes*
No XR	Comfort vs. Safety	0.87	[0.57, 0.99]	<0.0001	*Yes*
	Intuition vs. Safety	0.73	[0.31, 0.94]	0.0028	*Yes*
	Comfort vs. Intuition	0.86	[0.60, 0.97]	0.0001	*Yes*
No Visual	Comfort vs. Safety	0.92	[0.78, 0.98]	<0.0001	*Yes*
	Intuition vs. Safety	0.85	[0.54, 0.97]	0.0001	*Yes*
	Comfort vs. Intuition	0.20	[-0.21, 0.56]	0.4977	No
Path Visual	Comfort vs. Safety	0.77	[0.42, 1.00]	0.0014	*Yes*
	Intuition vs. Safety	0.40	[0.18, 0.70]	0.1564	No

an interdependency among them. Conversely, the `Path Visual` configuration exhibited weaker and partially non-significant correlations. This could indicate that providing visualisations may affect the user's perception of these metrics.

Table 2. Wilcoxon Signed-Rank Test results to assess statistical significance of metrics across different configurations, determined at the $\alpha = 0.05$ level.

Metric	Configuration Comparison	W Statistic	p-value
	No Visual vs. Path Visual	10.0	**0.0364**
Comfort	No XR vs. Path Visual	12.0	*0.1049*
	No XR vs. No Visual	12.0	*0.3657*
	No Visual vs. Path Visual	0.0	**0.0030**
Intuition	No XR vs. Path Visual	3.5	**0.0047**
	No XR vs. No Visual	9.0	*0.7389*
	No Visual vs. Path Visual	4.0	**0.0126**
Safety	No XR vs. Path Visual	8.0	*0.0702*
	No XR vs. No Visual	4.0	*0.3363*

The Wilcoxon Signed-Rank Test was performed to investigate ratings across the three configurations (Table 2). Significant differences were observed between the `No Visual` and `Path Visual` configuration across all three metrics, indicating that participants found visualisation to have a meaningful impact on their experience. Intuition ratings also differed significantly between the `No XR` and `Path Visual` configurations. No other comparisons reached statistical significance. The bootstrap resampling analysis also supported these findings (Table 3).

Table 3. Bootstrap Analysis of Mean Differences (5000 resamples used to derive 95% confidence intervals of mean differences), with statistical significance determined at the $\alpha = 0.05$ level.

Metric	Configuration Comparison	Mean Difference	95% CI	Significant
	Path Visual vs. No Visual	0.93	[0.21, 1.64]	*Yes*
Comfort	Path Visual vs. No XR	0.71	[-0.07, 1.43]	No
	No XR vs. No Visual	0.21	[-0.71, 1.14]	No
	Path Visual vs. No Visual	1.64	[0.93, 2.36]	*Yes*
Intuition	Path Visual vs. No XR	1.50	[0.79, 2.29]	*Yes*
	No XR vs. No Visual	0.14	[-0.86, 1.14]	No
	Path Visual vs. No Visual	0.79	[0.14, 1.43]	*Yes*
Safety	Path Visual vs. No XR	0.50	[-0.07, 1.14]	No
	No XR vs. No Visual	0.29	[-0.50, 1.07]	No

Qualitative Analysis. Participants reported that XR visualisations enhanced their spatial awareness and improved their understanding of the robot's intentions, leading to more intuitive interactions and better anticipation of robot movements. Many noted increased confidence and reduced uncertainty when interpreting the robot's behaviour. However, several challenges were also identified, including physical discomfort (such as eye strain, headset weight, and early signs of motion sickness), reduced peripheral vision, and concerns about the accuracy of visual alignment. Occasional feelings of being unsafe were reported, particularly when the robot approached closely without visual aids. To improve the overall user experience, participants recommended refining the XR interface to enhance both comfort and visual accuracy.

4.3   Evaluation

The results revealed nuanced patterns regarding the effects of XR configurations on user experience. Bootstrapped Spearman correlation analysis suggested that the relationship between all the metrics varied depended on the experimental configuration. Strong inter-correlations identified in the No XR and No Visual configurations, weakened significantly in the Path Visual configuration. This indicates that visualisations changed how participants interpreted these metrics and could suggest that as more information is provided through visual feedback, users may develop a clearer intuition about the robot's behaviour without this necessarily translating that experience into a stronger sense of comfort or safety, and vice versa. The additional contextual information could shift the user's focus, potentially decoupling the metrics that were otherwise related; an interesting observation worth further study.

The Wilcoxon Signed-Rank Test results showed that visualisations led to statistically significant improvements across all the metrics compared to the No Visual configuration. Intuition was the only metric that improved significantly when comparing the visualisation condition directly to the baseline No XR configuration. This suggests that visualisations do improve participants' intuition, but not their experience of comfort or safety interacting with the robot.

Across all metrics, the IQR was reduced when participants used the No Visual configuration, indicating less variability but also suggesting a negative shift in user experience. This trend is further supported by qualitative reports describing discomfort from the headset itself, which likely impacted ratings independently of the visualisation itself.

Participants consistently reported improvements in their spatial awareness when visualisations were enabled, supporting the hypothesis that visual feedback helps clarify robot motion and intent. This aligns with the results from the bootstrap mean difference analysis, which confirmed significant improvements in Intuition when visualisations were used, regardless of whether the baseline comparison was the No Visual or the No XR configuration.

5 Discussion

This paper demonstrates the feasibility of integrating XR technologies with robotics for improved HRI transparency. The technical implementation successfully established a real-time communication pipeline between an XR headset and the TIAGo robot via ROS, enabling visualisations of the robot's planned trajectory and current pose, addressing key HRI perception and interaction challenges.

One of the primary successes of this technical development is the seamless communication facilitated by the ROS TCP Connector. Although not explicitly quantified, the absence of user concerns regarding latency or lagging of the visualisations in XR suggests that, for this system, latency was sufficiently low to support experimentation. The system accurately transformed coordinate data, allowing for intuitive visualisations that aligned well with the physical robot's movement, thereby enhancing user awareness of robot actions. These advancements contribute to making robot interactions more transparent.

The pilot study demonstrated XR-based trajectory visualisations' promising potential for improving robot behaviour understanding using visual cues for improved spatial awareness and intuition, aligning with prior work [7,19]. While participants were predominantly technical/academic, this pilot validates the system's capability for future HRI studies with a wider demographic. Within these limitations, we were able to observed statistically significant intuition improvement and consistent reports on improved spatial awareness with visualisations.

Interestingly, a bootstrapped Spearman correlation analysis revealed visualisations led to participants interpreting Comfort, Intuition, and Safety metrics more independently. This might suggest a cognitive decoupling effect due to additional contextual information from visual cues changing how users process experience. While visualisations significantly improved participants' intuition about robot behaviour, this did not proportionally increase their comfort or safety. This forms a new hypothesis: intuition strengthens independently of responses to comfort/safety as explicit robot intention information is received. This offers novel insight into XR-mediated HRI user perception, distinguishing our empirical contribution. Even with increased predictability, a moving robot's inherent proximity might still evoke feelings not directly correlating with a clearer understanding of its actions. Overall, these findings suggest XR has strong potential to increase transparency and interpretability in robotic systems by shifting how users perceive different aspects of their experience.

Despite these encouraging results, some challenges emerged. Most notably, physical discomfort from the headset and occasional visual misalignments due to poor localisation likely contributed to the reduced user experience in the headset-only condition without visual content. Future technical work should prioritise improving headset ergonomics and alignment accuracy, alongside enhancing visual cues (e.g., thought bubbles indicating robot actions) and interactive functionalities (e.g., "chasing", object manipulation). Integrating XR into diverse scenarios, such as games, could also provide insights into safety and dynamic interaction capabilities.

Methodologically, future studies could benefit from increasing participant sample size to strengthen result robustness and generalisability. Expanding the variety and complexity of interaction tasks could provide more practical and engaging scenarios, enhancing overall system usability assessment. Furthermore, refining questionnaire design to eliminate redundancy and reduce partial correlations among survey items would improve the clarity and reliability of user feedback. Finally, further investigations into the observed decoupling of user experience metrics under XR conditions could deepen our understanding of how visual feedback influences perceptions of comfort, safety, and intuitiveness as distinct yet interconnected components of HRI.

6   Conclusion

This paper presents a novel framework for HRI research, leveraging XR to improve robotic system transparency and interpretability. By establishing a real-time communication pipeline between an XR headset and the TIAGo robot via ROS, the system enables intuitive visualisation of robot behaviour, addressing a core HRI challenge.

The pilot study critically validated the proposed framework. XR-enhanced trajectory visualisation significantly improved participants' robot intent interpretation, spatial awareness, and clarity, with statistically significant gains in perceived intuitiveness validating XR's potential to enhance robot transparency and interpretability. Notably, a bootstrapped Spearman correlation analysis revealed that the presence of visualisations altered the relationships among Comfort, Intuition, and Safety metrics. However, physical discomfort from XR headset use negatively influenced overall user experience, reflected in reduced median scores and narrower interquartile ranges for the XR headset-only condition. Addressing these ergonomic concerns in future research is crucial for fully realising XR's benefits in practical HRI applications.

Although the system successfully facilitates real-time data exchange and accurate visualisation, challenges such as physical discomfort and occasional misalignments highlight areas for refinement. From a technical standpoint, future research should focus on optimising user comfort, improving spatial alignment, and expanding the application of XR-driven interaction methods to broader HRI contexts. Additionally, incorporating digital twins and refining XR-based safety features could further enhance the effectiveness of these systems.

Ultimately, this work contributes to the ongoing advancement of human-centred robotics, supporting the development of safer, more intuitive, and more transparent robotic systems by leveraging XR as a tool for increasing interpretability in HRI.

Acknowledgments. This work was supported by the Engineering and Physical Sciences Research Council and AgriFoRwArdS CDT [EP/S023917/1].

References

1. Adel, A.: Future of industry 5.0 in society: human-centric solutions, challenges and prospective research areas. J. Cloud Comput. **11** (2022). https://doi.org/10.1186/s13677-022-00314-5
2. Ali, O.: XRVis_for_robots, May 2025. https://doi.org/10.5281/zenodo.15565848
3. Allspaw, J., LeMasurier, G., Yanco, H.: Comparing performance between different implementations of ros for unity. In: 6th International Workshop on Virtual, Augmented, and Mixed-Reality for Human-Robot Interactions. Stockholm, SE, March 2023
4. Arunachalam, H., et al.: LCASTOR 2024 team description paper, July 2024, https://repository.lincoln.ac.uk/articles/report/LCASTOR_2024_Team_Description_Paper/25853875
5. Bailenson, J.N., et al.: Seeing the world through digital prisms: psychological implications of passthrough video usage in mixed reality. Tech. Mind Behav. (TMB) (2024). https://doi.org/10.1037/tmb0000129
6. Chandan, K., Kudalkar, V., Li, X., Zhang, S.: Arroch: augmented reality for robots collaborating with a human. In: 2021 IEEE International Conference on Robotics and Automation (ICRA), pp. 3787–3793 (2021). https://doi.org/10.1109/ICRA48506.2021.9561144
7. Cogurcu, Y., Douthwaite, J., Maddock, S.: A comparative study of safety zone visualisations for virtual and physical robot arms using augmented reality. Computers **12**, 75 (2023). https://doi.org/10.3390/computers12040075
8. Gerkey, B., Lu, D., Ferguson, M., Hoy, A.: amcl ros wiki (2020), http://wiki.ros.org/amcl
9. Gruenefeld, U., Prädel, L., Illing, J., Stratmann, T., Drolshagen, S., Pfingsthorn, M.: Mind the arm: realtime visualization of robot motion intent in head-mounted augmented reality. In: Proceedings of Mensch Und Computer 2020, MuC 2020, pp. 259–266. ACM, New York, NY, USA (2020). https://doi.org/10.1145/3404983.3405509
10. Grzeskowiak, F., Babel, M., Bruneau, J., Pettre, J.: Toward virtual reality-based evaluation of robot navigation among people. In: 2020 IEEE Conference on Virtual Reality and 3D User Interfaces (VR), pp. 766–774 (2020). https://doi.org/10.1109/VR46266.2020.00100

11. Han, Z., Parrillo, J., Wilkinson, A., Yanco, H.A., Williams, T.: Projecting robot navigation paths: Hardware and software for projected ar. In: 2022 17th ACM/IEEE International Conference on Human-Robot Interaction (HRI), pp. 623–628 (2022). https://doi.org/10.1109/HRI53351.2022.9889354
12. Hiroi, Y., Miyawaki, K., Ito, A.: Development of a play-tag robot with human–robot contact. Appl. Sci. **13**(23) (2023). https://doi.org/10.3390/app132312909
13. Kaarlela, T., Padrao, P., Pitkäaho, T., Pieskä, S., Bobadilla, L.: Digital twins utilizing xr-technology as robotic training tools. Machines **11**(1) (2023). https://doi.org/10.3390/machines11010013
14. Leutert, F., Schilling, K.: Projector-based augmented reality support for shop-floor programming of industrial robot milling operations. In: 2022 IEEE 17th International Conference on Control & Automation (ICCA), pp. 418–423 (2022). https://doi.org/10.1109/ICCA54724.2022.9831840
15. Marder-Eppstein, E., Lu, D., Ferguson, M., Hoy, A.: Move_base ros wiki. (2020), http://wiki.ros.org/move_base
16. Meta Platforms: Meta Quest 3 Mixed Reality Headset – Specifications and Features. Product Documentation (2023), https://www.meta.com/quest/
17. Pages, J., Marchionni, L., Ferro, F.: Tiago: the modular robot that adapts to different research needs. In: International workshop on robot modularity, IEEE/RSJ International Conference on Intelligent Robots and Systems (IROS), vol. 290 (2016)
18. Quigley, M., et al.: Ros: an open-source robot operating system. In: IEEE International Conference on Robotics and Automation Workshop on Open Source Software, vol. 3, p. 5. Kobe (2009)
19. San Martin, A., Kildal, J., Lazkano, E.: Mixed reality representation of hazard zones while collaborating with a robot: sense of control over own safety. Virtual Reality **29**(1), 43 (2025). https://doi.org/10.1007/s10055-025-01107-2
20. Walker, M., Hedayati, H., Lee, J., Szafir, D.: Communicating robot motion intent with augmented reality. In: Proceedings of the 2018 ACM/IEEE International Conference on Human-Robot Interaction, pp. 316–324. ACM. https://doi.org/10.1145/3171221.3171253
21. Walker, M., Phung, T., Chakraborti, T., Williams, T., Szafir, D.: Virtual, augmented, and mixed reality for human-robot interaction: a survey and virtual design element taxonomy **12**(4), 1–39. https://doi.org/10.1145/3597623

Sensing and Perception

Leveraging Stable Diffusion for Monocular Depth Estimation via Image Semantic Encoding

Jingming Xia, Guanqun Cao, Guang Ma, Yiben Luo, Qinzhao Li, and John Oyekan$^{(\boxtimes)}$

University of York, York, UK
john.oyekan@york.ac.uk

Abstract. Monocular depth estimation involves predicting depth from a single RGB image and plays a crucial role in applications such as autonomous driving, robotic navigation, 3D reconstruction, etc. Recent advancements in learning-based methods have significantly improved depth estimation performance. Generative models, particularly Stable Diffusion, have shown remarkable potential in recovering fine details and reconstructing missing regions through large-scale training on diverse datasets. However, models like CLIP, which rely on textual embeddings, face limitations in complex outdoor environments where rich context information is needed. These limitations reduce their effectiveness in such challenging scenarios. Here, we propose a novel image-based semantic embedding that extracts contextual information directly from visual features, significantly improving depth prediction in complex environments. Evaluated on the KITTI and Waymo datasets, our method achieves performance comparable to state-of-the-art models while addressing the shortcomings of CLIP embeddings in handling outdoor scenes. By leveraging visual semantics directly, our method demonstrates enhanced robustness and adaptability in depth estimation tasks, showcasing its potential for application to other visual perception tasks.

Keywords: Monocular depth estimation · Stable diffusion · Semantic embedding · Generative model

1 Introduction

Estimating the distance between objects and the camera is crucial for many vision-based applications, including autonomous driving, virtual reality, robotic navigation and 3D reconstruction. Traditional depth sensing techniques often rely on specialized hardware like LiDAR and depth cameras (e.g., Kinect [1]), which can either be expensive or impractical for certain applications. Monocular depth estimation, which predicts depth from a single RGB image, offers a cost-effective and versatile alternative, eliminating the need for multiple cameras or complex hardware [2,3]. However, the lack of geometric cues in 2D images makes monocular depth estimation an inherently ill-posed problem.

© The Author(s), under exclusive license to Springer Nature Switzerland AG 2026
A. Cavalcanti et al. (Eds.): TAROS 2025, LNAI 16045, pp. 41–53, 2026.
https://doi.org/10.1007/978-3-032-01486-3_5

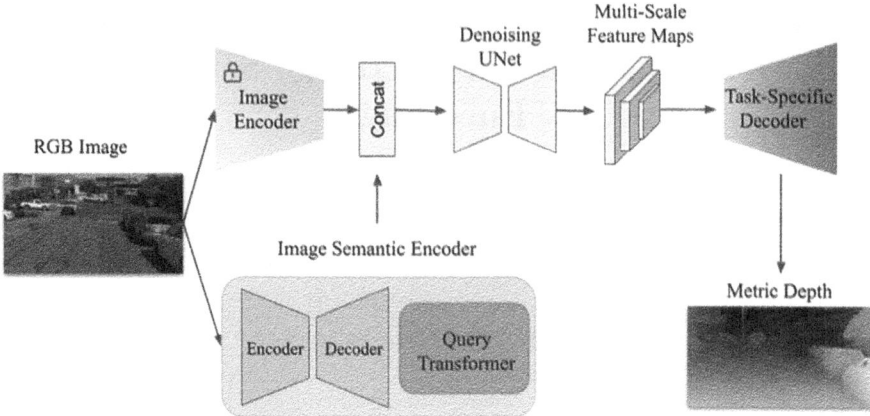

Fig. 1. The overview of our proposed framework: an input RGB image is processed through two parallel pathways, an Image Encoder and an Image Semantic Encoder. The Image Encoder extracts latent features, with its weights frozen during training and inference, while the Image Semantic Encoder produces a semantic vector that conditions these features. Both are integrated within a denoising UNet that fuses these modalities to produce multi-scale feature maps. Subsequently, a decoder upsamples these feature maps, generating the final metric depth map.

Deep learning has significantly advanced monocular depth estimation by learning complex mappings from images to depth maps. Eigen et al. pioneered this approach by introducing a convolutional neural network (CNN) that integrates global and local features [4]. Generative models have further enhanced depth estimation tasks by capturing more fine-grained details. As a result, researchers have increasingly shifted their focus toward leveraging generative models for depth prediction.

2 Related Work

Monocular depth estimation is pivotal in applications such as robotic navigation, autonomous driving, and virtual reality. Traditional methods based on geometric principles, like Scale-Invariant Feature Transform (SIFT) and Conditional Random Fields (CRFs), often struggle with feature matching and computational demands in complex scenes. The advent of deep learning has significantly enhanced accuracy and efficiency, establishing learning-based approaches as the mainstream in monocular depth estimation [2]. Among these, generative models have shown substantial potential in depth prediction tasks [5,7,8,16] including through the leveraging of generative models such as GANs [17]. Below we discuss related work that have made use of generative models in depth estimation.

2.1 Diffusion Models

Diffusion models have emerged as a promising approach, offering improved training stability by iteratively adding and removing Gaussian noise through a probabilistic process modeled as a Markov Chain [9]. This approach leverages the gradual introduction of noise during the forward process and its removal during the reverse process, allowing stable training dynamics [6]. Although diffusion models have a stable training process, they require a large number of iterations for training due to their multiple sampling steps. Furthermore, GANs like StyleGAN3 [18] produce high-fidelity output, however, they often face instability during training compared to diffusion models. To address high computational demands, Rombach et al. proposed applying diffusion processes in a lower-dimensional latent space, significantly enhancing efficiency without compromising accuracy [10]. Building on this approach, Zhao et al. introduced the Visual Perception with Diffusion (VPD) framework [11], extending Stable Diffusion to various vision tasks. VPD integrates a denoising UNet and a task-specific decoder, achieving state-of-the-art performance on the NYUv2 depth estimation dataset and the RefCOCO image segmentation dataset, demonstrating robust results across diverse tasks.

2.2 Semantic Embeddings in Diffusion Models

Semantic encoders play a important role in providing contextual information for depth estimation within diffusion models. The Contrastive Language-Image Pre-training (CLIP) model [12] has been leveraged to supply rich semantic guidance, as seen in models like VPD, which achieved leading results on the NYUv2 dataset. However, reliance on text prompts can be limiting in complex scenes where generating accurate textual descriptions is challenging. To overcome this limitation, researchers have explored alternatives. Prompt-free diffusion models [13] offer an alternative by removing the dependency on text inputs altogether, making them more robust in scenes where textual prompts may be unreliable or unnecessary. BLIP-2 [19] generates image captions to serve as scene descriptions, aiding semantic understanding. Some other studies treat semantic extraction as a classification task, utilizing pretrained image encoders like Vision Transformer (ViT) [20] alongside learnable embedding vectors. For more direct and flexible applications, models such as SeeCoder offer a promising solution by extracting semantic features directly from visual inputs without relying on text-image alignment or classification tasks. Similar to CLIP, SeeCoder is trained on large datasets like Laion2B-en [21] and COYO-700M [22], and its Transformer-based architecture enables it to capture rich, multi-scale semantic features, making it highly effective for various visual understanding tasks.

3   Methodology

As depicted in Fig. 1, our proposed framework consists of four main components: a latent feature extractor, a spatially enhanced semantic encoder (SeeCoder), a denoising UNet, and a task-specific decoder. The input RGB image is processed through two parallel pathways: the latent feature extractor compresses the image into a lower-dimensional space, while the semantic encoder generates high-level embeddings for contextual information. These features are integrated within the denoising UNet to reconstruct the depth map by combining visual and semantic cues. Finally, the task-specific decoder refines and upsamples the output to produce the final high-resolution depth map.

3.1   Latent Features Extraction

In our pipeline, we utilize the encoder of a pre-trained variational autoencoder (VAE) to convert the RGB image from pixel space into a lower-dimensional latent representation, as is commonly done in Stable Diffusion. Formally, the encoder maps the input image $x \in \mathbb{R}^{H \times W \times 3}$ to a compact latent vector z via $z = E_{\mathrm{VAE}}(x)$, by learning a probabilistic distribution for each image. This process captures essential features while discarding irrelevant details, reducing computational cost and easing convergence. The VAE encoder remains frozen during training to retain its learned features, allowing our model to leverage these compact and informative representations for the subsequent depth map generation.

3.2   Spatially Enhanced SeeCoder (Image Semantic Encoder)

Unlike traditional methods that extract semantics using CLIP, our proposed spatially enhanced SeeCoder embedding directly extracts semantic context from the visual features of the image. The input image is processed by the SWIN-L [23] backbone encoder of SeeCoder, converting it into multi-scale feature maps. These feature maps are then upsampled through the SeeCoder decoder to obtain refined multi-scale representations. Finally, a Query Transformer performs semantic extraction, generating 148 semantic vectors of dimension 768. Among them, 144 are local queries, each performing cross-attention with the decoder's multi-scale feature maps to focus on specific regions, while 4 are global queries that concatenate with the local queries and perform self-attention to capture overall context [24].

In order to enhance the model's spatial understanding, we add dilated convolution and spatial attention modules to each transformer layer in the SeeCoder backbone encoder. The spatial attention module helps the model focus on important regions by generating an attention map based on the input features. Specifically, the attention map is calculated by applying average pooling and max pooling along the channel dimension, concatenating the results, and passing them through a convolution layer.

During training, we utilize the pretrained SeeCoder, freezing its weight parameters to retain the learned representations, and only update the weights for the newly added dilated convolution and spatial attention modules.

3.3   Denoising UNet

The denoising UNet is a pivotal component in our framework, responsible for reconstructing the depth map from the noisy latent representations generated during the diffusion process. The UNet architecture comprises an encoder and a decoder connected through skip connections, enabling the network to capture both global context and fine-grained details effectively.

In the encoder path, the UNet progressively downsamples the input latent features z_t at each time step t, extracting hierarchical representations at multiple scales. Conversely, the decoder path upsamples these features to reconstruct the spatial dimensions, with skip connections merging corresponding encoder and decoder features. This design preserves essential information across different resolutions, facilitating accurate depth estimation.

In order to integrate semantic guidance, the denoising UNet incorporates cross-attention mechanisms that leverage the semantic embeddings s extracted by the spatially enhanced SeeCoder. At each resolution level, cross-attention layers enable the UNet to focus on relevant semantic information, enhancing the feature representations used for denoising. Specifically, the cross-attention operation is applied during both the upsampling and downsampling stages, allowing the model to align the latent features with the semantic context at multiple scales, improving the coherence and accuracy of the generated depth maps.

The UNet is trained to predict the noise ϵ added to the latent representation z_0 during the forward diffusion process. The training objective minimizes the mean squared error between the predicted noise $\epsilon_\theta(z_t, t, s)$ and the actual noise ϵ, formulated as:

$$L_{\mathrm{DM}} = \mathbb{E}_{z_0, \epsilon \sim \mathcal{N}(0,1), t} \left[\| \epsilon - \epsilon_\theta \left(z_t, t, s \right) \|_2^2 \right], \tag{1}$$

where z_t is obtained by the forward diffusion process defined as:

$$z_t = \sqrt{\bar{\alpha}_t} z_0 + \sqrt{1 - \bar{\alpha}_t} \epsilon, \tag{2}$$

with $\bar{\alpha}_t$ representing the accumulated product of the noise schedule parameters.

By optimizing this loss function, the denoising UNet learns to iteratively remove noise from the latent representations, progressively refining the depth map estimation. The incorporation of semantic embeddings via cross-attention enhances the denoising process, allowing the model to utilize high-level semantic cues alongside low-level visual features. This synergy between the latent features and semantic context enables our model to produce detailed and accurate metric depth maps, even in complex scenes.

During training, our denoising UNet is trained from scratch without relying on pre-trained weights. This allows the model to learn task-specific features tailored to monocular depth estimation directly from the data. By optimizing the entire network, the model learns to effectively utilize both the latent visual features and the high-level semantic cues to produce accurate depth maps. This end-to-end training approach ensures that all components of the model are finely tuned to the specific requirements of depth estimation, leading to better performance in complex scenes.

3.4 Task-Specific Decoder

In our task, the decoder serves to generate the final depth map. The decoder architecture comprises three primary components: a deconvolution module, a convolution module, and an upsampling module. It processes multi-scale feature maps as input, progressively refining and upsampling these features through deconvolution and convolution operations. For upsampling, we use bilinear interpolation with a scale factor of 2, ensuring smooth transitions between different resolutions. The final output is a high-resolution metric depth map, effectively capturing detailed spatial information from the input feature representations. The combination of deconvolution and bilinear upsampling enables efficient feature refinement and enhances spatial resolution without significantly increasing computational complexity.

4 Experiments

We conducted experiments across two datasets as mentioned below KITTI: has been used as a benchmark for autonomous driving and computer vision research. It features real-world driving scenes from urban and rural areas [14].

4.1 Outdoor Datasets

KITTI. As a benchmark for autonomous driving and computer vision research, KITTI featuring real-world driving scenes from urban and rural areas. We use the data split of Eigen et al., specifically, using 23,158 annotated depth map and RGB image pairs for training, with another 697 RGBD image pairs reserved for validation.

Waymo. In order to conduct more comprehensive testing across different environments, we employed the Waymo Open Dataset. This dataset includes a vast collection of scenes from various cities, suburban areas, and rural roads across the United States, offering a broader range of weather conditions (e.g., sunny, rainy, foggy) and lighting conditions (e.g., daytime, dusk, nighttime) [15]. The Waymo Open Dataset provides high-resolution sensor data from multiple cameras and LiDAR, along with accurate ground truth annotations. This diversity allows us to evaluate our model's performance under varied and challenging scenarios, assessing its robustness and generalization capabilities in real-world conditions.

4.2 Evaluation Metric

In this study, three experiments were conducted to evaluate the effectiveness and generalization ability of the proposed method. The model was assessed using a quantitative analysis approach by comparing predicted depth maps to ground truth depth maps in the validation set. In the process of comparing differences, we only perform the calculations on valid depth values in the ground truth, which are the non-zero regions. To evaluate the proportion of predictions within different accuracy ranges, we employ the metrics δ_1, δ_2, and δ_3, which represent the percentage of predictions where the relative error is within 1.25, 1.25^2, and 1.25^3 times the actual depth values, respectively. Additionally, other metrics such as absolute relative error (Abs Rel), squared relative error (Sq Rel), and root mean square error (RMSE) are also utilized to provide a comprehensive assessment of the model's performance. Collectively, these metrics offer insights into both the accuracy and robustness of the depth predictions, ensuring a thorough analysis of the proposed method's effectiveness.

4.3   Training and Evaluation on KITTI

Our model was primarily trained on the KITTI dataset, where we trained various embedding schemes for approximately 20 epochs each. We recorded the best performance on the validation set for each scheme (Fig. 2).

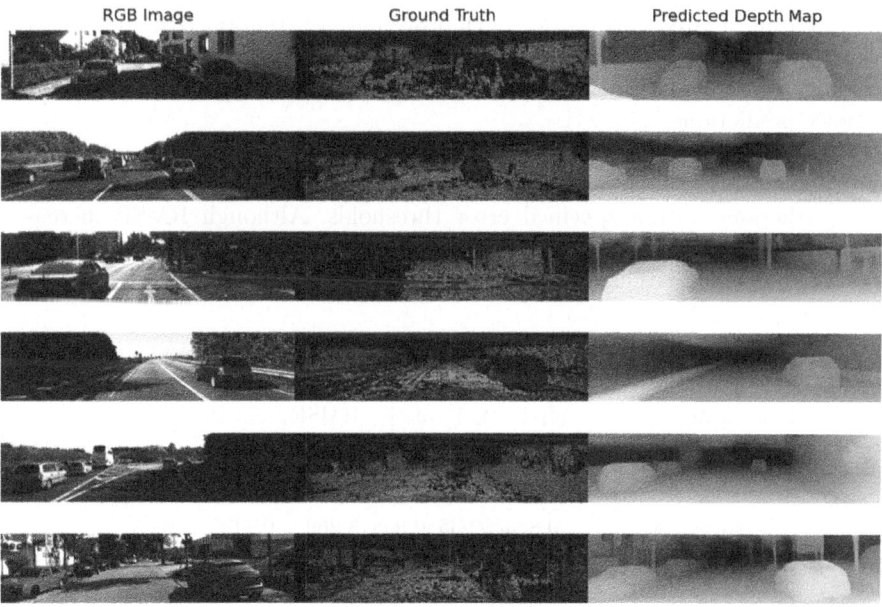

Fig. 2. The visualization of selected samples from the KITTI dataset. Several samples are shown, with each column from left to right representing the RGB image, the sparse ground truth depth map after visualization processing, and the dense depth map predicted by our model.

Data Augmentation and Preprocessing. The preprocessing approach employed is consistent with that used in VPD. During training, various data augmentation techniques are applied to the RGB images from the KITTI dataset. These augmentations include random horizontal flipping, random cropping, adjustments to brightness and contrast, gamma correction, and random modifications to hue, saturation, and brightness. The goal of these augmentations is to enhance the model's robustness across different scenes and lighting conditions. During evaluation, the original resolution of 1242×375 depth maps are split into left and right segments for separate prediction. Each segment is then subjected to horizontal flipping augmentation. Finally, the two segments are weighted and fused to generate the final depth map.

Implementation Details. Our model is implemented using PyTorch [25] and was trained end-to-end. We used AdamW as the optimizer with β_0 values of 0.9 and 0.999, a weight decay of 0.1. The model was trained on the KITTI dataset using eight NVIDIA L20 GPUs over approximately 13 h, with a batch size of 3 per GPU, resulting in a total batch size of 24. We employed a one-cycle training strategy, starting with an initial learning rate of 4e-5, gradually increasing the learning rate to a maximum of 6e-4, and then decreasing it throughout the iterations.

As shown in Table 1, we evaluated four different embedding schemes. Using SeeCoder alone yielded satisfactory performance across all metrics. However, incorporating dilated convolutions (DC) or spatial attention (SA) individually led to increased errors, indicating training instability. Specifically, δ metrics declined, and RMSE, Abs Rel, and Sq Rel increased, suggesting less accurate distance predictions.

Combining both DC and SA with SeeCoder resulted in slight performance improvements. Notably, δ_1 and δ_2 metrics improved, indicating more accurate predictions within specified error thresholds. Although RMSE increased marginally, the overall accuracy was enhanced, demonstrating that the combined approach managed larger errors more effectively.

Table 1. Performance comparison of different embedding combination.

Embeddings	$\delta_1 \uparrow$	$\delta_2 \uparrow$	$\delta_3 \uparrow$	RMSE$\downarrow$	Abs Rel$\downarrow$	Sq Rel$\downarrow$
SeeCoder	0.973	0.996	0.999	2.216	0.054	0.164
SeeCoder+DC	0.876	0.922	0.950	3.296	0.143	1.155
SeeCoder+SA	0.883	0.935	0.968	3.269	0.112	0.757
SeeCoder+DC+SA	**0.974**	**0.997**	**0.999**	**2.179**	**0.052**	**0.162**

Ablation Study. We conducted an ablation study to assess the impact of spatial enhancement modules on model performance, using SeeCoder as the baseline. Integrating dilated convolutions (DC) alone decreased prediction accuracy, with δ_1 dropping from 0.973 to 0.876 and Sq Rel increasing sixfold. Similarly, adding spatial attention (SA) alone did not improve performance significantly but was less detrimental than DC alone.

Interestingly, combining both DC and SA led to improved performance over the baseline. The δ_1 metric increased to 0.974, and RMSE decreased from 2.216

to 2.179, indicating enhanced accuracy. These results suggest that the combined effect of DC and SA benefits the model more than either module individually. This may be because their combination compensates for each other's shortcomings; for instance, DC might introduce excessive contextual information, while SA may struggle to fully capture both global and local features.

4.4   Evaluation on Waymo

Testing Details. During the testing process on the Waymo open dataset, we used the model weights that were trained on the KITTI dataset. We selectively chose depth maps from three distinct scene types for our testing. One of these scenes is a typical daytime outdoor scenarios similar to KITTI, serving as a reference for evaluating the model's generalization capability across different environments. The other two scenes are rainy and nighttime environments, each with nearly 600 test samples from the FRONT view. To maintain consistency with the KITTI training data, we first resized the resolution of 1920 × 1280 images proportionally. For RGB images, bilinear interpolation was used to smooth and preserve details, while for depth maps, nearest-neighbor interpolation was applied to maintain the accuracy of object edges. Consistent with the approach used for KITTI samples, we applied the Garg Crop [26] evaluation mask to minimize the influence of irrelevant information, such as the sky and the front of the vehicle, on the model's performance. Finally, performance metrics were calculated for each scene to observe the model's accuracy variation across different scenarios, and depth map visualizations were conducted to assess the model's performance.

Fig. 3. The visualization of model prediction differences across three different scenarios: normal daylight conditions, rainy weather, and nighttime.

Visualization Analysis. As illustrated in Fig. 3, the predicted dense depth maps across the three different scenes accurately capture the edges and contours of objects. Even in areas where visual cues are less prominent, such as poorly lit regions in nighttime scenes, our method successfully identifies and completes objects. However, we also observed some potential challenges for accurate predictions. For instance, in Normal conditions, predictions of the sky and distant forests appear blurred, and the model struggles to precisely delineate the edges of these elements. This issue becomes more frequent in Rainy and Nighttime environments. In Rainy conditions, water droplets on the camera lens affect the accuracy of local predictions, while in nighttime, large dark regions without illumination lead to prediction failures. Such textureless, large color blocks pose increased difficulty for the model's regional predictions, ultimately contributing to higher error rates (Table 2).

Table 2. Performance comparison among different scenarios.

Scenes	$\delta_1 \uparrow$	$\delta_2 \uparrow$	$\delta_3 \uparrow$	RMSE↓	Abs Rel↓
Normal	0.044	0.312	0.893	5.061	0.389
Rainy	0.012	0.198	0.862	4.600	0.415
Night	0.017	0.150	0.807	5.678	0.428

4.5   Comparison of Related Models

In the field of monocular depth estimation, we compared our model's performance with several state-of-the-art methods on the KITTI Eigen split test set to comprehensively evaluate its effectiveness. The selected models include early CNN-based approaches, self-supervised learning methods, and recent transformer-based architectures. The metrics reported represent the best results cited in their respective papers. For example, Eigen et al. [4] introduced one of the pioneering CNN architectures for monocular depth estimation, establishing a baseline for subsequent research. Their method utilized a multi-scale network to predict depth. In [16], Monodepth2 advanced the field with a self-supervised learning approach that leverages photometric consistency between stereo image pairs, significantly reducing the reliance on ground truth depth data and enhancing its practicality for real-world applications.

Recent transformer-based models have further pushed the boundaries of depth estimation performance. For example, Tu et al. [27], introduced adaptive binning, allowing the model to allocate depth prediction resources more efficiently across different depth ranges. DPT [28] leveraged vision transformers to capture global context, enhancing the model's understanding of complex scenes. ZoeDepth [29], particularly the ZoeDepth-M12-K version used in our comparison, focused on zero-shot generalization, demonstrating strong performance across various datasets without fine-tuning.

In the comparison with existing models, our model outperforms previous depth estimation methods across all evaluation metrics. This indicates that our approach, leveraging large-scale training and stable diffusion mechanisms, offers

Table 3. Performance comparison of different models on KITTI validation set.

Models	$\delta_1 \uparrow$	$\delta_2 \uparrow$	$\delta_3 \uparrow$	RMSE↓	Abs Rel↓	Sq Rel↓
Eigen et al.	0.702	0.898	0.967	6.307	0.203	1.517
Monodepth2	0.879	0.961	0.982	4.701	0.115	0.882
AdaBins	0.964	0.995	0.999	2.360	0.058	0.190
DPT	0.959	0.995	0.996	2.573	0.062	–
ZoeDepth	0.970	0.996	0.999	2.440	0.054	0.189
Ours	**0.974**	**0.997**	**0.999**	2.179	**0.052**	**0.162**

a significant advantage in capturing depth information from scenes. For instance, early CNN models had limitations in accuracy, while self-supervised models like Monodepth2, though reducing reliance on labeled data, still struggled to maintain high precision in certain complex scenarios. In contrast, recent transformer-based models such as AdaBins and DPT improved depth estimation by introducing adaptive binning and global context capturing. However, our model further enhances these performances, particularly in accurate estimation across different depth ranges and better global scene understanding, demonstrating its strong adaptability and generalization capabilities. By successfully repurposing SeeCoder for depth estimation, our model not only achieves near state-of-the-art performance on benchmark datasets but also shows potential for broader applications in future vision tasks (Table 3).

5   Conclusion and Future Work

We proposed a novel approach that integrates SeeCoder, an image-based semantic encoder, along with a spatial enhancement module into the Stable Diffusion framework for monocular depth estimation. By directly extracting semantic features from images and enhancing spatial features, our method addresses the limitations of text-based prompts in complex outdoor scenarios thereby improving depth estimation accuracy. Experiments on KITTI and Waymo datasets show that our approach achieves competitive performance when compared with state of the art techniques. Furthermore, spatially enhanced SeeCoder demonstrates robustness across conditions, including rain and night, suggesting that large-scale pre-trained models can be adapted to complex vision tasks. However, our model struggles with predicting depth in textureless regions and does not yet surpass current state-of-the-art models [8]. Future work includes improving SeeCoder's semantic accuracy beyond spatial enhancement, enhancing robustness to noise in textureless regions without cropping and extending our approach to other visual perception tasks to validate generalizability.

Acknowledgement. We would like to acknowledge the support of the Engineering and Physical Sciences Research Council (EPSRC) funding: DigiCORTEX

(EP/W014688/1), NanoMan (EP/V055089/1) and Launchpad Network+ Researcher in Residence scheme [grant numbers EP/W037009/1, EP/X528493/1].

References

1. Han, J., Shao, L., Xu, D., Shotton, J.: Enhanced computer vision with microsoft kinect sensor: a review. IEEE Trans. Cybern. **43**(5), 1318–1334 (2013)
2. Ming, Y., Meng, X., Fan, C., Yu, H.: Deep learning for monocular depth estimation: a Review. Neurocomputing **438**, 14–33 (2021)
3. Kumar, C.S., Bhandarkar, S.M., Prasad, M.: Monocular depth prediction using generative adversarial networks. In: Proceedings of the IEEE Conference on Computer Vision and Pattern Recognition Workshops, pp. 300–308 (2018)
4. Eigen, D., Puhrsch, C., Fergus, R.: Depth map prediction from a single image using a multi-scale deep network. In: Proceedings of the 27th International Conference on Neural Information Processing Systems (NIPS), vol. 2, pp. 2366–2374 (2014)
5. Jung, H., Kim, Y., Oh, C., Sohn, K.: Depth prediction from a single image with conditional adversarial networks. In: Proceedings of the IEEE International Conference on Image Processing (ICIP), Beijing, pp. 1717–1721 (2017)
6. Dhariwal, P., Nichol, A.: Diffusion models beat GANs on image synthesis. In: Proceedings of the 35th International Conference on Neural Information Processing Systems (NIPS), vol. 1, Article No. 672, pp. 8780–8794 (2024)
7. Saxena, S., Kar, A., Norouzi, M., Fleet, D.J.: Monocular depth estimation using diffusion models. arXiv preprint arXiv:2302.14816 (2023)
8. Patni, S., Agarwal, A., Arora, C.: ECoDepth: effective conditioning of diffusion models for monocular depth estimation. In: Proceedings of the IEEE/CVF Conference on Computer Vision and Pattern Recognition (CVPR), pp. 28285–28295 (2024)
9. Ho, J., Jain, A., Abbeel, P.: Denoising diffusion probabilistic models. In: Proceedings of the 34th International Conference on Neural Information Processing Systems (NIPS), vol. 1, Article No. 574, pp. 6840–6851 (2020)
10. Rombach, R., Blattmann, A., Lorenz, D., Esser, P., Ommer, B.: High-Resolution image synthesis with latent diffusion models. In: Proceedings of the IEEE/CVF Conference on Computer Vision and Pattern Recognition (CVPR), pp. 10684–10694 (2022)
11. Zhao, W., Yongming, R., Liu, Z., Liu, B., Zhou, J., Lu, J.: Unleashing text-to-image diffusion models for visual perception. In: Proceedings of the IEEE/CVF International Conference on Computer Vision, pp. 5729–5739 (2023)
12. Radford, A., et al.: Learning transferable visual models from natural language supervision. In: International Conference on Machine Learning, pp. 8748–8763. PMLR (2021)
13. Xu, X., Guo, J., Wang, Z., Huang, G., Essa, I., Shi, H.: Prompt-free diffusion: taking "text" out of text-to-image diffusion models. In: Proceedings of the IEEE/CVF Conference on Computer Vision and Pattern Recognition, pp. 8682–8692 (2024)
14. Geiger, A., Lenz, P., Stiller, C., Urtasun, R.: Vision meets robotics: the KITTI dataset. Int. J. Robot. Res. **32**(11), 1231–1237 (2013)
15. Sun, P., et al.: Scalability in perception for autonomous driving: waymo open dataset. In: Proceedings of the IEEE/CVF Conference on Computer Vision and Pattern Recognition, pp. 2446–2454 (2020)

16. Godard, C., Mac Aodha, O., Firman, M., Brostow, G.J.: Digging into self-supervised monocular depth prediction. In: Proceedings of the IEEE/CVF International Conference on Computer Vision (ICCV), p. 2019 (2019)
17. Goodfellow, I., et al.: Generative adversarial nets. In: Advances in Neural Information Processing Systems 27 (NIPS), pp. 2672–2680 (2014)
18. Karras, T., Aittala, M., Laine, S., Härkönen, E., Hellsten, J., Lehtinen, J., Aila, T.: Alias-free generative adversarial networks. In: Proceedings of the 35th International Conference on Neural Information Processing Systems (NeurIPS) (2021)
19. Li, J., Li, D., Savarese, S., Hoi, S.: BLIP-2: bootstrapping language-image pre-training with frozen image encoders and large language models. In: Proceedings of the 40th International Conference on Machine Learning (ICML), vol. 2023, Article No. 814, pp. 19730–19742 (2023)
20. A. Dosovitskiy et al.: An image is worth 16x16 words: transformers for image recognition at scale. arXiv preprint arXiv:2010.11929 (2021)
21. C. Schuhmann et al.: Laion-400m: open dataset of CLIP-filtered 400 million image-text pairs. arXiv preprint arXiv:2111.02114 (2021)
22. Byeon, M., Park, B., Kim, H., Lee, S., Baek, W., Kim, S.: Coyo-700 m: image-text pair dataset. https://github.com/kakaobrain/coyo-dataset, Accessed 26 Aug 2024 (2022)
23. Liu, Z., et al.: Swin transformer: hierarchical vision transformer using shifted windows. In: Proceedings of the IEEE/CVF International Conference on Computer Vision, pp. 9992–10002 (2021)
24. Vaswani, A., et al.: Attention is all you need. In: Advances in Neural Information Processing Systems (NIPS), pp. 6000–6010 (2017)
25. Paszke, A., et al.: PyTorch: an imperative style, high-performance deep learning library. In: Advances in Neural Information Processing Systems (NeurIPS) (2019)
26. Garg, R., Kumar, B.G.V., Carneiro, G., Reid, I.: Unsupervised CNN for single view depth estimation: geometry to the rescue. In: European Conference on Computer Vision (ECCV), pp. 740–756 (2016)
27. Z. Tu, X. Chen, P. Ren, and Y. Wang: AdaBin: Improving Binary Neural Networks with Adaptive Binary Sets. In: Proceedings of European Conference on Computer Vision (ECCV), Cham, vol. 13671, pp. 379–395 (2022)
28. Ranftl, R., Bochkovskiy, A., Koltun, V.: Vision transformers for dense prediction. In: Proceedings of the IEEE/CVF International Conference on Computer Vision, pp. 12179–12188 (2021)
29. Bhat, S.F., Birkl, R., Wofk, D., Wonka, P., Müller, M.: ZoeDepth: zero-shot transfer by combining relative and metric depth. arXiv preprint arXiv:2302.12288 (2023)

Marker Density of Optical Tactile Sensor for Moving Object Tracking

Bhoomika Gandhi$^{(\boxtimes)}$ ⓘ and Sanja Dogramadzi ⓘ

the University of Sheffield, England, UK
{bgandhi1,s.dogramadzi}@sheffield.ac.uk

Abstract. Soft tactile sensors have the ability to infer more physical properties of an object relative to classical optical motion-capture systems. Three marker densities in a tactile sensor array (the Motion Capture Pillow, MCP) were evaluated for tracking two rotary motions using a weighted mannequin head. The Kanade–Lucas–Tomasi algorithm was employed to track head movements using three silicone sheets, each embedded with different marker spacings (5, 10, and 15 mm). The averaged Spearman's correlation slightly changed from 0.80 (for 10 mm spacing) to 0.67 (for 5 mm spacing) for pitch motion and from 0.68 (for 10 mm spacing) to 0.59 (for 5 mm spacing) for roll motion of the mannequin head with respect to the MCP's frame. A correlation of +1.0 being the strongest positive correlation and 0.0 being weak correlation. The MAE reduced by 12.9% from matrix with 10 mm spacing to 5 mm spacing for pitch motion, and by 2.9% for roll motion. This established a foundation for further tuning the sensor using a higher density of the sensing matrix. The relatively sparsely dense sensor matrix with 15 mm spacing had minimal impact on the tracking performance of the sensor. Sources of noise were narrowed down to hysteresis, and boundary conditions. These results demonstrated the influence of marker density on the object tracking abilities of an optical soft tactile sensor, and established a basis for future optimisation.

Keywords: Motion capture · Tactile sensing · Head tracking · Spatial density

1 Introduction

1.1 Background and Aim

Motion Capture via Tactile Sensing. Tactile sensing in motion capture enables contact interactions with objects to obtain the physical properties, by mimicking features from the human sense of touch. This is widely used in robotics for tasks such as object manipulation, grasping, and shape recognition [17]. It does not rely on a field of view (FOV) of the target object, as seen in classical motion capture systems (e.g. VICON™), which are susceptible to errors from occlusions for such applications. Consequently, tactile sensing can provide more information about the physical properties of an object than a non-contact optical

A. Cavalcanti et al. (Eds.): TAROS 2025, LNAI 16045, pp. 54–67, 2026.
https://doi.org/10.1007/978-3-032-01486-3_6

motion capture system can, making them a valuable tool in the field of robotics and augmented/virtual reality.

Case Study. The Motion Capture Pillow (MCP) [5,7] is an optical tactile sensor that is being developed to track the head movements of patients during radiotherapy for brain and head and neck (H&N) cancer treatments using the Gamma Knife® by Elekta or Linear Accelerators (LINACs). These technologies often rely on the use of thermoplastic masks for patient immobilisation which is known to cause claustrophobia among patients, and negatively affects the accuracy of the radiotherapy treatment due to patient movement arising from discomfort [6]. The sensor can improve the accuracy of the treatments by providing real-time tracking of the patient's head, while improving the potential for patient comfort.

It uses a flexible deformable silicone sheet with an array of markers embedded underneath. The deformations of these markers indicate the motion of the head in contact with the MCP via a tracking algorithm. The organisation and orientation of these markers affects the accuracy of the tracking. This paper aims to investigate the effect of varying the size of the array (i.e. spacings between the markers) and builds on using the MCP with a fibrescope with greyscale image processing and Kanade-Lucas Tomasi (KLT) tracking algorithm, as was established in our previous paper [5].

1.2   Related Work

Motion capture can be achieved via contact or non-contact sensing techniques. Non-contact sensing typically uses cameras, or a marker based tracking with infrared (IR) cameras for motion tracking. Contact-based sensing methods as for example in slip detection with robotic grippers, capacitive or optical tactile sensors are commonly used for object manipulation.

Non-Contact Optical Sensing. Marker-based and markerless motion capture methods are widely used for applications in healthcare, robotics, entertainment, sports, and industrial safety measures. Although marker-based tracking provides higher accuracy over markerless systems [3,11,16], some recent developments with 3D vision cameras and deep learning algorithms for object tracking have improved the tracking accuracy of markerless vision systems to enable submillimeter accuracy. These systems overcome the limitations of marker-based tracking arising from marker occlusions since at least 4 markers are required at a point to obtain 6 DOF. An example of the markerless vision system includes markerless respiratory motion tracking for radiotherapy that used 4D deformation estimation with a mean reconstruction accuracy of ±0.23 mm [2]. Markerless tracking has also been used in the context of MRI and PET scans using an fiber-optic camera called Tracoline 2.0 which had an average RMS motion of 5.27 mm, with a resolution of ±0.5 mm to track respiratory movements [19].

Another commercialised approach, AlignRT™ by VisionRT [1,24] uses a markerless approach to track surface deformations using multiple ceiling mounted cameras and provides submillimeter accuracy in 3D translational movements. Occlusion still remains an issue requiring further development in these systems, along with brightness constancy issues with markerless systems [12,13,15,28].

Soft Tactile Sensing. Tactile sensing uses contact, which removes the restrictions related to occlusions and brightness constancy. These sensors include a range of sensors which may be capacitive, resistive, piezoelectric, thermoresistive, magnetic, or optical. Furthermore, soft tactile sensing enables non-linear deformations when interacting with objects that enables it to detect a wider range of properties such as force, object shape, slip, texture, and so on [9].

E-skins are soft flexible sensors that have been used in a variety of tactile sensing applications. For example, the eCushion [26] was designed for sitting posture monitoring. It used piezoelectric polymers to create a fabric with a 16×16 sensing grid, and obtained an accuracy of 85.9% using Naive Bayes Network based on Dynamic Time Warping used for classification. Due to the proximity of its sensing points and their structure, it suffered from inconsistency in calibration, lacked scalability due to variance in resistivity, and suffered from crosstalk. A force-sensing scalable tactile glove [20] overcame the issue of crosstalk using a custom signal isolation circuit. It was designed for object detection of a range of everyday use objects. It used conductive threads to create a knitted glove, embedded with an array of 548 piezoresistive sensors with the ability to detect 30 mN to 0.5 N each. It provided a classification accuracy of 89.4%using a ResNet-18-based architecture. A biomimetic tactile sensor, BioTAC [23], mimics the features of the human sense of touch including magnitude and direction of forces, and localising them. It used an array of electrodes embedded in a deformable finger shaped silicone elastomer. The elastomer used was Dragon Skin, along with a conductive fluid, i.e. NaCl. The electrodes were spaced 2 mm apart in a 4×5 grid. It measured the impedance variation in the conductive fluid via the embedded electrodes to estimate forces ranging from 0.1 to 30 N upon complex signal processing. The sensor suffers from hysteresis at high pressures (>4 N). At low pressures, the spring like nature of the elastomer and the low viscosity of the conductive fluid minimised any losses from hysteresis. It also suffered from the fluid diffusing into the elastomer due to its permeability.

Optics-based soft tactile sensors have the ability to further simplify the hardware and design mechanism, since they are assisted with computer vision techniques. They primarily rely on a camera, rather than complex electronics. This also reduces their chances of crosstalk, and enables interaction with an object to infer a range of physical properties that extend beyond force applied. GelSight [29] is a high resolution tactile sensor that captures the geometry, shape and contact forces. The elastomer used is soft, clear and deformable with a reflective coating and printed patterns. RGB LED sources illuminate the cavity, allowing a camera to capture the elastomers deformations to detect the target objects' depth and orientation. The photometric stereo algorithm was used to detect forces, as low as 0.05 N with 6 DOF. HiVTac [18] also uses a similar elastomer, called PDMS, of 500 μm which contains only 4 markers that are tracked by a camera that mimics a goniometer. It operates at a higher frequency than GelSight, at 100 Hz, enabling directional slip detection in real-time with a higher precision. It achieves a maximum error of magnitude $\pm 0.043N(\pm 1.547°)$. Another sensor uses PDMS with an embedded fiber ring resonator to read braille. It had an accuracy of 98.5%, using an MLP neural network and 100% accuracy with an LSTM neural network [21]. The use of a 2D elastomer can be restricting when sensing depth for larger objects. DenseTact [4] is similar to GelSight but used a dome-shaped clear elastomer (Silicone Inc. P-565 Platinum Clear Silicone) with a reflective metallic ink coating (Smooth-on Psycho Paint™). The dome shape increases its depth sensing range, and enables multidirectional sensing and 3D reconstruction with a higher accuracy than GelSight. The sensor highlights an average of 0.28 mm depth difference using a neural network. TacTip [25] is also a dome-shaped sensor, similar to DenseTact. It can sense a range of object properties such as texture, slip, grip, and shape recognitions. Its dome shape is maintained by an optically clear gel called GelSight, enclosed by a 3D printed black silicone sheet (Tango Black Plus). The markers on its silicone skin are also 3D printed in a hexagonal array of 127 pins. The dimensions of the sensor are 40 × 40 × 85. It uses monochrome illumination to capture the marker deformations to detect the object manipulation task using CNNs. Its small size provides a greater sensitivity to forces. The TacTip has since been developed in a range of shapes including cylinders, whiskers, and thumb [22]. Another version of TacTip improved the resolution of the sensor by using 532 pins in a geodesic pattern (with the same dimensions) [14]. This increased the object localisation accuracy of the sensor to 0.1 mm.

1.3   Contribution

The literature highlights that though marker-based systems have a higher accuracy, can be cumbersome due to limitations on the FOV. Markerless systems can overcome these limitations, however, this is at the expense of the accuracy of the tracking. Based on the related work, tactile sensors can provide more information (e.g. shape, texture, rigidity, location) about an object with a higher precision than markerless approaches. However, their accuracy based on marker density has not been thoroughly investigated, leaving a gap in the literature. In radiotherapy treatments, tactile sensors have the potential to improve the accuracy of a treatment by providing patient pose to radiographers using real-time tactile feedback.

The MCP is based on the technology behind the TacTip, where a deformable black silicone is used as the contact surface with markers embedded underneath for a camera to track the deformation of the markers. The TacTip relies on classification algorithms for interacting with a target object, rather than tracking its motion, while the MCP is being developed to track an objects' motion. The original version of the MCP [7] has a rectangular array of 19 × 9 markers, spaced 10 mm apart. This paper investigates the effects of the density of the sensory marker matrix on the MCP's head tracking accuracy. A mannequin based on the weight and size of a human head was used for tracking. Metrics such as Mean Absolute Error and Spearman's correlation are used to evaluate the performance of head pose tracking.

2   Materials and Methods

2.1   Modifications in MCP Design and Experimental Set-up

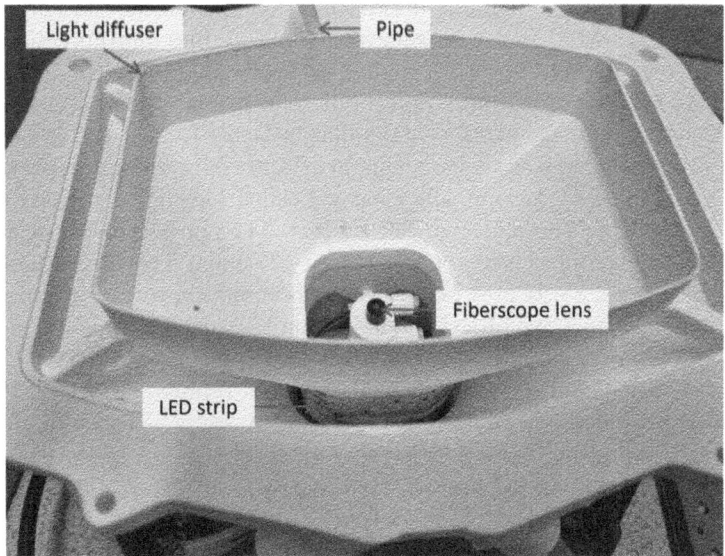

Fig. 1. The internal anatomy of the MCP. Pipe connects a PID controlled air pump mechanism to the pillow panel; LED strip illuminated the MCP to enable the camera to capture the markers on the silicone sheet via the fibrescope lens; Light diffuser minimised the light reflections captured by the fibrescope lens via the acrylic sheet.

The MCP set-up is based on a fibrescope for streaming images, and a 12V LED strip (1 m long) for illumination. The internal anatomy of the MCP can be seen in Fig. 1. Three silicone sheets were created with three different spacings between the markers, 5 mm, 10 mm, and 15 mm (see Fig. 2). Non-reflective acrylic screens and a 3D printed light diffuser were used to reduce noise from the reflection of the LEDs. The diffuser blocked the LEDs directly to reduce and scatter their intensity on the acrylic sheet, and the acrylic sheets' non-reflective coating dispersed the light further to reduce the intensity of the reflections.

3D Printed Silicone Sheets. A Stratasys J750 PolyJet 3D printer was used to manufacture three silicone sheets, which are used in the pillow panels of the

MCP. Here, Agilus 30 was used for the black silicone, and VeroWhite Plus for the embedded white markers.

Fig. 2. Three pillow panels with varying spacings in their silicone sheets: A. 5 mm spacing (38 × 19), B. 10 mm spacing (19 × 9), and C. 15 mm spacing (13 × 6), with non-reflective acrylic sheets.

Hardware Set-Up. A weighted 3D printed mannequin head of 3 kg was used to test the three sensing matrices of the MCP, since this is the lowest average human head weight [27], with the Franka Emika Panda robot arm for manipulation. The mannequin head manipulation involved its rotation in the x (roll) and y (pitch) axes of the MCP's frame, F_P. Custom attachments for the end-effector of the robot arm were also 3D printed using tough Polylactide (PLA) to secure the mannequin head. See Fig. 3 for the experimental set-up used for data collection. The air pressure in the pillow panels was set at 1.7 kPa using a PID controller. This maintains the pillow's concave shape and provides patient-comfort. A detailed explanation of this mechanism is described in our previous paper [5], the reader is encouraged to read it for a better understanding of the hardware set-up. For brevity, this is not repeated here.

2.2 Data Collection

The robot arm performs two motions on the mannequin, pitch and roll, respective to the MCP's frame, F_P. The pitch motion rotates the mannequin head by 20° each side from the home position (which is set to 0°), around the y-axis of F_P. Here, one cycle consists of four rotations in total since it starts from the home position, rotates 20° clockwise and anti-clockwise, followed by a further anti-clockwise and clockwise rotation by the same magnitude. The roll motion rotates it 7° in an anti-clockwise direction around the x-axis of F_P, followed by a clockwise rotation back to its home position, consisting of two rotations in total in one cycle. The end-effector pose data was recorded to provide ground truth, and the fibrescope in the MCP streamed the images at the same frequency along with the pressure sensor measuring the values inside the pillow panel. All the data were collected synchronously at a sampling frequency of 10 Hz, and

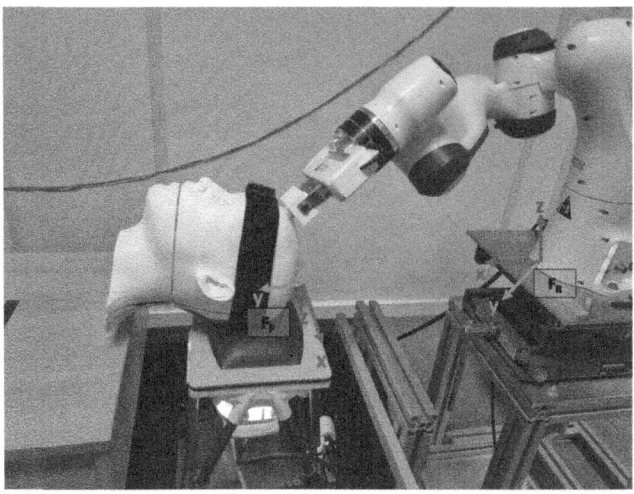

Fig. 3. Experimental set-up of MCP, Franka Emika Panda robot arm, and 3D printed weighted mannequin head in home position. F_P stands for frame of the pillow (MCP), and F_R for robots' base frame.

five recordings were taken for each motion (5 pitch rotation and 12 roll rotation cycles) using each pillow panel. The set-up used for this was the same as a previous study [5].

2.3   Data Analysis

KLT Tracking Algorithm. The KLT algorithm based on Shi-Tomasi corner detector was utilised for data analysis. The maximum corners parameter for this was modified to 300, 100, and 50, for the marker matrix spacings 5, 10, and 15 mm respectively, to effectively detect all the markers on the three different sensing arrays. These parameters were determined by trial and error, ensuring all the markers were being covered. Here, the maximum corners for the panel with 10 mm spacing was kept the same as in the previous work [5].

Spearman's Correlation. This metric calculates the correlation between two one-dimensional continuous numeric datasets, and is adaptable to non-linear data [8]. Here, the experimental values from the MCP were compared against the ground truth values from the robot arm. The correlation factor ranges from –1 to 1, where correlations close to zero signify poor correlation while correlations closer to 1 or –1 demonstrate a strong positive or negative correlation, respectively. This measure was used to establish a proof of how related the two variables are, using Eq. (1).

$$\rho = 1 - \frac{6 \sum d_i^2}{n(n^2 - 1)} \tag{1}$$

Here ρ is the Spearman's correlation coefficient, d_i is the difference between two ranks of each observation, and n is the number of observations.

Mean Absolute Error (MAE). This is a commonly used measure to obtain an average of the errors in the predicted values, compared to the ground truth. It is calculated in the same units as the target variable, simplifying its interpretation [10]. It was calculated using Eq. (2). A small error signifies good prediction, whereas a larger error signifies vice versa.

$$MAE = \frac{1}{N} \sum_{i=1}^{N} |y_i - x_i| \tag{2}$$

Here, y_i is the prediction from the MCP, and x_i is the ground truth from the robot arm.

Hysteresis. This was examined by splitting the motion cycles into loading and unloading phases for one trial and averaging them to obtain a mean loading and unloading curve. In the loading phase, the mannequin head moves away from its home position (at $0°$), while in the unloading phase, it moves back to the home position. The pitch motion was divided into four parts with one loading and unloading on each of the two sides (left and right sides of the home position), while the roll motion was divided into two parts (up and down) for loading and unloading.

3   Results

The results were obtained based on the KLT algorithm, using Spearman's correlation and MAE, both relative to the ground truth from the robot arm. The silicone sheet with 5 mm marker spacing has the lowest correlation with the ground truth for both, pitch and roll motions, along with the lowest yet most precise MAE score (minimum variation between samples) for roll with a mean of $1.34°$ for the five samples. The pitch motion data from the 5 mm sheet shows consistent noise at the maximum range of the motion, approximately above $9°$ in Fig. 6, so it was calculated again by adding a threshold to eliminate any motion beyond $9°$. Upon the removal of this noise, the MAE average for the trials changed from $12.88°$ to $4.99°$. For the same sheet the roll motion predictions remain consistent with a relatively higher precision than the other sheets, as is seen in Fig. 4.

The silicone sheets with 10 mm and 15 mm spacings show similar results to each other, signifying that reducing the density of the markers does not necessarily improve or reduce the performance of the MCP, but a higher density with 5 mm spacing can improve the performance.

The predictions from the MCP were in pixels and were scaled to the range of motion as established via the ground truth during post processing. A sample of the raw signals can be seen in Fig. 5.

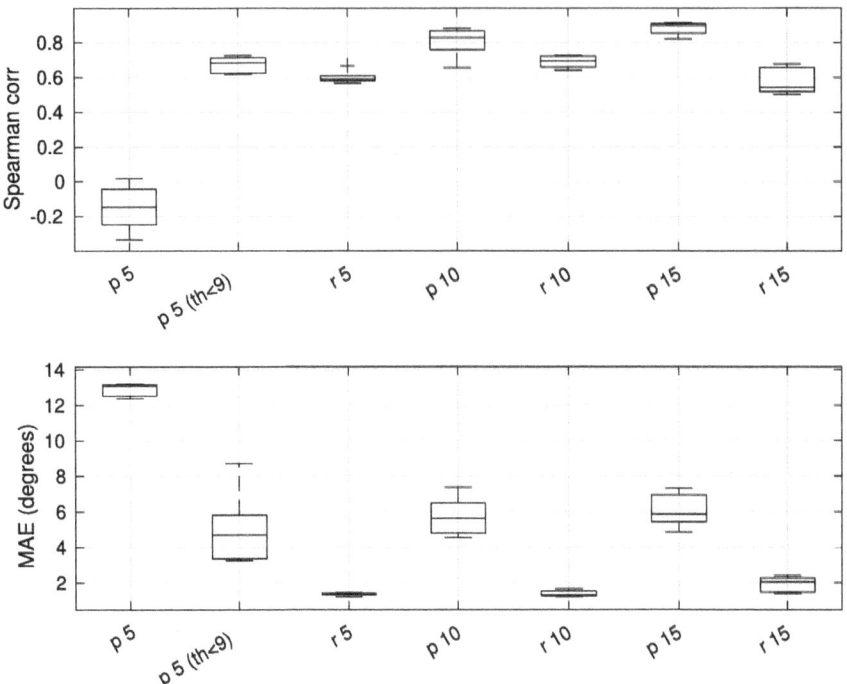

Fig. 4. Spearman's Correlation for the two rotational motions, pitch (p) and roll (r) of the mannequin for all three marker spacings - 5 mm, 10 mm and 15 mm, and Mean Absolute Error (MAE) in degrees for the same. Here, th refers to threshold, which was set to $9°$ and the other values were ignored for this calculation.

Spearman's correlation was also used to compare the results from the three pillow panels. Since the 10 mm spacing has been used in previous works, the correlations of the silicone sheets were calculated relative to this, see Fig. 7, where it shows roll motion from the 15 mm sheet with maximum correlation, followed by pitch from the 15 mm sheet. This is consistent with the previous results where the two sheets, 10 mm and 15 mm spacings show an insignificant difference. Roll from 5 mm shows a relatively lower correlation, and pitch from 5 mm shows the lowest correlation.

The hysteresis plots generated for the three marker densities for each motion can be seen in Fig. 8 and Fig. 9. These results show a slight lag in the MCP predictions relative to the ground truth data, with some discrepancy between the loading and unloading curves.

For pitch motion with 5 mm spaced markers, the maximum MCP predictions are approximately $10°$. This is related to the consistent noise, which was also reflected in its low spearman correlation and the raw data. This noise is also seen in the hysteresis plot in Fig. 8.

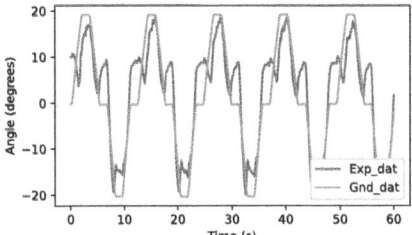 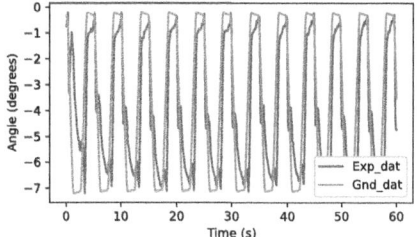

Fig. 5. A sample of pitch (left) and roll (right) motions from the silicone sheets with 10 mm marker spacing, with MCP predictions showing a consistent overshoot at 0° for pitch motion.

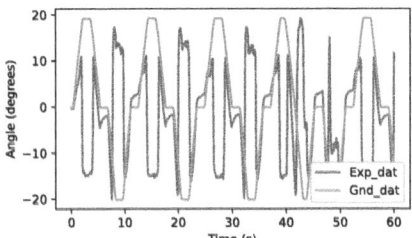 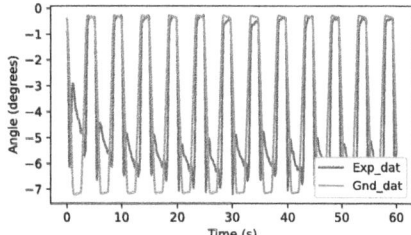

Fig. 6. A sample of pitch (left) and roll (right) motions from the silicone sheets with 5 mm marker spacing, showing more noise in pitch than roll motion.

4   Discussion

The results obtained from the three silicone sheets were as expected for the pitch motion, with the 5 mm marker spacing being an exception. This has noise induced at the extreme ends of the motion which could be due to a significant amount of markers that were being tracked leaving the FOV of the camera. The MAE for this was significantly improved when a threshold was set to consider head rotation angles below 9°. This demonstrates that a higher density of the marker matrix can provide more accuracy, although further testing is required upon improving the FOV of the sensor. These results are similar to the TacTip Superresolution model which had a higher marker density than the first TacTip, resulting in a higher accuracy [14]. To reach the maximal performance from this marker array, the sensor's design requires modifications to increase the distance between the camera lens and the silicone sheet to ensure a thorough coverage of all markers.

The spearman's correlation was strong (>0.6) for all of the motions and sensor densities, except for the boundaries of the silicone sheet with 5 mm spacing. This correlation metric cannot be used to establish a direct relationship between the MCP predictions and the ground truth, further work is required to obtain this using kalman filtering.

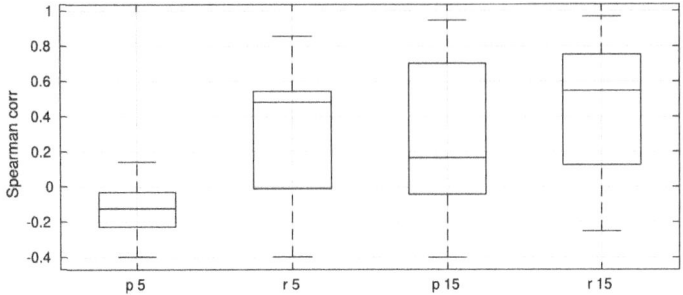

Fig. 7. Cross correlation between the silicone sheets with 5 mm and 15 mm spacing, with respect to 10 mm spacing for pitch, p, and roll, r, motions.

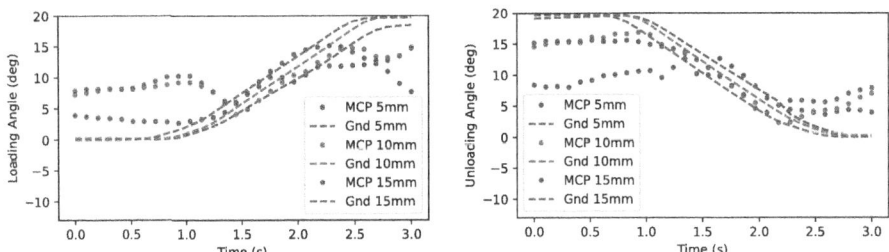

Fig. 8. Loading (left) and unloading (right) for pitch motion for the three silicone sheets with varying sensing matrix density, showing an average of the loading and unloading cycles from one trial.

The hysteresis graphs show the averaged loading and unloading phases for trials, providing more clarity to the raw data signals. The pitch motion shows similar trends for 10 mm and 15 mm spacing, but 5 mm spacing shows lower loading values at the initial resting stage and lower peak resting values. This solidified that the data from this sensor matrix was more consistent when the motion was below 9° where the sensor matrix was accurately captured by the camera. The roll motion had a smaller range, hence showed consistent results for the three sensing matrices. The MCP predictions show a stronger lag here than in the pitch motion. This could be due to larger air pressure variations within the MCP as the centre of mass of the mannequin head shifts along with the mannequin during the motion. Unloading had a larger lag than loading, which was due to hysteresis in the silicone used in the MCP. The effects of this could be reduced with slower loading and unloading with longer wait times between the two phases. Furthermore, using thinner silicone sheets with relatively lower pressure as seen in [23], or using chemical grafting such as polypyrrole on a porous PDMS substrate can reduce the effects of hysteresis further [17].

The noise in the pitch motion was more disruptive than the noise in the roll motion, which may be due to the range of motion being larger and the motion having more steps along the trajectory causing uneven pressure changes in the

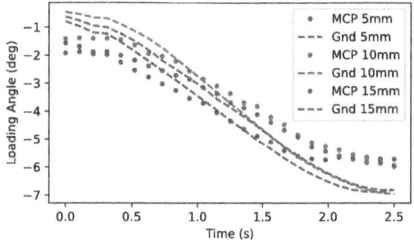 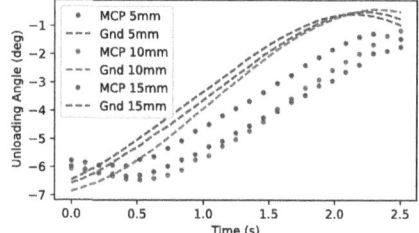

Fig. 9. Loading (left) and unloading (right) for **roll** motion for the three silicone sheets with varying sensing matrix density, showing an average of the loading and unloading cycles from one trial.

MCP. When it reached $0°$ in the pitch motion, the air pressure differences caused a small spike and a delay in the estimations stabilising again. This was not an issue with the roll motion since it was a more consistent motion.

5   Conclusion and Future Work

The MCP is a contact-based optical tactile sensor, that uses an array of markers. The optimal density of these markers has been evaluated in this work by comparing three spacing parameters (5 mm, 10 mm, and 15 mm) for the sensing matrix embedded in the silicone sheets of the pillow panels. This was used for tracking the motion of a 3D printed weighted mannequin head for two rotatory motions - pitch and roll with respect to F_P.

It shows that a higher density of the sensing matrix in the optical tactile sensor can improve the accuracy of the head tracking for rotational motions in the pitch and roll axes of F_P. This was established using performance metrics such as Spearman's correlation and MAE. Sources of noise in the data are due to hysteresis, air pressure changes in the MCP, and background noise, which require further processing to filter through. These results create a solid foundation to further investigate relationship between the KLT values from the dense sensing matrix and the head poses.

Future works also involve testing the MCP in a participant study to make it more versatile to the variations in human motions and the variations in their head types (e.g. weight, shape, and hair type); along with improving the robustness of the sensor with sensor fusion techniques using a gyroscope.

Acknowledgment. We are grateful to the EPSRC providing funding the PhD research of the first author of this work (Grant number: 2607213). This work was also supported by the Henry Royce Institute for Advanced Materials, funded through EPSRC grants EP/R00661X/1, EP/P025021/1 and EP/S019367/1.

References

1. AlignRT® Advance - Vision RT — visionrt.com. https://www.visionrt.com/alignrtadvance/, Accessed 01 Jun 2022
2. Berkels, B., Bauer, S., Ettl, S., Arold, O., Hornegger, J., Rumpf, M.: Joint surface reconstruction and 4d deformation estimation from sparse data and prior knowledge for marker-less respiratory motion tracking. Med. Phys. **40**(9), 091703 (2013)
3. Das, K., de Paula Oliveira, T., Newell, J.: Comparison of markerless and marker-based motion capture systems using 95% functional limits of agreement in a linear mixed-effects modelling framework. Sci. Rep. **13**(1), 22880 (2023)
4. Do, W.K., Kennedy, M.: Densetact: optical tactile sensor for dense shape reconstruction. In: 2022 International Conference on Robotics and Automation (ICRA), pp. 6188–6194. IEEE (2022)
5. Gandhi, B., Mihaylova, L., Dogramadzi, S.: Head tracking using an optical soft tactile sensing surface. Front. Robot. AI **11**, 1410858 (2024)
6. Goldsworthy, S., McNair, H., Dogramadzi, S.: Motion capture pillow (mcp): a novel method to improve comfort and accuracy in radiotherapy. Clin. Med. **19**(Suppl 2), 103 (2019)
7. Griffiths, G., Cross, P., Goldsworthy, S., Winstone, B., Dogramadzi, S.: Motion capture pillow for head-and-neck cancer radiotherapy treatment. In: 2018 7th IEEE International Conference on Biomedical Robotics and Biomechatronics (Biorob), pp. 813–818. IEEE (2018)
8. Hauke, J., Kossowski, T.: Comparison of values of pearson's and spearman's correlation coefficients on the same sets of data. Quaestiones geographicae **30**(2), 87–93 (2011)
9. Hughes, J., Culha, U., Giardina, F., Guenther, F., Rosendo, A., Iida, F.: Soft manipulators and grippers: a review. Front. Robot. AI **3**, 69 (2016)
10. Hyndman, R.J., Koehler, A.B.: Another look at measures of forecast accuracy. Int. J. Forecast. **22**(4), 679–688 (2006)
11. Kanko, R.M., Laende, E.K., Davis, E.M., Selbie, W.S., Deluzio, K.J.: Concurrent assessment of gait kinematics using marker-based and markerless motion capture. J. Biomech. **127**, 110665 (2021)
12. Le Moing, G., Ponce, J., Schmid, C.: Dense optical tracking: connecting the dots. In: Proceedings of the IEEE/CVF Conference on Computer Vision and Pattern Recognition, pp. 19187–19197 (2024)
13. Lee, B.Y., Liew, L.H., Cheah, W.S., Wang, Y.C.: Occlusion handling in videos object tracking: a survey. In: IOP Conference Series: Earth and Environmental Science, vol. 18, p. 012020. IOP Publishing (2014)
14. Lepora, N.F., Ward-Cherrier, B.: Superresolution with an optical tactile sensor. In: 2015 IEEE/RSJ International Conference on Intelligent Robots and Systems (IROS), pp. 2686–2691. IEEE (2015)
15. Li, K., He, F.Z., Yu, H.P.: Robust visual tracking based on convolutional features with illumination and occlusion handing. J. Comput. Sci. Technol. **33**, 223–236 (2018)
16. Puthenveetil, S.C., et al.: Comparison of marker-based and marker-less systems for low-cost human motion capture. In: International Design Engineering Technical Conferences and Computers and Information in Engineering Conference, vol. 55867, p. V02BT02A036. American Society of Mechanical Engineers (2013)
17. Pyo, S., Lee, J., Bae, K., Sim, S., Kim, J.: Recent progress in flexible tactile sensors for human-interactive systems: from sensors to advanced applications. Adv. Mater. **33**(47), 2005902 (2021)

18. Quan, S., Liang, X., Zhu, H., Hirano, M., Yamakawa, Y.: Hivtac: a high-speed vision-based tactile sensor for precise and real-time force reconstruction with fewer markers. Sensors **22**(11), 4196 (2022)

19. Slipsager, J.M., Ellegaard, A.H., Glimberg, S.L., Paulsen, R.R., Tisdall, M.D., Wighton, P., Van Der Kouwe, A., Marner, L., Henriksen, O.M., Law, I., et al.: Markerless motion tracking and correction for pet, mri, and simultaneous pet/mri. PLoS ONE **14**(4), e0215524 (2019)

20. Sundaram, S., Kellnhofer, P., Li, Y., Zhu, J.Y., Torralba, A., Matusik, W.: Learning the signatures of the human grasp using a scalable tactile glove. Nature **569**(7758), 698–702 (2019)

21. Wang, H., et al.: Optical tactile sensor based on a flexible optical fiber ring resonator for intelligent braille recognition. Opt. Express **33**(2), 2512–2528 (2025)

22. Ward-Cherrier, B., et al.: The tactip family: soft optical tactile sensors with 3d-printed biomimetic morphologies. Soft Rob. **5**(2), 216–227 (2018)

23. Wettels, N., Santos, V.J., Johansson, R.S., Loeb, G.E.: Biomimetic tactile sensor array. Adv. Robot. **22**(8), 829–849 (2008)

24. Wiersma, R.D., Tomarken, S., Grelewicz, Z., Belcher, A.H., Kang, H.: Spatial and temporal performance of 3d optical surface imaging for real-time head position tracking. Med. Phys. **40**(11), 111712 (2013)

25. Winstone, B., Griffiths, G., Melhuish, C., Pipe, T., Rossiter, J.: Tactip—tactile fingertip device, challenges in reduction of size to ready for robot hand integration. In: 2012 IEEE International Conference on Robotics and Biomimetics (ROBIO), pp. 160–166. IEEE (2012)

26. Xu, W., Huang, M.C., Amini, N., He, L., Sarrafzadeh, M.: ecushion: a textile pressure sensor array design and calibration for sitting posture analysis. IEEE Sens. J. **13**(10), 3926–3934 (2013)

27. Yoganandan, N., Pintar, F.A., Zhang, J., Baisden, J.L.: Physical properties of the human head: mass, center of gravity and moment of inertia. J. Biomech. **42**(9), 1177–1192 (2009)

28. Yu, J.J., Harley, A.W., Derpanis, K.G.: Back to basics: unsupervised learning of optical flow via brightness constancy and motion smoothness. In: Hua, G., Jégou, H. (eds.) ECCV 2016. LNCS, vol. 9915, pp. 3–10 Springer, Cham (2016). https://doi.org/10.1007/978-3-319-49409-8_1

29. Yuan, W., Dong, S., Adelson, E.H.: Gelsight: high-resolution robot tactile sensors for estimating geometry and force. Sensors **17**(12), 2762 (2017)

Automated USMN Integration for Precision Robotics and Large-Scale Metrology

Seemal Asif[1(✉)] (ID), Emmanuel Izuwa[1] (ID), Daniela Sawyer[2] (ID),
and Christopher Burkinshaw[2] (ID)

[1] Centre for Robotics and Assembly, Cranfield University, Cranfield MK43 0AL, UK
s.asif@cranfield.ac.uk
[2] University of Sheffield, AMRC, Factory 2050, Sheffield S9 1ZA, UK

Abstract. This study introduces a novel automation framework for the integration of the Unified Spatial Metrology Network (USMN) across Spatial Analyzer (SA) and PolyWorks (PW), addressing critical inefficiencies in manual metrology workflows. Traditional methods for USMN execution and data translation between platforms are labor-intensive, error-prone, and time-consuming. The proposed system automates data transfer, reference point alignment, and coordinate calibration, incorporating real-time error detection to ensure spatial coherence and enhance measurement accuracy. This approach significantly reduces processing time from days to minutes, mitigates human error, and standardizes inter-software interoperability, while maintaining residual RMS error within ≤ 0.02 mm. Application of this framework to large-scale robotic systems—common in aerospace, shipbuilding, and automotive manufacturing—demonstrates improved precision in automated tasks such as assembly, drilling, and alignment. By enabling seamless integration of multiple spatial instruments, the framework enhances the robustness and repeatability of high-precision measurements. This advancement represents a pivotal contribution to metrology automation and scalable, real-time calibration in complex industrial environments.

Keywords: Unified Spatial Metrology Network (USMN) · Spatial Analyzer · PolyWorks · Metrology Automation · Measurement Accuracy · Reference Point Calibration · Coordinate System Normalisation · Laser Tracker · High-Precision Metrology · Large-Scale Engineering · Robotic Automation

1 Introduction

Metrology serves as a fundamental pillar in precision engineering and manufacturing, providing essential measurement data necessary for quality assurance, process optimisation, and innovation.[1] The significance of metrology software in industrial applications cannot be overstated, as these tools provide the framework for accurate spatial measurements and data interpretation.[2].

Spatial Analyzer (SA) [3] is widely regarded as a comprehensive metrology tool, particularly due to its Unified Spatial Metrology Network (USMN) functionality. The

© The Author(s), under exclusive license to Springer Nature Switzerland AG 2026
A. Cavalcanti et al. (Eds.): TAROS 2025, LNAI 16045, pp. 68–79, 2026.
https://doi.org/10.1007/978-3-032-01486-3_7

USMN is essential in high-precision spatial measurement for large-scale engineering applications, as demonstrated in the EAST project [4]. The EAST project, a large super-conducting Tokamak device, required an advanced spatial metrology network to achieve precise alignment of its intricate components. Given its complex assembly involving both internal and external structures, a unified measurement framework was essential to maintain spatial consistency and accuracy. In large-scale engineering projects, USMN ensures seamless integration of multiple measurement systems, reducing discrepancies and improving precision. It mitigates environmental influences, such as temperature fluctuations, that can impact measurement stability. SA was used due to its compli-ance with ISO standards, robust uncertainty analysis capabilities, and ability to integrate data from diverse metrology instruments, ensuring high-precision measurements and traceability [4]. However, the dominance of SA in the metrology sector presents chal-lenges, particularly when integrating its outputs with other software solutions such as PolyWorks (PW) [5]. The absence of USMN capabilities in PW presents significant chal-lenges in large-scale metrology applications. USMN is essential for integrating multiple measurement instruments into a cohesive coordinate system, reducing uncertainties and ensuring precise calibration of reference points and large components. In contrast, PW, while renowned for its advanced scanning capabilities, lacks inherent USMN function-ality. Consequently, practitioners often perform USMN within SA and subsequently import the data into PW for further analysis. This process is time-consuming—poten-tially requiring a week for USMN execution in SA and an additional two days for data integration into PW, depending on the setup size. The absence of USMN in PW neces-sitates a more streamlined workflow to enhance efficiency and accuracy in metrological practices.

The traditional workflow, which requires executing USMN in SA, manually export-ing results, and subsequently reconfiguring them in PolyWorks, is not only time-intensive but also prone to errors that may compromise measurement accuracy. The need for an automated approach to facilitate data transfer, normalisation, and seamless software integration is evident. This paper presents a novel automation plugin that optimises this workflow, minimising human error, reducing processing time, and improving overall efficiency.

2   Unified Spatial Metrology Network (USMN) Process

The Unified Spatial Metrology Network (USMN) is a robust mathematical framework implemented within Spatial Analyzer (SA) to facilitate the integration of multiple mea-surement instruments into a cohesive and highly accurate spatial metrology system. The primary objective of the USMN methodology is to optimise the spatial alignment of measurement devices, thereby reducing systematic errors and enhancing measurement precision in large-scale engineering applications [6].

Large industrial robots operate over expansive workspaces, where a single measure-ment device, like a laser tracker or total station, cannot provide full coverage. USMN addresses this by combining multiple measurement instruments into a unified, opti-mized network, enabling continuous tracking of robotic movements across the entire assembly area. This is critical in applications like robotic drilling and riveting in air-craft fuselages, where even slight misalignments can lead to defects. Additionally, robot positioning errors due to mechanical flex, thermal expansion, and joint deflection can accumulate over time, impacting assembly quality. USMN mitigates these issues by optimising real-time measurement data, reducing positional drift, and improving calibration accuracy for automated systems. In adaptive manufacturing, where robots need to respond dynamically to variations in part geometry, USMN provides real-time feedback, ensuring automated assembly processes remain within tight tolerances. Moreover, in safety-critical environments, such as shipyard welding or spacecraft integration, USMN helps define precise collision avoidance zones, preventing robotic arms from interfering with other machinery or human operators. By continuously monitoring and minimizing uncertainty in robotic positioning, USMN ensures that large-scale robotic assembly processes remain accurate, efficient, and compliant with industry standards, ultimately improving production quality and reducing costly rework. Figure 1 showcase a setup of medium scale industrial robot with the metrology device. Realtime calibration of industrial robots is crucial for improving accuracy and efficiency in manufacturing, particularly in aerospace applications [7]. Traditional calibration methods often involve costly, static processes that interrupt robot operations. Recent research has focused on developing dynamic, realtime calibration techniques to address these limitations. Asif and Webb achieved error correction within 0.02 mm using a networked metrology device approach by using the laser tracker.[8] These advancements in realtime calibration techniques demonstrate significant potential for enhancing industrial robot performance and flexibility in complex manufacturing environments.

There are various methods for evaluating measurement system uncertainty. Calkins and Salerno [9] propose a practical approach using bundled observations from multiple instrument locations to determine uncertainties in spherical measurement systems. Damasceno and Couto provide an overview of methodologies, including the Guide to the Expression of Uncertainty in Measurement (GUM) and Monte Carlo methods [10]. Muelaner et al. (2015) introduce a hybrid approach combining Measurement Systems Analysis (MSA) with uncertainty evaluation, particularly useful for in-line measurements in industrial settings [11]. Keller and Sharpe (1992) describe a methodology for estimating uncertainty in electrical signal measurements using comparative measurements with reference meters [12]. These methods aim to quantify measurement uncertainties, considering factors such as environmental effects, operator technique, and instrument performance. The approaches presented offer practical tools for evaluating measurement uncertainty in various fields, from metrology to industrial applications.

The SA software employs the USMN method, which has been adopted through the pioneering work of New River Kinematics (NRK). This method is fundamentally based on the doctoral research of James Calkins [13], as presented in his dissertation on quantifying coordinate uncertainty fields in coupled spatial measurement systems. The USMN method utilises an iterative least-squares optimisation approach to integrate multiple coordinate acquisition systems while rigorously quantifying and propagating uncertainty. By assigning relative uncertainty weights to residual errors, the method ensures that higher-accuracy measurements exert a greater influence on the computed coordinate values. Unlike traditional sequential transformation methods, the USMN employs simultaneous bundle adjustment, dynamically updating the uncertainty fields as new measurements are introduced [9]. This approach enhances metrological precision by

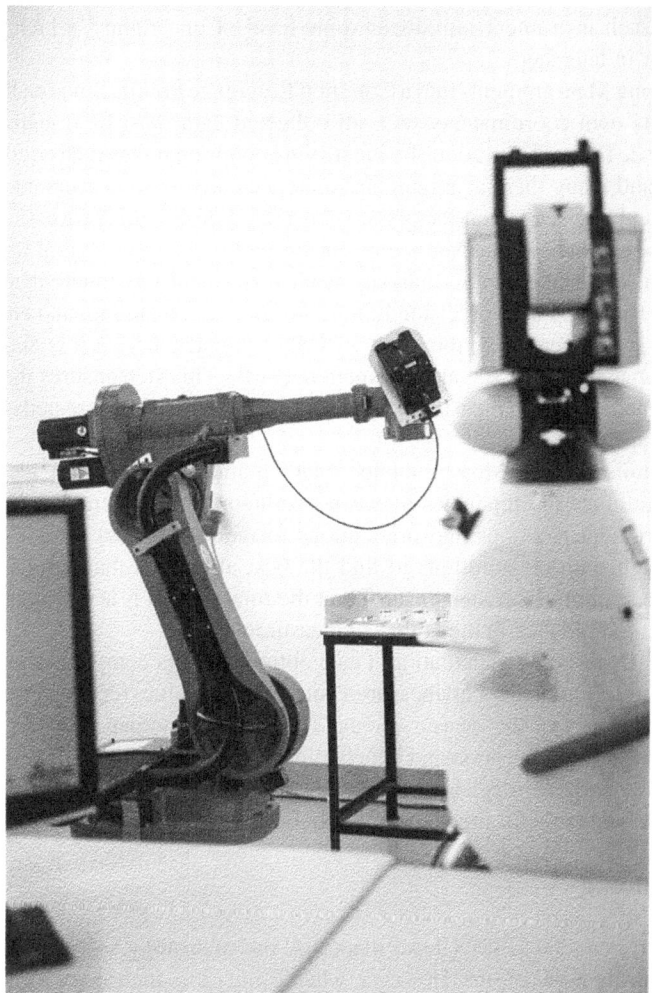

Fig. 1. Metroogy setup(Lasert Tracker) with Industrial Robot (Intelligent Automation Lab, Cranfield University)

optimising the spatial relationships between instruments and measured points, making it particularly effective in large-scale measurement applications where multiple systems, such as laser trackers, photogrammetry, and total stations, must be combined into a unified dataset with robust uncertainty quantification. Following are the steps in the USMN Process:

Step 1: Data Collection from Multiple Instruments: Measurements are gathered from different coordinate measurement systems (e.g., laser trackers, theodolites, CMMs). These instruments may capture overlapping data points to ensure redundancy. The collected data includes spatial coordinates, angles, and distances, which form the basis for further processing. Each instrument introduces some level of uncertainty, which needs to be accounted for in later steps.

Step 2: Aligning Measurements into a Common Reference Frame: Since each instrument operates in its own coordinate system, all collected data must be transformed into a single reference frame. This is done by identifying common points measured by multiple instruments and using them as alignment references. Errors in instrument positioning, orientation, and environmental factors are considered during this process. The result is a unified dataset where all measurements correspond to the same spatial framework.

Step 3: Error and Uncertainty Analysis: Each instrument has inherent measurement errors due to factors such as precision limitations, operator handling, and environmental variations (e.g., temperature, vibrations). USMN evaluates these errors and determines how they propagate across the measurement network. This step ensures that the uncertainty associated with each measurement is quantified and can be corrected or minimised in the next stage.

Step 4: Optimisation of Measurements: Mathematical optimisation techniques are applied to minimise discrepancies between overlapping measurements. This involves refining instrument positions and orientations to reduce residual errors. The process iterates through multiple solutions to find the best alignment that results in the least amount of uncertainty. This step ensures that the final dataset is as accurate as possible by leveraging redundancy in the collected measurements.

Step 5: Final Uncertainty Calculation: Once optimisation is complete, the final uncertainty values are computed for all measured points. These values represent the confidence level in the accuracy of the measurements. The uncertainty map provides insight into which areas have high precision and which might need additional verification. The final dataset is now ready for decision-making, ensuring that the combined measurements meet industry standards for precision and reliability.

3   Methodology

The ability to generate USMN have made SA the metrology software of choice for many engineering applications. However, when using other metrology software and the USMN is required for a given workspace, it can be performed in SA and the USMN composites can be imported to the metrology software of choice. Figure 2 illustrates the flow of the process:

The USMN integration workflow involves a combination of manual and automated steps to streamline the process of transferring and utilising USMN data in other metrology software. The process begins with generating USMN in SA, followed by exporting the USMN data from SA, and then importing the data into other metrology software (all of these steps, in light blue, require manual execution). It was ensured that the last position for the USMN was desired tracker position in the PolyWorks workspace. This can be any position with a good line of sight to the targets. Once the data is imported, the coordinate system is recreated, and reference points are aligned (yellow), a step that can be automated. Following this, the system can validate and normalise the imported USMN data (yellow), ensuring spatial consistency. The process then moves to configuring measurement parameters and calibrating the setup (yellow), which can also be automated to reduce manual intervention. Once calibrated, test measurements are performed to verify

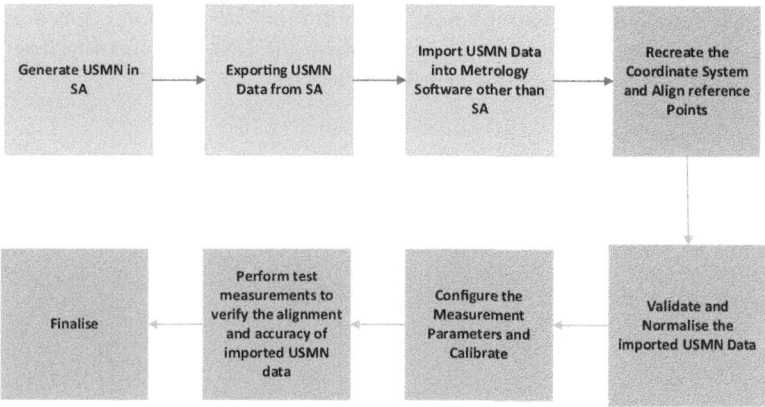

Fig. 2. USMN Importing Workflow Steps from SA to anyother metrology software

the alignment and accuracy of the imported USMN data (yellow), ensuring that the system meets the required precision standards. Finally, the process is finalised, marking the completion of the USMN integration workflow (yellow). The automation of the yellow-highlighted steps significantly reduces human effort, minimizes errors, and enhances overall measurement accuracy.

Using PolyWorks metrology software as a case study, the USMN for an assembly cell has been generated in SA and the results saved as a text file. This paper looks at the process required to automate the USMN data importation process.

The macros (modular programs) have been written to work with any open PolyWorks workspace like the one seen in the Fig. 3 below:

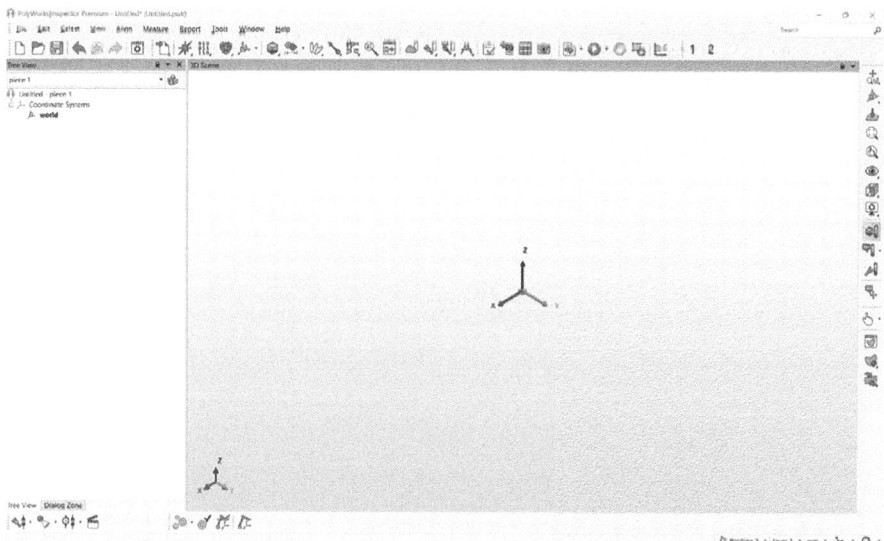

Fig. 3. PW Workspace

The operator clicks on button 1 highlighted in Fig. 4, the system opens a window, allowing the operator to select the directory where the USMN composite from SA is saved.

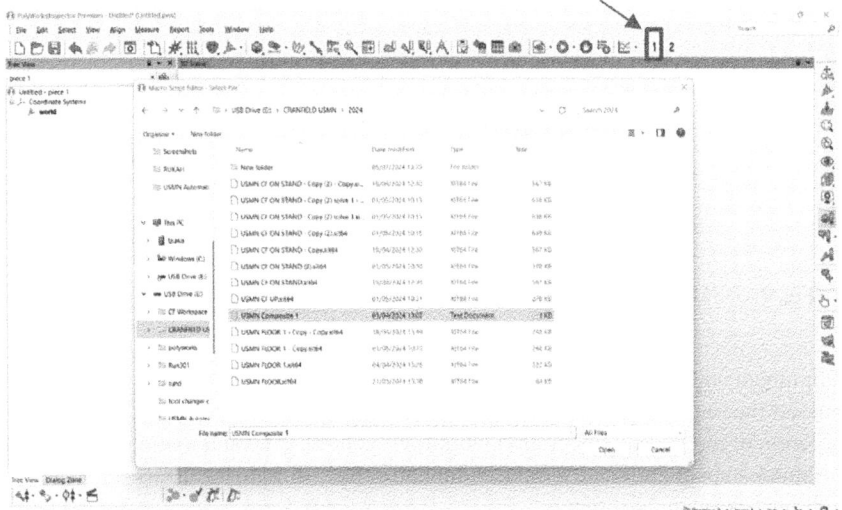

Fig. 4. USMN Composite Selection process

The USMN points are imported automatically into the PolyWorks workspace as elements as seen in the Fig. 5 below.

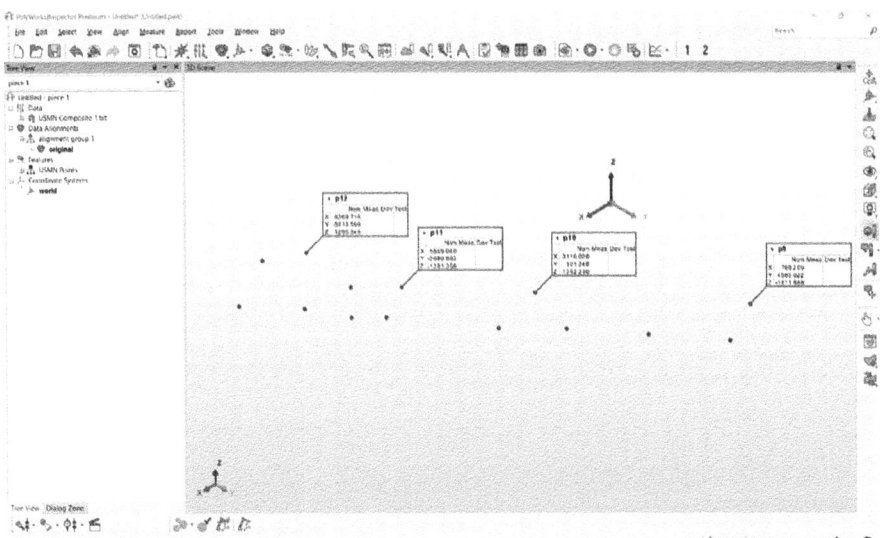

Fig. 5. Creating points from USMN Composite point cloud (elements)

The elements are used to create points. These points are grouped and then imported into the device position setup using the "Create global primitives from centers" option.

This imports the points as targets that can be used to create a new device position. The laser tracker is completely unaware of the positions of the targets in space at this point. Hence, there is a need to create a new device position to help lock it onto the targets. For this pupose, operator then click on the button 2. To aid in selecting the targets in the cell, the system activates the camera on the laser tracker as seen in Fig. 6 below. This helps eliminate the need to manually move the laser beam from target to target.

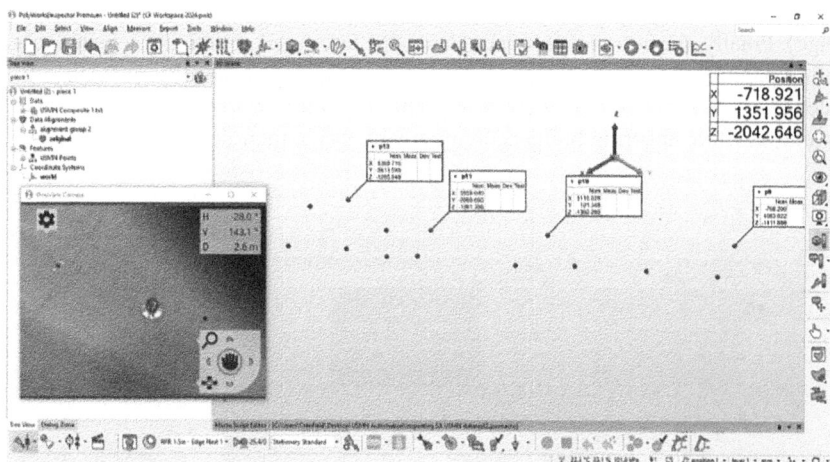

Fig. 6. Using laser tracker camera to select reflectors (Point targets)

Then the system then activates the new device position creation process. Combined with the laser tracker camera, the operator can select the targets in the workspace as seen in Fig. 7 below.

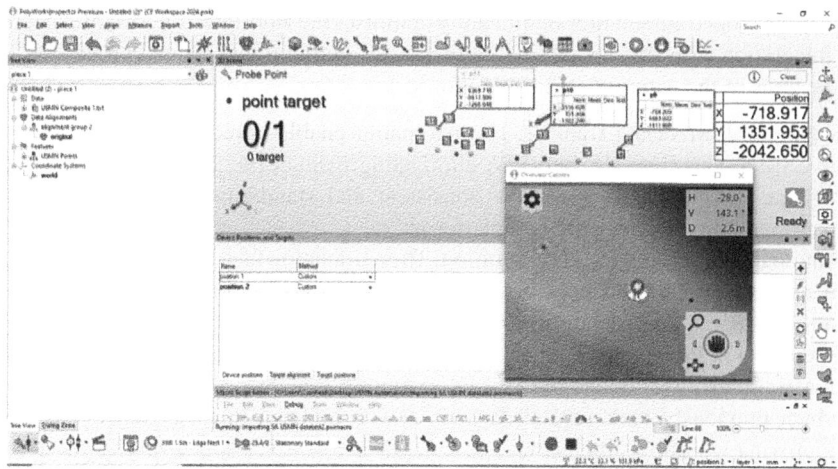

Fig. 7. Fitting the points to the Device Position

At this point, the laser tracker is fully locked into the cell and can now be used to take measurements.

The process is illustrated below in Fig. 8 consists of both operator-executed and system-driven steps to streamline measurement workflows. The process begins with the operator initiating USMN in SA to execute calibration and establish reference points (orange). The operator then clicks button 1 in PW to import the USMN text file (orange). Once imported, the system seamlessly automates alignment creation, generating alignment points in PW (blue). Following this, the operator clicks button 2(blue) in PW to create a device position on the imported points and group them, this is performed automatically. The system then prompts the operator to select targets on the screen (orange). Finally, the automated process locks the laser tracker onto the selected targets, enabling precise measurement (blue). The system then automatically normalise/fit the device (laser tracker) based on the USMN. This structured workflow minimises manual intervention while ensuring high accuracy in large-scale metrology applications.

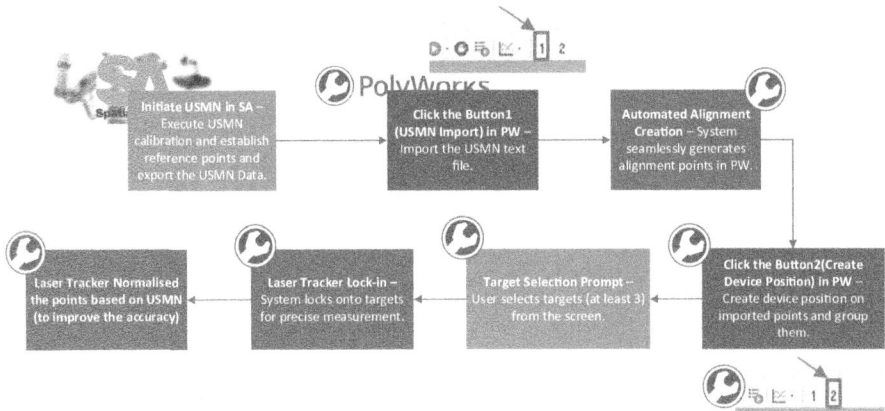

Fig. 8. Automated Process Setup

The developed automation significantly optimises the workflow for USMN execution and integration with PW, addressing inefficiencies in traditional manual processes. The key features of the automation are as follows:

- Seamless USMN Data Transfer: The automation enables direct and structured import of USMN data from SA into PW, eliminating manual file conversions and reducing data loss risks. It ensures a consistent and standardised format, enhancing interoperability between the two platforms.
- Automated Reference Point Calibration: The automation facilitates precise alignment of reference points and large components within the coordinate system. It ensures uniform spatial consistency, reducing the need for manual reconfiguration in PW.
- Reduction in Processing Time: By eliminating redundant manual steps, the automation significantly shortens the USMN execution timeline. The integration process, which previously took several days, is now completed in a fraction of the time, improving workflow efficiency.

- Minimisation of Human Errors: Manual data handling introduces inaccuracies due to potential misalignment, incorrect data input, or configuration errors. The automation mitigates these risks by implementing an error-checking mechanism that ensures data accuracy before integration.
- Enhanced Measurement Consistency: The automation maintains spatial integrity across different measurement systems by preserving original USMN parameters. It provides uniform calibration across multiple measurement setups, improving repeatability and reliability.
- User-Friendly Interface and Process Simplification: The automation features an intuitive interface that allows operators to execute USMN operations with minimal technical intervention. It streamlines the process, enabling metrology professionals to focus on high-value analysis rather than data handling.
- Scalability and Future Adaptability: The automated system is designed to accommodate various metrology setups, allowing for scalability across different measurement environments. It provides a foundation for future enhancements, including AI-driven optimisations and expanded software compatibility. By integrating these features, the automation significantly enhances the efficiency, accuracy, and usability of USMN execution within PW, making it a transformative solution in large-scale metrology applications.

4   Discussion and Conclusion

To test the system, it was important to compare the normal (manual) method and the new automated method using the same USMN run. The workspace for the test was set up, and reflectors were placed in position. The USMN was performed in SA using 11 stations, as seen in Fig. 9 below.

Fig. 9. USMN Workspace

Before exporting, the overall RMS was 0.03. The USMN composite was exported and imported manually using the stated procedure; the RMS in PolyWorks was 0.037. Due to the manual tasks involved in this process, the time taken to complete the import was approximately 36 min. The same task was performed using the automation program. The RMS after importing to PolyWorks was 0.029. And this only took about 4.5 min. The workspace used for this test is a relatively large space, but this can be replicated for smaller workspaces as well. The laser tracker used for this test was the Leica AT960.

It was observed that the syntax in the PolyWorks macro editor required modification when running the program on a different tracker. One key feature that contributes to significant time savings is the AT960's built-in camera, which can automatically lock onto reflectors. This functionality is difficult to implement on earlier models, such as the AT901-MR, as observed during testing. Figure 10 showcase the comparison of both mathods.

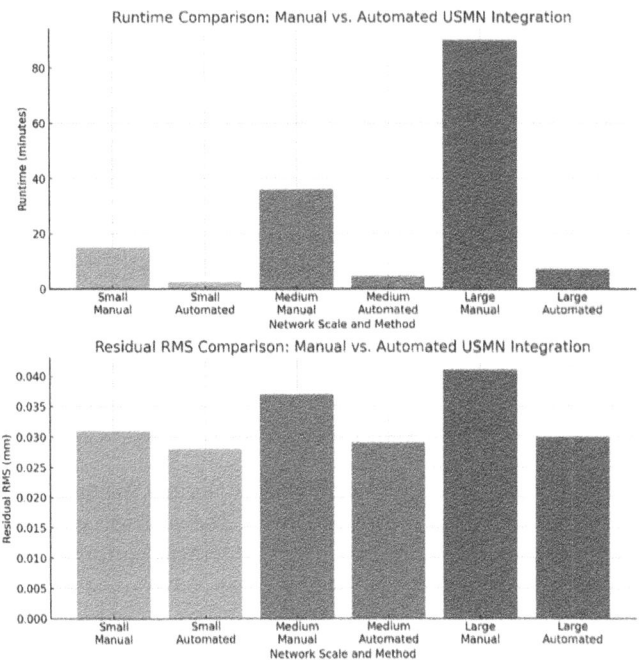

Fig. 10. Comparison Manual vs. Automated USMN Integration

The automation framework for USMN integration has markedly improved the efficiency, accuracy, and reliability of spatial metrology workflows. Tasks that previously required up to two days—such as importing USMN data into PW and aligning components—can now be completed in minutes, significantly enhancing productivity and reducing downtime.

Beyond accelerating workflow, the system reduces human error by standardising data transfer and alignment processes. Automated integration preserves spatial integrity and repeatability while real-time error detection mechanisms identify discrepancies early, improving overall measurement reliability.

The framework also enhances interoperability between SA and PW, enabling a consistent and scalable solution adaptable to diverse industrial environments. By removing manual dependencies, it ensures uniformity across varying metrology setups.

In summary, the proposed system offers a transformative step forward in large-scale metrology, delivering faster execution, improved accuracy, and robust process standardisation. Future work will explore algorithmic optimisation and cross-platform compatibility to extend its applicability across broader engineering contexts.

Acknowledgment. This work part of a collaboration with AMRC Sheffield, funded by the Engineering and Physical Sciences Research Council's Innovation Launchpad Network+ Researcher in Residence scheme [grant numbers EP/W037009/1, EP/X528493/1].

References

1. Olu-lawal, K.A., Olajiga, O.K., Ani, E.C., Adeleke, A.K., Montero, D.J.P.: The role of precision metrology in enhancing manufacturing quality: a comprehensive review. Eng. Sci. Technol. J. **5**(3), 728–739 (2024)
2. Jamshidi, J., Kayani, A., Iravani, P., Maropoulos, P.G., Summers, M.D.: Manufacturing and assembly automation by integrated metrology systems for aircraft wing fabrication. Proc. Inst. Mech. Eng. B J. Eng. Manuf. **224**(1), 25–36 (2010). https://doi.org/10.1243/09544054J EM1280
3. Spatial Analyzer, "Overview of SpatialAnalyzer." Accessed 13 Feb 2025. https://www.kin ematics.com/spatialanalyzer/
4. Liu, C., Gu, Y., Zheng, Y., Qin, S., Wang, J.: Study on precision spatial measurement network of EAST. In: Cui, J., Tan, J., Wen, X. (eds.) Ninth International Symposium on Precision Engineering Measurement and Instrumentation, SPIE, p. 94462C (2015). https://doi.org/10. 1117/12.2181108
5. InnovMetric Software Inc, "3D Dimensional Analysis and Quality Control SW." Accessed 13 Feb 2025. https://www.innovmetric.com/products/polyworks-inspector
6. New River Kinematics (NRK), "Unified Spatial Metrology Network (USMN)." Accessed 13 Feb 2025. https://www.kinematics.com/spatialanalyzer/usmn.php
7. Asif, S., Webb, P.: Realtime Calibration of an Industrial Robot, MDPI: Applied System Innovation (2022). https://doi.org/10.3390/asi5050096
8. Asif, S., Webb, P.: Managing delays for realtime error correction and compensation of an industrial robot in an open network. Machines **11**(9) (2023). https://doi.org/10.3390/machin es11090863
9. Calkins, J.M., Salerno, R.J.: A practical method for evaluating measurement system uncertainty. In: Boeing Large Scale Metrology Conference (2000)
10. Damasceno, J.C., Couto, P.R.G.: Methods for evaluation of measurement uncertainty. In: Metrology, A. (ed.) Rijeka: IntechOpen (2018), ch. 2. https://doi.org/10.5772/intechopen. 74873
11. Muelaner, J., Francis, A., Chappell, M., Maropoulos, P.: A hybrid Measurement systems analysis and uncertainty of measurement approach for industrial measurement in the light controlled factory (2015)
12. Keller, S., Sharpe, D.T.: A practical methodology for estimating uncertainty in electrical signal measurements. In: 1992 Conference Record IEEE Instrumentation and Measurement Technology Conference, pp. 623–628 (1992). https://doi.org/10.1109/IMTC.1992.245064
13. Calkins, J.: Quantifying coordinate uncertainty fields in coupled spatial measurement systems (2002)

Frequency Map Enhancement Revisited and Extended for Biohybrid Robotics

Tomas Vintr[1]([⊠]) [iD], Vanda Vintrova[2] [iD], Martin Stefanec[4] [iD],
Zdenek Rozsypalek[3] [iD], Fatemeh Rekabi-Bana[1] [iD], and Farshad Arvin[1] [iD]

[1] Computer Science Department, Durham University, Durham, UK
{tomas.vintr,fatemeh.rekabi-bana,farshad.arvin}@durham.ac.uk
[2] Prague, Czech Republic
[3] Artificial Intelligence Center, Department of Computer Science, Faculty of
Electrical Engineering, Czech Technical University in Prague, Prague, Czechia
zdenek.rozsypalek@fel.cvut.cz
[4] Artificial Life Lab, Department of Zoology, Institute of Biology, University of Graz,
Graz, Austria
martin.stefanec@uni-graz.at

Abstract. Frequency Map Enhancement with its ability to forecast periodic dynamics is a crucial step forward in robotic autonomy. We propose an extension that allows the modelling of phenomena that can be quantified by rational numbers, thus broadening its usability and applicability. We are evaluating its functionality in a simulation using data from the extensive robotic field experiment currently underway as part of the RoboRoyale project, which aims to help slow the global pollination crisis by supporting the most important pollinators - honeybees. The project performs vast amounts of robotic experiments around honeybee colony with thousands of bees interacting in a densely populated and ever-changing system, individual bees performing distinct tasks simultaneously. A honey bee colony is a challenging environment for autonomous robotics and spatio-temporal modelling. It opens questions on spatio-temporal modelling that were in the pure robotic experiments hidden or quietly bypassed.

Keywords: Maps of Dynamics · Honeybee Hive Observation · Long-term Autonomous Robotics

1 Introduction

Recent advances in computational hardware, coupled with rapid progress in artificial intelligence and machine learning, have led to growing expectations that intelligent robots will soon be available to assist people in their daily activities. These robots are envisioned to operate effectively in various environments for extended periods, not only taking on repetitive tasks but also helping with tasks

---

V.Vintrova—Independent researcher.

A. Cavalcanti et al. (Eds.): TAROS 2025, LNAI 16045, pp. 80–93, 2026.
https://doi.org/10.1007/978-3-032-01486-3_8

where human efficiency may be limited due to slow reactions, low dexterity, or emotional stress. Moreover, robots are expected to assist in tasks that require sustained focus or that involve infrequent actions, which demand swift and precise responses when they occur. In addition, due to the significant increase in data flow and advancements in database technologies, autonomous systems are now regarded as knowledge repositories that can support inexperienced humans in making informed decisions during unusual situations.

Currently, robots are proficient in operating autonomously within controlled, structured, or known environments. However, outside of industrial plants—designed specifically for robotic operations—most environments remain unstructured and unpredictable. To address this challenge, significant efforts in robotics have focused on mapping techniques in which a robot, either supervised or directly controlled by a human, creates a model of its environment using its onboard sensors. This allows the robot to transform an unknown environment into a known one, enabling its deployment in spaces that are not predefined.

Despite this, many environments are dynamic, which means that changes over time can render the robot's created model obsolete. This presents a major challenge for the long-term autonomous operation of intelligent robots in environments that are subject to change. The issue of long-term operations in changing environments has traditionally been explored through the lenses of robot mapping and self-localization. Some methods have focused on eliminating [4] or accounting for changes in the environment [33], while others have sought to update models based on observed changes [9]. In addition, some approaches have aimed to learn from environmental changes by modelling persistence, periodicity, or the effects of those changes [28]. A notable example of this is the STRANDS project [17], which utilized the Frequency Map Enhancement (FreMEn) [26] technique to model environmental dynamics and human behaviours, improving robot performance during long-term deployments in dynamic environments. The STRANDS project showed that modelling and forecasting changes induced by human working routines and derived from the Sun's illumination improve robot efficiency [11]. Consequently, the STRoLL project demonstrated that understanding human habits significantly improves the acceptance of robots in real world environments [42]. In general, temporal models that capture periodic dynamics offer significant advantages over more static approaches, particularly when applied in real-world settings where predictability of human actions plays a key role [18,19].

Because robots are subject to real-world limitations, such as battery downtime and irregular data collection, one of the most effective methods for incorporating temporal dynamics into robotic mapping is Frequency Map Enhancement (FreMEn), which uses frequency analysis to model environmental changes. It is based on non-uniform Fourier transforms [6] and, therefore, able to process irregular data. This approach allows robots to focus on periodic changes while ignoring trends that have minimal impact over the medium term. The FreMEn method was integrated into various robotic tasks, enhancing the performance in navigation [14,45], exploration [31,34] and task scheduling [44]. It was successfully applied to long-term robot deployments [16], demonstrating its effectiveness in dynamic environments. The method's ability to forecast periodic dynamics has been crucial in improving robot autonomy.

Despite the success of FreMEn, challenges remain, especially concerning the spatial independence of neighbouring cells in the model. To address these challenges, continuous spatio-temporal representations have been explored, allowing for more accurate modelling of environmental dynamics. The key challenge remains computational efficiency, as many continuous models require substantial resources [15]. This was addressed by incorporating FreMEn's spectral analysis into continuous models building [27] providing computationally and memory effective models [43]. Although the robotics continue to evolve, the original FreMEn's idea, focusing on time-based dynamics, is still vital in enabling robots to handle complex dynamic environments or unknown environments under the research.

Such advanced methods developed to manage complex, dynamic, and data-rich environments in robotics can be adapted for use in other fields facing similar challenges. Many disciplines contend with the task of processing vast amounts of irregular data in intricate environments. Honeybee ethology serves as a prime example: within a colony, thousands of bees interact in a densely populated and ever-changing system, each individual performing distinct tasks simultaneously [22, 46]. A recently developed robotic system designed to monitor honeybee behaviour has already demonstrated the potential for high-quality data collection in such settings [41]. Transferring and adapting proven robotic methods, such as real-time mapping and dynamic modelling, could significantly improve the control and efficiency of these systems.

We propose a definition of the FreMEn variant that can deal with rational number time series. We evaluated it in an actual robotic task of high interest, currently under investigation in the RoboRoyale project [38].

2   Motivation

FreMEn was originally developed for visual sensory data processed by image feature detection methods [25]. Such data consist of spatio-temporal position with a binary label whether some specific phenomenon had been detected or not. When applied to Lidar data consisting only of detections, it needed to be reimplemented (with disputable success) [42] or applied to heavily preprocessed datasets [43]. In the RoboRoyale project, the robot's imaging system scans honeybee combs, classifying multiple features in each section and yielding a high density of detections. The resulting data are highly heterogeneous and cannot be effectively captured using a binary classification approach. As binary class labelling does not make sense, we cannot use FreMEn directly for modelling the dynamics of robot's environment.

The RoboRoyale project uses robots to support honeybee colonies, to improve pollination efficiency, addressing the ongoing pollination crisis [3,7,38,39]. The system tracks the queen and observes worker bees and comb cells using a robotic gantry with a moving camera [41].

The system focuses on the queen to capture details such as feeding events, movement patterns, and interactions with worker bees, while also gathering data on overall hive condition—including comb integrity, brood health, and resource distribution. This requires high-quality visual data captured by a robotic system that continuously follows the queen, recording detailed images. However, this limits the robot's field of view, preventing it from capturing the entire colony state in a single observation. Therefore, a comprehensive image of the comb can only be constructed by combining multiple images taken from different locations, which necessitates careful planning of the robot's movements and observation schedule to account for the dynamic behaviour of both the queen and the workers. By gaining a deeper understanding of the queen's behaviour, we can eventually introduce a robotic systems capable of interacting with her to modify her behaviour - a process we refer to as ecosystem hacking [20, 38]. This could, for example, enhance the queen's egg-laying performance, which could accelerate colony growth, ultimately leading to improved pollination services [12]. In the honeybee colony, the queen plays a pivotal role in colony growth through egg laying [1, 32]. As the only female capable of producing fertilized eggs, her continued presence is essential for colony survival [46]. To ensure the colony remains aware of her status, the queen actively distributes pheromones while moving through the hive to identify suitable cells for egg deposition [8, 30, 37]. Concurrently, she maintains continuous interactions with worker bees that provide necessary feeding and grooming [2, 13, 36]. Periodically, the queen enters a resting, sleep-like, state—characterized by minimal movement and a distinct head-up posture— which can last from a few minutes to several hours [35]. These resting periods are detectable via vision-based tracking and provide windows during which the robotic system can capture images of the comb [24]. However, these intervals may be too brief to survey the entire comb comprehensively, especially given that worker bees often occlude significant portions of the structure. This requires either staying at each scanning location long enough for the bees to move around or revisiting these locations several times throughout one day.

FreMEn was not applied to the task of collecting a complete image of the underlying comb, because the data from the individual images with bee detections do not correspond to FreMEn's original design. The original FreMEn was designed to continually observe some detectable phenomenon that occurred irregularly. For example, usually closed doors are opened, empty place was traversed by a human, empty chair was occupied by a person. To apply FreMEn directly means to fragmentize every image into grid and detect whether each cell contains bee or not. However, due to robot's design and the task, the question is not when and where specifically a bee occurs, but whether the image is expected to be full of bees or relatively empty. Moreover, contrary to people that use their personal space and, therefore, the grid can have meaningfully large cells, worker bees are crawling one over another and the resolution of grid should be very fine-grained. Applying grid to each image would also lead to high computational demand with a minimum or no information gained.

As this is not an exceptional situation and we faced it multiple times in past (for example in project FreMEn contra COVID [29]), we decided to extend FreMEn usability and additionally defined it for situations where the information from the detector consists of number of detections and not only detection of phenomenon's occurrence.

3   Method

A similar problem was discussed in [23]. However, we were not able to success-fully reimplement their solution, Addition Amplitude Model. The main reason consists in averaging of angles that led to poor results on our traditional evaluat-ing datasets. Their search for dominant frequencies is iterative and they propose a multiple choice of identical frequency. They claim that this way the method reaches more precise estimation of amplitude. Our implementation, when choos-ing one frequency multiple times, led to computational instability. We speculate that their results were influenced by incorrect calculation of amplitudes due to imprecision in original FreMEn's definition (note the difference in Eq. (2) and Eq. (11) in [26]).

Therefore, we provide a different definition, very similar to the original app-roach. Contrary to the original definition, for the sake of simplicity, we omit in our equations calculation of partial, weighted averages, and calculate those averages over batch of data.

FreMEn uses for the frequency analysis two parameters, a set of candidate angular frequencies $\omega_k \in \Omega$ and the order of the model m. The set of angular fre-quencies is derived from either data or expert's opinion. Model order defines how many angular frequencies will be used for modelling phenomena. It is advised to estimate model order by cross-validation, but due to computational demands, it is in usual scientific experiments also defined by expert's opinion. It was shown that for forecasting models in office-like environments the right choice of model order value is between 2 and 5, preferably 5, while optimised set of angular fre-quencies is $\Omega = \{2\pi k/604800\}_{k=1}^{168}$, which reflects workweek routines of people.

Let us assume a set of candidate angular frequencies $\omega_k \in \Omega$, model order m, and n observations consisting of rational numbers $r(t_i)$ acquired at different times t_i, $i = 1 \ldots n$. The proposed method builds the model parameters in the following way:

– calculate the mean

$$\mu = \frac{1}{n} \sum_{i=1}^{n} r(t_i), \tag{1}$$

– $\forall \omega_k$ calculate the spectrum

$$\gamma_k = \frac{2}{n} \sum_{i=1}^{n} \left(r(t_i) - \mu \right) e^{jt_i \omega_k}, \tag{2}$$

– and estimate the maximum value that can occur

$$r_{max} \geq \max_{i=1}^{n} r(t_i).$$ (3)

The model can then forecast value $r(t_0)$ at specific time t_0:

$$r(t_0) = \mu + \sum_{1}^{m} |\gamma_c| \cos(t_0\omega_c - \arg(\gamma_c))$$ (4)

or estimate relative crowdedness:

$$p(t_0) = \frac{1}{r_{max}} \left(\mu + \sum_{1}^{m} |\gamma_c| \cos(t_0\omega_c - \arg(\gamma_c)) \right).$$ (5)

Note that the presented calculation can be also used for the data labelled by zeros and ones. We will use the acronym *FreMEnext* for this extension to Frequency Map Enhancement in the following text.

4 Evaluation

We evaluate the proper functioning in a simulation consisting of data from the extensive robotic field experiment performed under currently running project RoboRoyale. The design of the evaluation is directly derived from a former evaluation published in [5]. The technical details of the evaluation can be found in the original article, which also presents the results of testing different algorithms. The deep technical details of a robot that observes the honeybee hive can be found in [41]. For the sake of simplicity, we avoid a description of parts of the very complex system, that are not closely connected to this evaluation.

We did not include comparison of qualitatively different spatio-temporal models, because the models cannot forecast the right time for observation in this scenario design. Therefore, any comparison of spatio-temporal models would be speculative and subjected to the scenario parameters setup. The primary hypothesis we are testing in this evaluation is whether the proposed method is capable of deployment in challenging tasks [5,41]. The secondary hypothesis is derived from conclusions in [23] - does the iterative approach to choice of dominant frequencies in data significantly influences quality of the model?

4.1 Observing Honeybee Comb

Our hive is specifically designed for observing bee colonies. It consists of two stacked wooden combs, enclosed by glass panels on both sides (see Fig. 1). Our system focuses on two objectives. The primary objective is to continuously captur highly detailed images of the honeybee queen within the hive. This is achieved using a positionable FullHD camera.

The secondary objective is to capture a complete, occlusion-free image of the comb on a daily basis. Since the full brood evolution takes about three

Fig. 1. System used in the RoboRoyale project for studying and interacting with honeybee colonies [41]. (a) The full system setup features two robots equipped with cameras that observe both sides of an observation honeybee hive. The area is illuminated by infrared lighting, which is invisible to honeybees. (b) Perspective from one robot, capable of navigating to various functional locations within the hive. (c) Close-up colour photo of the comb surface, illustrating the dense congregation of bees and their diverse interactions.

weeks and filling the combs with honey takes several days, observations of the comb cells once per day are sufficient to capture their long-term dynamics. The system achieves a daily comb snapshot by performing a full hive scan cycle each time the queen is at rest. This involves systematically moving the camera across a pre-defined grid covering the honeycomb and collecting local image data. The gathered data are then combined with previous observations to filter out occlusions caused by bees. The challenge is to optimize the selection of scanning locations to maximize coverage while minimizing the number of observations. In our experiments, we simulate selective data collection using a dataset recorded by the system.

The dataset consists of one month of full scans collected by our robotic system [41]. These scans contain honeybee comb images arranged in a regular rectangular grid from both sides of the comb, denoted as "side 0" and "side 1." Bee detection is performed using a fine-tuned YOLOv8 model [21], and the bee orientations are estimated using a custom convolutional neural network (CNN) [41]. In total, data consist of nearly five million detections of bees. We split the dataset into the first 21 days for training and the following 8 days for testing the coverage methods.

4.2   Methods in Evaluation

Every day d the robot executes a number of scanning cycles indexed as c. Every scan S_i is a set of bee observations at the tile i. Location l_i of tiles, $i = 1, \ldots, N$, are given by the predefined positions of the camera and its field-of-view. For purposes of collecting the complete image of (almost) empty comb, we define for every location l in every day d after every scanning cycle c a state $s_l^{(c)}$ that represents proportion of area in camera's field-of-view captured free of bees.

Each mapping method differs in how it determines the ranking $R^{(c)}$ at each cycle. For a cycle c, a method proposes a ranking $R^{(c)}$ of all tiles. According to this ranking, camera visits the first $a \cdot 100\%$ of locations. The ratio a is referred to as "areas ratio" and was introduced to the original evaluation scheme to assess the necessity of full scanning cycles. The ranking R reflects the method's preferences. For example, Greedy prefers locations with low state s_l and FreMEnext locations with a low state with forecasted low number of bees. The rules for the ranking R of locations l of individual methods can be formally expressed:

Random proposes a random reshuffle of location indexes, and is expected to provide the worst performance,

$$R_{\text{random}} \sim \text{Permutation}(\{1, \ldots, N_l\}). \tag{6}$$

Sequential performs a snake-like motion, which is a default motion of camera when performing the scanning of the comb,

$$R^{(c)}_{\text{sequential}}(x) = (x + c \cdot a \cdot N_x) \mod N_x. \tag{7}$$

Greedy prefers to visit locations with the lowest state,

$$\forall (i, j) : s_i^{(c-1)} < s_j^{(c-1)} \Rightarrow R^{(c)}_{\text{greedy}}(i) < R^{(c)}_{\text{greedy}}(j). \tag{8}$$

FreMEnext uses model $f_{\text{FreMEnext}}$ to forecast crowdedness p of individual locations l at time t during current cycle c

$$\forall l : p_l = f_{\text{FreMEnext}}(t, l) \tag{9}$$

From this forecast, we estimate information gain at the location l and time t

$$e^{(c-1)}_{\text{FreMEnext}, l} = (1 - s_l^{(c-1)})(1 - q p_l), \tag{10}$$

as the product of unobserved portion of area and expected free space, where q is a parameter expressing the ratio between an intention to observe locations with the lowest state (like Greedy) and not to observe crowded locations. The ranking R is then directly derived from the expected information gain e

$$\forall (i, j) : e_i^{(c)} < e_j^{(c)} \Rightarrow R^{(c)}_{\text{FreMEnext}}(i) < R^{(c)}_{\text{FreMEnext}}(j). \tag{11}$$

The model order m was set to $m = 5$ and a set of candidate angular frequencies was derived from a day, $\Omega = \{2\pi k/86400\}_{k=1}^{24}$. Model forecasted relative crowdedness, Equation (5). To avoid rejection of hypothetically contributing ideas, we also implemented an iterative version of FreMEnext, denoted simply as *Iterative*.

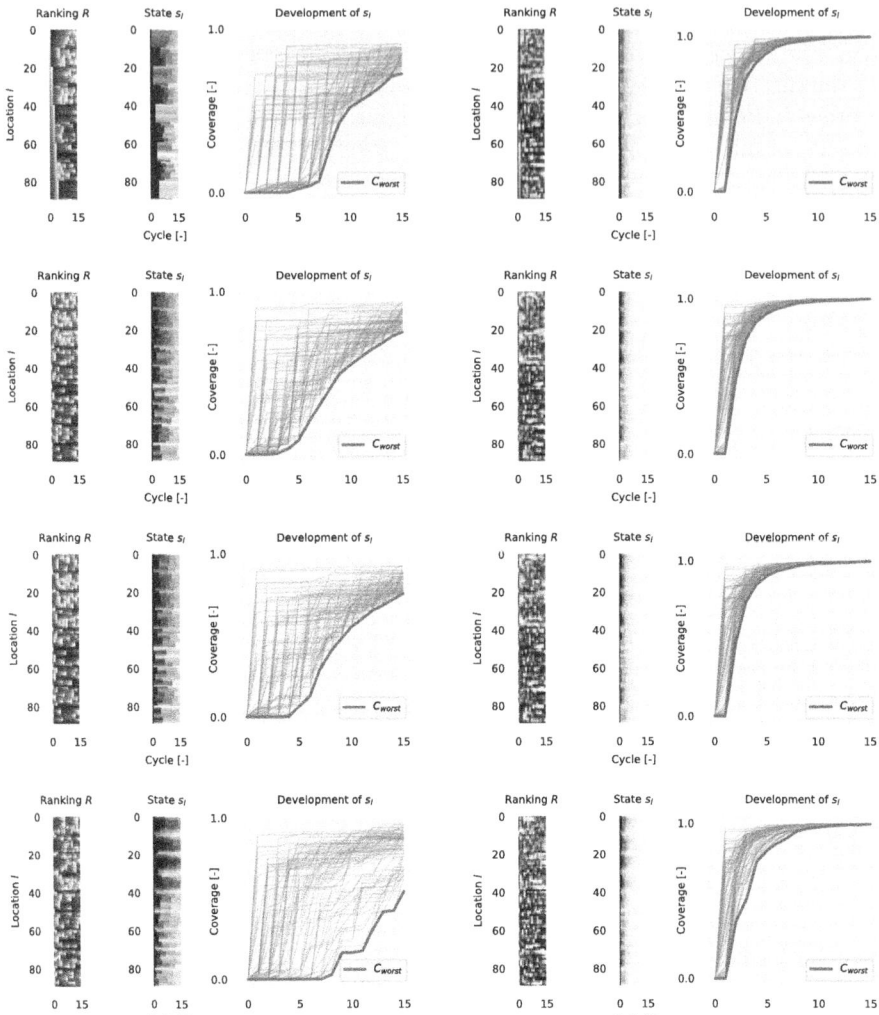

Fig. 2. Comparison of AUC of FreMEnext and Greedy at randomly chosen day d with different values of areas ratio a and ratio of influence of forecast q. **Left column** shows AUC of methods with $a = 0.1$, **right column** shows AUC of methods with $a = 0.5$. **Top row** shows results of Greedy, **other three** rows shows results of FreMEnext with $q = 0.01$, $q = 0.10$, $q = 1.00$, respectively (top-down). **Each graph** shows ranking R in every cycle c, evolution of states s_l over all locations l, and evolution of coverage of every location after every cycle (thin lines), together with evolution of a minimum coverage over all locations C_{worst} (thick red line). AUC is an area under the thick red line. **Bottom row** shows poor results of FreMEnext when using $q = 1$. **Right column** shows very low difference between results when area ratio is $a = 0.5$.

4.3   Evaluation Metric

To determine the completeness of the "image of empty comb" we define achieved coverage C of the whole comb as a minimum state s_l over all locations l in a day d,

$$C_{\text{worst},d}(c) = \min_l s_l^{(c)}, \tag{12}$$

where c is a number of the scanning cycles performed on day d.

To compare the methods performance in the evaluation, we compute the AUC for every combination of areas ratio and day (a, d) defined as

$$AUC_{a,d} = \int_i C_{\text{worst},(a,d)}(i)\, di \tag{13}$$

and use an implementation [40] of the Quade statistical test for complete block design studies [10], with Šidák's correction [47] and significance level set to 5%.

4.4   Impact of Parameters

We use two parameters that influence the results of the evaluation; area ratio a and ratio of spatio-temporal model influence q. The area ratio defines how many locations are visited during a scanning cycle. The original setting uses $a = 1$ which means that the camera visits all locations during each scanning cycle. The authors of [5] studied an influence of partial scans ($0 < a \leq 1$). Their analysis showed that it is not possible to reach the required coverage 99% for values below $a = 0.1$ in reasonable time (one day). Values higher than $a = 0.5$ lead to indifference between results of non-random methods and values higher then $a = 0.8$ between all methods. As the task is to scan the comb in limited time, we calculate and compare $AUC_{a,d}$ of each method for every day and for 10 evenly distributed values of a only for $0.1 \leq a \leq 0.5$, and omit scenarios with $a > 0.5$ that lead to good results even without optimisation of decision-making. This restriction strengthens the differences between methods while preserves original goal.

Parameter q is not part of the analysis in [5]. However, this influence ratio is concealed in normalisation of crowdedness forecasts p_l. Recalculated to q, the normalisation gives us low values, usually $q < 0.01$. We do not want to speculate whether the normalisation or parameter q is mathematically more meaningful, but the interpretation of q is easier. It defines the degree of influence of forecasts on the resulting decision-making. Moreover, its impact on results is interesting and should be taken into account in the future work, see Fig. 2.

From the Fig. 2, we can infer that decisions derived only from the spatio-temporal model do not lead to acceptable results. Such system would avoid "always crowded" areas which leads to inability to cover the whole comb. Choosing the best value of q extends beyond the scope of this work. However, we can estimate that results of FreMEnext for $0.01 \leq q \leq 0.1$ look quite promising. For our evaluation, we chose, partly arbitrary, $q = 0.1$.

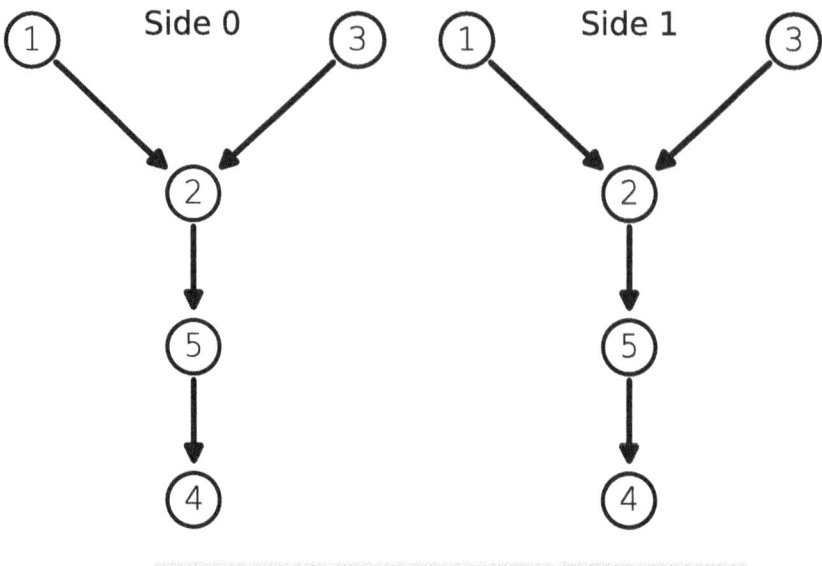

Fig. 3. Diagram showing a comparison of values of AUC for each combination of tested area ratios and day. An arrow shows statistically significant difference between methods obtained from Quade test with Šidák correction. We can see that there is no significant difference between Iterative and FreMEnext, and that the inclusion of forecasts from these models improved the performance of the system. Even though the queen is expected to behave differently on each side (her presence is disjunctive) and the number of locations on each side differs, significance of difference between methods is identical on both sides.

4.5   Results

We evaluated functionality of the proposed FreMEnext in hundreds of cycles of presented task. We can see in Fig. 3 that FreMEnext met the expectation. Similarly to other methods derived from Maps of Dynamics and presented in the original paper [5], FreMEnext forecasts helped the system to make better preferences. Therefore, we expect that the proposed method is capable of deployment in challenging tasks.

We exploited the expectation that the queen behaves differently on each side of the comb and the fact that the hardware setting is not identical, and divided the evaluation into two different tasks - scanning side 0 and scanning side 1. The difference in forecast quality between Iterative and FreMEnext in both schemes is statistically indifferent, while both approaches are significantly better than other methods in both schemes, see Fig. 3. Therefore, we state that our iterative variant implementation, which is also more computationally intensive, did not perform differently.

5 Conclusion

We proposed an extended variant of Frequency Map Enhancement, FreMEnext, suitable for modelling cyclic phenomena quantifiable by rational numbers. It broadens usability of Frequency Map Enhancement in modelling spatio-temporal dynamics and allows for an application in very challenging scientific field— autonomous robotics in biological experiments. We showed its successful implementation in the robotic task that is currently under research. The proposed method following its definition processed millions of observations and built hundreds of models in a simulation consisting of data from the extensive robotic field experiment. Similarly to the original definition [26], FreMEnext has an asymptotic computational complexity $O(n)$. Therefore, we expect it to be applicable in large-scale real-world scenarios, particularly in biohybrid robotics.

Acknowledgements. This work was partially supported by EU project RoboRoyale (964492) and SENSORBEES (101130325). MS was supported by the Field of Excellence COLIBRI (Complexity of Life in basic Research and Innovation) of the University of Graz.

References

1. Abou-Shaara, H.F., Adgaba, N., Al-Ghamdi, A.A.: Current knowledge about behaviors of honey bee queens with highlighting of the importance future studies. J. Basic Appl. Zoology **82**(1), 1–7 (2021). https://doi.org/10.1186/s41936-021-00234-x
2. Allen, M.D.: The honeybee queen and her attendants. Anim. Behav. **8**(3–4), 201–208 (1960)
3. Althaus, S.L., Berenbaum, M.R., Jordan, J., Shalmon, D.A.: No buzz for bees: media coverage of pollinator decline. Proc. Natl. Acad. Sci. **118**(2), e2002552117 (2021)
4. Austin, D., Fletcher, L., Zelinsky, A.: Mobile robotics in the long term-exploring the fourth dimension. In: Proceedings 2001 IEEE/RSJ International Conference on Intelligent Robots and Systems. Expanding the Societal Role of Robotics in the the Next Millennium (Cat. No. 01CH37180), vol. 2, pp. 613–618. IEEE (2001)
5. Blaha, J., et al.: Toward perpetual occlusion-aware observation of comb states in living honeybee colonies. In: 2024 IEEE/RSJ International Conference on Intelligent Robots and Systems (IROS), pp. 5948–5955. IEEE (2024)
6. Bland, D.M., Laakso, T.I., Tarczynski, A.: Analysis of algorithms for nonuniform-time discrete fourier transform. In: 1996 IEEE International Symposium on Circuits and Systems (ISCAS), vol. 2, pp. 453–456. IEEE (1996)
7. Buchmann, S.L., Nabhan, G.P.: The pollination crisis. Sciences **36**(4), 22–27 (1996)

8. Butler, C., Fairey, E.M.: Pheromones of the honeybee: biological studies of the mandibular gland secretion of the queen. J. Apic. Res. **3**(2), 65–76 (1964)

9. Churchill, W., Newman, P.: Experience-based navigation for long-term localisation. Int. J. Rob. Res. **32**(14), 1645–1661 (2013)

10. Conover, W.J.: Practical Nonparametric Statistics, 3rd edn. Wiley, New York (1999)

11. Fentanes, J.P., Lacerda, B., Krajník, T., Hawes, N., Hanheide, M.: Now or later? predicting and maximising success of navigation actions from long-term experience. In: 2015 IEEE International Conference on Robotics and Automation (ICRA), pp. 1112–1117. IEEE (2015)

12. Fèvre, D.P., Dearden, P.K.: Influence of nutrition on honeybee queen egg-laying. Apidologie **55**(4), 53 (2024)

13. Free, J., Ferguson, A., Simpkins, J.: The behaviour of queen honeybees and their attendants. Physiol. Entomol. **17**(1), 43–55 (1992)

14. Ge, Z., Jiang, J., Coombes, M., Liang, S.: Enhancing swift and socially-aware navigation with continuous spatial-temporal routing. Int. J. Soc. Robot. **17**(1), 87–98 (2025)

15. Guizilini, V.C., Ramos, F.T.: A nonparametric online model for air quality prediction. In: AAAI, pp. 651–657 (2015)

16. Hanheide, M., Hebesberger, D., Krajník, T.: The when, where, and how: an adaptive robotic info-terminal for care home residents. In: ACM/IEEE International Conference on Human-Robot Interaction, HRI '17, pp. 341–349. ACM, New York (2017). https://doi.org/10.1145/2909824.3020228

17. Hawes, N., et al.: The strands project: long-term autonomy in everyday environments. IEEE Rob. Autom. Maga. **24**(3), 146–156 (2017)

18. Hebesberger, D., Koertner, T., Gisinger, C., Pripfl, J., Dondrup, C.: Lessons learned from the deployment of a long-term autonomous robot as companion in physical therapy for older adults with dementia a mixed methods study. In: 2016 11th ACM/IEEE International Conference on Human-Robot Interaction (HRI), pp. 27–34. IEEE (2016)

19. Hebesberger, D., Koertner, T., Gisinger, C., Pripfl, J.: A long-term autonomous robot at a care hospital: a mixed methods study on social acceptance and experiences of staff and older adults. Int. J. Soc. Robot. **9**(3), 417–429 (2017)

20. Ilgün, A., et al.: Bio-hybrid systems for ecosystem level effects. In: ALIFE 2021: The 2021 Conference on Artificial Life, p. 41. Artificial Life Conference Proceedings (2021).https://doi.org/10.1162/isal_a_00396

21. Jocher, G., Chaurasia, A., Qiu, J.: Ultralytics yolov8 (2023). https://github.com/ultralytics/ultralytics

22. Johnson, B.R.: Division of labor in honeybees: form, function, and proximate mechanisms. Behav. Ecol. Sociobiol. **64**, 305–316 (2010)

23. Jovan, F., Wyatt, J., Hawes, N., Krajník, T.: A poisson-spectral model for modelling temporal patterns in human data observed by a robot. In: 2016 IEEE/RSJ International Conference on Intelligent Robots and Systems (IROS), pp. 4013–4018. IEEE (2016)

24. Klein, B.A., Stiegler, M., Klein, A., Tautz, J.: Mapping sleeping bees within their nest: spatial and temporal analysis of worker honey bee sleep. PLoS ONE **9**(7), e102316 (2014)

25. Krajník, T., Fentanes, J., Cielniak, G., Dondrup, C., Duckett, T.: Spectral analysis for long-term robotic mapping. In: International Conference on Robotics and Automation (ICRA), pp. 3706–3711. IEEE (2014)

26. Krajník, T., Fentanes, J.P., Santos, J.M., Duckett, T.: Fremen: frequency map enhancement for long-term mobile robot autonomy in changing environments. IEEE Trans. Robot. **33**(4), 964–977 (2017)
27. Krajník, T., et al.: Warped hypertime representations for long-term autonomy of mobile robots. IEEE Rob. Autom. Lett. **4**(4), 3310–3317 (2019)
28. Kucner, T.P., et al.: Survey of maps of dynamics for mobile robots. Int. J. Rob. Res. **42**(11), 977–1006 (2023)
29. Laboratory of Chronorobotics: Kdynakoupit.cz (2019). https://kdynakoupit.cz. Accessed 28 Nov 2022
30. Maisonnasse, A., et al.: New insights into honey bee (apis mellifera) pheromone communication: is the queen mandibular pheromone alone in colony regulation? Front. Zoology **7**, 1–8 (2010)
31. Molina, S., Cielniak, G., Duckett, T.: Go with the flow: exploration and mapping of pedestrian flow patterns from partial observations. In: 2019 International Conference on Robotics and Automation (ICRA), pp. 9725–9731. IEEE (2019)
32. Moore, P.A., Wilson, M.E., Skinner, J.A.: Honey bee queens: evaluating the most important colony member. Bee Health **7**(10) (2015)
33. Rosen, D.M., Mason, J., Leonard, J.J.: Towards lifelong feature-based mapping in semi-static environments. In: 2016 IEEE International Conference on Robotics and Automation (ICRA), pp. 1063–1070. IEEE (2016)
34. Santos, J.M., Krajník, T., Duckett, T.: Spatio-temporal exploration strategies for long-term autonomy of mobile robots. Robot. Auton. Syst. **88**, 116–126 (2017)
35. Sauer, S., Kinkelin, M., Herrmann, E., Kaiser, W.: The dynamics of sleep-like behaviour in honey bees. J. Comp. Physiol. A **189**, 599–607 (2003)
36. Slessor, K.N., Kaminski, L.A., King, G., Borden, J.H., Winston, M.L.: Semiochemical basis of the retinue response to queen honey bees. Nature **332**(6162), 354–356 (1988)
37. Slessor, K.N., Winston, M.L., Le Conte, Y.: Pheromone communication in the honeybee (apis mellifera l.). J. Chem. Ecol. **31**, 2731–2745 (2005)
38. Stefanec, M., et al.: A minimally invasive approach towards "ecosystem hacking" with honeybees. Front. Rob. AI **9**, 791921 (2022)
39. Steffan-Dewenter, I., Potts, S.G., Packer, L.: Pollinator diversity and crop pollination services are at risk. Trends Ecol. Evol. **20**(12), 651–652 (2005)
40. Terpilowski, M.: scikit-posthocs: pairwise multiple comparison tests in Python. J. Open Source Softw. **4**(36), Art. no. 1169 (2019)
41. Ulrich, J., et al.: Autonomous tracking of honey bee behaviors over long-term periods with cooperating robots. Sci. Rob. **9**(95), eadn6848 (2024)
42. Vintr, T., et al.: Toward benchmarking of long-term spatio-temporal maps of pedestrian flows for human-aware navigation. Front. Rob. AI **9** (2022)
43. Vintr, T., et al.: Time-varying pedestrian flow models for service robots. In: 2019 European Conference on Mobile Robots (ECMR), pp. 1–7. IEEE (2019)
44. Vintr, T., et al.: Natural criteria for comparison of pedestrian flow forecasting models. In: 2020 IEEE/RSJ International Conference on Intelligent Robots and Systems (IROS), pp. 11197–11204. IEEE (2020)
45. Wang, Y., Fan, Y., Wang, J., Chen, W.: Long-term navigation for autonomous robots based on spatio-temporal map prediction. Robot. Auton. Syst. **179**, 104724 (2024)
46. Winston, M.L.: The Biology of the Honey Bee. Harvard university press, Harvard (1991)
47. Šidák, Z.: Rectangular confidence regions for the means of multivariate normal distributions. J. Am. Stat. Assoc. **62**(318), 626–633 (1967)

Towards a Modular Compliant Actuator Toolkit

Oliver Smith[(✉)], Swen E. Gaudl[iD], and Pablo Borja[iD]

School of Engineering, Computing and Mathematics, University of Plymouth,
Drake Circus, Plymouth PL4 8AA, UK
oliver.smith@students.plymouth.ac.uk,
{swen.gaudl,pablo.borjarosales}@plymouth.ac.uk

Abstract. Compliant Actuators differ from traditional Servo Actuators via the ability to sense and control for forces, in addition to position and velocity. A multitude of concepts exist: force-torque control of brushless DC motors, Series Elastic Actuators (SEAs) featuring a physical elastic element, and Variable Stiffness Actuators (VSA), which use a stiffness control mechanism to modulate the physical stiffness of the elastic element. However, due to the complexity, variety, and prohibitive cost of parts and fabrication, there is a lack of reproduction, which hinders the, development, adoption, and application of such devices.

This paper introduces the concept of a Modular Compliant Actuator Toolkit (MCAT), intended to facilitate cost-effective design, control, fabrication, and testing. The MCAT comprises of 3D printed panels and parts which assemble to form a box-shaped compliant actuator, using off-the-shelf components, supplemented with associated hardware and code. By identifying the challenges pertaining to the research and development of compliant actuators , and segmenting them into discrete aspects of the MCAT, a user can focus their efforts on their specific research, without the upfront cost of time, labour, and finance. Additionally presents on-going progress towards a low cost SEA prototype, and discusses the lessons learned from development.

Keywords: compliance · variable stiffness · series elastic actuator · robotics

1 Introduction

Robots during the 20th century were mainly used in manufacturing applications, requiring the ability to handle large payloads with repeatable precision. These robots were designed for position control exclusively. As such, their limbs, joints, transmissions, and end-effectors were all designed to be as rigid as possible, understanding that any form of elasticity in the system will contribute to positional error.

By contrast, humans and animals feature elasticity as part of their joint actuation, enabling them to perceive and control for forces, through modulating

A. Cavalcanti et al. (Eds.): TAROS 2025, LNAI 16045, pp. 94–107, 2026.
https://doi.org/10.1007/978-3-032-01486-3_9

the joint stiffness. Accordingly, robots lacking stiffness control are unsuitable for many real-world applications, and unsafe for operation in shared human robot environments. Researchers have pioneered different concepts for realising joint stiffness control, broadly referred to as *Compliant Actuators*, endowing robots with advantageous capabilities, including force control, shock absorption, energy efficiency, harmonic and explosive motions. However there are limitations to existing research, principally the cost of development, and lack of reproduction. To facilitate cost-effective research and development of compliant actuators, this paper introduces work towards a modular compliant actuator toolkit (MCAT).

The rest of this paper is as follows: A background of compliant actuator technology is given, followed by the design of the MCAT and demonstrative Series Elastic Actuator (SEA) prototype. Successive iterations to the design, fabrication, code based and control schema, are discussed. Specifically, calibration data for position and force, are presented and discussed, from which future work aims are set.

2   Background

There is a diverse range of concepts to realise compliant actuation.

Brushless DC motor control via current modulation, known as *Force Torque Control*, achieved using Field-Orientated-Control or Direct-Torque-Control. Such devices use larger, more expensive motors to generate the desired torque, either as *Direct-Drive* actuators with no gearing, or *Quasi-Direct* with a low enough gear ratio, so that the actuator remains *Backdrivable*. These devices require custom or expensive control boards for real-time response to external forces, but are a mature technology, used today in robot arms and quadrupeds. The major drawback of these devices is the lack of physical elasticity, and as such, a much larger motor is required to absorb shock forces. External force backdrive the motor, which generates significant heat during use, and can wear gears over time.

Subsequently, there are *Series Elastic Actuators*, which place a spring between the actuator/transmission and the output joint, using sensors to measure the external force. To achieve the desired stiffness, the position of the actuator can be modulated. The name given for this method is *Equilibrium Stiffness Control* but is also known as *Virtual Stiffness* control, noting that the physical stiffness constant of the spring is unchanged. SEAs are advantageous over brushless motors for their shock tolerance, force control, safety, and energy conservation. There have been attempts at commercialisation; the collaborative robot arm Baxter of Rethink Robotics, and the Hebi X-Series SEA. One key drawback of SEAs is the fixed stiffness constant of the elastic element, which unlike muscles, cannot be modulated. Virtual stiffness control methods such as direct force-torque control of brushless motors, or equilibrium position control of SEAs passive elastic element.

Variable Stiffness Actuators (VSAs) iterate upon series elastic actuators through the introduction of a stiffness control mechanism. There are many different VSA concepts for modulating the physical stiffness of the elastic element:

Agonist-antagonist VSAs are bio-inspired, using two non-linear SEAs working in opposition to achieve control of the output joint stiffness, akin to muscles pairs such as the human bicep and tricep [1,12,13,13]. Lever arm mechanisms adjust the effective length of the elastic element [6,11,15,17], often using a leaf spring [4,5], and, pre-tensioner mechanisms use a second servo motor to pre-load the spring [8,20,21,24].

Research across these concepts has explored many different aspects of design and control: Actuation, transmission, the elastic element, sensor choice and location, non-linearity, arrangement, modelling, and the method of control. There are a wide variety of concepts for realising control of force, torque, and physical stiffness of robot joints [8,18,19,22,23]. Compliant Actuators come in many kinds, all shapes, sizes, arrangements, mehanical complexity, and it has been argued by leaders of the field that compliant actuators require a task-specific design, tailoring the design of the mechanism and choice of components, to the intended application [18]. This is supported by the most successful examples, which were designed from the ground up for a specific task. This is reflected in the research, with the majority of which is either a test bench rig [4,6,16,17,21] - unsuited for application, an actuator embodied as part of a robot limb [2,9,13] or prosthesis [12], or one-off devices, which frequently make use of custom fabricated parts, often using high-end CNC or 3D printing machines [3,10,11,14], and thus are prohibitively expensive. These task-specific and one-off builds present a limitation of academia, and result in a lack of reproduction. To create a compliant actuator requires the practice of a variety of technical skills, including CAD modelling, math modelling, electronics, coding and control theory. The development requires many iterations, and fabrication is often prohibitively expensive for smaller projects/teams. Whether for the purpose of academic research and development of prototypes, commercial or industry applications, the investment of time and labour to realise a compliant actuator is often not cost-effective.

3   Design

3.1   The Modular Compliant Actuator Toolkit

The MCAT is in essence, a box, assembled from four panels, with each panel segmenting aspects of the design and control of compliant actuators. The concept of the MCAT is to create a free and open-source toolkit for the research and development of compliant actuators. As such, the MCAT uses affordable and commonly available parts and hardware, with all original parts 3D printed on a low-end FDM machine, to be assembled using hand tools. The only custom work required is soldering pull-up resistors for the encoders, and cutting the shafts to length.

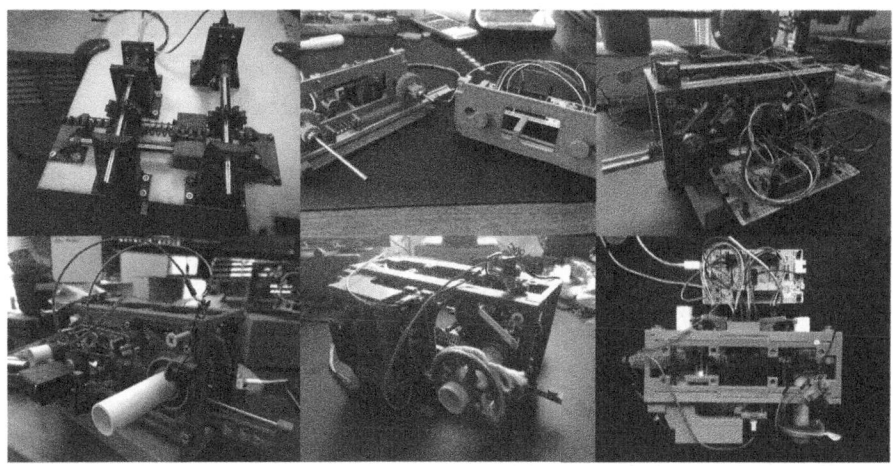

Fig. 1. Successive iterations towards a Modular Compliant Actuator Toolkit (MCAT), and a SEA prototype. From top left to bottom right: Top Left: The SEA test bench which motivated the MCAT concept. Middle: A rejected concept, lacking negative space. Right: The first functional MCAT-SEA device. Bottom left: Version two. Bottom middle and right: Version 3.5, presented in this paper.

Two "Template Panels" are used to define the MCAT exterior dimensions, a 60×200 mm horizontal panel, and 100×200 mm vertical panel. Walls are 5×5 mm in thickness to balance structural rigidity against printing times, and 5mm increments are used in the design whenever possible for a cohesive design. The size is deliberate: to take advantage of the 3D printer workspace, and provide users with a generous amount of internal space to work with. Users should be able to draw from a "library" of CAD models for different components, as well as assemblies, reducing the amount of original work.

Ultimately, the use of the MCAT is driven by the user's own goals. However, a general high-level workflow for using the MCAT is as follows: A user would start by printing the template box and selecting their hardwarem making use of reusing known components (e.g., bearings, shafts, sensors). It is expected that the user will already have a desired torque source, elastic element, and stiffness mechanism in mind. Using the MCAT box, the user should develop one panel at a time, first the actuator panel, then the opposing sensor panel, - from which a closed-loop position control system can be constructed. Afterward, the saliant stiffness mechanism can be designed, which will thus define the mechanical geometry of the overall system.

The MCAT is intended to take a user from concept to functional prototype, and then support iterative development. Once a user is satisfied with their choice of hardware, stiffness mechanism, control strategy, and other design parameters, they can move beyond the MCAT. At that point, the knowledge gained can be used to design a one-off actuator built from high-quality materials, compact, enclosed, and tailored for the final application.

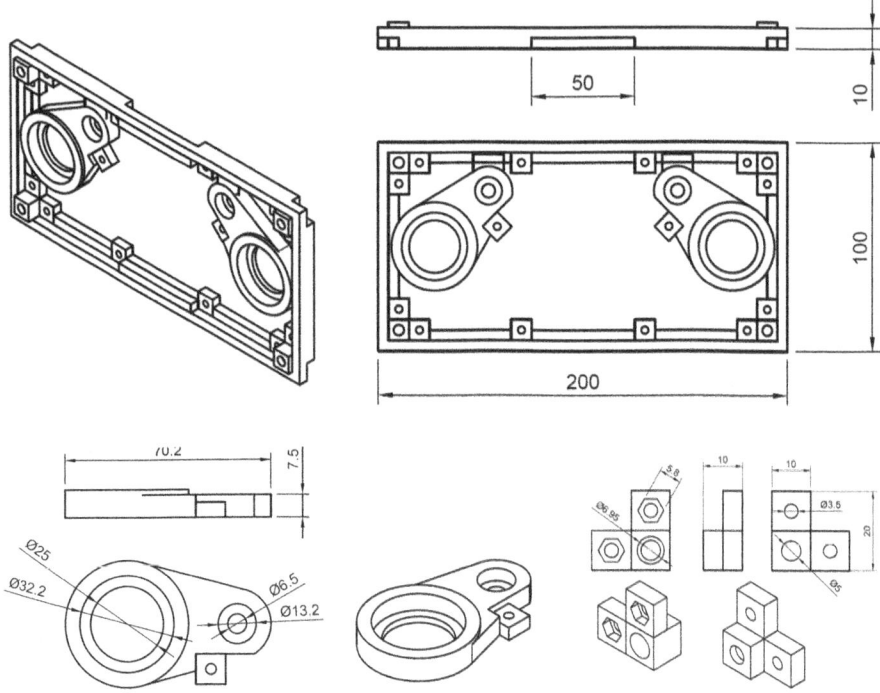

Fig. 2. Vertical Template Panel Drawing. Top: full panel; Bottom left: bearing assembly; Bottom right: "corner piece" featuring hex M3 hex huts and M5 brass insert, used in Template Panel assembly, and printing calibration.

The Actuator Panel features the torque source (servo, stepper, brushless DC), pertaining hardware (motor driver, voltage regulator, power jack), and gearing to the input shaft. Space is given for a reduction gearing or full gearbox.

The Sensor Panel Includes the control hardware (typically a microcontroller), relevant sensors (encoders, potentiometers, strain gauges), and space for any additional electronics.

The Stiffness-Mechanism panel should include the elastic element, transmission, and mechanism for stiffness control.

The Attachment Panel Only serves as a means for integrating an MCAT box with a larger system. For example, a 50 mm carbon fibre shaft, or 20 mm aluminium extrusion.

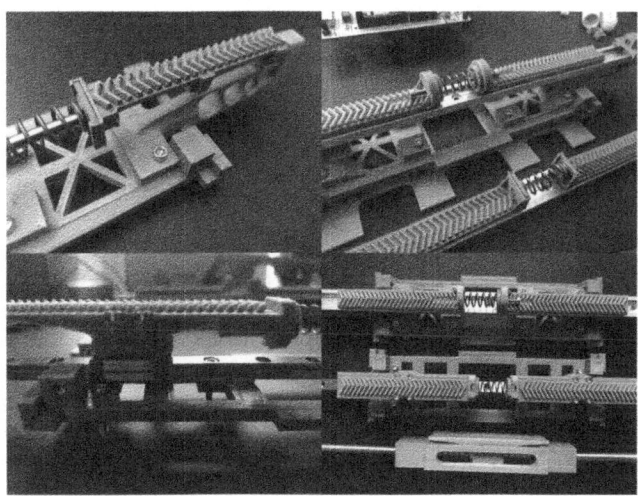

Fig. 3. Iterations of the stiffness mechanism. Top Left: Use of a 4 mm shaft to reduce friction by minimizing points of contact. Top Right: Replacing a friction fit spring with a bolted version to reduce play. Bottom Left: A close up of the current stiffness mechanism. Bottom Right: Successive iterations, with the bottom most being in development.

Parts List				
Item Name	Thread / Diameter	Length / Width	Material	Quantity
Threaded Insert	M5 / 6.4mm	9.35mm	Brass	16
Countersunk Machine Screw	M5	25mm	Stainless Steel	8
Hex Nut	M3	2.2mm	Stainless Steel	44
Hex Socket Cap Screw	M3	16mm	Stainless Steel	21
Hex Socket Cap Screw	M3	25mm	Stainless Steel	4
Encoder Bearings	4mm I.D 13mm O.D	5mm	Stainless Steel	8
Shaft Bearings	20mm I.D 32mm O.D	7mm	Stainless Steel	8
Joint Shafts	20mm	100mm	PVC	2
Encoder Shafts	4mm	100mm	Stainless Steel	2
Mounting Hub	4mm I.D	5mm	Aluminium	5
Linear Guide Rail	N/A	300mm	Aluminium	1
Compression Spring	Spring rate 4.51N/mm	29.5mm / 11.25mm	Steel	1

Fig. 4. Table of parts used.

3.2   The MCAT SEA Variant

A Series Elastic Actuator is being developed, using the MCAT. The SEA prototype is useful both in refining the MCAT, and realising an affordable device that can serve as a benchmark for future work. The MCAT-SEA presented uses off-the-shelf hardware including the voltage regulator, servomotor, steel compression spring, guide rail, two hall-effect encoders, and microcontroller. The servo has a reported stall torque of 16 Kgcm at 6 volts, operating speed of 0.16 s/60 and uses a pulse width modulation (PWM) signal with a period of 20 ms. The steel compression spring used has a free length of 26 mm, maximum deflection of 14.8 mm, spring rate of 1.85 N/mm, and thus a maximum force of 27.38 N. The magnetic hall effect encoders used have a count per revolution of 4096, a 1:1 gearing is used between the input joint and encoder shaft. To improve measurement accuracy, a 2:1 reduction was implemented for the output joint. A rack and pinion mechanism is used to translate the rotation into linear translation, with a guide rail used to provide smooth motion. Helical gears are used for the joint shafts to transmit a larger force and minimise backlash. A bevel was added to reduce the risk of misprinted parts meshing improperly.

Iterative Development. The development of a Series Elastic Actuator using the MCAT shows the value of a dedicated resource for compliant actuator prototyping. Noteworthy iterations include: The joint shafts were upgraded from 4 mm steel to 20 mm PVC, and subsequently, better joint shaft bearing with reduced friction were used. The compression spring was swapped for a lower stiffness constant, for easier measurement of spring deflection characteristics. Additionally, the method of attaching the spring to the internal stiffness mechanism was improved, using 3 mm bolts instead of a friction fit which resulted in 1 mm of backlash. The output encoder shaft was modified to use a 2:1 gear reduction, effectively doubling the joint encoder precision. A servo motor alignment tool uses a 5 mm bolt for manual fine tuning of the input shaft and servo spur gears. Numerous stiffness mechanisms were tested, alternating from a 8 mm steel shaft to an aluminium guide rail, back to a 4 mm steel shaft, and then again to a more expensive guide rail with linear ball bearing guide carriages.

4   Control

The use of an elastic element as part of an otherwise rigid mechanical system introduces new challenges in control.

4.1   Equilibrium Stiffness Control (EqSC)

For Series Elastic Actuators, there exists a proven method of controlling for the desired stiffness and position of the output joint, Equilibrium position stiffness control.

In our context, Hooke's law can be written as follows:

$$F = -k_{act} * (\ell - s - a), \tag{1}$$

where F represents the force due to the spring; k_{act} denotes the spring constant; ℓ is the total actuator length; a represents the free spring length; s denotes the translational displacement of the actuator.

From (1), we compute the external force F_0 acting on the spring, and subsequently K_{des}, the desired "virtual" stiffness: (2)

$$F - F_0 = -k_{des} * (l - l_0) \tag{2}$$

Equations (1) and (2) can be substituted and resolved for the desired position s_{des} of the actuator (3), an equation known as equilibrium stiffness control (EqSC).

$$s_{des} = l - a + (F_0 - K_{des}(l - l_0))/k_{act} \tag{3}$$

4.2   Control Schema

The user specifies a desired position and stiffness setting, which are input to the EqSC function, along with an estimate of the spring deflection and output joint force, from which a target position for the actuator is generated. A Proportional-Integral- Derivative (PID) controller is used to generate an output value which is used to modulate the Pulse-Width-Modulation (PWM) signal, reading from the output joint encoder to improve accuracy. Last, a simple threshold is used post-calibration to account for any remaining, spring deflection error. The control schema presented is simplistic, as the current focus is on building robust control functionality.

4.3   Code Base

As part of the MCAT, a C++ library is in development, with a class of functions pertaining compliant actuators. Converting between linear and rotational translation, calculating spring deflection and force estimates, mapping the actuator and torque source PWM ranges. EqSC and PID functions are included, along with logging functionality for experimentation. The main application code is multi-threaded, enabling the user to separate and better understand aspects of control; *sense*, *process*, and *actuate*. Further development remains; ideally, a user should be able to create an instance of an MCAT object from the library, setting key parameters regarding geometric and physical properties.

5   Calibration Experiments

It is important to understand the advantages and disadvantages of compliant actuators, whether compared against traditional servo motor actuators, or the many SEA and VSA concepts. "Variable stiffness actuators: The user's point of view" [7] explains the salient experiments and performance metrics for a compliant actuator. These include the actuator's speed vs torque, torque vs stiffness profiles, from which a three-dimensional workspace of the torque-speedstiffness volume, plus torque-deflection curves, used to measure hysteresis. However, as the MCAT-SEA prototype is still in development, the value of the data presented identifying and understanding issues, used to evidence future development decisions.

5.1 Experiment Setup

The experiments devised plot target position against a measured variable, wherein the servo motor is "sweeps" the full $0 - 180°$ range of the actuator in increments of $5°$, in both directions. For constant load conditions, a mass is attached to a shaft via string and pulley (see 1), spooling in order to maintain a constant load. These preliminary experiments investigate two key error metrics; output shaft position error, and the spring deflection error. By measuring these variables over the range of the stiffness mechanism, unwanted characteristics can be observed and better understood. Attention is given to hysteresis, the variance in error for the given direction, and cogging, the behaviour where gears or motors experience jerky, uneven movement due to improper teeth engagement.

5.2 Position Calibration

Figure 5 shows the different characteristics between recent iterations plotting the joint angle error from the target position, using PWM values without any PID correction. The Version 3 (Fig 5a) uses a $IGUS$ aluminum channel guide rail with plastic and brass guide carriages, whilst 3.5 (Fig 5b) uses a higher quality $MGN9B$ linear guide rail complete with ball bearing carriage (see 3). Additionally, 3.5 uses a 2:1 reduction gear ratio for the output encoder shaft, and lower friction shaft bearings.

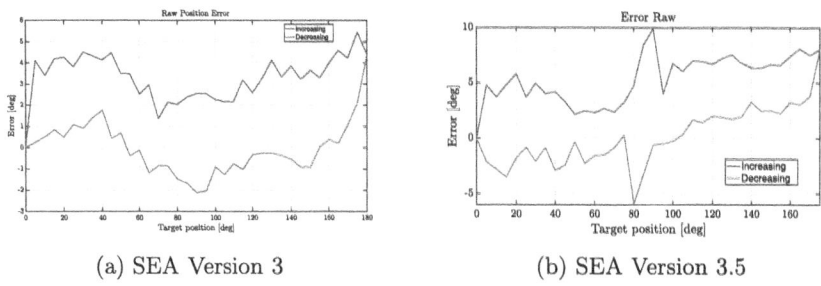

(a) SEA Version 3   (b) SEA Version 3.5

Fig. 5. Measured encoder position error, comparing differences between stiffness mechanisms.

Comparing the two, it can be observed that both prototypes exhibit a large hysteresis, which is the result of a compression spring being used as an extension spring, when the servo is in reverse. Version 3 has a smaller error overall than 3.5 Version 3.5 exhibits a severe cogging, with a noticeable spike in the error. By printing the gears with a tooth profile that is too small, minor errors in printing result in a significant meshing inconsistency, and a gear reduction amplifies this problem.

Figure 6 shows the raw position error, compared against the result of PID correction, from which a significant reduction both in error and cogging.

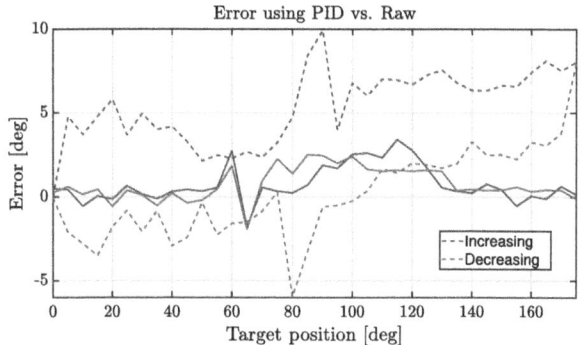

Fig. 6. The reduction of position error using PID control.

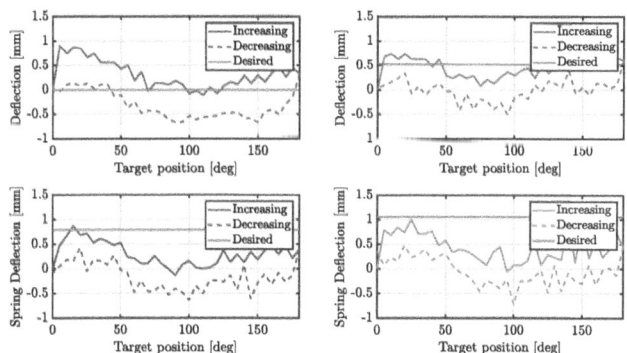

Fig. 7. An average spring error (mm) over the range of actuator, for different constant loads (degrees). From top left to bottom right: 0 g, 100 g, 150 g, 200 g.

5.3 Spring Calibration

Figures 7 and 8 show the spring deflection profiles of Version 3 and 3.5, respectively, in response to different constant loads , with the horizontal red line indicating the desired response, as a ground truth. For the profiles in 7, the deflection error is an average of three trials.

Ideally, the deflection would be consistent and with negligible error across the full range of scenarios, but this is not the case. Mechanical design and fabrication issues, mainly the tolerance and alignment of printed parts, introduce friction, stiction, backlash, which manifest as hysteresis and cogging characteristics. However, it can be observed that the shape of the error profile is consistent for different constant loads, and experiment repetitions.

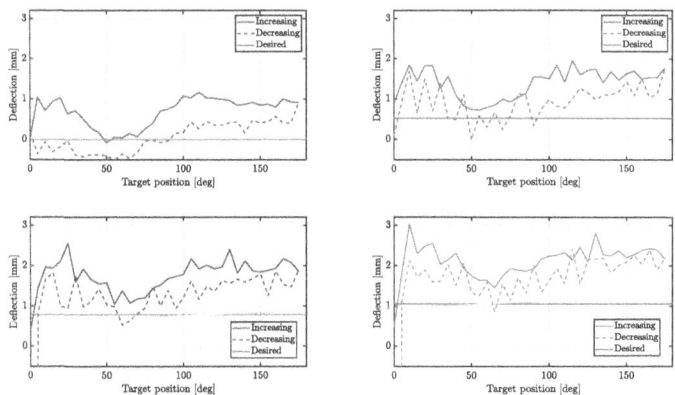

Fig. 8. Spring deflection (mm) profiles over the position range for Version 3.5. Load conditions, from top left to bottom right: 0 g, 100 g, 150 g, 200 g. Red line indicates the desired deflection.

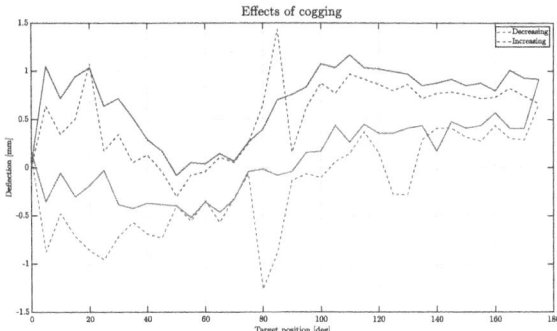

Fig. 9. The effects of cogging, caused by a misaligned encoder spur gear.

In Fig. 9 mis-alignment of the output encoder shaft spur gear causes improper meshing, resulting in the presence of a large spike in position error. This highlights the importance of gear modulus and alignment, and also suggests that other spikes are also the result of less noticeable cogging effects.

6   Conclusion and Future Work

This paper introduces work towards a Modular Compliant Actuator Toolkit, a resource intended to facilitate cost-effective research and development of compliant actuator prototypes. Development progress of a Series Elastic Actuator is presented and discussed. The results of these experiments demonstrate successful iterations using the MCAT and a prototyping resource, and identify areas in need of further development. Currently, the SEA prototype has limitations owing thequality of the torque source, and the cogging of the gear-trains, whilst MCAT concept itself is only limited insofar as the quality of the 3D printed parts. Improvements for the next version include: Both chevron and spurs gears should use a larger modulus and bevelled walls to minimise cogging. Encoder gear reductions should be fitted to both joints, with a larger gear ratio, and code to handle position rollover. A stiffness mechanism featuring consistent, bi-directional stiffness constant is highly desirable, to reduce hysteresis. The error profiles could be modeled and used to calibrate the device. Further improvements to system modelling control schema, such as adaptive gains or nested PID loops can be used to optimise performance. The long term aim is to release the MCAT as an open source project, including CAD files, schematics, code, and documentation for design, fabrication, assembly, and testing.

References

1. Azadi, M., Behzadipour, S., Faulkner, G.: Antagonistic variable stiffness elements. Mech. Mach. Theory **44**(9), 1746–1758 (2009)
2. Bigras, P., Lambert, M., Perron, C.: New formulation for an industrial robot force controller: Real-time implementation on a kuka robot. In: 2007 IEEE International Conference on Systems, Man and Cybernetics, pp. 2794–2799 (2007). https://doi.org/10.1109/ICSMC.2007.4413645
3. Catalano, M.G., et al.: Vsa-cubebot: a modular variable stiffness platform for multiple degrees of freedom robots. In: 2011 IEEE International Conference on Robotics and Automation, pp. 5090–5095 (2011). https://doi.org/10.1109/ICRA.2011.5980457
4. Choi, J., Hong, S., Lee, W., Kang, S.: A variable stiffness joint using leaf springs for robot manipulators. In: 2009 IEEE International Conference on Robotics and Automation, pp. 4363–4368 (2009). https://doi.org/10.1109/ROBOT.2009.5152716
5. Choi, J., Hong, S., Lee, W., Kang, S., Kim, M.: A robot joint with variable stiffness using leaf springs. IEEE Trans. Rob. **27**(2), 229–238 (2011). https://doi.org/10.1109/TRO.2010.2100450
6. Dežman, M., Gams, A.: Rotatable cam-based variable-ratio lever compliant actuator for wearable devices. Mech. Mach. Theory **130**, 508–522 (2018)
7. Grioli, G., Wolf, S., Garabini, M., Catalano, M., Burdet, E., Caldwell, D., Carloni, R., Friedl, W., Grebenstein, M., Laffranchi, M., et al.: Variable stiffness actuators: the user's point of view. Int. J. Robot. Res. **34**(6), 727–743 (2015)

8. Guo, J., Tian, G.: Conceptual design and analysis of four types of variable stiffness actuators based on spring pretension. Int. J. Adv. Rob. Syst. **12**(5), 62 (2015)
9. Hirzinger, G., Brunner, B., Dietrich, J., Heindl, J.: Sensor-based space robotics-rotex and its telerobotic features. IEEE Trans. Robot. Autom. **9**(5), 649–663 (1993). https://doi.org/10.1109/70.258056
10. Kashiri, N., Caldwell, D.G., Tsagarakis, N.: A self-adaptive variable impedance actuator based on intrinsic non-linear compliance and damping principles. In: 2017 IEEE International Conference on Robotics and Automation (ICRA), pp. 1248–1254 (2017). https://doi.org/10.1109/ICRA.2017.7989148
11. Kim, B.S., Song, J.B.: Hybrid dual actuator unit: a design of a variable stiffness actuator based on an adjustable moment arm mechanism. In: 2010 IEEE International Conference on Robotics and Automation, pp. 1655–1660 (2010). https://doi.org/10.1109/ROBOT.2010.5509264
12. Martinez-Villalpando, E., Herr, H.: Agonist-antagonist active knee prosthesis: a preliminary study in level-ground walking. J. Rehabil. Res. Dev. **46**, 361–73 (2009). https://doi.org/10.1682/JRRD.2008.09.0131
13. Petit, F., Friedl, W., Höppner, H., Grebenstein, M.: Analysis and synthesis of the bidirectional antagonistic variable stiffness mechanism. Robotics Research. In: The Eleventh International Symposium. Springer Tracts in Advanced Robotics, vol. 20, no. 2, pp. 684–695 (2015)
14. Pratt, J., Krupp, B., Morse, C.: Series elastic actuators for high fidelity force control. Ind. Robot: Int. J. (2002)
15. Sardellitti, I., Medrano-Cerda, G.A., Tsagarakis, N., Jafari, A., Caldwell, D.G.: Gain scheduling control for a class of variable stiffness actuators based on lever mechanisms. IEEE Trans. Rob. **29**(3), 791–798 (2013). https://doi.org/10.1109/TRO.2013.2244787
16. Sulzer, J., Peshkin, M., Patton, J.: Marionet: an exotendon-driven rotary series elastic actuator for exerting joint torque. In: 9th International Conference on Rehabilitation Robotics, 2005. ICORR 2005, pp. 103–108 (2005). https://doi.org/10.1109/ICORR.2005.1501062
17. Sun, J., Zhang, Y., Zhang, C., Guo, Z., Xiao, X.: Mechanical design of a compact serial variable stiffness actuator (svsa) based on lever mechanism. In: 2017 IEEE International Conference on Robotics and Automation (ICRA), pp. 33–38 (2017). https://doi.org/10.1109/ICRA.2017.7988687
18. Van Ham, R.: Compliant actuator designs. IEEE Robot. Autom. Mag. **12**(9–10), 1157–1171 (2009)
19. Vanderborght, B., et al.: Variable impedance actuators: a review. Robot. Auton. Syst. **61**(12), 1601–1614 (2013)
20. Vanderborght, B., Tsagarakis, N.G., Semini, C., Van Ham, R., Caldwell, D.G.: Maccepa 2.0: adjustable compliant actuator with stiffening characteristic for energy efficient hopping. In: 2009 IEEE International Conference on Robotics and Automation, pp. 544–549 (2009). https://doi.org/10.1109/ROBOT.2009.5152204
21. Vanderborght, B., Van Ham, R., Lefeber, D., Sugar, T.G., Hollander, K.W.: Comparison of mechanical design and energy consumption of adaptable, passive-compliant actuators. Int. J. Robot. Res. **28**(1), 90–103 (2009)
22. Veale, A.J., Xie, S.Q.: Towards compliant and wearable robotic orthoses: a review of current and emerging actuator technologies. Medical Eng. Phys. **38**(4), 317–325 (2016)

23. Wolf, S., et al.: Variable stiffness actuators: review on design and components. IEEE/ASME Trans. Mechatron. **21**(5), 2418–2430 (2016). https://doi.org/10.1109/TMECH.2015.2501019
24. Wolf, S., Hirzinger, G.: A new variable stiffness design: matching requirements of the next robot generation. In: 2008 IEEE International Conference on Robotics and Automation, pp. 1741–1746 (2008). https://doi.org/10.1109/ROBOT.2008.4543452

Locomotion and Control

Multi-Contact Posture Generation Using Vector Field Inequalities

Daniel S. J. Derwent$^{(\boxtimes)}$ [ID], Simon Watson[ID], and Bruno Vilhena Adorno[ID]

Manchester Centre for Robotics and AI, University of Manchester, Oxford Rd,
Manchester M13 9PL, UK
{daniel.johnson-2,simon.watson,bruno.adorno}@manchester.ac.uk

Abstract. We present a novel method for solving posture generation problems in multi-contact motion planning for legged robots. Our approach builds on the state of the art by generating not only optimal contact placement locations but also simultaneously verifying the existence of a feasible trajectory allowing the robot to make those contacts. By optimising the robot's velocity rather than its configuration, we are able to replace what would otherwise be a highly constrained non-linear optimisation problem with a series of linearly constrained quadratic programs, which are comparatively much faster to solve. We implement our posture generator as part of a receding horizon multi-contact planning algorithm to generate several motion plans in challenging environments, including chimney climbing and negotiating narrow passages by forming contacts on walls. Using Bayesian data analysis, we find that the mean execution time of our planner is faster than the state of the art in all scenarios tested (ranging from 10 s to 10 min faster), while in two of four scenarios it returns shorter paths (ranging from 23.4 stance changes longer to 53.9 stance changes shorter).

Keywords: Contact planning · Legged robots · Vector-field inequalities

1 Introduction

A unique challenge of legged motion planning is the need to plan how the robot will make and break contacts with its environment. If the desired form of motion is known and approximately cyclical (*e.g.*, walking across uneven terrain), it may suffice to use a pre-specified or adaptive gait. However, if robots are to perform acyclic motions such as navigating sparse irregular footholds [2] or very rough terrain where the precise contact locations are critical [7], then they must explicitly plan where, and in what sequence, individual contacts should be made or broken. This is referred to as multi-contact motion planning.

To guarantee that a given contact combination (*i.e.*, a *stance* [2]) is feasible, multi-contact planners must find safe whole-body configurations (referred to as *witness postures* [4]) that allow the robot to realise the intended stance

© The Author(s), under exclusive license to Springer Nature Switzerland AG 2026
A. Cavalcanti et al. (Eds.): TAROS 2025, LNAI 16045, pp. 111–123, 2026.
https://doi.org/10.1007/978-3-032-01486-3_10

while respecting certain constraints (*e.g.*, avoiding collisions, maintaining balance, *etc.*). The task of finding a witness posture for a given stance is known as the '*posture generation problem*'.

1.1 Related Works

Multi-contact planners are typically divided into Motion-Before-Contact (MBC) and Contact-Before-Motion (CBM) approaches [2]. MBC algorithms plan a collision-free torso trajectory and then solve the posture generation problem to find witness postures for each resulting torso pose. For example, the planner in [14] generates a large offline dataset of randomly sampled limb configurations that is searched at runtime to assemble witness postures. MBC planners typically execute faster than CBM planners, needing only to consider the robot's torso pose rather than the full configuration. However, MBC approaches must assume what kinds of motion the robot can execute and constrain the trajectory search to regions where such motions are most likely possible, leading to a loss of generality (*e.g.*, [14] does not consider configurations where all contacts are on vertical surfaces).

Alternatively, CBM algorithms plan a series of stances that are combined to form an overall motion, solving the posture generation problem for each stance to verify their feasibility. Early CBM planners solve the posture generation problem using random sampling [2,6] that is biased in later works by user-defined primitives [7]. Another approach by Mordatch *et al.* uses numerical optimisation to select optimal contacts from a set of candidate footholds while simultaneously generating witness postures for each [11]. However, these approaches are all limited by their reliance on possible footholds being pre-surveyed.

The CVBFP algorithm [4] improves upon that in [11] by allowing the optimiser to choose contact locations from anywhere on a given surface. However, CVBFP assumes that whole-body trajectories between witness postures exist without verifying this to be the case. This is partially addressed by the multi-stage framework presented in [5], wherein the first stage computes a sequence of stances and witness postures, and the second stage generates a whole body trajectory which executes the motion. However, because the stance sequence is planned prior to the trajectory, it remains possible that a stance sequence may be returned for which a feasible trajectory cannot be found.

1.2 Statement of Contributions

We propose a novel posture generator that improves upon the state-of-the-art by:

- Guaranteeing that kinematically feasible whole-body trajectories between witness postures exist *before* they are added to the search tree, verifying assumptions made in [4,5].
- Generating the stance, witness posture, and whole-body trajectory *simultaneously*, removing the need for any additional stages of planning.

We also incorporate our posture generator into a novel receding horizon planning architecture that allows the robot to iteratively re-plan as it explores. We demonstrate our approach by planning several challenging motions for the Corin hexapod [15], including scenarios where some or all of the robot's contacts are on vertical surfaces (see Fig. 1). Finally, we use Bayesian data analysis techniques to compare our planner's performance to that of CVBFP [4].

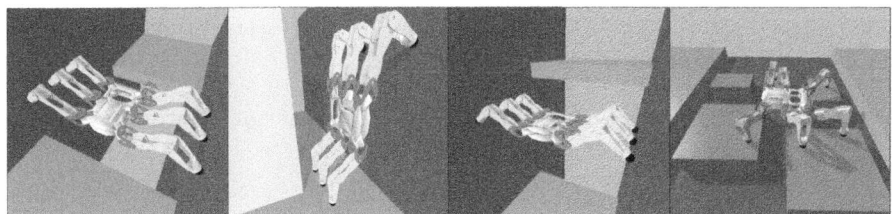

Fig. 1. Simulated example scenarios used in this work. We refer to these scenarios (from left to right) as '*chimney walking*', '*wall walking*', '*chimney climbing*', and '*stepping stones*'.

2   Mathematical Preliminaries

The proposed posture generator relies heavily on geometrical primitives, such as planes, lines, and points, in addition to rigid transformations, twists, and wrenches, all of which are elegantly represented using dual quaternion algebra. Additionally, several robot modelling and control techniques that are useful for solving posture generation problems have been developed that utilize the strong algebraic properties of dual quaternion algebra, making this an attractive choice. Quaternions belong to the set $\mathbb{H} \triangleq \{h_1 + \hat{i}h_2 + \hat{j}h_3 + \hat{k}h_4 \; : \; h_1, h_2, h_3, h_4 \in \mathbb{R}\}$, where $\hat{i}$, $\hat{j}$, and $\hat{k}$ denote imaginary units such that $\hat{i}^2 = \hat{j}^2 = \hat{k}^2 = \hat{i}\hat{j}\hat{k} = -1$. Quaternions can represent 3D orientations and rotations using elements of the subset $\mathbb{S}^3 \triangleq \{h \in \mathbb{H} \; : \; \|h\| = 1\}$, as well as positions using elements of the subset $\mathbb{H}_p \triangleq \{h \in \mathbb{H} \; : \; \text{Re}(h) = 0\}$ [16]. *Dual* quaternions extend quaternions and belong to the set $\mathcal{H} \triangleq \{h + \varepsilon h' \; : \; h, h' \in \mathbb{H}, \varepsilon^2 = 0, \varepsilon \neq 0\}$. The set of *unit* dual quaternions, $\underline{\mathcal{S}} \triangleq \{\underline{h} \in \mathcal{H} \; : \; \|\underline{h}\| = 1\}$, represent rigid transformations in 3D space, and any $\underline{x} \in \underline{\mathcal{S}}$ can be written as $\underline{x} = r + \varepsilon \frac{1}{2}pr$, where $r \in \mathbb{S}^3$ and $p \in \mathbb{H}_p$ denote the rotation and translation components of the rigid transformation respectively [16]. Analogously to $\mathbb{H}_p$, we also define the subset $\mathcal{H}_p \triangleq \{h + \varepsilon h' : h, h' \in \mathbb{H}_p\}$, which is useful for modelling certain primitives.

The coefficients of elements of any of the aforementioned sets can be bijectively mapped into vectors. For example,

$$\text{vec}_3\left(\hat{i}h_1 + \hat{j}h_2 + \hat{k}h_3\right) = \begin{bmatrix} h_1 & h_2 & h_3 \end{bmatrix}^T, \quad \text{vec}_4\left(h_1 + \hat{i}h_2 + \hat{j}h_3 + \hat{k}h_4\right) = \begin{bmatrix} h_1 & h_2 & h_3 & h_4 \end{bmatrix}^T.$$

This is particularly convenient when using task-space constrained controllers with geometrical constraints because they can be formulated as quadratic programs with linear constraints in the control inputs. For example, consider the robot configuration $q(t) \triangleq \left[\text{vec}_4\left(r(t) \right) \; \text{vec}_3\left(p(t) \right) \; \theta(t) \right]^T$ where $r(t) \in \mathbb{S}^3$ and $p(t) \in \mathbb{H}_p$ denote the torso orientation and position at time t, respectively, such that the torso pose may be given as $\underline{x}(t) = r(t) + \varepsilon\frac{1}{2}p(t)r(t)$, and $\theta(t)$ is the vector of joint configurations. Consider a task vector $x \triangleq x\left(q \right)$, which might represent, for instance, the robot pose, position, or orientation, and a constant desired task vector $x_d \in \mathbb{R}^m$. We can define an error vector $\tilde{x} \triangleq x - x_d$ and minimise the error using the control law

$$
\begin{aligned}
u \in \underset{\dot{q}}{\arg\min} \quad & \left\| J_{\tilde{x}}\dot{q} + \eta_o\tilde{x} \right\|_2^2 + \lambda^2 \left\| \dot{q} \right\|_2^2 \\
\text{subject to} \quad & W\left(q \right)\dot{q} \preceq w\left(q \right),
\end{aligned}
\tag{1}
$$

where $J_{\tilde{x}} = \partial\tilde{x}/\partial q$, $\eta_o \in (0, \infty)$, $\lambda \in [0, \infty)$, and $W\left(q \right) \in \mathbb{R}^{\ell \times n}$ and $w\left(q \right) \in \mathbb{R}^\ell$ impose ℓ linear constraints on $\dot{q}$ [10].

The vector field inequality (VFI) framework allows us to transform non-linear geometric constraints on q into linear constraints on $\dot{q}$, which ensure that the original constraints on q are met [10]. This requires only a differentiable signed distance function $d \triangleq d(q)$ between a geometrical entity kinematically coupled to the robot and another geometrical primitive in the task space, and the Jacobian matrix $J_d \in \mathbb{R}^{1 \times n}$ such that $\dot{d} = J_d\dot{q}$ [10]. To keep a robot entity outside of a given region, e.g., for collision avoidance, we can define $\tilde{d}(q) \triangleq d(q) - d_{\text{safe}}$ and formalise this requirement as $\tilde{d}(q) \geq 0$. Using the VFI framework, we can restate this as the constraint

$$
\dot{\tilde{d}}(q) \geq -\eta_d\tilde{d}(q) \iff -J_d\dot{q} \leq \eta_d\tilde{d}(q),
\tag{2}
$$

where $\eta_d \in (0, \infty)$ determines the maximum approach velocity [10]. Similarly, to keep a robot entity inside a given region, e.g., keeping the centre of mass inside a support polygon, we restate the requirement as $\tilde{d}(q) \leq 0$ to obtain the constraint $J_d\dot{q} \leq -\eta_d\tilde{d}(q)$. Robot entities and zones of interest (i.e., restricted zones and safe zones) can take on a wide variety of forms, with distance functions and corresponding Jacobians defined in the literature for combinations of points, lines, planes and many others [10,12,13]. Throughout this paper, the relevant signed distance function between two primitives $\underline{a}, \underline{b} \in \mathcal{H}$ is denoted by $d_{a,b}$ and the *square* distance by $D_{a,b}$. In both cases the Jacobian matrix is denoted $J_{a,b}$. The formulations for each distance function and Jacobian are found in [10], unless otherwise stated.

3   Proposed Posture Generation Approach

The core idea behind our approach is to use a VFI-constrained controller like (1), which drives the robot into an appropriate stance/witness posture. This allows us to simultaneously generate new stances while implicitly generating the witness posture and whole-body trajectory, which can then be tracked by a closed-loop controller on the real robot.

The posture generator receives the initial configuration and stance, the foot being moved (the *foot of interest*, or FOI) and the surface to place it upon. The posture generator works in three stages—the lifting stage, transition stage, and placement stage. The lifting stage finds a configuration where the robot can safely break the existing contact with the FOI. The transition stage then moves the FOI to the desired contact surface, and the placement stage optimises its location on that surface. Our formulation considers all three stages as part of the same movement, which is simpler than [4] and [5], where lifting and placing are distinct actions generated by separate posture generator calls. Often the FOI can be lifted from the initial configuration, in which case the lifting stage is skipped. Likewise, if the FOI already lies on the desired surface then the transition stage is also skipped.

Thanks to our simpler formulation, we replace one non-linear optimisation problem in the configuration space [4,5] with a series of linearly constrained quadratic programs in the tangent space, which considerably reduces execution times. Once the control input for a given sampling period is computed, we use numerical integration to generate the next configuration, recalculate the functions of q (*e.g.*, the Jacobian matrices), and then generate the next control input. This continues until either the stage's stopping criteria are satisfied or an evaluation limit is reached.

The VFIs guarantee that if the robot entities are outside of their restricted zones at time $t = 0$, then they will continue to be so for all times $t > 0$ [10] when operating in *continuous time*. Since we use *discrete* numerical integration steps, the robot can briefly enter the restricted zone between consecutive time steps, potentially resulting in unsafe behaviour or an unfeasible optimisation problem. To address this, we artificially inflate the boundaries of each restricted zone by a buffer $b_d \in (0, \infty)$, which can be given as a function of the robot's maximum speed and the integration period, and terminate the optimisation if the non-inflated boundaries are crossed. We thus re-write the constraint (2) for keeping outside a given region as

$$\dot{\tilde{d}}(q) \geq -\eta_d \left(\tilde{d}(q) - b_d \right) \implies -J_d \dot{q} \leq \eta_d \left(\tilde{d}(q) - b_d \right). \tag{3}$$

Analogously, the tightened constraint to stay inside a safe region is given as

$$\dot{\tilde{d}}(q) \leq -\eta_d \left(\tilde{d}(q) + b_d \right) \implies J_d \dot{q} \leq -\eta_d \left(\tilde{d}(q) + b_d \right). \tag{4}$$

Furthermore, to ensure that there is always at least one solution to problem (1), we design our constraints such that they are always satisfied by $\dot{q} = 0$. When q violates the inflated boundaries but does not violate the original boundaries (*i.e.*, $0 \leq \tilde{d}(q) < b_d$), we have $\tilde{d}(q) - b_d < 0$ and $\dot{q} = 0$ does not satisfy (3). To overcome this problem, we add a slack variable $s_d \in [0, \max(0, -\eta_d(\tilde{d}(q) - b_d))]$ to the constraint, resulting in

$$- J_d \dot{q} \leq \eta_d \left(\tilde{d}(q) - b_d \right) + s_d. \tag{5}$$

Therefore, $0 \leq \tilde{d}(\boldsymbol{q}) < b_d$ implies $s_d = -\eta_d(\tilde{d}(\boldsymbol{q}) - b_d)$, and (5) becomes $-\boldsymbol{J}_d\dot{\boldsymbol{q}} \leq 0$, to which $\dot{\boldsymbol{q}} = \boldsymbol{0}$ is a valid solution, disallowing any further progress towards the restricted zone. Analogously, when staying inside a safe region but beyond the tightened boundary, we have that $-b_d < \tilde{d}(\boldsymbol{q}) \leq 0$ and the slack variable is rewritten as $s_d \in [0, \max(0, \eta_d(\tilde{d}(\boldsymbol{q}) + b_d))]$ so that (4) is relaxed as $\boldsymbol{J}_d\dot{\boldsymbol{q}} \leq -\eta_d\left(\tilde{d}(\boldsymbol{q}) + b_d\right) + s_d$, making $\dot{\boldsymbol{q}} = \boldsymbol{0}$ a feasible solution. Finally, problem (1) is rewritten as

$$\boldsymbol{u} \in \underset{\dot{q},s}{\operatorname{argmin}} \quad \Psi(\dot{\boldsymbol{q}}) + \Phi(\dot{\boldsymbol{q}}, \boldsymbol{s}) \tag{6}$$
$$\text{subject to} \quad \dot{\boldsymbol{q}} \in \mathcal{C}_{\dot{q}} \text{ and } \boldsymbol{s} \in \mathcal{C}_s$$

with

$$\Phi(\dot{\boldsymbol{q}}, \boldsymbol{s}) = \lambda^2 \|\dot{\boldsymbol{q}}\|_2^2 + \alpha^2 \|\boldsymbol{s}\|_2^2, \tag{7}$$

where $\alpha, \lambda \in [0, \infty)$ and $\boldsymbol{s} = \begin{bmatrix} s_1 \cdots s_\ell \end{bmatrix}^T$, with s_i denoting the ith slack variable. The task function $\Psi(\dot{\boldsymbol{q}})$ defines the task for a given stage in the form of (1), whereas $\mathcal{C}_{\dot{q}}$ and $\mathcal{C}_s$ denote the sets of variables $\dot{\boldsymbol{q}}$ and $\boldsymbol{s}$, respectively, that respect the relevant task constraints.

4   Constraints and Objectives

4.1   Common Constraints

Five types of constraints apply to all stages of the posture generator: avoiding collisions and self-collisions; maintaining balance; preventing contacts from sliding; respecting the limits and underlying topologies of the optimisation variables; and avoiding excessive torso tilting.

Collisions Avoidance and Self-Collision Constraints: We describe the surfaces in the environment as a set $\Pi_{\text{obj}}(\boldsymbol{q}) \subseteq \{\boldsymbol{\pi}_{O_1}, \ldots, \boldsymbol{\pi}_{O_n}\}$, wherein each element $\boldsymbol{\pi}_{O_i} \in \boldsymbol{\mathcal{S}}$ is a plane, such that $\boldsymbol{\pi}_{O_i} = \boldsymbol{n}_{O_i} + \varepsilon d_{O_i}$, with $\boldsymbol{n}_{O_i} \in \mathbb{S}^3 \cap \mathbb{H}_p$ being the plane normal and d_{O_i} being the distance between the plane and the origin of the reference frame [16]. Since the planes are infinite, to represent non-convex free spaces (such as the wall walking environment shown in Fig. 1), the planes in Π_{obj} are selected based on the robot's configuration $\boldsymbol{q}$, similar to the approach in [12]. We define $\mathcal{A} \subset \mathcal{H}$ as the set of dual quaternion primitives representing each robot body, which may be planes, lines or points [16]. Hence, the collision avoidance constraints are defined as

$$-\boldsymbol{J}_{\underline{\boldsymbol{a}}_i\boldsymbol{\pi}_{O_j}}\dot{\boldsymbol{q}} \leq \eta_d\left(\tilde{d}_{\underline{\boldsymbol{a}}_i\boldsymbol{\pi}_{O_j}} - b_d\right) + s_{\underline{\boldsymbol{a}}_i\boldsymbol{\pi}_{O_j}}, \ \forall\underline{\boldsymbol{a}}_i \in \mathcal{A}, \forall\boldsymbol{\pi}_{O_j} \in \Pi_{\text{obj}}(\boldsymbol{q}). \tag{8}$$

The process for self-collision avoidance is similar. We denote by $\mathcal{B}(\underline{\boldsymbol{a}}) \subset \mathcal{A}$ the subset of primitives in $\mathcal{A}$ which are forbidden from colliding with $\underline{\boldsymbol{a}} \in \mathcal{A}$. The self-collision constraint is thus written as

$$-\boldsymbol{J}_{\underline{\boldsymbol{a}}\underline{\boldsymbol{b}}}\dot{\boldsymbol{q}} \leq \eta_d\left(\tilde{d}_{\underline{\boldsymbol{a}}\underline{\boldsymbol{b}}} - b_d\right) + s_{\underline{\boldsymbol{a}}\underline{\boldsymbol{b}}}, \ \forall\underline{\boldsymbol{b}} \in \mathcal{B}(\underline{\boldsymbol{a}}), \forall\underline{\boldsymbol{a}} \in \mathcal{A}. \tag{9}$$

Balance Constraint: We use the generalised support polygon proposed by Bretl and Lall [3] that describes the set of (x, y)-coordinates that the robot's centre of mass $\boldsymbol{p}_C \in \mathbb{H}_p$ must occupy to maintain static balance without sliding for contacts on arbitrary surfaces. We define a set of planes $\Pi_{\text{balance}} \triangleq \{\boldsymbol{\pi}_{B_1}, \ldots, \boldsymbol{\pi}_{B_m}\}$ describing a vertical prism whose (x, y) cross section is the support polygon. Hence, we obtain the VFI constraint

$$\boldsymbol{J}_{\boldsymbol{p}_C \boldsymbol{\pi}_{B_i}} \dot{\boldsymbol{q}} \leq -\eta_d \left(\tilde{d}_{\boldsymbol{p}_C \boldsymbol{\pi}_{B_i}} + b_d \right) + s_{\boldsymbol{p}_C \boldsymbol{\pi}_{B_i}}, \ \forall \boldsymbol{\pi}_{B_i} \in \Pi_{\text{balance}}. \tag{10}$$

Preventing Foot Sliding: We constrain each foot to remain inside a sphere centred on its desired location. Defining the set $\mathcal{P}_{\text{feet}} \subset \mathbb{H}_p$ containing the position of the frame attached to each foot, and denoting by $\boldsymbol{p}_{d_i} \in \mathbb{H}_p$ the desired location of foot i, we write

$$\boldsymbol{J}_{\boldsymbol{p}_i \boldsymbol{p}_{d_i}} \dot{\boldsymbol{q}} \leq -\eta_d \left(\tilde{D}_{\boldsymbol{p}_i \boldsymbol{p}_{d_i}} + b_d \right) + s_{\boldsymbol{p}_i \boldsymbol{p}_{d_i}}, \ \forall \boldsymbol{p}_i \in \mathcal{P}_{\text{feet}}, \tag{11}$$

where $\tilde{D}_{\boldsymbol{p}_i \boldsymbol{p}_{d_i}} (\boldsymbol{q}) \triangleq D_{\boldsymbol{p}_i \boldsymbol{p}_{d_i}} (\boldsymbol{q}) - R_{\text{sphere}}^2$, with R_{sphere} being the sphere's radius.

Respecting Variable Limits and Topologies: Since the configuration vector $\boldsymbol{q}$ includes the term $\boldsymbol{r} \in \mathbb{S}^3$, the optimisation must be constrained to ensure that $\dot{\boldsymbol{q}}$ respects the properties of the underlying topology of unit quaternions—*i.e.*, the condition $\|\boldsymbol{r}\| = \text{vec}_4 (\boldsymbol{r})^T \text{vec}_4 (\boldsymbol{r}) = 1$ must be maintained. By taking the time derivative of this expression, we obtain the constraint

$$\text{vec}_4 (\dot{\boldsymbol{r}})^T \text{vec}_4 (\boldsymbol{r}) = 0. \tag{12}$$

We also constrain $\boldsymbol{s}$ to respect its limits, and constrain $\dot{\boldsymbol{q}}$ to respect limits on $\boldsymbol{q}$ (similar to [13]). Given limits on $\boldsymbol{q}$ in the form $\boldsymbol{q}_{\min}, \boldsymbol{q}_{\max} \in \mathbb{R}^n$, we also define $\boldsymbol{s}_{\max} \subset \mathbb{R}^\ell$ as an upper limit on $\boldsymbol{s}$ such that each element i of $\boldsymbol{s}_{\max}$ is given by $s_{\max_i} = \max \left(-\eta_d (\tilde{d}_i - b_d), \eta_d (\tilde{d}_i + b_d) \right)$. Thus we write the constraints

$$\eta_d \left(\boldsymbol{q}_{\min} - \boldsymbol{q} + b_d \right) \leq \dot{\boldsymbol{q}} \leq \eta_d \left(\boldsymbol{q}_{\max} - \boldsymbol{q} - b_d \right), \qquad \boldsymbol{0}_\ell \leq \boldsymbol{s} \leq \boldsymbol{s}_{\max}, \tag{13}$$

where $\boldsymbol{0}_\ell \in \mathbb{R}^\ell$ is a vector of zeros.

Preventing Robot Tilting: Finally, we constrain the robot's orientation to lie within a maximum tolerance from a desired value. Like CVBFP [4], our planner incorporates a guide path that may be generated autonomously or by the user. Therefore, the desired torso orientation is defined as that of the closest point on the guide path to the current configuration. We then obtain lines describing the x, y and z axes of the robot's torso frame with respect to the world frame $(\underline{\boldsymbol{l}}_x, \underline{\boldsymbol{l}}_y, \underline{\boldsymbol{l}}_z \in \mathcal{H}_p \cap \underline{\boldsymbol{\mathcal{S}}}$, respectively) as well as those for the desired torso orientation (denoted $\underline{\boldsymbol{l}}_{d_x}, \underline{\boldsymbol{l}}_{d_y}, \underline{\boldsymbol{l}}_{d_z} \in \mathcal{H}_p \cap \underline{\boldsymbol{\mathcal{S}}}$). Using the angular distance function between two lines $d_{\phi_{L_1} \phi_{L_2}}$ and its Jacobian matrix $\boldsymbol{J}_{\phi_{L_1} \phi_{L_2}}$ as described in [13], we write

$$\boldsymbol{J}_{\phi_{L_i} \phi_{L_{d_i}}} \dot{\boldsymbol{q}} \leq -\eta_d \left(\tilde{d}_{\phi_{L_i} \phi_{L_{d_i}}} + b_d \right) + s_{\phi_{L_i} \phi_{L_{d_i}}}, \ \forall \underline{\boldsymbol{l}}_i \in \{\underline{\boldsymbol{l}}_x, \underline{\boldsymbol{l}}_y, \underline{\boldsymbol{l}}_z\}. \tag{14}$$

4.2 Lifting Stage

In the lifting stage, the posture generator moves the robot into a configuration where the FOI is not required for the robot's balance and can thus be safely lifted. We compute two generalised support polygons [3], one *with* and one *without* the FOI, whose respective sets of planes are denoted Π_{with} and Π_{without}, and we define the line $\underline{l}_{\text{cent}} \in \mathcal{H}_p \cap \underline{\mathbf{S}}$ that is parallel to the world frame's z-axis and intersects the centroid of the region Π_{without}. Thus, we define the task function for the lifting stage as $\Psi_L(\dot{\mathbf{q}}) = \left\| \mathbf{J}_{\mathbf{p}_C \underline{l}_{\text{cent}}} \dot{\mathbf{q}} + \eta_o \tilde{d}_{\mathbf{p}_C \underline{l}_{\text{cent}}} \right\|_2^2$, which drives the robot's CoM, $\mathbf{p}_C$, towards $\underline{l}_{\text{cent}}$ until $\tilde{d}_{\mathbf{p}_C \underline{\pi}_i} \leq -b_d$ for all $\underline{\pi}_i \in \Pi_{\text{without}}$. If this condition is already met, then the lifting stage is skipped. We define the sets $\mathcal{C}_{\dot{q}}$ and $\mathcal{C}_s$ for the lifting stage as the values of $\dot{\mathbf{q}}$ and $\mathbf{s}$, respectively, that respect constraints (8) to (14). Note that (10) uses $\Pi_{\text{balance}} = \Pi_{\text{with}}$ for the lifting stage, but all subsequent stages use $\Pi_{\text{balance}} = \Pi_{\text{without}}$.

4.3 Transition Stage

In the transition stage, the FOI is brought into contact with the desired surface if it is not already. The desired contact surface is a plane $\underline{\pi}_{\text{con}} \in \underline{\mathbf{S}}$ with boundaries defined by the set of planes Π_{bound}. Thus, denoting the position of the FOI $\mathbf{p}_F \in \mathbb{H}_p$, we consider the transition stage satisfied if and only if $\tilde{d}_{\mathbf{p}_F \underline{\pi}_i} \leq -b_d$ for all $\underline{\pi}_i \in \Pi_{\text{bound}}$ and $\tilde{D}_{\mathbf{p}_F \underline{\pi}_{\text{con}}} \leq -b_d$. The objective function for this stage depends on whether $\mathbf{p}_F$ respects the boundaries in Π_{bound}. If all the boundary planes are respected, then we constrain $\mathbf{p}_F$ to continue respecting them by applying the constraint

$$\mathbf{J}_{\mathbf{p}_F \underline{\pi}_i} \dot{\mathbf{q}} \leq -\eta_d \left(\tilde{d}_{\mathbf{p}_F \underline{\pi}_i} + b_d \right) + s_{\mathbf{p}_F \underline{\pi}_i}, \ \forall \underline{\pi}_i \in \Pi_{\text{bound}}, \tag{15}$$

while the task function $\Psi_{T_r}(\dot{\mathbf{q}}) \triangleq \left\| \mathbf{J}_{\mathbf{p}_F \underline{\pi}_{\text{con}}} \dot{\mathbf{q}} + \eta_o \tilde{D}_{\mathbf{p}_F \underline{\pi}_{\text{con}}} \right\|_2^2$ drives $\mathbf{p}_F$ towards $\underline{\pi}_{\text{con}}$. Alternatively, if one or more boundary plane in Π_{bound} is not respected, then constraint (15) is not applied and the task function is re-written as $\Psi_{T_n}(\dot{\mathbf{q}}) \triangleq \left\| \mathbf{J}_{\mathbf{p}_F \underline{l}_{\text{con}}} \dot{\mathbf{q}} + \eta_o \tilde{D}_{\mathbf{p}_F \underline{l}_{\text{con}}} \right\|_2^2 + \Psi_{T_r}(\dot{\mathbf{q}})$, where $\underline{l}_{\text{con}} \in \mathcal{H}_p \cap \underline{\mathbf{S}}$ is a line through the centroid of the contact plane which is perpendicular to its surface, similar to that used in the lifting case. Thus this task function also brings $\mathbf{p}_F$ into the region described by Π_{bound}.

Finally, $\mathbf{p}_F$ is constrained to prevent it from crossing in-front of any preceding legs. For example, the middle left foot cannot cross in-front of the front left foot (designated the *blocking foot*). To define this constraint, we first define a plane $\underline{\pi}_x$ that intersects the blocking foot with a normal vector parallel to the x-axis of the robot's torso frame, which points forward with respect to the body. Thus, we define the constraint

$$\mathbf{J}_{\mathbf{p}_F \underline{\pi}_x} \dot{\mathbf{q}} \leq -\eta_d \left(\tilde{d}_{\mathbf{p}_F \underline{\pi}_x} + b_d \right) + s_{\mathbf{p}_F \underline{\pi}_x}. \tag{16}$$

As before, we define $\mathcal{C}_{\dot{q}}$ and $\mathcal{C}_s$ for the transition stage as the values of $\dot{\mathbf{q}}$ and $\mathbf{s}$, respectively, that respect constraints (8) to (16).

4.4   Placement Stage

The placement stage optimises the position of p_F on π_{con} by minimising a potential field $U(q) : Q \to \mathbb{R}$ that is based on a guide path composed of line segments linking waypoint positions for each foot. Here, we consider only the potential field associated with the FOI, denoted $U_F(q)$, as no other foot is free to move. Let us denote the closest point on the relevant guide path to p_F as $p_U \in \mathbb{H}_p$ and the point that terminates the line segment containing p_U as $p_T \in \mathbb{H}_p$. Thus, $U_F(q)$ is given as $U_F(q) \triangleq \beta D_{p_F p_U} + \gamma D_{p_U p_T}$, where $\beta, \gamma \in [0, \infty)$. Thus, to minimise $U_F(q)$, the posture generator forms contacts as close to the guide path as possible by minimising $D_{p_F p_U}$ while making as much progress towards the goal as possible by minimising $D_{p_U p_T}$. Writing the Jacobian of $U_F(q)$ with respect to q as $J_{U_F}(q) \triangleq \beta J_{p_F p_U} + \gamma J_{p_U p_T}$, the task function for the placement stage is given as $\Psi_P(\dot{q}) = \|J_{U_F}\dot{q} + \eta_o U_F(q)\|_2^2$. Finally we limit the maximum square distance from p_F to π_{con} by applying the constraint

$$J_{p_F \pi_{\text{con}}} \dot{q} \leq -\eta_d \left(\tilde{D}_{p_F \pi_{\text{con}}} + b_d \right) + s_{p_F \pi_{\text{con}}}. \tag{17}$$

The sets $C_{\dot{q}}$ and C_s are thus given for the placement stage as the values of $\dot{q}$ and s respectively which respect constraints (8) to (17).

5   Other Considerations

5.1   Numerical Integration

Once a control input is generated by using (6), the robot configuration is updated via numerical integration as follows. First, the configuration velocity vector $\dot{q} \triangleq \left[\text{vec}_4(\dot{r}(t)) \ \text{vec}_3(\dot{p}(t)) \ \dot{\theta}(t)\right]^T$ is extracted from $u = (\dot{q}, s)$, and the torso pose derivative is calculated as $\dot{\underline{x}}(t) = \dot{r}(t) + \varepsilon \frac{1}{2}(\dot{p}(t)r(t) + p(t)\dot{r}(t))$. Then, the next torso pose $\underline{x}(t + \tau)$ and joint angle vector $\theta(t + \tau)$, where $\tau \in (0, \infty]$ is the integration step, are calculated as

$$\underline{x}(t + \tau) = \exp\left(\tau \dot{\underline{x}}(t)\underline{x}(t)^*\right)\underline{x}(t), \qquad \theta(t + \tau) = \theta(t) + \tau\dot{\theta}(t), \tag{18}$$

where the (dual quaternion) exponential map and group operation are used in the first expression to ensure that the underlying topological space of unit dual quaternions [16] is respected. The pose $\underline{x}(t + \tau)$ can hence be decomposed into $r(t + \tau)$ and $p(t + \tau)$, and used to form the overall configuration $q(t + \tau)$. As mentioned in Sect. 3, the integration step may bring the robot into the restricted region, necessitating cancelling the control input generation. This happens most often with the contact sliding constraint (11), which is typically very tight. We partially address this by using the following constrained controller to correct drift in the foot positions resulting from the numerical step,

$$u \in \underset{\dot{q}}{\text{argmin}} \qquad \|J_{\text{drift}}\dot{q} + \eta_o D_{\text{drift}}\|_2^2 + \lambda^2 \|\dot{q}\|_2^2$$

$$\text{subject to} \quad \text{vec}_4(\dot{r})^T \text{vec}_4(r) = 0, \tag{19}$$

where $D_{\mathrm{drift}} \in \mathbb{R}^6$ is the stacked vector of square distances between each foot and its desired location, and $J_{\mathrm{drift}} = \partial D_{\mathrm{drift}}/\partial q$. This reduces the frequency of violations but still necessitates small values of τ to avoid violating the remaining constraints on (6). We resolve this by varying τ between $\tau_{\min}$ and $\tau_{\max}$, making large steps where possible and smaller steps where necessary.

When a value of u is returned by solving (6), the posture generator calculates $q(t + \tau)$ using $\tau = \tau_{\max}$. The controller in (19) is used to correct any contact drifts, and the resulting configuration is checked to verify that the constraints are satisfied. If so, then the posture generator progresses to the next optimisation. If, however, $q(t+\tau)$ is invalid, then $\tau \leftarrow \tau - \Delta\tau$ and $q(t+\tau)$ is recalculated. To maintain non-oscillatory numerical stability, we must ensure that $\eta_o \tau \leq 1$ [1], thus each time τ is changed, η_o is re-calculated as $\eta_o = {^{\tau_\eta}}/\tau$, where $\tau_\eta \in (0, 1]$ is a user-defined constant. This continues until either a valid step is found or $\tau = \tau_{\min}$, in which case the posture generator terminates and returns a failure.

5.2   Receding Horizon Planning Strategy

The posture generator is implemented as part of our receding horizon contact planning (RHCP) algorithm. We do not give a full account of RHCP here, but it is described more fully in [8]. For the purposes of this paper, the main feature of RHCP is that it performs a local breadth-first search wherein one call to the posture generator is made for each combination of a foot and a contact surface in the environment. The resulting child nodes, each containing a feasible stance and an associated witness posture, are expanded in the same way to produce a second generation of children, and so on until a horizon depth $k_{\max}$ is reached. At that point, the node on the horizon whose witness posture best minimises the potential field is chosen, the first foot step towards the stance contained in that node is executed, and the process repeats until the robot reaches the goal.

6   Experiments and Results

Our planner and posture generator were compared to CVBFP in the four simulated scenarios depicted in Fig. 1. Both planners generated 130 motion plans for Corin in each scenario using the same starting configurations for both planners sampled from a normal distribution for each motion plan. RHCP used a two-step planning horizon. All tests used an IntelÂ® Core™ i9-7900X Processor. Bayesian data analysis techniques were used to compare the number of stance changes in each plan and the total planning time, assuming that both metrics can be modelled by t-distributions [9]. Note that lifting and then placing a foot counts as two stance changes. The probability distributions of the difference in means and the effect size for each scenario are shown in Fig. 2. A region of practical equivalence (ROPE) of ± 0.1 was used to determine which effect sizes are statistically significant and is shown in *red* in Fig. 2.

In 57 wall walking tests and one stepping stones test, CVBFP failed to return a plan within two hours and was timed out. These cases are therefore excluded

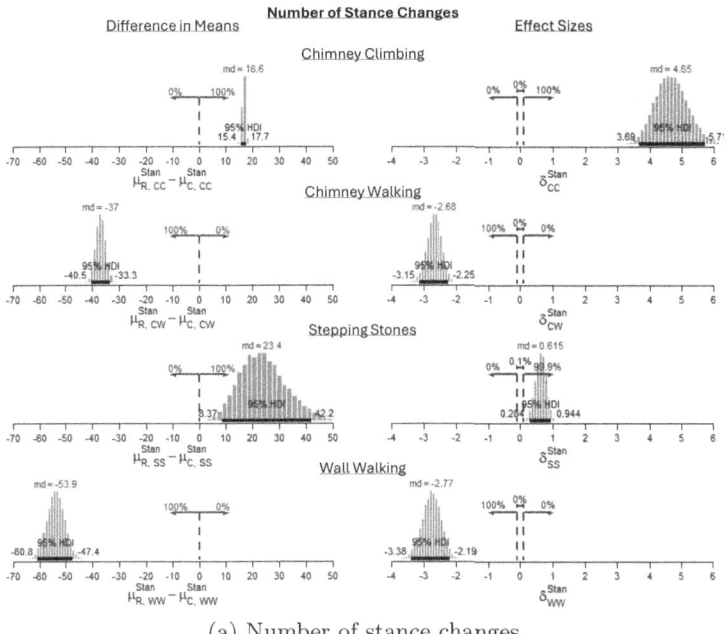

(a) Number of stance changes.

(b) Planning time.

Fig. 2. Probability distributions for the stance changes (*top*) and planning time (*bottom*) in each environment. The difference in means $\mu_R - \mu_C$ between RHCP and CVBFP (*left*) and effect sizes σ (*right*) are given in each case.

from the analysis in Fig. 2. We hypothesise that in these cases CVBFP became stuck because the robot had assumed a configuration where its balance was critically dependent on a particular foot, preventing that foot from being lifted and thus preventing the robot from making forward progress. Backing up in the search tree could resolve this problem, but due to its policy of sibling node generation [4], CVBFP is slow to consider this option, preferring to try alternative placements for the remaining feet until it exhausts its options and is forced to backtrack. Our planner does not suffer from this problem because we only explore a single contact location for a given foot and surface pair, making RHCP comparatively quicker to give up on unproductive lines of exploration and accept backing up. Further research is required to provide more confidence in this hypothesis, but we note that similar problems were also encountered in our preliminary work [8].

As one might expect, given that our planner is local while CVBFP is global, Fig. 2a shows a statistically significant increase in the number of stance changes made in the chimney climbing and stepping stones scenarios, with RHCP making 16.6 and 23.4 more stance changes than CVBFP on average, respectively. However, in the chimney walking and wall walking scenarios, RHCP made 37.0 and 53.9 *fewer* stance changes on average, respectively. Additionally, Fig. 2b shows a statistically significant decrease in planning time for all scenarios, with RHCP completing approximately 10 s faster than CVBFP in the chimney climbing scenario, 5.5 min faster in the chimney walking and stepping stones scenarios, and 10 min faster in the wall walking scenario on average. Furthermore, as the slowest CVBFP results, those which timed out, have been excluded from the analysis in Fig. 2b the true improvement in execution time, particularly in the wall walking scenario, may be greater than that shown.

7   Conclusions

This paper presented a novel posture generator for legged robots to successfully generate several motions in challenging environments. With a two-step planning horizon, our approach was faster than the state-of-the-art in all scenarios tested, in some cases generating shorter paths despite being a local planner, all while adding new capabilities—namely, the ability to simultaneously plan whole-body trajectories.

Future works will analyse in more detail how different environments and horizon depths affect the performance of the two planners and validate the paths produced by executing them in realistic simulations and on the physical robot.

Acknowledgments. This work was supported by a grant from the University of Manchester and by the Royal Academy of Engineering under the Research Chairs and Senior Research Fellowships programme. Corin was developed by Hassan Hakim Khalili and Wei Cheah [15]. R code to generate Fig. 2 was based on scripts released by John K. Kruschke, with adaptations by Ana Christina Almada Campos and the authors.

Disclosure of Interests. The authors have no competing interests to declare that are relevant to the content of this article.

References

1. Bjerkeng, M., Falco, P., Natale, C., Pettersen, K.Y.: Stability analysis of a hierarchical architecture for discrete-time sensor-based control of robotic systems. IEEE Trans. Rob. **30**(3), 745–753 (2014). https://doi.org/10.1109/TRO.2013.2294882
2. Bretl, T.: Motion planning of multi-limbed robots subject to equilibrium constraints: the free-climbing robot problem. Int. J. Robot. Res. **25**(4), 317–342 (2006). https://doi.org/10.1177/0278364906063979
3. Bretl, T., Lall, S.: Testing static equilibrium for legged robots. IEEE Trans. Rob. **24**(4), 794–807 (2008). https://doi.org/10.1109/TRO.2008.2001360
4. Escande, A., Kheddar, A., Miossec, S.: Planning contact points for humanoid robots. Robot. Auton. Syst. **61**(5), 428–442 (2013). https://doi.org/10.1016/j.robot.2013.01.008
5. Ferrari, P., et al.: Multi-contact planning and control for humanoid robots: design and validation of a complete framework. Robot. Auton. Syst. **166**, 104448 (2023). https://doi.org/10.1016/j.robot.2023.104448
6. Hauser, K., Bretl, T., Latombe, J.C.: Non-gaited humanoid locomotion planning. In: 5th IEEE-RAS International Conference on Humanoid Robots, 2005, pp. 7–12 (2005). https://doi.org/10.1109/ICHR.2005.1573537
7. Hauser, K., Bretl, T., Harada, K., Latombe, J.C.: Using Motion Primitives in Probabilistic Sample-Based Planning for Humanoid Robots, pp. 507–522. Springer, Berlin (2008). https://doi.org/10.1007/978-3-540-68405-3_32
8. Johnson, D.S., Adorno, B.V., Watson, S.: Receding horizon contact planning for advanced motions in hexapod robots. In: Towards Autonomous Robotic Systems Extended Abstracts: 24th Annual Conference, TAROS 2023 Cambridge, UK, pp. 34–37 (2023). https://research.manchester.ac.uk/en/publications/receding-horizon-contact-planning-for-advanced-motions-in-hexapod
9. Kruschke, J.K.: Bayesian estimation supersedes the t test. J. Exp. Psychol. Gen. **142**(2), 573–603 (2013)
10. Marinho, M.M., Adorno, B.V., Harada, K., Mitsuishi, M.: Dynamic active constraints for surgical robots using vector-field inequalities. IEEE Trans. Rob. **35**(5), 1166–1185 (2019). https://doi.org/10.1109/TRO.2019.2920078
11. Mordatch, I., Todorov, E., Popović, Z.: Discovery of complex behaviors through contact-invariant optimization. ACM Trans. Graph. **31**(4) (2012). https://doi.org/10.1145/2185520.2185539
12. Pereira, M.S., Adorno, B.V.: Manipulation task planning and motion control using task relaxations. J. Control Autom. Electr. Syst. **33**(4), 1103–1115 (2022)
13. Quiroz-Omaña, J.J., Adorno, B.V.: Whole-body control with (self) collision avoidance using vector field inequalities. IEEE Robot. Autom. Lett. **4**(4), 4048–4053 (2019). https://doi.org/10.1109/LRA.2019.2928783
14. Tonneau, S., Del Prete, A., Pettré, J., Park, C., Manocha, D., Mansard, N.: An efficient acyclic contact planner for multiped robots. IEEE Trans. Robot. **34**(3), 586–601 (2018). https://doi.org/10.1109/TRO.2018.2819658
15. University of Manchester: Corin: Mobile hexapod for remote inspection and object manipulation (2022). https://uomrobotics.com/robots/corin.html
16. Vilhena Adorno, B.: Robot Kinematic Modeling and Control Based on Dual Quaternion Algebra — Part I: Fundamentals (2017). https://hal.science/hal-01478225. working paper or preprint

Acrobotics: A Generalist Approach to Quadrupedal Robots' Parkour

Guillaume Gagné-Labelle[✉], Vassil Atanassov, and Ioannis Havoutis

Dynamic Robot Systems Group (DRS), University of Oxford, Oxford, UK
{guillaume.gagne-labelle,vassil.atanassov,
havoutis}@oxfordrobotics.institute

Abstract. Climbing, crouching, bridging gaps, and walking up stairs are just a few of the advantages that quadruped robots have over wheeled robots, making them more suitable for navigating rough and unstructured terrain. However, executing such manoeuvres requires precise temporal coordination and complex agent-environment interactions. Moreover, legged locomotion is inherently more prone to slippage and tripping, and the classical approach of modeling such cases to design a robust controller thus quickly becomes impractical. In contrast, reinforcement learning offers a compelling solution by enabling optimal control through trial and error. We present generalist reinforcement learning algorithm for quadrupedal agents in dynamic motion scenarios. The learned policy rivals state-of-the-art specialist policies trained using a mixture of experts approach, while using only 25% as many agents during training. Our experiments also highlight the key components of the generalist locomotion policy and the primary factors contributing to its success. Supplementary material and video can be found here.

Keywords: Reinforcement learning · Quadrupedal robots · Generalist policy

1 Introduction

Within the area of reinforcement learning, there are various methods for controlling quadruped robots. In the context of dynamic locomotion, the mixture of experts approach is nowadays considered the state of the art [3,12,19,28]. The technique consists of training one machine learning model per targeted ability, for example, walking, climbing, trotting, etc., and then training an upstream model to select the appropriate skill at any given moment. From an explainability perspective, decoupling the learning process into sub-parts allows an easier analysis of the derived policy. Additionally, splitting the problem into smaller components simplifies the overall solution and the engineering choices required, since reinforcement learning (RL) algorithms are known to be mroe sensitive to design choices than other machine learning paradigms [11,26].

Nevertheless, the mixture of experts technique is not devoid from substantial drawbacks. Three of them are particularly worth addressing. First, the mixture

A. Cavalcanti et al. (Eds.): TAROS 2025, LNAI 16045, pp. 124–137, 2026.
https://doi.org/10.1007/978-3-032-01486-3_11

of experts does not make optimal usage of the neural networks' parameters. For example, the limb coordination required to jump on a box or to leap over a gap is very similar. Therefore, some information accumulated in each specialized network parameter is repeated. Decoupling these actions in separated models [28] can lead to a sub-optimal architecture where a larger than necessary set of parameters is needed to achieve the same performance.

Another downside of the mixture of experts approach is that the algorithm pipeline can be overly complex and difficult to optimize and improve. This is especially true for RL problems since often other inference models (e.g. critics) are involved during the training phase. Furthermore, for legged locomotion, it is already common to split the problem into a planning module (to generate trajectories) and another path-following module or controller (to steer the robot towards the generated path) [22]. In this setting where networks are inevitably entangled in the algorithm, splitting the task into multiple specialized networks becomes even more challenging.

Lastly, the mixture of experts introduces inductive biases by defining what constitutes a specific skill and how information flows, which can lead to sudden, non-smooth, transitions between policies [3]. As argued in Richard Sutton's The Bitter Lesson [25], history shows that generalist methods often outperform approaches based on domain knowledge, highlighting the need for better algorithms rather than human-driven designs.

These observations motivate the work presented throughout this paper. We propose a generalist policy with a less convoluted algorithm pipeline. Our goal is to analyze the algorithm thoroughly by conducting ablation studies and implementing prominent generalist policies' ideas.

1.1 Approach

We develop a generalist policy that uses deep reinforcement learning (DRL) to control quadruped robots. In this context, a generalist policy, as opposed to a specialist one, is a single unified policy that can tackle all presented obstacles without the need for ad hoc switching between different specialized policies when encountering specific obstacles.

Despite their promising potential for generalization, generalist policies have multiple weaknesses. In particular, they tend to be less stable and more sensitive to design choices [3,4,12]. Consequently, the goal of this work is not to outperform the state-of-the-art with arbitrary engineering choices. Instead, this paper aims to study and analyze the foundational elements necessary for the convergence and optimal performance of generalist agents while focusing on simplicity and stability. These findings aim to offer valuable insights for developing larger and more powerful generalist agents by leveraging greater computational resources and integrating the best-performing methods from this work into future projects.

1.2 Contribution

Our contribution has two parts. First, we propose a simple yet competitive generalist algorithm for training quadruped robots. Our pipeline requires fewer computational resources than concurrent methods, the proposed algorithm is simple and easy to implement, and the performance is comparable to state-of-the-art specialist policies for agile locomotion. Second, we present a rigorous and thorough ablation study of the main implementation components. This analysis of the algorithm helps identify the critical design choices and ideas that are helpful for the convergence of reputedly unstable RL algorithms. This can greatly help researchers in designing learning-based locomotion approaches and develop systems significantly faster.

2 Related Work

Legged Locomotion: Addressing the challenge of legged locomotion has long relied on complex model-based methods [2,10] that only offer partial solutions. Recently, DRL has shown to be a compelling alternative and demonstrated state-of-the-art results on both proprioceptive [1,8,13,16,18] and perceptive [5,9,20, 21] locomotion on difficult terrain. Many recent methods follow a "privileged learning" approach [6], where a "teacher" agent is first trained with privileged information (e.g., environment parameters, mass and ground friction), and then distilled into a "student" network that is trained to replicate the teacher's actions given non-privileged observations [15,20].

Robot Parkour: Given the success of DRL for locomotive policies, recent research has focused on demonstrating ever-more agile parkour-like behaviors [3,7,28]. As these skills are more challenging to learn, prior work often trains a discrete set of specialist policies for different parkour sub-tasks, and either distills them into one generalist policy [3,28] or trains a high-level skill selector [12]. This adds a significant overhead, partially due to designing and tuning the rewards for each specialist policy, and due to the computational cost of the distillation step, especially for perceptive controllers that requires depth camera images.

3 Method

Our approach uses a generalist policy trained on Isaac Gym [17] via Proximal Policy Optimization (PPO) [24]. The training phase requires about four hours on an NVIDIA RTX 3060 GPU. The critic network is modeled with a multilayer perceptron with three hidden layers of size 512, 256 and 128 that outputs a scalar. The policy π uses the same architecture as the critic, but the output is of size 12.

Each value in the policy output corresponds to the mean of a Gaussian distribution for each joint from which the action is sampled at every timestep. The standard deviation of these distributions is modeled with a single parameter updated via gradient descent on the RL objective. The standard deviation

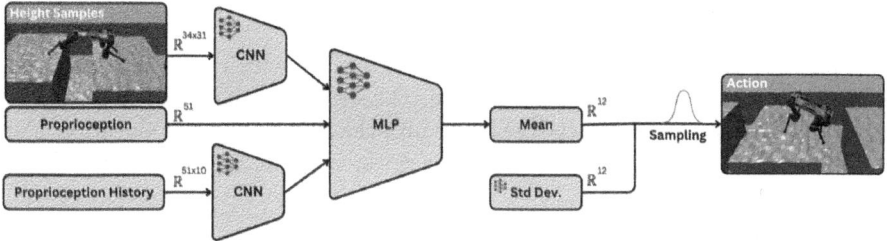

Fig. 1. Training overview. The height samples and observation history are encoded through a convolutional neural network to reduce their dimensionality before being concatenated and given to the main actor.

is limited to a maximum value of 1.0 to prevent an unrestrained increase in the parameter. This adjustment prevents pathological snowballing effects of the standard deviation observed in [7] and stabilizes the overall algorithm.

The reward function structure is available in the supplementary material. Notably, as encouraging steady large steps has been a successful approach in other works [14,23], there is a heavy penalty for having all four limbs in the air at the same time and a reward for promoting a trotting gait with long stride only in the flat environment.

For the agent to learn a stable gait before engaging in parkour, a small pretraining phase of 1k iterations on a flat terrain is introduced. It takes about 5k total iterations for an agent to learn to behave stably in every environment. The training is extended to 20k iterations before assessing the performance.

The Barkour benchmark [3] introduced standardized metrics to evaluate the performance of quadruped robots through an obstacle course inspired by dog agility competitions. The course incorporates elevated pause tables, weave poles, a 30° A-frame, and a jump board. The scoring system considers both the completion time and penalties. Unlike Barkour, the goal of this work is not to maximize agility directly but rather to overcome obstacles at a given steady pace. Our work thus adapts the benchmark by adjusting the difficulty to one that is challenging yet achievable for the ANYmal robot: that is, about 70% of the maximal difficulty. The proposed adaptation of the score R_{adapted} is

$$R_{\text{adapted}} = 1.0 - |t_{\text{run}} - \mathbb{E}(t_{\text{command}})| * 0.01 - \text{penalties}$$

where t_{run} is the time required to complete the 18 m of the parkour course and $\mathbb{E}(t_{command})$ is the expected time to complete it given the input of an arbitrary velocity command. A penalty of -0.1 is added to the final score every time the robot trips or fails an obstacle. An agent unable to complete the course receives a score of 0. The reported adapted Barkour score is an average over 30 runs evaluated manually for each experiment.

3.1   Input

The policy π and the critic share the same input, which is a concatenation of three components: the proprioception, the elevation map and a history of previous proprioceptive states. Both the proprioception and the elevation map are provided by the ANYmal robot framework, in both simulation and on the real robot platform.

Proprioception. This part of the input is a 51-dimensional concatenation of the following: base linear velocity $\mathbf{v} \in \mathcal{R}^3$, base angular velocity $\omega \in \mathcal{R}^3$, roll and pitch angles $\alpha \in \mathcal{R}^2$, oracle heading $\psi \in \mathcal{R}^2$, velocity command $v_{cmd} \in \mathcal{R}^1$, joint position $\mathbf{q} \in \mathcal{R}^{12}$, joint velocity $\dot{\mathbf{q}} \in \mathcal{R}^{12}$, previous action $\mathbf{a} \in \mathcal{R}^{12}$, and feet contact state $\mathbf{c} \in \{0,1\}^4$. The oracle heading represents the yaw angle between the heading of the robot and the target. We provide the following two targets to achieve better performance. The velocity command is sampled in the range $[0.4, 0.8]$ m/s. The position of each joint is given in radians from the respective articulation, where the origin corresponds to the nominal position of the robot.

Elevation Map Encoding. The elevation map corresponds to 1054 evenly spaced height samples. The samples come from 34×31 points from a 1.6×1 m^2 region under the robot. The region is slightly shifted forward from the center of the robot. The height samples are the only available external perception of the robot in the algorithm. To leverage the spatial coherence of the samples, they are encoded into a vector of 32 dimensions by a convolutional neural network (CNN).

History of Proprioceptive States. The history is a buffer of the ten previous proprioceptive states of the robot. The 51×10 dimensional input is first reduced to a 30×10 dimensional matrix by the means of a linear layer before being encoded with a CNN sliding in the temporal dimension. The output is encoded in a 20-dimensional vector.

3.2   Training Environments

1024 ANYmal agents are trained in parallel in a variety of eight categories of different environments presented in Fig. 2. Each terrain is modelled as an 18×4 m^2 area that the agent has to overcome. The flat terrain is used mainly during the pretraining phase, but also sparsely during the training phase to avoid any forgetting issue after the distribution shift from pretraining to training [27]. The difficulty ranges are reported in Table 1.

The difficulties of the terrains are modeled as a discrete curriculum of 20 levels. Let $[\alpha, \beta]$ be a difficulty range for an arbitrary obstacle (as shown in Table 1), the difficulty $\mathcal{D}$ of level l is calculated as $\mathcal{D} = \alpha + l \cdot (\beta - \alpha)/20$. Once an agent has completed the last level, it is reassigned to a random level of the same category.

To get promoted to a more challenging terrain, an expected distance is computed from the velocity command and a time window of 20 s. The robot gets promoted to a harder level if it crosses more than 80% of this expected distance and gets demoted if it doesn't traverse more than 40%.

Table 1. Difficulty range of the training obstacles.

Obstacle	Steps	Boxes	Stairs		Gaps
Parameter	height (m)	height (m)	tread (m)	riser (m)	gap size (m)
Difficulty	$[0.1, 0.8]$	$[0.1, 1.0]$	$[0.3, 0.5]$	$[0.05, 0.25]$	$[0.1, 1.0]$
	Inclined Boxes		Slopes	Weave Poles	
Parameter	tilt (°)	stone length (m)	angle (°)	spreading (m)	
Difficulty	$[0, 50]$	$[0.9, 1.8]$	$[10, 30]$	$[0.1, 0.7]$	

Fig. 2. IsaacGym simulation setup of the eight environments used during the training phase represented at 75% of their maximal difficulty.

4   Results & Discussion

Table 2 displays the 90% prediction intervals for the success rate, adapted Barkour score, and average sum of squared torques[1] after 5k learning iterations. For comparison purposes, Table 2 also displays the performance after 20k learning iterations of the algorithm as well as the performance of the first phase ("teacher" training) of the Extreme Parkour with Legged Robots algorithm [7] after the same number of iterations.

Table 2. Performance of the main algorithm on the adapted Barkour environment.

Algorithm	Completion (%)	Barkour Score	Avg. Torque (N^2m^2)
Base model - 5k	$[87.26, 100+]$	$[0.73, 0.97]$	$[14'526, 15'990]$
Base model - 20k	99.61	0.90	13'989
Ex. Parkour - 20k	0.00	0.00	N.A.

After 20k learning iterations, the completion percentage is not significantly different from the model at 5k iterations as it falls into the prediction interval, but this is likely due to the evaluation environment being slightly too easy for both models in that particular case. The 20k model provides better completion percentage than every individual 5k model[2]. Moreover, the average sum of squared torques is significantly below the prediction interval, indicating improvement in terms of unnecessary movements. After 20k iterations, the agent learns to gallop over gaps rather than crossing them one foot at a time, and the gait is generally much smoother.

The adapted Barkour score is 0.90, where a single penalty was observed over thirty runs when the robots struggled to climb on the ending table. The main factor in lowering the score is the speed of the robot. The agent speed consistently exceeds the velocity command by $(41 \pm 16)\%$ on average. This behavior is most probably a consequence of the goal-tracking reward. Indeed, as can be seen in the provided supplementary material, the agent can ensure a maximal goal-tracking reward by aiming almost directly at the next goal at a speed greater than the velocity command. Nonetheless, observation shows that the velocity command still affects the agent's speed, probably because crossing obstacles at lower speeds is generally easier. As for the agent trained with the Extreme Parkour with Legged Robot algorithm, although it is able to complete some of the parkour obstacles with low probability (see Fig. 3), completing all five obstacles consecutively proved too difficult and no successful run was observed after 30 attempts.

---

[1] The average sum of squared torques on successful agents serves as a proxy for energy loss—which is itself a proxy for natural locomotion of quadruped animals [22].

[2] The exact results of the four models from which the prediction intervals are derived are presented in the supplementary material: https://drive.google.com/drive/fold ers/18h25azbCFfPF4fhSsRfxKrnZo3dPKs_j?usp=sharing.

4.1   Fundamental Skills

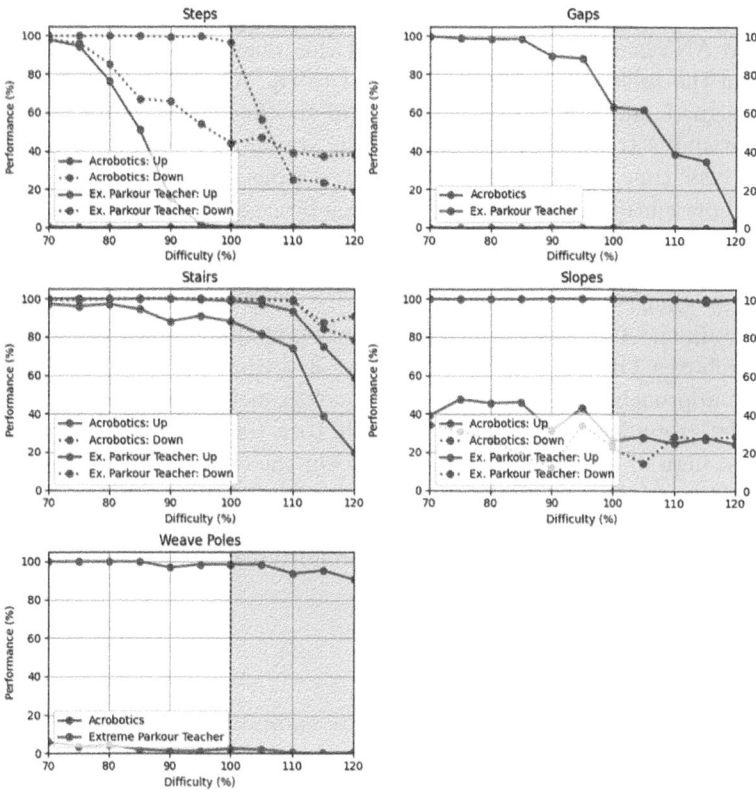

Fig. 3. Performance of the algorithm on the basic skills developed through the training environments.

Figure 3 depicts the empirical probability of overcoming the obstacle for each skill. The robot achieves about 90%+ performance on every single obstacle at 95% of the training difficulty besides the climbing up skill. The performance is still excellent for obstacles up to approximately 75cm, corresponding to the robot's height to its hips. The drop in performance at this height is intuitive: when observing the policy for boxes above this threshold, it seems like the robot struggles to put its knee on the box to push itself up. Even when fully opening its hip, its knee is only about 75 cm high.

As for gaps, there seems to be two limiting factors. The first one is the robot's reach, but the second one is the extent of the elevation map in front of the robot, which is roughly 90cm and where the performance seems to drop. Past that point, as the elevation map is the only exteroception of the agent, it is difficult to discern between an edge and a gap. Moreover, to bridge wide gaps, the robot benefits from linear momentum. This momentum is difficult to obtain at low velocities when the detection the other side of the gap happens late.

Without using any form of privileged information, Acrobotics consistently outperforms the teacher of the algorithm presented in Extreme Parkour [7] when applied to ANYmal. A probable reason for this phenomenon is the lower joint velocity of the limbs of ANYmal compared to the A1 robots for which Cheng et al. designed and applied their algorithm to. As discussed in Sect. 3, during the teacher's training phase, the average standard deviation of the actions increases over time, yielding almost random actions after an extensive training phase and preventing any meaningful learning process. By clipping the said standard deviation of each action, the exploration is limited, but this seems to be an advantageous trade-off in the long run.

At first glance, it appears in Fig. 3 that Extreme Parkour outperforms Acrobotics in the 100%+ difficulty regime when climbing down stairs and stepping down boxes. Observation shows that our algorithm tends to be more meticulous when approaching those obstacles and a clear inclination to keep the robot's feet on the ground is noticeable. This leads to a tendency to tip over when a step is too high or a staircase, too shallow. On the other hand, the behavior of the robot trained with the Extreme Parkour approach seems more impulsive: it tends to jump off or fall off the box or staircase. The robot sometimes "survives" the fall (it doesn't violate any termination condition), but such carelessness can limit real world deployment in practice.

4.2 Ablation Study

All the policies presented in this section are compared and evaluated after 5k iterations. In each table, a value that lies within the 90% confidence prediction interval of the base model performance is presented in green: no statistically significant impact on performance is observed from the ablation. An utterly green row signifies that no evaluated metric is altered from the ablation; the component is superfluous to the algorithm's performance.

Proprioception. The results reported in Table 3 highlight that, with 90% certainty, the algorithm extracted from the ablation of each part of the proprioception input comes from a different distribution than the one resulting from the default algorithm. In particular, the linear velocity of the base of the robot, the position of the robot's joints and the previous sampled action are unequivocally the most important components of the proprioception as the performance quickly deteriorates without these inputs. On the other hand, although necessary, the information provided by the angular velocity and the detection of the feet contacts with the ground seems to be less important pieces of information in proprioception. In both cases, the null hypothesis is rejected in favor of the alternative hypothesis: the ablation of the feet contacts detection has a statistically significant impact on the performance of the algorithm.

Table 3. Performance of the algorithm on the adapted Barkour environment after training with ablation of the input. An ablation is done by masking the according input with zeros in the input vector.

Ablation	Completion (%)	Barkour Score	Avg. Torque (N^2m^2)
Base Model	$[87.26, 100+]$	$[0.73, 0.97]$	$[14'526, 15'990]$
Linear Vel. (3D)	9.77	0.06	19'197
Angular Vel. (3D)	82.13	0.85	15'533
Roll & Pitch (2D)	75.29	0.75	15'547
Joints Pos. (12D)	0.00	0.00	N.A.
Joints Vel. (12D)	76.86	0.60	16'007
Prev. Action (12D)	18.65	0.12	19'795
Feet Contact (4D)	86.04	0.64	15'045
History (510D)	88.18	0.80	14'901

History of Proprioceptive States. As per Table 3, the results from the proprioception history input seem to be nuanced. Generally, every evaluated metric falls inside the prediction interval and the null hypothesis can not be rejected. However, both the completion rate and the adapted Barkour score fall not only in the lower part of the prediction interval but are individually equal or worse than every reported metric of the individual models. Therefore, it might be that the impossibility of rejecting the status quo hypothesis is due to the small amount of under-trained default models rather than equal performances. In other words, only four default models were trained for only 5k iterations to build the prediction intervals. This creates uncertainty with respect to the performance that is reflected in the prediction intervals. Since the performance of the ablation rests in the lower part of the intervals, it is possible that the performance is affected but not quantifiable in this context.

Reward Function. Quantifying the role of specific terms in the reward function is not straightforward. Some of the terms aim not to increase the overall performance directly but rather to improve the policy's natural-looking behavior. Even though the average sum of squared torques tries to quantify precisely this, it is only a proxy for the minimization of energy which is itself only a proxy for natural-looking behavior. The conclusions extracted from this subsection thus provide valuable insights, but should be considered within the context of the outlined constraints.

Table 4 shows unequivocally that the roles of the torque and action rate penalty are crucial to the success of the derived policy. These two penalties are subtly different from one another. The action rate term penalizes the agent for taking actions that are widely different at two sequential timesteps. On the other hand, the torque is directly proportional to the angular acceleration of the joint. Therefore, the torque penalty constrains the robot into taking actions that

Table 4. Performance of the algorithm on the adapted Barkour environment after training with ablation of the reward function.

Ablation	Completion (%)	Barkour Score	Avg. Torque (N^2m^2)
Base Model	$[87.26, 100+]$	$[0.73, 0.97]$	$[14'526, 15'990]$
Base Angular Vel.	79.10	0.62	15'970
Joint Acceleration	91.99	0.81	16'677
Collision	44.92	0.43	17'535
Action Rate	0.20	0.00	16'136
Torques Variation	89.45	0.80	14'996
Torques	1.17	0.00	31'588
DOF Error	83.59	0.81	15'953
Stumbling	92.77	0.85	16'148
Trotting	65.82	0.47	14'300
Feet in Air	83.40	0.67	14'899
Feet Air Time	60.16	0.60	14'314

limit the acceleration of its joints. This means, for example, that two subsequent actions that accelerate a limb in the same direction are greatly penalized by the torque penalty but not by the action rate penalty. Both terms seem to be critical to the functionality of the algorithm.

Surprisingly, the penalty associated with torque variation does not significantly influence performance. The meaning of this penalty is very similar to the action rate: it penalizes the agent for taking subsequent actions that create widely different torques. A possible explanation of the negligible consequences of the ablation of the torque variation is the reward's coefficient, as it is one million times smaller than the action rate's coefficient.

For the same reason of being multiplied by a very small coefficient, the ablation of the joint acceleration penalty, with a reward coefficient only 2.5 times greater than the torque variation penalty, does not affect the performance. Nevertheless, the ablation of both the joint acceleration and torque variation has a statistically significant impact on the average sum of squared torques and might promote the natural-looking behavior of the agent.

Pretraining, Standard Deviation Limit & Batch Size. This ablation study focuses on assessing the role of three higher-level design choices of the algorithm. It questions the necessity of the pretraining phase, which lasts 1k iterations, or 20% of the total training duration. It also challenges the idea of introducing a maximal limit of 1.0 for the standard deviation of each action distribution and the importance of the batch size in the RL pipeline.

Table 5 shows that above all else, batch size is the most crucial design choice. Decreasing the batch size from 1024 to 512 implies that the policy encounters only half as many scenarios per learning iteration. When there are not enough

Table 5. Performance of the algorithm on the adapted Barkour environment after training with ablation of high-level design choices.

Ablation	Completion (%)	Barkour Score	Avg. Torque ($N^2 m^2$)
Base Model	[87.26, 100+]	[0.73, 0.97]	[14'526, 15'990]
STD Clipping	63.96	0.61	24'852
Pretraining	94.14	0.88	16'007
Batch Size 512	0.39	0.00	17'141

agents at any given time in the environment, the reward signal is noisier and the variance hinders the learning process. More experiments were performed with even fewer agents, but the results are not reported as the performance completely deteriorated. It is reasonable to believe that increasing the number of agents by leveraging more computational power could significantly improve performance.

The ablation of the standard deviation clipping also has a statistically significant impact on performance according to every metric. Potentially, as the standard deviation increases over training time, rather than promoting exploration, the actions become increasingly jittery and almost random. By limiting the standard deviation magnitude, some exploration is still possible, but the sampled actions are still meaningful.

Finally, the ablation of the pretraining phase does not provide a significant difference in performance. The average sum of squared torques is slightly above the prediction interval, but only by 1.16% and including or not the value in the interval is approximately arbitrary. Consequently, the ablation of the pretraining phase does not have a noticeable effect on performance, and the pretraining phase can be removed from the pipeline to promote simplicity at 90% certainty.

5   Conclusion

In this paper we proposed a competitive generalist locomotion policy for the ANYmal robot. Our approach achieves competitive results, on average about 90% success rate at 95% difficulty, on a set of experimental parkour trials of increasing complexity and difficulty.

To summarize, the mixture of experts approach currently leads in solving quadruped robots' agile locomotion challenges. However, history shows that inductive biases are suboptimal for long-term machine learning solutions.

Our ablation study highlights that every proprioception component is crucial for the end-result performance, while the history of proprioceptive states offers mixed results. Penalties on joint acceleration and stumbling improve behavior, but torque variation penalties are mostly redundant. Clipping standard deviation and batch sizes are vital for convergence, while pretraining appears inessential.

Future work includes refining design choices, such as training environments, standard deviation limits, and neural network architecture. Testing fully trained models and expanding the experiments for reproducibility are our next steps.

Additionally, leveraging more computational power could improve competitiveness while transitioning to hardware implementation to validate real-world performance.

References

1. Atanassov, V., Ding, J., Kober, J., Havoutis, I., Santina, C.D.: Curriculum-based reinforcement learning for quadrupedal jumping: a reference-free design. IEEE Robot. Autom. Mag. 2–15 (2024). https://doi.org/10.1109/MRA.2024.3487325
2. Bouman, A., et al.: Autonomous spot: long-range autonomous exploration of extreme environments with legged locomotion (2020). https://arxiv.org/abs/2010.09259
3. Caluwaerts, K., et al.: Barkour: benchmarking animal-level agility with quadruped robots. arXiv preprint arXiv:2305.14654 (2023)
4. Campanaro, L., De Martini, D., Gangapurwala, S., Merkt, W., Havoutis, I.: Roll-drop: accounting for observation noise with a single parameter. In: Proceedings of Machine Learning Research, pp. 718–730. Proceedings of Machine Learning Research (2023)
5. Campanaro, L., Gangapurwala, S., Merkt, W., Havoutis, I.: Learning and deploying robust locomotion policies with minimal dynamics randomization. In: Proceedings of Machine Learning Research, pp. 578–590. Proceedings of Machine Learning Research (2024)
6. Chen, D., Zhou, B., Koltun, V., Krähenbühl, P.: Learning by cheating. In: Proceedings of the Conference on Robot Learning, pp. 66–75. PMLR (2020). https://proceedings.mlr.press/v100/chen20a.html
7. Cheng, X., Shi, K., Agarwal, A., Pathak, D.: Extreme parkour with legged robots. arXiv preprint arXiv:2309.14341 (2023)
8. Gangapurwala, S., Campanaro, L., Havoutis, I.: Learning low-frequency motion control for robust and dynamic robot locomotion. In: 2023 IEEE International Conference on Robotics and Automation (ICRA), pp. 5085–5091. IEEE, London (2023). https://doi.org/10.1109/ICRA48891.2023.10160357. https://ieeexplore.ieee.org/document/10160357/
9. Gangapurwala, S., Geisert, M., Orsolino, R., Fallon, M., Havoutis, I.: RLOC: terrain-aware legged locomotion using reinforcement learning and optimal control. IEEE Trans. Rob. **38**(5), 2908–2927 (2022). https://doi.org/10.1109/TRO.2022.3172469. Conference Name: IEEE Transactions on Robotics
10. Gehring, C., Fankhauser, P., Isler, L., Diethelm, R., Bachmann, S., Potz, M., Gerstenberg, L., Hutter, M.: ANYmal in the field: solving industrial inspection of an offshore HVDC platform with a quadrupedal robot. In: Ishigami, G., Yoshida, K. (eds.) Field and Service Robotics. SPAR, vol. 16, pp. 247–260. Springer, Singapore (2021). https://doi.org/10.1007/978-981-15-9460-1_18
11. Henderson, P., Islam, R., Bachman, P., Pineau, J., Precup, D., Meger, D.: Deep reinforcement learning that matters. In: Proceedings of the AAAI Conference on Artificial Intelligence, vol. 32 (2018)
12. Hoeller, D., Rudin, N., Sako, D., Hutter, M.: Anymal parkour: learning agile navigation for quadrupedal robots (2023). https://arxiv.org/abs/2306.14874
13. Hwangbo, J., et al.: Learning agile and dynamic motor skills for legged robots. Science Robotics **4**(26), eaau5872 (2019). https://doi.org/10.1126/scirobotics.aau5872. https://www.science.org/doi/full/10.1126/scirobotics.aau5872. publisher: American Association for the Advancement of Science

14. Hwangbo, J., et al.: Learning agile and dynamic motor skills for legged robots. Sci. Robot. **4**(26), eaau5872 (2019)
15. Kumar, A., Fu, Z., Pathak, D., Malik, J.: RMA: rapid motor adaptation for legged robots. In: Robotics: Science and Systems XVII. Robotics: Science and Systems Foundation (2021). https://doi.org/10.15607/RSS.2021.XVII.011. http://www.roboticsproceedings.org/rss17/p011.pdf
16. Lee, J., Hwangbo, J., Wellhausen, L., Koltun, V., Hutter, M.: Learning quadrupedal locomotion over challenging terrain. Sci. Robot. **5**(47), eabc5986 (2020). https://doi.org/10.1126/scirobotics.abc5986. https://www.science.org/doi/10.1126/scirobotics.abc5986. Publisher: American Association for the Advancement of Science
17. Makoviychuk, V., et al.: Isaac gym: high performance GPU-based physics simulation for robot learning (2021). https://arxiv.org/abs/2108.10470
18. Margolis, G.B., Agrawal, P.: Walk these ways: tuning robot control for generalization with multiplicity of behavior. In: Proceedings of The 6th Conference on Robot Learning, pp. 22–31. PMLR (2023). https://proceedings.mlr.press/v205/margolis23a.html
19. Merel, J., et al.: Hierarchical visuomotor control of humanoids. arXiv preprint arXiv:1811.09656 (2018)
20. Miki, T., Lee, J., Hwangbo, J., Wellhausen, L., Koltun, V., Hutter, M.: Learning robust perceptive locomotion for quadrupedal robots in the wild. Sci. Robot. **7**(62), eabk2822 (2022).https://doi.org/10.1126/scirobotics.abk2822. https://www.science.org/doi/full/10.1126/scirobotics.abk2822. publisher: American Association for the Advancement of Science
21. Miki, T., Lee, J., Wellhausen, L., Hutter, M.: Learning to walk in confined spaces using 3D representation (2024). https://arxiv.org/abs/2403.00187
22. Rudin, N., Hoeller, D., Bjelonic, M., Hutter, M.: Advanced skills by learning locomotion and local navigation end-to-end. In: 2022 IEEE/RSJ International Conference on Intelligent Robots and Systems (IROS), pp. 2497–2503. IEEE (2022)
23. Rudin, N., Hoeller, D., Reist, P., Hutter, M.: Learning to walk in minutes using massively parallel deep reinforcement learning. In: Conference on Robot Learning, pp. 91–100. PMLR (2022)
24. Schulman, J., Wolski, F., Dhariwal, P., Radford, A., Klimov, O.: Proximal policy optimization algorithms (2017). https://arxiv.org/abs/1707.06347
25. Sutton, R.: The bitter lesson (2019). http://www.incompleteideas.net/IncIdeas/BitterLesson.html
26. Sutton, R.S., Barto, A.G.: Reinforcement Learning: An Introduction. 2nd edn. The MIT Press, Cambridge (2018). http://incompleteideas.net/book/the-book-2nd.html
27. Wang, Z., Yang, E., Shen, L., Huang, H.: A comprehensive survey of forgetting in deep learning beyond continual learning (2023). https://arxiv.org/abs/2307.09218
28. Zhuang, Z., et al.: Robot parkour learning. arXiv preprint arXiv:2309.05665 (2023)

An Integrated LQR and Sliding Mode Controller for Balance and Motion Control of a Five-Link Two-Wheel Legged Robot

Ziyue Wang, Chenyi Li, and Long Zhang$^{(\boxtimes)}$

School of Engineering, University of Manchester, Manchester M13 9PL, UK
`long.zhang@manchester.ac.uk`

Abstract. Two-wheel legged robots combine the mechanical structures of both wheeled and legged robots, achieving higher mobility speeds than legged-only robots while offering superior obstacle-crossing capabilities compared to wheeled-only robots. However, balance control remain challenges due to the inaccuracies of system model and external disturbances, particularly when operating under changes of robot height, mass and load. This paper proposes a novel fusion controller combining a single layer State-Fused Sliding Mode Controller (SF-SMC) and Linear Quadratic Regulator (LQR). The proposed approach retains the optimality of LQR while incorporating the robustness of SMC, thereby reduces the reliance on model accuracy and simplifies the complexity of SMC design. Meanwhile, the proposed fusion control algorithm only requires a simplified wheeled inverted pendulum model rather than a complex and accurate model, making it well-suited for low-cost robots with limited sensors and low computational capacity. The balance performance of the proposed method is extensively tested on a low-cost five-link two-wheel legged robot. The results demonstrate that, compared to the standalone LQR, the proposed fusion control algorithm could reduce system overshoot, expand the stability region, and enhance robustness against external disturbances.

Keywords: Wheel Legged Robot · Sliding Mode Control · Linear Quadratic Regulator · Robust Nonlinear Control

1 Introduction

Two-wheel legged robots integrate the efficiency and mobility of wheeled robots with the versatility of legged systems [1]. Through articulated leg joints and driving wheels, they reduce motion impact via continuous wheel-ground contact; meanwhile, it enables obstacle crossing and traversal in unstructured terrains [2]. Moreover, their compact size, light weight design, and low energy consumption make them suitable for narrow environments. Therefore, they are increasingly used in search-and-rescue, field exploration and other scenarios, such as last-mile delivery [3]. It could also serve as mobile platforms for manipulation tasks. Due

© The Author(s), under exclusive license to Springer Nature Switzerland AG 2026
A. Cavalcanti et al. (Eds.): TAROS 2025, LNAI 16045, pp. 138–151, 2026.
https://doi.org/10.1007/978-3-032-01486-3_12

to their underactuated and nonlinear dynamics, maintaining balance requires active wheel control, making robust motion and balance control essential for reliable performance [4].

For two-wheel legged robots balance and motion control, one of conventional methods is Proportional-Integral-Derivative (PID) control. PID control is often preferred due to its low computational overhead, and ease of implementation. The most basic form concentrates only on tilt angle [2,5], but tends to yield short balance durations and positional drift. Cascade PID strategies have been used to integrate balance control with velocity or position regulation [6], with some robustness to height variations [7]. However, these PID-based methods may struggle with the strong coupling and nonlinearity of two-wheel legged systems, often failing under excessive tilt, height or load changes, or external distrubances.

Another conventional approach is the Linear Quadratic Regulator (LQR), which uses a linear wheeled inverted pendulum model. LQR offers optimal control and low energy consumption, effectively handling coupling and demonstrating strong real-world performance [8]. However, its effectiveness depends heavily on accurate model and linear assumptions, making it vulnerable to large state deviations from equilibrium point or system variations.

Modern methods include some nonlinear robust control methods. For nonlinear robust control, Sliding Mode Control (SMC) is one of the most representative methods. SMC designs a desired manifold in the state space named sliding surface, then control the system converge to this desired manifold. This sliding surface defines the desired system dynamics under control and the system on sliding surface can slide and finally reach the equilibrium point, offering strong robustness against uncertainties and external disturbances [9]. However, standard SMC is not directly applicable to underactuated two-wheel legged robots, because both balance and velocity or position must be controlled and one sliding surface often proves insufficient to achieve all objectives. To address this limitation, decoupled sliding mode control designs separate surfaces for balance and position [10], however the interference between these surfaces may degrade performance and stability. Hierarchical SMC has also been introduced to mitigate coupling, but it increases parameter-tuning complexity and prolongs the control design process [11].

Recent works proposed some fusion methods, like integrating LQR with Whole-Body Control [12], Nonlinear Feedforward Control [13], Model Predictive Control [14], or Active Disturbance Rejection Control [15] to improve robustness and adaptability. Nevertheless, these approaches demand substantial computational power and extra sensors, reducing their suitability for low-cost robotics systems with limited computational capacities.

Overall, existing balance and motion control methods for two-wheel legged robots present three major challenges:

1. LQR is often vulnerable to model inaccuracies and nonlinearities. On low-cost robots with limited sensor quality, precise system modeling becomes challenging. Real-world disturbances also degrade LQR performance on such platforms.

2. In coupled systems (e.g., two-wheel legged robots), SMC typically employs multi-layer sliding surfaces, resulting in extensive parameter tuning and increased design complexity.
3. Existing fusion methods that integrate LQR or SMC with other algorithms often requires significant computations, which may not be suitable for low cost and computation limited systems.

To address above challenges, this paper proposes a novel fusion approach combining LQR and a single-layer State-Fused Sliding Mode Controller (SF-SMC), which simultaneously controls both position and balance. By linearly integrating, the framework retains optimality of LQR while adding robustness of SMC against model inaccuracies and external disturbance. Experimental results confirm the method's strong robustness and stability.

The main contributions of this paper are summarized as follows:

1. Proposes a novel SF-SMC algorithm to control both balance and position simultaneously. Compared with conventional SMC, it reduces the number of parameter. Uses fixed weight to integrate SF-SMC with LQR, the fusion controller enhances robustness against system model inaccuracy and external disturbances.
2. The proposed fusion controller keeps low computational cost. It is deployed on low-cost robotics systems with limited computational capacities to validate its adaptability and feasibility in low cost robot practical applications.

2   System Model

A two-wheel legged robot can be modeled as two wheeled inverted pendulums connected by the robot body. The rods of these inverted pendulums form a planar five-link structure. When ignoring leg joint movements and focusing only on the robot's straight-line motion, small turning and balance, the system can be simplified to a planar wheeled inverted pendulum model [16]. Figure 1 illustrates how the body, leg, and wheel are connected.

In order to model dynamics of the system, Newton-Lagrangian method is used [17], which is given by

$$L = T - V = T_{body} + T_{wheel} - V_{body} - V_{wheel} \qquad (1)$$

where L denotes the Lagrangian, T is the kinetic energy, and V is the potential energy of the system, T_{body} denotes the kinetic energy of the robot body, T_{wheel} denotes the kinetic energy of the driving wheel, V_{body} denotes the potential energy of the robot body, V_{wheel} denotes the potential energy of the wheel.

The kinetic energy and potential energy terms of both the body and the wheel are given by

$$T_{body} = \frac{1}{2}m(\dot{\theta}^2 r^2 + l^2\dot{q}^2 - 2\dot{\theta}rl\cos q \cdot \dot{q}) \qquad (2)$$

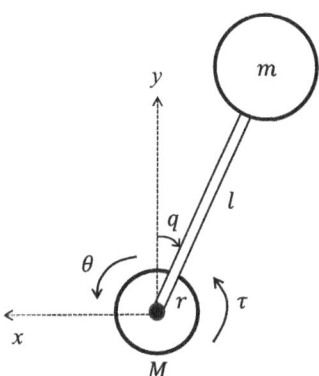

Fig. 1. Diagram of the wheel legged inverted pendulum model. The model consists of a circular driving wheel (mass M, radius r), a simplified leg (length l), and an upper body (mass m). The tilt angle of the body is q, while θ denotes the wheel's rotation angle and τ is driving torque.

$$T_{wheel} = \frac{3}{4}M\dot{\theta}^2 r^2 \tag{3}$$

$$V_{body} = -mgl(1 - \cos q) \tag{4}$$

$$V_{wheel} = 0 \tag{5}$$

Then using Newton-Lagrangian method, the complete dynamics are given by [18]

$$\tau = (m + M)r^2\ddot{\theta} + mrl\sin q \cdot \dot{q}^2 - mrl\cos q \cdot \ddot{q} + \frac{1}{2}Mr^2\ddot{\theta} \tag{6}$$

and

$$0 - ml^2\ddot{q} \quad mrl\cos q \cdot \ddot{\theta} - mgl\sin q \tag{7}$$

3 Control Algorithms

In this section, we propose a novel fusion method, which linearly combine a single layer SF-SMC with LQR to enhance the robustness and stability of a two-wheel legged robot. The overall control framework, as shown in the Fig. 2, where $\mathbf{x} = [\theta \ \dot{\theta} \ q \ \dot{q}]^T$ is the state vector of the dynamic model.

3.1 Linear Quadratic Regulator

LQR is a typical optimal control method based on a linear model, which requires the linear state-space model of the robot for computation. From (6) and (7), the state-space model could be derived and given by

$$\frac{d}{dt}\mathbf{x} = F(\mathbf{x}) + G(\mathbf{x}) \cdot \tau \tag{8}$$

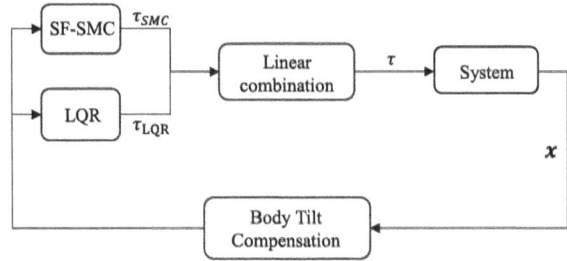

Fig. 2. Diagram of control frame. τ_{SMC} and τ_{LQR} denotes the control signal of SMC and LQR, τ denotes the total controller signal. $\mathbf{x} = [\theta\ \dot{\theta}\ q\ \dot{q}]^T$, is the state vector of the dynamic model.

where

$$F(\mathbf{x}) = \begin{bmatrix} f_1(\mathbf{x}) & f_2(\mathbf{x}) & f_3(\mathbf{x}) & f_4(\mathbf{x}) \end{bmatrix}^T$$

$$G(\mathbf{x}) = \begin{bmatrix} g_1(\mathbf{x}) & g_2(\mathbf{x}) & g_3(\mathbf{x}) & g_4(\mathbf{x}) \end{bmatrix}^T$$

$$f_1(\mathbf{x}) = \dot{\theta},\ f_2(\mathbf{x}) = \frac{-2mrl\sin q\dot{q}^2 + 2mrg\cos q\sin q}{-2\,mr^2\cos^2 q + 3Mr^2 + 2\,mr^2}$$

$$f_3(\mathbf{x}) = \dot{q},\ f_4(\mathbf{x}) = \frac{-2mrl\cos q\sin q\dot{q}^2 + 3Mgr\sin q + 2mrg\sin q}{-2mrl\cos^2 q + 3Mrl + 2mrl}$$

$$g_1(\mathbf{x}) = 0,\ g_2(\mathbf{x}) = \frac{2}{-2\,mr^2\cos^2 q + 3Mr^2 + 2\,mr^2}$$

$$g_3(\mathbf{x}) = 0,\ g_4(\mathbf{x}) = \frac{2\cos q}{-2mrl\cos^2 q + 3Mrl + 2mrl}$$

Then, by linearizing around equilibrium point $(q = 0)$, the linear model is given by

$$\frac{d}{dt}\mathbf{x} = A\mathbf{x} + B\cdot\tau \tag{9}$$

where

$$A = \begin{bmatrix} 0 & 1 & 0 & 0 \\ 0 & 0 & \frac{2mg}{3Mr} & 0 \\ 0 & 0 & 0 & 1 \\ 0 & 0 & \frac{2mg+3Mg}{3Ml} & 0 \end{bmatrix},\ B = \begin{bmatrix} 0 \\ \frac{2}{3Mr^2} \\ 0 \\ \frac{2}{3Mrl} \end{bmatrix}$$

Using the Algebraic Riccati Equation (ARE) [19], a standard method for computing LQR gain given by

$$0 = A^T P + PA - PBR^{-1}B^T P + Q \tag{10}$$

where Q and R are the state and control cost matrices, P is the solution to the Algebraic Riccati Equation. Then the LQR gain K could be derived and given by

$$K = R^{-1}B^T P \tag{11}$$

Finally, the LQR output is given by [20]

$$\tau_{LQR} = -K \cdot \mathbf{x} \tag{12}$$

where K is LQR gain and τ_{LQR} denotes the output of LQR.

3.2   State-Fused Sliding Mode Control

To handle nonlinearities and uncertainties, we introduce Sliding Mode Control (SMC). SMC aims to design a manifold in state space, this manifold determines the desired system dynamics under control of SMC. SMC controls system to converge to the manifold, then the system can converge to equilibrium point in finite time. Here the manifold is also called sliding surface. However, because the two-wheel legged robot is underactuated and coupled, the input torque τ influences both position and balance, complicating the design of the sliding surface. To address this issue, this study adopts a state-fused approach. When the robot maintains a nonzero tilt angle, gravity naturally induces motion in the direction of inclination. Utilizing this characteristic, the position control could be converted into an equivalent desired tilt angle, this process is called state-fused and allows the sliding surface to focus only on tilt angle control. By directly controlling the tilt angle, the sliding surface indirectly regulates the robot's position and movement. In this merging process, using the proportional and derivative terms of the position error to determine the desired tilt angle, ensure convergence of the robot's position. The sliding mode surface of SF-SMC is given by

$$q_d = k \cdot \theta + k_d \cdot \dot{\theta} \tag{13}$$

and

$$S = \lambda_1 (q - k\theta - k_d\dot{\theta}) + \lambda_2 (\dot{q} - k\dot{\theta} - k_d\ddot{\theta}) \tag{14}$$

where q_d is the desired tilt angle and S is the sliding surface variable, k, k_d, λ_1, λ_2 are the parameters of sliding mode surface.

This sliding mode surface design not only reduces the number of control parameters but also need lower computational complexity and simplifies parameter tuning, making the control implementation more efficient.

To make system Lyapunov stable, a positive definite Lyapunov function is given by [10]

$$V = \frac{1}{2}S^2 \tag{15}$$

where V denotes the Lyapunov function.

The $\dot{S}$ and $\dot{V}$ are given by

$$\dot{S} = -PS - Q_1 \cdot sign(S) \tag{16}$$

and

$$\dot{V} = -PS^2 - Q_1|S| \tag{17}$$

$\dot{V}$ is negative definite, so the system is Lyapunov stable. Next, the controller output of SMC is derived, given by

$$\tau_{SMC} = \frac{-PS - Q_1 sgn(S) - \lambda_1 \dot{q} + \lambda_1 k\dot{\theta} + (\lambda_1 k_d + \lambda_2 k)f_2 - \lambda_2 f_4 + \lambda_2 k_d \theta^{(3)}}{\lambda_2 g_4 - (\lambda_1 k_d + \lambda_2 k)g_2} \tag{18}$$

where P and Q_1 are the parameters of SMC and u_{SMC} is the output of SMC. The proposed SF-SMC includes q, $\dot{q}$, θ, $\dot{\theta}$, $\ddot{\theta}$, $\theta^{(3)}$ state variables and P, Q_1, k, k_d, λ_1, λ_2 parameters.

3.3   Linear Combination of LQR and SF-SMC

Because LQR often relies on accurate system model and linear assumption, system nonlinearities or variations may result in degraded control performance. To solve this, we linearly combine the outputs of LQR and SF-SMC using fixed weights, given by

$$\tau = w_1 \cdot \tau_{LQR} + w_2 \cdot \tau_{SMC} \tag{19}$$

where w_1 is the weight of LQR output and w_2 is the weight of SMC output.

This approach retains the LQR's optimality in near-linear regimes while leveraging the robustness of SMC, thus improving the overall controller performance. For standalone LQR or SMC, it is easy to prove their stability. However, due to the presence of nonlinear switching terms in combination with linear feedback, it is challenging to conduct a unified stability analysis using conventional Lyapunov methods. Although a theoretical proof has not yet been established, MATLAB simulations and real-world control experiments in next section demonstrate that the system consistently converges to the desired state under various system parameters and external disturbance, indicating good robustness and stability. For the weight allocation between the two controllers, lower weight for LQR and higher weight for SMC have stronger robustness but worse optimality while higher weight for LQR and lower weight for SMC have less robustness but stronger optimality.

4   Results

To evaluate the feasibility and performance of the proposed algorithm, we compared the proposed control strategy with standalone LQR in both a simulation environment and on a physical robot platform.

4.1   Simulation Experiment

We simulated the two-wheel legged robot system in MATLAB. Robot systems parameters are given in Table 1. Meanwhile, the values for the controller parameters are determined by multiple trails and tuning, which are also listed in Table 1, where Q is a 4×4 diagonal matrix. To prevent potential instability caused by excessive total gain in the fusion controller, a conservative weight combination strategy (0.7 and 0.7) was adopted in both simulation and physical experiments. Although this weight setting results in a total gain slightly higher than the standard unit-gain LQR, the introduction of the SMC component fundamentally changes the control structure and mechanism. Therefore, it is regarded as a comparison between different control strategies rather than a simple gain adjustment. The main focus of the experiments is evaluating the fusion controller improvement in robustness to system variations.

Table 1. Parameters of Robot System

Parameter	Value	Parameter	Value	Parameter	Value
M (kg)	0.1	Q	diag(0.1,0.1,0.1,0.1)	λ_2	0.01
m (kg)	0.5	R	100	w_1	0.7
r (m)	0.025	P	10	w_2	0.7
l (m)	0.055	Q_1	1	k	0.001
		λ_1	1	k_d	0.0003

The controller is designed based on these nominal values. Then varied the system actual values of mass m and height l to evaluate the robustness and stability of both the proposed controller and the standalone LQR under parameter deviations. The simulation experimental scenarios are listed in Table 2 and the simulation results are presented in Fig. 3.

Table 2. Simulation Experimental Scenarios and Conditions

Scenario	Control Algorithm	Height	Mass	Initial Tilt (°)
Different heights with initial tilt angle	Single LQR	l	$4m$	40
	Proposed	l	$4m$	40
	Single LQR	$1.5l$	m	40
	Proposed	$1.5l$	m	40
	Single LQR	$1.5l$	$4m$	40
	Proposed	$1.5l$	$4m$	40

4.2 Hardware Experiment

We use a robot platform designed at the University of Manchester [21], which is a planar five-link two-wheel legged robot. The robot is equipped with two PM3010 brushless motors for the driving wheels, four 8120MG servos for the hip joints, two ESP32 microcontrollers for real-time control and a MPU6050 IMU to measure the robot's tilt angle. Photographs of the robot prototype are shown in Figs. 4a–4d.

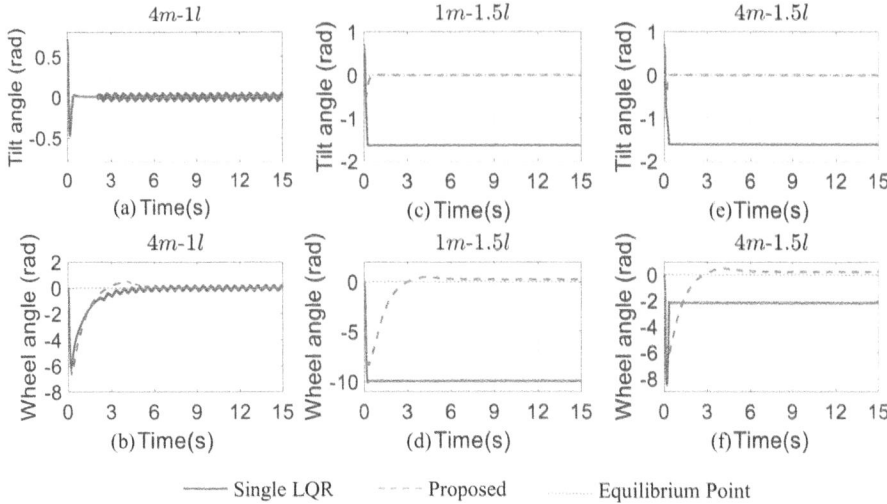

Fig. 3. Simulation results comparing the proposed method and single LQR under various parameter deviations. Subfigures (a) and (b) correspond to mass $4m$ and height $1l$; (c) and (d) to $1m$ and $1.5l$; and (e) and (f) to $4m$ and $1.5l$.

(a) The original robot with nominal height.

(b) The robot with 1.5 times height.

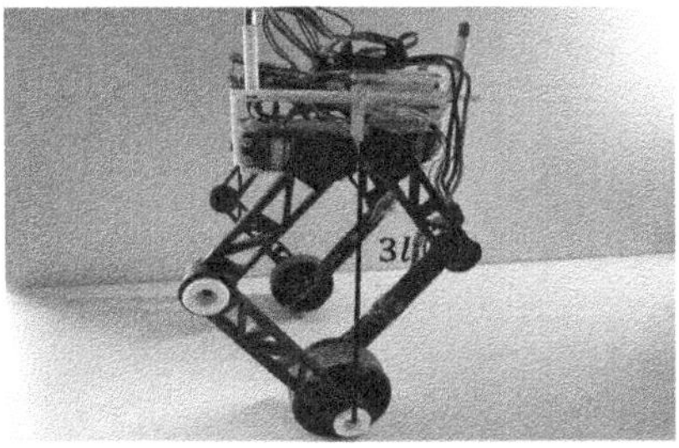

(c) The robot with 3 times height.

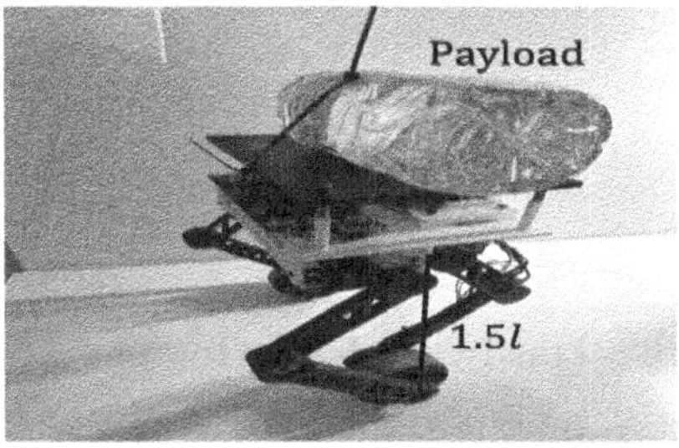

(d) 1.5 times height robot with payload.

Fig. 4. Photographs of the robot prototype at different heights: (a) $1l$, (b) $1.5l$, (c) $3l$, (d) $1.5l$ with payload.

Table 3 summarizes three experimental scenarios. Here kick disturbances were introduced at a defined time, but they were manually applied and not precisely quantified, efforts were made to ensure consistency across trials. The proposed fusion approach and the standalone LQR controller are tested separately. The results are presented in Figs. 5–6. The summary of practical performance is listed in Table 4 and the detailed analysis is given below:

Table 3. Practical Experimental Scenarios and Conditions

Scenario	No.	Controller	Height	Initial Tilt (°)	External Disturbance (Applied Time)	Payload
Different heights with initial tilt angle	1	Single LQR	l	15	N/A	N/A
		Proposed	l	15	N/A	N/A
	2	Single LQR	$1.5l$	11	N/A	N/A
		Proposed	$1.5l$	11	N/A	N/A
	3	Single LQR	$3l$	7	N/A	N/A
		Proposed	$3l$	7	N/A	N/A
Different heights with kick disturbance	4	Single LQR	$1.5l$	0	2 s	N/A
		Proposed	$1.5l$	0	2 s	N/A
	5	Single LQR	$3l$	0	3 s	N/A
		Proposed	$3l$	0	3 s	N/A
With payload	6	Single LQR	$1.5l$	6	N/A	0.75 kg
		Proposed	$1.5l$	6	N/A	0.75 kg

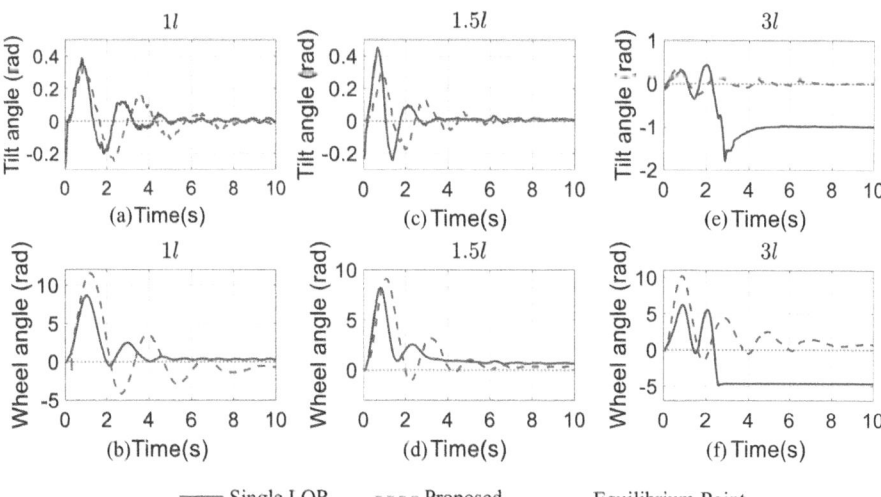

Fig. 5. Practical results comparing the proposed method and single LQR under different heights with initial tilt angle. Subfigures (a) and (b) correspond to Scenario 1; (c) and (d) to Scenario 2; and (e) and (f) to Scenario 3.

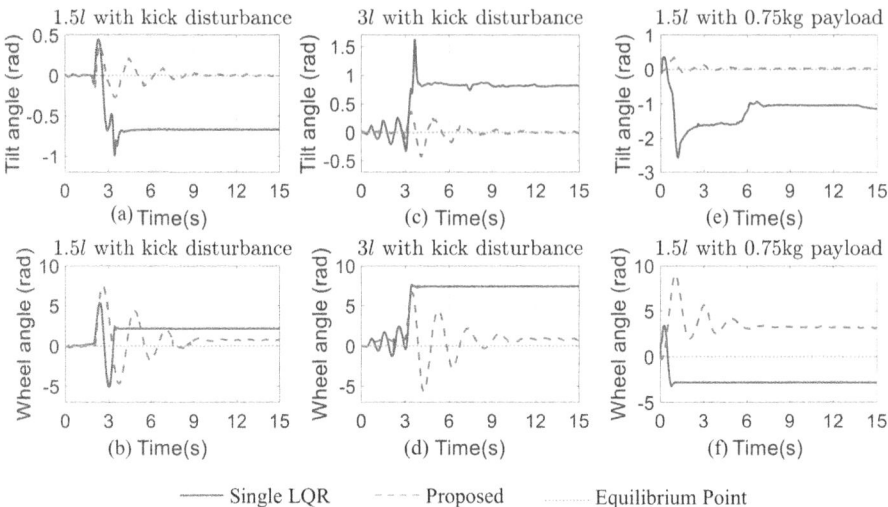

Fig. 6. Practical results comparing the proposed method and single LQR under different heights with kick disturbance and payload. Subfigures (a) and (b) correspond to Scenario 4; (c) and (d) to Scenario 5; and (e) and (f) to Scenario 6.

Table 4. Practical Performance Comparison under Different Heights

Scenario No.	Controller	Settling Time (s)	Overshoot (rad)	Oscillation/Stability
1	Single LQR	4 (Fast)	0.4 (Large)	Slight oscillation
	Proposed	7 (Slow)	0.3 (Small)	No oscillation
2	Single LQR	4 (Fast)	0.45 (Large)	Slight oscillation
	Proposed	7 (Slow)	0.3 (Small)	No oscillation
3	Single LQR	N/A	N/A	Unstable
	Proposed	7	0.38	Stable
4	Single LQR	N/A	N/A	Poor robustness
	Proposed	7	0.35	Great robustness
5	Single LQR	N/A	N/A	Poor robustness
	Proposed	7	0.35	Great robustness
6	Single LQR	N/A	N/A	Unstable
	Proposed	6	0.3	Stable

Scenario 1, 2 and 3: Scenario 1,2 and 3 aim to validate the stability of the proposed method under different height configurations. When the robot height remain unchanged or vary within a 1.5 times, the fusion control algorithm exhibits longer settling time compared to standalone LQR, but with reduced tilt angle overshoot and slighter steady state oscillations. So there is a trade-off between settling time and overshoot. The reason is that the system departs significantly from equilibrium point at the beginning, the performance of LQR is degraded by the nonlinearities, resulting in a higher overshoot. However, the fusion method uses SF-SMC to rapidly pull the system tilt back toward the equilibrium point, mitigating overshoot. When system is close to equilibrium point, the optimality of LQR might be degraded by inaccuracy of system model, resulting in steady state oscillations, while SF-SMC could enforce system move to equilibrium point, therefore reduces the stable state oscillations. However, it also compromises part of LQR's optimality, thereby prolonging the settling time. When the robot height vary to 3 times, the standalone LQR controller could not keep stable with an initial tilt angle while the proposed fusion controller performs strong stability. It is because that the fusion method is bolstered by the additional robustness contributed by SF-SMC and effectively complements LQR's optimal performance.

Scenario 4 and 5: Scenario 4 and 5 aim to evaluate the robustness of the proposed method when the height changes and external disturbances are also introduced. When the robot height vary 1.5 or 3 times, the standalone LQR controller could not reject kick disturbances while the proposed fusion controller performs strong robustness. It is also because robustness of SF-SMC.

Scenario 6: Scenario 6 aims to evaluate the stability of the proposed method when both the mass and height of the robot vary, as adding a payload alters both the total mass and the position of the center of mass. In this case, the proposed method perform strong stability, while standalone LQR fails to keep balance.

These outcomes align with the simulation results and further validate the proposed method merging SF-SMC with LQR via linear combination significantly enhances the system's robustness and reliability against parameter variations, modeling inaccuracies, and external disturbances. Although the fusion approach may slightly increase the settling time, reliability and robustness are generally more critical for two-wheel legged robots facing manufacturing tolerances, unknown payloads, and external disturbances. Hence, the extra cost in settling time is a reasonable trade-off.

5   Conclusion

The proposed SF-SMC regulates both balance and position, with only few parameters compared with conventional SMC. The fusion controller integrating SF-SMC and LQR combines both linear optimality and nonlinear robustness. It effectively handles parameter mismatches and disturbances while maintaining a moderate response speed, offering a balanced and reasonable solution for two-wheel legged robots, especially under significant mass or height changes.

This study focuses on planar balance and motion, future extensions to 3D tasks such as trajectory tracking could further enhance its practical applicability. In addition, although the proposed method reduces the steady state oscillations, some still remain due to chattering caused by SMC. Future work could address via smoothing functions or adaptive boundary layers. Moreover, our proposed method could be compared with other fusion method like LQR-MPC or LQR-ADRC to validate its performance in future work.

References

1. Liu, X., et al.: Development of wheel-legged biped robots: a review. J. Bionic Eng. **21**(2), 607–634 (2024). https://doi.org/10.1007/s42235-023-00468-1
2. Chate García, K.V., Prado Ramírez, O.E., Rengifo Rodas, C.F.: Comparative analysis between fuzzy logic control, LQR control with kalman filter and PID control for a two wheeled inverted pendulum. In: Chang, I., Baca, J., Moreno, H.A., Carrera, I.G., Cardona, M.N. (eds.) Advances in Automation and Robotics Research in Latin America. LNNS, vol. 13, pp. 144–156. Springer, Cham (2017). https://doi.org/10.1007/978-3-319-54377-2_13
3. Lee, J., Bjelonic, M., Reske, A., Wellhausen, L., Miki, T., Hutter, M.: Learning robust autonomous navigation and locomotion for wheeled-legged robots. Sci. Rob. **9**(89), eadi9641 (2024). https://doi.org/10.1126/scirobotics.adi9641
4. Zhu, Q., et al.: Overview of structure and drive for wheel-legged robots. Robot. Auton. Syst. **181**, 104777 (2024). https://doi.org/10.1016/j.robot.2024.104777
5. T, N., K T, P.: PID controller based two wheeled self balancing robot. In: 2021 5th International Conference on Trends in Electronics and Informatics (ICOEI), pp. 1–4 (2021). https://doi.org/10.1109/ICOEI51242.2021.9453091
6. Yang, Z., Zhang, L.: Balancing control of low-cost wheel-leg robotics for control and robotics education. In: 2024 29th International Conference on Automation and Computing (ICAC), pp. 1–5 (2024). https://doi.org/10.1109/ICAC61394.2024.10718853
7. Zhang, C., Liu, T., Song, S., Meng, M.Q.H.: System design and balance control of a bipedal leg-wheeled robot. In: 2019 IEEE International Conference on Robotics and Biomimetics (ROBIO), pp. 1869–1874 (2019). https://doi.org/10.1109/ROBIO49542.2019.8961814
8. Klemm, V., .: Ascento: a two-wheeled jumping robot. In: 2019 International Conference on Robotics and Automation (ICRA), pp. 7515–7521 (2019). https://doi.org/10.1109/ICRA.2019.8793792
9. Pisano, A., Usai, E.: Sliding mode control: a survey with applications in math. Math. Comput. Simul. **81**(5), 954–979 (2011). https://doi.org/10.1016/j.matcom.2010.10.003
10. Park, M.S., Chwa, D.: Swing-up and stabilization control of inverted-pendulum systems via coupled sliding-mode control method. IEEE Trans. Ind. Electron. **56**(9), 3541–3555 (2009). https://doi.org/10.1109/TIE.2009.2012452
11. Hou, M., Zhang, X., Chen, D., Xu, Z.: Hierarchical sliding mode control combined with nonlinear disturbance observer for wheeled inverted pendulum robot trajectory tracking. Appl. Sci. **13**(7), 4350 (2023). https://doi.org/10.3390/app13074350
12. Klemm, V., et al.: LQR-assisted whole-body control of a wheeled bipedal robot with kinematic loops. IEEE Rob. Autom. Lett. **5**(2), 3745–3752 (2020). https://doi.org/10.1109/LRA.2020.2979625
13. Raza, F., Hayashibe, M.: Towards robust wheel-legged biped robot system: combining feedforward and feedback control. In: 2021 IEEE/SICE International Symposium on System Integration (SII), pp. 606–612 (2021). https://doi.org/10.1109/IEEECONF49454.2021.9382678

14. Cui, Z., Xin, Y., Liu, S., Rong, X., Li, Y.: Modeling and Control of a Wheeled Biped Robot. Micromachines **13**(5), 747 (2022). https://doi.org/10.3390/mi13050747
15. Feng, X., Liu, S., Yuan, Q., Xiao, J., Zhao, D.: Research on wheel-legged robot based on LQR and ADRC. Sci. Rep. **13**(1), 15122 (2023). https://doi.org/10.1038/s41598-023-41462-1
16. Huang, C.H., Wang, W.J., Chiu, C.H.: Design and implementation of fuzzy control on a two-wheel inverted pendulum. IEEE Trans. Ind. Electron. **58**(7), 2988–3001 (2011). https://doi.org/10.1109/TIE.2010.2069076
17. Silver, W.M.: On the equivalence of lagrangian and newton-euler dynamics for manipulators. Int. J. Rob. Res. **1**(2), 60–70 (1982). https://doi.org/10.1177/027836498200100204
18. Wang, S., et al.: Balance control of a novel wheel-legged robot: design and experiments. In: 2021 IEEE International Conference on Robotics and Automation (ICRA), pp. 6782–6788 (2021). https://doi.org/10.1109/ICRA48506.2021.9561579
19. Anderson, B.D.O., Moore, J.B.: Optimal Control: Linear Quadratic Methods. Courier Corporation (2007)
20. Marton, Lö., Hodel, A.S., Lantos, Bé., Hung, J.Y.: Underactuated robot control: comparing LQR, subspace stabilization, and combined error metric approaches. IEEE Trans. Ind. Electron. **55**(10), 3724–3730 (2008). https://doi.org/10.1109/TIE.2008.923285
21. Yang, Z., Li, C., Zhang, L.: Self balancing performance of wheel-legged robots under disturbance and faulty conditions. In: 2024 International Conference on Intelligent Robotics and Automatic Control (2024)

Analysis of Adaptive Passive Technologies for the Robot Traversal in Unstructured Environments

Robert Liam Stevenson$^{(\boxtimes)}$ (iD) and Alexandr Klimchik (iD)

Lincoln Centre for Autonomous Systems (L-CAS), University of Lincoln,
Brayford Pool Campus, Lincoln LN6 7TS, UK
28260769@students.lincoln.ac.uk, AKlimchik@lincoln.ac.uk

Abstract. This paper evaluates adaptive passive technologies for improving robotic locomotion in unstructured environments, focusing specifically on the Passively-Transformable Single-Part Wheel (PaTS-Wheel) and our novel variant, the "DogBone-Wheel." We assessed these wheel designs in authentic woodland environments, measuring their energy efficiency, vibration profiles, and traversal capabilities in comparison to traditional wheels. Our findings demonstrate that the PaTS-Wheel achieved a superior obstacle-climbing ability (70% of wheel diameter vs. 25% for standard wheels), while maintaining remarkably consistent energy consumption across varied terrain types—only a 4% variation compared to 35.7% for standard wheels. The wheel exhibits predictable mechanical behaviour and balanced vibration characteristics, though with 39.8% higher baseline energy consumption than traditional wheels. However, practical limitations, including debris entrapment between flexure components and the need for adequate robot ground clearance, constrain real-world performance. The DogBone-Wheel's modular construction offered manufacturing flexibility, but it reduced traction due to the use of PLA components. These results validate the potential of passive transformation mechanisms to enhance robotic mobility in challenging terrain with consistent energy performance and minimal active control. Repo with print files, data and processing code:
https://github.com/robert-stevenson-1/DogBone-Wheels.

Keywords: Unstructured Environments · Compliant joints · Robotics · Real-world · Wheel Robots · 3D Printing

1 Introduction

In the era of Industry 4.0, manufacturing and agricultural sectors are increasingly adopting autonomous robotic systems to enhance productivity, efficiency, and sustainability. This digital transformation has led to growing global energy demand, with industries contributing to more than 40% of global greenhouse gas emissions, resulting in mounting pressures to develop more sustainable approaches to improve energy efficiency across their operations [6, 14].

© The Author(s), under exclusive license to Springer Nature Switzerland AG 2026
A. Cavalcanti et al. (Eds.): TAROS 2025, LNAI 16045, pp. 152–164, 2026.
https://doi.org/10.1007/978-3-032-01486-3_13

Mobile robots, such as those in agricultural settings, often face challenges navigating unstructured environments. Unlike the structured conditions of factory floors, environments such as crop fields, orchards, and vineyards present unpredictable terrain and conditions with numerous obstacles that impede locomotion [10]. The inefficiencies that emerge when robots encounter such environments result in increased energy consumption, reduced operational speed, and ultimately higher emissions, which contradict goals for more sustainable practices.

While various locomotion methods exist for mobile robots, wheel-based approaches remain predominant in agricultural and industrial applications due to their relative efficiency on structured surfaces. However, traditional circular wheels perform poorly on uneven terrain, lacking the necessary traction and obstacle traversal capabilities for reliable operation in complex environments. This fundamental limitation restricts the deployment potential of autonomous systems in many practical settings where they could provide significant value, as recent advances in terrain traversability analysis have highlighted the importance of adaptive mechanisms for unstructured environments in terrain with dense vegetation and uncertain ground conditions [3,16].

Two primary approaches exist for addressing these mobility challenges: improving navigation algorithms or redesigning locomotion systems. The Passively-Transformable Single-Part Wheel (PaTS-Wheel) developed by Godden et al. represents an innovative direction in the latter category [7]. This wheel uses a flexure-based design that passively transforms when encountering obstacles, enabling improved climbing capabilities without active mechanisms or additional energy consumption. While promising in laboratory testing, the PaTS-Wheel's performance in authentic outdoor environments remains largely unexplored – a critical gap between theoretical innovation and practical application.

This research addresses this gap by evaluating the PaTS-Wheel in real-world unstructured environments and introducing a modified design, the "DogBone-Wheel", which explores alternative manufacturing approaches and material combinations through its modular assembly. Our objectives include measuring energy efficiency, vibration profiles, and overall traversal capabilities compared to traditional wheel designs and identifying practical limitations and potential improvements for deployment in real, outdoor environments. Through comparative testing of the PaTS-Wheel, DogBone-Wheel, and traditional wheels, we will bridge the gap between laboratory innovation and field deployment and create more effective robotic mobility solutions for outdoor robotics and inspection tasks.

2   Related Works

2.1   Wheel-Based Locomotion

While extensive research has focused on perception-based traversability estimation [3], fewer studies address mechanical adaptation to terrain variability. Considering Wheel-based locomotion remains the predominant method for mobile robots, particularly in agricultural and industrial applications, due to its efficiency on structured terrains [9]. However, traversal through unstructured environments presents significant challenges for wheeled robots, with the difficulties around wheel slippage and small debris that reduce contact/friction between the wheel and the ground, which prevents the mobile system from generating sufficient traction for effective motion [1,11]. It is because of these inefficiencies that wheel-based locomotion is not able to exceed the higher, more efficient speeds that are possible on flat terrains compared to other locomotion methods [2,11].

However, Kashiri et al. suggest that carefully designing actuating components in wheel drive systems can enhance energy efficiency by reducing the power required for traversing uneven terrains [8]. Though primarily focused on legged robots, their research offers valuable insights for wheel-based systems, with potential benefits seen in hybrid locomotive designs and passive elastic elements that store and reuse energy during movement.

2.2   Morphing Wheel Technologies

Morphing wheels dynamically alter their geometry to improve traction and obstacle traversal capabilities. The PaTS-Wheel is a passive wheel design that, unlike other adaptive wheel designs, requires no active components and transforms its shape purely through passive mechanical response to obstacles [7]. The design utilises a flexure mechanism that, when pressed against an obstacle, extends "claws" from the "pad" and presses inwards, allowing it to hook onto obstacles and pull itself up and over previously insurmountable ones. This principle of using mechanical compliance for adaptation is explored in other recent passive designs, such as novel centipede-inspired robots that also adapt to terrain without active control systems [18].

In testing, the PaTS-Wheel could traverse obstacles $\approx 70\%$ of the wheel's diameter (120 mm), significantly outperforming traditional 4-spoke circular wheels and 4-legged wheels (wheg) hybrid wheels of the same size, which manage only $\approx 25\%$, while also showing comparable energy efficiency to circular wheels on rigid surfaces and superior efficiency to wheg-type wheels. However, the original study's testing environment featured relatively uniform, deliberately positioned obstacles rather than the heterogeneous, randomly distributed obstacles typical in natural, unstructured environments. This raises questions about the wheel's performance in real deployment scenarios and how it handles smaller debris in these environments.

Other morphing wheels have incorporated active mechanisms for improving their terrain adaptabilities. Zeng et al.'s variable-diameter wheels comprise six equally spaced pantographs that use helical torsion springs to vary the diameter, allowing for a more compact and lightweight mechanism over conventional rigid-body expandable designs [17]. Contracting for flat surfaces minimises the rolling resistance, whereas expanded operation for uneven terrain improves its surmounting capabilities. The "wheel-foot" also increases traction on soft surfaces, reducing slippage. However, concerns about material fatigue from repeated deformations highlight the challenges of deploying such mechanisms in harsh conditions. Together with the incorporation of active components alongside compliant elements, this results in additional energy usage. The obstacle traversal approach resembles wheg-wheels, lifting the robot's body upward and forward toward obstacles. However, the effectiveness of this approach is critical for the balance between wheel diameter and stabiliser length to be properly calibrated, as the robot may fail to contact obstacles with the wheel tip or lose ground contact after initial climbing. Nagatani, Kuze and Yoshida developed similar variable-diameter wheels for small search and rescue robots navigating narrow, bumpy environments [13]. Their design includes a variable-length stabiliser to address the instability issues that can arise with expanded wheel diameters that Zeng et al. point out. Similarly, the Rim Shape Changeable (RSC) wheel by Fu et al. uses a motor-driven four-bar linkage to actively transform its shape, enabling bi-directional obstacle-crossing [5].

While these systems improve adaptability, they require additional actuators, increasing energy consumption and mechanical complexity. This highlights how wheel mechanism effectiveness often depends more on the overall robot design than the wheel technology itself, emphasising the importance of holistic system design when implementing novel wheel technologies.

2.3   Research Gap and Objectives

The existing literature reveals several key gaps. First, most morphing wheel technologies require active components, increasing energy consumption and complexity. Second, the testing of these technologies, including the PaTS-Wheel, has occurred mainly in controlled environments rather than natural, unstructured settings. Third, practical considerations such as manufacturing methods, material selection, and real-world operational constraints remain an area of constant exploration.

We address these gaps by evaluating the purely passive PaTS-Wheel in real-world outdoor environments, developing and testing a modified design, "DogBone-Wheel," that explores alternative material combinations and manufacturing approaches, measuring energy efficiency and vibration profiles in real-world conditions, and identifying practical limitations and improvements for deployment.

This work aims to bridge the gap between laboratory demonstrations and field-deployable passive wheel technologies for agricultural and outdoor robotic applications by extending previous research into more realistic testing environments and exploring practical implementation considerations.

3   Wheel Design and Manufacturing Methodology

This chapter presents the design and manufacturing approaches for three wheel variants: the reproduced PaTS-Wheel, the novel DogBone-Wheel, and standard circular wheels used as controls, using polylactic acid (PLA) and thermoplastic polyurethane (TPU) as the core materials. All wheel designs where made with a 120 mm diameter and 20 mm thickness.

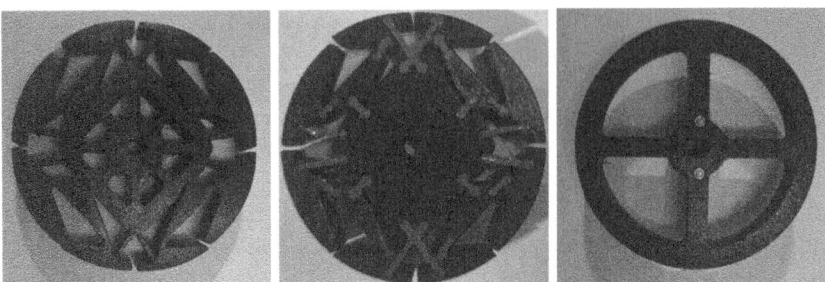

Fig. 1. Left: Reproduced PaTS-Wheel printed in eSUN eTPU-95A showing integrated flexure mechanism. **Middle:** Modified PaTS-Wheel, called "DogBone-Wheel", with modular construction using flexible joints (NinjaFlex TPU) and rigid structural components (PLA) for claws and pads. **Right:** Standard circular wheel with four spokes printed in identical TPU material serving as experimental control. **All:** 120 mm diameter and 20 mm thickness.

PaTS-Wheel Reproduction. The PaTS-Wheel in Fig. 1 (left image) was reproduced using the shared 3D file on a Sovol SV06 3D printer using eSUN eTPU-95A, with a 0.20 mm layer height, 2 perimeter walls, and 20% Gyroid infill pattern at ≈ 20 mm/s [7]. This approach maintained consistency with the original design parameters to establish a validated baseline for comparative analysis.

DogBone-Wheel Development. Initial attempts to enhance the PaTS-Wheel involved creating a hybrid construction with TPU flexures and stiffer PLA central sections. A single flexure printed in PLA proved too rigid to compress at 4 mm thickness, with joint fatigue occurring after fewer than 20 compressions. Multi-material printing, combining TPU flexure layers with PLA central layers, encountered poor layer adhesion and required excessive manual intervention due to filament changes.

These constraints led us to develop the "DogBone-Wheel", which separates the flexure mechanism's *bones* from the structural components. This modular design allows for additional manufacturing flexibility by printing components in appropriate materials (E.g. varying the 'bone' material hardness) and assembling the components, rather than requiring multi-material printing. The DogBone-Wheel in Fig. 1 (center image) consisted of flexible *bones* printed in NinjaFlex TPU (85A Shore hardness) and structural components printed in PLA. While requiring additional assembly time, this approach offered greater control over the wheel's mechanical properties. It behaved similarly to the PaTS-Wheel regarding stiffness with our chosen materials, but risked reducing available traction.

Control Wheel Design. Standard circular wheels with four central spokes in Fig. 1 (right image) were manufactured using identical TPU material (95A Shore hardness) as the PaTS wheel.

4 Experimental Setup and Testing Process

Test Platform Overview. A four-wheeled robot platform (Similar in size to the one from the PaTS=Wheels paper) with Ackermann steering evaluated wheel performance in unstructured environments [7]. The platform featured independent drive motors with a max RPM of 159 enabling individual wheel rotation necessary for engaging flexure claws. A 4S lithium-ion battery provided 12 V via DC voltage regulator to motors and control systems. Data collection occurred at 100 Hz using a Raspberry Pi 4 with BNO085 IMU (linear acceleration, angular velocity) and INA260 sensor (current draw, voltage monitoring). The platform was driven at full speed to the motor during testing, resulting in a traversal speed of ≈1 m/s. The total weight of the platform is ≈2.3 kg with the PaTS-Wheel installed, and therefore may vary slightly depending on the installed wheel type.

 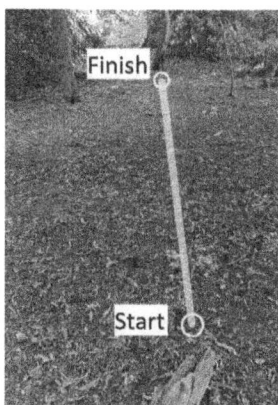

Fig. 2. Area 1 (Left) and 2 (Right) of the test sites at Hartsholme Country Park.

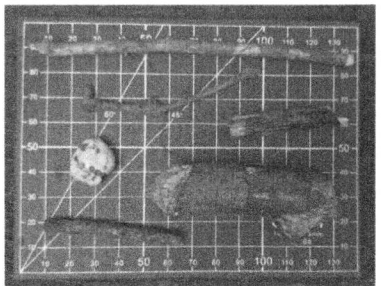 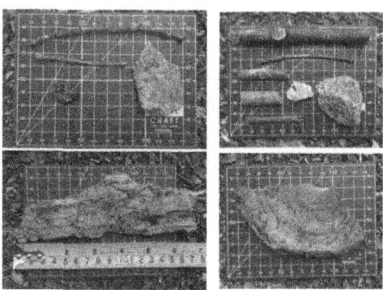

Fig. 3. Example debris found in Area 1.

Fig. 4. Example debris found in Area 2.

Testing Environment and Procedure. Testing was conducted at Hartsholme Country Park in two woodland areas shown in Fig. 2: Area 1 (moderate debris (examples in Fig. 3), level terrain) and Area 2 (complex terrain (examples in Fig. 4), dense vegetation, roots, logs). Each wheel completed three teleoperated runs per area along predetermined paths (8.9 m Area 1, 12.5 m Area 2). All testing occurred on the same day to minimise environmental variability.

Data Processing and Analysis Methods. Energy efficiency analysis examined current draw distributions and mean values across test runs. Vibration analysis employed Fast Fourier Transform (FFT) and Power Spectral Density (PSD) using Welch's method on linear acceleration data, the same as the PaTS-Wheel's paper, with an additional high-pass filtering removing DC components below 0.5 Hz [4,7,15].

Additionally, qualitative observations were made during the collection of these tests, such as interactions and wheel deformation behaviour with different terrain features (roots, logs, loose debris), debris entrapment in wheel mechanisms, traction during operation, and ground clearance limitations. These observations complemented our quantitative measurements for assessing the PaTS-style wheels' real-world performance characteristics, practical limitations, and potential applications in similar outdoor environments.

5   Results and Discussion

Table 1 presents comprehensive performance comparisons across all wheel designs and testing environments, revealing distinct trade-offs between energy efficiency, obstacle traversal capabilities, and practical deployment considerations.

The current draw distributions, as illustrated in Fig. 5, across both testing environments, provide detailed insight into the energy consumption patterns summarised in Table 1. The PaTS-Wheel demonstrated remarkable terrain adaptability, with energy consumption varying only 4% between moderate (Area 1) and complex (Area 2) environments. This consistency contrasts sharply with the standard wheel's 35.7% energy increase when transitioning between areas, highlighting the adaptive advantage of passive transformation mechanisms. The distribution patterns in Fig. 5 reveal that while the DogBone-Wheel maintained similar energy profiles to the PaTS-Wheel in Area 1, its performance degraded significantly in Area 2 due to reduced traction from PLA contact surfaces, leading to increased slippage on loose terrain.

The FFT and PSD analyses in Fig. 6 and Fig. 7 reveal that all wheels exhibited dominant vibration frequencies within the 0–5 Hz range, characteristic of low-frequency terrain interactions. The detailed frequency spectra demonstrate the PaTS-Wheel's superior mechanical stability through more consistent frequency patterns compared to the DogBone-Wheel's multi-part construction. Area 2's detritus layer, visible in Fig. 2 (Right), acted as a damping medium, reducing peak vibration amplitudes across all wheel types compared to Area 1.

Table 1. Comprehensive Performance Comparison of Wheel Designs

Performance Metric	Standard	PaTS-Wheel	DogBone-Wheel
Energy Consumption			
Area 1 (Mean Current)	473.16 mA	661.58 mA (+39.8%)	**572.75 mA (+21.0%)**
Area 2 (Mean Current)	641.86 mA	**669.77 mA (+4.0%)**	762.93 mA (+18.8%)
Obstacle Traversal			
Max. Obstacle Height	~30 mm	**~84 mm**	**~84 mm**
	(25% diameter)	**(70% diameter)**	**(70% diameter)**
Climbing Mechanism	None	Passive claws	Passive claws
Vibration Characteristics			
Dominant Freq. Range	0–5 Hz	0–5 Hz	0–5 Hz
Vibration Amplitude	**Lowest**	Moderate	Elevated
Mechanical Stability	**High**	Good	Reduced
Manufacturing			
Construction Type	Single TPU	Single TPU	Modular TPU/PLA
Print Complexity	**Low**	Moderate	High
Material Customization	Limited	Limited	**High**
Practical Performance			
Traction (Loose Terrain)	**Good**	**Good**	Reduced
Debris Entrapment Risk	**Low**	Moderate	Moderate
Ground Clearance Req.	Standard	Moderate	Moderate
Key Trade-offs			
Primary Advantages	Energy efficient, simple design	Consistent energy, obstacle climbing	Manufacturing flexibility
Primary Limitations	Poor obstacle traversal	Debris entrapment, energy penalty	Reduced traction, assembly complexity
Recommended Use	Structured environments	Moderate terrain complexity	Research, specialized materials

The PSD analysis (Fig. 7) shows this damping effect was most pronounced for the DogBone-Wheel, suggesting that loose terrain may partially compensate for its structural limitations.

Field testing in authentic woodland environments (Fig. 2) revealed practical constraints not identified in laboratory studies. Both PaTS-style wheels experienced debris entrapment, with Fig. 8 documenting organic material lodging in flexure mechanisms during operation. The debris characteristics shown in Fig. 3 and Fig. 4 highlight the varying challenges between test environments, with Area 1's larger debris causing wheel lock-up and Area 2's smaller debris increasing vibrations. Ground clearance limitations frequently prevented full utilisation of the obstacle traversal capabilities demonstrated in Table 1, emphasising the importance of integrated platform design for passive transformation wheels. The modular DogBone-Wheel design (Fig. 1) showed particular vulnerability to debris accumulation at component interfaces.

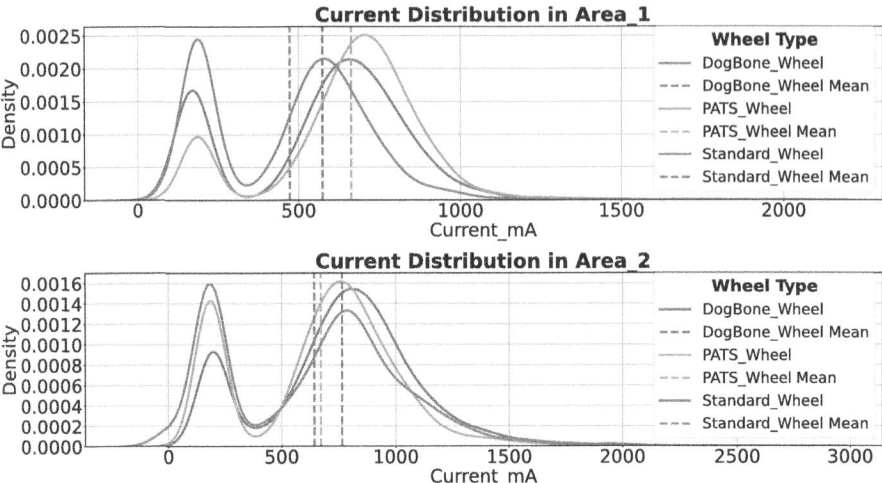

Fig. 5. Current draw distributions of the Standard Wheel, PaTS-Wheel and DogBone-Wheel of Area 1 (Left) and Area 2 (Right)

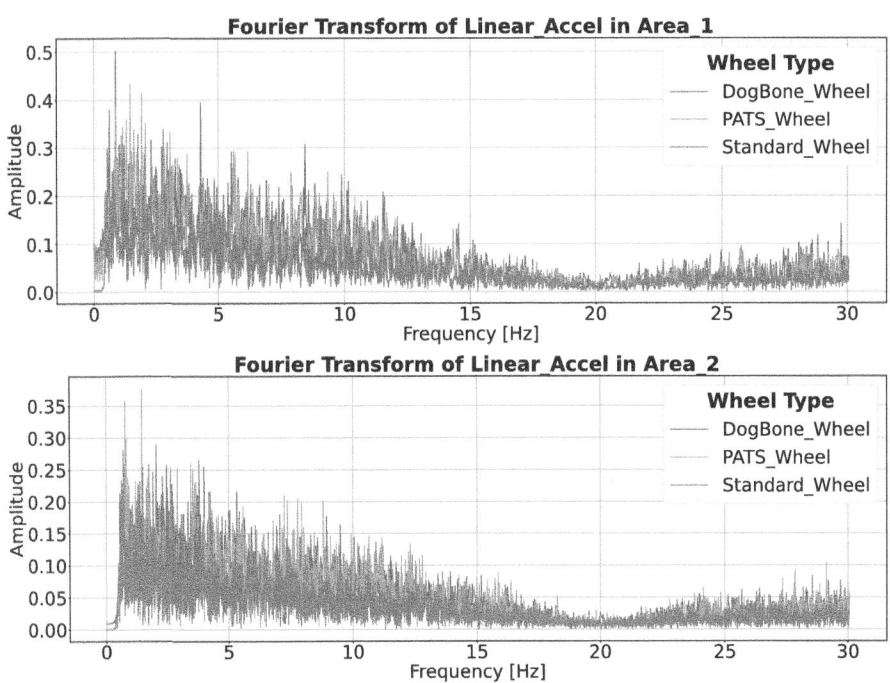

Fig. 6. Fourier series of the linear acceleration for the Standard Wheel, PaTS-Wheel and DogBone-Wheel of Area 1 (Top) and Area 2 (Bottom)

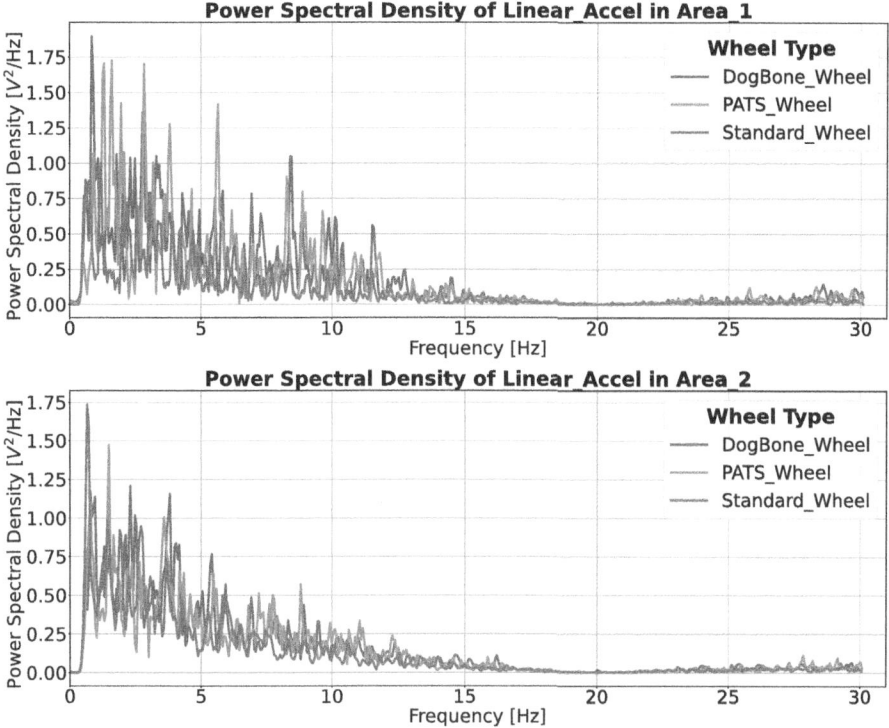

Fig. 7. Power Spectral Density (PSD) plots of linear acceleration magnitude for the Standard Wheel, PaTS-Wheel and DogBone-Wheel of Area 1 (Top) and Area 2 (Bottom)

Fig. 8. Debris in Areas 1 (Left) and Areas 2 (Right) getting stuck in the DogBone-Wheel during testing.

Our energy efficiency results align closely with Godden et al.'s laboratory findings [7]. The 4% energy penalty observed in complex terrain (Area 2, Fig. 5) closely matches the 2.4% difference reported for artificial grass testing, confirming minimal energy overhead for passive transformation in challenging environments. However, the authentic outdoor testing environment revealed debris vulnerability (Fig. 8) and ground clearance dependencies not apparent in controlled laboratory conditions, highlighting the critical importance of real-world validation for morphing wheel technologies.

The DogBone-Wheel's modular approach, while offering manufacturing flexibility, demonstrated through both energy analysis and practical deployment, that material interface optimisation remains critical for competitive performance. The vibration analysis suggests that while modular construction increases mechanical complexity, the fundamental passive transformation principles remain viable. The consistent energy performance of PaTS-style wheels across terrain complexity (Table 1) validates passive transformation as an energy-efficient approach to enhanced mobility, with practical deployment requiring careful consideration of debris management strategies and integrated platform design It is also worth noting that the obstacle traversal capability of 70% of the wheel's diameter is highly competitive, approaching the 76% clearance of recently developed active shape-changing wheels, but without the associated complexity and energy overhead of additional actuators, of the Rim Shape Changeable Wheels by Fu et al. [5].

6   Conclusion

This study evaluated passive adaptive wheel technologies in real-world unstructured environments, focusing on the PaTS-Wheel design and our modified DogBone-Wheel variant. Our research bridges the gap between laboratory testing and practical field deployment by assessing these wheel designs across natural woodland terrains with varying complexity. Our findings demonstrate that the PaTS-Wheel offers significant advantages for robots operating in challenging unstructured environments. In complex terrain, the PaTS-Wheel required only 4% more energy than the standard wheel while providing superior obstacle traversal capabilities. This minimal energy penalty represents an acceptable trade-off for enhanced mobility. The PaTS-Wheel maintained consistent energy consumption across terrain types, contrasting with the standard wheel's 35.7% energy increase when moving from moderate to complex terrain. Both PaTS-style wheels successfully climbed obstacles up to 84 mm radius (70% of wheel diameter), validating laboratory findings in real-world conditions. The DogBone-Wheel's modular design offered manufacturing flexibility but did not outperform the PaTS-Wheel, showing 13.9% higher energy consumption in complex terrain due to reduced traction from PLA components.

Vibration analysis revealed that PaTS-style wheels generate higher amplitude vibrations than standard wheels, with dominant frequencies in the 0–5 Hz range. However, the PaTS-Wheel's single-piece construction demonstrated more consistent frequency patterns than the DogBone-Wheel's multi-part design.

Field testing revealed several practical constraints that were not apparent in laboratory studies. PaTS-style wheels exhibited vulnerability to debris entrapment, with organic material becoming lodged in flexure mechanisms. Ground clearance limitations of the robot chassis often prevented full utilisation of the wheels' obstacle traversal capabilities. Material selection proved critical, with TPU construction providing better traction than PLA/TPU combinations.

In conclusion, passive transformation wheel technologies demonstrate promising capabilities for enhancing robot mobility in unstructured environments with minimal energy penalties in challenging terrain. However, successful deployment requires careful consideration of environmental factors, particularly debris, and an integrated platform design to leverage their obstacle traversal capabilities fully.

Future work should address practical deployment limitations by developing debris-resistant claw geometries and investigating variations in TPU Shore hardness to optimise a balance of traction and flexibility. Long-term durability studies through extended fatigue testing are essential for establishing maintenance requirements, complementing the design improvements identified in our study, while also providing insight into how to deploy wheels of this design more effectively onto systems. Extended field trials in authentic agricultural environments are necessary to validate findings under operational conditions and assess the effects of seasonal variation. Co-design optimisation of robot platforms to maximise passive wheel benefits represents another priority area. Furthermore, integrating advanced perception, such as the multi-modal sensing frameworks (WildFusion) proposed by Liu et al., could enable a platform to better anticipate and approach obstacles, maximising the effectiveness of the passive transformation mechanism [12]. By addressing these challenges, we can bridge the gap for passive transformation wheels to transition from laboratory demonstrations to field-deployable solutions, enabling more efficient robotic mobility in unstructured environments where energy-efficient locomotion is critical for sustainable autonomous operations.

Acknowledgments. This work was supported by the Engineering and Physical Sciences Research Council and AgriFoRwArdS CDT [EP/S023917/1].

References

1. Binbin, X., Jizhan, L., Meng, H., Jian, W., Zhujie, X.: Research progress on autonomous navigation technology of agricultural robot. In: 2021 IEEE 11th Annual International Conference on CYBER Technology in Automation, Control, and Intelligent Systems (CYBER), pp. 891–898 (2021). https://doi.org/10.1109/CYBER53097.2021.9588152
2. Bruzzone, L., Quaglia, G.: Review article: locomotion systems for ground mobile robots in unstructured environments. Mech. Sci. **3**(2), 49–62 (2012). https://doi.org/10.5194/ms-3-49-2012
3. Carvalho, A., Portugal, D., Peixoto, P.: On terrain traversability analysis in unstructured environments: recent advances in forest applications. Intell. Serv. Rob. **18**, 195–213 (2025). https://doi.org/10.1007/s11370-025-00591-4
4. Cooley, J.W., Tukey, J.W.: An algorithm for the machine calculation of complex fourier series. Math. Comput. **19**(90), 297–301 (1965)

5. Fu, Z., Xu, H., li, Y., Guo, W.: Design of a novel wheel-legged robot with rim shape changeable wheels. Chin. J. Mech. Eng. **36** (2023). https://doi.org/10.1186/s10033-023-00974-7

6. Ghobakhloo, M.: Industry 4.0, digitization, and opportunities for sustainability. J. Clean. Prod. **252**, 119869 (2020). https://doi.org/10.1016/j.jclepro.2019.119869

7. Godden, T., Mulvey, B.W., Redgrave, E., Nanayakkara, T.: Pats-wheel: a passively-transformable single-part wheel for mobile robot navigation on unstructured terrain. IEEE Rob. Autom. Lett. **9**(6), 5512–5519 (2024). https://doi.org/10.1109/LRA.2024.3389828

8. Kashiri, N., et al.: An overview on principles for energy efficient robot locomotion. Front. Rob. AI **5** (2018). https://doi.org/10.3389/frobt.2018.00129

9. Kelly, S.D., Murray, R.M.: Geometric phases and robotic locomotion. J. Robot. Syst. **12**(6), 417–431 (1995). https://doi.org/10.1002/rob.4620120607

10. Le, T.D., Ponnambalam, V.R., Gjevestad, J.G., From, P.J.: A low-cost and efficient autonomous row-following robot for food production in polytunnels. J. Field Rob. **37**(2), 309–321 (2020)

11. Lee, J., Bjelonic, M., Reske, A., Wellhausen, L., Miki, T., Hutter, M.: Learning robust autonomous navigation and locomotion for wheeled-legged robots. Sci. Rob. **9**(89), eadi9641 (2024). https://doi.org/10.1126/scirobotics.adi9641

12. Liu, Y., Chen, B.: Wildfusion: multimodal implicit 3d reconstructions in the wild (2024). https://arxiv.org/abs/2409.19904

13. Nagatani, K., Kuze, M., Yoshida, K.: Development of a transformable mobile robot with a variable wheel diameter. J. Rob. Mechatron. **19**(3), 252–257 (2007). https://doi.org/10.20965/jrm.2007.p0252

14. US EPA, O.: Global Greenhouse Gas Overview (2016). https://www.epa.gov/ghgemissions/global-greenhouse-gas-overview

15. Welch, P.: The use of fast fourier transform for the estimation of power spectra: a method based on time averaging over short, modified periodograms. IEEE Trans. Audio Electroacoust. **15**(2), 70–73 (1967)

16. Yoon, H.S., Hwang, J.H., Kim, C., Son, E.I., Yoo, S.W., Seo, S.W.: Adaptive robot traversability estimation based on self-supervised online continual learning in unstructured environments. IEEE Rob. Autom. Lett. **9**(6), 4902–4909 (2024). https://doi.org/10.1109/LRA.2024.3386451

17. Zeng, W., Gao, F., Jiang, H., Huang, C., Liu, J., Li, H.: Design and analysis of a compliant variable-diameter mechanism used in variable-diameter wheels for lunar rover. Mech. Mach. Theory **125**, 240–258 (2018). https://doi.org/10.1016/j.mechmachtheory.2018.03.003

18. Zhang, T., et al.: A centipede-inspired robot with passive terrain adaptation: optimized design and performance analysis. Sci. Rep. **15** (2025). https://doi.org/10.1038/s41598-025-97457-7

Practical Handling of Dynamic Environments in Decentralised Multi-Robot Patrol

James C. Ward[1]([⊠])[iD], Arthur Richards[1,2][iD], and Edmund R. Hunt[1][iD]

[1] University of Bristol, Bristol, UK
{james.c.ward,edmund.hunt}@bristol.ac.uk
[2] Bristol Robotics Laboratory, Bristol, UK

Abstract. Persistent monitoring using robot teams is of interest in fields such as security, environmental monitoring, and disaster recovery. Performing such monitoring in a fully on-line decentralised fashion has significant potential advantages for robustness, adaptability, and scalability of monitoring solutions, including, in principle, the capacity to effectively adapt in real-time to a changing environment. We examine this through the lens of multi-robot patrol, in which teams of patrol robots must persistently minimise time between visits to points of interest, within environments where traversability of routes is highly dynamic. These dynamics must be observed by patrol agents and accounted for in a fully decentralised on-line manner. In this work, we present a new method of monitoring and adjusting for environment dynamics in a decentralised multi-robot patrol team. We demonstrate that our method significantly outperforms realistic baselines in highly dynamic scenarios, and also investigate dynamic scenarios in which explicitly accounting for environment dynamics may be unnecessary or impractical.

Keywords: Multi-Robot Systems · Autonomous Agents · Surveillance Robotic Systems

1 Introduction

Effective deployment of multi-robot teams to hazardous or communication denied environments is of obvious applicability to a range of fields including security [13], environmental monitoring [7], and disaster recovery [11]. One desirable behaviour in these scenarios is persistent monitoring—the long-term repeated observation of points of interest in an environment. This is especially relevant in scenarios where human presence may be undesirable due to the presence of environmental hazards [5], and those in which traditional static surveillance systems may be impractical due to the absence of power or communication infrastructure. It is possible that the traversability of such environments varies significantly over the course of a monitoring scenario—in these cases, handling unknown environmental dynamics is of vital importance to the effective deployment of a

A. Cavalcanti et al. (Eds.): TAROS 2025, LNAI 16045, pp. 165–179, 2026.
https://doi.org/10.1007/978-3-032-01486-3_14

multi-robot team. Here, we introduce a method to adapt patrol behaviour to time-varying route traversability for arbitrary patrol strategies.

1.1 The Multi-Robot Patrolling Problem

The Multi-Robot Patrolling Problem (MRPP) is a popular formalisation of this problem, and has seen considerable attention in the literature [4,12]. The goal of this problem is typically framed as the persistent minimisation of maximum or average idleness [14], defined as the time between successive visits to a point of interest in an environment, by a team of mobile autonomous robots. Points of interest in the environment are used to define a patrol graph, where the vertices of the graph represent points to be frequently visited, the edges represent traversable routes between these points, and the edge weights correspond to the time taken for an agent to traverse an edge. A common variant of this problem is "adversarial" patrol [12], where rather than idleness minimisation, the goal of the patrol team is to prevent a hostile agent from gaining undetected access to the environment, but in this work we only consider idleness-minimising patrol.

1.2 Centralised Versus Decentralised Patrol

In the single-agent case, the patrol tour that persistently minimises maximum idleness on a patrol graph can be found by solving the Travelling Salesman Problem (TSP) on the patrol graph [6]. Expanding this to multiple agents adds considerable complexity—approaches exist that attempt to solve the n-agent case by partitioning the patrol graph into $m \leq n$ subgraphs and assigning one or more agents to follow a TSP tour on each subgraph [1,2], at considerable computational cost and with large approximation factors. If $m = n$, this is known as the "min-max vertex cycle cover problem" [22], and has been examined considerably in the literature, including within the context of multi-robot patrol [18]. Regardless of their proximity to optimality, any attempts to pre-compute optimal cyclic agent trajectories have significant downsides. Any agent failures or changes to the environment have the potential to invalidate a pre-planned solution, and adding new agents to improve performance would require recalculating all trajectories, possibly at significant computational cost.

Consequently, fully on-line approaches, based on real-time, short-horizon decision making are seen as practical approaches and are popular in the literature. Many on-line approaches have the additional advantage of being easily decentralisable, which is potentially advantageous [8] in communication denied environments (i.e. environments in which long range communication may be impossible or only intermittently possible) due to removing any reliance on communication with a central controller. A large number of high performing on-line strategies have been previously published [10,16,17,20,21], based on a range of heuristic approaches to idleness minimisation and inter-agent coordination. Typically these strategies operate with short-horizon online decision making, whereby upon arriving at a vertex of the patrol graph, they select a neighbouring vertex to next travel to based on edge weights and vertex idlenesses of the patrol graph and any information or intentions communicated by other agents. In this way, decentralised online patrol strategies treat the patrol problem as a POMDP. However, while potential adaptability to dynamic environments is a key benefit of these solutions, little work exists that tackles it explicitly. Examination has been made of modifying some existing strategies to adapt to random edge removal on the patrol graph [15], and "environment dynamics" within the context of an environment containing dynamically varying reward has been considered [23]. However, to our knowledge no attempts have been made to introduce robustness to general time-varying environments to arbitrary patrol methodologies.

1.3   Our Contributions

We address this gap in the literature by presenting a practical approach for handling environments with time-varying traversability in multi-robot patrolling. Our proposed methods are supplemental to existing on-line decentralised patrol algorithms, allowing for existing patrol strategies to be used without modification in the presence of dynamic environments. We also present examination of scenarios in which explicitly accounting for environment dynamics may or may not be necessary—in some cases, heavily time-varying environments can be treated as if they were static without loss of performance, as we discuss later.

2   Problem Definition

2.1   Idleness-Minimising Patrol

We model the environment to be monitored as a patrol graph $\mathcal{G}$, comprising a set of vertices $\mathcal{V}$ connected by edges $\mathcal{E}$ with weights $\mathcal{W}$. $\mathcal{V}$ corresponds to points of interest in the environment to be frequently visited, $\mathcal{E}$ corresponds to traversable routes between these points, and $\mathcal{W}$ corresponds to the travel times along these routes. $\mathcal{G}$ may be considered undirected under the assumption that routes have the same travel times in each direction, but may also be considered directed when this assumption does not hold, for example in the case of road networks, as we examine in Sect. 4.2. The idleness $I_{v,t}$ of a vertex v at time t is defined as the time in seconds since that vertex was most recently visited by a patrol agent. Mean graph idleness $\overline{I}_{\mathcal{G}}$ is defined as $\frac{1}{T|\mathcal{V}|} \sum_{t=0}^{T} \sum_{v=0}^{|\mathcal{V}|} I_{v,t}$, i.e. the mean idlenesses of all vertices over the entire scenario time duration. Maximum graph idleness, denoted $\max I_{\mathcal{G}}$, is the maximum idleness over all vertices over the entire scenario time duration. A patrol team of n agents employs a fixed patrol strategy with the intention of minimising either $\overline{I}_{\mathcal{G}}$ or $\max I_{\mathcal{G}}$.

2.2   Environment Dynamics

We model environment dynamics as time-dependent variation of $\mathcal{W}$, potentially around some assumed baseline value, reflecting changes in the time taken to traverse an edge. These variations may result in agents taking longer to traverse an edge, for example when modelling congestion or obstructions, or may result in agents taking less time to traverse an edge, for example in cases where agent speed is influenced by wind speed and direction. The baseline value may not be known accurately by the patrol team, or may reflect some prior belief about the environment—in this way, the handling of *dynamic* environments can be considered adjacent to the handling of *uncertain* environments. We consider that an agent can only truly know the weight of an edge at any given time by traversing it—while it may not be generally possible to predict the travel time of a route in advance, it can be known post-hoc after observation. This leads us to the concept of "uncertainty" within the context of a dynamic patrolling scenario. Under the assumptions that edge weights vary according to an unknown time-dependent model and can only be observed by traversing the edge, any edge which has not been traversed in a long time (and so may have varied significantly since it was last observed) can be considered to have high uncertainty, and any edge which has been recently traversed has a low uncertainty.

3   Methods of Handling Dynamic Environments

3.1   Key Principles and Constraints

Two key principles guided the approaches taken in this work. Firstly, that the goal is to improve idleness-minimising behaviour in the presence of environment dynamics, rather than to develop the best model or understanding of the environment. This is a subtle line to walk—literature interest in exploration of dynamic or uncertain environments often considers the understanding of the environment to be the goal. We, in contrast, already have an established goal in this case—we cannot compromise idleness minimisation in order to collect information, unless we are confident that information would lead to improved idleness minimisation performance. Our second key principle is that any method developed should operate seamlessly alongside existing idleness-minimising decentralised multi-agent patrol strategies, in order to be deployable without requiring modification of patrol strategies. To this end, our method cannot directly interfere with decision making, as this is entirely controlled by the patrol strategy, and must therefore influence agent behaviour by modifying the inputs to the patrol strategy—specifically, observations and beliefs in the state of the environment.

We constrain ourselves further by noting that a desirable method to address this problem should be model-free. Any method that involves building an internal model of environment dynamics has the flaw that, in general, there is no reason to assume that the environment dynamics are controlled or modellable by a persistent underlying model. The nature of the dynamics may change rapidly and unpredictably, resulting in a previously fit model now being entirely inappropriate. The lack of a model limits our ability to predict future behaviors, steering us towards a purely reactive approach. This also precludes the use of a Bayesian or Kalman filter-based approach, both of which are otherwise obvious choices for modelling uncertain scenarios.

3.2   The Decay Method

To satisfy these principles, we use the *decay* method, a case of the three-parameter RE (Roth/Erev) method [9], a classical game-theoretical model-free reinforcement learning approach. This method has seen attention in the literature as a decision making method in uncertain environments [3,19], and our naming of it follows these works. Here we show that our particular problem is a natural fit for a special case of this method. Following [9], the three-parameter RE method for decision making in uncertain environments is as follows:

$$q_{nj}(t+1) = (1 - \phi)q_{nj}(t) + E_k(j, R(x)) \tag{1}$$

where $q_{nj}(t)$ is the propensity for player n to play strategy j at time t, ϕ is a recency parameter to gradually reduce the importance of past experience, and $E(j, R(x))$ is an update to each strategy j according to the experience of playing strategy k and receiving reward $R(x)$. Fitting this method to our scenario affords us a natural approach to handling the tradeoff between exploration (observing uncertain edge weights) and exploitation (using knowledge to minimise idleness).

First, we argue that the propensity to play a strategy can be substituted for the belief of an agent in the weight of an edge of the patrol graph. A rational idleness-minimising agent will, all other things being equal, preferentially traverse a lower-weight edge than a higher-weight edge in order to sooner reduce the idleness of a vertex. This then allows us to encourage or discourage certain actions by modifying an agent's belief in the weight of an edge—for example, reducing the weight belief on a certain edge will encourage an agent to traverse it at a time when doing so will still appear to be rational idleness minimising behaviour. In this way it is possible to encourage exploration without requiring any modification of an idleness-minimising patrol strategy, and avoid forcing exploratory actions without considering idleness minimisation.

We must then select $E_k(j, R(x))$ such that upon traversing an edge j, q_j is set to the observed edge weight (as the agent now has high certainty in the edge weight) and all other edge weights are updated to reflect the increase in uncertainty caused by time passing without traversal. In this problem, the best representation of "higher uncertainty" in an edge weight is that in decision making its value is moved closer to the mean average current edge weight belief over the entire graph, as this represents the "zero information" state when comparing edges to each other. This ensures that, all other things being equal, a high uncertainty edge will be considered more desirable than one that is known to have a larger (worse) than average weight, and less desirable than one that is known to have a smaller (better) than average weight. This formulation of the three-parameter RE method has previously been seen in the literature [3,19] within the context that in a scenario in which rewards are symmetrically distributed around zero, expected values of actions decay towards zero (i.e. no information) the longer they are unchosen.

Our implementation of this, which we refer to as the *decay* method, is as follows. When an agent finishes traversing an edge, it records the time taken as the weight of that edge. This is transmitted to other agents, who do the same upon receipt of the message. The agent's beliefs of all other edge weights then decay towards the collective mean $\overline{W}$ based on a decay factor ϕ, such that:

$$W_i = (1 - \phi)^t W_{i-1} + \phi^t \overline{W} \tag{2}$$

where t is the time since the agent last updated its belief in (or received new information of) a given edge weight. These weight beliefs are input to the patrol strategy being used by the patrol team. Our final addition to this method is a time-dependent decay factor to account for varying time between observations. In this work, $\phi = 0.0025$ was used, tuned on two maps not used in our testing.

3.3   Baseline Methods

Alongside our decay method, the following baseline methods are considered:

- **Lazy**: The patrol agents do not monitor the environment, and make all decisions on the basis of their prior belief of environment edge weights.
- **Simple**: When a patrol agent finishes traversing an edge, it records the time taken as the weight of that edge. This is communicated to other agents, who do the same. Edge weight beliefs only change when the edge is traversed.
- **Omniscient**: The patrol agents have perfect knowledge of the environment dynamics and edge weights at all times.

4   Testing

4.1   Constructed Scenarios

To examine the performance of our decay method, we selected three leading literature patrol strategies to handle idleness-minimising decision making. State Exchange Bayesian Strategy (SEBS) [16], Expected Reactive (ER) [21], and Minimal Network Strategy (MNS) [20] were selected as all three are fully online decentralised strategies offering high levels of idleness minimisation performance. Also, all three have sufficiently different mechanisms, such that we are combining the dynamic environment handling methods with a range of idleness minimising behaviours. The four dynamic environment handling methods ("lazy", "simple", "omniscient", and "decay") and three patrol strategies were implemented in MAGESim[1], a simulator used for examining multi-agent behaviours in graph structured environments.

Two maps, "Grid" and "DIAG floor 1" (originally from ROS Patrolling Sim[2]), shown in Fig. 1, were selected. To model a range of environment dynamics, we generated three sets of dynamic profiles to apply to the edge weights of the patrol graphs. These operate by scaling the speed at which agents are able to

---

[1] https://github.com/jward0/magesim. Our implementations can be found on the "dynamic_environment" branch.

[2] http://wiki.ros.org/patrolling_sim.

move along an edge by a time-varying factor, to reflect edges becoming more or less easy to traverse at different times. The first, "blockages", applies a speed scale factor of 0.1 for long, randomly selected periods of time. The second, "fast walk", scales agent speed according to a fast-moving noisy random walk clamped to the range (0, 1]. The third, "smooth walk", scales agent speed according to a slower-moving random walk with momentum with a rolling average applied, clamped to all positive values (the smooth walk is then the only profile that can *increase* agent speed along an edge). Examples of these profiles are shown in Figs. 2, 3 and 4. When one of these profiles is generated for a patrol graph, the speedup for each edge is generated randomly and independently, such that the average correlation between speedups on different edges is close to 0.

Patrol teams of size $n = 1, 2, 4, 8$, and 16 were simulated for all combinations of map, dynamic profile, dynamic handling method, and patrol strategy, for 2500 s. The prior edge weight beliefs for the lazy handling method were set to the edge weights in the absence of dynamics. For each combination of parameters, the simulation was repeated 5 times with different initial agent positions. We additionally simulated all scenarios with no environment dynamics present.

To assess the robustness of the patrol strategies to incorrect information, these tests were repeated with no dynamics present, the lazy dynamic handling method, and multiplicative Gaussian noise ($\mu = 1$, $\sigma = 0.05$ to 1.60) applied to the patrol team's beliefs in the edge weights. This allowed us to measure performance in the cases where the patrol teams were making decisions based on consistently incorrect information.

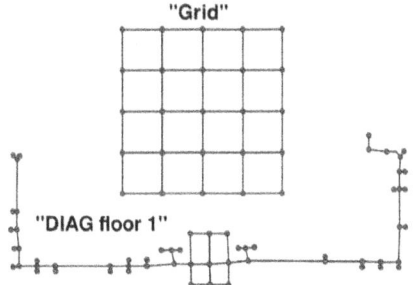

Fig. 1. The two patrol graphs used in our constructed scenarios (not to scale)

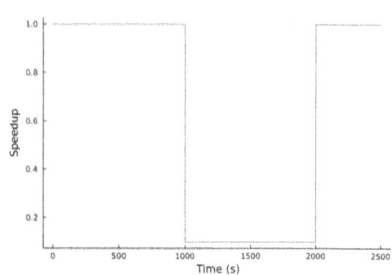

Fig. 2. Example "blockages" dynamics

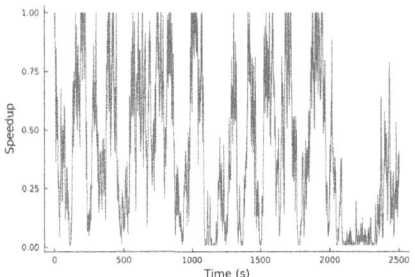

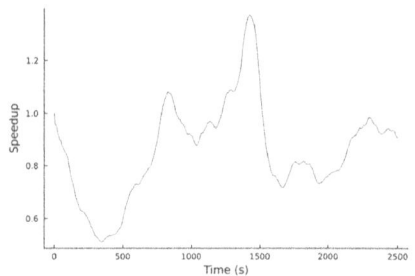

Fig. 3. Example "fast walk" dynamics

Fig. 4. Example "smooth walk" dynamics

4.2   Real-World Scenario

In order to examine the behaviour of patrol teams in a real-world dynamic environment, we constructed a scenario based on real-world traffic data. 16 points were selected throughout the city of Bristol from locations of University accommodation and used to construct a patrol graph, shown in Fig. 5[3]. Edge weights corresponding to vertex-to-vertex travel times were then obtained from predicted traffic data over a 24 h period starting at midnight, using the Google Maps Routes API to estimate travel times along all edges at 10 min intervals, following the fastest predicted routes at those times. These edge weights are shown in Fig. 6. These weights were then converted to a dynamic profile and imported into MAGESim, to allow for simulation based on real-world traffic data. As before, we selected SEBS, ER, and MNS as our patrol strategies, and examined the lazy, simple, omniscient, and decay dynamic environment handling methods. We simulated patrol teams of size $n = 1$, 2, 4, and 8 (16 agents on a 16-vertex graph was deemed unrealistically crowded) for the full 24 h (86400 s) period. As before, we also simulated this environment with no dynamics (generated by artificially setting all edge weights to their smallest observed values to reflect travel times with no congestion). It is worth noting that in this scenario, the adjacency matrix of the patrol graph is not symmetric, meaning that traversal times along an edge vary depending on the direction of travel—this was not the case in our constructed scenarios (Sect. 4.1), but is obviously possible in a real-world scenario.

---

[3] Map image provided by Ordnance Survey under the Open Government License (https://www.nationalarchives.gov.uk/doc/open-government-licence/version/3/.

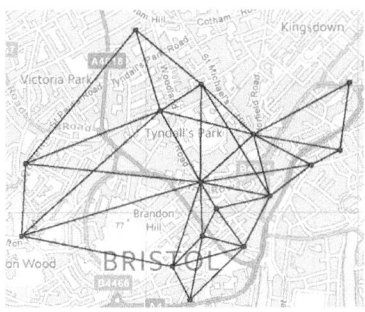
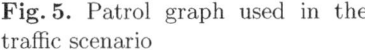

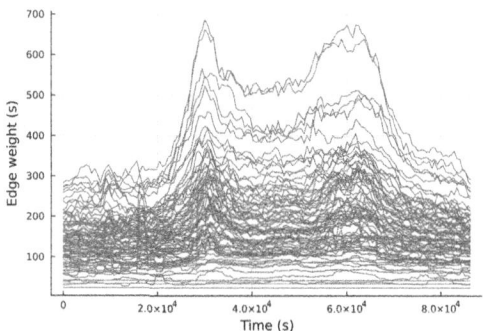

Fig. 5. Patrol graph used in the traffic scenario

Fig. 6. Edge weights over time for the traffic scenario (each line represents one edge)

While our constructed scenarios involved generating dynamic profiles for all edges randomly and independently, edge weights in this scenario are strongly correlated, with average correlation coefficient between any two edges of 0.736. This had a significant impact on behaviour, as we will discuss in the next sections.

5   Results

5.1   Constructed Scenarios

Table 1 shows the relative average idlenesses (measured average idlenesses divided by those observed with no environment dynamics) averaged across both maps for all scenarios considered for our three dynamic profiles, using the lazy baseline method. This is a measure of the impact of the environment dynamics in the case that nothing is done to account for them, to quantify the degree to which they interfere with idleness minimising behaviour. This shows that fast walk is the most disruptive profile, followed by blockages and then smooth walk, and also that relative idleness generally increases with the number of agents—we attribute this to the fact that as the number of agents increases so does the importance of effective inter-agent coordination, which is compromised by having incorrect environmental information. In the case where no environment dynamics were present, none of the dynamic handling methods tested were observed to significantly alter performance.

Table 1. Average idlenesses relative to no environmental dynamics for lazy baseline, varying with team size n

	Blockages			Fast walk			Smooth walk		
n	SEBS	ER	MNS	SEBS	ER	MNS	SEBS	ER	MNS
1	3.10	2.54	2.49	4.14	3.71	3.65	1.19	1.18	1.13
2	3.01	2.67	2.84	4.66	5.12	5.07	1.20	1.22	1.19
4	3.06	3.12	2.97	5.77	5.38	5.47	1.22	1.22	1.26
8	3.40	3.76	3.12	5.94	6.28	5.86	1.30	1.37	1.28
16	3.37	4.26	2.98	7.20	7.70	6.70	1.27	1.45	1.26

Dynamic Handling

The results in this section consist of average idlenesses normalised against those observed using the aforementioned lazy baseline in identical scenarios. This allows us to directly examine the degree to which the methods considered present an improvement over default patrol behaviour that makes no effort to account for varying environments.

Tables 2 and 3 show relative average idlenesses observed with the simple and omniscient baselines and our decay method, varying with dynamic profile and team size. Relative idlenesses averaged over every variable for the three methods are 0.934 for the simple method, 0.920 for the decay method, and 0.846 for the omniscient method, representing improvements over the lazy baseline of 6.6%, 8.0%, and 15.4% respectively. The full un-averaged results were examined using the Wilcoxon signed-rank test, as this allows us to match results from identical scenarios for each method. This found that while the omniscient method unsurprisingly outperforms the others, our decay method outperforms the simple method with p-value of 0.038. While statistically significant to within $p = 0.05$, the effect size (8.0% versus 6.6% reduction in average idleness) is not large. We discuss this further in Sect. 6.

Table 2. Average idlenesses relative to lazy baseline varying with dynamic profile

	Simple			Decay			Omniscient		
Profile	SEBS	ER	MNS	SEBS	ER	MNS	SEBS	ER	MNS
Blockages	0.78	0.79	0.97	0.77	0.79	0.96	0.68	0.71	0.93
Fast walk	1.05	1.09	1.01	0.99	1.02	1.01	0.82	0.86	0.95
Smooth walk	0.89	0.86	0.96	0.89	0.87	0.97	0.86	0.84	0.96

Table 3. Average idlenesses relative to lazy baseline varying with team size n

	Simple			Decay			Omniscient		
n	SEBS	ER	MNS	SEBS	ER	MNS	SEBS	ER	MNS
1	1.01	1.01	0.98	0.95	0.97	0.99	0.87	0.91	0.92
2	0.99	1.00	0.98	0.94	0.96	1.01	0.86	0.90	0.93
4	0.93	0.97	1.01	0.90	0.94	0.99	0.81	0.83	0.98
8	0.83	0.83	0.98	0.84	0.82	0.98	0.71	0.71	0.97
16	0.79	0.76	0.95	0.79	0.76	0.94	0.71	0.66	0.93

Robustness to Incorrect Information

Table 4 shows average relative idleness against the standard deviation of the multiplicative 1-mean Gaussian noise applied to the patrol team's belief of edge weights with no environment dynamics. The performance of SEBS and ER was observed to not significantly worsen until $\sigma = 0.4$ (corresponding to an average error magnitude of roughly 32%) after which performance gradually decayed at a similar rate for both, while MNS was observed to have extremely effective noise-rejection behaviour, as no degradation in performance was observed even with the largest noise magnitude tested. This high level of apparent robustness is discussed in Sect. 6.

5.2   Real-World Scenario

Table 5 shows the relative average idlenesses of the observed real-world traffic scenario compared to the same environment with congestion artificially removed (i.e. edge weights are constant at their smallest observed values) in order to quantify the impact of the environment dynamics. Table 6 shows the relative average idlenesses observed with the simple, decay, and omniscient methods compared to the lazy baseline for all patrol strategies and team sizes tested. While the observed average slowdown from the environment dynamics was larger than was observed for smooth walk in our constructed scenarios, omniscient handling only offered an average improvement of 1.8% over lazy handling, despite having access to perfect information. We also observe that neither the simple baseline nor our decay method offer improved performance over the lazy

Table 4. Average relative idleness against noise standard deviation (constructed scenarios)

σ	SEBS	ER	MNS
0.05	1.00	0.99	1.00
0.10	1.00	0.99	0.99
0.20	1.00	0.99	0.99
0.40	1.06	1.04	0.98
0.80	1.09	1.10	0.99
1.60	1.14	1.16	0.99

Table 5. Average idlenesses relative to no dynamics for lazy baseline, varying with team size n (real-world scenario)

n	SEBS	ER	MNS
1	1.33	1.33	1.35
2	1.24	1.27	1.30
4	1.27	1.31	1.29
8	1.29	1.28	1.31

baseline. This suggests that, in this real-world scenario, improved access to information does not significantly improve performance. We discuss this phenomenon in Sect. 6. As with our constructed scenarios, none of the dynamic handling methods were observed to significantly alter performance in the absence of environment dynamics.

Table 6. Average idlenesses relative to lazy baseline varying with team size n

	Simple			Decay			Omniscient		
n	SEBS	ER	MNS	SEBS	ER	MNS	SEBS	ER	MNS
1	1.00	1.00	1.05	0.94	0.94	1.01	0.94	0.94	1.01
2	1.20	1.18	1.05	1.04	1.01	1.00	1.01	0.99	1.01
4	1.18	1.13	1.05	1.07	1.00	1.01	0.99	0.96	1.00
8	1.06	1.14	1.01	0.97	1.04	1.00	0.98	0.96	0.99

6   Discussion

We have presented a practical and effective method of handling environments with time-varying traversability in decentralised on-line multi-robot patrol. Our results from our proposed decay method show an average idleness reduction of 8% compared to the lazy baseline over our constructed scenarios. While the omniscient baseline offered better performance, it is impractical to implement in a real patrol scenario. The simple baseline performed only slightly (but statistically significantly) worse than the decay method, with average idleness reduction of 6.6% compared to the lazy baseline. We attribute the small difference of effect size to the similarity between our decay method and the simple baseline combined with the robustness of the patrol strategies to incorrect information. Our examination of this, by adding multiplicative Gaussian noise to the edge weight belief of patrol teams, demonstrates that the patrol strategies used are highly robust to incorrect patrol weight belief, with no observed drop in performance for SEBS or ER until $\sigma = 0.40$, corresponding to an average error magnitude of roughly 32%. As such, the disregard for information staleness by the simple method could be largely absorbed by the robustness of the patrol strategies.

MNS, meanwhile, demonstrated no performance degradation even for the largest noise magnitudes examined—this apparent rejection of edge weight information was reflected in our dynamic environment handling results, for which all methods show the least improvement for MNS. To investigate this, we examined the neural network weights used in the pre-trained, published instance of MNS that was used in this work, finding that MNS assigns only very small weights to edge information. This is counter-intuitive, as it suggests that leading levels of idleness minimisation are attainable while paying very little attention to the actual structure of the patrol graph, and instead making decisions purely on the basis of vertex idlenesses. Its apparent robustness to incorrect information was also observed in the average idlenesses relative to no dynamics for lazy baseline, shown in Table 1—MNS suffers a smaller degradation in performance as a result of unaccounted environment dynamics than either SEBS or ER.

A second observation from our constructed scenarios is that the fast walk dynamics proved challenging for non-omniscient methods to deal with (though our decay method did still outperform the simple baseline). This is unsurprising, as these dynamics vary sufficiently quickly (see Fig. 3) that any observed edge weights are invalidated almost immediately. In this case, then, ignoring the environment dynamics altogether may be a reasonable approach—it may also be true that the fast walk dynamic model presents an unrealistically harsh scenario that would be unlikely to appear in a real deployment.

In our simulation of a real-world traffic scenario, the omniscient baseline was found to outperform the lazy baseline by only a tiny margin, and neither of the other methods offered improvements. We attribute this to the strong inter-correlation ($\overline{\rho} = 0.736$) between observed edge weights over time. In Fig. 6, this can be observed as all edge weights following similar patterns of variation, just at different scales. The consequence of this is that the relative attractiveness of the different edges varied very little over time—edges that were attractive for low congestion were still attractive for high congestion, so decisions can be made effectively on the basis of a snapshot of the edge weights without time-varying information. This has important implications for assessing when environment dynamics in a patrol scenario can be safely ignored—even if there is significant variation in edge weights over time, if these variations for all edges are strongly correlated with each other then none of the methods discussed in this paper are necessary to achieve high performance.

Based on our results, we suggest that, in a potential real-world deployment, plausible models of environmental dynamics should be considered to see whether an explicit dynamic handling approach is useful. If dynamics are too highly variable, as in our fast walk profile, or too highly inter-correlated, as in our real-world traffic scenario, on-line adaptation may simply not be an effective or necessary tool to improve performance. However, in cases where dynamics vary on a timescale that observations made by one agent can be useful to another and are not strongly inter-correlated, as was observed in our blockages and smooth walk profiles, the model-free decay method presented in this work is a practical and effective on-line, decentralised approach to maintaining high levels of performance, when used in tandem with an existing patrol strategy.

7 Conclusions

In this work, we have examined how dynamic environments might be practically handled in a decentralised, fully on-line multi-robot patrol deployment. Considering several models of environment dynamics, we have identified scenarios in which intelligent handling of said dynamics are either unnecessary or impractical. In cases where the environment dynamics can be effectively addressed with a practically implementable method, we have shown that our proposed "decay" method outperforms plausible baselines. This method can integrate with existing idleness-minimising patrol strategies with no modification required, can operate in a fully decentralised, on-line fashion, requires no additional observation or inter-agent communication beyond that already carried out during patrolling, and does not compromise performance in dynamically inactive environments. As such, our proposed method presents a practical, effective approach to improving performance in potential real-world deployments.

Acknowledgments. This work was supported by the Engineering and Physical Sciences Research Council via the FARSCOPE-TU CDT (grant no. EP/S021795/1) and by the Royal Academy of Engineering under the Research Fellowship programme.

Disclosure of Interests. The authors have no competing interests to declare that are relevant to the content of this article.

References

1. Afshani, P., et al.: Approximation algorithms for multi-robot patrol-scheduling with min-max latency. In: 14th International Workshop on the Algorithmic Foundations of Robotics (2020)
2. Afshani, P., et al.: On cyclic solutions to the min-max latency multi-robot patrolling problem. In: 38th International Symposium on Computational Geometry (2022)
3. Ahn, W.Y., Busemeyer, J.R., Wagenmakers, E.J., Stout, J.C.: Comparison of decision learning models using the generalization criterion method. Cogn. Sci. **32**, 1376–1402 (2008)
4. Basilico, N.: Recent trends in robotic patrolling. Curr. Robot. Rep. **3**(2), 65–76 (2022)
5. Bird, B., et al.: A robot to monitor nuclear facilities: using autonomous radiation-monitoring assistance to reduce risk and cost. IEEE Robot. Autom. Mag. **26**(1), 35–43 (2019)
6. Chevaleyre, Y.: Theoretical analysis of the multi-agent patrolling problem. In: Proceedings of the IEEE/WIC/ACM International Conference on Intelligent Agent Technology, pp. 302–308 (2004)
7. Dunbabin, M., Marques, L.: Robots for environmental monitoring: significant advancements and applications. IEEE Robot. Autom. Mag. **19**(1), 24–39 (2012)
8. Durfee, E.H., Lesser, V., Corkill, D.D.: Trends in cooperative distributed problem solving. IEEE Trans. Knowl. Data Eng. **1**, 63–83 (1989)
9. Erev, I., Roth, A.E.: Predicting how people play games: reinforcement learning in experimental games with unique, mixed strategy equilibria. Am. Econ. Rev. **88**(4), 848–881 (1998)
10. Farinelli, A., Iocchi, L., Nardi, D.: Distributed on-line dynamic task assignment for multi-robot patrolling. Auton. Robot. **41**(6), 1321–1345 (2017)
11. Ghassemi, P., Chowdhury, S.: Multi-robot task allocation in disaster response: addressing dynamic tasks with deadlines and robots with range and payload constraints. Robot. Auton. Syst. **147**, 103905 (2022)
12. Huang, L., Zhou, M., Hao, K., Hou, E.: A survey of multi-robot regular and adversarial patrolling. IEEE/CAA J. Autonm. Sinica **6**(4), 894–903 (2019)

13. Jakob, M., Vaněk, O., Pěchouček, M.: Using agents to improve international maritime transport security. IEEE Intell. Syst. **26**(1), 90–96 (2011). https://doi.org/10.1109/MIS.2011.23
14. Machado, A., Ramalho, G., Zucker, J., Drogoul, A.: Multi-agent patrolling: an empirical analysis of alternative architectures. In: Proceedings of the 3rd International Conference on Multi-Agent Based Simulation II, Bologna, Italy, pp. 155–170 (2002)
15. Othmani-Guibourg, M., El Fallah-Seghrouchni, A., Farges, J.L., Potop-Butucaru, M.: Multi-agent patrolling in dynamic environments. In: 2017 IEEE International Conference on Agents (ICA), pp. 72–77. IEEE (2017)
16. Portugal, D., Rocha, R.P.: Distributed multi-robot patrol: a scalable and fault-tolerant framework. Robot. Auton. Syst. **61**(12), 1572–1587 (2013)
17. Portugal, D., Rocha, R.P.: Cooperative multi-robot patrol with Bayesian learning. Auton. Robot. **40**(5), 929–953 (2016)
18. Scherer, J., Schoellig, A.P., Rinner, B.: Min-max vertex cycle covers with connectivity constraints for multi-robot patrolling. IEEE Robot. Autom. Lett. **7**(4), 10152–10159 (2022)
19. Speekenbrink, M., Konstantinidis, E.: Uncertainty and exploration in a restless bandit problem. Top. Cogn. Sci. **7**, 351–367 (2015)
20. Ward, J.C., McConville, R., Hunt, E.R.: Lightweight decentralized neural network-based strategies for multi-robot patrolling. In: Proceedings of the 40th ACM/SIGAPP Symposium on Applied Computing, SAC 2025, pp. 823–831 (2025)
21. Yan, C., Zhang, T.: Multi-robot patrol: a distributed algorithm based on expected idleness. Int. J. Adv. Robot. Syst. **13**(6) (2016)
22. Yu, W., Liu, Z.: Improved approximation algorithms for some min-max and minimum cycle cover problems. Theor. Comput. Sci. **654**, 45–58 (2016)
23. Zhou, X., Wang, W., Wang, T., Lei, Y., Zhong, F.: Bayesian reinforcement learning for multi-robot decentralized patrolling in uncertain environments. IEEE Trans. Veh. Technol. **68**(12), 11691–11703 (2019)

Manipulation and Dexterous Interaction

Acquiring Tactile Skills on a Quadruped Robot Using Vision-Based Soft Tactile Sensors

Zeyu Chen, Luchen Li⬤, Jianwei Liu⬤, Valerio Modugno⬤,
Dimitrios Kanoulas⬤, and Thomas George Thuruthel$^{(\boxtimes)}$⬤

Department of Computer Science, University College London, London, UK
{zeyu.chen.23,luchen.li.23,jianwei.liu.21,v.modugno,d.kanoulas,
t.thuruthel}@ucl.ac.uk

Abstract. Modern quadruped robots commonly rely on visual feedback and proprioceptive sensors for control and environmental analysis. However, these sensors lack the ability to perceive fine level contact information with the environment. To overcome these challenges, this paper introduces an innovative solution that integrates vision-based soft tactile sensors with a quadruped robot, providing the robot with enriched environmental feedback while maintaining compliant interactions. We present the design and modelling of our proposed solution on a commercially available quadruped robot. Through a learning based modelling pipeline, we equip the robot to estimate the magnitude and direction of contact forces in interaction with the ground. We believe such tactile information can significantly enhance the robot's perception and interaction capabilities, offering deeper insights into surface properties and improving its adaptability in diverse conditions.

Keywords: Soft sensing · Machine learning · Legged locomotion

1 Introduction

Quadruped robots, modeled after the locomotion of four-legged animals, have emerged as a pivotal category in intelligent robotics, valued for their adaptability and stability across varied terrains. Unlike wheeled or tracked robots, quadrupeds excel at navigating obstacles and rugged landscapes, such as slopes, rocky paths, and uneven ground. This unique capability makes quadrupeds particularly suitable for demanding applications in search and rescue, exploration, agriculture, and military operations. Pioneering developments in this field include Boston Dynamics' BigDog [1,2], designed in collaboration with DARPA, which demonstrated robust mobility on diverse terrains.

The advancement of quadruped robots is strongly facilitated by comprehensive sensory feedbacks that capture and process essential environmental

---

Z. Chen and L. Li—These authors contributed equally to this work.

ⓒ The Author(s), under exclusive license to Springer Nature Switzerland AG 2026
A. Cavalcanti et al. (Eds.): TAROS 2025, LNAI 16045, pp. 183–194, 2026.
https://doi.org/10.1007/978-3-032-01486-3_15

information [19]. While traditional robotic systems have often relied on visual and proprioceptive feedback for movement and navigation, tactile feedback has become increasingly critical for quadruped robots seeking to achieve stable, adaptive mobility and intricate environmental interactions [20]. It provides real-time insights into surface characteristics, enabling them to sense and respond to ground textures, obstacles, and force variations with precision. In particular, vision-based soft tactile sensors, such as TacTip and GelSight [3,4], have recently received increasing attention for their ability to capture fine details of surface texture, force, and contact points [5,6]. Originally applied to robotic manipulators for object gripping, vision-based tactile sensors are now being integrated into quadruped systems for terrain identification [21]. These sensors enable quadrupeds to make fine adjustments in response to real-time tactile data, resulting in enhanced control over movement, especially on unstructured and unpredictable terrains. However, estimating contact information from raw image data over diverse surfaces is still a challenging problem.

Estimating force magnitude and direction from tactile images is a complex problem, which is dependent on the contact area, surface properties, lighting conditions, etc. In recent years, deep learning has emerged as a transformative tool for interpreting tactile data, allowing for the extraction of intricate features from high-dimensional tactile images [23–26]. However, these works are still limited to marker-based tactile sensors and are restricted to contacts of known surface areas.

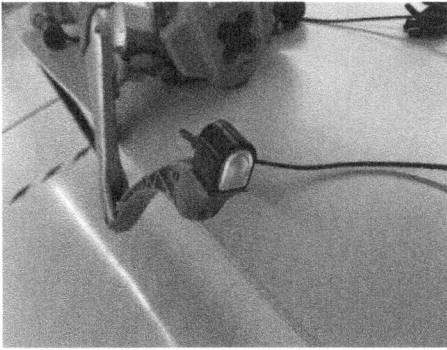

Fig. 1. Go1 quadruped robot with newly designed feet with a vision-based tactile sensor.

This works aims to build upon these advancements by developing a modelling pipeline to estimate force magnitude and direction from images collected by a vision-based soft tactile sensor mounted on a robotic quadruped. Given the high variability in contact scenarios—such as changes in force, tilt angles, directions, and surface roughness—the model must generalize across diverse conditions. To this end, we collected a comprehensive dataset covering a range of contact conditions, including variations in force, angle, and materials, which was used to train a deep neural network. By leveraging data and deep learning techniques, our model can process and learn from subtle visual cues within the tactile images, making it capable of estimating force information that can play a crucial role for agile quadruped locomotion.

2   Setup and Methodology

2.1   Installation of Tactile Sensor

The Go1 quadruped robot, developed by Unitree Robotics, was selected for this experiment due to its exceptional flexibility and robust performance, which align well with the demands of our testing scenarios. Integrating the tactile sensor into the robot required careful consideration of placement to ensure reliable ground contact and accurate environmental data collection, including measurements of surface texture, force distribution, and inclination. To achieve this, the robot's foot connector was redesigned to securely house the tactile sensor. By replacing the original foot with a custom connector, the sensor maintains consistent contact with diverse surfaces throughout the robot's movements, ensuring reliable data capture in real time (Fig. 1).

2.2   Data Collection Setup with UR5

In order to address the stability and control challenges inherent in using a full quadruped robot for data collection, we developed a setup with a UR5 robotic arm attached with the DIGIT tactile sensor to simulate the motion and interaction of a single quadruped leg, as shown in Fig. 2. This provided a controlled environment that eliminates balance and gait-related issues, which would otherwise introduce noise and compromise data quality. By controlling the robotic arm to make the sensor surface contact with a plate under varying conditions, we created a dataset containing paired tactile images and force values that form a reliable foundation for model training, before eventual deployment on the quadruped robot. To obtain accurate force data, we used a setup of four TE Connectivity force sensors (Fig. 2(a)), each measuring up to 22.6 kgf with a ±1% nonlinearity error [7]. A customizable plate was secured over the sensors (Fig. 2) to ensure consistent contact and reliable force transmission while providing the ability to change surface properties.

2.3   Dataset Overview

In real-world settings, quadruped robots are often required to navigate complex terrains, including inclined surfaces with varied angles and orientations, as well as surfaces composed of different materials. To capture these variations and improve the model's ability to generalize across a broad range of conditions, our dataset includes four primary variables: the magnitude of the applied force, the angle of the tilt, the direction of the tilt, and the type of contact material. We aim to simulate diverse interaction scenarios, ensuring the model is robustly

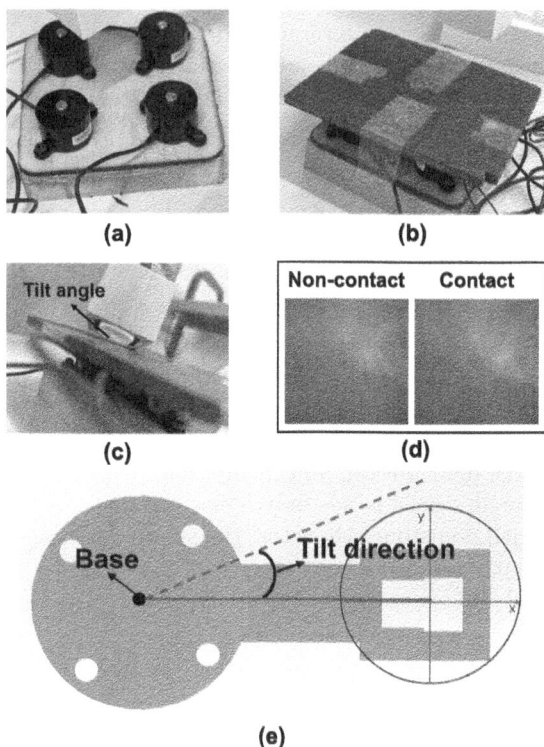

Fig. 2. Experiment setup:Experiment setup: (a) A four load cell setup for estimating force magnitude and direction. (b) The customizable contact plate mounted on the load cells. (c) The tactile sensor is mounted on a UR5 arm to collect data for training, performing tilted touch the contact plate. (d) Raw tactile image from the DIGIT sensor. (e) Illustration of the tilt direction, which is defined as the angle between the baseline (aligned with the x-axis) and the direction of inclination.

trained and adaptable to real-world applications where quadruped robots must respond accurately to dynamic and unpredictable environments.

The dataset contains a total of 44,161 samples, each consisting of synchronized measurements of tactile image frames, force magnitude, direction, and tilt angle. Five levels of tilt angles (1, 3, 5, 7, and 9°) were selected to measure the angle between the plane of the tactile sensor's contact membrane and the plate, simulating interactions with inclined surfaces. For each tilt level, the end-effector was rotated horizontally in 10-degree increments across a full 360-degree range, providing 36 orientation levels from 0 to 350°. In addition, three distinct plate materials (smooth acrylic, fabric, and anti-slip tape) were used to introduce varying contact surface roughness.

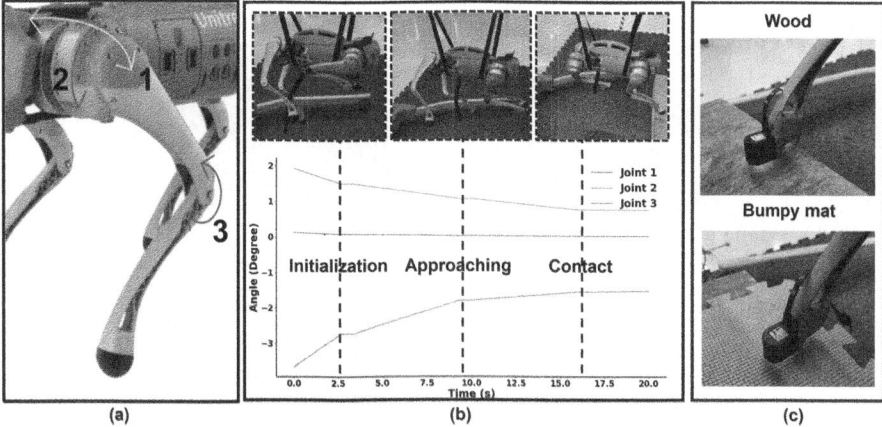

Fig. 3. Experiment setup with the Quadruped Robot: (a) Rotation direction of the robot leg joints, the colored lines refer to corresponding joint 1, 2, and 3. (b) The variation of rotation angles for three joints during the control process are plotted against time, showing the three stages of robot leg motion. (c) Two kinds of contact surface material: wood and bumpy mat.

2.4 Experiment Setup on the Quadruped Robot

To evaluate the performance and robustness of the force estimation model in a real-world environment, we integrated the DIGIT tactile sensor onto a modified leg of the Go1 quadruped robot, as shown in Fig. 1. Given potential issues with tactile gel damage from the robot's weight and the balancing challenges, we simplified the setup: the quadruped robot is suspended horizontally while the modified leg is controlled to descend and contact the target surface.

The motion of the robot leg is achieved through control of the three joints (as illustrated in Fig. 3(a)), including two hip joints that control the Pitch (joint 1)and Yaw (joint 2) movements, respectively, and a knee joint (joint 3) for pitch movement. The entire motion phases are illustrated in Fig. 3(b), during which the desired angle position of each joint for initializing, approaching and reach the target surface is identified to generate a linear interpolated trajectory. A proportional-derivative (PD) controller is designed to managed joint angles for steady movement. The entire movement duration is around 20 s, which varies in real experiments as a result of various interference (such as position error). Tactile images were recorded throughout the process, capturing data both before and after contact. The experiment trials contain three different contact patterns, with different target contact position: directly under the leg, 5 cm to the left, and 5 cm to the right. As displayed in Fig. 3(c), wooden board and bumpy mat are selected as contact surface to evaluate the model's generalization on diverse materials.

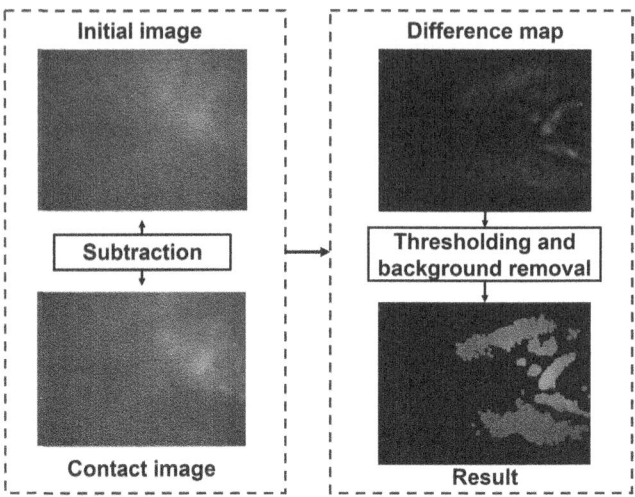

Fig. 4. Preprocessing on the tactile image to highlight contact features.

2.5   Image Processing and Model Architecture

Image processing is essential to highlight distinctive features in tactile sensor images, as indentation locations can be challenging for neural networks to detect from the raw tactile image. To address this, we preprocess images by calculating the pixel-wise difference between the initial non-contact image and subsequent contact images [8], highlighting changes in contact areas, which is formulated as:

$$\text{diff}(x, y) = |\text{gray\_base}(x, y) - \text{gray\_img}(x, y)| \tag{1}$$

The resulting image is shown in Fig. 4. This also makes the model robust to changes in ambient light conditions. To further emphasize key features, we applied Otsu's Thresholding technique. This method segments the image into foreground (contact area) and background based on grayscale values. By calculating the grayscale histogram, we identified the optimal threshold t^* that maximizes the variance between classes $\sigma_B^2(t)$:

$$\sigma_B^2(t) = w_0(t) \cdot w_1(t) \cdot [\mu_0(t) - \mu_1(t)]^2 \tag{2}$$

where $w_0(t)$ and $w_1(t)$ are the probabilities, and $\mu_0(t)$ and $\mu_1(t)$ are the means of the foreground and background classes [9]. Pixels with values above t^* are set to white, while those below are set to black, resulting in high-contrast images that enhance significant features for the model.

We selected VGG16 architecture for training our model. One key reason is its simple and straightforward architecture, which primarily relies on a series of stacked 3×3 convolutional layers. This consistent use of same-sized convolution kernels makes the structure of VGG16 highly regular and predictable [10]. Additionally, the smaller convolution kernels help reduce the number of parameters,

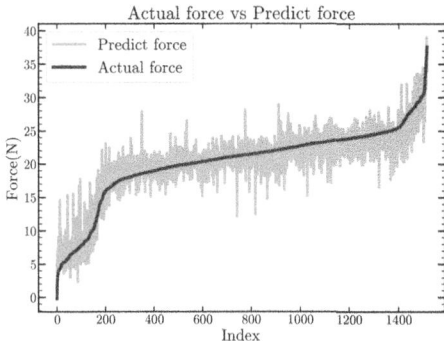

Fig. 5. Predicted forces versus the actual forces on the test set on various surface materials.

Table 1. Summary of force prediction accuracy.

Index	Mean Absolute Error (N)	MSE
Global	1.6490	4.8449
0–200	1.6997	5.4793
200–600	1.6454	4.6531
>600	1.6394	4.7893

thereby minimizing the risk of overfitting [11]. With its 16-layer depth, VGG16 is also capable of capturing complex feature hierarchies.

3   Results

3.1   Training Results Using the UR5 Robot Arm

During the training process, the entire dataset was split into 80% for training and 20% for testing. The test performance of our perception model is summarized here.

Figure 5 shows the force prediction performance of the perception model on various surfaces. The data is sorted to see the prediction trend. Overall, the model demonstrates a strong capability to follow the general trend of actual force changes, capturing the key patterns of contact force dynamics. Table 1 shows the average error in predictions. We can see that the prediction become slightly more accurate at higher forces.

Tilt estimation results (Fig. 6) further highlight the model's effectiveness across varying conditions, maintaining an average difference of 0.71° and consistent performance within the 1–7° tilt range (Table 2). However, at the upper tilt limit of 9°, the model's error rate increases, attributed to the sensor's tilt constraints and edge-related image artifacts. To enhance performance at these higher tilt angles, edge enhancement techniques like Sobel or Canny filters may

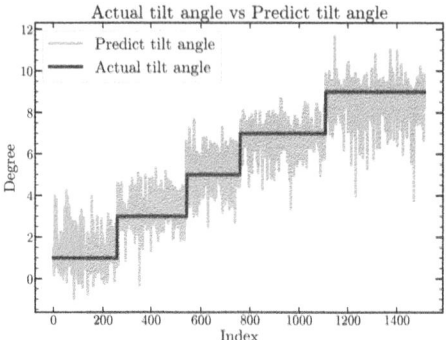

Fig. 6. Comparison of Predicted and Actual Tilt Angle.

Table 2. Summary of tilt angle prediction.

Degree	Mean Absolute Error (°)	MSE
Global	0.71	0.8736
1–7°	0.6802	0.7728
9°	0.7742	1.1517

be beneficial for improving the clarity of boundary features, especially where the indentation approaches the sensor's edge.

Similarly, the model performs consistently in estimating the tilt direction in all direction (Fig. 7). On average, we can determine the direction of contact with an accuracy of 17° (Table 3).

Table 3. Summary of tilt direction prediction accuracy.

Index	Mean Absolute Error (°)	MSE
Global	17.0571	580.2456
0–400	17.3760	606.9978
400–1200	16.9245	574.0903
>1200	16.9874	561.7635

3.2 Experiment Results on the Quadruped Robot

Next, we access performance of the optimized force estimation model in a real-world interaction scenario where the quadruped robot makes controlled contact with various surfaces. Figure 8 presents the prediction results of contact force magnitude over time across six distinct experimental trials, including the force

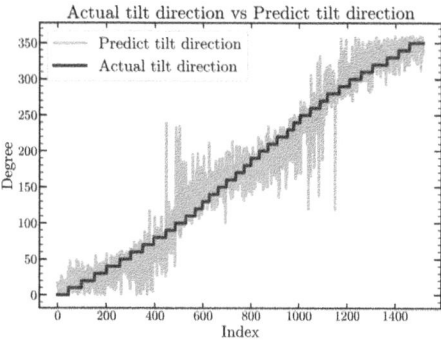

Fig. 7. Comparison of Predicted versus Actual tilt direction with respect to the ground plate.

values estimated from the vision-based tactile images throughout the motion phase as described in Fig. 3. Due to experimental limitations, ground truth for force measurements are unavailable, which restricts the quantitative assessment of the prediction accuracy. Nevertheless, the model's performance can still be qualitatively evaluated by examining the trends in predicted forces.

As can be observed in Fig. 8, the fluctuation of the original predicted force curves reflect the interference occurring in the experiment, including the shaking and instability of robot leg, periodic environment noise. In particular, during shaking, the robotic leg may momentarily lose contact with the surface, leading the sensor to record a lower force value. Alternatively, sudden increases in applied force during shaking could cause the sensor to record an excessively high value. These abrupt variations result in inaccurate force readings. To enhance the clarity of the force trends, we applied Savitzky-Golay filtering [22], which smooths the curve while preserving important features, making the trend more discernible.

The overall trend across all estimated force curves effectively captures the motion pattern of the quadruped robot's leg. During the initialization and approach phases, where the robot's leg has not yet contacted the surface, the predicted force values remain low (approximately zero). Following surface contact, the force readings increase gradually, reflecting the expected progression of the interaction. It is also worth noting the decreasing trend at the end of each predicted force curve, which aligns with the robot's movement as it lifts from the contact surface. This suggests that the model can adaptively infer contact force in response to the robot's dynamic motion.

The model demonstrated sensitivity to surface variations, as evidenced by the results on the bumpy mat, where force predictions showed more fluctuations due to the uneven texture. In contrast, on the smooth wooden surface, the force readings were steadier, matching the expected behavior for regular contact surfaces. This consistency suggests that the model can generalize across diverse

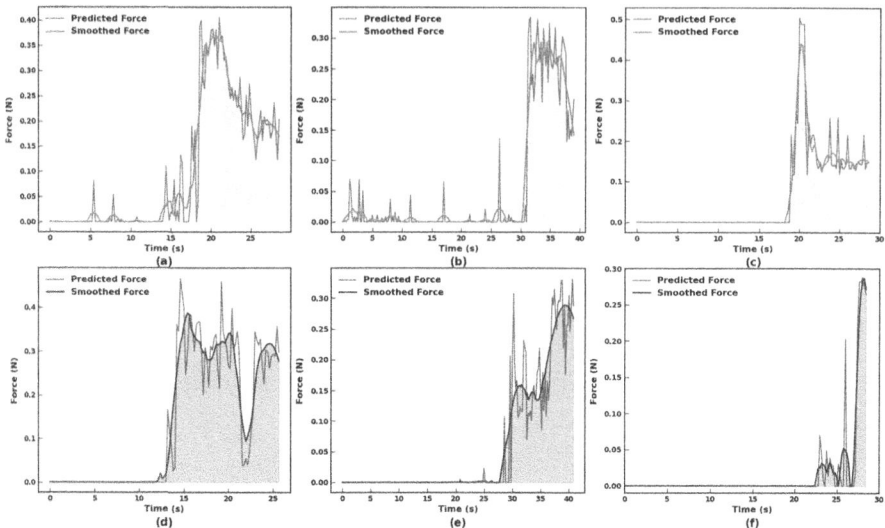

Fig. 8. Force prediction results during quadruped robot experiments are plotted over time. The first row shows results on a bumpy mat, while the second row presents results on a wooden surface. Each column corresponds to a different contact position: (a) and (d) show results 5 cm left of the leg, (b) and (e) directly beneath the leg, and (c) and (f) 5 cm right.

surface textures and potentially improve the robot's adaptability in varying environments.

In summary, the findings underscore the model's potential for estimating contact forces in real-world scenarios with quadruped robots. The model's ability to capture force dynamics across different surfaces demonstrates its robustness and adaptability to varying textures and movement phases. Future work should incorporate ground truth measurements to quantitatively assess accuracy, which would solidify the model's reliability and extend its application in diverse, real-world terrains. This advancement holds promise for improving tactile feedback and adaptive navigation in robotic systems engaging with complex environments.

4   Conclusion

In this work, we present a comprehensive modeling approach to estimate force information in quadruped robotic interaction using a vision-based soft tactile sensor. By leveraging advanced vision-based tactile sensing and deep learning techniques, we aim to endow the robot with tactile skills that contribute to adaptive and precise locomotion in complex, real-world scenarios.

The proposed UR5-based dataset captures a wide range of interaction information, constructing a robust and diverse training foundation. By including diversity in force magnitudes, tilt directions, and surface roughness, this dataset offers comprehensive coverage of scenarios a quadruped robot might encounter, enhancing the model's adaptability and across various conditions, including complex, dynamic interactions typical in quadruped robotics. Promising results are obtained from the preliminary experiments, which indicate the model's capability for providing accurate inference of essential force information.

The real-world validation on the quadruped robot qualitatively demonstrates the model's capacity to generalize across material textures and respond adaptively to movement dynamics. Although ground truth data for force measurements was unavailable, the predicted trends aligned well with the expected motion phases, showcasing the model's potential for real-world deployment.

In conclusion, this study provides a promising exploration of enhancing the perception and control of quadruped robot with fine-level tactile information, which could contribute to force estimation that is essential in precise navigation and control in complex scenario such as unstructured and unpredictable terrain. Future work will integrate advanced control strategies to further enhance the robot's interactions and robustness in complex environments.

Acknowledgments. This work was partially supported by the UKRI FLF [MR/V025333/1] (RoboHike). For the purpose of Open Access, the author has applied a CC BY public copyright license to any Author Accepted Manuscript version arising from this submission.

References

1. Raibert, M., Blankespoor, K., Nelson, G., Playter, R.: Bigdog, the rough-terrain quadruped robot. In: IFAC Proceedings Volumes, vol. 41, no. 2, pp. 10822–10825 (2008)
2. Hutter, M., et al.: Anymal a highly mobile and dynamic quadrupedal robot. In: 2016 IEEE/RSJ International Conference on Intelligent Robots and Systems (IROS), pp. 38–44. IEEE (2016)
3. Lepora, N.F.: Soft biomimetic optical tactile sensing with the TacTip: a review. IEEE Sens. J. **21**(19), 21131–21143 (2021)
4. Yuan, W., Dong, S., Adelson, E.H.: Gelsight: high-resolution robot tactile sensors for estimating geometry and force. Sensors **17**(12), 2762 (2017)
5. Andrussow, I., Sun, H., Kuchenbecker, K.J., Martius, G.: Minsight: a fingertip-sized vision-based tactile sensor for robotic manipulation. Adv. Intell. Syst. **5**(8), 2300042 (2023)
6. Yamaguchi, A., Atkeson, C.G.: Tactile behaviors with the vision-based tactile sensor FingerVision. Int. J. Humanoid Rob. **16**(03), 1940002 (2019)
7. TE Connectivity: FC2231-0000-0050-L Datasheet. https://www.datasheets.com/te-connectivity-fc2231-0000-0050-l. Accessed 5 Oct 2024
8. Gonzalez, R.C., Woods, R.E.: Digital Image Processing, 3rd edn. Prentice-Hall, Inc. (2002)
9. Otsu, N.: A threshold selection method from gray-level histograms. IEEE Trans. Syst. Man Cybern. **9**(1), 62–66 (1979). https://doi.org/10.1109/TSMC.1979.4310076

10. Simonyan, K., Zisserman, A.: Very deep convolutional networks for large-scale image recognition. In: Proceedings of the International Conference on Learning Representations (ICLR) (2015)

11. Razavian, A.S., Azizpour, H., Sullivan, J., Carlsson, S.: CNN features off-the-shelf: an astounding baseline for recognition. In: Proceedings of the IEEE Conference on Computer Vision and Pattern Recognition Workshops, pp. 806–813 (2014)

12. LeCun, Y., Bottou, L., Bengio, Y., Haffner, P.: Gradient-based learning applied to document recognition. Proc. IEEE **86**(11), 2278–2324 (1998). https://doi.org/10.1109/5.726791

13. Nair, V., Hinton, G.E.: Rectified linear units improve restricted Boltzmann machines. In: Proceedings of the 27th International Conference on Machine Learning (ICML 2010), pp. 807–814 (2010)

14. Rumelhart, D.E., Hinton, G.E., Williams, R.J.: Learning representations by back-propagating errors. Nature **323**(6088), 533–536 (1986). https://doi.org/10.1038/323533a0

15. Bridle, J.S.: Probabilistic interpretation of feedforward classification network outputs, with relationships to statistical pattern recognition. In: Neurocomputing, pp. 227–236 (1990). https://doi.org/10.1007/978-3-642-76153-9_28

16. Le, K.: An Overview of VGG16 and NIN Models. https://lekhuyen.medium.com/an-overview-of-vgg16-and-nin-models-96e4bf398484. Accessed 5 Oct 2024

17. Sobel, I., Feldman, G.: A 3x3 isotropic gradient operator for image processing. In: Stanford Artificial Intelligence Project (SAIL) (1968)

18. Canny, J.: A computational approach to edge detection. IEEE Trans. Pattern Anal. Mach. Intell. **8**(6), 679–698 (1986)

19. Wang, K., Chen, T., Bi, J., Li, Y., Rong, X.: Vision-based terrain perception of quadruped robots in complex environments. In: 2021 IEEE International Conference on Robotics and Biomimetics (ROBIO), pp. 1729–1734. IEEE (2021)

20. Mudalige, N.D.W., et al.: Dogtouch: CNN-based recognition of surface textures by quadruped robot with high density tactile sensors. In: 2022 IEEE 95th Vehicular Technology Conference (VTC2022-Spring), pp. 1–5. IEEE (2022)

21. Song, Z., et al.: TacTID: high-performance visuo-tactile sensor-based terrain identification for legged robots. IEEE Sens. J. (2024)

22. John, A., Sadasivan, J., Seelamantula, C.S.: Adaptive savitzky-golay filtering in non-gaussian noise. IEEE Trans. Signal Process. **69**, 5021–5036 (2021). https://doi.org/10.1109/TSP.2021.3106450

23. Sun, H., Kuchenbecker, K.J., Martius, G.: A soft thumb-sized vision-based sensor with accurate all-round force perception. Nat. Mach. Intell. **4**(2), 135–145 (2022)

24. Kakani, V., Cui, X., Ma, M., Kim, H.: Vision-based tactile sensor mechanism for the estimation of contact position and force distribution using deep learning. Sensors **21**(5), 1920 (2021)

25. Chen, Z., Ou, N., Zhang, X., Luo, S.: TransForce: Transferable Force Prediction for Vision-based Tactile Sensors with Sequential Image Translation. arXiv preprint arXiv:2409.09870 (2024)

26. Zhang, T., Cong, Y., Li, X., Peng, Y.: Robot tactile sensing: vision based tactile sensor for force perception. In: 2018 IEEE 8th Annual International Conference on CYBER Technology, pp. 1360–1365. IEEE (2018)

MultiClear: Multimodal Soft Exoskeleton Glove for Transparent Object Grasping Assistance

Chen Hu[1], Timothy Neate[1], Shan Luo[1], and Letizia Gionfrida[1,2]

[1] King's College London, London WC2R 2LS, UK
{tyrone.hu,timothy.neate,shan.luo,letizia.gionfrida}@kcl.ac.uk
[2] Harvard University, Cambridge, MA, USA
gionfrida@seas.harvard.edu

Abstract. Grasping is a fundamental skill for interacting with the environment. However, this ability can be difficult for some (e.g. due to disability). Wearable robotic solutions can enhance or restore hand function, and recent advances have leveraged computer vision to improve grasping capabilities. However, grasping transparent objects remains challenging due to their poor visual contrast and ambiguous depth cues. Furthermore, while multimodal control strategies incorporating tactile and auditory feedback have been explored to grasp transparent objects, the integration of vision with these modalities remains underdeveloped. This paper introduces *MultiClear*, a multimodal framework designed to enhance grasping assistance in a wearable soft exoskeleton glove for transparent objects by fusing RGB data, depth data, and auditory signal. The exoskeleton glove integrates a tendon-driven actuator with an RGB-D camera and a built-in microphone. To achieve precise and adaptive control, a hierarchical control architecture is proposed. For the proposed hierarchical control architecture a high-level control layer provides contextual awareness, a mid-level control layer processes multimodal sensory inputs, and a low-level control executes PID motor control for fine-tuned grasping adjustments. The challenge of transparent object segmentation was managed by introducing a vision foundation model for zero-shot segmentation. The proposed system achieves a Grasping Ability Score of $70.37 \pm 3.96\%$, demonstrating its effectiveness in transparent object manipulation.

Keywords: Wearable robots · Grasping assistance · Multimodal sensing

1 Introduction

Grasping is a fundamental skill required for interacting with objects in daily life. However, individuals with hand impairments [24], such as those resulting from stroke, spinal cord injury, or neuromuscular disorders, often experience significant difficulties in generating stable and controlled grasps [24,29]. These impairments limit autonomy and quality of life, necessitating assistive solutions

A. Cavalcanti et al. (Eds.): TAROS 2025, LNAI 16045, pp. 195–209, 2026.
https://doi.org/10.1007/978-3-032-01486-3_16

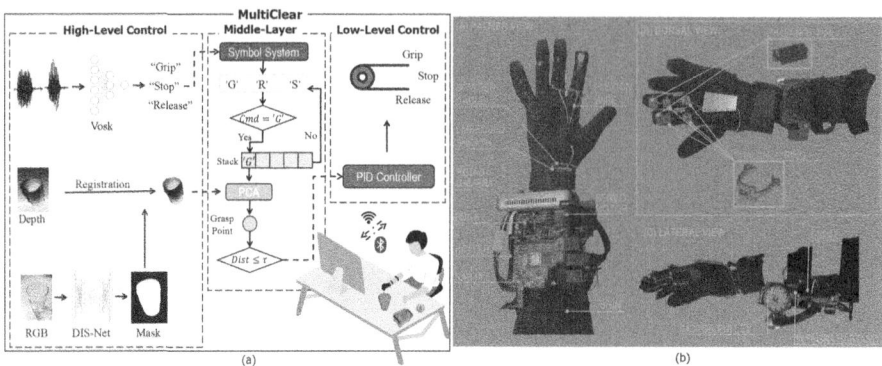

Fig. 1. (a) **Overview of *MultiClear*:** The proposed multimodal framework captures RGB, depth, and auditory inputs through sensors mounted on the exoglove. The high-level control module processes the RGB frames using DIS-Net [23] for forward inference, generating a mask of the target object. The mask is aligned with the current depth frame to extract depth information, which is then passed to the middle layer. Simultaneously, voice input is processed by the Vosk ASR model [1], which converts predefined prompt words into control commands. These commands are fed into the middle layer. By integrating the data from all three modalities, the middle layer makes decisions and sends target commands to the low-level PID controller for motor rotation, executing grasp or release actions. (b) **Hardware setup:** The soft exoglove consists of three main components: an actuator, a tendon-driven glove, and sensing equipment. 3D-printed custom components were designed for routing the wires, connected to the motor to trigger grasp and release actions. After gathering data from the three modalities, client-server interaction is facilitated via Wi-Fi and Bluetooth modules in the microcontrollers.

to restore hand function. Wearable robots, particularly exogloves (exogloves), have been developed to augment grasping ability by applying external torque to facilitate finger flexion and extension towards a more stable grasp [9,14]. Compared to rigid ones, soft exogloves constructed from flexible materials offer enhanced comfort and adaptability, making them suitable for prolonged use in daily activities [4,6].

Recent advancements in wearable robotics have explored the integration of vision to enhance adaptability and environmental awareness in robotic assistance [19,26]. Visual cues can provide contextual information that enables intent recognition and real-time grasp modulation, reducing reliance on direct user input. However, existing vision-assisted exogloves primarily focus on opaque objects, struggling with transparent objects due to low visual contrast and ambiguous depth cues. This limitation impacts their applicability in real-world scenarios, where transparent objects such as glassware are common.

Depth completion and estimation have been studied [27,31,32]. ClearGrasp [27] predicts the surface normal and the transparent boundary to solve the depth estimation. Duisterhof et al. [7] use NeRF to recover depth to grasp transparent objects. Approaches based on generative models, such as GANs [32] and

Diffusion models [31], were proposed to generate sparse parts of the depth map. Although significant progress has been made for depth completion, these methods remain computationally expensive, preventing real-time deployment, and they are primarily designed for robotic manipulation. In robotic grasping tasks, complete depth information of transparent objects is essential for computing critical grasp-related parameters, such as 6D poses of both the target object and the robotic arm, as well as grasp planning. However, in grasp assistance, intent originates from the user rather than an autonomous system. This implies that the intent detection algorithm only needs to leverage a limited amount of environmental information to timely trigger user intent, rather than performing comprehensive depth reconstruction.

Futhermore, while multimodal control strategies incorporating tactile and auditory feedback have been investigated to improve intent detection and grasping stability [25,33], the integration of vision with these modalities remains underexplored. Current control paradigms often rely on single-modality inputs, such as surface electromyography signals [28] or force-sensing resistors [25], which provide limited contextual awareness and require explicit user effort to initiate grasping actions.

To address these challenges, *MultiClear*, a multimodal framework designed to enhance grasping accuracy for transparent objects by integrating RGB, depth, and auditory modalities was introduced. The system consists of a tendon-driven soft exoglove equipped with an RGB-D camera and a built-in microphone. A hierarchical control architecture that operates across three layers to achieve precise and adaptive control was proposed to: 1) High-level control provides contextual awareness by processing multimodal sensory inputs. 2) Mid-level control fuses data from RGB, depth, and auditory sources for intent recognition. 3) Low-level control executes fine-tuned grasping adjustments using proportional-integral-derivative (PID) motor control. The contributions of this work are:

1. We propose *MultiClear*, a multimodal control framework designed for grasping assistance with transparent objects, integrating zero-shot segmentation and multimodal perception for robust object manipulation.
2. To enhance generalizability, we employ a vision foundation model for zero-shot segmentation, accurately detecting and segmenting transparent object boundaries. The alignment of these boundaries with depth maps facilitates precise grasp point extraction and reliable intent triggering.
3. We introduce a hierarchical multimodal control architecture integrating RGB, depth, and auditory inputs. The architecture comprises a high-level layer for contextual awareness, a mid-level for sensor fusion, and a low-level for precise motor execution through PID control.
4. *MultiClear* is implemented on a custom-designed tendon-driven soft exoglove. Extensive experiments, including evaluations using the Grasp Ability Score (GAS), demonstrate significant advances in transparent object grasping assistance.

2   Related Work

2.1   Controllers for Soft Exoglove

Recent advancements in upper-limb wearable robots have introduced a variety of control strategies aimed at improving user interaction, adaptability, and task specificity [6,35]. Traditional joystick-based methods remain prevalent due to their simplicity and reliability [28], but their limited dexterity constrains them in executing fine or complex movements [2]. Similarly, force-feedback controllers have shown promise in telemanipulation by providing haptic cues [3]; however, they require prior contact with objects, which reduces adaptability in unstructured environments.

Neuromuscular interface-based strategies, particularly those decoding electromyographic (EMG) signals, allow for proportional and adaptive assistance [17,28]. These approaches hold promise for intuitive control, though challenges remain in ensuring robustness during real-world deployment.

To improve autonomy and responsiveness, recent approaches have integrated contextual sensing into control pipelines. Vision-based perception, in particular, enables systems to infer environmental context and user intent, facilitating adaptive assistance planning [9]. Compared to other modalities, vision has been shown to reduce inter-user variability and improve consistency across trials [14,34]. These findings highlight the emerging importance of perceptually driven, context-aware controllers in advancing soft exoglove functionality and usability.

2.2   Multimodal Fusion

Humans perceive the world through multiple sensory modalities, such as vision, and hearing, allowing them to form a wide understanding of their environment [39]. With advancements in sensor technology, it has become increasingly feasible to collect and analyze diverse forms of data for downstream tasks. However, integrating these heterogeneous data streams effectively remains a challenge, particularly in real-world environments where such data may be noisy, imbalanced, or even corrupted. For traditional assistive devices, empirical and theoretical studies have demonstrated that multimodal fusion approaches may fail under such conditions due to their inability to effectively manage the complexity of heterogeneous sensory inputs and dynamically adapt to variations in data quality [12,21,37].

This failure often arises because conventional approaches treat multimodal data at a single decision level, making it difficult to prioritize or reweight sensory information based on contextual relevance or reliability. These limitations highlight the need for a hierarchical control architecture that can decompose the decision-making process across multiple levels, enabling more robust and adaptive responses by contextualizing high-level information, fusing multimodal data efficiently, and ensuring precise low-level motor execution. To address these challenges, the proposed multimodal framework introduces a hierarchical control architecture that integrates RGB, depth, and auditory data, to enhance contextual awareness and ensure robust, adaptive control during grasping tasks. By incorporating a high-level control layer for contextual understanding, a mid-level control layer for multimodal sensor fusion, and a low-level control layer for precise motor execution through PID control, the proposed framework aims to deliver reliable assistive control strategies, even in complex and uncertain scenarios.

3 Hardware Design and Control

3.1 Hardware Design

The implemented soft exoglove, based on an existing design [25], consists of three primary components (Fig. 1 (b)): 1) an embedded actuator utilizing a Tendon-Sheath Mechanism (TSM), 2) a custom glove that transfers force to the finger joints, and 3) a sensing module for interaction feedback. The actuation system, powered by a LiPo battery (Crazepony, 1400 mAh, 11.1 V, 64.1 g, Shenzhen, China), weighs 0.5 kg and is mounted on a forearm-worn shin guard (Super Comfortable Shin Pad, Northdeer, China). A flat servo motor (Digital Servo, 4.8 V, 24 kgcm, CHICIRIS, China) drives a 30 mm diameter pulley, around which the actuation cable is wound.

The system employs a microcontroller (Raspberry Pi 4B, 1.5 GHz, 4 GB RAM, Broadcom, UK) for acquiring RGB-D data with a main control chip (ESP32, 2.4 GHz, 4 GB, Bluetooth, Shanghai, China). A voice module (MARKELL, China) converts analogue inputs into digital signals for further processing.

The TSM connects the actuation system to the glove and is designed to remain fixed, reducing the impact of dynamic sheath bending angles. To maintain a tight, straight connection between the actuation system and the palm-supporting pieces, the sheaths are slightly tensioned, which minimizes sheath bending during operation. This approach reduces unwanted contact between the tendon wires and the sheath, effectively stabilizing fingertip force against dynamic changes in the sheath's bending angle.

The glove itself features 3D-printed rings and nails, fabricated using general PLA material through an FDM 3D printer, installed on the metacarpophalangeal (MCP), proximal interphalangeal (PIP), and distal interphalangeal (DIP) joints, simulating the passage of human flexion tendons through these joints. This design enables the glove to perform grasping and releasing motions. Flexion tendons are routed through the palm, while extension tendons are positioned on the back of the hand. These tendons are pulled and released antagonistically, driven by the motor's clockwise and counterclockwise revolutions, allowing the index and middle fingers to curl inward and release, respectively.

A RealSense D415 camera (Intel RealSense, California, USA) is mounted beneath the wrist to capture environmental data. The camera, attached to the shin pad via a miniature gimbal, sends color and depth images through the Raspberry Pi's Wi-Fi module to a server (Dell, Precision 7680, US) for multimodal inference. A microphone (Uxcell, China) is integrated into the actuation system to capture system inputs.

Algorithm 1. middle layer Control Algorithm

```
1: Initialize stack for storing commands
2: Initialize torqueDeadZone ← predefined value
3: Initialize pendingGripCommand ← False
4: while True do
5:      # Check if "grip" command is received
6:      if receivedCommand == "grip" then
7:          Push "grip" to stack
8:          pendingGripCommand ← True
9:          # Process depth information if a "grip" command is active
10:         currentDepth ← Get current depth from Depth Frame
11:         dist ← Calculate distance between graspingPoint and camera
12:         if dist ≤ distThreshold then
13:             Wait for 2 seconds
14:             Send "grip" command via Bluetooth to low-level PID Controller
15:             pendingGripCommand ← False
16:         end if
17:     end if
18:     # Check if "release" command is received
19:     if receivedCommand == "release" then
20:         Send "release" command to PID Controller
21:         if "grip" exists in stack then
22:             Remove "grip" from stack
23:         end if
24:     end if
25:     # Check if "stop" command is received
26:     if receivedCommand == "stop" then
27:         Send "stop" command to PID Controller
28:         pendingGripCommand ← False
29:     end if
30:     # Discard depth and torque values unless a "grip" command is active
31:     if pendingGripCommand == False then
32:         Discard current depth and torque values
33:     end if
34: end while
```

3.2   Hierarchical Control Strategy

With the integration of an RGB-D camera and a microphone, the actuation system supports multimodal inputs (Fig. 1 (a)), including RGB frames, depth frames, and voice signals. The high-level control module within the multimodal framework processes visual and auditory data concurrently. Once the RGB-D camera mounted on the exoglove receives the data stream, the system transmits it via Wi-Fi to the server, where the data is processed frame by frame. To optimize efficiency, one frame is selected for inference every three frames. The selected RGB frame is processed by the dichotomous image segmentation network (DIS-Net), generating a mask of the target object. This mask is then aligned with the current depth frame to extract depth information of the object's boundary, which is forwarded to the middle layer for further processing. At the edges of transparent objects, abrupt normal variations and thickness changes create high-contrast features, resulting in depth sparsity rarely occurring at the edges, while it is predominantly observed in the interior regions of transparent objects. Consequently, the RealSense camera can still capture depth information at the object's edges.

Voice signals, after analog-to-digital conversion, are input into the Vosk ASR model [1] for real-time transcription. Vosk leverages a Time-Delay Neural

Network (TDNN) [36] and Long Short-Term Memory (LSTM) [10] architecture to map the voice input into text. The three command prompts defined as – "*grip*", "*release*", and "*stop*" – are sent to the middle layer for interpretation.

The middle layer discards depth information and torque values unless a "*grip*" command is received. Upon receiving the "*grip*" command, it starts processing the object's depth information and pushes the command onto a stack. According to depth information at the object's boundaries, the object centroid using Principal Component Analysis (PCA) [20] is computed and defined as the grasp point. The grasp point is continuously detected in real-time to update the distance between the exoskeleton glove and the object, thereby adapting to and autonomously triggering the user's grasp intent. The middle layer delays for two seconds before sending the "grip" command via Bluetooth to the low-level velocity PID Controller. Upon receiving a "*release*" command, the middle layer forwards it to the PID controller and removes any pending "*grip*" command from the stack. If a "*stop*" command is received, it is immediately transmitted to the PID Controller.

The low-level PID Controller, when receiving the "*grip*" command, initiates forward motor rotation, applying a constant torque of 24 kgcm ($\approx$ 2.35 Nm) for fine-tuned grasping adjustment when the power system provides 4.8 V voltage. Based on the benchmarking comparison, this precise torque aids users in grasping objects. According to [22], the required force to grasp objects during ADLs does not exceed 15 N, and the pinch forces required to execute most of the daily life tasks are lower than 10.5 N [30]. When the "*Maintain*" command is active, the system ignores all other voice inputs except "release," preventing environmental noise from interfering with PID control and causing grasp failure or slippage. Upon receiving the "*release*" command, the controller reverses motor rotation to release the object. The "*stop*" command halts motor operation immediately.

4   Research Protocol

To evaluate the performance of *MultiClear* with users, a case study involving six participants with approval (*MRPP-23/24-40750*) from the University and the College Research Ethics Committee (CREC) at King's College London, to test the implemented exoglove was conducted. All participants were instructed to keep their hands relaxed and refrain from applying any force to the six transparent objects during the Grasping Ability Score (GAS) test. To demonstrate the effectiveness of the vision foundation model for grasping assistance, the intermediate results from *MultiClear* was also visualized.

4.1   Dataset

Six objects used in the study were chosen to represent three distinct grasp types: cylindrical grip, spherical grasp, and pinch (Fig. 2). These classifications are based on the object set described by Jiang et al. [13], to ensure heterogeneity across attributes such as shape, mass, dimensions, and material composition.

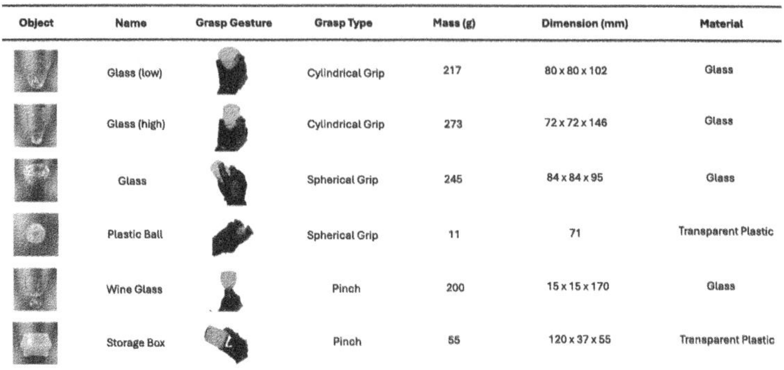

Object	Name	Grasp Gesture	Grasp Type	Mass (g)	Dimension (mm)	Material
	Glass (low)		Cylindrical Grip	217	80 x 80 x 102	Glass
	Glass (high)		Cylindrical Grip	273	72 x 72 x 146	Glass
	Glass		Spherical Grip	245	84 x 84 x 95	Glass
	Plastic Ball		Spherical Grip	11	71	Transparent Plastic
	Wine Glass		Pinch	200	15 x 15 x 170	Glass
	Storage Box		Pinch	55	120 x 37 x 55	Transparent Plastic

Fig. 2. The dataset comprises six transparent objects, categorized into three groups, with users performing grasps using three distinct grip types, including Cylindrical Grip, Spherical Grip, and Pinch. The mass, dimensions, and material composition of the objects can significantly impact grasping performance.

Specifically, the cylindrical grip included the glass (low) and glass (high), the spherical grip was used for the small plastic ball and the glass in an upside-down orientation, and the pinch grasp was assigned to the wine glass and small storage box. These grasp types were specifically selected because they represent the most common grasping patterns in human daily activities (ADLs), as established by comprehensive grasp taxonomies presented in prior literature [5,8]. Thus, this selection ensures diverse object properties and provides a realistic and representative assessment of grasping performance across typical daily usage scenarios.

4.2   Participants

To evaluate the grasping performance of the designed multimodal exoglove, six healthy, right-handed participants were recruited, including four males and two females, with an average age of 25.0 ± 6 years, weight of 75 ± 14 kg, and height of 1.80 ± 0.22 m. All participants demonstrated normal hand motor function. They were instructed to perform grasping tasks while ensuring that these actions caused no discomfort or pain.

The study received ethical approval (*MRPP-23/24-40750*) from the University and the College Research Ethics Committee (CREC) at King's College London. Participants were thoroughly briefed on the study's objectives and procedures, and all provided written informed consent prior to participation.

4.3   Research Procedure

During the protocol, participants were seated next to a table (Fig. 1). They were instructed to keep their hands relaxed without applying any force on the object during the grasp. A researcher handed the objects to the participants, who were then asked to hold the grasp for three seconds (Fig. 3). Afterwards, they rotated

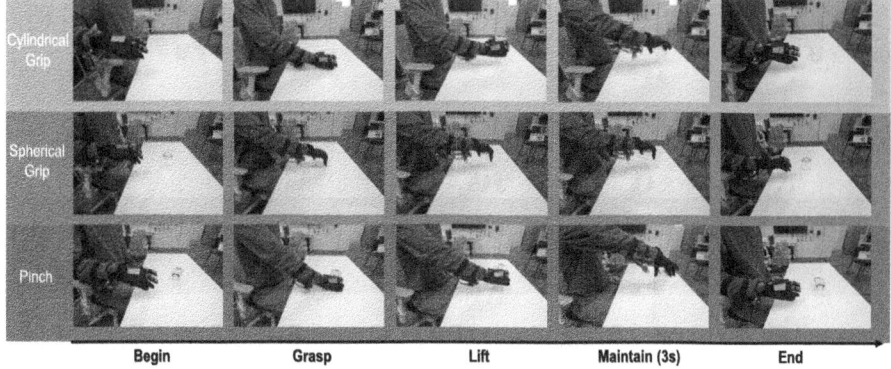

| | Begin | Grasp | Lift | Maintain (3s) | End |

Fig. 3. Five stages of the research procedure: (1) **Begin:** The user starts seated at a table, gives the "grip" command, and moves their hand toward the object. (2) **Grasp:** When the distance between the camera and the object is less than 400mm for 2 s, the system triggers the grasp. (3) **Lift:** Once the motor stops and the grasp stabilizes, the user lifts the object. (4) **Maintain:** For the Cylindrical and Spherical grips, the user rotates their wrist to a palm-down position and holds this for three seconds. (5) **End:** The user places the object back on the table, gives the "release" command to reverse the motor, and then issues the "stop" command to halt the motor.

their hand 90° to a palm-down position, maintaining the grasp for an additional three seconds before the system initiated the release. Additionally, the researcher recorded how often the camera made contact with the desk to evaluate whether placing the sensor underneath caused any discomfort to users.

Following the protocol proposed by [18], each object was grasped three times under each control mode to evaluate the multimodal exoglove's performance in two aspects: grasp initiation (Grasping) and object retention (Maintaining). Grasping was scored on a scale of 0, 0.5, and 1, where 0 indicated failure, 0.5 an incorrect grasp type but successful lift, and 1 a correct grasp. Maintaining was similarly rated from 0 (dropped) to 1 (stable), with 0.5 assigned for noticeable movement. Scores across objects of the same grasp type were averaged to produce a type-specific score. A cumulative Grasping Ability Score (GAS) [16] was then calculated and expressed as a percentage, where 100% reflects performance equivalent to that of a healthy individual unaided by an exoskeleton.

4.4   Transparent Object Segmentation

Figure 4 visualizes the segmentation outputs for six transparent objects using DIS-Net with the pre-trained weights. Despite not being specifically fine-tuned on transparent objects, DIS-Net accurately captures their contours. It achieves zero-shot segmentation across a range of transparent objects with diverse shapes, laying the groundwork for grasping tasks in open-world environments. Moreover, when tested on an RTX 2000 Ada laptop GPU, DIS-Net achieves an inference

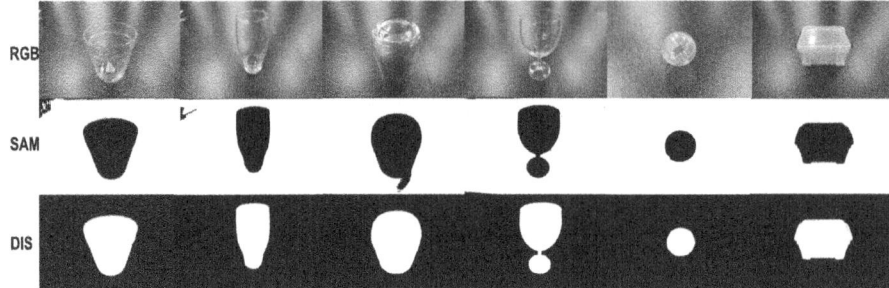

Fig. 4. The first row displays RGB images of six transparent objects from the dataset. The second row shows masks generated by Segment Anything (SAM), where SAM demonstrates sensitivity to image edges (e.g., Glass (high), Glass (low), and Wine Glass) and object contours, leading to inaccurate segmentation. In contrast, the third row illustrates the masks produced by DIS-Net, which focuses specifically on the outer contours of the transparent objects.

speed of 10 fps. In addition, the Segment Anything Model (ViT-B SAM) [15] was applied to segment the same six objects in the dataset. The results indicate that SAM struggles with contour inference for transparent objects (e.g., an upside-down glass) and certain image frames (e.g., a wine glass). Furthermore, SAM's model size is more than twice that of DIS-Net, making it less suitable for downstream grasping tasks when evaluated on both accuracy and performance.

4.5 Grasping Ability Score

The GAS for six participants using the multimodal soft exoglove to perform three types of grasps on six transparent objects (Fig. 5). On average, the proposed framework achieved a grasping score of $80.4 \pm 5.4\%$, a maintaining score of $60.41 \pm 6.18\%$, and an overall GAS of $70.37 \pm 3.96\%$. Compared to the exoglove presented in [38], which achieved a GAS score of 53%, the proposed system demonstrated an improvement of $17.37 \pm 3.96\%$. While [38] included participants with mild hand impairments, in the study, users did not apply any force during the grasping tasks. Similarly, when compared to the exoglove designed in [18], which achieved a GAS of $80.18 \pm 0.23\%$, the performance is lower by 9.18%. However, it is important to note that both [38] and [18] evaluated grasping non-transparent objects. Given the material characteristics of transparent objects, such as lower surface friction and distinct weight distribution, grasping them poses additional challenges.

The distance (mm) was measured from the wrist to the tips of the thumb, index finger, and middle finger. The soft exoglove was built using a 2XL-sized glove, with 3D-printed units attached at the finger joints to route wires. Consequently, the fit between the user's hand size and the glove significantly impacted grasping success rates. Participants with larger hands, such as User1 and User4, achieved higher GAS scores (Fig. 5). This issue was particularly evident in the

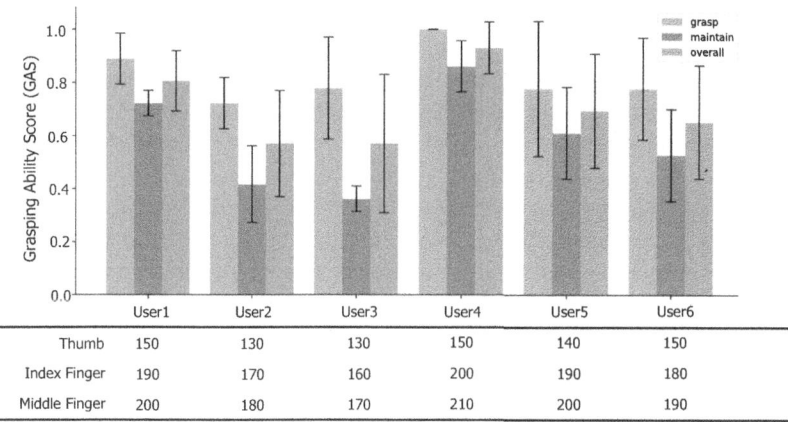

Fig. 5. The average GAS for six users performing three different grip types on six transparent objects. Grey, red, and blue bars represent the Grasping, Maintaining, and overall GAS, respectively. The table below provides the measured distances (mm) from each user's palm to the tips of the thumb, index finger, and middle finger. (Color figure online)

Table 1. Comparison of the grasping, maintaining, and overall GAS scores for three grasp types using the multimodal soft exoglove.

Grasp type	Grasping score (%)	Maintaining score (%)	GAS score (%)
Cylindrical grip	94.44 ± 3.93	68.06 ± 5.8	81.25 ± 3.37
Spherical grip	61.11 ± 7.46	48.61 ± 7.32	54.86 ± 4.72
Pinch	91.66 ± 4.81	58.33± 5.42	75.00 ± 3.78
Average	80.4 ± 5.4	60.41± 6.18	70.37 ± 3.96

maintaining task, where participants rotated their wrists to a palm-down position. The low friction coefficient of the transparent object surfaces led to frequent slippage or object drops. Moreover, the success rate for grasping transparent plastic objects was higher than that for glass objects.

For the spherical grip, where the palm is consistently positioned downward during both grasping and maintaining tasks, the challenge for the exoglove in grasping transparent objects is heightened. As shown in Table 1, the GAS score for the spherical grip was 54.86±4.72%, significantly lower than that of the cylindrical grip (81.25±3.37%) by approximately 26%, and lower than the pinch grip (75.00±3.78%) by around 20%. The primary reason for this lower performance is that in the spherical grip, the palm faces downward, causing only the fingertips to provide friction. In contrast, other grip types such as the cylindrical grip allow the palm to partially contribute friction, enhancing stability. Repeated trials also exhibited relatively high variability due to this limitation.

5 Discussion

This study presents a multimodal soft exoglove designed to assist grasping transparent objects for individuals with neurodegenerative diseases. Grasping Ability Score (GAS) evaluations with six healthy participants demonstrated effective assistive grasping despite incomplete depth information. The system successfully identified grasp points using edge-based normal discontinuities and thickness variations; however, relying solely on edge-based depth is insufficient for certain transparent objects. Future research will incorporate advanced depth completion methods, such as diffusion-based or GAN-based models, to enhance grasp reliability.

The current prototype lacks adaptive sizing, which could hinder practical deployment. To address this, we will develop multiple glove sizes (XS to XXL) to accommodate diverse hand anatomies.

Quantifying individual modality contributions (vision, depth, speech) remains necessary. Although prior studies [11] compared force-sensing and joystick control modes, comprehensive ablation studies evaluating vision-only, speech-only, and combined vision-plus-speech conditions are planned to quantify each sensor's contribution to GAS and latency.

Potential occlusions, a common issue for camera-based systems, were not explicitly evaluated in this study. Feedback from Stroke Patient and Public Involvement (PPI) sessions suggested survivors prefer separately arranging objects to facilitate access, reducing occlusion occurrences. Nevertheless, future research will enhance system robustness against occlusion.

As this work is the first to explore transparent object grasping in exogloves, direct literature comparisons were limited. To support community reproducibility, we will publicly release our object dataset.

Lastly, acknowledging the limitation of testing solely with healthy participants, subsequent studies will involve clinical populations to better evaluate therapeutic and assistive effectiveness. Integration with digital self-management tools for neurodegenerative disorder patients also represents an important future research direction.

6 Conclusion

As the importance of exogloves for assisting individuals with neurodegenarative disorders in completing daily activities tasks continues to grow, the design and development of soft exogloves with intuitive, user-friendly interaction to effectively support transparent object grasping remains an open challenge. This paper presents a multimodal framework *MultiClear* designed to improve the efficiency of grasping transparent objects by combining RGB, depth, and auditory modalities. The framework is embedded into a soft exoglove that bridges the gap between high-level contextual awareness and low-level PID control. Experimental results show that the proposed exoglove achieves a GAS of 70.37±3.96%, illustrating the possible effectiveness of zero-shot segmentation for transparent objects using a vision foundation model based on dichotomous segmentation. Future work aims to explore whether integrating depth completion into the *MultiClear* framework can further enhance the accuracy of assistive grasping in individuals with motor disorders, testing the system's effectiveness on post-stroke survivors for instance, refining both the design and functionality to better support daily tasks.

References

1. Vosk - github. https://github.com/alphacep/vosk-api
2. Alicea, R., Xiloyannis, M., Chiaradia, D., Barsotti, M., Frisoli, A., Masia, L.: A soft, synergy-based robotic glove for grasping assistance. Wearable Technologies **2**, e4 (2021)
3. Baselli, C., Missiroli, F.E.A.: Tendon-driven haptic glove for force feedback tele-manipulation. IEEE RAS/EMBS Biomed. Robot. Biomechatronics **10**, 1043–1050 (2024)
4. Coyle, S., Majidi, C., LeDuc, P., Hsia, K.J.: Bio-inspired soft robotics: material selection, actuation, and design. Extreme Mech. Lett. **22**, 51–59 (2018)
5. Cutkosky, M.R.: On grasp choice, grasp models, and the design of hands for manufacturing tasks. IEEE Trans. Robot. Autom. **5**(3), 269–279 (1989). https://doi.org/10.1109/70.34763
6. Du Plessis, T., Djouani, K., Oosthuizen, C.: A review of active hand exoskeletons for rehabilitation and assistance. Robotics **10**(1), 40 (2021)
7. Duisterhof, B.P., Mao, Y., Teng, S.H., Ichnowski, J.: Residual-nerf: learning residual nerfs for transparent object manipulation. In: 2024 IEEE International Conference on Robotics and Automation (ICRA), pp. 13918–13924. IEEE (2024)
8. Feix, T., Romero, J., Schmiedmayer, H.B., Dollar, A.M., Kragic, D.: The grasp taxonomy of human grasp types. IEEE Trans. Hum.-Mach. Syst. **46**(1), 66–77 (2016). https://doi.org/10.1109/THMS.2015.2470657
9. Gionfrida, L., Kim, D., Scaramuzza, D., Farina, D., Howe, R.D.: Wearable robots for the real world need vision. Sci. Robot. **9**(90), eadj8812 (2024)
10. Hochreiter, S., Schmidhuber, J.: Long short-term memory. Neural Comput. **9**(8), 1735–1780 (1997)
11. Hu, C., et al.: Point cloud-based grasping for soft hand exoskeleton (2025). https://arxiv.org/abs/2504.03369
12. Huang, Z., et al.: Learning with noisy correspondence for cross-modal matching. Adv. Neural Inf. Process. Syst. **34**, 29406–29419 (2021)
13. Jiang, J., Cao, G., Deng, J., Do, T.T., Luo, S.: Robotic perception of transparent objects: a review. IEEE Trans. Artif. Intell. (2023)
14. Kim, D., et al.: Eyes are faster than hands: a soft wearable robot learns user intention from the egocentric view. Sci. Robot. **4**(26), eaav2949 (2019)
15. Kirillov, A., et al.: Segment anything. arXiv:2304.02643 (2023)
16. Llop-Harillo, I., Pérez-González, A., Starke, J., Asfour, T.: The anthropomorphic hand assessment protocol (AHAP). Robot. Auton. Syst. **121**, 103259 (2019)
17. Lotti, N., et al.: Intention-detection strategies for upper limb exosuits: model-based myoelectric vs dynamic-based control. In: IEEE International Conference on Biomedical Robotics and Biomechatronics (BioRob), pp. 410–417 (2020)
18. Maldonado-Mejía, J.C., et al.: A fabric-based soft hand exoskeleton for assistance: the exhand exoskeleton. Front. Neurorobot. **17**, 1091827 (2023)

19. Missiroli, F., et al.: Integrating computer vision in exosuits for adaptive support and reduced muscle strain in industrial environments. IEEE Robot. Autom. Lett. (2023)
20. Pearson, K.: On lines and planes of closest fit to systems of points in space. Lond. Edinb. Dublin Philos. Mag. J. Sci. **2**(11), 559–572 (1901). https://doi.org/10.1080/14786440109462720
21. Peng, X., Wei, Y., Deng, A., Wang, D., Hu, D.: Balanced multimodal learning via on-the-fly gradient modulation. In: Proceedings of the IEEE/CVF Conference on Computer Vision and Pattern Recognition, pp. 8238–8247 (2022)
22. Polygerinos, P., et al.: Soft robotic glove for combined assistance and at-home rehabilitation. Robot. Auton. Syst. **73**, 135–143 (2015)
23. Qin, X., Dai, H., Hu, X., Fan, D.P., Shao, L., Van Gool, L.: Highly accurate dichotomous image segmentation. In: European Conference on Computer Vision, pp. 38–56. Springer (2022)
24. Raghavan, P.: The nature of hand motor impairment after stroke and its treatment. Curr. Treat. Options Cardiovasc. Med. **9**(3), 221–228 (2007)
25. Rho, E., Kim, D., Lee, H., Jo, S.: Learning fingertip force to grasp deformable objects for soft wearable robotic glove with tsm. IEEE Robot. Autom. Lett. **6**(4), 8126–8133 (2021)
26. Rho, E., et al.: Multiple hand posture rehabilitation system using vision-based intention detection and soft-robotic glove. IEEE Trans. Ind. Inform. (2024)
27. Sajjan, S., et al.: Clear grasp: 3d shape estimation of transparent objects for manipulation. In: 2020 IEEE International Conference on Robotics and Automation (ICRA), pp. 3634–3642. IEEE (2020)
28. Sierotowicz, M., et al.: Emg-driven machine learning control of a soft glove for grasping assistance and rehabilitation. IEEE Robot. Autom. Lett. **7**(2), 1566–1573 (2022)
29. Silver, S., et al.: Peripheral nerve entrapment and injury in the upper extremity. Am. Family Physician **103**(5), 275–285 (2021). https://www.aafp.org/pubs/afp/issues/2021/0301/p275.html
30. Smaby, N., et al.: Identification of key pinch forces required to complete functional tasks. J. Rehabil. Res. Dev. **41**(2) (2004)
31. Sun, T., Hu, D., Dai, Y., Wang, G.: Diffusion-based depth inpainting for transparent and reflective objects. IEEE Trans. Circuits Syst. Video Technol. (2024)
32. Tang, Y., Chen, J., Yang, Z., Lin, Z., Li, Q., Liu, W.: Depthgrasp: depth completion of transparent objects using self-attentive adversarial network with spectral residual for grasping. In: 2021 IEEE/RSJ International Conference on Intelligent Robots and Systems (IROS), pp. 5710–5716. IEEE (2021)
33. Tran, P., et al.: Flexotendon glove-iii: voice-controlled soft robotic hand exoskeleton with novel fabrication method and admittance grasping control. IEEE/ASME Trans. Mechatron. **27**(5), 3920–3931 (2022)
34. Tricomi, E., et al.: Environment-based assistance modulation for a hip exosuit via computer vision. IEEE Robot. Autom. Lett. **8**(5), 2550–2557 (2023)
35. Triwiyanto, T., et al.: A review on robotic hand exoskeleton devices: state-of-the-art method. In: Proceedings of the 1st International Conference on Electronics, Biomedical Engineering, and Health Informatics: ICEBEHI 2020, 8-9 October, Surabaya, Indonesia, pp. 331–341. Springer (2021)
36. Waibel, A., Hanazawa, T., Hinton, G., Shikano, K., Lang, K.J.: Phoneme recognition using time-delay neural networks. In: Backpropagation, pp. 35–61. Psychology Press (2013)

37. Xu, B., et al.: Different data, different modalities! Reinforced data splitting for effective multimodal information extraction from social media posts. In: Proceedings of the 29th International Conference on Computational Linguistics, pp. 1855–1864 (2022)
38. Yurkewich, A., Ortega, S., Sanchez, J., Wang, R.H., Burdet, E.: Integrating hand exoskeletons into goal-oriented clinic and home stroke and spinal cord injury rehabilitation. J. Rehabil. Assist. Technol. Eng. **9**, 20556683221130970 (2022)
39. Zhang, Q., et al.: Multimodal fusion on low-quality data: a comprehensive survey. arXiv preprint arXiv:2404.18947 (2024)

Towards Accurate Shape Prediction for Compact Spring Backbone Tendon-Driven Continuum Robots

Burak Ozdemir$^{(\boxtimes)}$ (ID), Pietro Valdastri (ID), and James H. Chandler (ID)

Science and Technologies of Robotics in Medicine Laboratory, School of Electronic and Electrical Engineering, Faculty of Engineering and Physical Sciences, University of Leeds, Leeds, UK
ml20bo@leeds.ac.uk

Abstract. Continuum robots deliver exceptional dexterity and adaptability in confined environments, making them highly suitable for tasks such as minimally invasive surgery and inspection. Among various configurations, tendon-driven designs represent a common approach that relies on an elastic backbone and one or more drive tendons. Utilising springs for the backbone element offers specific design advantages, including wide availability, tuneable mechanical properties, and an open central channel. However, this approach increases axial compliance, leading to reduced actuation efficiency, increased tendon friction, and a reduction in the validity of common model assumptions. This paper considers the applicability of two modelling approaches to a compact spring backbone tendon-driven continuum robot design. Specific comparison is made between a geometric model based on the constant curvature assumption and a force-based analytical elastic model that considers axial compression and tendon friction under actuation loading. Experimental validation via a single-tendon prototype indicates that, while the geometric model offers simplicity and can be optimised for predicting tip position (mean error of 2.4 mm), large discrepancies exist when predicting the full shape of the robot (RMSE of 9.3 mm). Conversely, the analytic model achieves substantially improved accuracy for both tip (mean error of 1.4 mm) and shape (RMSE of 5.3 mm), and may offer an improved model for informing design and control of this class of continuum robot.

Keywords: Continuum Robots · Tendon-Driven Manipulators · Constant Curvature · Force-Based Modelling · Experimental Validation

1 Introduction

Continuum robots (CR) are an established class of robots that offer exceptional dexterity and adaptability, enabling them to navigate confined or cluttered environments [1,2]. Although several actuation approaches have been proposed for CRs, tendon-driven continuum robots (TDCRs) have attracted considerable

© The Author(s), under exclusive license to Springer Nature Switzerland AG 2026
A. Cavalcanti et al. (Eds.): TAROS 2025, LNAI 16045, pp. 210–222, 2026.
https://doi.org/10.1007/978-3-032-01486-3_17

interest [3]. This is in part due to their potential for compact designs, simple drive mechanisms, and relatively high output forces [4]. These characteristics make TDCRs well-suited for a range of applications, from endoscopic surgery [5] to complex industrial manipulation [6].

In general, TDCRs are designed to facilitate continuous bending by employing a soft or compliant backbone and routing drive tendons through the robot's body to a distal termination point. If the backbone behaves as an ideal elastic inextensible rod, and tendons retain precise routing and low friction, the robot (or robot segment) may form constant radius curves under actuation [7]. However, limitations imposed by material selection and interaction, component fabrication methods, and assembly processes often move designs away from these ideal characteristics [3]. This can also be exacerbated when meeting additional application-specific requirements such as a small diameter, a specific stiffness, or functional component integration [8].

If the assumption of constant radius bending is valid, geometric models allow the robot (or robot segment) to be treated as a circular arc [9]. The geometric *constant curvature* model is extensively used in continuum robotics as it considerably simplifies the kinematics, allowing robot-specific mappings to be readily derived to relate tendon lengths to arc parameters and robot end-effector poses. However, model simplifications do not directly accommodate aspects such as tendon friction or backbone compression/extension/torsion [7].

In contrast, force-based analytical models can explicitly account for tendon tension, compression, frictional losses, and backbone elasticity to represent the manipulator more accurately and facilitate design optimisation [10,11]. Although these models usually require more parameters and detailed calibration, they promise greater precision in predicting robot shape and end-effector pose under actuation loading. In addition, Cosserat-rod models [12] have emerged as a powerful alternative framework in continuum robotics. These models treat the robot as a continuous elastic rod, capturing complex deformations such as bending, torsion, shear, and axial extension, although at the cost of increased computational complexity [13]. Together, force-based analytical models and Cosserat-rod models provide complementary insights into the robot's behaviour, with the choice of model typically reflecting a trade-off between computational tractability and the level of fidelity required.

In the presented work, we focus on model development and validation for a compact single tendon spring backbone TDCR. Utilising spring elements for the TDCR's backbone can deliver efficient assembly, extension/compression and provide an open central channel [14–16]. However, this design approach introduces high axial compliance and increased tendon friction. We evaluate the impact of these factors on the robot's bending performance, and develop and compare two modelling paradigms to estimate the tip pose and body shape of this type of TDCR.

The remainder of the paper is organised as follows. Section 2 introduces the general TDCR design. Section 3 describes the two modelling approaches applied to the TDCR design. Section 4 outlines the experimental setup and data capture.

Section 5 presents the experimental results and discussion, and Sect. 6 concludes the paper with suggestions for future work.

2   Spring Backbone TDCR Design Architecture

As shown in Fig. 1, we consider a TDCR design comprised of a spring backbone and evenly spaced tendon routing discs. The TDCR has a total length of 110 mm with a 1.6 mm tendon offset, a helical steel spring backbone, and a series of continuum discs spaced evenly at 10 mm intervals. The spacer discs provide structural support and guide tendons from the actuation unit at the robot's proximal end to anchor points at its distal tip. While the current design employs a single tendon for in-plane deflection, additional tendons may be readily integrated around the central axis to achieve three-dimensional bending.

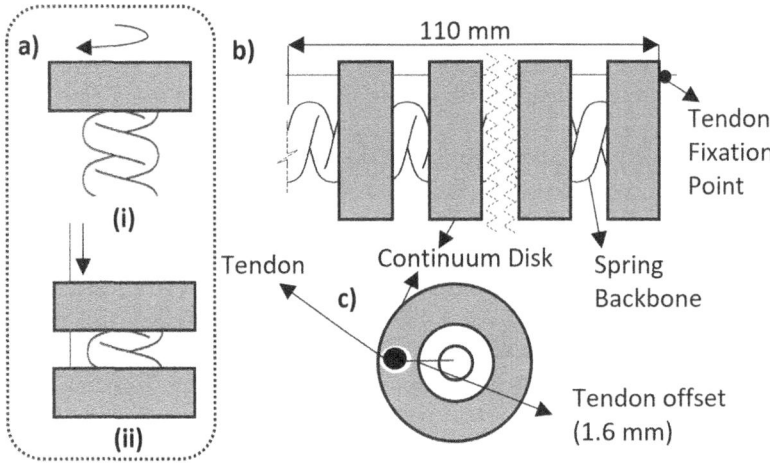

Fig. 1. Schematic view of the spring backbone TDCR design, showing: (a) Assembly steps: (i) rotating the disc onto the spring and (ii) threading the tendon through the disc channel, (b) side view, and (c) top view, with main structural components and dimensions indicated.

3   Modelling Approach

Modelling the TDCR aims to allow prediction of the static tip position and body shape during tendon actuation. Two distinct modelling approaches are considered to understand their suitability to this type of TDCR. We first consider the common geometric approach that assumes that the robot can be approximated as bending with constant curvature [9]. We consider possible parameter adaptation to this model that may allow for errors in tendon displacements (e.g., tendon slack, lateral movement and/or elongation [8]) to be accounted for. The second approach employs a force-based analytical elastic model to account for applied tendon force, tendon friction, and axial compression.

3.1 Modelling Under Constant Curvature

The constant curvature (CC) model approximates the bending of a continuum robot (or robot segment) as a circular arc [7]. Here, we describe the model for general co-planar tendon configurations, as seen in Fig. 2, as well as for our simplified single-tendon manipulator.

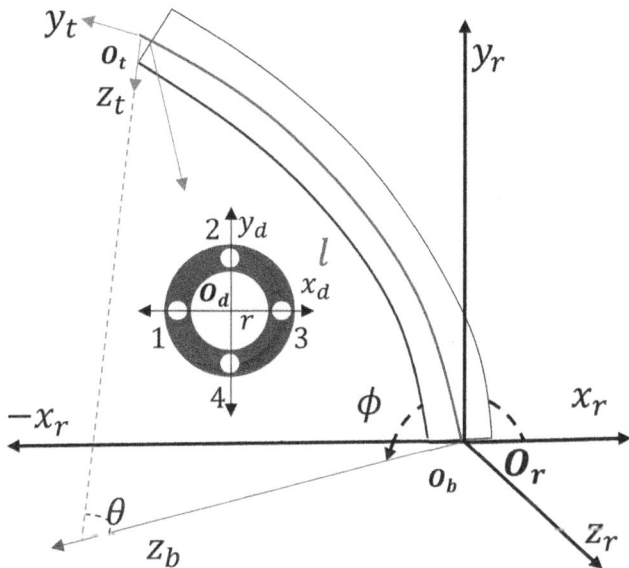

Fig. 2. Illustration of the coordinate systems applied to the manipulator. The reference frame (O_r) is fixed at the base, while the disc frame (O_d) is defined on each disc to represent tendon alignment. The bending plane frame (O_b) represents the fixed bending plane, which remains constant due to the single-tendon actuation (set at $\phi = \pi$ based on the frame convention shown). The end-effector frame (O_t) is located at the tip, defining its position and orientation.

In the basic CC model, the configuration of the manipulator is characterised by three key parameters: the curvature of the arc, k, the arc length, l, and the angle of the bending plane, ϕ. Additionally, a fixed radial distance r from the disc centres to the tendon is assumed to be 1.6 mm for the given design. For a system with four symmetrically arranged tendons, the length of the ith tendon is given by

$$l_i = l + \Delta l_i, \quad i = 1, 2, 3, 4, \tag{1}$$

with the tendon length change due to bending expressed as

$$\Delta l_i = -r\,\theta \left[\cos\left(\phi_i - \phi\right)\right], \tag{2}$$

where ϕ_i are the fixed angular positions of the tendon holes (e.g., $0°$, $90°$, $180°$, and $270°$ for two coplanar tendon pairs).

Equation (2) represents the forward relation from bending angle to individual tendon length change, however, the inverse mapping from input Δl to θ can also be considered. In the presented experiments, we employ a single-tendon actuation strategy (tendon 1 as seen in Fig. 2), which induces bending in the x_r–y_r plane, as defined by our reference coordinate system (x_r, y_r, z_r). The arc curvature corresponding to a given tendon displacement Δl_1 is then determined as

$$k = \frac{\Delta l_1}{l\,r}. \tag{3}$$

Optimised Constant Curvature Model. Although the basic CC model provides a straightforward mapping from tendon displacements to the robot's configuration, its predictive accuracy may be limited by the assumption of a fixed nominal arc length l. In practice, factors such as tendon slack, tendon extension, and material compliance can cause deviations from the ideal circular arc, meaning that the measured tendon displacement may not correspond directly to the motion of the actuator. To address these discrepancies, we introduce an optimisation procedure that adjusts the effective arc length, denoted l_{opt}, and accounts for tendon loss— defined as the difference between the actuator displacement and the effective tendon displacement.

In the *Optimised Constant Curvature Model*, we compute the effective curvature as

$$k_{\mathrm{eff}} = f(l_{\mathrm{opt}}, \Delta l_{\mathrm{opt}}), \tag{4}$$

where l_{opt} is the optimised (effective) arc length and Δl_{opt} represents the effective tendon displacement optimised for each configuration. The function $f(l_{\mathrm{opt}}, \Delta l_{\mathrm{opt}})$ maps these parameters to the effective curvature, thereby accounting for variations in both the arc length and tendon loss.

Assuming the bending plane is fixed at $\phi = 180°$, the homogeneous transformation matrix simplifies to:

$$T(k_{\mathrm{eff}}, l_{\mathrm{opt}}, \theta) = \begin{bmatrix} -\cos\theta & \sin\theta & 0 & 0 \\ \sin\theta & \cos\theta & 0 & -\dfrac{1}{k_{\mathrm{eff}}}\left(1 - \cos\left(k_{\mathrm{eff}} l_{\mathrm{opt}}\right)\right) \\ 0 & 0 & -1 & \dfrac{1}{k_{\mathrm{eff}}}\sin\left(k_{\mathrm{eff}} l_{\mathrm{opt}}\right) \\ 0 & 0 & 0 & 1 \end{bmatrix}, \tag{5}$$

so that the tip position is given by

$$\begin{bmatrix} x_t \\ y_t \\ z_t \\ 1 \end{bmatrix} = T(k_{\mathrm{eff}}, l_{\mathrm{opt}}) \begin{bmatrix} 0 \\ 0 \\ 0 \\ 1 \end{bmatrix}. \tag{6}$$

This optimisation approach effectively evaluates the best-fit model under the assumption of CC, compensating for both deviations in the arc length and tendon loss.

3.2   Analytical Elastic Model

In contrast to the purely geometric approach, the force-based analytical model explicitly accounts for the physical effects of tendon actuation, friction, and axial compression [10]. In this formulation, the continuum robot is discretised into N segments of nominal length Δs. For our system, $\Delta s = 5\,\text{mm}$ and the total nominal length is $110\,\text{mm}$ (i.e., $N = 22$).

Let F_a denote the force applied to the tendon. Due to friction along the tendon path, the force transmitted to the jth segment is reduced according to:

$$F_{\text{eff},j} = F_\text{a} - (j-1)\Delta F, \tag{7}$$

where $\Delta F = F_{\text{f,total}}/N$ is the friction loss per segment. Given a fixed tendon offset r, the bending moment at the jth segment is

$$M_j = r\, F_{\text{eff},j}. \tag{8}$$

Assuming the backbone behaves as a linear elastic beam, the bending increment (in radians) for a segment is computed by:

$$\Delta\psi_j = \frac{\Delta s}{E_\text{bend}\, I}\, M_j, \tag{9}$$

where E_bend and I are the effective Young's modulus for bending and the second moment of area, respectively. The bending stiffness factor is thus defined as:

$$k_\text{bend} = \frac{\Delta s}{E_\text{bend}\, I}.$$

In addition, axial compression is considered by defining the axial stiffness

$$K_\text{axial} = E_\text{axial}\, A, \tag{10}$$

with E_axial as the Young's modulus in axial compression and A as the cross-sectional area. The axial shrinkage in the jth segment is:

$$\Delta s_{c,j} = \frac{\Delta s}{E_\text{axial}\, A}\, \left(\mathbf{z}_j^\top \mathbf{f}_j\right), \tag{11}$$

where $\mathbf{f}_j = F_{\text{eff},j}\, \mathbf{n}_j$ (with $\mathbf{n}_j$ representing the tendon force direction) and $\mathbf{z}_j$ is the local tangent direction. The effective segment length is then:

$$\Delta s_{\text{eff},j} = \Delta s + \Delta s_{c,j}. \tag{12}$$

Starting from a fixed base position $\mathbf{p}_1 = [0\,0\,0]^T$ and an initial orientation R_1, the position of the $(j+1)$th node is updated recursively by

$$\mathbf{p}_{j+1} = \mathbf{p}_j + R_j\, \Delta s_{\text{eff},j}\, \mathbf{e}_z,$$

where $\mathbf{e}_z = [0\,0\,1]^T$ is the nominal backbone direction. The orientation is updated according to

$$R_{j+1} = R_j\,\Delta R_j,$$

with ΔR_j being the incremental rotation matrix corresponding to a rotation of $\Delta\psi_j$ about the appropriate local axis. This incremental rotation is applied at each step to capture the bending of the robot.

Table 1 summarises the key system parameters used in the force-based analytical model.

Table 1. System Parameters for the Force-Based Analytical Model

Variable	Parameter	Value
L	Overall nominal length	110 mm
Δs	Nominal segment length	5 mm
N	Number of segments	22
E_{bend}	Young's modulus (bending)	50×10^3 Pa
I	Second moment of area	$7.85 \times 10^{-9}\,\text{m}^4$
k_{bend}	Bending stiffness factor	$\Delta s/(E_{\text{bend}}\,I)$
A	Cross-sectional area	$1.314\text{E}{-}3\,\text{m}^2$
E_{axial}	Young's modulus (axial)	120×10^3 Pa
K_{axial}	Axial stiffness	$157.68\,\text{N/m}$
r	Tendon offset	1.6 mm
t_d	Tendon diameter	0.2 mm

4   Experimental Setup

To evaluate the bending behaviour of our spring backbone TDCR, a miniature linear actuator (L12, Actuonix Motion Devices Inc.) with 100 mm of travel and integrated positional feedback was connected to the drive tendon (Fig. 3). The actuator was connected to a power supply and its position was controlled and measured via a data acquisition system (cDAQ, National Instruments). A high-speed camera (Basler aCA2040-120um) was used to image the shape and tip pose of the robot during actuation. The camera setup provided sub-millimetre resolution through close-range imaging, high pixel density (2048×1536), and in-plane scale calibration using reference markers. Based on the pixel-to-length ratio derived from the calibration, the system enabled reliable error measurements on the order of 0.1 mm.

Starting from an unactuated configuration (0 mm tendon displacement, no slack), the tendon was successively shortened to target absolute displacements of 6, 8, 10, 12, 14, and 16 mm (based on the CC model and robot's geometry, these correspond to predicted bending angles (θ) of between $20°$ and $180°$). For each

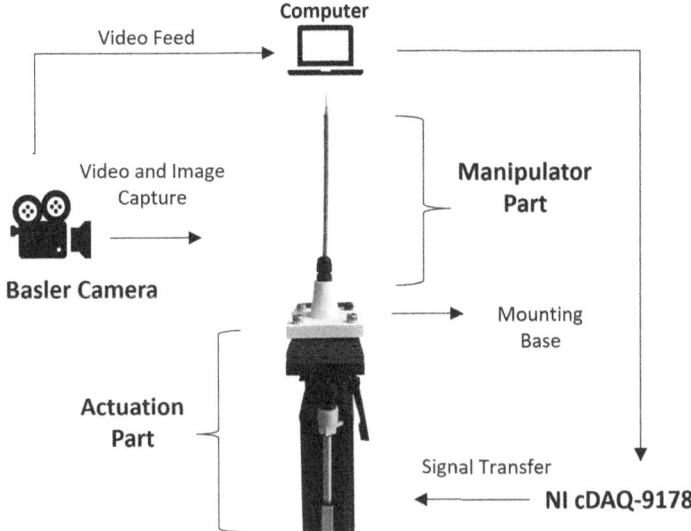

Fig. 3. The experimental setup includes a manipulator and actuator system, a Basler camera for real-time motion capture, NI cDAQ-9178 for data acquisition, and a computer running LabVIEW, ImageJ, and MATLAB for signal control and data analysis.

displacement, three repeat trials were conducted. For each actuated configuration, the linear displacement was captured via the integrated position transducer and the robot's deformation was captured via the camera. For each tendon displacement, the disc centre positions were extracted using image segmentation and averaged over the three trials for comparison with the proposed models. The corresponding estimated applied force (F_a) and total tendon friction (F_f) values were obtained by fitting Model-2 to the experimental data over the full shape profile using MATLAB's curve fitting toolbox.

5   Results and Discussion

Experimentally captured data were evaluated against three model configurations: (1) the basic CC model (Model 1), (2) the optimised CC model (Optimised Model 1), and (3) the force-based analytical elastic model (Model 2). In the following sections, we first compare the tip positions (defined by the position of the most distal disc) for each tendon displacement. We then compare the full manipulator shapes (defined by the positions of 10 discs along the robot's length).

5.1   End-Tip Comparison

Figure 4 shows the end-tip positions for each tendon displacement. Model 1 (Fig. 4(a)) over predicts the bending angle and thus tip positions, while the

Optimised Model 1 demonstrates a significant improvement in end-tip prediction by allowing length and effective tendon displacement to vary. The end-tip positions predicted by Model 2 (Fig. 4 (b)) further improve the agreement with the experimental data, showing minimal deviation across all displacement levels. This comparison underscores that, while optimising the geometric model can enhance tip prediction, the comprehensive inclusion of physical effects in Model 2 more reliably captures the robot's tip position.

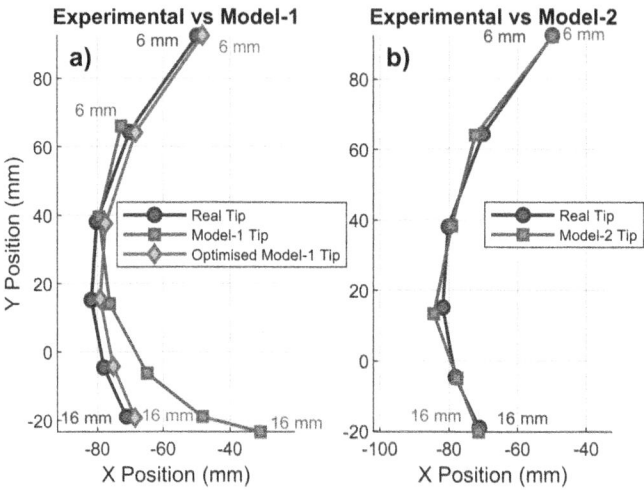

Fig. 4. End-tip position comparisons for tendon displacements of 6–16 mm. **a)** Experimentally measured end-tip positions ("Real Tip (Experimental Result)") are compared with predictions from the basic CC model ("Model 1 Tip") and the optimised CC model ("Optimised Model 1 Tip"). **b)** The force-based model ("Model 2 Tip") predictions are contrasted with the experimental data, demonstrating the model's accuracy in capturing the end-tip location.

5.2   Full Curve Comparison

Figure 5 compares the full manipulator shapes determined experimentally with the predictions of Model 1 and Optimised Model 1 for the discrete tendon displacements evaluated. As with the tip position, Model 1 over predicts bending causing significant deviation from the robot's real shape. The Optimised Model 1 achieves improved shape approximation, however, some discrepancies remain, indicating the unsuitability of the CC assumption for shape estimation of the robot design.

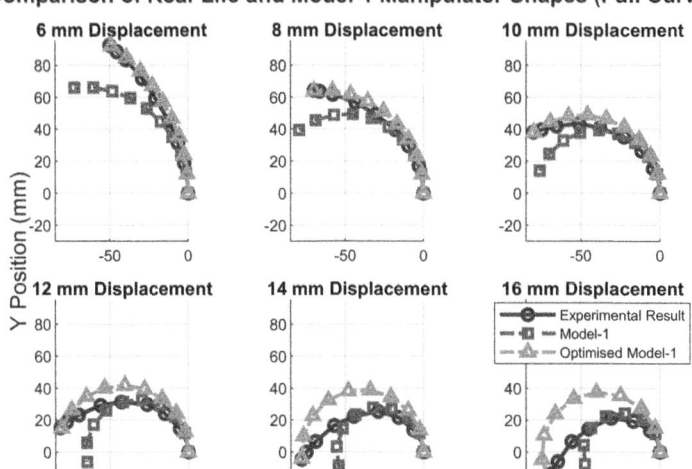

Fig. 5. Full curve comparison between the experimental manipulator shape and the predictions of the two geometric models. The plot shows the positions of 10 discs along the continuum robot for tendon displacements ranging from 6 mm to 16 mm.

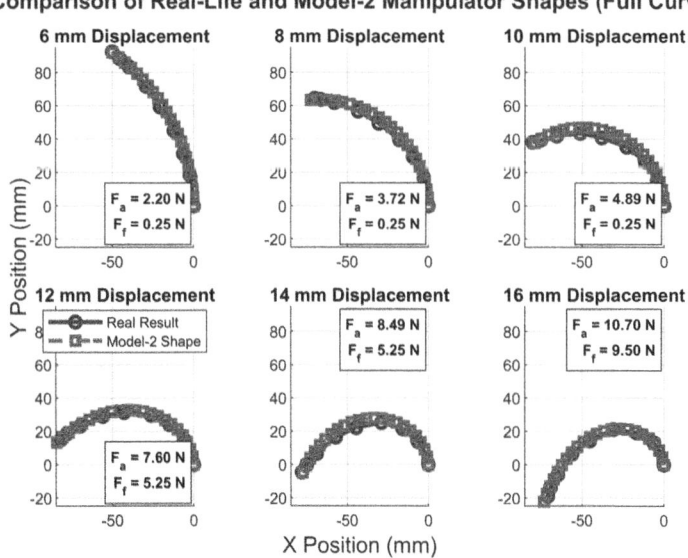

Fig. 6. Full curve comparison between Model 2 and the experimental results. The plot shows the entire manipulator shape across tendon displacements of 6–16 mm, with estimated Applied Force (F_a) and Tendon Friction (F_f) values indicated in each subplot.

Figure 6 shows Model 2 results, which produce a close approximation of the full shape of the robot. The inclusion of backbone compression and tendon friction within Model 2 allows the non-constant curves formed under experimental actuation to be closely approximated.

5.3   RMS Error Analysis

To evaluate the shape prediction accuracy of the three modelling approaches, we computed the root mean square error (RMSE) between the model-predicted and experimentally measured disc positions in the 2D xy-plane over all 10 discs:

$$\text{RMSE} = \sqrt{\frac{1}{N} \sum_{i=1}^{N} \left\| \mathbf{p}_i^{\text{exp}} - \mathbf{p}_i^{\text{model}} \right\|^2} \tag{13}$$

where $\mathbf{p}_i^{\text{exp}}$ and $\mathbf{p}_i^{\text{model}}$ denote the 2D (x, y) coordinates of disc i, and $N = 10$. Figure 7 shows that Model 2 consistently exhibits the lowest RMS error, demonstrating its superior accuracy in replicating the robot's shape. Additionally, the Optimised Model 1 substantially reduces the RMS error compared to the basic Model 1, though some full-curve discrepancies persist.

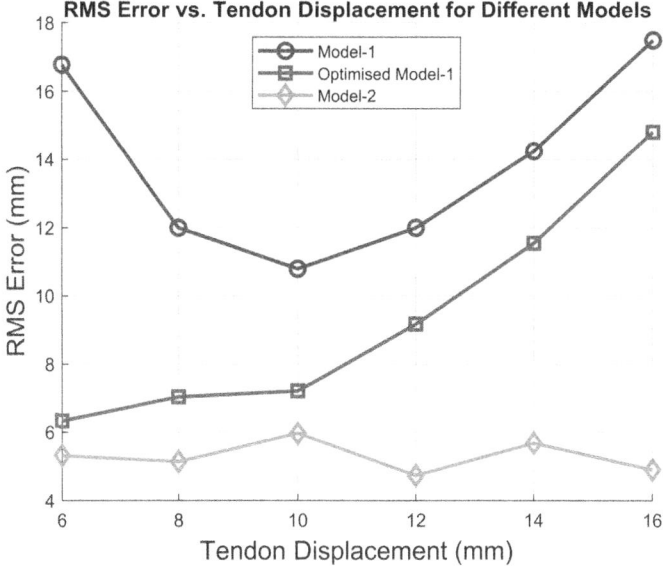

Fig. 7. RMS error comparison for the three modelling approaches (Model-1, Optimised Model-1, Model-2) across tendon displacements from 6 mm to 16 mm. The RMS error, computed as the root mean square of the Euclidean distances between the predicted and experimental disc coordinates (for all 10 discs), demonstrates that Model 2 consistently yields lower error values, indicating its superior predictive accuracy over the other approaches.

Overall, our results indicate that while the CC model provides a simple and computationally efficient mapping from tendon displacement to robot configuration, its accuracy is limited. Refinement through compensating parameters (Optimised Model 1) markedly improves tip prediction (mean tip error of 2.4 mm); however, it still exhibits high errors in capturing the full manipulator shape (mean RMSE of 9.3 mm). In contrast, by explicitly incorporating the effects of tendon actuation, friction, and axial compression, the force-based analytical model (Model 2) captures nonlinear behaviour and delivers a detailed prediction of the continuum robot's configuration. This model reliably estimates both the end-tip position (mean tip error of 1.4 mm) and the overall shape, achieving a mean RMSE of 5.3 mm over all tendon displacements. These findings suggest that although geometric models offer computational simplicity, the force-based approach is better suited for applications requiring high shape accuracy, such as those within delicate environments.

6   Conclusion

In this study, we present a comparative evaluation of two modelling approaches for a spring backbone TDCR. As the axial compression and tendon friction are appreciable within this type of design, we consider the suitability of the commonly employed CC assumption. Although the modification of the actuator mapping and the configuration parameters improves agreement, the resultant robot shape is poorly captured via the necessary assumptions. Conversely, the proposed force-based analytical elastic model allows for the impacts of tendon tension, friction and compressive effects to be accounted for, delivering improved shape predictions. Future work will extend the application of this model through direct tendon load measurements and experimental parameter calibrations and will consider multi-tendon actuation for three-dimensional motion. We also aim to integrate this model into a real-time feedback control loop to enhance its applicability in dynamic and practical settings. Consideration of the physical phenomena within non-ideal TDCR designs, such as those proposed here, is critical for enhancing design and control accuracy.

Acknowledgments. This work was supported in part by the Engineering and Physical Sciences Research Council (EPSRC) under grants EP/Y037235/1, EP/V047914/1, and EP/V009818/1; the European Research Council (ERC) through the European Union's Horizon 2020 Research and Innovation Programme under grant 818045; and the National Institute for Health and Care Research (NIHR) Leeds Biomedical Research Centre (BRC) (NIHR203331). Any opinions, findings, and conclusions or recommendations expressed in this article are those of the authors and do not necessarily reflect the views of the EPSRC, the ERC or the NIHR. B. Ozdemir was also supported by a scholarship from the Turkish Ministry of National Education, Republic of Turkiye.

References

1. da Veiga, T., et al.: Challenges of continuum robots in clinical context: a review. Progress Biomed. Eng. **2**(3), 032003 (2020)
2. Burgner-Kahrs, J., Rucker, D.C., Choset, H.: Continuum robots for medical applications: a survey. IEEE Trans. Robot. **31**(6), 1261–1280 (2015)
3. Russo, M., et al.: Continuum robots: an overview. Adv. Intell. Syst. **5**(5), 2200367 (2023)
4. Nguyen, T.D., Burgner-Kahrs, J.: A tendon-driven continuum robot with extensible sections. In: 2015 IEEE/RSJ International Conference on Intelligent Robots and Systems (IROS), pp. 2130–2135. IEEE, 2015
5. Kato, T., Okumura, I., Song, S.E., Golby, A.J., Hata, N.: Tendon-driven continuum robot for endoscopic surgery: preclinical development and validation of a tension propagation model. IEEE/ASME Trans. Mechatron. **20**(5), 2252–2263 (2014)
6. Uthayasooriyan, A., Vanegas, F., Jalali, A., Digumarti, K.M., Janabi-Sharifi, F., Gonzalez, F.: Tendon-driven continuum robots for aerial manipulation—a survey of fabrication methods. Drones **8**(6), 269 (2024)
7. Rao, P., Peyron, Q., Lilge, S., Burgner-Kahrs, J.: How to model tendon-driven continuum robots and benchmark modelling performance. Front. Robot. AI **7**, 630245 (2021)
8. Amanov, E., Nguyen, T.-D., Burgner-Kahrs, J.: Tendon-driven continuum robots with extensible sections–a model-based evaluation of path-following motions. Int. J. Robot. Res. **40**(1), 7–23 (2021)
9. Webster III, R.J., Jones, B.A.: Design and kinematic modeling of constant curvature continuum robots: a review. Int. J. Robot. Res. **29**(13), 1661–1683 (2010)
10. Zhang, J., Simaan, N.: Design of underactuated steerable electrode arrays for optimal insertions. J. Mech. Robot. **5**(1), 011008 (2013)
11. Thuillier, A., Krut, S., Zemiti, N., Poignet, P.: Optimal bending stiffness design of a soft micro-robot for cochlear implantation. In: 2024 IEEE 7th International Conference on Soft Robotics (RoboSoft), pp. 492–497. IEEE, 2024
12. Till, J., Aloi, V., Rucker, C.: Real-time dynamics of soft and continuum robots based on cosserat rod models. Int. J. Robot. Res. **38**(6), 723–746 (2019)
13. Janabi-Sharifi, F., Jalali, A., Walker, I.D.: Cosserat rod-based dynamic modeling of tendon-driven continuum robots: a tutorial. IEEE Access **9**, 68703–68719 (2021)
14. Kim, Y., Cheng, S.S., Diakite, M., Gullapalli, R.P., Simard, J.M., Desai, J.P.: Toward the development of a flexible mesoscale mri-compatible neurosurgical continuum robot. IEEE Trans. Robot. **33**(6), 1386–1397 (2017)
15. Li, M., Kang, R., Geng, S., Guglielmino, E.: Design and control of a tendon-driven continuum robot. Trans. Inst. Meas. Control. **40**(11), 3263–3272 (2018)
16. Garbin, N., Wang, L., Chandler, J.H., Obstein, K.L., Simaan, N., Valdastri, P.: Dual-continuum design approach for intuitive and low-cost upper gastrointestinal endoscopy. IEEE Trans. Biomed. Eng. **66**(7), 1963–1974 (2019)

Locomotion of Multi Arm Robot for In-Orbit Operations (MARIO) in Lab Environment

Praveen Elavazhagan$^{(\boxtimes)}$ ⓘ, Cameron Leslie ⓘ, Saurabh Upadhyay ⓘ, Gilbert Tang ⓘ, and Leonard Felicetti ⓘ

Faculty of Engineering and Applied Sciences, Cranfield University, College Rd, Wharley End, Bedford MK43 0AL, UK
{Praveen.Elavazhagan.489,Cameron.Leslie,Saurabh.Upadhyay,g.tang, Leonard.Felicetti}@cranfield.ac.uk
https://www.cranfield.ac.uk/

Abstract. This paper presents the control architecture and experimental validation of MARIO, a multi-arm robotic platform developed by Cranfield University for In-Orbit Servicing and Manufacturing (IOSM) task demonstration in a laboratory environment. MARIO comprises three ROS-enabled, 6-degree-of-freedom robotic arms with a 5 kg payload capacity, mounted on a pneumatic air-bearing platform that enables near-frictionless planar movement over an epoxy floor. Each arm is equipped with onboard cameras and end-effectors to perform locomotion, assembly, and manipulation tasks with high precision. The developed ROS2-based control framework integrates a multi-layered architecture, combining a collision-free trajectory planner, synchronized multi-arm coordination, and hardware-level execution for smooth and accurate motion. The platform is experimentally validated in the laboratory through arm-based locomotion and coordinated base-arm movements using standard interfaces. The resulting control architecture can be used as the foundation for developing a common framework of the multi-arm robot in orbital application.

Keywords: Space Robotics · Control framework · Multi-Arm Robot · Assembly · Locomotion · ROS2 · IOSM

1 Introduction

Multi-arm space robotics have gained prominence in In-orbit Servicing, Assembly and Manufacturing (ISAM) due to their dexterity and capability to perform complex tasks [1]. These robotic systems enable precise manipulation, making them suitable for applications such as satellite servicing, space station maintenance, and large-scale assembly [2]. The advantages of multi-arm robots over traditional single-arm systems include redundancy, improved payload handling, and the ability to execute coordinated motions [3].

A. Cavalcanti et al. (Eds.): TAROS 2025, LNAI 16045, pp. 223–234, 2026.
https://doi.org/10.1007/978-3-032-01486-3_18

The development of on-orbit servicing technologies has been extensively reviewed in prior studies, which highlight advancements in robotic autonomy, manipulation, and system-level architectures that support multi-arm robotic systems in space [4]. Research on in-orbit robotic control has highlighted the importance of optimal motion planning and task execution [5]. Closed-chain manipulation techniques have been explored to enhance stability in multi-arm coordination [6]. Moreover, real-time simulations in physics engines have provided insights into robotic behaviors in space and simulated space environments [2]. These facilitate the evaluation of control algorithms before real-world deployment, reducing mission risks and costs.

Inverse kinematics and optimization techniques have been utilized to enhance the performance of space robotic manipulators [7]. These are essential for tasks such as docking, component replacement, and structural assembly for ISAM. Furthermore, reconfigurable robotic arms have been proposed to enhance adaptability in dynamic space environments [8]. Thronson et al. discussed the transformative potential of robotic in-space servicing and how future systems could evolve toward higher levels of autonomy and modularity [9].

Despite these advancements, real-world validation of multi-arm locomotion remains a challenge. The in space simulation of the multi-arm robot's locomotion and tasks for ISAM are being explored in multiple studies [10] [11]. Current studies emphasize simulation without extensive hardware testing [3]. While multiple areas like cable-suspended robotic systems or robotic platforms with tracks are being explored to recreate space locomotions on the ground [12]. At Cranfield university, a Multi Arm Robot for In-orbit Operations (MARIO) has been developed to support the validation and verification of robotic and space systems in lab environment. This research aims to develop a ROS 2 control framework for a realistic representation of MARIO interactions using an easily extensible software architecture for research. This framework allows for efficient path planning and collision modelling for MARIO, ensuring that locomotion planning and execution are easier.

By leveraging ROS2 and moveit2, this study seeks to establish an efficient method for validating multi-arm locomotion strategies in a laboratory setup. The findings will contribute to future advancements in in-orbit assembly and servicing, improving the operational efficiency of space robotic systems.

Key Contribution: In the following sections we will first provide an overview of the critical issues of multi-arm robotic platforms for in-orbit assembly tasks, in particular to MARIO (Sect. 2), moving towards the control architecture of the robotic system (Sect. 3). Next, we describe the locomotion sequence adapted for the lab experimentation (Sect. 4), then the results and observation are discussed in detail (Sect. 5). Final remarks conclude the paper (Sect. 6).

2   Problem Overview

Significant progress has been made in space robotics, but several key challenges remain. A primary difficulty is the accurate replication of zero-gravity conditions in laboratory environments, which is essential for the effective execution of loco-motion and space operations with robotic systems. Current methods typically involve suspending robots from above and using manipulators to simulate space operations [13].

However, these approaches restrict the robot's motion and dynamic behavior. Achieving free-floating behavior, where the robot's base and arms interact solely through internal forces without external constraints, cannot be accomplished with cables or tracks. As a result, it fails to fully capture the inertial effects and free body dynamics experienced in real space conditions, limiting the proper evaluation of the robot's locomotion capability and overall system performances.

MARIO overcomes these limitations using an on-board pneumatic air-bearing platform, used in conjunction with a flat epoxy floor. This allows for the friction between the platform and the floor to be reduced to near zero, enabling a simulated planar microgravity environment. MARIO is then free to perform locomotion by docking to fixed structures in said environment. From a control perspective, in-situ planning of collision-free trajectories around these structures is non-trivial. The planner must consider collisions between MARIO's body, three six-degree-of-freedom manipulators, and structures that MARIO moves relative to.

To solve this problem efficiently, a multi-layered control architecture is used to facilitate locomotion tasks: firstly, individual controllers are employed for each manipulator, enabling simple and solvable kinematic solutions. Secondly, a virtual environment representing the lab as collision objects is used to represent the planning space. This enables robust and efficient planning within an accurate representation of MARIO's environment.

3   ROS Control Architecture Overview

The control system of MARIO is built on the Robot Operating System 2 (ROS2) framework, which provides a modular, real-time control system for coordinating the movements of the robotic platform. Each arm operates independently but is synchronized through ROS2 move group control nodes, ensuring smooth coordination during task execution. The control architecture is shown in Fig. 1. It supports real-time communication between the sensors and actuators, providing continuous feedback for controlling the robot's movement and task execution. The control architecture is divided into three macro-blocks:

- a *path-planner*, computes joint trajectories for the manipulators with self and environmental collision avoidance.
- the *ROS2 controllers*, the software-based controllers which calculate the required joint targets to execute and follow the target trajectories
- the *MARIO hardware interfaces*, a software layer that passes the joint targets calculated by the ROS2 controllers to the onboard hardware.

The experimental setup of MARIO in the Laboratory of Autonomous Navigation and Demonstration (LAND) is shown in Fig. 2. Mario is positioned in

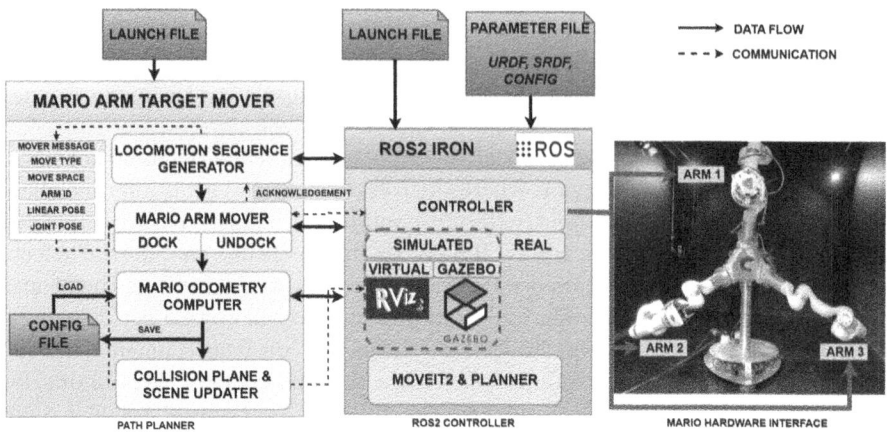

Fig. 1. MARIO Control Architecture

front of the spacecraft mock-up with multiple latching/docking points that are modelled into the ROS2 Framework for MARIO to do anchored arm-based loco-motion. The SIROM interface from SENER [14] will take care of these anchoring interactions through visual servoing and ArUco markers. The locomotion is generated with the LAND walls and the spacecraft mock-up (except the docking points T1 to T10) as collision objects.

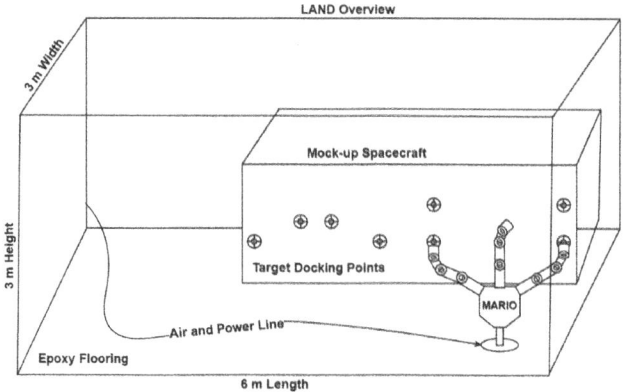

Fig. 2. MARIO Experimental Setup

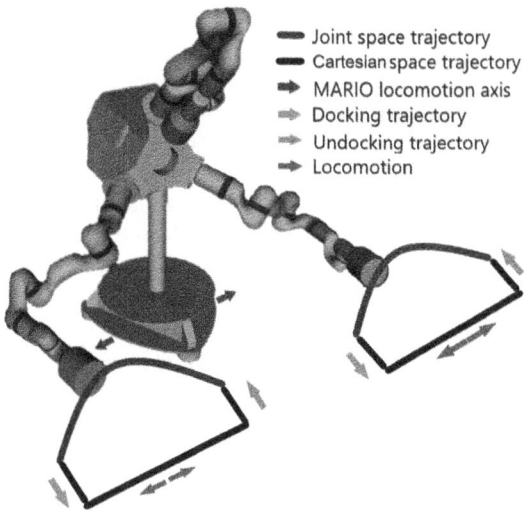

Fig. 3. MARIO control workflow

3.1 Locomotion Workflow for In-Lab Setup

The MARIO system employs a locomotion strategy that leverages its multi-arm configuration to "crawl" along surfaces. This method involves the robot using its arms to grab and release structural elements, pulling or pushing itself forward with the help of the SIROM interfaces. This approach allows MARIO to navigate complex space structures, such as the exterior of a satellite or space station, without relying on external propulsion or wheels. The same is replicated in the testing lab for MARIO to move along the surface of the spacecraft mock-up as shown in Fig. 2.

MARIO's control system facilitates both docking and movement of the arms to achieve locomotion. When it needs to relocate, the system follows a precise sequence: firstly, the docked arm follows a trajectory that positions MARIO's body for the subsequent movements. The undocked arm then latches to a nearby interface allowing the other arm to release. This coordinated docking and undocking process allows MARIO to traverse the structure while maintaining stability during transitions. While one arm is docked, the control system determines the optimal path to the next docking interface for the undocked arm Fig. 3. It uses real-time feedback from the manipulator controllers to monitor the robot's position, ensuring accurate movement between docking points. As MARIO moves, the system continuously updates the collision environment to prevent obstacles. In order to ensure collision locomotion we need the position of collision objects used by the planner to be updated after each phase of MARIO's movement. This is achieved by with a localisation process that tracks MARIO's position using an odometry system.

3.2   MARIO Transformation Tree

MARIO's configuration consists of three manipulators connected to a central hub that often interact with shared objects or with each other. Each arm's motion impacts the others, creating a system of interdependent movements. This type of kinematic chain is complex to model and control, as it requires ensuring that all arms work in harmony without causing internal stresses or collisions. The frame description in Fig. 4 shows the base frame that is tracked relative to the world frame. All trajectories and component meshes are modelled relative to this frame which serves as the origin for the entire MARIO assembly. The locomotion sequence of the MARIO robot follows a structured workflow to ensure smooth and precise multi-arm movement, odometry computation, and collision avoidance. The basics behind the MARIO's crawling or inchworm movement along with the computational logic is explained in detail on the following sections.

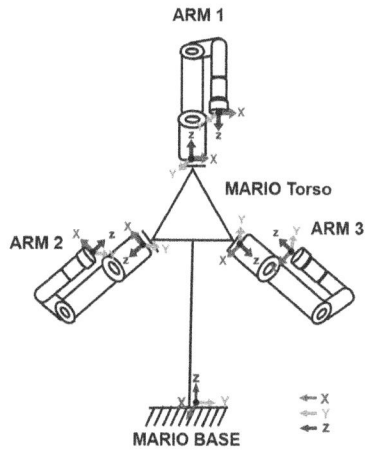

Fig. 4. MARIO Transformation Tree

4   MARIO Locomotion Sequence

The overall workflow which provides the path and target points for MARIO's locomotion and manipulation is illustrated in Fig. 5, along with its message flow and subscriptions. The Moveit controller uses the OMPL planner with RRT algorithm for path planning. For the manipulator arm, the URDF provided with the XArm packages provided by Ufactory is being used for robotic controls.

4.1   Locomotion Sequence

The target points are modelled as target 1 to 10 in the controller and are used for locomotion.

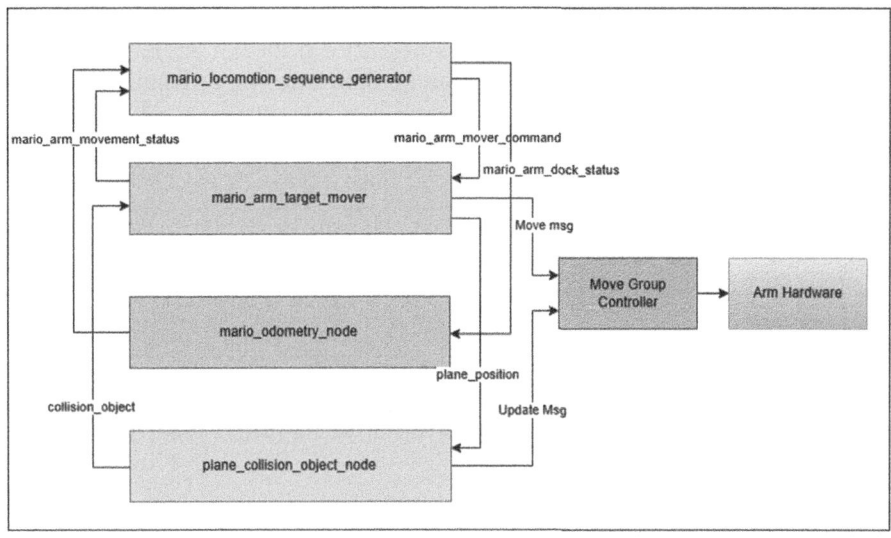

Fig. 5. MARIO Locomotion workflow

Step 1: Compute Arm Movements and Update Dock Status

The *mario_locomotion_sequence_generator* logs initial positions, calculates displacement, and updates transformation matrices: Mathematically, the transformation matrix T for the arm is represented as:

$$\left[R(q) \, | \, p(q) \right] \tag{1}$$

where R is the rotation matrix and p is the translation vector. The base position update in the global coordinate frame is obtained as:

$$p_{new} = T \cdot p_{old} \tag{2}$$

where p_{old} is the previous position vector and p_{new} is the updated position.

Step 2: Verify Reachability and Execute Movement

The *mario_arm_target_mover* checks reachability in Cartesian or Joint space, updates collision planes, and determines movement using inverse kinematics: Mathematically, given a target position p_t, the required displacement in Cartesian space is given by:

$$\Delta p = p_t - p_{current} \tag{3}$$

If the movement is executed in joint space, inverse kinematics is used:

$$q = IK(p_t) \tag{4}$$

where q represents the joint configuration.

Step 3: Detect and Avoid Collisions
The *plane_collision_object_node* identifies obstacles from last updated collision objects poisitons via the Odometry data and refines trajectory planning by maintaining a minimum safe distance:

$$d_{min} \geq \epsilon \tag{5}$$

where d_{min} is the minimum distance from the arm to the obstacle and ϵ is a predefined safety threshold. Since LAND is a constrained lab environment, the minimum distance criterion is considered rather than the minimum energy for the trajectory calculations.

Step 4: Track Odometry and Apply Corrections
The *mario_odometry_node* records arm positions(Tool Center Point) before and after docking through joint values and FK, correcting the odometry model for the new update:

$$p_{odom} = T_{odom} \cdot p_{prev} \tag{6}$$

where T_{odom} represents the accumulated transformation matrix for odometry corrections.

Step 5: Execute Motion Commands
The Move Group Controller transmits precise motion commands to the MoveIt2 controller, executing coordinated transformations:

$$T_{final} = T_{base} \cdot T_{arm} \cdot T_{end-effector} \tag{7}$$

where T_{base} represents the transformation from the world to the robot base, T_{arm} represents the transformation from the base to the arm joint, and $T_{end-effector}$ represents the final transformation to the end-effector.

This sequencer module and nodes will send the commands to MARIO controller to perform the planned trajectories of the locomotion sequence. The results are discussed in detail in the sections below.

5   Results and Discussion

The results of the MARIO locomotion sequence, as demonstrated using the proposed control architecture, will illustrate the robot's ability to perform controlled and repeatable movements. The virtual representation of the controller path planning and collision objects are given in the Rviz view as shown in 6. The locomotion sequence involved left and right movements of 350 mm, with collision objects dynamically updated to reflect MARIO's new positions.

The sequence begins with MARIO positioned at the center of the workspace, where Arm 2 docks and Arm 3 undocks, preparing for movement. Once Arm 2 is securely docked, only linear motion is executed to prevent potential damage to the setup. During the movement phase, Arm 2 moves to the right while MARIO's base shifts left. After returning to the initial position, the robot performs the reverse motion, where Arm 2 moves left and the base shifts right.

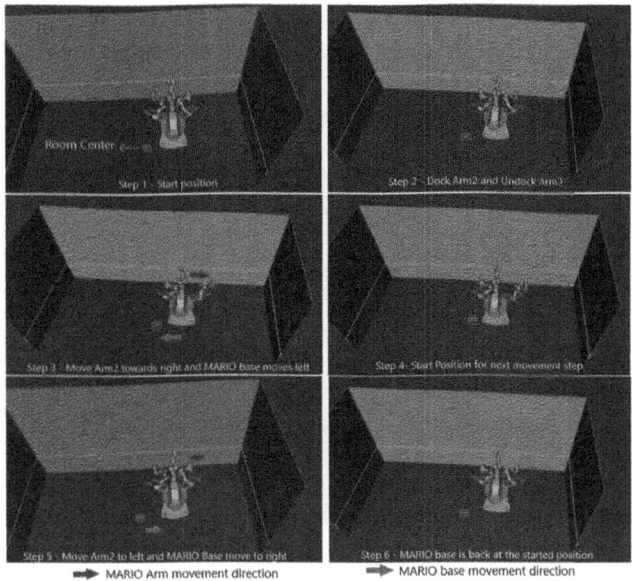

Fig. 6. MARIO locomotion simulation

This update mechanism ensures that the collision objects and information shifts around MARIO using odometry data, allowing the system to maintain an accurate position reference within the LAND environment.

The Fig. 7 highlights key movements in the sequence with the hardware. The MARIO, once docked to one of the target points in the spacecraft mock-up, then receives a linear command to move Arm 2 750 mm along the negative y-axis in the tool frame, and the base is translated 750 mm along the positive Y axis which is described in detail on the mario transformation tree shown in 4. It is done in 5 steps, with 150 mm or 250 mm movement commands being sent to the controller from the locomotion sequencer, while the collision information is being updated at the end of each set with the updated MARIO's base position. This controlled localization within the LAND environment enables the control system to execute and validate MARIO's locomotion effectively. Furthermore, this approach ensures that the MARIO system can perform real-time locomotion with its hardware counterpart.

The joint state analysis illustrated in Fig. 8 will provide the overview of the anchored locomotion sequence representation in MARIO's Arm-2. The provided linear movements of the anchored locomotion will provide the smooth trajectory needed for the locomotion of MARIO since the joint space movement will be between the transition of initial points before each anchored motion and then the planner will slowly transition to the linear or Cartesian space coordinated movement, which is described in the plot.

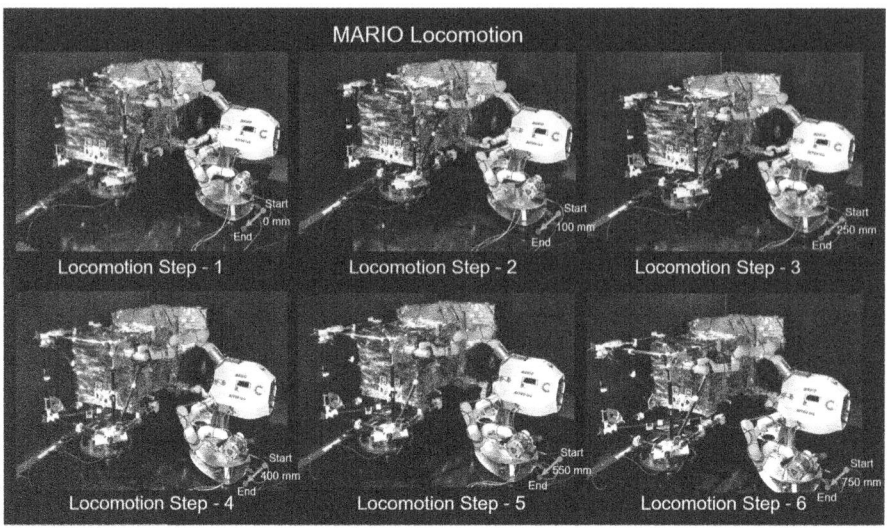

Fig. 7. MARIO Locomotion

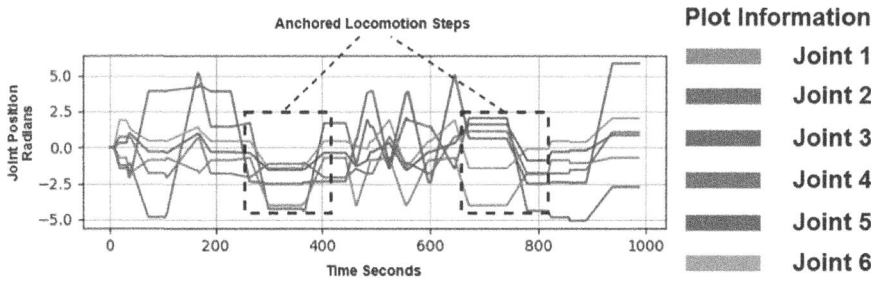

Fig. 8. Joint state plot of Arm-2 for Anchored Motion

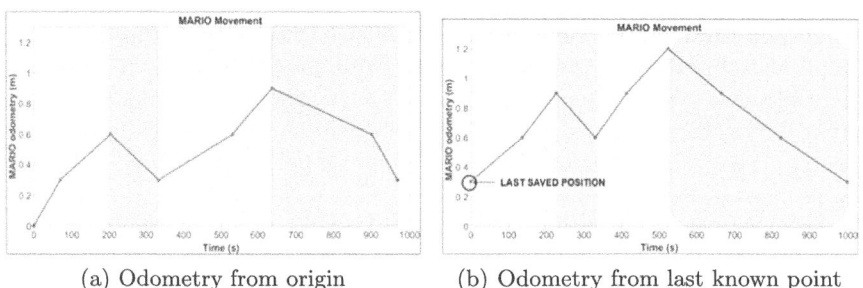

(a) Odometry from origin   (b) Odometry from last known point

Fig. 9. Odometry Plot of MARIO locomotion

The two key graphs, 9(a) and 9(b), illustrate MARIO's trajectory and odometry data within the LAND floor. These visualizations depict MARIO's planar localization details, emphasizing displacement variations along the Y-axis. In the plot, pale green region represents leftward displacement (+Y direction), while the pale orange region denotes rightward displacement (-Y direction) of the MARIO base during the locomotion simulation. This distinction helps MARIO process relative objects and collision data, feeding essential path computation details into its controller. By leveraging odometry data, the LAND environment is computed as a collision object within the MoveIt control framework. This setup enables the environment to be translated within the plane while keeping the MARIO system fixed at the center, serving as both the world frame and origin. Additionally, this approach allows the system to verify planned paths and detect potential collisions through the in-situ planner before executing physical movements, ensuring safer operations. This alternative significantly enhances the robot's awareness of the LAND environment and the positioning of interactive objects for path planning within the control framework, enabling more accurate validation of locomotion strategies.

6 Conclusion

The paper presented the control architecture for virtual simulation of the multi-arm robot to perform the locomotion and manipulation necessary for the ISAM application in a more adaptable framework for in-lab environment like the LAND. The collected odometry data during the tests demonstrated the effectiveness of the localization system in tracking MARIO's position. The ability to update relative objects and collision information on MARIO's arm movement after each step provides a dynamic and accurate representation of the operational lab(LAND) environment. This system allowed MARIO to maintain a known relative position to the structure and navigate efficiently within the simulated workspace. The results prove the feasibility of replicating frictionless conditions for MARIO and its environment for space robotics testing. This supports the development and validation of in-orbit servicing and manipulation tasks in laboratory environments. Future work will focus on introducing autonomy in MARIO's locomotion and incorporating impedance control for docked interactions, further improving the platform's capability to perform complex assembly and servicing operations with higher precision and safety.

References

1. McBryan, K.: Comparing multi-arm robotics for in-space assembly. Front. Space Technol. **3** (2022). https://doi.org/10.3389/frspt.2022.702614.
2. Xue, Z., Liu, J., Wu, C., Tong, Y.: Review of in-space assembly technologies. Chin. J. Aeronaut. **34**(11), 1–20 (2021). https://doi.org/10.1016/j.cja.2020.09.043
3. Ma, B., Jiang, Z., Liu, Y., Xie, Z.: Advances in space robots for on-orbit servicing: a comprehensive review. Adv. Intell. Syst. **5**(1) (2023). https://doi.org/10.1002/aisy.202200397.

4. Flores-Abad, A., Ma, O., Pham, K., Ulrich, S.: A review of space robotics technologies for on-orbit servicing. Prog. Aerosp. Sci. **68**, 1–26 (2014). https://doi.org/10.1016/j.paerosci.2014.03.002

5. Lutze, J.P., Schuller, R., Mishra, H., Rodríguez, I., Roa, M.A.: Optimization of multi-arm robot locomotion to reduce satellite disturbances during in-orbit assembly. In: IEEE Aerospace Conference Proceedings. IEEE Computer Society (2023). https://doi.org/10.1109/AERO55745.2023.10115776

6. Chu, X., Hu, Q., Zhang, J.: Path planning and collision avoidance for a multi-arm space maneuverable robot. IEEE Trans. Aerosp. Electron. Syst. **54**(1), 217–232 (2018). https://doi.org/10.1109/TAES.2017.2747938

7. Zhao, J., Yang, X., Zhao, Z., Yang, G., Zhao, L.: Inverse kinematics and multi-objective configuration optimization of the SSRMS manipulator. Adv. Space Res. **72**(9), 3580–3594 (2023). https://doi.org/10.1016/j.asr.2023.06.058

8. Mishra, H., De Stefano, M., Ott, C.: Dynamics and control of a reconfigurable multi-arm robot for in-orbit assembly. In: IFAC-PapersOnLine, Elsevier B.V., pp. 235–240, July 2022. https://doi.org/10.1016/j.ifacol.2022.09.101

9. Thronson, H., Akin, D., Grunsfeld, J., Lester, D.: The evolution and promise of robotic in-space servicing. In: AIAA SPACE,: Conference and Exposition. Reston, Virginia: American Institute of Aeronautics and Astronautics, September 2009. https://doi.org/10.2514/6.2009-6545

10. Bhadani, S., Dillikar, S.R., Pradhan, O.N., et al.: A ROS-based simulation and control framework for in-orbit multi-arm robot assembly operations. Presented at: ASTRA 2023: 17th Symposium on Advanced Space Technologies in Robotics and Automation, 18–20 October 2023, Leiden, The Netherlands (2023). https://dspace.lib.cranfield.ac.uk/handle/1826/20622

11. Dillikar, S.R., Leslie, C., Upadhyay, S., Felicetti, L., Tang, G.: A ROS-based control framework for simulating locomotion of a multi-arm space assembly robot. In: Huda, M.N., Wang, M., Kalganova, T. (eds.) Towards Autonomous Robotic Systems. TAROS 2024. LNCS, vol. 15052, pp. 93–105. Springer, Cham (2025). https://doi.org/10.1007/978-3-031-72062-8_9

12. Gao, Y., Chien, S.: Review on space robotics: toward top-level science through space exploration, 2017. https://www.science.org

13. Deremetz, M., et al.: MIRROR-a modular and relocatable multi-arm robot demonstrator for on-orbit large telescope assembly. In: 17th Symposium on AASTRA At: Leiden link: https://roboshare.esa.int/ASTRA/Astra2023/2023PAPERS/80_Deremetz_Design and Validation of a Modular Multi-arm Relocatable Robot for in-space Servicing and large Structure Assembly.pdf

14. Díaz-Carrasco, M., Lázaro, A., Ruiz, A., Centeno, M., Gala, J., Viñals, J.,: SIROM roadmap for future in-orbit servicing applications. In: Proceedings of the ESA/ESTEC Workshop on Advanced Space Technologies for Robotics and Automation (ASTRA), Noordwijk, Netherlands, 2023

Software Engineering for Robotics

Surveying Deliberation Practices and Methodological Needs in Robotics Software Engineering

Michaela Klauck[1]([⊠]) [ID], Christian Henkel[1] [ID], Marco Lampacrescia[1] [ID],
and Ginny Jorgensen[2]

[1] Bosch Research, Robert Bosch GmbH, Renningen, Germany
{michaela.klauck,christian.henkel2,marco.lampacrescia}@de.bosch.com
[2] Inventya Ventures, Dublin, Ireland
g.jorgensen@inventya.com

Abstract. This paper presents findings from two surveys on challenges and preferences in developing robust deliberation for autonomous robots. The first survey targeted robotics experts and software developers to understand workflows and methodological needs in developing deliberation systems, guiding the development of an open-source toolbox for robust deliberation technology within the EU project CONVINCE. The toolbox includes AS2FM, enabling formal modeling of robotic systems for quantitative verification. The second survey, conducted at ROSCon 2024, evaluated AS2FM and other deliberation tools, providing feedback for further development. This work advances user-centric robotics software design and fosters collaboration in autonomous deliberation technologies.

1 Introduction

The rapid advancement of robotics and autonomous systems raises the need for robust and reliable deliberation for long-term autonomy, enabling informed decision-making in dynamic environments. Deliberation technologies, as behavior trees (BTs), finite-state machines (FSMs), and task planning, are essential for autonomy but present challenges in integration, usability, and verifiability, esp. for robot-environment interaction and internal system communication.

Ensuring robust autonomy in novel or rare situations remains a key research goal. Most efforts focus on testing individual software components for safety and reliability [8], often neglecting environment and system-wide interactions as in Robot Operating System (ROS) applications [15]. While current deliberation techniques combine preprogrammed behaviors, logical inference, and learning-based approaches [9], they lack formal verification, making it hard to guarantee correct behavior [8], e.g., in terms of temporal logic properties. Existing approaches validate components in isolation, rely on resource-intensive system-wide testing, or use extensive software-hardware models [5]. This highlights the need for tools ensuring robustness through formal modeling with verification and

A. Cavalcanti et al. (Eds.): TAROS 2025, LNAI 16045, pp. 237–244, 2026.
https://doi.org/10.1007/978-3-032-01486-3_19

validation (V&V) [3,4,14]. Projects like Papyrus for Robotics [16] and Smart-Soft [17] haven been extended to support verification in CARVE [3], SCOPE [2], and SafeCC4Robotics [12]. However, no existing tool combines deliberation, learning, perception, and control while offering modelling languages and verification tools. This gap hinders the adoption of advanced cognitive capabilities in industry. Ensuring robustness requires verifying entire robotic systems within their environment, as classic testing alone cannot provide guarantees of correct long-term operation and efficient anomaly handling at design time.

To address these challenges, the CONVINCE EU Horizon project developed an open-source toolbox [10,18] for application-specific deliberation systems, enabling robust long-term operation in dynamic environments. A survey among robotics experts and developers captured insights into workflows, preferences, and needs in autonomous deliberation. Based on these findings, AS2FM [7] (Autonomous Systems to Formal Models) was developed to translate ROS 2 system components (e.g., BTs, skills, and communication features) into a formal model (in terms of a Markov Decision Process (MDP)) of the entire robotic system for statistical model checking of temporal logic properties with Storm [11]. A follow-up survey at the ROSCon 2024 workshop *Hands-on with ROS 2 Deliberation Technologies* assessed AS2FM and other deliberation tools through real-world applications, identifying strengths, limitations, and ideas for future improvements of the deliberation technologies of CONVINCE.

This paper synthesizes insights from both surveys, offering an overview of deliberation practices and methodological needs in robotics software engineering. By addressing developers' preferences and challenges, we aim to increase tools' capabilities and foster collaboration in the robotics community. Section 2 presents findings from the initial survey, Sect. 3 details AS2FM's evaluation at ROSCon 2024, and Sect. 4 discusses future tool development needs.

2 CONVINCE Autonomous Systems Developer Survey

To support the development of robust deliberation capabilities in autonomous robots, a quantitative survey was conducted between January and April 2024. It gathered insights from robotics experts and developers on deliberation practices, models, and the use of formal verification. Participants were acquired online via public calls for participation on LinkedIn, ROS discourse, mailing lists, at robotics and verification conferences, etc. The survey received 91 responses, with 60 fully completed. Respondents were introduced to key terminology: *Deliberation logic* describes the specific instance of logic executed by the system (e.g., point-to-point navigation). *Deliberation language* refers to the language used to define a deliberation logic (e.g., BTs, FSMs, Markov Chains). *Deliberation engine* is the software or library running a deliberation language (e.g., SMACC, BehaviorTree.CPP, FlexBE [19]). An interactive page with plots illustrating the results is available online with a summary in a flyer. The full dataset is accessible on Zenodo [1]. The findings highlight current trends and areas for improvement, guiding the development of the CONVINCE open-source software toolbox.

Participants' Background. The survey was completed by software developers (60%), application and system engineers (25%), researchers (6.67%) or managers (8.33%). They work in SMEs (43.33%), academia (36.67%), and large corporations (10%). Most respondents focus on mobile ground robot navigation (41.67%) or mobile manipulation (28.33%), others are working on stationary industrial manipulation (8.33%), aerial (8.33%), and underwater robots (6.67%). Their robots mainly operate in outdoor unstructured environments (30%), industrial settings (25%), or warehouses (16.67%); dynamic, uncertain environments where the CONVINCE toolbox aims to enhance deliberation robustness. A majority (76.66%) identifies as experts or proficient in autonomous system deliberation, ensuring the study's representativeness. Most use deliberation for task planning (84.75%) and implementing system skills (61.02%), others apply it to fallback logic, navigation, behavior selection, and configuring robot architecture. This confirms that CONVINCE's focus on robust deliberation through task and motion planning, and system-wide modeling (ROS communication, BTs, BT plugins, skills, environment of robot) in AS2FM aligns with user needs.

Deliberation Languages. Fig. 1 (left) shows that BTs (77.97%), FSMs (64.41%), and hand-coded if-else structures (54.24%) are the most regularly used deliberation languages, highlighting the tendency to use well-designed, accessible deliberation languages. However, the high percentage implementing logics by hand suggests that existing tools do not provide specific deliberation strategies, that developers end up implementing themselves.

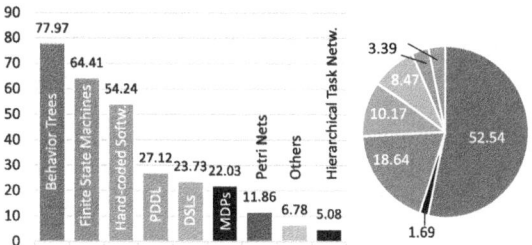

Fig. 1. Used (left) and preferred (right, same color scheme) deliberation languages in % of answers.

When evaluating preferences of deliberation languages (Fig. 1, right), a significant shift was observed wherein over 52.5% of respondents prefer BTs, compared to 18.64% who prefer FSM. Moreover, on a scale 0–10 ((not) interested using BTs), 71.66% rated them between 7 and 10. This highlights not only a strong preference for BTs as a deliberation language but also reinforces CONVINCE's decision to center its tooling around it. Cross-analysis (Fig. 2, right) reveals BTs are favored because they are easy to understand (83.8%, (strongly) agree), modify (83.9%), and implement (74.2%), though debugging (64.6%) and comparison with other implementations (42%) remain challenging. These deficiencies could be improved with verification. Those not currently using BTs are still open to trying them, with the majority rating their willingness above 5 (0–10 scale). Free-text answers highlight key requirements for practical deliberation languages: clear visualization of functional logic, direct language integration in APIs of interfacing tools, easy real-world deployment, clear documentation, formal guarantees, scalability, extendability, composability, debugging, and modifiability. With the open source toolbox of CONVINCE including comprehensive documentation and tutorials, we try to satisfy these needs.

Debugging & Testing. For debugging deliberation logic, 61.02% use ROS diagnostic tools (e.g., rostopic, rqt_console), followed by language specific debugging tools for Python (52.54%) and C++ (49.15%). Logging BT traces (45.76%) and using Groot from BehaviorTree.cpp (37.29%) are also common. Testing of the deliberation logic is primarily done in simulation (88.14%) or manually on the actual system (77.97%), with fewer using unit tests (44.07%) or model checking (15.25%). These results highlight a gap in generic debugging, and verification tools, especially since none of the tools referenced to be used by the participants provide formal correctness guarantees. However, it also shows that model checking is not completely unknown to this community. To handle unforeseen events, 68.97% rely on generic fallbacks, while 25.86% implement blocking reactions. However, these methods do not ensure robust long-term autonomy in unknown environments, reinforcing the need for formal verification and situation learning with feedback loops to planning and navigation, that is the goal of CONVINCE.

Participants were asked to rate their satisfaction with currently used testing methods (Fig. 2, left). Both simulation and manual testing were rated highly (≥ 4 on a 1–5 scale) by 69.49% and 61.4% of participants respectively. Model checking was lesser-known (34.55% were unable to rate it), yet 21.82% of those familiar with it expressed high satisfaction. This suggests that while model checking is underutilized due to lack of tools, it is worth supporting the need to make it more accessible. Only 33.33% were satisfied with available testing methods for their preferred deliberation logic, leaving room for strengthening methods currently underexplored in robotics, like model checking. This is underpinned by 77.58% expressing a need for more systematic testing and verification of deliberation engines. Free-text responses emphasized that developers want to 'make [their] system more robust' and handle the complexity of robot systems. They also mentioned 'The big missing part is to [make] the context of the decision making [process] more explicit[...] So, any progress in making verification more systematic is a gain'. This further supports CONVINCE's goal of enhancing verification for robust, long-term robot autonomy.

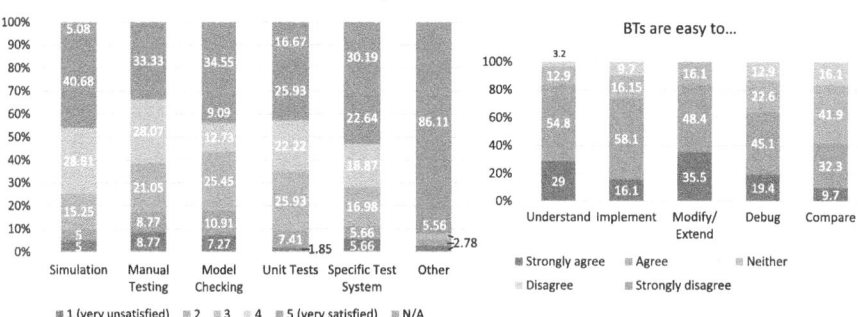

Fig. 2. Satisfaction with testing methods for deliberation logics and rating of BTs.

Formal Models. The introduction of model checking is hindered by the lack of formal representations of deliberation logics. 81.03% of developers do not use formal models (e.g., Markovian Processes, Channel Systems) to develop them. Even among those who claimed to have a formal model, many responses could not be classified as such, suggesting the actual percentage is even higher. Despite this, 43.86% of developers are willing to invest effort in writing a formal model if it enables systematic testing and verification. 36.84% were undecided, highlighting the need to raise awareness of formal methods in robotics. Cross-analysis shows that 52% of those seeing the need for systematic verification would invest time, though some recognize high effort without better tooling. Participants reluctant to adopt formal models cited high effort, code changes, and expert knowledge as barriers, yet many are open to explore them. Most respondents (36.36%) would dedicate 10–20% of their total development time to systematic verification, with 67.27% willing to invest up to 30%, highlighting the desire for tools targeting effective and accessible formal verification. Asked for their preferred format or language in writing a formal model, developers favored a BT-compatible approach, ideally close to BT.cpp XML and a language like Python. These insights inspired the development of AS2FM, allowing to model a system based on ROS 2 communication and BT.cpp, including the robot's environment. In general, the findings suggest there is demand amongst the robotics community for robust, verifiable robotic systems. The CONVINCE toolbox addresses this problem by formally modelling the complete robotic architecture in AS2FM using familiar formalisms (BTs, MDPs), lowering the entry barrier for developers.

3   ROSCon 2024 ROS 2 Deliberation Technologies Survey

At ROSCon 2024, the *ROS Deliberation Community Group* hosted a *Hands-on with ROS 2 Deliberation Technologies* workshop showcasing the diversity of deliberation technologies, including BTs, FSMs, task planning, and verification and validation systems. Participants tackled predefined tasks using BehaviorTree.CPP, FlexBE [19], ros_bt_py, SkiROS2 [13], and AS2FM [7], guided by the tools' maintainers. A survey [6] conducted at the end gathered feedback on these tools, identifying strengths and limitations in different areas. The full results are available online [6]. In the following, we mostly focus on results concerning AS2FM. The survey received 86 responses with 65 fully completed.

Participants' Background. Respondents' demographics align with the first study: 43% work in small & mid-sized enterprises, 26.7% in large corporations, and 23.3% in research institutes, the rest is self-employed or in other associations. Experience in AI and robotics is high, with 66.2% having worked there for at least three years. However, experience with robotic deliberation is lower, with 53.9% being beginners, 33.7% proficient, and only 7% experts. Familiarity with tools for implementing deliberation is very limited (around 5% or lower), except for BT.cpp (26.7%), while newer tools (AS2FM, SkiROS2) are largely unfamiliar.

Tool Comparisons. A meta-observation from the survey is that 20–40% of participants often marked N/A when rating tools, i.e., did not feel confident in answering the question, indicating a need for greater exposure to recent deliberation technologies. Overall, setup procedures were rated well across tools (scale 1–5, 5 = very easy), with many participants voting $\geq$4: BT.cpp (64.7%), FlexBE (58.8%), AS2FM (45.9%), SkiROS2 (40%), and ros_bt_py (38.8%). Notably, AS2FM received the most 5 point ratings (36.47%), directly followed by BT.cpp (35.3%) (all others only 15–20%), reporting a positive installation process despite the tool's complexity. There were no technical issues with AS2M. For the other tools they could be fixed by the workshop instructors. Execution speed and responsiveness were generally well received, with satisfaction levels highest for BT.cpp (73%), followed by AS2FM (59.2%), FlexBE (50%), ros_bt_py (28.8%), and SkiROS2 (27%) ($\geq$ 4 on scale 1–5, very unsatisfied to very satisfied).

Feedback on AS2FM underscored its uniqueness and potential: participants valued its ability to 'provide reliability insights otherwise unavailable', noted that 'no other tool like this exists', and that 'it [covers] far more scenarios/edge-cases than one could realistically write otherwise'. However, they recognized the challenge of requiring a formal system model, which adds effort and poses risks of discrepancies between the model and reality. Some found the syntax challenging, while others considered it 'simple to use', highlighting a need for tailored onboarding resources. To address these concerns, we provide online documentation and tutorials, will focus on improving model traceability, and increase interpretability of the results by visual inspection tools.

As expected, AS2FM was rated the hardest tool to learn, similar to SkiROS2, reflecting the complexity of both tools, indicating that more awareness and training of developers for formal verification is needed. All of that has to be interpreted in the light that many participants were beginners in robotic deliberation. Many respondents (41.5%) were uncertain about recommending AS2FM for future projects, more than for other tools. However 24.6% indicated they would consider it after improvements were implemented, the highest proportion among all tools. Given its early development stage and the participants' limited prior exposure to formal verification, this cautious optimism reinforces the need for more training and awareness within the community.

4   Conclusion

The surveys provide valuable insights into deliberation in robotics and its challenges. BTs are the most widely used deliberation language, while the reliance of developers on manual validation and simulation, reveals a gap in systematic verification tools. Formal models are underutilized despite their recognized value, emphasizing the need for accessible, well-supported verification tooling centered around BTs. Newer tools like AS2FM show strong potential but require better onboarding and usability. While participants appreciate its unique verification capabilities, they highlight challenges in modeling effort, syntax complexity, and interpretability of the results. Future work will focus on these points to increase the awareness of formal methods to bridge the gap between research advancements and benefits in robotics engineering. By addressing these challenges, CONVINCE aims to make systematic verification more accessible, ultimately enhancing the reliability of autonomous systems.

Acknowledgements. The work was supported by the European Union's Horizon Europe Research & Innovation Program, Grant 101070227 (CONVINCE).

References

1. Chen-Jorgensen, G., Klauck, M., Lampacrescia, M., Henkel, C., Wallis, D.: Results of the convince autonomous systems developer survey (2024). https://doi.org/10.5281/zenodo.13382222
2. Colledanchise, M., Cicala, G., Domenichelli, D.E., Natale, L., Tacchella, A.: Formalizing the execution context of behavior trees for runtime verification of deliberative policies. In: Proceedings of the IEEE/RSJ International Conference on Intelligent Robots and Systems (IROS), pp. 9841–9848. IEEE (2021)
3. Colledanchise, M., Cicala, G., Domenichelli, D.E., Natale, L., Tacchella, A.: A toolchain to design, execute, and monitor robots behaviors. arXiv preprint arXiv:2106.15211 (2021)
4. Espiau, B., Kapellos, K., Jourdan, M.: Formal verification in robotics: why and how? In: Proceedings of Robotics Research: The Seventh International Symposium, pp. 225–236. Springer (1996)
5. Foughali, M., Berthomieu, B., Zilio, S.D., Hladik, P.E., Ingrand, F., Mallet, A.: Formal verification of complex robotic systems on resource-constrained platforms. In: Proceedings of the 6th Conf. on Formal Methods in Software Engineering (2018)
6. Henkel, C., et al.: Results of the roscon24 workshop survey 'hands-on with ros2 deliberation technologies' (November 2024). https://doi.org/10.5281/zenodo.14051492
7. Henkel, C., Lampacrescia, M., Klauck, M., Morelli, M.: AS2FM: Enabling statistical model checking of ROS 2 systems for robust autonomy. Accepted at IROS 2025
8. Ingrand, F.: Recent trends in formal validation and verification of autonomous robots software. In: Proceedings of the IEEE International Conference on Robotic Computing (IRC), pp. 321–328. IEEE (2019)
9. Ingrand, F., Ghallab, M.: Deliberation for autonomous robots: a survey. Artif. Intell. **247**, 10–44 (2017). https://doi.org/10.1016/j.artint.2014.11.003
10. Klauck, M., Lange, R., Henkel, C., Kchir, S., Palmas, M.: Towards robust autonomous robots using statistical model checking. In: Secchi, C., Marconi, L. (eds.) European Robotics Forum 2024, pp. 137–142. Springer Nature Switzerland, Cham (2024)
11. Lampacrescia, M., Klauck, M., Palmas, M.: Towards verifying robotic systems using statistical model checking in STORM. In: Steffen, B. (ed.) Bridging the Gap Between AI and Reality - Second International Conference, AISoLA 2024, Crete, Greece, October 30 – 3 November 2024, Proceedings. LNCS, vol. 15217, pp. 446–467. Springer, Cham (2024). https://doi.org/10.1007/978-3-031-75434-0_28

12. Martinez, J., Ruiz, A., Radermacher, A., Tonetta, S.: Assumptions and guarantees for composable models in papyrus for robotics. In: Proceedings of the IEEE/ACM International Workshop on Robotics Software Engineering (RoSE), pp. 1–4. IEEE (2021)
13. Mayr, M., Rovida, F., Krüger, V.: Skiros2: a skill-based robot control platform for ROS. In: IROS, pp. 6273–6280 (2023). https://doi.org/10.1109/IROS55552.2023.10342216
14. Meywerk, T., Walter, M., Herdt, V., Kleinekathöfer, J., Große, D., Drechsler, R.: Verifying safety properties of robotic plans operating in real-world environments via logic-based environment modeling. In: Proceedings of the International Symposium on Leveraging Applications of Formal Methods, pp. 326–347. Springer (2020)
15. Quigley, M., et al.: Ros: an open-source robot operating system. In: Proceedings of the ICRA Workshop on Open Source Software, vol. 3, p. 5 (2009)
16. Radermacher, A., Morelli, M., Hussein, M., Nouacer, R.: Designing drone systems with papyrus for robotics. In: Proceedings of Drone Systems Engineering and Rapid Simulation and Performance Evaluation: Methods and Tools, pp. 29–35 (2021)
17. Schlegel, C., Haßler, T., Lotz, A., Steck, A.: Robotic software systems: from code-driven to model-driven designs. In: Proceedings of the International Conference on Advanced Robotics, pp. 1–8. IEEE (2009)
18. Street, C., et al.: Towards a verifiable toolchain for robotics. In: Proceedings of the AAAI Symposium Series, vol. 4, no. 1, pp. 398–403 (November 2024). https://doi.org/10.1609/aaaiss.v4i1.31823
19. Zutell, J.M., Conner, D.C., Schillinger, P.: Ros 2-based flexible behavior engine for flexible navigation. In: SoutheastCon 2022, pp. 674–681 (2022). https://doi.org/10.1109/SoutheastCon48659.2022.9764047

SAFLITE: Fuzzing Autonomous Systems via Large Language Models

Taohong Zhu[1]([✉])(iD), Adrians Skapars[1], Fardeen Mackenzie[1], Declan Kehoe[1], William Newton[1], Suzanne Embury[1], and Youcheng Sun[1,2]

[1] The University of Manchester, Manchester, UK
taohong.zhu@manchester.ac.uk
[2] MBZUAI, Abu Dhabi, UAE

Abstract. Fuzz testing is a widely adopted testing methodology in software engineering that offers efficient means of testing software and identifying vulnerabilities. This paper presents a universal framework aimed at improving the efficiency of fuzz testing for Autonomous Systems (AS), particularly Unmanned Aerial Vehicle (UAV) autonomous systems. At its core is SAFLITE (Safe Flight Testing), a predictive component that evaluates whether a test case meets predefined safety criteria. By leveraging the large language model (LLM) with information about the test objective and the AS state, SAFLITE assesses the relevance of each test case. We evaluated SAFLITE by instantiating it with various LLMs, including GPT-3.5, Mistral-7B, and Llama2-7B, and integrating it into four fuzz testing tools: PGFuzz, DeepHyperion-UAV, CAMBA, and TUMB. These tools are designed specifically for testing autonomous drone control systems. The experimental results demonstrate that, compared to PGFuzz, SAFLITE increased the likelihood of selecting operations that triggered bug occurrences in each fuzzing iteration by an average of 93.1%. Additionally, after integrating SAFLITE, the ability of DeepHyperion-UAV, CAMBA, and TUMB to generate test cases that caused system safety violations increased by 234.5%, 33.3%, and 17.8%, respectively. The benchmark used in evaluation was from CPS-UAV Tool Competition 2024.

Keywords: Fuzzing · Autonomous System · LLM

1 Introduction

Autonomous Systems (AS) are increasingly used in sectors such as transportation, healthcare, and industrial automation [8]. Ensuring their reliability and safety is essential, as failures pose significant risks to human life and infrastructure [13,20].

While the testing approach proposed in this paper is applicable to general AS, we focus specifically on AS for Unmanned Aerial Vehicles (UAVs). Figure 1 illustrates the functioning of such a system: ❶ Mission-specific configurations are provided to the control algorithm module. ❷ As the UAV operates, its

sensors collect environmental data, forming the current state, which is relayed
to the control algorithm module to calculate the next actions [6,12]. ❸ Commands are generated based on whether the mission is complete or if certain
conditions hinder further progress. If the mission continues, the system outputs
commands according to a predefined safety policy for the UAV to execute. The
UAV then carries out these commands and sends updated sensor data back.
External factors, such as wireless remote control or changing wind conditions,
can also influence the UAV, and the AS adjusts accordingly based on the sensor
feedback.

Fuzz testing is a software testing method that involves supplying
invalid, unexpected, or random data
inputs to a program in order to
uncover bugs and vulnerabilities [3].
This approach has been applied to
fuzzing AS [11], where seeds such as
configuration parameters relevant to
the safety properties under test are
selected. A seed is randomly chosen
for mutation, assigned random values, and input into a UAV simulator.
Kim et al. [11] define a metric that

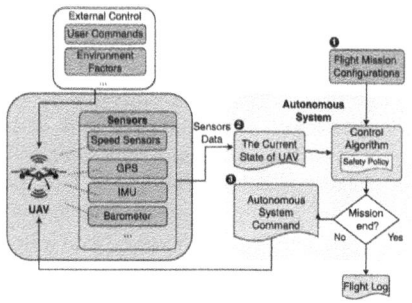

Fig. 1. An Illustrative Workflow of an
Autonomous System for UAVs

measures how closely an input leads to the triggering of a bug. This metric is
computed after the simulator executes the input, and its increase or decrease is
used to assess whether the seed is valuable for future use, rather than generating
entirely new random values.

Motivated by [11], instead of relying on user-specified heuristics, we leverage
the LLM's understanding of safety properties as the metric for automatically
determining the relevance of a test case. In other words, our focus is on how
"interesting" a test case is in relation to specific testing objectives via LLMs.
This approach shifts the emphasis of AS fuzzing to properly defining the system's
safety properties and ensuring that the LLM accurately interprets these safety
properties as the key objectives for testing.

For example, testers may evaluate whether a drone control system violates
its hover policy by defining "Drone altitude changes during hover mode" as an
interesting test condition. Our approach transforms an LLM into a predictor
that identifies which test cases are most likely to meet this condition, deeming
those as interesting test cases.

In summary, this paper offers the following contributions: 1) The design of a
universal fuzzing framework that integrates LLMs for testing AS, 2) The development of SAFLITE as a predictor for test case relevance, and 3) Its application
to real-world fuzzing tools. We release SAFLITE at [1] for developers to test their
own fuzzing tools.

2   Approach

We developed a framework called UNIVERSAL AUTONONMOUS SYSTEM FUZZING WITH LLMs to leverage large language models' understanding of safety properties in fuzzing tests for AS. This framework allows all AS fuzzing tools to integrate with large language models, facilitating comprehensive fuzzing tests on these systems.

2.1   Universal AS Fuzzing with LLMs

To establish a universal fuzzing framework for AS that integrates with large language models, we initiated our approach by analysing current AS fuzzing tools including PGFuzz [11], DeepHyperion-UAV [25], CAMBA [4], and TUMB [16]. These tools primarily utilise mutation-based fuzzing techniques. By abstracting and refining their processes, we designed a universal AS fuzzing framework that encapsulates the methodologies of these tools. This process is shown in Fig. 2, excluding the SAFLiTE component which represents the proposed LLM integration in this study.

The fuzzing process begins with randomly selected/generated test cases being stored as initial inputs in the seed pool within the seed manager module. The seed manager selects a test case, known as a seed, from the seed pool based on a predefined seed scheduling strategy. This seed is then transferred to the mutation module, where it is

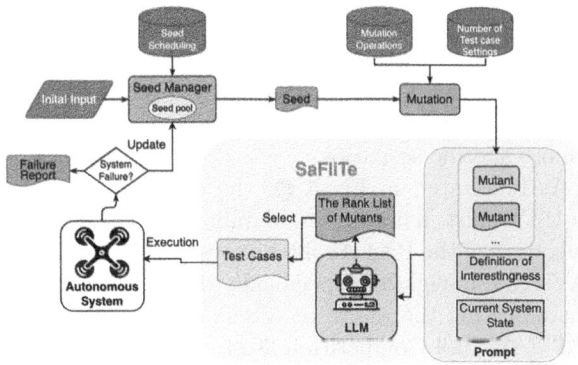

Fig. 2. Workflow of universal AS fuzzing with LLMs

subjected to predefined mutation operations, such as randomly changing a value of parameter in the test case. This mutation creates a new test case that is executed by AS. Optionally, there could be a "number of test case settings" in the mutation module to control the number of new test cases generated at each step by the fuzzing tool. In the event of a system failure, i.e., the violation of some safety property, a report is generated for detailed analysis. Otherwise, if the new test case does not result in a system failure, it is used by the seed manager to update the seed pool, for example, in PGFuzz, based on the defined metric, seeds that lead to an increase in the metric are given a higher probability of being selected from the seed pool by the seed manager, thereby increasing the likelihood of triggering bugs.

Following the formulation of the universal AS fuzzing framework as illustrated in Fig. 2, we include the SAFLiTE module prior to the AS executing the test cases, which are now first analysed through LLMs. Further details on this integration are explained in Sect. 2.2.

2.2 SaFliTe

In fuzz testing, fuzzing tools for AS often produce a high volume of ineffective test cases due to the expansive input space of AS. These tools traditionally mutate seeds using predefined mutation operations, such as randomly changing the value of a parameter, which leads to inefficiency in discovering system safety issues. To address this, we have introduced an automated tool SaFliTe, designed to improve testing efficiency without the manual review burden. SaFliTe employs a large language model to assess the relevance of generated test cases to predefined conditions. A visual depiction of SaFliTe's framework is provided in the highlighted box of Fig. 2.

SaFliTe adapts the LLM as its reasoning engine for fuzzing, featuring the following essential pieces:

Definition of Interestingness. Based on the safety specifications of an AS, some test cases are deemed more "interesting" than others due to their potential to breach safety requirements. This interestingness is defined by the expected behavior of the AS when it violates these safety properties. The scope of this definition can vary from broad objectives, such as causing a control system crash, to more specific scenarios.

As illustrated in Fig. 3 ⓐ, the definition of interestingness stipulates that the UAV must maintain a minimum distance of 1.5 m from obstacles during the navigation of the PX4-Avoidance system's mission. This criterion emphasizes the UAV's safe navigation, specifically designed to prevent collisions with obstacles, thus reflecting the safety requirements for operation. This example is from the CPS-UAV Tool Competition 2024 [10].

Current System State. It refers to the condition of the AS immediately before SaFliTe analyses the test cases. For example, when testing a UAV control system, the current system state might include details such as the current location of drone and additional parameters like GPS coordinates or pitch angle. The selection of specific information to include can be informed by the definition of interestingness, which interprets the safety specifications, aiming for improving the accuracy of the assessment regarding how closely the system aligns with the predefined test conditions.

The example in Fig. 3 ⓑ shows the coordinates of the UAV under testing, which represent the current state information essential for the navigation task.

Mutants. These represent the outcomes of mutations performed by the fuzzing tool. It is helpful to include a more detailed description of these results when presenting them, as this will assist the LLM in accurately understanding each test case.

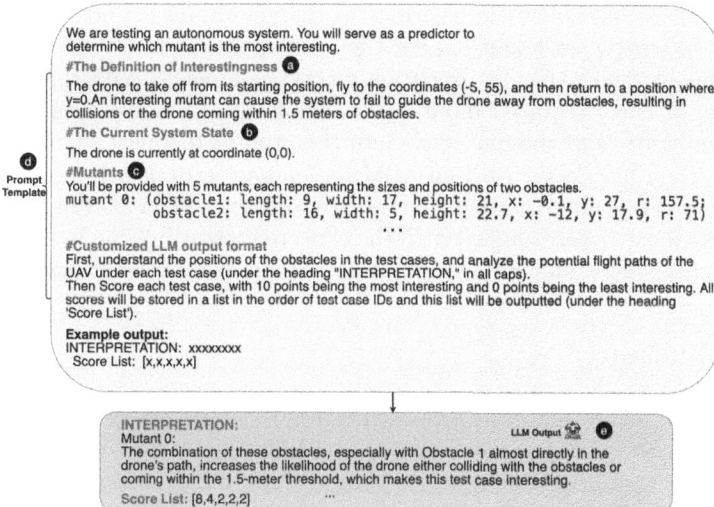

Fig. 3. A concrete example of SAFLITE applied to a fuzzing tool testing a UAV obstacle avoidance system, PX4-Avoidance.

Figure 3 ⓒ provides a concrete example of constructing a Mutants piece. Information from five mutants is extracted and formatted in a structured way, informing the LLM that each mutant represents the sizes and positions of two obstacles.

Prompt Template. To enable SAFLITE to work effectively with different LLMs as the prediction core while ensuring consistent output, we developed a prompt template that systematically incorporates all relevant information to be provided to the LLM and standardises its output. As shown in Fig. 3, the template (ⓓ) is populated using the definition of interestingness (ⓐ), the current system state (ⓑ), and the corresponding mutants (ⓒ).

Moreover, SAFLITE employs the CoT (Chain of Thoughts) approach to customise the LLM output format. The LLM should interpret the meaning of each mutant, then evaluate how each mutant will impact the current system state, based on the information provided about the current state. The LLM should produce a brief explanation for each thought process and assign a score to each mutant. A score of 10 indicates that the test case is the most interesting, meaning it is highly likely to meet the test conditions outlined in the definition of interestingness after execution, while a score of 0 signifies the opposite.

The final part of the prompt template is an *Example Output*, which helps ensure the LLM consistently formats its responses. When SAFLITE is applied to the AS fuzzing tools (as shown in Fig. 2), the default expected output is a selection of test cases from a ranked list of mutants.

In addition, the LLM provides insights for each test case in its output, upon which it generates a final ranked list of test case scores. As illustrated in Fig. 3

●, the LLM assesses obstacle positions in the environment and evaluates how proximity to waypoints might impact the avoidance system of UAV.

In summary, the SAFLITE execution process commences with the automated population of three required inputs—the definition of interestingness, the current system state, and the mutants—into the prompt template. This populated prompt is then interfaced with an LLM to generate a ranked list of test cases. Finally, SAFLITE employs a defined strategy to select test cases from this ranked list that are most closely aligned with the expected test condition in the AS, such as setting thresholds for interestingness and uninterestingness values.

3   Evaluation

In this section, we evaluate the proposed SAFLITE approach by addressing three research questions (RQs): validating that LLMs can indeed identify interesting test cases (Sect. 3.1), showing that a more specific definition of interestingness can further improve its effectiveness (Sect. 3.2), and, utmost, confirming that SAFLITE significantly improves the performance of existing fuzzing tools (Sect. 3.3).

3.1   RQ1: How Effectively do LLMs Predict the Interestingness of Test Cases?

Experimental Setup. For RQ1, we provided SAFLITE with a labelled dataset for prediction and evaluation. The dataset comprises 117 log files representing both flight issues (interesting) and normal flights (non-interesting), sourced from a combination of real-world and synthesised flights [10,18]. The logs that feature flight issues are considered test cases by developers, used to reproduce bugs, identify, and resolve issues within the PX4 system. The interesting logs were drawn either from the PX4 GitHub issue tracker, where users had uploaded logs that were accepted as demonstrating buggy behaviour requiring code changes, or from simulated flights replicating similar issues. The non-interesting logs were sourced from two places: simulated flights conforming to a standardised test card used by PX4 developers to validate code changes, and flights completed during the development of a new navigation submodule. These non-interesting logs showed standard mission completions and adhered to the policy requirements of the additional submodule. We broadly define interestingness as the occurrence of uncommon, difficult-to-understand, or significantly unexpected behaviors in drones, which may potentially lead to high-risk flights.

To assess the effectiveness of SAFLITE across different LLMs, we selected three models: GPT-3.5 [14], Mistral-7B [9], and Llama-2-7B [19] such that Mistral-7B and Llama-2-7B are deployed locally. The evaluation was conducted using four metrics: Accuracy (*Acc*), Precision (*Prec*), Recall, and F1-score (*F1*).

Table 1. Performance comparison of different LLMs for predicting the interestingness of flight log benchmarks.

LLMs	Acc	F1	Prec	Recall
LLAMA-2-7B	47.1%	54.3%	48.9%	61.1%
Mistral-7B	62.9%	66.7%	61.9%	**72.2%**
GPT-3.5	**68.6%**	**68.6%**	**70.6%**	66.7%
GPT-3.5 (temp=1)	52.4%	46.4%	55.9%	39.8%

Results. The results for the four metrics are summarised in Table 1, showing that GPT-3.5 achieves the highest performance in three metrics, with an accuracy of 68.6% and an F1 score of 68.6%. Its precision of 70.6% underscores GPT-3.5's strong ability to identify interesting test cases. The overall accuracy metric indicates that Llama-2-7B, the local LLM, performs the least effectively. However, another local LLM, Mistral-7B, performs comparably to GPT-3.5 and even surpasses it in recall, suggesting a strong capability to distinguish between interesting and non-interesting test cases. This demonstrates that smaller, locally deployed LLMs can achieve performance comparable to GPT-3.5. Given the advantages of local LLMs for secure, local deployments, task-specific fine-tuning of Mistral-7B could further enhance its potential as the reasoning engine for SAFLiTE.

An analysis of the recall metric reveals that GPT-3.5's recall drops significantly when its temperature is set to 1, indicating confusion in distinguishing between interesting and non-interesting test cases. This suggests that a high temperature results in overly random outputs and fabricated responses without adequate reasoning. Therefore, we recommend avoiding high-temperature settings when using SAFLiTE.

> Answer to RQ1: LLMs, such as GPT-3.5 and Mistral-7B, demonstrate effectiveness in predicting the interestingness of the flight log benchmark, though their performance is not exceptional. The broad definition of interestingness likely plays a key role in limiting their effectiveness.

3.2 RQ2: How Does a More Specific Definition of Interestingness Impact the Effectiveness of SAFLiTE?

Experimental Setup. To examine the impact of using a more specific definition of interestingness on the effectiveness of SAFLiTE, we conducted experiments by integrating SAFLiTE with the existing fuzzing tool PGFuzz [11].

PGFuzz can perform fuzzing tests on ArduPilot [17] and PX4 [18] systems based on safety policies to detect policy violations. We obtained a list of bugs from the PGFuzz repository[1]. Since most bugs in the list lacked details about

---

[1] The bug list is available in Sect. 4 of the README on the PGFuzz GitHub repository at https://github.com/purseclab/PGFuzz.

the system state or violated policies, we selected 8 bugs for our experiment. For each bug, we translated the associated policy violation into a natural language description, which served as a definition of interestingness for SAFLITE. We then provided SAFLITE with the control system's state at the time of the bug occurrence (details are in Sect. 5 of the README in [1]). Given that PGFuzz randomly selects a parameter from a list related to the target policy as a test case, we extracted all possible parameters from this list and provided them to SAFLITE for analysis. Each test case was scored: below 4 as non-interesting, 5 to 7 as mid-interesting, and above 7 as interesting. If the test case that caused the bug was rated mid-interesting or interesting, it indicates that SAFLITE improves the likelihood of selecting bug-causing test cases over PGFuzz's random selection, thereby enhancing efficiency and demonstrating the value of using more specific Definitions of Interestingness.

Results. The results of this experiment are presented in Fig. 4. Each pie chart represents the outcomes of using SAFLITE to analyse a specific violated safety property. For example, Fig. 4a shows that, for the selected safety property and across all test cases generated by PGFuzz, SAFLITE classified 58.8% of test cases as non-interesting, 36.5% as mid-interesting, and only 4.9% as interesting. Although the proportion of interesting test cases is the smallest, the test cases that changed the UAV flight mode and caused the system to violate the policy requiring a minimum altitude check (e.g., 10 m) to trigger the FLIP flight mode were accurately classified as interesting. Therefore, compared to PGFuzz's random selection of all possible test cases, using SAFLITE to select only from the interesting category increases the likelihood of selecting a test case that leads to a policy violation by 93.1% in each fuzzing round. Overall, SAFLITE effectively classified most test cases that resulted in policy violations as interesting, with only two classified as mid-interesting and none as non-interesting. On average, the probability of selecting a bug-causing test case in each fuzzing round increased by 94.7%.

Additionally, we observed that GPT-3.5 accurately understands the function of each test case and its impact on drone control systems. For example, GPT-3.5 correctly identified the test case MAV_CMD_DO_PARACHUTE as a command to deploy the UAV parachute (for full test case analyses, refer to Sect. 5 of the README in [1].). This suggests that GPT-3.5's training data might include considerable information about ArduPilot and PX4 systems. However, the test cases that caused bugs No.24 and No.25 were categorised as mid-interesting instead of Interesting. Upon review, this occurred because GPT-3.5 lacked knowledge of the specific values assigned to these test cases, making it difficult to predict their exact impact. As correct classification is challenging without specific values, this demonstrates that GPT-3.5 recognises that some value assignments may not cause bugs, while others might.

New Bugs. Both PGFuzz and PGFuzz+SAFLITE were given 24 h to perform fuzzing tests on each policy. The results were compared based on the number of bugs discovered and the number of fuzzing rounds completed. Notably, when

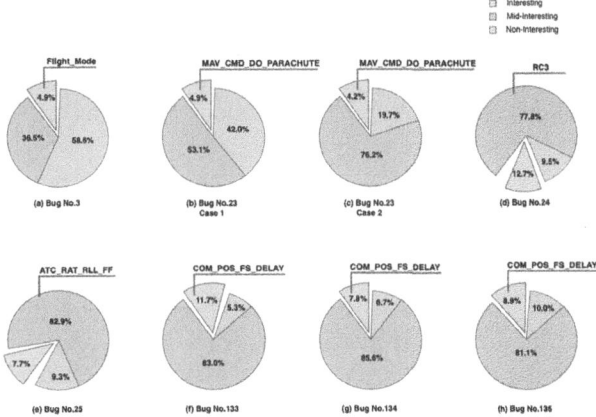

Fig. 4. For each bug, SAFLITE categorizes all potential test cases generated by PGFuzz into three groups based on the corresponding Current State and Definition of Interestingness. The figure highlights which category the test case that triggered the bug was assigned to.

testing the policy requiring the vehicle to maintain constant location, heading, and altitude in Hold mode, both PGFuzz and PGFuzz+SAFLITE identified the same policy violation.

However, PGFuzz+SAFLITE achieved this in just 126 rounds of fuzzing, significantly fewer than the 269 rounds required by PGFuzz. Additionally, the bug identified by PGFuzz+SAFLITE is a new bug in the PX4 system that had not been previously identified and was absent from the bug list presented by PGFuzz. As shown in Fig. 5, the UAV, which is supposed to hover at point L in Hold mode, keeps moving in one direction. The process of discovering the bug is as follows: ❶ The drone was initially in Hold mode, hovering in place. ❷ SAFLITE analysed the test cases, and the MAV_CMD_DO_REPOSITION test case was assigned a score of 7. ❸ When the PX4 system executed the MAV_CMD_DO_REPOSITION test case, the drone began moving northwest but

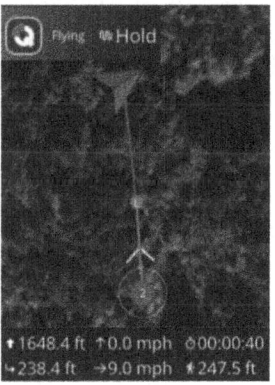

Fig. 5. UAV keeps moving in Hold mode.

remained in Hold mode. Through investigation, it was found that the implementation of the MAV_CMD_DO_REPOSITION command in the PX4 system lacks a capability check to ensure that the command is allowed in the current flight mode.

Answer to RQ2: Using SAFLITE with a specific definition of interestingness as the test condition can enhance the effectiveness of existing fuzzing tools, particularly by improving their ability to understand the relevance of test cases to predefined conditions.

3.3 RQ3: How Effectively Does SAFLITE Improve the Performance of Existing AS Fuzzing Tools?

Experimental Setup. To assess whether SAFLITE can successfully integrate with fuzzing tools and improve their performance in a full fuzzing test process, we followed the structure of UNIVERSAL AUTONONMOUS SYSTEM FUZZING WITH LLMs and combined SAFLITE with fuzzing tools from the SBFT UAV Testing Competition [10]: DeepHyperion-UAV [25], TUMB [16], and CAMBA [4]. The competition tasked these fuzzing tools with testing the PX4-Avoidance system, where a UAV navigates missions in a virtual environment under the control of PX4-Avoidance. The competition rule requires participating fuzzing tools to generate as many valid test cases as possible. A test case defines the size and coordinates of obstacles in the environment and is considered valid if the UAV either collides with an obstacle or comes too close. We translated this valid test case rule into the definition of interestingness for SAFLITE, as in Fig. 3❶.

In our experiments, we adhered strictly to the competition rule and ran all fuzzing tools in the designated environment. Since automated control systems may behave differently across various missions, we provided six distinct missions (Mission 2–7) to compare the performance of the fuzzing tools in different scenarios. Mission 1 was excluded, as it was intended for participants to test their tools during development. Each mission, defined by the competition organisers, varied only in specific waypoints, requiring the system to guide the drone through them in sequence. We compared the number of valid test cases generated by the modified tools (integrated with SAFLITE) to those produced by the original tools used in the competition.

Results. The experimental results, presented in Table 2, demonstrate that SAFLITE successfully integrates with various fuzzing tools, completing the full fuzzing process and improving their performance. Each integrated tool generated more valid test, with improvements observed in all the missions.

Among the three tools, DeepHyperion-UAV exhibited the most significant improvement in the number of valid test cases. However, the gains for CAMBA and TUMB were more modest. Upon reviewing their code, we believe this is due to their approach of making only minor mutations to each test case when generating new ones. As a result, the test cases produced are often very similar, and the LLM assigns similar scores, reducing the ability of the tools to rank test cases effectively based on their relevance to the Definition of Interestingness.

Notably, all three fuzzing tools integrated with SAFLITE showed significant improvements in the number of valid test cases generated in Mission 2. In the

Table 2. Comparison of the number of valid test cases generated by DeepHyperion-UAV, CAMBA, and TUMB in on the UAV Testing Competition benchmark before and after the integration of SaFliTe. Each valid test case represents a unique scenario that causes the UAV mission to fail.

Tool Name	Number of Valid Test Cases					
	Mission 2	Mission 3	Mission 4	Mission 5	Mission 6	Mission 7
DeepHyperion-UAV	2	10	8	4	0	5
DeepHyperion-UAV + **SaFliTe**	**17**	**15**	8	**10**	**25**	**22**
CAMBA	7	9	0	1	6	10
CAMBA + **SaFliTe**	**11**	**11**	**2**	**3**	6	**11**
TUMB	2	15	11	7	18	20
TUMB + **SaFliTe**	**5**	15	**18**	7	**20**	**21**

other missions, at least one tool either showed no increase or achieved only a single additional valid test case. This variability in performance across missions may be attributed to the complexity of the tasks. Mission 2, being the simplest, involves the drone navigating to a waypoint and returning, which could explain the more consistent performance. However, as the missions become more complex, the LLM may struggle to fully understand the mission, leading to unstable test case predictions and inconsistent performance. To address this, fine-tuning the LLM for specific missions or providing more detailed descriptions of the mission in the Current System State within the prompt might help improve its understanding and improve the accuracy of test case predictions.

Table 3. Results of the number of valid test cases generated by DeepHyperion-UAV + SaFliTe using different LLMs.

LLM	Number of Valid Test Cases					
	Mission 2	Mission 3	Mission 4	Mission 5	Mission 6	Mission 7
GPT3.5	17	15	8	10	25	22
Mistral-7B	13	11	13	8	33	14
Llama-2-7B	12	10	8	4	16	8

Different LLMs. We further investigate the outcomes from DeepHyperion-UAV + SaFliTe, using different LLMs as the prediction core. As shown in Table 3, overall, GPT-3.5 still delivers the most significant improvement in the capabilities of DeepHyperion-UAV, while Llama-2-7B offers relatively less improvement. Notably, Mistral-7B demonstrates performance improvements that are nearly on par with GPT-3.5 and even surpasses GPT-3.5 in Mission 4 and Mission 6. The performance rankings of the three LLMs in fuzzing align with the results from RQ1, with GPT-3.5 leading, Mistral-7B close behind, and Llama-2-7B showing the weakest performance.

Given the results, Mistral-7B's strong performance is particularly impressive, considering it is a local LLM that has not undergone fine-tuning. This highlights the suitability of locally deployed, smaller LLMs for AS fuzzing tasks, and further improvements could unlock even greater potential for such models in this domain.

> Answer to RQ3: SAFLITE can successfully integrate with various fuzzing tools, execute a full fuzzing test, and significantly improve their performance.

4   Related Work

In fuzzing AS, most tools rely on mutation-based techniques. For example, Hu et al. mutated traffic scenarios by changing traffic light colors or vehicle starting positions for testing the autonomous driving systems [7]. Additionally, there is also a lot of research focused on fuzzing UAV AS. For example, Khatiri et al. organized a fuzzing competition for the PX4-avoidance system, aiming to generate test cases that cause policy violations [10]. This led to the development of several fuzzing tools for UAV systems. Zohdinasab et al. introduced a novel algorithm to rank seeds, selecting the best ones for mutation and test case generation [25]. Tang et al. developed TUMB, which uses Monte Carlo Tree Search (MCTS) to explore the UAV environment and generate diverse test cases [16]. Similarly, Winsten et al. [21] applied Wasserstein generative adversarial networks [2] to generate UAV test cases, comparable to Zhong et al.'s use of neural networks in fuzzing autonomous driving systems to predict whether new seeds would trigger traffic violations [24]. Both approaches exploit neural networks' ability to manage complex relationships. However, training neural networks can pose significant stability and convergence issues [15]. In contrast, we leverage LLMs to predict test cases, offering a more adaptive approach. Current research on LLMs in AS focuses on environmental understanding. For instance, Jiahui et al. showed that LLMs can assess the realism of driving environments [23]. Similarly, PromptTrack, introduced by Dongming et al., enables LLMs to predict object trajectories [22], while HiLM-D predicts risk object locations from images [5]. Our research differs by focusing on using LLMs to predict interesting test cases based on their environmental understanding.

5   Conclusion

In this paper, we introduce SAFLITE, a predictor that uses an LLM to determine whether a test case aligns with a user-defined test condition. We designed a framework for SAFLITE that integrates with any fuzz testing tool for AS, using its predictive capabilities to filter out irrelevant test cases and enhance performance. We evaluated the prediction accuracy of SAFLITE using real flight logs and tested it with four fuzz testing tools on three automated systems. The results show that SAFLITE significantly improves fuzz testing efficiency.

References

1. *SAFLITE* (2024). https://github.com/Trusted-AI-in-System-Test/SaFliTe-Test-Interestingness-Predictor
2. Arjovsky, M., Chintala, S., Bottou, L.: Wasserstein generative adversarial networks. In: ICML, pp. 214–223. PMLR (2017)
3. Cha, S.K., Woo, M., Brumley, D.: Program-adaptive mutational fuzzing. In: Symposium on Security and Privacy, pp. 725–741. IEEE (2015)
4. De Liso, M., Soi, Z.W.: CAMBA CPS-UAV at the SBFT tool competition 2024: CAMBA: cost-aware mutation-based test case generation for unmanned aerial vehicles. In: Proceedings of the 17th International Workshop on SBFT, pp. 47–48 (2024)
5. Ding, X., Han, J., Xu, H., Zhang, W., Li, X.: Hilm-d: towards high-resolution understanding in multimodal large language models for autonomous driving. arXiv preprint arXiv:2309.05186 (2023)
6. Giering, M., Venugopalan, V., Reddy, K.: Multi-modal sensor registration for vehicle perception via deep neural networks. In: HPEC, pp. 1–6. IEEE (2015)
7. Hu, Z., Guo, S., Zhong, Z., Li, K.: Coverage-based scene fuzzing for virtual autonomous driving testing. arXiv preprint arXiv:2106.00873 (2021)
8. Jahan, F., Sun, W., Niyaz, Q., Alam, M.: Security modeling of autonomous systems: a survey. ACM Comput. Surv. (CSUR) **52**(5), 1–34 (2019)
9. Jiang, A.Q., et al.: Mistral 7b. arXiv preprint arXiv:2310.06825 (2023)
10. Khatiri, S., Saurabh, P., Zimmermann, T., Munasinghe, C., Birchler, C., Panichella, S.: SBFT tool competition 2024: CPS-UAV test case generation track. In: 17th International Workshop on SBFT. ZHAW Zürcher Hochschule für Angewandte Wissenschaften (2024)
11. Kim, H., Ozmen, M.O., Bianchi, A., Celik, Z.B., Xu, D.: Pgfuzz: policy-guided fuzzing for robotic vehicles. In: NDSS (2021)
12. Korthals, T., Kragh, M., Christiansen, P., Karstoft, H., Jørgensen, R.N., Rückert, U.: Multi-modal detection and mapping of static and dynamic obstacles in agriculture for process evaluation. Front. Robot. AI **5**, 28 (2018)
13. Mejri, M.N., Ben-Othman, J., Hamdi, M.: Survey on vanet security challenges and possible cryptographic solutions. Veh. Commun. **1**(2), 53–66 (2014)
14. Ouyang, L., Wu, J., Jiang, X., Almeida, D., et al.: Training language models to follow instructions with human feedback. Adv. NeurIPS **35**, 27730–27744 (2022)
15. Pascanu, R., Mikolov, T., Bengio, Y.: On the difficulty of training recurrent neural networks. In: ICML, pp. 1310–1318. Pmlr (2013)
16. Tang, S., Zhang, Z., Cetinkaya, A., Arcaini, P.: TUMB at the SBFT 2024 tool competition-CPS-UAV test case generation track. In: Proceedings of the 17th International Workshop on SBFT, pp. 53–54 (2024)
17. Team, A.D.: ArduPilot (2009). https://ardupilot.org/
18. Team, P.D.: PX4 autopilot (2012). https://px4.io/
19. Touvron, H., et al.: Llama 2: open foundation and fine-tuned chat models. arXiv preprint arXiv:2307.09288 (2023)
20. Wakabayashi, D.: Uber's self-driving cars were struggling before arizona crash. International New York Times pp. NA–NA (2018)
21. Winsten, J., Soloviev, V., Peltomäki, J., Porres, I.: Adaptive test generation for unmanned aerial vehicles using WOGAN-UAV. In: Proceedings of the 17th ACM/IEEE International Workshop on SBFT, pp. 43–44 (2024)

22. Wu, D., Han, W., Wang, T., Liu, Y., Zhang, X., Shen, J.: Language prompt for autonomous driving. arXiv preprint arXiv:2309.04379 (2023)
23. Wu, J., Lu, C., Arrieta, A., Yue, T., Ali, S.: Reality bites: assessing the realism of driving scenarios with large language models. arXiv preprint arXiv:2403.09906 (2024)
24. Zhong, Z., Kaiser, G., Ray, B.: Neural network guided evolutionary fuzzing for finding traffic violations of autonomous vehicles. IEEE Trans. Softw. Eng. (2022)
25. Zohdinasab, T., Doreste, A.: DeepHyperion-UAV at the SBFT tool competition 2024-CPS-UAV test case generation track. In: Proceedings of the 17th International Workshop on SBFT, pp. 49–50 (2024)

Varanus: Runtime Verification for CSP

Matt Luckcuck[1]([✉]) [iD], Angelo Ferrando[2] [iD], and Fatma Faruq[3] [iD]

[1] University of Nottingham, Nottingham, UK
matt.luckcuck@nottingham.ac.uk, aferrando@unimore.it
[2] University of Modena and Reggio Emilia, Modena, Italy
[3] Manchester, UK

Abstract. Autonomous systems are often used in changeable and unknown environments, where traditional verification may not be suitable. Runtime Verification (RV) checks events performed by a system against a formal specification of its intended behaviour, making it highly suitable for ensuring that an autonomous system is obeying its specification at runtime. Communicating Sequential Processes (CSP) is a process algebra usually used in static verification, which captures behaviour as a trace of events, making it useful for RV as well. Further, CSP has more recently been used to specify autonomous and robotic systems. Though CSP is supported by two extant model checkers, so far it has no RV tool. This paper presents VARANUS, an RV tool that monitors a system against an oracle built from a CSP specification. This approach enables the reuse without modifications of a specification that was built, e.g. during the system's design. We describe the tool, apply it to a simulated autonomous robotic rover inspecting a nuclear waste store, empirically comparing its performance to two other RV tools using different languages, and demonstrate how it can detect violations of the specification. VARANUS can synthesise a monitor from a CSP process in roughly linear time, with respect to the number of states and transitions in the model; and checks each event in roughly constant time.

1 Introduction

Robotic and Autonomous Systems (RAS) must operate reliably in unpredictable, dynamic environments, where design-time assumptions may not hold and traditional verification techniques often fall short. Runtime Verification (RV) addresses this challenge by comparing events performed by a System Under Analysis (SUA) to a formal specification of its intended behaviour; this specification, or *oracle*, determines whether the SUA has complied with it. RV can be performed *online*, on a running program, or *offline*, by analysing a logged execution trace. It enables the behaviour of an autonomous SUA to drive exploration of the specification's state space, providing ongoing assurance during operation and bridging the *reality gap* between design-time models and real-world execution [19].

This paper presents VARANUS, an RV tool that meets the challenges of autonomous systems. It uses a Communicating Sequential Processes (CSP) specification as its oracle. Although CSP is a well-established process algebra with

---

F. Faruq—Independent Researcher.

A. Cavalcanti et al. (Eds.): TAROS 2025, LNAI 16045, pp. 259–272, 2026.
https://doi.org/10.1007/978-3-032-01486-3_21

two model checkers – the Failures-Divergences Refinement checker (FDR) [15] and the Process Analysis Toolkit [31] – it previously lacked dedicated support for RV. Though this work focusses on autonomous systems, we note that VARANUS can also be used for the RV of non-autonomous systems.

CSP is a rich, flexible language often used to model requirements or high-level designs, and has more recently been used to specify autonomous and robotic systems [26]. Specifications at varying abstraction levels can be linked through refinement, and CSP enables reasoning about concurrency, synchronisation, and message-passing. VARANUS synthesises its oracle directly from a CSP process, in contrast to approaches that rely on CSP implementations or dialects (see Sect. 2).

A key advantage of our approach is that VARANUS verifies behaviour against a detailed process model, not just individual properties. This enables the reuse of formally verified specifications from earlier development stages and supports validating existing CSP models against implementations, closing the verification loop. Reusing a verified model lends confidence that the oracle is correct, and helps amortise the time spent building the model [30].

RAS are typically component-based (e.g., Robot Operating System (ROS)) and involve complex communication patterns. CSP is particularly suited to this context, allowing modular specifications and supporting detailed reasoning about message ordering. VARANUS leverages these features to detect violations such as incorrect sequencing or mismatched communication.

We demonstrate VARANUS using a simulated autonomous rover patrolling a nuclear waste store, monitored against a CSP specification that captures the minimal behaviour required to meet four system requirements. We evaluate VARANUS by checking traces from this simulation against the CSP model.

We also stress-test VARANUS using randomly generated CSP models and traces of increasing size to empirically show its linear performance. Additionally, we compare VARANUS' synthesis times with two state-of-the-art RV tools. While our evaluations are performed offline, VARANUS also supports online RV; however instrumenting this case study for online use proved difficult, so this is left as future work. Nonetheless, we show that the CSP oracle can be synthesised in roughly linear time, and each event checked in roughly constant time (see Sect. 5).

The rest of the paper is structured as follows: Sect. 2 covers related work; Sect. 3 introduces CSP and VARANUS; Sect. 4 presents the rover case study; Sect. 5 reports the evaluation; and Sect. 6 concludes with future work.

2   Related Work

Many robotics Domain Specific Languages (DSLs) prioritise code generation or simulation over verification [28], highlighting the need for verification in robotic systems. Our survey on Formal Methods for Autonomous Robotic Systems [20] identifies a notable exception: the Behaviour Interaction Priority (BIP) approach, which supports both specification and verification [5–7], and has been extended with RV-BIP [10]. More recently, RoboChart [26] offers a diagrammatic modelling language with a (timed) tock-CSP semantics; the structure and timing constructs provided by RoboChart models are a future target for VARANUS.

Our approach uses a CSP model directly as the RV oracle. Cavalcanti et al. [8] proposed translating divergence-free CSP processes into Kripke structures for RV, but no tool has resulted from this work. Other approaches rely on CSP dialects or implementations. For example, the **Jass** system [4] includes an assertion for permissible method traces using a CSP dialect tailored to Java [27], limiting its general reuse. Our work is agnostic of the SUA's implementation. Similarly, CSP_E [33], a Scala-based shallow-embedded DSL, requires converting models and lacks full CSP support, limiting its reusability.

Dynamic verification has also been applied to mobile robotics, such as predicting collisions with humans [18] or safe robot arm operation [29]. These are online methods, but do not provide static validation.

By contrast, ModelPlex [25] combines offline verification of hybrid models in differential dynamic logic (dL) with online validation, triggering safe behaviour when deviations occur. Another approach checks runtime behaviour of an autonomous robot against a model of its deployment environment [13], revealing where real-world interactions break design-time assumptions. While similar in goal, our case study is human-controlled and does not model its environment.

Rule-based systems are popular in RV for efficient event matching, particularly those using the Rete algorithm [14]. LogFire [16], a Scala-based tool, and Drools[1], a widely-used rule engine, use Rete to minimise re-evaluation by structuring rules as networks. These frameworks are efficient and flexible, by contrast VARANUS avoids rule-centric design by using CSP.

Temporal logic-based RV tools, such as LogScope [2] and TraceContract [3], support complex event monitoring via parameterised temporal logic. While expressive, they may struggle with performance on large event sets. VARANUS offers a more scalable alternative by modelling concurrency and dependencies directly in CSP, enabling efficient handling of complex sequences.

The Monitoring Oriented Programming (MOP) framework [24] improves efficiency through parametric trace slicing, creating independent traces per event parameter. In contrast, VARANUS achieves linear performance without slicing, offering a simpler solution aligned with CSP models.

Complex Event Processing (CEP) [22] targets real-time event pattern recognition in large data streams. Drools integrates CEP-like features for adaptive rule processing. However, VARANUS takes a deterministic approach focused on structured event sequences, making it better suited for ordered process models.

Finally, Runtime Monitoring Language (RML) [1] specifies monitors with complex temporal and state-based conditions. Unlike VARANUS, which uses CSP directly, RML emphasises rule-based and state-machine monitoring. VARANUS targets structured verification in concurrent and distributed systems, where strict event ordering and concurrency control are essential. Its model-driven approach complements RML's flexibility, offering robust support for high-assurance environments.

---

[1] https://www.drools.org/.

Table 1. Summary of CSP operators used in this paper.

Action	Syntax	Description
Skip	*Skip*	The terminating process
Simple Prefix	$a \rightarrow Skip$	Simple synchronisation on a with no data, followed by *Skip*
Input Event	$a?in$	Synchronisation that binds a the input value to *in*
Restricted Input Event	$a?in : (valid)$	Restricts the possible values of *in* to members of *valid*
Parameter Event	$c.value$	Synchronisation matching the given *value*
Guarded Event	$(boolean\ expression)\&c.var$	Guards communication on c with a boolean expression
External Choice	$P \square Q$	Choice between two processes P and Q

3   Varanus: CSP Runtime Verification

This section describes VARANUS, our CSP verification tool[2]. VARANUS is capable of monitoring the SUA against a CSP process that specifies its intended behaviour. While the CSP model captures only the intended behaviour of the SUA, not its environment, failures at runtime can expose where the environment does not behave as the SUA assumes. The current version of VARANUS (v0.9.4) uses FDR's API to parse the CSP specification and to check if the CSP process is suitable, given the events in the SUA that are visible, via a determinism check (described in Sect. 3.2). We aim to remove the dependency on FDR and limitation of the tool to deterministic processes in future work.

The SUA can be monitored *online*, where VARANUS listens for events performed by a running SUA; or *offline*, where VARANUS reads events from a logged trace of the SUA's behaviour. Our evaluation focusses on offline RV. In either case, VARANUS checks if the event is valid, given the current trace of events and returns a verdict (pass or fail); for a failing trace, VARANUS will warn the user, then display the failing trace and acceptable events (a counterexample). In the rest of this section, we briefly describe CSP (Sect. 3.1) to give the reader an understanding of the language used to specify the system's intended behaviour, and give an overview of how VARANUS works (Sect. 3.2).

3.1   CSP Overview

This section provides a brief overview of CSP as a primer for the reader. Table 1 shows the operators that we use in this paper. CSP specifications are built from processes, which may take parameters. A process describes a sequence of events; for example $a \rightarrow b \rightarrow Skip$ is the process where the events a and b happen sequentially, followed by *Skip* which is the terminating process. An event is an instantaneous communication on a *channel*, and each event marks something that we are interested in during the system's execution. Channels enable message-passing between processes, they are synchronous, non-lossy, and may

---

[2] VARANUS, named for the biological genus of Monitor Lizards, is available at https://github.com/autonomy-and-verification/varanus/releases/tag/v0.9.4.

have multiple end-points; but a process may also perform an event (communicate an event on a channel) independently without a cooperating process.

A channel may declare typed parameters, for example *channel c : int* declares a channel c with one integer parameter. Parameters communicated on c may be inputs ($c?in$), outputs ($c!out$), or a given value ($c.value$); here *in*, *out*, and *value* are all of type *int* to match the parameter type. Input parameters bind to the parameter name, and output parameters must already exist in the scope of the process. Inputs can be restricted ($c?p : (set)$) to only parameters (p) in a given *set* – since c takes an *int* parameter, *set* is a set of *ints*. $P \ \Box \ Q$ offers the alternative of either P or Q, once the first event of either P or Q occurs, the other becomes unavailable.

FDR's input language, CSP_M, is a machine-readable version of CSP that adds basic set functions like $member(e, S)$, which returns true if e is a member of the set S; and $diff(S, T)$, which returns the set S with the elements from set T removed. For verification, FDR has in-built assertions and can check *refinement* between processes. The in-built assertions are used to check for *deadlock*, where a process can no longer perform any events; *divergence*, where a process may perform an infinite sequence of internal events; and *non-determinism*, where a process can both accept and refuse to perform an event after some initial trace. A refinement assertion compares the behaviour of the processes. For example, if we have two processes P and Q, then P is refined by Q ($P \sqsubseteq Q$) if every behaviour of Q is also a behaviour of P. This can be thought of as Q implementing P, like a software component implementing an interface.

3.2 Varanus Overview

VARANUS provides a terminal interface and most of its options can be set using a YAML configuration file. When we are confident that the CSP specification accurately represents the system's intended behaviour, we can use it for RV. As previously mentioned, VARANUS uses FDR to parse CSP specification, explore the Labelled-Transition System (LTS) produced by FDR to synthesise our RV oracle (which is also an LTS). We do not directly use the data structure produced by FDR because its own documentation says that "the methods that are used to visit transitions of this machine are not high-performance"[3]. VARANUS assumes that the CSP specification can be correctly parsed by FDR and has been verified as a correct specification of the intended behaviour of the SUA.

To monitor the SUA, VARANUS processes each event performed by the SUA, either by reading a file of logged events or listening over sockets/WebSockets. The information/events that VARANUS can read is, clearly, dependent on the SUA itself. But if the event names do not match the events in the CSP model, then VARANUS can read a JSON file that contains mappings between the SUA events and the CSP events. This must be written manually, because it is highly dependent on the SUA and specification.

---

[3] https://cocotec.io/fdr/manual/api/c++/class_f_d_r_1_1_l_t_s_1_1_machine.html.

VARANUS checks the behaviour of the SUA against the formal model being used as the oracle. In this formal model, M, a transition from one state to another is labelled by the event that triggers that transition; the set of all the events that the model can perform is called its alphabet, and we use the function $Alpha(M)$ to get the alphabet of model M. The SUA can be thought of as a 'hidden' model, the transitions of which are revealed one event at a time.

For each new event, e, produced by the SUA, VARANUS checks if e is the label of one of the transitions leaving the current state; we represent this set of events using the function $Events(s)$, which produces the events of the transitions leaving state s. If the event is in the model's alphabet ($e \in Alpha(M)$) and in the set of event labels for the current state ($e \in Events(s)$) then the event is valid and the current state in the LTS moves to the transition's destination state, s'.

If the event is in the model's alphabet but is not available in this state ($e \in Alpha(M)$ but $e \notin Events(s)$), then VARANUS will always conclude that this is a failing trace of events. However, if the event is not in the model's alphabet ($e \notin Alpha(M)$ and, presumably, $e \notin Events(s)$ either) then we have a problem, because we don't know why the alphabets of the model and SUA are different. Maybe:

1. the model is complete and the SUA is misbehaving; or,
2. the model is partial and the correctness of the SUA does not depend on e.

So VARANUS provides two modes, *strict* and *permissive*, to deal with these two possibilities. Strict mode handles situation 1, above; if VARANUS receives an event that is not in the model's alphabet, then it sees this as an error in the SUA. Permissive mode handles situation 2: if VARANUS receives an event not in the alphabet, then it simply stays in the current state.

In strict mode, we assume that the CSP model is complete, it captures exactly what the system should do. In this mode, if an event from the SUA is not in $Alpha(M)$, then VARANUS reports an error because the model does not have a corresponding transition, therefore the SUA must be misbehaving. Definition 1 shows the next-state function for VARANUS's strict mode.

Definition 1. (Next-State in Strict Mode)

$$next_{strict}(s, e) = \begin{cases} Error & if\ e \notin Alpha(M) \\ Error & if\ e \notin Events(s) \\ s' & otherwise \end{cases}$$

In permissive mode we assume that the model is an patrial, or abstract specification of what the system should do. Here, if an event from the SUA is not in $Alpha(M)$, then VARANUS ignores it and stays in the current state. Definition 2 shows the next-state function for permissive mode.

Definition 2. (Next-State in Permissive Mode)

$$next_{permissive}(s, e) = \begin{cases} s & if\ e \notin Alpha(M) \\ Error & if\ e \notin Events(s) \\ s' & otherwise \end{cases}$$

For offline RV, VARANUS processes each event from the logged events in the trace file, checking it and transitioning to the next state, until it either reaches the end of the trace file or finds a failing event. For online RV, VARANUS listens for, and checks, events until the SUA disconnects or it finds a failing event. In both cases, if a new event produces a trace that fails, VARANUS will report this to the user. In future work, we want to improve the interaction between VARANUS and the SUA to enable runtime *enforcement*, where behaviour that violates the specification can be corrected. We discuss this more in Sect. 6.

A current limitation of VARANUS (v0.9.4) is that it can only use deterministic CSP processes, this is to simplify how VARANUS deals with a mismatch between the alphabets of the CSP model and the SUA; we aim to remove this limitation in future work. This mismatch causes a problem when the alphabet of the CSP model is a larger than the SUA; CSP lets us hide the events that the model can perform but the SUA cannot, but these hidden events can cause non-determinism which makes it hard to decide if the SUA has violated the specification or not. VARANUS checks that the CSP process is deterministic, while hiding the events that the SUA cannot perform. If the process is non-deterministic, VARANUS aborts before even synthesising the oracle.

4   Case Study

Our case study involves an autonomous ground rover patrolling a simulated nuclear waste store [21]. The rover must inspect five waypoints and take radiation readings – categorised as *red* (high), *orange* (medium), or *green* (low). A human operator uses this data to assess safety, while autonomous patrolling reduces human exposure to harmful radiation.

If the rover detects high or medium radiation, it returns to the entry point (waypoint 0) for decontamination, preventing damage and avoiding human retrieval in hazardous conditions.

The rover's high-level requirements are:

REQ1: Inspect each waypoint unless radiation is high.
REQ2: Inspect each waypoint at least once.
REQ3: Abort and return to entry on high radiation.
REQ4: Complete all inspections or abort due to high radiation.

The system comprises four components: **Localisation**, which estimates the rover's position; **Navigation**, which handles path planning and movement tracking; the **Agent**, which makes decisions based on the rover's position and radiation level (*radiationStatus*); and the **Radiation Sensor**, which monitors radiation and confirms inspections. Built using ROS, the system supports trace collection via a global clock.[4] Future work will explore decentralised RV.

Our CSP model captures the minimal behaviour satisfying REQ1–REQ4. We verify it with FDR and reuse it directly in VARANUS as the RV oracle. Since the

---

[4] https://wiki.ros.org/Clock.

SUA may perform additional, irrelevant events, we use VARANUS in permissive mode, requiring only that events from the model's alphabet occur in the specified order and with correct parameters.

$ROVER(\emptyset, \_) =$
  $mission\_complete \rightarrow Skip$
  $\square$
  $radiation\_level?\,Green \rightarrow ROVER(\emptyset, Green)$
  $\square$
  $radiation\_level?r : (Red, Orange) \rightarrow ROVER\_ABORT$

$ROVER(WaypointSet, Rad) =$
  $inspect?wp : (WaypointSet) \rightarrow ROVER\_INSPECTING(WaypointSet, Rad, wp)$
  $\square$
  $radiation\_level?\,Green \rightarrow ROVER(WaypointSet, Green)$
  $\square$
  $radiation\_level?r : (Red, Orange) \rightarrow ROVER\_ABORT$
  $\square$
  $(member(0, WaypointSet))\&move.0 \rightarrow ROVER(diff(WaypointSet, 0), Rad)$

$ROVER\_INSPECTING(WaypointSet, Rad, wp) =$
  $move.wp \rightarrow ROVER(diff(WaypointSet, wp), Rad)$
  $\square$
  $radiation\_level?\,Green \rightarrow ROVER\_INSPECTING(WaypointSet, Green, wp)$
  $\square$
  $radiation\_level?r : (Red, Orange) \rightarrow ROVER\_ABORT$

$ROVER\_ABORT = move.0 \rightarrow mission\_abort \rightarrow Skip$

Fig. 1. Specification of the rover's abstract behaviour. Using pattern-matching $ROVER(\emptyset, \_)$ defines the processes behaviour when the $WaypointSet$ is empty (in CSP $\_$ is a wildcard) otherwise the process behaves as $ROVER(WaypointSet, Rad)$.

Figure 1 shows the main CSP processes. If $WaypointSet = \emptyset$, $ROVER(\emptyset, \_)$ ends the mission. Otherwise, $ROVER(WaypointSet, Rad)$ forms the main loop: the rover issues an *inspect* command for a waypoint $wp \in WaypointSet$, then transitions to $ROVER\_INSPECTING(WaypointSet, Rad, wp)$ to perform *move.wp*. After moving, it returns to $ROVER$ with wp removed $(diff(WaypointSet, \{wp\}))$.

A guarded *move.0* event represents entry into the store and is only enabled if 0 is in $WaypointSet$. The *radiation_level* event is always available. If the level is Red or $Orange$, the process transitions to $ROVER\_ABORT$, which triggers *move.0* and aborts the mission. If the level is $Green$, then the rover continues with the Rad parameter updated to match.

The specification in Fig. 1 satisfies REQ1–REQ4. It checks radiation before inspection (REQ1), removes inspected waypoints from the set (REQ2), returns to waypoint 0 on Red or $Orange$ readings (REQ3), and terminates only when all waypoints are inspected or high radiation is detected (REQ4).

The model begins with $mission\_start \rightarrow ROVER(waypointID, Green)$, where $waypointID$ is the full set of waypoints and $Green$ is assumed at the entry point. Upon termination via $mission\_complete$ or $mission\_abort$, a new mission can begin. The events $mission\_start$, $mission\_complete$, and $mission\_abort$ help identify mission boundaries in traces.

VARANUS synthesises an LTS from this model and monitors traces as described in Sect. 3.2. For example, the trace ⟨*mission_start*, *inspect*.2, *radiation_level*. *Green*, *move*.2, ...⟩ passes, as *inspect* and *move* target the same waypoint and radiation is safe. In contrast, the trace ⟨*mission_start*, *inspect*.2, *radiation_level*. *Red*, *move*.2, ...⟩ fails, since the rover should return to waypoint 0 after detecting high radiation. In the next section, we evaluate VARANUS's performance and its ability to catch such violations.

5 Evaluation

We evaluate VARANUS via two experiments. First, we stress-test it using generated models and traces of increasing size. Then, we demonstrate its effectiveness by monitoring event traces from the simulated rover case study – first using a passing trace, then injecting faults. While VARANUS supports online RV, instrumenting this particular case study proved challenging, so making it easier to map ROS messages into events in the model is left for future work.

5.1 Stress Testing

We stress-test VARANUS's performance during LTS synthesis and verification by using increasingly large CSP models and traces. Our experiments were run on a machine with an Intel Core i7 2.80 GHz 4-core CPU and 16 GiB RAM, and record the timings using the `time` module in Python's standard library.

To create a 'worst-case process', we generate CSP models of size N such that the corresponding LTS has N states, each with transitions to all others – e.g., a model of size 10 yields 10 states and 100 transitions. These maximal-transition models subsume any other finite LTS of the same size and alphabet. Figure 2 shows that synthesis time grows roughly linearly with model size. Each data point represents the average of 10 runs.

We generate traces of varying lengths, using the alphabet of the CSP models from the previous test, to evaluate how VARANUS's performance varies by trace length. Any generated trace is valid, since the CSP models always accept any event in the alphabet. Figure 3 shows the time to verify complete traces for models of different sizes. The x-axis represents trace length; the y-axis, verification time. Each line corresponds to a model size (e.g., 100 to 10,000 states). As expected, verification time increases linearly with trace length, indicating VARANUS's suitability for online RV. Figure 4 reorganises the same data, here the lines corresponds to a different trace length. The results show linear scaling with both model size and trace length.

Figure 5 presents the average time to verify individual events. Unlike previous plots, it highlights that VARANUS can process each event in constant time – an essential property for online RV, where events arrive incrementally.

We also compare VARANUS's synthesis time with two existing approaches: Linear-time Temporal Logic (LTL) via the Spot library [9] and RML via SWI-Prolog [32]. Figure 6 shows synthesis times for over 1,000 randomly generated

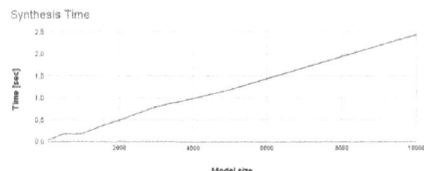

Fig. 2. Monitor synthesis time.

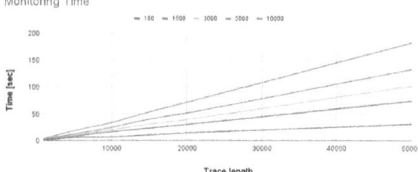

Fig. 3. Verification time (whole trace).

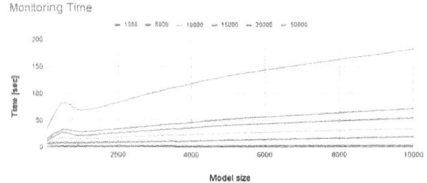

Fig. 4. Verification time (whole trace) but varying the model size.

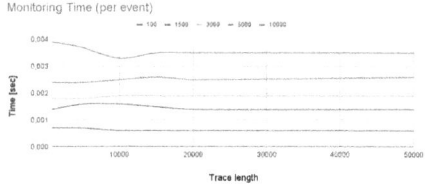

Fig. 5. Verification time (single event).

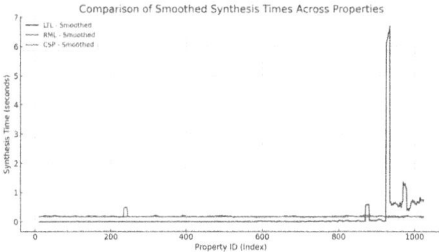

Fig. 6. Comparison of Synthesis Time for LTL, RML, and (our synthesis of) CSP. The Property ID is the identifier of the LTL properties analyses, in which higher is the ID, bigger is the size of the LTL property.

LTL formulae, with equivalent CSP and RML specifications derived from each[5]. RML [1] is included due to its process algebra roots and conceptual similarities to VARANUS. As Fig. 6 shows, LTL synthesis time degrades with formula size, but both VARANUS and RML maintain stable, scalable performance.

5.2   Monitoring the Case Study

To evaluate VARANUS on the simulated rover from Sect. 4, we collected a 243-event trace from a run where the rover patrolled five waypoints with all radiation levels reported as *Green*. We included *mission_start* and *mission_complete* events to mark the trace boundaries. The **Radiation Sensor** in the simulation continuously emits *radiation_level* events, which the model accommodates.

---

[5] Restricted to the safety fragment of LTL to enable translation, following [17].

Table 2. Summary of approximate total time, synthesis time, checking time, and mean checking time per event, for the four experiments in Sect. 5.2. The final column shows the number of events that were checked and the total number of events in the trace, for each experiment, and if the trace passed or failed.

Total Time	Synthesis Time	Checking Time	Mean Time/Event	Events/Total Events
0.39 s	0.22 s	0.14 s	0.0004 s	243/243 (Pass)
0.27 s	0.19 s	0.05 s	0.0004 s	51/243 (Fail)
0.30 s	0.22 s	0.05 s	0.0004 s	49/243 (Fail)
0.31 s	0.20 s	0.08 s	0.0004 s	121/243 (Fail)

These experiments assess whether VARANUS produces correct verdicts, rather than focusing on synthesis or verification time. Table 2 summarises performance metrics. We ran our experiments on a machine with an Intel Xeon 3.50GHz 8-core CPU and 32 GiB RAM on Ubuntu 22.04.4.

Running VARANUS on the full 243-event trace yields no violations, completing in ∼0.39 s. This is expected, as all events are correctly ordered and radiation levels remain *Green*. The LTS synthesis took ∼0.22 s, and trace checking ∼0.14 s, with an average of 0.0004 s per event. To test failure detection, we inject a fault where the rover encounters *radiation_level.Red* but continues the mission, violating REQ3. VARANUS aborts after 51 events, correctly expecting *move.0*, and completes in ∼0.27 s (synthesis: ∼0.19 s; checking: ∼0.05 s).

We also evaluate VARANUS's ability to detect incorrect event ordering and parameter mismatches. Reversing *inspect.1* and *move.1* causes a failure after 49 events (total time: ∼0.30 s; synthesis: ∼0.22 s; checking: ∼0.05 s). Injecting a mismatch (e.g., *inspect.3* followed by *move.5*) causes VARANUS to abort after 121 events, completing in ∼0.31 s (synthesis: ∼0.20 s; checking: ∼0.08 s). In all cases, the average checking time remains ∼0.0004 s per event.

As shown in Table 2, the mean checking time per event is ∼0.0004 s, even for the full passing trace. Figure 5 shows that even under pessimistic conditions, this time remains below 0.004 s for models with up to 10,000 states and 50,000 events. These results suggest that VARANUS is suitable for online RV, with minimal runtime overhead. Although LTS synthesis is relatively slow, it occurs only once before monitoring begins and does not affect runtime performance. Future work aims to improve synthesis speed (Sect. 6). VARANUS effectively detects deviations from the CSP model, including violations of system requirements and incorrect event ordering or parameter mismatches.

6   Conclusion and Future Work

This paper presents VARANUS, a novel RV tool that verifies a system's behaviour against a CSP specification. VARANUS builds an LTS from a CSP process and uses it as an oracle to validate the SUA's actions. While the specification is parsed using FDR, event checking is performed independently on the synthesised LTS.

We demonstrated VARANUS using a simulated autonomous rover and stress-tested it with worst-case models and traces of increasing size. VARANUS synthesises the LTS it uses as its oracle in roughly linear time and checks each event in constant time. In the rover case study, the mean event checking time was ∼0.0004 s, indicating that VARANUS introduces minimal overhead and is suitable for online RV. Reusing unmodified CSP specifications simplifies the modelling process, which is often the primary bottleneck in applying formal methods [30].

CSP enables the specification of both high-level requirements and detailed designs, linked by refinement, and is sensitive to event order – essential for message-based systems. This makes it particularly useful for RV of RAS, because it bridges the gap between design-time models and dynamic real-world behaviour. VARANUS also enhances the CSP toolset by supporting validation of existing models against real implementations.

In future work, we aim to remove the dependency on FDR by developing a stand-alone CSP parser. This would improve synthesis time and enable support for platforms where FDR is unavailable, such as ARM-based systems. We also plan to enable runtime *enforcement*, where incorrect behaviours are corrected by selecting valid alternatives from the model. This requires system architectures that consult VARANUS before executing behaviours [19], as well as support for replanning or automated selection of valid next steps from counterexamples. To facilitate this, we will link VARANUS to the ROSMonitoring framework [12], which will also support future demonstrations of online RV.

We further intend to demonstrate VARANUS on more complex examples, including larger models and scenarios with multiple monitors (e.g., one per component). This will allow us to explore the impact on synthesis and checking time at scale. Additionally, we are interested in using VARANUS for predictive RV, where the CSP model is used to detect behaviours that inevitably lead to failure. Combined with multiple monitors, this opens the door to multi-monitor predictive RV [11]. Finally, we plan to use VARANUS to monitor CSP mission specifications, ensuring robotic systems adhere to their intended missions [23].

Acknowledgements. Some of Luckcuck's initial work was done while working for the Universities of Liverpool, Manchester, and Maynooth. We are grateful to Faruq for her work on this paper *in her spare time*, and to Pedro Ribeiro for his help fixing FDR and his general interest in the work.

References

1. Ancona, D., Franceschini, L., Ferrando, A., Mascardi, V.: RML: theory and practice of a domain specific language for runtime verification. Sci. Comput. Program. **205**, 102610 (2021). https://doi.org/10.1016/J.SCICO.2021.102610
2. Barringer, H., Groce, A., Havelund, K., Smith, M.H.: Formal analysis of log files. J. Aerosp. Comput. Inf. Commun. **7**(11), 365–390 (2010). https://doi.org/10.2514/1.49356

3. Barringer, H., Havelund, K.: TRACECONTRACT: a scala DSL for trace analysis. In: Butler, M., Schulte, W. (eds.) FM 2011. LNCS, vol. 6664, pp. 57–72. Springer, Heidelberg (2011). https://doi.org/10.1007/978-3-642-21437-0_7

4. Bartetzko, D., Fischer, C., Möller, M., Wehrheim, H.: Jass – java with assertions. Electron. Notes Theor. Comput. Sci. **55**(2), 103–117 (2001). https://doi.org/10.1016/S1571-0661(04)00247-6

5. Basu, A., et al.: Rigorous component-based system design using the BIP framework. IEEE Softw. **28**(3), 41–48 (2011). https://doi.org/10.1109/MS.2011.27

6. Basu, A., et al.: Incremental component-based construction and verification of a robotic system. Front. Artif. Intell. Appl. **178**, 631–635 (2008). https://doi.org/10.3233/978-1-58603-891-5-631

7. Bensalem, S., Gallien, M., Ingrand, F., Kahloul, I., Thanh-Hung, N.: Designing autonomous robots. IEEE Robot. Autom. Mag. **16**(1), 67–77 (2009). https://doi.org/10.1109/MRA.2008.931631

8. Cavalcanti, A., Huang, W., Peleska, J., Woodcock, J.: CSP and Kripke structures. In: Leucker, M., Rueda, C., Valencia, F.D. (eds.) ICTAC 2015. LNCS, vol. 9399, pp. 505–523. Springer, Cham (2015). https://doi.org/10.1007/978-3-319-25150-9_29

9. Duret-Lutz, A., et al.: From spot 2.0 to spot 2.10: what's new? In: Shoham, S., Vizel, Y. (eds.) Computer Aided Verification - 34th International Conference, CAV 2022, Haifa, Israel, 7–10 August 2022, Proceedings, Part II. LNCS, vol. 13372, pp. 174–187. Springer, Heidelberg (2022). https://doi.org/10.1007/978-3-031-13188-2_9

10. Falcone, Y., Jaber, M., Nguyen, T.-H., Bozga, M., Bensalem, S.: Runtime verification of component-based systems. In: Barthe, G., Pardo, A., Schneider, G. (eds.) SEFM 2011. LNCS, vol. 7041, pp. 204–220. Springer, Heidelberg (2011). https://doi.org/10.1007/978-3-642-24690-6_15

11. Ferrando, A., et al.: Bridging the gap between single- and multi-model predictive runtime verification. Formal Methods Syst. Des. **59**(1), 44–76 (2021). https://doi.org/10.1007/S10703-022-00395-7

12. Ferrando, A., Cardoso, R.C., Fisher, M., Ancona, D., Franceschini, L., Mascardi, V.: ROSMonitoring: a runtime verification framework for ROS. In: Mohammad, A., Dong, X., Russo, M. (eds.) TAROS 2020. LNCS (LNAI), vol. 12228, pp. 387–399. Springer, Cham (2020). https://doi.org/10.1007/978-3-030-63486-5_40

13. Ferrando, A., Dennis, L.A., Cardoso, R.C., Fisher, M., Ancona, D., Mascardi, V.: Toward a holistic approach to verification and validation of autonomous cognitive systems. ACM Trans. Softw. Eng. Methodol. **30**(4), 43:1–43:43 (2021). https://doi.org/10.1145/3447246

14. Forgy, C.: Rete: a fast algorithm for the many patterns/many objects match problem. Artif. Intell. **19**(1), 17–37 (1982). https://doi.org/10.1016/0004-3702(82)90020-0

15. Gibson-Robinson, T., Armstrong, P., Boulgakov, A., Roscoe, A.W.: FDR3—a modern refinement checker for CSP. In: Ábrahám, E., Havelund, K. (eds.) TACAS 2014. LNCS, vol. 8413, pp. 187–201. Springer, Heidelberg (2014). https://doi.org/10.1007/978-3-642-54862-8_13

16. Havelund, K.: Rule-based runtime verification revisited. Int. J. Softw. Tools Technol. Transf. **17**(2), 143–170 (2015). https://doi.org/10.1007/S10009-014-0309-2

17. Leuschel, M., Currie, A., Massart, T.: How to make FDR spin LTL model checking of CSP by refinement. In: Oliveira, J.N., Zave, P. (eds.) FME 2001. LNCS, vol. 2021, pp. 99–118. Springer, Heidelberg (2001). https://doi.org/10.1007/3-540-45251-6_6

18. Liu, S.B., Roehm, H., Heinzemann, C., Lutkebohle, I., Oehlerking, J., Althoff, M.: Provably safe motion of mobile robots in human environments. In: 2017 IEEE/RSJ International Conference on Intelligent Robots and Systems (IROS). IEEE (2017). https://doi.org/10.1109/iros.2017.8202313
19. Luckcuck, M.: Using formal methods for autonomous systems: five recipes for formal verification. Proc. Inst. Mech. Engineers Part O: J. Risk Reliabil. (2021). https://doi.org/10.1177/1748006X211034970
20. Luckcuck, M., Farrell, M., Dennis, L.A., Dixon, C., Fisher, M.: Formal specification and verification of autonomous robotic systems: a survey. ACM Comput. Surv. **52**(5), 1–41 (2019). https://doi.org/10.1145/3342355
21. Luckcuck, M., Farrell, M., Ferrando, A., Cardoso, R.C., Dennis, L.A., Fisher, M.: A compositional approach to verifying modular robotic systems (2023). https://arxiv.org/abs/2208.05507
22. Luckham, D.: The power of events: an introduction to complex event processing in distributed enterprise systems. In: Bassiliades, N., Governatori, G., Paschke, A. (eds.) RuleML 2008. LNCS, vol. 5321, pp. 3–3. Springer, Heidelberg (2008). https://doi.org/10.1007/978-3-540-88808-6_2
23. MacConville, D., Farrell, M., Luckcuck, M., Monahan, R.: Csp2turtle: verified turtle robot plans. Robotics **12**(2), 62 (2023). https://doi.org/10.3390/ROBOTICS12020062
24. Meredith, P.O., Jin, D., Griffith, D., Chen, F., Rosu, G.: An overview of the MOP runtime verification framework. Int. J. Softw. Tools Technol. Transf. **14**(3), 249–289 (2012). https://doi.org/10.1007/S10009-011-0198-6
25. Mitsch, S., Platzer, A.: ModelPlex: verified runtime validation of verified cyber-physical system models. Formal Methods Syst. Des. **49**(1–2), 33–74 (2016). https://doi.org/10.1007/s10703-016-0241-z
26. Miyazawa, A., Ribeiro, P., Li, W., Cavalcanti, A., Timmis, J., Woodcock, J.: Robochart: modelling and verification of the functional behaviour of robotic applications. Softw. Syst. Model. **18**(5), 3097–3149 (2019). https://doi.org/10.1007/s10270-018-00710-z
27. Moller, M.: Specifying and checking java using CSP. In: Workshop on Formal Techniques for Java-like Programs, Málaga, Spain, p. 9 (2002). http://www.cs.ru.nl/ftfjp/2002/MichaelMoeller.pdf
28. Nordmann, A., Hochgeschwender, N., Wigand, D., Wrede, S.: A survey on domain-specific languages in robotics. J. Softw. Eng. Robot. **7**(July), 195–206 (2016). https://doi.org/10.1007/978-3-319-11900-7_17
29. Pereira, A., Althoff, M.: Safety control of robots under computed torque control using reachable sets. In: 2015 IEEE International Conference on Robotics and Automation (ICRA). IEEE (2015). https://doi.org/10.1109/icra.2015.7139020
30. Rozier, K.Y.: Specification: the biggest bottleneck in formal methods and autonomy. In: Blazy, S., Chechik, M. (eds.) VSTTE 2016. LNCS, vol. 9971, pp. 8–26. Springer, Cham (2016). https://doi.org/10.1007/978-3-319-48869-1_2
31. Sun, J., Liu, Y., Dong, J.S.: Model checking CSP revisited: introducing a process analysis toolkit. In: Margaria, T., Steffen, B. (eds.) ISoLA 2008. CCIS, vol. 17, pp. 307–322. Springer, Heidelberg (2008). https://doi.org/10.1007/978-3-540-88479-8_22
32. Wielemaker, J., Schrijvers, T., Triska, M., Lager, T.: Swi-prolog. Theory Pract. Log Program. **12**(1–2), 67–96 (2012). https://doi.org/10.1017/S1471068411000494
33. Yamagata, Y., et al.: Runtime monitoring for concurrent systems. In: Falcone, Y., Sánchez, C. (eds.) RV 2016. LNCS, vol. 10012, pp. 386–403. Springer, Cham (2016). https://doi.org/10.1007/978-3-319-46982-9_24

Preliminary Study of DSL Code Generation for Robotics with LLMs

Alberto Tagliaferro$^{(\boxtimes)}$ (ID), Livia Lestingi (ID), and Matteo Rossi (ID)

Politecnico di Milano, Milan, Italy
{alberto.tagliaferro,livia.lestingi,matteo.rossi}@polimi.it

Abstract. Code generation through Large Language Models (LLMs) has made significant progress in recent years. However, when the code generation involves a lesser-known Domain-Specific Language (DSL), a standard tool in software development for cyber-physical systems, LLMs' performance significantly decreases. We present an exploratory study assessing LLMs' performance in generating LIrAs (Language for Interactive Agents) code, a DSL for robotic and multi-agent tasks specification. This work is a stepping stone towards improving LLM-generated DSL code through iterative specification repair techniques driven by formal verification results.

Keywords: Domain-Specific Languages (DSLs) · DSL Code Generation · Multi-Agent Systems · Large Language Models

1 Introduction

Software-intensive systems—e.g., autonomous driving, assistive robotics, and smart manufacturing—are increasingly integrated into our lives. These systems rely on intelligent cyber agents that gather and process environmental data, and act according to their tasks and analyzed inputs. Human interaction in Multi-Agent Systems (MASs) further complicates these complex systems, requiring stakeholders to mitigate various risks, including financial and, crucially, physical harm. Consequently, specifying interactive tasks in MASs is a significant challenge for software engineers [6], demanding specialized expertise, time, and effort, and it is error-prone.

Domain-Specific Languages (DSLs) have become essential tools in robotics to specify tasks [8]. Their high-level nature makes them effective for expressing complex behaviors and configurations in a concise, human-readable form. They can also be translated into formal models, enabling formal verification of task specifications. However, users must learn both the syntax and semantics of each DSL and each application often requires a custom DSL, as shown by the large number of such languages developed for different domains [13].

The advancements in Large Language Models (LLMs) have capabilities in understanding and generating human language, as well as code in widely used languages like Python, C, and C++ [21]. This opens up opportunities to automate software development from natural language specifications to implementation. However, when tasked with generating code in lesser-known DSLs, LLMs performance drops noticeably [3,11]. Hallucinations and syntax errors increase, and the generated DSL code often fails to capture the intended specification.

LLMs have shown strong performance in complex code generation tasks [10], including those traditionally considered challenging [7,21,22], thanks to the large amount of training data. Beyond general-purpose languages, recent research investigates their potential in generating code with DSL. For example, LLMs have been used to generate textual modeling languages like PlantUML [16] for UML diagrams [4,18]. Bassamzadeh and Methani [3] compare fine-tuning and Retrieval Augmented Generation (RAG) for DSL code generation; fine-tuning reduces hallucinations, while RAG improves syntax correctness. LLMs have also been applied in robotics, particularly for task planning and execution. Singh et al. [17] propose ProgPrompt, which uses LLMs to generate executable task plans from program-like specifications, showcasing the potential to bridge human-readable task descriptions and robot-executable plans.

This work investigates the use of LLMs for DSL code generation in robotics, starting from real-world scenario descriptions. As a testbed, we use the LIrAs DSL, a language designed for specifying MAS tasks via agents' atomic abilities [19]. Listing 1.1 [20] illustrates a basic example of LIrAs, introducing some of the language's key elements to aid in understanding the experimental campaign described in Sect. 2. In this example, a `Human` and a `Robot` must reach the first Point of Interest (PoI), namely `poi1`, but the `Robot` begins its movement only once the `Human` has reached the destination. After both agents arrive at the destination, the `Human` proceeds towards `poi2`, followed by the `Robot`.

In the first line of Listing 1.1 (as in any LIrAs specification), we define the name of the pattern, followed by the required input parameters—agents, locations, and any necessary resources (Lines 2, 3, 4, 5). Next, separate sequences are defined (Line 6 and Line 9), one for each agent involved in the pattern. These sequences specify the actions that the corresponding agent must perform, e.g., the actions listed on Line 7 and Line 8 for the `Human` agent. The concurrent execution of these sequences, synchronizes according to specific rules, the most important of which are described here.

Each sequence may contain an arbitrary number of sub-sequences, labeled using the notation `i:`, where `i` is a natural number. Within a sequence, sub-sequences must have unique numbers and must be in ascending order. When the pattern starts, all sub-sequences labeled `1:` begin simultaneously across all agents. Execution of sub-sequences labeled `2:` starts only after all agents have completed their first sub-sequence. Notably, a sub-sequence may contain multiple actions, and its duration is not predetermined.

In LIrAs, it is also possible to handle empty or missing sub-sequences, loops, and a property known as continuation, which allows an agent to skip certain synchronizations with others. Finally, as shown in Line 10, conditional statements can be used to control actions. The conditional constructs available in LIrAs

Listing 1.1. LIrAs specification of the motivating example.

```
RobotFollower
agents:
    humans: Human
    robots: Robot
locations: poi1, poi2
Human:
1: moveTo poi1
2: moveTo poi2
Robot:
1: moveTo poi1 if position(Human,poi1) else stop
2: follow Human (poi2)
```

include if/else, until, and their combinations. Each conditional statement depends on one or more atomic predicates, combined using unary or Boolean operators (e.g., and, or, not).

In this work, we explore various system prompt configurations—including the DSL grammar, textual descriptions, and in-context learning. This last technique means that we provide one or more user-assistant examples, more specifically we provide a specification in natural language and the expected associated LIrAs code that the LLM should generate. Experiments were conducted using a locally deployed LLM, and the generated LIrAs code was manually evaluated. Our goal is to leverage LLMs to lower the cost and complexity of writing DSL specifications, making them more accessible to the robotics community.

The experimental setup and the results are presented in Sect. 2. While Sect. 3 concludes and outlines the envisioned future developments.

2   Probing LLMs for LIrAs Code Generation

This section presents the experimental campaign supporting our exploratory study, which addresses the following research questions:

RQ1. How accurate is the selected LLM in generating LIrAs specifications?
RQ2. What is the time overhead of using the LLM for DSL code generation?

To address these questions, we developed the pipeline shown in Fig. 1[1]. We tested the generation of LIrAs code for four scenarios (SC_k where $k \in \{1, 2, 3, 4\}$ in Fig. 1) drawn from the literature on real-world robotic applications [1,2,15]. Each natural language specification was pre-processed to remove superfluous

---

[1] Experimental details, results, and evaluations are available at https://github.com/albiferro99/TAROS25-Paper74. All experiments were performed on a machine with an Apple M3 chip and 16 GB RAM, using Meta-Llama-2-7B with Q4 quantization [14].

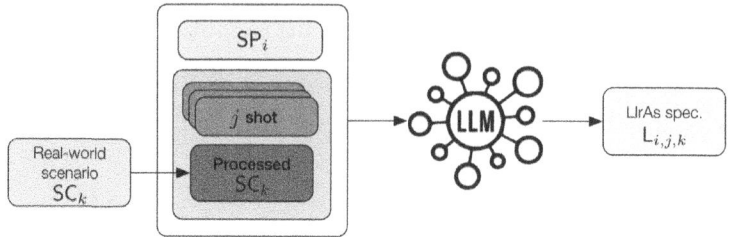

Fig. 1. Pipeline overview, from a real-world scenario up to its LIrAs specification.

Table 1. Questions used to evaluate LLM-generated specifications for **RQ1**.

Q1	Is the name of the Scenario consistent with the specification?
Q2	Are the inputs syntactically well structured?
Q3	Are the input agents consistent with the specification?
Q4	Are the input locations consistent with the specification?
Q5	Are the input resources consistent with the specification?
Q6	Is there a sequence for each Agent?
Q7	Is there any additional Sequence?
Q8	Are the used actions coherent with the specification?
Q9	Are the used atomic predicates coherent with the specification?
Q10	Are sub-sequences numbered increasingly?
Q11	Do sub-sequences contain continuations?
Q12	Are actions that must be executed simultaneously in the same sub-sequence?
Q13	Is the specification syntactically correct?
Q14	Are there no hallucinations? (Extra information, sub-sequence for locations...)

context and ambiguous details, ensuring that inputs matched what a user might realistically provide. Statements like "Infections caught during hospital stays account for around $37,000$ deaths per year in Europe and almost $100,000$ in the U.S." were removed, as they do not contribute to robotic specifications.

To define the LLMs' behavior across all interactions [9] we initialized it with five different system prompts (SP_i, $i \in \{1, 2, 3, 4, 5\}$). SP_1 and SP_2 have textual descriptions of LIrAs's features, e.g., agent synchronization and conditional statements. SP_3 provides the grammar of LIrAs, while SP_4 includes the grammar and explanatory comments. Lastly, SP_5 is a pseudo-code version of LIrAs. We also adopted in-context learning [5] with j-shot configurations ($j \in 0, 1, 2$). Each shot included (i) a user prompt describing a scenario from real-world robotics applications [12] and (ii) the corresponding expected DSL code. This approach is especially useful when the model is not fine-tuned for the task, as it helps reduce hallucinations, syntax errors, and unnecessary textual elaboration.

In summary, we combined 5 system prompts, 4 scenarios, and 3 shots configurations. This resulted in 60 generated LIrAs instances, denoted as $L_{i,j,k}$.

To address **RQ1**, we evaluated the accuracy of each generated LIrAs code against the original scenario description using 14 quantitative metrics (Table 1) tailored to LIrAs. Each metric was scored by a human expert using a simplified 0–2 Likert scale: 0 (missing or incorrect), 1 (partially correct), and 2 (fully correct and aligned with the expectations). These metrics provide a general overview of

Table 2. RQ1 average results among the four different tested scenarios.

	SP1			SP2			SP3			SP4			SP5		
	0-shot	1-shot	2-shot	0-shot	1-shot	2-shot	0-shot	1-shot	2-shot	0-shot	1-shot	2-shot	0-shot	1-shot	2-shot
Q1	1.5	1	2	0.5	0.5	2	0	0.5	2	0	0.5	1	1.75	0.75	2
Q2	0	2	2	0	1.5	2	0	1.75	2	0	2	2	0	1.75	2
Q3	0.5	1	1.5	0	1.25	1.25	0	0.75	1.25	0	0.75	1.25	0	1	1.5
Q4	0.5	0.75	1.75	0	0.75	1.5	0	0.5	1.5	0	0.5	1.75	0	0.75	1.5
Q5	0.25	0.25	1	0	0.25	1.25	0	0.75	1	0	0.25	1	0	0.75	1.5
Q6	0	2	2	0.75	1.5	2	0	1.75	2	0	1.5	1.5	0.5	2	2
Q7	0.5	0.5	0.5	0.5	1.5	0.5	0.5	0.5	0	1	0	0.5	0.5	0.5	1
Q8	1.25	1	1.5	1.25	0.75	1.75	0	0.75	2	0.25	0.75	0.75	0.75	1.5	1
Q9	0.25	0	0.75	0	0	1	0	0	0	0	0	1	0	0	0.25
Q10	0.75	2	1.75	1.25	2	2	0	2	2	0	1.75	2	0	2	2
Q11	0	2	1.75	0.25	1.5	2	0	1.5	1.25	0	1	2	0	1.75	2
Q12	0	0	0	0	0	0	0	0	0	0	0	0	0	0	0
Q13	0	0.5	1.5	0	1	1	0	0.75	1.25	0	0	0.75	0	0.25	1.75
Q14	0	0	0.5	0.5	0.5	0.75	0.25	0	0.5	0	0	0.5	0	0.5	1.5
Average	0.393	0.929	1.321	0.357	0.929	1.357	0.054	0.821	1.196	0.089	0.643	1.143	0.25	0.964	1.429
Overall	0.25	0.5	1.25	0	0.25	1	0	0	1.75	0	0.25	0.75	0	0.5	1.75

the quality of the generated LIrAs code, focussing on syntax correctness and alignment with the specification. An exception is the *Overall evaluation*, a more subjective metric, which uses a 0–5 scale to capture broader qualitative judgments. For **RQ2**, we track the time required to generate each $L_{i,j,k}$.

Table 2 reports the results for **RQ1**, specifically the average score across the four input scenarios and all the possible configurations previously described.

The most important trend observed in the figures reported in Table 2 is the always growing score both on the *Avarege value* and the *Overall evaluation* for each *SP* from 0-shot up to 2-shots. This shows the importance of in-context learning when dealing with applications the LLMs are not trained for.

Several trends emerge from the results. On the positive side, pattern names are usually consistent, and input sections are generally captured well, both syntactically and semantically. Sub-sequences are almost always numbered in ascending order, aligning with LIrAs conventions. However, a key feature—agent synchronization through sub-sequence labels—was never accurately captured, as shown by the zeros in Q12 of Table 2. Similarly, the property called "continuation" was frequently used in a syntactically correct manner but never meaningfully deployed, as it appears almost randomly rather than being driven by the scenario's requirements. Actions were mostly well-aligned and ordered correctly within each agent's sequence. Conditional statements and atomic predicates were less frequent than expected and often failed to match scenario details. Hallucinations (Q14 in Table 2) also surface in the generated code. However, these are mitigated in two-shot learning, where the model shows fewer extraneous additions. Table 2 shows that in-context learning (1- or 2-shot) consistently improved syntax, scenario alignment, and reduced hallucinations. Finally, in 0-shot cases with grammar-based prompts (SP_3 and SP_4), the model often misunderstood the task, sometimes outputting only the grammar or irrelevant natural language sentences.

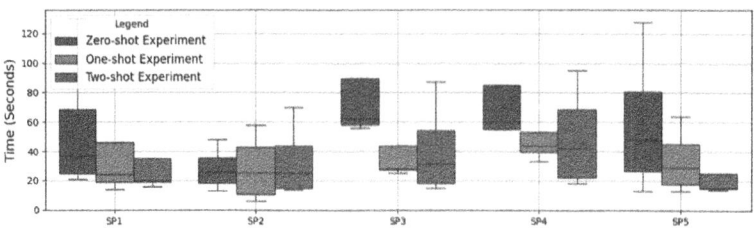

Fig. 2. RQ2 results: time [s] to generate the DSL code, grouped by SP and number of shots.

Figure 2 shows a grouped box plot of generation times. On average, generating a result takes about 45 seconds, with times ranging from 6 to 164 seconds. Notably, 0-shot examples took longer and were less accurate, indicating this approach is less effective than 1- or 2-shot learning.

Because this is a preliminary study, it is not exhaustive. Rather, it lays the groundwork for future research and more extensive empirical evaluations. For instance, future work could explore different models (including those not deployed locally) with more parameters to enhance LLMs performance, consider a wider array of scenarios and more-shot examples, employ metrics to capture semantic correctness more precisely, and automate the evaluation process to increase objectivity and reduce time overhead.

3   Future Research Outlook

This preliminary work is a baseline for future research. The envisioned framework begins with a user providing a natural language prompt to the Generative AI, describing the agents' goals and the operational environment. The Generative AI, potentially using the foundational DSL syntax and semantics (in this case, LIrAs), generates a textual DSL specification for the mission. Next, the AI-generated DSL specification is translated into a formal model (or programming language) and undergoes formal verification (or program verification). The resulting specification is then subjected to a data analysis step, which generates a repair action specification to be sent to a *Prompt Refiner*. The Prompt Refiner, starting with the initial natural language prompt, implements the repair action and updates the prompt for the Generative AI (LLM) to produce a revised specification. This iterative process can be repeated multiple times to ensure the final specification aligns with the user's requirements.

Summarizing, this framework allows users to generate DSL specifications for robotic missions via LLM, laying the groundwork for future research in automated mission specification through an iterative refinement process.

References

1. Askarpour, M., et al.: Robomax: robotic mission adaptation exemplars. In: 2021 International Symposium on Software Engineering for Adaptive and Self-Managing Systems (SEAMS), pp. 245–251. IEEE (2021)
2. Baraka, K., Veloso, M.M.: Mobile service robot state revealing through expressive lights: formalism, design, and evaluation. Int. J. Soc. Robot. **10**, 65–92 (2018)
3. Bassamzadeh, N., Methani, C.: A comparative study of dsl code generation: fine-tuning vs. optimized retrieval augmentation. arXiv preprint arXiv:2407.02742 (2024)
4. De Bari, D., Garaccione, G., Coppola, R., Torchiano, M., Ardito, L.: Evaluating large language models in exercises of UML class diagram modeling. In: Proceedings of the 18th ACM/IEEE International Symposium on Empirical Software Engineering and Measurement, ESEM '24, pp. 393–399. Association for Computing Machinery (2024)
5. Dong, Q., et al.: A survey on in-context learning (2024). arXiv:2301.00234 [cs]
6. Dragule, S., Gonzalo, S.G., Berger, T., Pelliccione, P.: Languages for specifying missions of robotic applications. In: Software Engineering for Robotics, pp. 377–411 (2021)
7. Feng, Z., et al.: Codebert: a pre-trained model for programming and natural languages. arXiv preprint arXiv:2002.08155 (2020)
8. Fowler, M.: Domain-Specific Languages. Pearson Education, Boston (2010)
9. Giray, L.: Prompt engineering with ChatGPT: a guide for academic writers. Ann. Biomed. Eng. **51**(12), 2629–2633 (2023)
10. Jana, S., Biswas, R., Pal, K., Biswas, S., Roy, K.: The evolution and impact of large language model systems: a comprehensive analysis. Alochana J. **13** (2024)
11. Joel, S., Wu, J.J., Fard, F.H.: A survey on llm-based code generation for low-resource and domain-specific programming languages. arXiv preprint arXiv:2410.03981 (2024)
12. Menghi, C., Tsigkanos, C., Pelliccione, P., Ghezzi, C., Berger, T.: Specification patterns for robotic missions. IEEE Trans. Softw. Eng. (2019)
13. Nordmann, A., Hochgeschwender, N., Wrede, S.: A survey on domain-specific languages in robotics. In: Brugali, D., Broenink, J.F., Kroeger, T., MacDonald, B.A. (eds.) SIMPAR 2014. LNCS (LNAI), vol. 8810, pp. 195–206. Springer, Cham (2014). https://doi.org/10.1007/978-3-319-11900-7_17
14. Ollama: Llama 2 (2025). https://ollama.com/library/llama2
15. of Robotics IFR, I.F.: Case studies - service robots (2025). https://ifr.org/case-studies/service-robots-case-studies
16. Roques, A., Contributors, P.: PlantUML Software (2009). https://github.com/plantuml/plantuml
17. Singh, I., et al.: Progprompt: generating situated robot task plans using large language models. In: 2023 IEEE International Conference on Robotics and Automation (ICRA), pp. 11523–11530 (2023)
18. Tagliaferro, A., Corbo, S., Guindani, B.: Leveraging llms to automate software architecture design from informal specifications. In: 9th International Workshop on Formal Approaches for Advanced Computing Systems (FAACS), pp. 291–299. IEEE (2025)
19. Tagliaferro, A., Lestingi, L., Rossi, M.: Towards verifiable multi-agent interaction pattern specification. In: Proceedings of the 2024 IEEE/ACM 12th International Conference on Formal Methods in Software Engineering (FormaliSE), pp. 122–126 (2024)

20. Tagliaferro, A., Lestingi, L., Rossi, M.: Verification-oriented specification of multi-agent interaction patterns. In: Workshop on Agents and Robots for reliable Engineered Autonomy, pp. 38–53. Springer, Heidelberg (2024). https://doi.org/10.1007/978-3-031-73180-8_3
21. Wang, J., Chen, Y.: A review on code generation with llms: application and evaluation. In: IEEE International Conference on Medical Artificial Intelligence (MedAI), pp. 284–289. IEEE (2023)
22. Xu, F.F., Vasilescu, B., Neubig, G.: In-ide code generation from natural language: promise and challenges. ACM Trans. Softw. Eng. Methodol. (TOSEM) **31**(2), 1–47 (2022)

A Verification Methodology for Safety Assurance of RAS

Mustafa Adam[1]([envelope]) [ID], David A. Anisi[1,2] [ID], and Pedro Ribeiro[3] [ID]

[1] Faculty of Science and Technology, Norwegian University of Life Sciences (NMBU),
Ås, Norway
mustafa.adam@nmbu.no
[2] Department of Mechatronics, University of Agder (UiA), Kristiansand, Norway
[3] Department of Computer Science, University of York, York, UK
https://www.nmbu.no, http://www.UiA.no, https://www.york.ac.uk/

Abstract. Autonomous robots deployed in shared human environments, such as agricultural settings, require rigorous safety assurance to meet both functional reliability and regulatory compliance. These systems must operate in dynamic, unstructured environments, interact safely with humans, and respond effectively to a wide range of potential hazards. This paper presents a verification workflow for the safety assurance of an autonomous agricultural robot, covering the entire development life-cycle, from concept study and design to runtime verification. The outlined methodology begins with a systematic hazard analysis and risk assessment to identify potential risks and derive corresponding safety requirements. A formal model of the safety controller is then developed to capture its behaviour and verify that the controller satisfies the specified safety properties with respect to these requirements. The proposed approach is demonstrated on a field robot operating in an agricultural setting. The results show that the methodology can be effectively used to verify safety-critical properties and facilitate the early identification of design issues, contributing to the development of safer robots and autonomous systems.

Keywords: Formal Verification (FV) · Runtime Verification (RV) · Robots and Autonomous Systems (RAS)

1 Introduction

The deployment of Robots and Autonomous Systems (RAS) in agriculture is rapidly accelerating, offering substantial improvements in efficiency, sustainability, and productivity across diverse tasks [20]. As these systems transition from controlled environments to real-world agricultural settings, assuring their safety and reliability becomes essential for regulatory compliance and stakeholder trust. Dynamic and unstructured conditions—such as variable terrain, changing weather, and human presence—introduce complex safety challenges that demand robust risk mitigation and verifiable assurance frameworks [4].

© The Author(s), under exclusive license to Springer Nature Switzerland AG 2026
A. Cavalcanti et al. (Eds.): TAROS 2025, LNAI 16045, pp. 281–294, 2026.
https://doi.org/10.1007/978-3-032-01486-3_23

Standards like ISO 18497 [22], IEC 61508 [23] provide foundational guidance for safety-critical systems. In this context, the IEEE 7009–2022 standard [11] provides a more focused framework for addressing fail-safe design in autonomous and semi-autonomous systems. However, these standards often target conventional, deterministic systems and may not fully address the autonomy and complexity of modern robotic platforms. A key challenge, as noted by Fisher et al. [7], is translating high-level, textual standards into formal, machine-verifiable specifications suitable for automated analysis.

Formal verification (FV) ensures that a system fulfils given specifications in all circumstances regardless of input possibilities [18]. FV methods extend beyond traditional testing approaches, such as unit testing or hardware-in-the-loop simulation, which lack formal guarantees and do not scale well with the increased complexity of autonomous systems [4]. Luckcuck *et al.* address the rationale for employing FV of RAS [13], providing a survey of the state-of-the-art on formalism and challenges. While FV methods like Model Checking (MC) and theorem proving offer rigorous verification, many existing approaches focus solely on offline or static analysis, limiting their applicability in real-world scenarios. In fact, a very recent, structured literature review regarding use of FV methods for RAS, which has also been submitted to TAROS [3], reveals that merely 8% of all relevant papers consider an "integrated approach", combining offline MC and online Runtime Verification (RV).

This paper presents a formal verification (FV) methodology for RAS that combines formal modelling, safety requirement traceability, and explicit treatment of uncertainty across the engineering lifecycle. Our approach supports the verification of safety properties from hazard analysis through to runtime verification and operational assessment. To complete an important but missing piece in our earlier works [1,2], we place particular emphasis on the Safety Controller (SC) in this paper, a key component responsible for enforcing runtime safety responses.

The remainder of this paper is structured as follows: Sect. 2 introduces the overall verification methodology. Section 3 details the formal modelling and verification of the Safety Controller. Finally, Sect. 4 concludes the paper and highlights directions for future work.

2   Formal Verification Methodology

This section introduces the overall verification methodology and outlines the activities for the safety assurance of RAS. An agricultural robot performing UVC-light treatment in strawberry plants is used as a representative case study to illustrate the application of the methodology [1]. The proposed approach builds upon the workflow introduced in [9]. While the specific hazards addressed in the case study pertain to UVC treatment, the methodology itself is generalizable and applicable to a broad range of RAS.

The figure below illustrates the lifecycle-oriented verification methodology, detailing each engineering phase and its verification-specific steps within the broader development process. It also highlights complementary engineering activities to show how verification is integrated throughout the system lifecycle.

Next, we detail the workflow, activities and artifacts of each engineering phase.

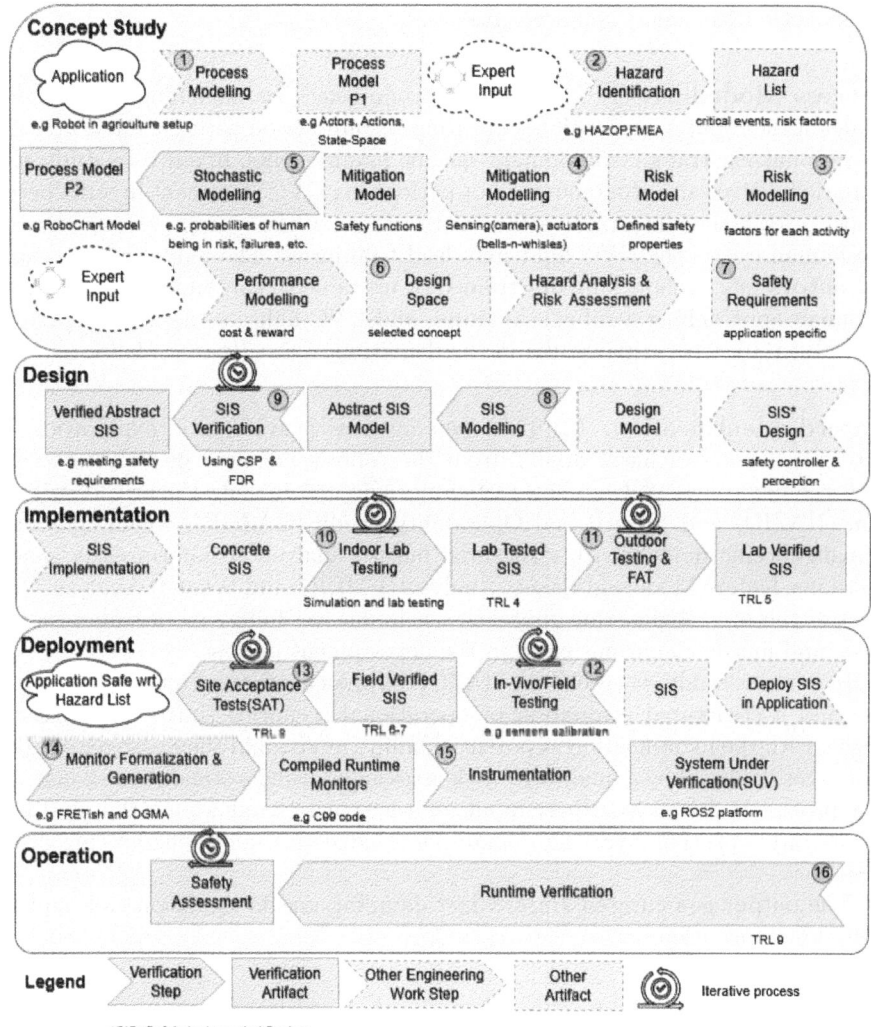

Fig. 1. Overview of the verification methodology across the engineering lifecycle. Iterative steps allow returning to the relevant previous phase based on the failure's root cause. All artifacts shown have been produced and exemplified in our agricultural case study.

2.1   Concept Study

The concept-study phase, which for larger projects may occur several years before system deployment and operation, lays the foundation for safety verification by defining the application, identifying hazards, modelling processes, and evaluating risks. It combines expert domain knowledge with formal analysis to extract critical safety requirements.

Process Modelling. ① The workflow commences by modelling a high-level model of the robotic application, capturing its interaction with the environment, operational constraints, and domain-specific requirements. In our case study, the scenario involves an autonomous robot performing UVC treatment in strawberry crops—a task that underscores the safety nature of the system, as exposure of the human eye to the UVC light may lead to injuries. The model incorporates key **actors** (e.g., robot, human - trained or untrained), core **activities** (such as a human approaching a robot), **actions**, and UVC light as the main source of risk. Taken together, this results in the definition of the *Process Model*.

Hazard Identification. ② This step involves a systematic exploration of potential sources of harm arising from the robot's behavior or its interaction with the environment. Common techniques adopted include Hazard Identification (HAZID) and Hazard and Operability Study (HAZOP), which combines domain-specific models with structured hazard analysis to inform early safety decisions, Failure Mode and Effects Analysis (FMEA), and What-If Analysis [23]. These structured engineering approaches help uncover failure modes, operational risks, and unsafe conditions early in the development process.

In our case study, we adopt the HAZOP approach informed by domain expertise and a structured evaluation of operational scenarios [1,10]. The process begins with the identification of potential failure modes and their associated consequences, followed by a qualitative risk assessment using a standard risk matrix. The process is driven by expert input, and it typically follows a structured but collaborative process involving domain knowledge and safety engineering practices.

The output is a curated *Hazard List* detailing unsafe conditions relevant to the UVC application.

Risk Modelling. ③ After identifying hazards, risks are assessed based on likelihood and severity to prioritize safety requirements. Approaches such as Preliminary Risk Analysis (PRA), probabilistic risk modelling, and activity-based risk graphs can be applied. In our work, we utilize activity-based risk modeling with a custom matrix that captures the likelihood of human presence, sensor failure rates, and robot behavior patterns. This results in a Risk Model that supports formal requirement derivation and highlights a critical scenario: the robot, during UVC treatment, fails to detect a human entering a hazardous zone during row transition.

Mitigation Modelling. ④ Based on identified hazards and associated risk-level, *Mitigation Models* specify system reactions to risks. These are used to shape a design space where alternative mitigation actions are analysed to achieve the desired Safety Integrity Level (SIL). The output is a detailed mitigation model which will be integrated later in the safety controller design.

Stochastic Modelling. ⑤ Probabilistic aspects such as human intrusion, sensor failure, and actuator uncertainty are captured in a *Process Model*, developed using RoboChart's [14] probabilistic modelling facilities. The robot's UVC treatment behaviour, the object detection system (ODS), and human presence are each represented as individual probabilistic state machines synchronised through a discrete-time tick mechanism [1]. The combined model is automatically translated into PRISM's input language. Formal properties, such as the probability of a human being exposed to UVC light in a danger zone during the transition, are verified using PCTL queries in PRISM. In ⑥ we provide estimates for cost and reward of the different mitigation approaches, their disruption of the UVC treatment process, and the effort required for their execution.

Safety Requirements. ⑦ Here we formalise the system level requirements based on the SIL quantification from previous steps. The level of risk ranging from SIL 1 to SIL 4, each increasing level corresponds to a 10-fold decrease in Probability of Failure on Demand (PFD), hence the higher the SIL, then the more stringent requirements. Our probabilistic model checking enables estimation of whether system configurations (e.g., sensor performance or human awareness levels) can meet target SIL thresholds.

2.2   Design Phase

In the design phase of our methodology, safety requirements are translated into concrete component-level specifications based on identified hazards and risk analyses. The Safety Instrumented Functions (SIFs) is designed, incorporating sensors, internal logic, and actuators to fulfil the required SILs. In ⑧ we model the SIS using RoboChart to represent the system as independent processes that interact via message-passing communication channels. In step ⑨, offline model-checking is used to verify formally these designs with respect to the defined safety requirement before implementation begins, ensuring early-stage correctness.

2.3   Implementation Phase

The verified design is implemented as integrated hardware and software components on a Thorvald platform robot. The SIS is realized using ROS2 for the controller, and the Obstacle Detection System (ODS) is based on a YOLO model running with input from an Intel RealSense D435 camera. These choices are direct consequences of the verification and analysis results obtained during the earlier concept-study and design phases. Their performance, however, needs to be tested and verified in increasingly more realistic settings.

In ⑩, we conduct indoor lab testing to empirically assess the classification model's accuracy. The dataset is partitioned into training, testing, and validation sets, achieving a classification accuracy of 94%, well above the 70% threshold defined in the concept study to achieve the desired SIL [1]. Additionally, the SIS is simulated using ROS2 and Gazebo, where Gazebo serves as the virtual environment for the robot. Custom plugins were developed to enable bi-directional interaction between the Gazebo simulation and the ROS2 nodes. The goal of this stage is to achieve Technology Readiness Level (TRL) 4.

In ⑪, outdoor testing is performed in the intended deployment environment. This phase confirms the system's performance. The outcome of both indoor and outdoor lab testing is a SIS, demonstrating compliance with the system requirements and achieving TRL 5.

2.4   Deployment Phase

The SC is deployed on a real agricultural robot and evaluated in dynamic outdoor environments to ensure its performance under real-world conditions, including varying lighting, terrain, and environmental dynamics. The setup is presented in Fig. 2.

Fig. 2. The robot was deployed in a polytunnel for simulated UVC operation.

In ⑫, the sensors are calibrated according to the mission profile, and the robot is deployed for prototype demonstration in relevant environments. Testing is conducted in intended operational conditions, ideally at the final deployment site. The focus at this stage is on ensuring correct integration, and confirming basic functionality—such as in open fields that mimic actual farms. This on-site verification of SIS raises the TRL to 6–7.

In (13), the complete system is tested and accepted at the actual operational site. This stage emphasizes the assessment of the system's reliability, robustness, and compliance with operational and safety requirements under real deployment conditions. The system tested here is the production-ready version, with all components finalized and integrated for use in the real world. Conducting Site Acceptance Test (SAT) yields TRL of 8. In (14) we generate runtime monitors from formalized properties of interest. We used the Formal Requirement Elicitation Tool (FRET) [6], to capture requirements in structured natural language and automatically translate into monitor specifications. These are then processed by OGMA [17] to generate C99 monitor code, which can be synthesized and integrated in ROS 2 platform in step (15).

2.5   Operation Phase

In the operation phase, the robot performs its agricultural tasks in a real-world environment. To ensure compliance with safety requirements at runtime, a runtime verification (RV) framework is utilized [2]. It employs monitors generated from formal safety specifications to observe system behavior and verify adherence to safety properties. In (14), the RV framework evaluates both temporal and state-based safety conditions during live operation. Upon detecting potential or actual violations, it triggers predefined mitigation actions, such as halting motion, issuing alerts, or transitioning the system into a safe state. This proactive mechanism enhances operational safety, particularly in dynamic and uncertain field environments. Step (15) provides an assessment and feedback loop leveraging runtime data to uncover unexpected scenarios, edge cases, and near-misses. This feedback is used both to evaluate the effectiveness of the proposed methodology and iteratively improve the system's models, safety requirements, and implementation, thus supporting a continuous and adaptive safety assurance lifecycle.

3   Safety Controller (SC)

A *Safety Controller* ensures system safety by monitoring conditions and executing mitigation actions when necessary. Unlike general-purpose control systems, it acts independently to detect hazards and prevent unsafe behavior, even with component faults or degraded performance [12].

In autonomous agricultural robotics, SC is vital due to the complex and dynamic nature of farm environments. Terrain, weather, lighting, unexpected human or animal presence, and hazardous equipment demand context-aware safety responses. The controller evaluates situational data to manage risks in real-time. However, agricultural robots must also maintain high operational efficiency to perform time-sensitive, energy-intensive tasks. Overly conservative safety actions, like unnecessary stops, can lower throughput, waste energy, and erode trust. The core challenge is balancing safety with efficiency—designing controllers that respond proportionally to context and risk is key to scalable deployment

3.1 Modelling in RoboChart

This section details the formal modeling and verification of the SIS safety controller using RoboChart [14], a state-machine-based formalism for reactive robotic systems. Abstraction and modularization techniques manage complexity and ensure all critical safety requirements are covered. The model is verified through refinement checks to confirm compliance with safety properties before deployment. The RoboChart model in Fig. 3 reflects the system architecture while abstracting hardware details [16].

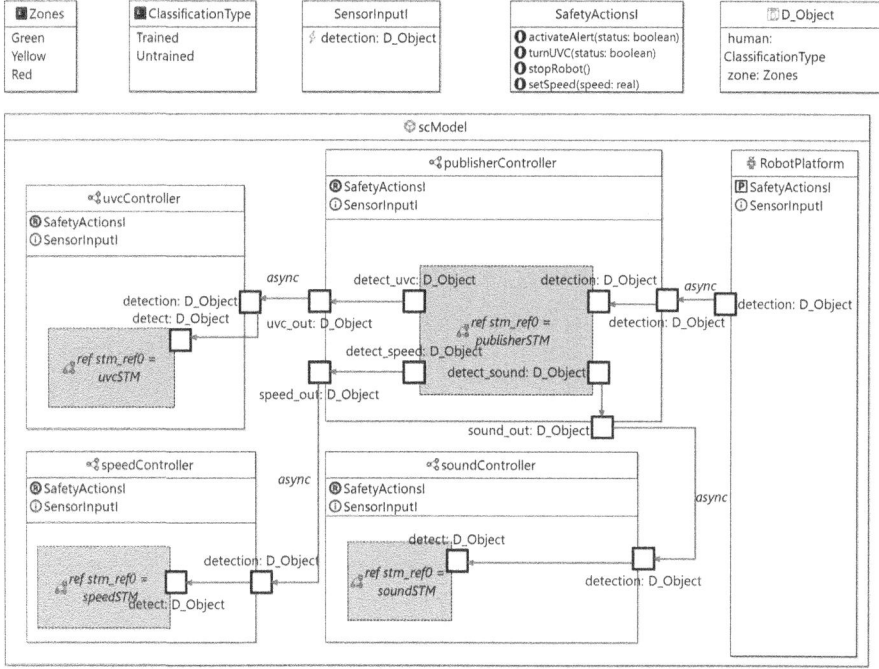

Fig. 3. Overview of the RoboChart model of the SIS architecture, generated using RoboTool.

The robotic platform, denoted as `RobotPlatform`, defines the external interfaces available to the safety software. It uses the `SensorInputI` interface to receive environment-derived classification events from perception modules, and provides the `SafetyActionsI` interface for invoking critical mitigation actions, such as `activateAlert`, `turnUVC`, `stopRobot`, and `setSpeed`. These operations originate from the mitigation strategies introduced in Sect. 2.1.

To support semantic classification of detected objects, we define two enumerated types: Zones (with values Green, Yellow, Red) and ClassificationType (with values Trained, Untrained). These are composed into a record type D_Object, representing classified detections from the perception system and used as inputs to the RoboChart controllers.

Figure 3 is composed of four interacting controllers: publisherController, uvcController, speedController, and soundController. The publisherController serves as a dispatcher that receives detection events and asynchronously relays them to the remaining controllers via typed events. Each controller encapsulates a state machine that governs its decision-making logic. The state machines are shown in Fig. 4. The uvcSTM disables the UVC light when a human is detected in high-risk proximity zones, depending on their classification. The speedSTM either reduces the robot's velocity or halts it based on proximity and human training level. The soundSTM triggers alerts in lower-risk situations to increase awareness. This illustrates the balancing act between risk level and safety on one hand, and operational efficiency on the other.

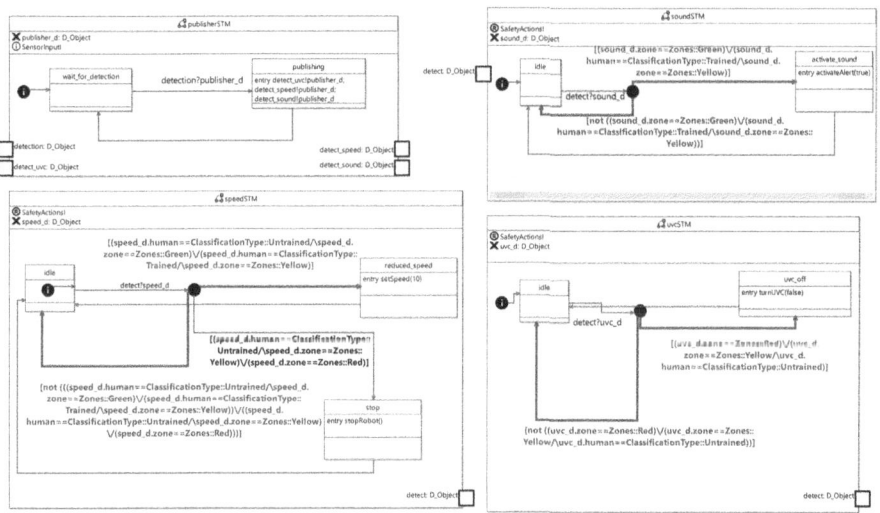

Fig. 4. State machines defining the safety response logic for UVC control, speed management, and alerting (sound).

Transitions between states are triggered by events and guarded by Boolean conditions over the fields of D_Object. Logical conditions are derived from hazard mitigation rules and encoded into transition guards, ensuring deterministic and safe behaviour. This structure follows the separation-of-concerns principle advocated in [15], where physical execution is abstracted into service operations and software safety logic is isolated in controller-specific state machines. The verification process is discussed in Sect. 3.2.

3.2   Verification of Safety Properties

To ascertain that the RoboChart model complies with the safety requirements, we first capture the requirements as timed behaviours in *tock*-CSP [5], a discrete timed process algebra. Then, we verify that the behaviour of the RoboChart model, whose formal semantics is defined as a *tock*-CSP process, is that permitted by the specification via the notion of refinement that captures conformance. For automated verification, we leverage RoboTool's integration with the CSP [21] model-checker FDR [8], following the methodology outlined in [14].

We focus on verifying Safety Requirements, **R1** to **R5** as specified in Table 1, which require that an appropriate mitigation action must occur within a bounded time interval upon the detection of a human in the robot's vicinity. Each case specifies one or more actions (e.g., alert, speed reduction, stopping, or UVC shutdown) that must be completed within a defined deadline. Next, we illus-

Table 1. Safety Requirements, R_i, and mitigation actions.

ID	Human detected	Zone	Mitigation Actions
R_1	Trained	Green	Activate sound
R_2	Untrained	Green	Activate sound & slow down
R_3	Trained	Yellow	Activate sound & slow down
R_4	Untrained	Yellow	Turn off UVC & Stop robot
R_5	Trained/Untrained	Red	Turn off UVC & Stop robot

trate how the requirements are captured in *tock*-CSP. Listing 1.1 sketches the process `SpecR15`, which captures the safety requirements using CSP events by describing the required pattern of interaction via a set of equational definitions. Here, we capture all requirements in a single process, so that they can all be checked at once, although they could have equivalently been captured via separate processes. As the requirements are timed, `SpecR15` is defined within a `Timed` section ..... and uses a function `timed_priority` to ensure the correct timed semantics are calculated by FDR[1]. Initially, it behaves as specified by `Initial`, that accepts an input (?) event `scModel::detection.in` with an arbitrary value i typed according to the RoboChart event `detection`, and then (->) behaves as `Response(i,2)` followed (;) by the recursion, that handles a new input. Here, i is the value communicated and 2 the maximum number of time units for the response to occur. The `Response` is defined by another process `within` a context where h and z take the value of the human and zone components of i in a `let` definition. Then, there is an `if` case for each possible input. In Listing 1.1 we sketch the first two requirements and omit the others as they are of a similar nature. For **R1**, a `Green` zone detection of a `Trained` person triggers an alert, here specified using a deadline operator (`EndBy`) that requires that the process

---

[1] https://cocotec.io/fdr/manual/cspm/definitions.html.

in the first argument, representing the call to the operation `activateAlert` with value `True`, terminates (`SKIP`) within d time units. The construction is similar for **R2**, but instead the response triggers both `activateAlert` and `setSpeed`, so in that case we use interleaving (|||) as their order is irrelevant.

```
timed csp SpecR15 csp-begin
Timed(OneStep) { -- For calculation of tock-CSP semantics
  SpecR15 = timed_priority(Initial)
  -- Top-level specification process
  Initial = scModel::detection.in?i -> Response(i,2) ;
    Initial
  -- Response after an input detection is received
  Response(i,d) = (
  let h = D_Object_human(i)
      z = D_Object_zone(i)
  within -- One case per input value
  if (z==Zones_Green and h==ClassificationType_Trained)
  then (EndBy(scModel::activateAlertCall.True -> SKIP,d))
  else if (z==Zones_Green and h==
    ClassificationType_Untrained)
  then (EndBy(scModel::activateAlertCall.True -> SKIP,d)
       ||| EndBy(scModel::setSpeedCall.10 -> SKIP,d))
  ... ) } csp-end
```

Listing 1.1. Sketch of *tock*-CSP specification of safety requirements R1 and R2.

For verification, we consider the RoboChart model in a context where we assume that the `detection` input does not change more often than once every time unit to reflect realistic sensing intervals. This is captured in *tock*-CSP by the process `CSc`, defined in Listing 1.2, as the parallel composition ([|...|]) of `scModel::O__`, the *tock*-CSP semantics automatically calculated by RoboTool for the RoboChart model, and `Inp` synchronising on the channel set ({|...|}) that includes the event `detection` with any value. In process `Inp`, we require that at least one time unit elapses (`WAIT(1)`) between each `detection` input.

```
timed csp CSc associated to scModel csp-begin
Timed(OneStep) {
  CSc = timed_priority(
    let Inp = scModel::detection.in?x__ -> WAIT(1) ; Inp
        Def = scModel::O__(1) [|{|scModel::detection.in|}|]
            Inp
    within Def) }
csp-end
```

Listing 1.2. System model with constrained timed input for refinement checking.

We then formulate a refinement **assertion A1**, as shown in Listing 1.3, to check whether the system behavior of `CSc` **refines** the expected specification `SpecR15` in the CSP **traces** semantic model, that is adequate for reasoning about safety and timeliness. Here, safety means that all possible timed executions of the implementation are allowed by the safety specification (`SpecR15`).

```
timed assertion A1 : CSc refines SpecR15 in the traces
    model.
```

Listing 1.3. Timed refinement assertion for safety verification.

In addition to this refinement check, we verify key correctness properties of the RoboChart model, including *deadlock freedom* and *determinism*. Such assertions can be written effortlessly without having to define a CSP process, and similarly to the previous assertion are checked using RoboTool's integration with FDR.

In our particular example, due to the relatively small size and complexity, the model was successfully verified within a few seconds with all assertions passing and, therefore, no counterexamples generated. This confirms that safety mitigation actions are correctly triggered and completed within the defined 2-unit time bound after a corresponding detection event. The verification was completed within a few seconds and involved a modest number of states and transitions, posing no scalability issues. These properties ensure that the system does not enter a state from which no further progress is possible and that its behaviour is deterministic, that is, a particular detection input leads to a specific response.

4 Conclusion

This work presents an integrated, methodology for RAS verification that combines probabilistic modelling, formal methods, and RV across the engineering lifecycle. Using RoboChart, we formally model and verify the SIS, with safety properties encoded in *tock*-CSP and verified via FDR through RoboTool. Evaluating the methodology's effectiveness involves both adherence to established standards [23] and empirical performance in an actual operation setting. While alignment with best practices and workflows builds confidence, real-world performance—captured through RV, near-misses, and safety incidents—ultimately determines success. In our methodology, these steps have been incorporated in the Operation phase (see ⑮), where operational data is used to evaluate the effectiveness of the overall methodology and iteratively refine the models, further strengthening assurance over time. This step also helps addressing a challenge within all model-based methods, namely ensuring that the formal model accurately reflects the real-world system. While abstractions are needed to manage complexity, they must be carefully balanced to avoid oversimplification and minimise the *reality gap* between the model and the deployed system.

Future work will focus on advancing from online RV to *predictive* RV, where monitors proactively anticipate potential hazards based on system and environmental state [19,24]. This predictive power enables earlier mitigation and deeper integration with autonomous decision-making, enhancing overall system safety and responsiveness.

Acknowledgments. The research presented in this paper has received partial funding from the Norwegian Research Council (RCN) RoboFarmer, project number 336712, the UK EPSRC Grants EP/M025756/1, EP/R025479/1, and EP/V026801/2, and the Royal Academy of Engineering Grant No CiET1718/45.

Disclosure of Interests. The authors have no competing interests to declare that are relevant to the content of this article.

References

1. Adam, M., Ye, K., Anisi, D.A., Cavalcanti, A., Woodcock, J., Morris, R.: Probabilistic modelling and safety assurance of an agriculture robot providing light-treatment. In: Proceedings of the 19th IEEE International Conference on Automation Science and Engineering (CASE), pp. 1–7 (2023). https://doi.org/10.1109/CASE56687.2023.10260395

2. Adam, M., Hartmark, E.E., Andersen, T., Anisi, D.A., Cavalcanti, A.: Safety assurance of autonomous agricultural robots: from offline model-checking to runtime verification. In: Proceedings of the 20th IEEE International Conference on Automation Science and Engineering (CASE), pp. 2511–2516 (2024). https://doi.org/10.1109/CASE59546.2024.10711810

3. Azaiez, A., Anisi, D.A., Farrell, M., Luckcuck, M.: Revisiting formal methods for autonomous robots: a follow-up survey. In: Submitted to TAROS 2025. Zenodo (2025). https://doi.org/10.5281/zenodo.15100775

4. Bakirtzis, G., Carr, S., Danks, D., Topcu, U.: Dynamic certification for autonomous systems. arXiv preprint (2023). https://arxiv.org/abs/2203.10950

5. Baxter, J., Ribeiro, P., Cavalcanti, A.: Sound reasoning in tock-csp. Acta Informatica **59**(1), 125–162 (2022). https://doi.org/10.1007/S00236-020-00394-3

6. Conrad, E., et al.: A compositional proof framework for FRETish requirements. CoRR arxiv:2201.03641 (2022)

7. Fisher, M., Dennis, L.A., Webster, M.P.: Towards a framework for certification of reliable autonomous systems. Auton. Agent. Multi-Agent Syst. **35**(1), 1–55 (2021). https://doi.org/10.1007/s10458-020-09468-y

8. Gibson-Robinson, T., Armstrong, P., Boulgakov, A., Roscoe, A.W.: FDR3—a modern refinement checker for CSP. In: Ábrahám, E., Havelund, K. (eds.) TACAS 2014. LNCS, vol. 8413, pp. 187–201. Springer, Heidelberg (2014). https://doi.org/10.1007/978-3-642-54862-8_13

9. Gleirscher, M.: Yap: Tool support for deriving safety controllers from hazard analysis and risk assessments. In: Electronic Proceedings in Theoretical Computer Science, vol. 329, pp. 31–47 (2020).https://doi.org/10.4204/eptcs.329.4

10. Guevara, L., Khalid, M., Hanheide, M., Parsons, S.: Assessing the probability of human injury during uv-c treatment of crops by robots. In: Proceedings of a Workshop or Conference (2021). https://doi.org/10.31256/Pj6Cz2L

11. IEEE Standards Association: IEEE Standard for Fail-Safe Design of Autonomous and Semi-Autonomous Systems (IEEE Std 7009-2022). https://standards.ieee.org/ieee/7009/7096/ (2022)

12. International Electrotechnical Commission: IEC 61508: Functional Safety of Electrical/Electronic/Programmable Electronic Safety-related Systems. IEC (2010)

13. Luckcuck, M., Farrell, M., Dennis, L.A., Dixon, C., Fisher, M.: A summary of formal specification and verification of autonomous robotic systems. In: Ahrendt, W., Tapia Tarifa, S.L. (eds.) IFM 2019. LNCS, vol. 11918, pp. 538–541. Springer, Cham (2019). https://doi.org/10.1007/978-3-030-34968-4_33

14. Miyazawa, A., Ribeiro, P., Li, W., Cavalcanti, A., Timmis, J., Woodcock, J.: RoboChart: modelling and verification of the functional behaviour of robotic applications. Softw. Syst. Model. **18**(5), 3097–3149 (2019). https://doi.org/10.1007/s10270-018-00710-z

15. Murray, Y., Nordlie, H., Anisi, D.A., Ribeiro, P., Cavalcanti, A.: Model checking and verification of synchronisation properties of cobot welding. In: Electronic Proceedings in Theoretical Computer Science, vol. 411, pp. 91–108 (2024). https://doi.org/10.4204/EPTCS.411.6

16. Murray, Y., Sirevåg, M., Ribeiro, P., Anisi, D.A., Mossige, M.: Safety assurance of an industrial robotic control system using hardware/software co-verification. Sci. Comput. Program. (2022). https://doi.org/10.1016/j.scico.2021.102766

17. NASA: Ogma: Operational goal-based mission analysis (2024). https://github.com/nasa/ogma. Accessed 27 June 2024

18. Peled, D.A.: Formal methods. In: Handbook of Software Engineering, pp. 193–222. Springer, Cham (2019). https://doi.org/10.1007/978-3-030-00262-6_5

19. Pinisetty, S., Jéron, T., Tripakis, S., Falcone, Y., Marchand, H., Preoteasa, V.: Predictive runtime verification of timed properties. J. Syst. Softw. 353–365 (2017)

20. Rahmadian, R., Widyartono, M.: Autonomous robotic in agriculture: a review. In: Proceedings of the Third International Conference on Vocational Education and Electrical Engineering (ICVEE), pp. 1–6 (2020). https://doi.org/10.1109/ICVEE50212.2020.9243253

21. Roscoe, A.W.: Understanding Concurrent Systems. Texts in Computer Science. Springer, Heidelberg (2010). https://doi.org/10.1007/978-1-84882-258-0

22. Secretary, I.C.: Agricultural machinery and tractors – safety of highly automated agricultural machines – principles for design. ISO Standard 18497:2018 (2018)

23. Smith, D., Simpson, K.: The Safety Critical Systems Handbook. Elsevier, Amsterdam (2020). https://doi.org/10.1016/C2019-0-00966-1

24. Zhang, X., Leucker, M., Dong, W.: Runtime verification with predictive semantics. In: Goodloe, A.E., Person, S. (eds.) NFM 2012. LNCS, vol. 7226, pp. 418–432. Springer, Heidelberg (2012). https://doi.org/10.1007/978-3-642-28891-3_37

Towards Digital Twin Aided Autonomy for a UR3e Robotic Manipulator
(Invited Paper)

Andreas Kaag Thomsen$^{(\boxtimes)}$ ⬤, Buster Salomon Rasmussen ⬤,
Mirgita Frasheri ⬤, Santiago Gil ⬤, and Peter Gorm Larsen ⬤

DIGIT, Department of Electrical and Computer Engineering, Aarhus University,
Aarhus, Denmark
{akt,bsr,mirgita.frasheri,sgil,pgl}@ece.au.dk

Abstract. Robots have become a key technology in the manufacturing domain by replacing manual labour, while speeding up, increasing accuracy, and reducing the costs of production processes. Nevertheless, unexpected faults can happen anytime during production, potentially leading to component or system failure, resulting in lower productivity, increased costs, and additional manual maintenance burdens. In this context, Digital Twins (DTs) represent a promising technology that aims to improve the performance and reduce robot downtime. DTs leverage the integration of real robot and simulated data during run-time to monitor the robots and deploy mitigating actions when faults are detected. In this paper, we explore the development of a DT for the Universal Robots UR3e robotic arm, seeking to enhance its capabilities, allowing it to autonomously adapt when faults are detected during the execution of pick-and-place tasks. A proof-of-concept is presented, leveraging the principles of self-adaptation through the Monitor-Analyse-Plan-Execute over a Knowledge base (MAPE-K) loop. Results show that the proposed DT framework effectively detects and mitigates faults in real time, reducing task execution interruptions and improving robotic autonomy. These findings highlight the potential of DTs for enhancing fault tolerance and autonomy in robotic manipulators.

Keywords: Digital Twins · Self-Adaptation · Cyber-Physical Systems

1 Introduction

Digital Twins (DTs) are digital replicas of (cyber-)physical systems, often referred to as Physical Twins (PTs) [11]. Unlike traditional simulations, DTs enable bi-directional communication with their PTs during run-time. A PT continuously shares its own state (e.g., joint positions), while the DT can influence

---

A. K. Thomsen and B. S. Rasmussen—Co-first authors.

A. Cavalcanti et al. (Eds.): TAROS 2025, LNAI 16045, pp. 295–309, 2026.
https://doi.org/10.1007/978-3-032-01486-3_24

the PT's operation by assigning tasks or reconfiguring it. A DT includes models, simulators, and monitors that use real PT data to support services like self-adaptation. While a PT can function without a DT, a DT-enabled PT benefits from these services, reducing downtime, cutting costs, and improving efficiency [5]. This is particularly notable in manufacturing, the focus of this paper, due to its alignment with Industry 4.0 goals and the attention it has received in recent research surveys [15,19]. Beyond efficiency improvements, DTs provide a model-centric approach that supports fault detection through continuous synchronisation and adaptation to evolving system states, enhancing dependability and robustness in dynamic, uncertain environments [5]. However, challenges remain in the generalisation and sharing of DTs, due to the lack of standardisation partly stemming from the bespoke nature of DT case studies [7,16]. This paper demonstrates the practical application and advantages of a DT-based approach in manufacturing.

Self-Adaptation refers to the ability of a system to adapt to changing conditions without external influence (e.g., human intervention), enabling a system to operate with some autonomous[1] functions. One well-known architecture that supports the implementation of self-adaptation is the *Monitor-Analyse-Plan-Execute over a Knowledge base* (MAPE-K) loop, introduced in 2003 by Kephart and Chess [10]. It represents four stages in which data propagates through to drive the self-adaptation process, relying on knowledge that includes models and incoming data. As pointed out in [4], there are similarities between such systems and DT-enabled systems that make the MAPE-K realisable in a DT-setting. Specifically, the managed element in autonomic systems can be compared to the PT, while the autonomic manager aligns with one of the DT's services. Moreover, the bi-directional communication between the autonomic manager and managed element is akin to the interaction between a PT and its DT, facilitating the integration of the MAPE-K loop into the DT framework.

This paper summarises the core results of [20], and examines the development of a DT for a robotic manipulator to achieve self-adaptation capabilities, using the UR3e as a manufacturing case study, which is programmed to execute a pick-and-place task. We propose a DT prototype[2] that employs the MAPE-K loop for self-adaptation, handling faults like gripper collisions and missing blocks. Gripper collisions are detected using spatial data, while joint trajectory divergence between the DT and PT identifies missing blocks. For mitigation, the gripper wrist rotates to resolve collisions, while missing blocks are managed using either the next available block or a separate stock area. Results show successful fault detection and mitigation in 3 out of 4 experiments, with the fourth producing a false positive, highlighting detection limits.

---

[1] Defined by Truszkowski et al. [21] as: *"A system's capacity to act according to its own goals, precepts, internal states, and knowledge, without outside intervention."*.

[2] Our code is publicly available at: https://tinyurl.com/gitlabsrc.

2   Related Work

DT technology has gained traction in robotics as a means enabling real-time monitoring, fault detection, and self-adaptation [5,9,14]. A key aspect of DT-based autonomy is the ability to detect and mitigate faults dynamically, often through frameworks like the MAPE-K loop. Feng et al. [4] investigated the use of MAPE-K in a DT for an incubator system, demonstrating its potential for self-adaptive responses to abnormal conditions. However, challenges remain in ensuring sufficient data availability and maintaining safety during adaptation. This study extends these concepts to robotic manipulation, exploring how MAPE-K can be leveraged in a DT framework for fault-tolerant automation.

Bruno et al. [1] investigated DTs for dynamic task allocation using two UR3e robots. They employed manual task duration measurements to detect time failures and trigger dynamic task reallocation. In contrast, our work focuses on fault detection and mitigation for a single robot, enabling autonomous reconfiguration. Rather than addressing time failures, our DT detects trajectory divergences by estimating trajectories based on angular kinematics.

A key challenge in DT-enabled robotics is the trade-off between kinematic and dynamic models, where kinematic models provide computational efficiency but may not fully capture system dynamics [3,25,26]. To address the limitations of kinematic modelling, Yang et al. [25] proposed a dynamic model for harmonic drive-based robot joints, enhancing DT capabilities with real-time dynamic simulations. Additionally, research by Zhou et al. [26] developed a dynamic DT for a non-holonomic mobile manipulator, incorporating Lagrange formulation to account for physical interactions between the robot and its environment or humans. This work demonstrated the effectiveness of dynamic models in improving real-time simulation and performance evaluation. While integrating advanced dynamic models could further refine the DT's representations, our work takes a pragmatic approach by leveraging kinematic modelling for fault detection and mitigation in a UR3e robotic manipulator.

3   Case Study: Pick-and-Place with UR3e

The robot is programmed to perform simple pick-and-place tasks, which involve picking up blocks of equal size and weight and placing them to form a predetermined shape (e.g. a square or a letter). The setup of the robot and its environment is illustrated in Fig. 1. Relevant aspects of the case study are covered in detail in the following paragraphs, particularly the required bi-directional data flow between the DT and PT, the description format and execution of the tasks, and the faults considered in this paper.

3.1   Digital Twin Data Integration

This study employs two communication interfaces for remote interaction with the UR3e: the Real-Time Data Exchange (RTDE) and the Dashboard Server

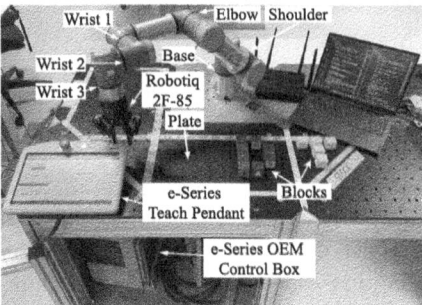

Fig. 1. The UR3e and its environment

(DBS), both operating over a standard TCP/IP connection. The RTDE interface facilitates bidirectional data exchange with the Control Box, while the DBS interface allows interaction with the Teach Pendant , enabling program loading, execution, and state retrieval. The *robot data* is collected from the PT through the RTDE connection with a frequency of 20Hz. This frequency was selected due to limitations in the library used on the DT side for trajectory generation, which only supports this frequency (Sect. 4.1). The data fields used are:

- `timestamp`: Time elapsed since the Control Box was started [s].
- `actual_q`: Actual joint positions [rad].
- `output_bit_register_65`: Control Box register used by the DT to detect when the task has started.
- `output_bit_register_66`: Control Box register used by the DT to detect when a block has been gripped.

3.2 Task Description and Execution

The robot executes a task consisting of N subtasks, each moving a block from its origin O_i to its target T_i. The arrangement of all subtasks within a task is referred to as the *task configuration*. Each subtask follows four joint positions to ensure collision avoidance with neighbouring blocks and base plate: Above Grip, Grip, Above Target, and Target. A UR-specific script (`.urp` format) uses joint-based `movej` commands, utilising trapezoidal time scaling, consisting of acceleration, constant velocity, and deceleration phases [13]. According to the UR Remote Operation Guide [24], joint positions are transmitted to the robot's general-purpose registers via RTDE, making them accessible during execution.

3.3 Potential Faults

Faults are broadly categorised into *operational* and *pre-operational* faults. Operational faults are those detected and solved during task execution while pre-operational faults are detected and solved before the initiation of the task.

Table 1 summarises the two faults under consideration and their respective mitigation strategies. *Gripper Collision* faults occur when the gripper collides with a neighbouring block while attempting to grip a block at its origin or place a block at its target. This triggers the safety system to release a *Protective Stop*, halting the robot. Therefore, our goal is to prevent this fault. *Missing Block* faults occur when a block is not present at its expected origin position. The detection and mitigation of these faults are presented in Sect. 4. In manufacturing numerous faults can occur such as power outages and collisions with the environment. In [20], the Protective Stop was also treated as a separate fault and mitigated manually. However, this paper narrows the scope to focus only on the two aforementioned faults.

Table 1. Types of Faults

Fault Category	Fault Name	Mitigation Strategy
Pre-operational	Gripper Collision	Wrist Rotation
Operational	Missing Block	1. Stock, 2. Shift

4   Digital Twin-Enabled Fault Detection and Mitigation

This section details how the DT-enabled UR3e system detects and mitigates faults in pick-and-place tasks using a MAPE-K-based self-adaptation mechanism. Fault detection and mitigation occur in the *Analyse* and *Plan* stages, while the *Execute* stage updates task configurations and joint positions in response to detected faults. The following subsections outline the DT models used for fault detection and describe the mitigation processes.

4.1   Digital Twin Models

The DT employs three models for fault detection: spatial, kinematic, and timing, which are subsequently elaborated. To aid fault detection, the models are combined to leverage the individual strengths each one offers, resulting in the joint positions of the robot when executing a task. This process is illustrated in Fig. 2.

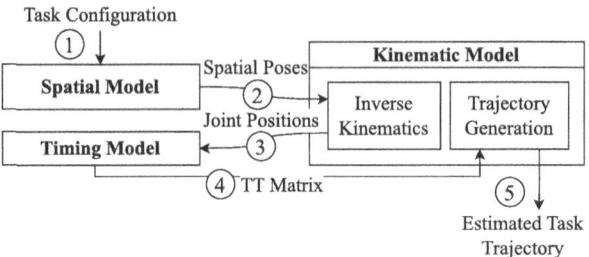

Fig. 2. Task trajectory generation using DT models. A Task Configuration is sent to the Spatial Model (1), producing spatial poses (2). These are converted to joint positions (3) by the kinematic model. The Timing Model uses these to compute the TT Matrix (4), enabling estimation of the final trajectory (5).

Spatial Model. The spatial model integrates spatial information relating to the physical environment, following the approach proposed by Gil et al. [6,8]. Its key functionality is to facilitate the transformation of each task specification coordinate $P_G = (x_G, y_G)$ into a spatial pose S, where $P_G \in G$ and $G \subset \mathbb{Z}^2$. G is identified as the *grid* and represents the positions on the plate. The translational component of S is denoted $P_R = (x_R, y_R, z_R) \in W$ where $W \subset \mathbb{R}^3$ is the robot's workspace, defined as the specification of the configurations that the end-effector of the robot can reach [13]. The rotational component of S is fixed, ensuring that the robot's third wrist remains perpendicular to the plate. The transformation from P_G to P_R is achieved by augmenting P_G with a coordinate $z \in \mathbb{R}$ representing the height above the plate in meters, resulting in the new coordinate $P_{G,A} = (P_G, z)$. Subsequently, $P_{G,A}$ is mapped to P_R using the measured distance between discrete grid points δ_H and the offset $P_{R,0}$ measured at $P_G = (0,0)$, using the approach in Eq. (1).

$$P_R = P_{R,0} + P_{G,A} \cdot \delta_H = ((x_{R,0} + x_G \cdot \delta_H),$$
$$(y_{R,0} + y_G \cdot \delta_H),$$
$$(z_{R,0} + z)) \tag{1}$$

Timing Model. The timing model estimates the duration of each robotic operation and their sequence within a task. Based on joint positions the model generates a *Timed Task* (TT) matrix, shown in Eq. (2), that encodes the temporal properties.

$$TT = \begin{bmatrix} \boldsymbol{\theta}_{S,0} & \boldsymbol{\theta}_{E,0} & TI_0 \\ \boldsymbol{\theta}_{S,1} & \boldsymbol{\theta}_{E,1} & TI_1 \\ \vdots & \vdots & \vdots \\ \boldsymbol{\theta}_{S,K-1} & \boldsymbol{\theta}_{E,K-1} & TI_{K-1} \end{bmatrix} \tag{2}$$

The ith row consists of: start joint positions $\boldsymbol{\theta}_{S,i}$, end joint positions $\boldsymbol{\theta}_{E,i}$ and a *Timing Interval* (TI) object TI_i. The latter consists of three attributes: a value $(TI_i.v)^3$, which is the estimated time of the ith operation; a type $(TI_i.t)$, which tells if the robotic manipulator is moving (MTI) or freezing (FTI); and a subtype $(TI_i.st)$ that provides specific information about the operation, such as whether the robot is moving with a block, or the gripper is releasing a block. The MTIs are estimated using angular kinematics and each FTI is established either empirically or deterministically, as elaborated in [20]. The order of operations within a task is established by utilising the prescribed sequence of operation types that occur when executing a subtask (e.g., move down to block at origin i, grip block at origin i, etc.), also elaborated in [20].

Kinematic Model. The kinematic model is used to compute Inverse Kinematics (IK), realised by the Levenberg-Marquardt (LM) algorithm, and to generate *task trajectories*, which we define as the estimated trajectories of all the robot's joints during the execution of a full task. These trajectories are estimated based on kinematics and are time-fixed. Each joint trajectory, from a start joint position θ_S to an end joint position θ_E, is modelled using a quintic polynomial time scaling generated from n time steps. The number of steps n for the ith operation is calculated by $n_i = \lfloor TI_i.v/dt \rfloor$ where $dt = 0.05s$. The rationale for employing quintic polynomial time scaling, rather than the trapezoidal time scaling used on the UR3e, stems from the specifications provided by UR. According to these specifications, only the leading axis is guaranteed to follow the given maximum velocity ω and acceleration α [23]. Consequently, the motion characteristics of the remaining five joints are not explicitly defined, making their behavior unpredictable under trapezoidal time scaling. The model is configured using the modified Denavit-Hartenberg (DH) convention with the DH parameters provided by UR [22]. It is implemented using the 'Robotics-Toolbox for Python' (RTB) library [2], where necessary computations for IK and trajectory generation are carried out within this framework.

4.2 Detection and Mitigation of the Missing Block Fault

Two approaches are considered to detect Missing Block faults, both based on the TT matrix from the timing model: a *timing threshold* approach, aiming to detect the fault based on a timer, and a *model divergence* approach, aiming to detect the fault based on divergence from the DT's estimated task trajectory. In this paper, we focus on the model divergence approach, as prior experiments show it outperforms the timing threshold approach in efficiency and data richness [20]. Greater data richness provides deeper insight into the modelled element, enhancing fault detection by helping to identify what fault occurred and why.

Detection of the Missing Block Fault Based on Model Divergence. The fault detection service monitors the trajectory error e between the DT and PT and the duration t that e exceeds a threshold. The error is the difference

---

³ $O.a$ denotes retrieval of the attribute a from the object O.

between the latest `actual_q` value and the expected trajectory point at the nearest `timestamp`. A fault is detected if e exceeds ε_e for more than ε_t as given by Eq. (3). Specifically, ε_e represents the maximum allowable positional deviation, while ε_t defines the maximum duration for which this deviation can persist. If $TI_i.st$ indicates the robot should carry a block, the fault is classified as Missing Block; otherwise, it is unknown, triggering a system shutdown.

$$\text{Fault} = \begin{cases} \text{True, if } e > \varepsilon_e \wedge t > \varepsilon_t \\ \text{False} \qquad \text{otherwise} \end{cases} \tag{3}$$

These thresholds are applied to counteract the small discrepancies that emerge between the DT and PT as illustrated in Fig. 3. As it will be covered in Sect. 5,

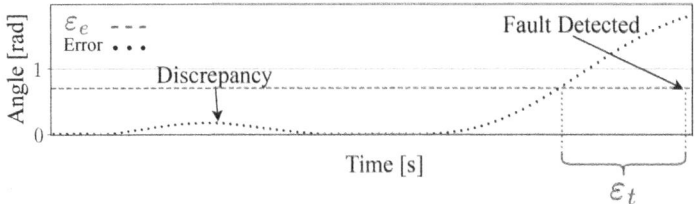

Fig. 3. Missing Block fault detection based on model divergence

ε_e and ε_t can be fine-tuned to increase efficiency and robustness. In this case study, it was also necessary to fine-tune the parameters of the Timing Model to account for an accumulating drift, thereby placating the issue [20].

Mitigation of the Missing Block Fault. Two strategies are proposed to handle a Missing Block fault: *Stock* and *Shift*. For a missing block n at subtask origin O_n:

- *Stock* reassigns O_n to a new position in the stock area $\Gamma = [\gamma_0, \ldots, \gamma_{M-1}]$, where $\gamma_j \in G$. Positions are incrementally tested until a block is found or M is reached. Thus: $O_n \leftarrow \gamma_j$.
- *Shift* moves subtask origins $O_n, \ldots, O_{N-2}$ to their next positions, removing the last subtask such that: $O_m \leftarrow O_{m+1}, \quad \forall m \in [n, \ldots, N-2]$. This prevents full shape completion.

4.3   Detection and Mitigation of the Gripper Collision Fault

To detect pre-operational Gripper Collision faults, the goal is to identify and mitigate potential collisions before they occur. This ensures that the gripper's tip does not collide with neighbouring blocks during picking or placing. Fault detection is based on the task configuration and utilises information from the spatial model. Additionally, each subtask includes a Boolean parameter, $RotateWrist$ (RW), which specifies whether wrist 3 should be rotated by $90°$.

Consider two blocks $b1$ and $b2$ with grid coordinates $P_1 = (x_1, y_1)$ and $P_2 = (x_2, y_2)$ and RW values RW_1 and RW_2. A fault is detected if the blocks are critically close to each other during picking or placing. The critical distance, D, depends on the RW value and the dimension (x or y) in which the blocks align. D is given by the distance from the centre of the block of interest to the edge of the neighbouring block. To compute D, the width w of each block and the hole distance δ_H are considered. The critical distance is given by:

$$D_y = |y_1 - y_2|\delta_H - \frac{w}{2} = \delta_y - \frac{w}{2} \tag{4}$$

when the blocks align in the x-dimension, and by:

$$D_x = |x_1 - x_2|\delta_H - \frac{w}{2} = \delta_x - \frac{w}{2} \tag{5}$$

when they align in the y-dimension. These distances are compared to the gripper's width δ_G in the following way: When the wrist is rotated ($RW = True$), the gripper expands along the y-axis, necessitating the examination of D_y. Conversely, when $RW = False$, the gripper extends along the x-axis, making D_x relevant. The feasibility F of picking or placing a block is governed by the following equation, assuming blocks are placed centrally on grid points:

$$F = \begin{cases} \text{False,} & \text{if } (RW_1 \wedge x_1 = x_2) \wedge \left(D_y \leq \frac{\delta_G}{2}\right) \\ \text{False,} & \text{if } (\neg RW_1 \wedge y_1 = y_2) \wedge \left(D_x \leq \frac{\delta_G}{2}\right) \\ \text{True,} & otherwise \end{cases} \tag{6}$$

The check in Eq. (6) is performed against all pairs of relevant block origins and targets. Let $O(i)$ and $T(i)$ define the sets of relevant origins and targets, respectively, for the ith subtask where $0 \leq i < N$. Then:

$$O(i) = \begin{cases} \{O_j \mid i+1 \leq j \leq N - 1\} & \text{if } 0 \leq i < N - 1 \\ \emptyset & \text{if } i = N - 1 \end{cases} \tag{7}$$

and:

$$T(i) = \begin{cases} \{T_j \mid 0 \leq j \leq i - 1\} & \text{if } 0 < i \leq N - 1 \\ \emptyset & \text{if } i = 0 \end{cases} \tag{8}$$

The fault is mitigated by updating the RW parameter of the specific subtask. If Eq. (6) yields $F = False$ then $RW_i \leftarrow \neg RW_i$ for the ith subtask.

5   Experimental Results and Discussion

We showcase the capabilities of the DT through a series of experiments. The experimental design methodology involves evaluating various combinations of variables to determine their fault detection capabilities. This approach focuses on identifying the limits of these variables to establish conditions under which all faults are detected, while simultaneously assessing performance metrics. Due to space constraints, only a subset of the extensive testing conducted is presented in this paper. The reader can refer to [20] for further information on the full set of experiments. In the following, the experimental setup, the results and the analysis hereof are presented.

5.1   Experimental Setup

The experimental setup involves configuring a task and injecting the two types of faults in Table 1 to evaluate the system's fault detection and mitigation capabilities. The task configuration remains consistent across all experiments and consists of assembling $N = 8$ blocks into a square shape. The Gripper Collision faults are induced by arranging the task configuration such that blocks are positioned closely enough to require wrist rotation. Specifically, the task is configured to include 11 potential Gripper Collision faults that must be detected and mitigated, i.e. the picking or placing of these blocks require wrist rotation. The Missing Block faults are enforced by removing blocks from their designated origins and in each experiment, blocks 1, 3 and 4 are removed from the plate. The experiments are carried out in the Digital Twin Lab at Aarhus University and are run on an Apple M4 Pro with 28 GB RAM.

5.2   Analysis of Results

We consider the following parameters for our experiments: the mitigation strategy ms and the two previously defined thresholds, ε_e and ε_t, for detecting Missing Block faults. We evaluate the experiments using the following metrics: the duration t (average over 5 runs) of executing the task, the number of Missing Block faults mitigated MB_{rate}, and the number of Gripper Collision faults mitigated GC_{rate}. Table 2 shows the results of the four experiments[4].

Table 2. Design and Results of the Experiments

	Parameters			Metrics		
	ε_e	ε_t	ms	t [s]	MB_{rate}	GC_{rate}
E1	0.7	1.0	stock	133.7	3/3	11/11
E2	0.7	1.0	shift	77.4	3/3	11/11
E3	0.7	0.1	stock	128.3	3/3	11/11
E4	0.3	1.0	stock	–	2/3	4/11

---

[4] Videos of the experiments are available at: https://tinyurl.com/3zxkk4p5.

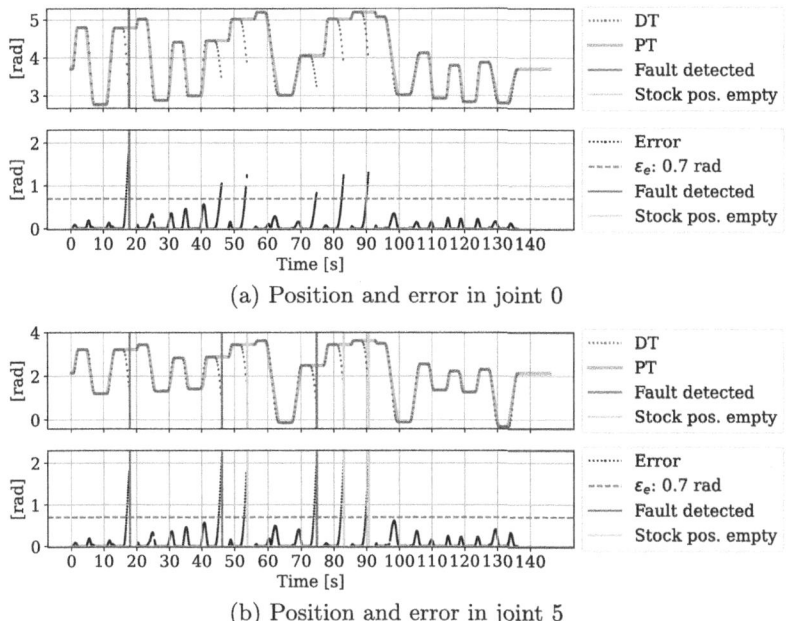

(a) Position and error in joint 0

(b) Position and error in joint 5

Fig. 4. Results from experiment E1, showing the DT's expected trajectory and the PT's measured trajectory for joints 0 and 5, along with the real-time error. Three Missing Block faults are detected: at $t_1 \approx 17$s in both joints, and at $t_2 \approx 46$s and $t_3 \approx 75$s in joint 5. Other joint trajectories are omitted as faults occur only in joints 0 and 5.

Stock Mitigation Strategy: Experiment E1 highlights an instance where all faults are detected and mitigated successfully using the stock mitigation strategy and conservative values for ε_e and ε_t. The associated figure in Fig. 4 presents a comparative analysis of the estimated trajectory as predicted by the DT and the actual trajectory measured from the PT in joints 0 (Fig. 4a) and 5 (Fig. 4b) alongside the real-time measured error between them. The figure reveals that the position curves of the PT and DT align closely until time $t \approx 17$s, with a maximum deviation ≈ 0.2 rad. At time $t \approx 17$s, a fault is detected when block 1 is not gripped. The DT continues to monitor this fault for a duration of 1 s ($\varepsilon_t = 1$s) and directs the PT to pause until a new task is prepared. By the time $t \approx 20$s, the updated task begins and block 1 is secured in the first stock position. A similar situation arises at time $t \approx 46$s, but in this case, there is no block in stock position 1. As a result, another fault is triggered at time $t \approx 53$s, after which block 3 is gripped in stock position 2 at time $t \approx 57$s. The same pattern is observed when block 4 is absent at time $t \approx 75$s. In this instance, neither stock positions 1 nor 2 are refilled, and block 4 is secured in stock position 3 at time $t \approx 95$s. By the time $t \approx 136$s the task has finished with all faults detected and mitigated, as observed by the first row in Table 2.

Shift Mitigation Strategy: In experiment E2 the values for ε_t and ε_e are consistent with those in experiment E1. However, the shift mitigation strategy is employed instead. This change in mitigation strategy results in a significant reduction in task completion time, with the task finishing ~56 s faster due to the need to reach only 5/8 target positions and not having to move to any stock positions. Despite this efficiency gain, it is important to note that the experiment does not result in the assembly of the desired square shape. As observed by the second row in Table 2, all faults are mitigated.

Reduced ε_t: In the third experiment, ε_t is reduced from 1s to 0.1 s. Compared to experiment E1, this results in faster detection of Missing Block faults, reducing task completion time by ≈ 5 s, as shown in the third row of Table 2. While this increase in efficiency is advantageous, ε_t should not be set too low, as doing so allows fewer data points to exceed ε_e, rendering the parameter ineffective. Specifically, the number of data points allowed to exceed ε_e before triggering a fault can be expressed as $\lfloor f \cdot \varepsilon_t \rfloor + 1$, where $f = \frac{1}{T}$ is the PT sampling frequency. In E3, where $\varepsilon_t = 0.1$s, this allows $\lfloor 0.1\text{s}/0.05\text{s} \rfloor + 1 = 3$ data points to exceed ε_e. If $\varepsilon_t < dt$, the fault is triggered before the next data point arrives, limiting the threshold to a single exceedance and effectively nullifying the temporal aspect of the fault detection. As discussed in Sect. 4.2, this is undesirable since errors between the DT and PT can occur even in the absence of faults, as illustrated in Fig. 4, possibly leading to fault detection based on inherent model error rather than actual faults. However, if ε_e is significantly higher than the typical error in fault-free conditions, the role of ε_t diminishes, as large deviations alone become sufficient indicators of a fault, regardless of duration.

Reduced ε_e: In the fourth experiment, ε_e is reduced from 0.7 rad to 0.3 rad while ε_t remains 1 s. As shown in Table 2, this led to premature termination after detecting 2/3 Missing Block faults due to a false positive. The fault was detected while the gripper held a block, triggering another Missing Block fault and causing system shutdown due to trajectory divergence between the DT and PT. This highlights the importance of selecting ε_e carefully to avoid false positives. Here, ε_e was set well below the maximum observed error (≈ 0.6 rad, see Fig. 4b). Two primary factors contribute to this error: (1) Uncertainty in the DT's timing model, as some FTIs are empirically estimated, leading to gradual drift if miscalculated. (2) Differences in trajectory scaling—while the DT uses quintic polynomial scaling, the PT employs trapezoidal scaling, causing increased trajectory discrepancy with distance travelled [20]. For instance, in Fig. 4b, a 3.7 rad movement in joint 5 at $t \approx 60$ s results in a 0.35 rad error due to scaling differences, leaving only a 0.05 rad margin for other uncertainties. The trajectory generation in this study does not account for robot dynamics, limiting precision. Incorporating dynamics into the DT model could reduce errors but requires accurate parameters, higher computational resources, and increased implementation complexity. Given these trade-offs, a kinematic model was used despite its lower accuracy. If dynamics were included, ε_e and ε_t could likely be reduced, improving task efficiency and enhancing the DT's predictive capabilities.

6   Concluding Remarks

In this paper, we presented a practical approach for enhancing the autonomy and fault tolerance of a UR3e robotic manipulator by leveraging a DT and the MAPE-K loop, which allow for real-time fault detection and self-adaptation. This combination of a DT and the MAPE-K loop improves the robotic system's ability to handle unexpected faults during task execution, thus reducing system downtime. One of the key aspects of the system is the introduction of multiple models - kinematic, timing and spatial - to support the fault detection mechanism. These models are integrated with the monitoring of the robot's state and allow the system to detect faults before they happen (pre-operational) and during operation (operational), providing both predictive and corrective capabilities. Overall, our experiments have validated the feasibility of a DT-based approach for robotic autonomy in manufacturing settings, showing that it is possible to detect and mitigate faults in real time.

However, efforts can be made to reduce the trajectory errors to increase fault detection speed and enhance robustness, potentially using a different time scaling or dynamic modelling. Additionally, to increase applicability, the system could be generalised for compatibility with other robots, and incorporated into a DT sharing platform such as the Digital Twin as a Service (DTaaS) software platform [17,18]. Future work on DT-aided autonomy for the UR3e robotic manipulator could benefit from advancements introduced in the RoboSAPI-ENS project, particularly its MAPLE-K framework for safe and trustworthy robotic self-adaptation [12]. Incorporating a validation step before executing adaptation strategies could enhance fault detection and mitigation, ensuring safer responses to unexpected faults. Additionally, formal verification techniques from RoboSAPIENS could improve the robustness of DT models by providing guarantees of safe operation during real-time adaptation.

References

1. Bruno, G., Aliev, K.: Digital twin application for dynamic task allocation. In: Borgianni, Y., Matt, D.T., Molinaro, M., Orzes, G. (eds.) Towards a Smart, Resilient and Sustainable Industry, pp. 145–154. Springer, Cham (2023). https://doi.org/10.1007/978-3-031-38274-1_13
2. Corke, P., Haviland, J.: Not your grandmother's toolbox – the Robotics Toolbox reinvented for Python. In: 2021 IEEE International Conference on Robotics and Automation (ICRA), pp. 11357–11363 (2021). https://doi.org/10.1109/ICRA48506.2021.9561366
3. Edrisi, F., Perez-Palacin, D., Caporuscio, M., Giussani, S.: Adaptive controllers and digital twin for self-adaptive robotic manipulators. In: 2023 IEEE/ACM 18th Symposium on Software Engineering for Adaptive and Self-Managing Systems (SEAMS), pp. 56–67 (2023). https://doi.org/10.1109/SEAMS59076.2023.00017
4. Feng, H., et al.: Integration Of The MAPE-K loop in digital twins. In: 2022 Annual Modeling and Simulation Conference (ANNSIM), pp. 102–113 (2022). https://doi.org/10.23919/ANNSIM55834.2022.9859489

5. Fitzgerald, J., Gomes, C., Larsen, P.G.: The Engineering of Digital Twins. Springer, Heidelberg (2024). https://doi.org/10.1007/978-3-031-66719-0

6. Gil, S., Mikkelsen, P.H., Tola, D., Schou, C., Larsen, P.G.: A modeling approach for composed digital twins in cooperative systems. In: 2023 IEEE 28th International Conference on Emerging Technologies and Factory Automation (ETFA), pp. 1–8 (2023). https://doi.org/10.1109/ETFA54631.2023.10275601

7. Gil, S., Oakes, B.J., Gomes, C., Frasheri, M., Larsen, P.G.: Toward a systematic reporting framework for digital twins: a cooperative robotics case study. Simulation **101**(3), 313–339 (2025). https://doi.org/10.1177/00375497241261406

8. Gil, S., Schou, C., Mikkelsen, P.H., Larsen, P.G.: Integrating skills into digital twins in cooperative systems. In: 2024 IEEE/SICE International Symposium on System Integration (SII), pp. 1124–1131 (2024). https://doi.org/10.1109/SII58957.2024.10417610

9. Huang, Z., Shen, Y., Li, J., Fey, M., Brecher, C.: A survey on ai-driven digital twins in industry 4.0: smart manufacturing and advanced robotics. Sensors **21**(19) (2021). https://doi.org/10.3390/s21196340. https://www.mdpi.com/1424-8220/21/19/6340

10. Kephart, J., Chess, D.: The vision of autonomic computing. Computer **36**(1), 41–50 (2003). https://doi.org/10.1109/MC.2003.1160055

11. Kritzinger, W., Karner, M., Traar, G., Henjes, J., Sihn, W.: Digital twin in manufacturing: a categorical literature review and classification. IFAC-PapersOnLine **51**(11), 1016–1022 (2018). https://doi.org/10.1016/j.ifacol.2018.08.474

12. Larsen, P.G., et al.: Robotic safe adaptation in unprecedented situations: the RoboSAPIENS project. Res. Direct. Cyber-Phys. Syst. **2**, e4 (2024). https://doi.org/10.1017/cbp.2024.4

13. Lynch, K., Park, F.: Modern Robotics: Mechanics, Planning, and Control. Cambridge University Press, Cambridge (2017)

14. Mazumder, A., et al.: Towards next generation digital twin in robotics: trends, scopes, challenges, and future. Heliyon **9**(2) (2023). https://doi.org/10.1016/j.heliyon.2023.e13359

15. Mihai, S., et al.: Digital twins: a survey on enabling technologies, challenges, trends and future prospects. IEEE Commun. Surv. Tutor. **24**(4), 2255–2291 (2022). https://doi.org/10.1109/COMST.2022.3208773

16. Niederer, S.A., Sacks, M.S., Girolami, M., Willcox, K.: Scaling digital twins from the artisanal to the industrial. Nat. Comput. Sci. **1**(5), 313–320 (2021). https://doi.org/10.1038/s43588-021-00072-5

17. Talasila, P., Gomes, C., Mikkelsen, P.H., Arboleda, S.G., Kamburjan, E., Larsen, P.G.: Digital twin as a service (DTaaS): a platform for digital twin developers and users. In: 2023 IEEE Smart World Congress (SWC), pp. 1–8 (2023). https://doi.org/10.1109/SWC57546.2023.10448890

18. Talasila, P., et al.: Composable digital twins on Digital Twin as a Service platform. Simulation **101**(3), 287–311 (2025). https://doi.org/10.1177/00375497241298653

19. Tao, F., Zhang, H., Liu, A., Nee, A.Y.C.: Digital twin in industry: state-of-the-art. IEEE Trans. Ind. Inf. **15**(4), 2405–2415 (2019). https://doi.org/10.1109/TII.2018.2873186

20. Thomsen, A.K., Rasmussen, B.S.: Towards Digital Twin Aided Autonomy for a Robotic Arm. Bsc thesis, Aarhus University (2024). https://tinyurl.com/AB-BSc-thesis

21. Truszkowski, W., et al.: Autonomous and Autonomic Systems: With Applications to NASA Intelligent Spacecraft Operations and Exploration Systems. NASA Mono-

graphs in Systems and Software Engineering, 1 edn. Springer, London (2009). https://doi.org/10.1007/b105417

22. Universal Robots A/S: DH Paramaters for calculations of kinematics and dynamics. https://tinyurl.com/URdhparam. Accessed 20 July 2024

23. Universal Robots A/S: Universal Robots e-Series User Manual - UR3e. https://tinyurl.com/UR3e-user-manual

24. Universal Robots A/S: Remote operation guide (2024). https://tinyurl.com/ReOpGuide. Accessed 4 Sept 2024

25. Yang, X., Qiang, D., Chen, Z., Wang, H., Zhou, Z., Zhang, X.: Dynamic modeling and digital twin of a harmonic drive based collaborative robot joint. In: 2022 International Conference on Robotics and Automation (ICRA), pp. 4862–4868 (2022). https://doi.org/10.1109/ICRA46639.2022.9812458

26. Zhou, Z., Yang, X., Wang, H., Zhang, X.: Digital twin with integrated robot-human/environment interaction dynamics for an industrial mobile manipulator. In: 2022 International Conference on Robotics and Automation (ICRA), pp. 5041–5047 (2022). https://doi.org/10.1109/ICRA46639.2022.9812004

Scenario-Based System Testing for Distributed Robotics Applications
(Invited Paper)

Jan Peleska[1]([⊠]) (iD), Felix Brüning[2] (iD), Anne E. Haxthausen[3] (iD), and Wen-ling Huang[1] (iD)

[1] Department of Mathematics and Computer Science, University of Bremen, Bremen, Germany
{peleska,huang}@uni-bremen.de

[2] Verified Systems International GmbH, Bremen, Germany
fbruening@verified.de

[3] DTU Compute, Technical University of Denmark, Kongens Lyngby, Denmark
aeha@dtu.dk

Abstract. Using a typical system test application for distributed robots operating in a joint mission for illustration, the **SC**enario **S**pecification Language SCSL is introduced. The design of the SCSL is motivated by the fact that according to the current state of the art, highly complex systems are no longer specified by comprehensive, monolithic models. Instead, relevant behaviours are represented separately in parameterised scenarios, and the overall system behaviour is derived from the library containing the complete scenario collection. For the specification of system tests, the scenario-based approach is particularly attractive, since only the test-specific behaviours need to be modelled, so that a comprehensive monolithic model is not needed. SCSL syntax and semantics are explained by means of a system test example for robots performing a salvage mission, and we sketch the tools for automated test data generation, test execution, and test evaluation.

1 Introduction

1.1 Objectives

The objective of this paper[1] is to present a scenario specification language for defining and executing functional system tests for complex cyber-physical systems (CPS). The presentation uses a typical example of a system test for several robots collaborating in a joint mission. When comparing "classical" model-based system testing (MBT) to the scenario-based approach, the crucial differences are as follows.

---

[1] A part of Sect. 1 has been taken verbatim from a preliminary description of SCSL syntax and semantics [22].

© The Author(s), under exclusive license to Springer Nature Switzerland AG 2026
A. Cavalcanti et al. (Eds.): TAROS 2025, LNAI 16045, pp. 310–337, 2026.
https://doi.org/10.1007/978-3-032-01486-3_25

- MBT aims to capture all admissible system behaviours within a comprehensive system model. From this model, test cases, test data, and test procedures are derived to achieve a certain level of coverage. This model coverage may also be related to requirements coverage, if the underlying formalism allows for tracing model elements to requirements and vice versa [21].
- Scenarios are more restrictive behavioural models, each scenario describing a relevant behavioural aspect of the system, for example, a traffic scenario for an autonomous vehicle. Each relevant system behaviour should be covered by at least one scenario. The collection of all scenarios, referred to as the *scenario library*, serves as a structured specification of system behaviour for testing purposes. A separate validation activity not discussed in this paper ensures that all relevant behaviours are covered by the library [11].
- Typically, scenarios are parameterised, so that they can be instantiated in different system test situations with different parameter values. A scenario instance is a concrete behavioural specification, where all parameters have been associated with concrete values.
- The objects under test – in the example presented here, the collaborating robots and a command centre supervising the mission – are input parameters to the test scenarios, and their expected behaviour is specified in the scenario, since only the scenario-specific behavioural aspects need to be described.
- A scenario-based system test consists of a set of scenario instances that define a meaningful end-to-end system behaviour in alignment with specific test objectives.

Consequently, scenarios are easier to specify than the reference models needed in MBT, where the expected behaviour of a system under test (SUT) needs to be modelled for *all* operational situations.

Typical test configurations for the scenario-based approach advocated by the authors will be variants of the one depicted in Fig. 1. The CPS under test is a distributed system where control computers communicate with each other and may act on electro-mechanical peripherals. In a system test configuration, some of these control computers will be present as *original equipment* OE, while others are replaced by *simulations* SIM. Hardware peripherals could also be replaced by other simulations, or they could be present as original *peripherals* PER. The solid lines between boxes each represent one or more interfaces for data exchange. Interfaces (to be introduced in Sect. 3.7) realise uni-directional data flows between components participating in a system test.

The objective of system tests is to check the functional behaviour of all original equipment and peripherals, as well as their interactions. The "local" behaviour of original equipment is monitored by *original equipment harnesses* OEH. These harnesses run test-specific *elementary scenarios* specifying the expected behaviour of their OE during the system test, as well as the stimulations to be provided for some OE input interfaces, as far as these are not provided by other OE or by simulations or peripherals.

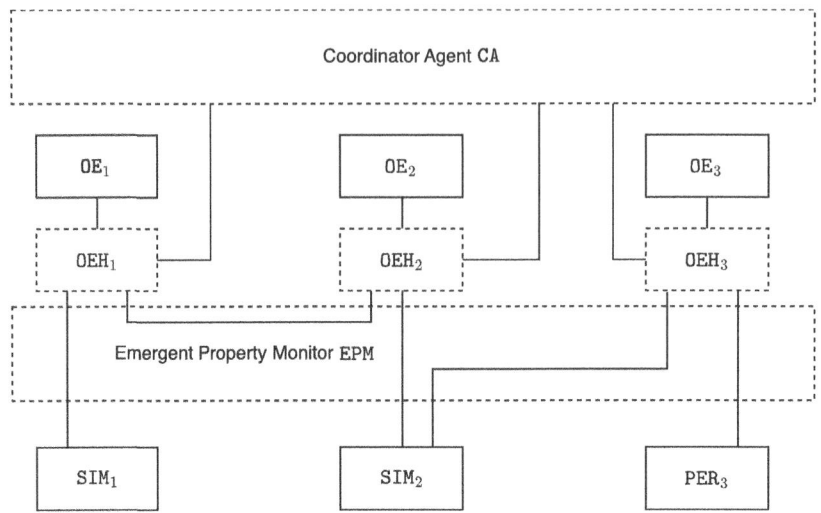

Fig. 1. System test configuration.

The succession of elementary scenarios to be executed by each OEH is coordinated by a *coordinator agent* CA. The CA receives status information about ongoing elementary scenario executions performed by each OEH and provides further elementary scenarios to be scheduled by the associated OEH. The collaboration between all components of the CPS will result in certain *emergent properties* [17] achieved by the overall system. These can be checked by an *emergent property monitor* EPM observing all communications between CPS sub-components and its operational environment (typically replaced by simulations during a system test).

1.2   Main Contributions

In this paper, we present the new **SC**enario **S**pecification **L**anguage SCSL. It provides language constructs for specifying *data types, constants, object types, elementary scenario types,* and *composite scenarios* describing *system test configurations*. Objects specify original equipment, peripherals, or simulations thereof. Typically, objects are just represented by their interface parameters, since their behaviour will be specified in a "situation-specific way" inside elementary scenarios. The latter are used for describing (a) a small number of behaviours to be expected in specific operational situations, or (b) the expected interactions of certain objects in such situations, or (c) an expected emergent behaviour of the CPS for the system test under consideration.

Elementary scenarios are specified using a parameter declaration, a precondition describing when an instance of the scenario will become active, a behavioural specification in Linear Temporal Logic (LTL), and an action language facilitating the use of LTL. The combination of temporal logic and action language allows to express behavioural aspects in *mixed declarative and imperative style*. From our experience, this facilitates behavioural modelling in a considerable way.

- Declarative specifications are good for including all acceptable behaviours without having to enumerate them algorithmically. On the downside, it may be quite hard to produce declarative specifications that capture all acceptable behaviours without inadvertently including some unwanted behaviours.
- Imperative specifications, when designed with a focus on simple readability, may exclude alternative acceptable solutions.

A distinguishing feature of SCSL is that its semantics takes explicitly into account that typical controllers in a CPS run in *execution cycles* of constant duration. New inputs are read and outputs are written at the beginning of each cycle. Therefore, they no longer behave like perfect physical models whose differential equations specify piecewise smooth evolutions for each real-valued observable (such as location or velocity). Instead, controllers produce variable updates at each cycle that should be close approximations of the discretised differential equations of the underlying physical models. Our position (which is also shared by other authors working in the field of CPS [4]) is that formalisms using a semantics close to physical models (like, for example, the Multi-Lane Spatial Logic MLSL [12]) should only be used to describe the idealised physical view of a CPS, while modelling formalisms used to derive test cases for the implemented system should take into account the cyclic nature of the controllers involved.

Elementary scenarios are complemented by operators to create composite scenarios, describing all aspects of a system test.

We introduce the formal syntax and semantics of SCSL. In contrast to wide spectrum language like UML and SysML [18,19] that can be specialised for the purpose of scenario specification, the SCSL syntax and semantics is very compact. Moreover, SCSL is executable for the purpose of automated test data generation and checking of actual SUT behaviour against the expected behaviour specified in SCSL.

While existing scenario specification languages are usually domain-specific [1] the SCSL is applicable to arbitrary application domains. Domain-specific support can be easily created by elaborating domain-specific elementary scenarios that are collected in a re-usable library [22]. This is advantageous for CPS engineers working in more than one domain, e.g. automotive, railways, aviation, and robotics. Instead of having to become familiar with several different domain-specific formalisms, they can always use SCSL, each time with different domain-specific libraries. Likewise, tool builders for scenario-based modelling and test support can focus on building one tool and provide domain-specific libraries, to be imported into the tool's scenario library.

1.3   Related Work

Gipps [10] created a mathematical specification formalism for computer-based car-following simulation. *Gipps' model* captures the behaviour of a single vehicle in a traffic stream, specifically how it reacts to the vehicle in front. The model specifies each braking and acceleration action of the following vehicle. Building on Gipps' work, the *Intelligent Driver Model (IDM)* [29] introduces time-continuous traffic flow scenario specification with environmental aspects. This enables the simulation of braking manoeuvres or minimum spacing between cars. This was further extended by additional physical simulations of longitudinal dynamics, expressed by the *Optimal Velocity Model (OVM)* [3]. OVM enables the dynamical adjustment of the acceleration after the lead vehicle brakes. The model uses mathematical equations to specify acceleration and braking values. Ulbrich et al. introduced fundamental formal definitions and examples for *scene*, *situation* and *scenario*, where a scene is considered as a snapshot of the environment including static and dynamic elements, a situation is defined as a context-specific scene and a scenario as a description of a temporal evolution of multiple scenes [30]. Hilscher et al. developed an abstract model using spatial interval logic to represent multi-lane roadways with potential lane changes of ego vehicles, called *Multi-Lane Spatial Logic* (MLSL). The formalism enables the verification of lane changes for a single vehicle in an environment with multiple ego vehicles, while a distance controller ensures safe spacing between vehicles [12]. Schwammberger [26] extended MLSL by incorporating property checks into the lane-changing controller for motorway scenarios, ensuring that undesirable events never occur, as initially proposed by Hilscher et al. [12]. Schwammberger implemented the line-change controller in UPPAAL to verify the implemented timed automaton and the line changing protocol. Damm et al. introduced *Traffic Sequence Charts* (TSC) as a formal and visual specification language for designing traffic scenarios in the context of autonomous vehicle testing [9]. TSCs are designed textually or visually, enabling structure-based validation to improve safety assurance by creating a scenario catalogue.

For scenario specification of distributed event-based systems, *Petri Nets* [23] are employed to define scenarios in form of subsequent events. Petri Nets facilitate the formal description of system requirements which are then used as input models for test generation, as outlined in Sarmiento et al. [25]. Today's scenario modelling is primarily graphic-based, like *ASAM OpenSCENARIO* [2], which is designed for the automotive domain, focusing on defining real-world traffic scenarios and simulating automotive components. Simulations of traffic behaviours are then utilised to test automotive components.

In addition to that, there are several proprietary car traffic simulation platforms, such as *PT-VISSIM* [24], which is designed for trajectory modelling. Beyond automotive applications, the latest *SysML V2* Standard [20] offers syntactic support for domain-independent test scenario definitions, based on occurrences, verification definitions, constraint definitions, interactions, and state machines. SysML V2 introduces enhancements over its predecessor to better support system-level modelling. The strengths of SysML V2 is in defining system interactions, state-driven behaviour and high-level operational scenarios.

In the aviation sector, the graphical *Aviation Scenario Definition Language (ASDL)* [13] supports formal specification of comprehensive aircraft landing scenarios. Scenario specification is also explored through Time Modelling, particularly for system requirements verification. For example, the *Clock Constraint Specification Language (CCSL)* [15] translates specifications into clock graphs. These graphs facilitate constraint-solving using SMT solvers.

Each existing scenario specification formalism has disadvantages: formalisms like ASAM OpenSCENARIO, IDM, or PT-VISSIM offer strong domain-dependent capabilities for behaviour specification and simulations but lack support for behaviour simulation of arbitrary domains and test generation. On the other hand, SysML V2, Petri-Nets and the Clock Constraint Specification Language (CCSL) are primarily domain-independent, but lack a simple, expressive syntax. Additionally, they are not fully suitable for formal behaviour specification. While test and code generation is possible with these formalisms, it often requires significant resources.

SCSL, however, offers a highly simple and more expressive syntax for formal scenario specification. By leveraging existing formalisms from UML/SysML and VDM, the LTL syntax is extended by using condition-actions on state transitions and frames to restrict variable modifications. SCSL is intentionally designed to be domain-independent, supporting specification of re-usable, parametrised scenario models that can be assembled into domain-specific libraries. The state-based behaviour of LTL is a notable feature that enables straightforward test and code generation from specified scenarios.

It is worth mentioning that the idea to combine declarative and imperative specification styles in one formal modelling language is actually quite old: we first came across this concept when studying the Vienna Design Method VDM, where declarative specifications were called *implicit* and imperative ones *explicit* [14].

1.4 Overview

In Sect. 2, the system test used as an example for introducing the SCSL is described in natural language. The SCSL objects and scenarios involved, as well as the resulting system test configuration are presented in Sect. 3. In this section, the basics of SCSL syntax and semantics are explained as well. Tool support for SCSL is discussed in Sect. 4. Section 5 contains a conclusion and discusses future work.

2 A System Test for Verifying Distributed Collaborating Robots

Mission. The robots' mission is to salvage goods from a known location in a hazardous area, where a salvage by humans is deemed to be impossible, due to various adverse environmental conditions.

Goods to be Salvaged. The goods consist of $m > 0$ items (like boxes or barrels) that can be picked up by a robot arm and loaded onto a transport-capable robot. Each item has a unique id, which can be spotted by the robots.[2]

Terrain. We assume that the terrain where the goods are located has several exclusion zones (such as cliff edges), so that the robots cannot reach their destination on a straight path from their starting points.

Robots. There are n robots of the *rover* type: they move on wheels that are suitable for the terrain. Each rover is identically equipped and has the same capabilities: (1) A robot arm to pick up an item. (2) A cargo bed where an item can be placed. (2) Sensors allowing to detect the boundaries of exclusion zones. (3) A GPS sensor to determine its location. (4) Autonomous moving capabilities to circumvent exclusion zones and find a path to a given destination, if such a path exists from their actual location. (5) Cameras, image recognition functions, RFID readers to detect and pick up an item and place it on a robot's flatbed. (6) Communication equipment to send status information to a command centre and receive commands from there. (7) Controllers to process the commands received.

Mission Planning. As the optimal path to the goods is unknown, rovers are deployed from different starting points, but they all get the same destination coordinates where all items to be salvaged are located. It is expected that some rovers will get stuck on their path and be unable to reach the destination. Others may have hardware faults, and some might be destroyed by inadvertently entering an exclusion zone. Therefore, n rovers are initially sent on the mission, while only $m < n$ rovers are needed to pick up and return the salvaged goods. The first m to reach the destination will be commanded to pick up the goods. To this end, the command centre sends different item ids to the rovers, so that they all approach and load different items. As soon as a rover has managed to load an item onto its flatbed, it is commanded to return to a specific location. All rovers that get stuck or fail during their mission are commanded to return (even if it is uncertain whether they will be able to return at all). The same holds for operative rovers that are no longer needed since all items to be salvaged have been picked up by other robots. Return locations may vary between rovers, especially for those that failed to reach the destination and can exit the hazardous area more quickly via alternative paths.

Pass Criterion. The system test passes if at least $m \leq n$ rovers arrive before time t_{atDst} (arrival deadline) and at least $k \leq m$ rovers return carrying salvaged items before time $t_{\mathrm{end}} > t_{\mathrm{atDst}}$ (mission completion deadline).

---

[2] Typical identification techniques could be QR codes or RFID tags.

3   Scenario-Based System Test Specification in SCSL

3.1   Overview

A complete SCSL system test specification consists of (1) elementary type specifications, such as enumerations, (2) composite data type specifications, similar to mathematical data types in Z or VDM [14,27], (3) global constants and function definitions, (4) object type specifications for the types of components participating in a system test, (5) elementary scenario type specifications, and (6) a system test configuration.

A system test configuration references all the participants in the test execution, as well as their means of interaction, and the test execution schedule. The participants are instances of object type specifications. Each object represents original equipment, peripherals, or simulations thereof, as introduced before in Sect. 1. The means of interaction between objects are provided by *interfaces*. Objects and interfaces are comprised in a *collaboration*[3] which is the first part of a system test configuration.

The execution schedule (second part of the system test configuration) shows how original equipment *should* and how simulations *will* evolve over time during the system test execution. This is specified by means of composing instances of elementary scenario types, using sequential and parallel operators. An elementary scenario refers to one or more objects and specifies how these should/will behave *in the specific circumstances captured by the scenario*. This is an essential feature of the SCSL:

> Instead of specifying all possible behaviours of an object type, the specific behaviour of each object in a situation captured by a scenario is described in the elementary scenario.

In the terms introduced in Sect. 1, elementary scenarios runs on an original equipment harness (OEH). Note that system test schedules usually involve more than one elementary scenario, since this type of test aims at verifying end-to-end functionality, as perceived by end users of the system. In the system test of the robots described in this paper, for example, separate elementary scenarios are used to describe robots approaching the salvage destination, robots loading items to be salvaged, and robots returning with or without items.

In the remainder of this section, illustrations for each of the six SCSL language elements will be given, using the system test described in Sect. 2 as an example.

3.2   Primitive Types and Composite Data Types

Each rover accepts commands from the command centre: initially, command goToDst will set a rover into motion, trying to reach the specified destination. Command pickUpItem orders a rover that has reached the target destination

---

[3] The notion of collaborations has been introduced in UML [19] for the purpose of showing which objects interact in specific situations.

to pick up an item to be salvaged. Command `returnToDst` directs a rover to return to a specific position.[4]

In the other communication direction, each rover sends status information to the command centre. While trying to reach the specified target destination, a rover is in state `approaching`, but it may also get broken along the way (state `fault`) or get stuck such that it will be unable to reach the destination (state `stuck`). After a rover has successfully picked up an item at the target destination, it transits to state `itemLoaded`, and then to `returningWithItem` after having been commanded to return to a specified position. After arrival at the return position, the final state of rovers carrying items is `returnedWithItem`. Some rovers will have to return without carrying items; for these, the states `returning` and `returned` apply.

These enumeration types are declared as shown in Listing 1.1.

Listing 1.1. Enumeration types.

```
1 enum
2   RoverCommands : {goToDst, returnToDst, pickUpItem};
3   Status : {initial, approaching, stuck, fault, atDst, itemLoaded,
4               returning, returningWithItem, returned, returnedWithItem};
5 end enum
```

We need a composite data type `Location` for specifying geographic coordinates (e.g. GPS) used for target and return destinations sent to the rovers. Also, each rover can establish its own position in coordinates of type `Location`. Another composite data type is `Zone` for specifying the exclusion zones that are present in the system testing area and should never be entered by any rover.[5]

3.3   Global Constants

The constants needed for our system test are specified in Listing 1.2.

Listing 1.2. Global constants.

```
1 global const
2   n : ℕ; -- initial number of rovers
3   m : ℕ; -- number of items to be salvaged
4   k : ℕ; -- minimal number of items to be salvaged
5   constraint
6     k ≤ m ≤ n
7   end constraint
8   t_atDst : ℝ≥0; -- arrival deadline when at least m rovers should
9                  -- have arrived at destination
10  t_end : ℝ≥0; -- mission deadline when at least
11                -- k items should have been salvaged
```

---

[4] In principle, commands `goToDst` and `returnToDst` have the same effect. We use two distinct commands, however, to clarify that first the target destination is specified to direct the robots to the goods to be salvaged (command `goToDst`), and after that the destination is specified to let the robots return to a home base (command `returnToDst`).

[5] Typically, a `Zone` element would be represented as a simple polygon.

```
12  constraint
13    t_atDst ≤ t_end
14  end constraint
15  targetDst : Location; -- target destination where the
16                        -- items to be salvaged can be found
17  numZones : ℕ; -- number of exclusion zones in the testing range
18  exclusionZone : Zone[numZones]; -- array of exclusion zones
19  startPos : Location[n]; -- start positions for each rover
20  returnDst : Location[n]; -- return destinations for each rover
21  allIds : ItemId*; -- List of item identifiers
22                    -- for each item to be salvaged
23  constraint
24    #allIds = m -- there are m items to be salvaged
25  end constraint
26 end const
```

3.4 Object Types

The object types for our system test are rovers and command centres. Rovers accept commands *cmd* from the control centre, the specification of destinations *dst* to be reached by each rover, identifications *id* of items to be picked up and salvaged, and their actual position *pos* provided by some external positioning system like GPS. As output, each rover communicates its current status *s* to the command centre. This interface specification is given in Listing 1.3, lines 1 and 2.

As motivated in Sect. 1, original equipment, peripherals, and simulations thereof operate in fixed processing cycles that may differ between object types. Therefore a *cycle time* is specified in relation to the (faster) observation and stimulation cycles that can be performed by the test equipment. The specification cycletime 20 states that any instance of type *Rover* performs one processing cycle in 20 observation cycles of the test equipment.

Listing 1.3. Object type 'Rover'.

```
1  object type Rover(in cmd : RoverCommands, in dst : Location, in id : ItemId,
2                    in pos : Location, out s : Status)
3    cycletime 20
4  end type
```

Command centres accept an array $s[i], i : 0..(n-1)$, of status values, one from each rover, as inputs. They communicate possibly different commands $cmd[i]$, destination specifications $dst[i]$, and item identifications $id[i]$ to the rovers. This is specified in Listing 1.4.

Listing 1.4. Object type 'CommandCentre'.

```
1  object type CommandCentre( in s : Status[n],
2                             out cmd : RoverCommands[n],
3                             out dst : Location[n],
4                             out id : ItemId[n] )
5    cycletime 10
6  end type
```

Note that these object type specifications do not indicate how outputs of some objects will be linked to inputs of others, since this cannot be determined once and for all on type level. Instead, the mapping from outputs to inputs is specified on object level in the collaboration part of the system test configuration (see Sect. 3.7).

3.5 Global Function Declaration

For evaluating the system test, a counting function is needed: $\texttt{numRovers}(r, S)$ counts the number of rovers in array r whose state has one of the values specified in set S. Boolean function $\texttt{inExclusionZone}(pos, \texttt{exclusionZone})$ returns true if and only if the geographic position pos is in one of the exclusion zones $\texttt{exclusionZone}[i]$, $i : 0..(\texttt{numZones} - 1)$.[6] Boolean function $\texttt{isCloseTo}(pos, dst)$ returns true if and only if a robot's actual position pos is close to the destination coordinate dst, so that the robot is in the position to load an item.

Listing 1.5. Global functions.

```
1  global function
2    numRovers : Rover[n] × ℙ(Status) ⟶ ℕ;
3    (r, S) ↦ #{i : 0..(n − 1) | r[i] ≠ null ∧ r[i].s ∈ S};
4    inExclusionZone : Location × Zone[numZones] ⟶ 𝔹;
5    -- inExclusionZone(pos, exclusionZone) = true iff pos is contained in one
6    -- of the exclusion zones exclusionZone[i]
7    -- (application of the ray casting algorithm)
8    isCloseTo : Location × Location ⟶ 𝔹;
9    -- isCloseTo(pos, dst) = true iff pos is close to dst
10  end function
```

For functions $\texttt{inExclusionZone}$ and $\texttt{isCloseTo}$, the detailed specifications have been ommitted in Listing 1.5. They would also be specified in Z-style, as illustrated in the case of the function $\texttt{numRovers}$.

3.6 Elementary Scenario Types

Scenario Structure and Behavioural Specification. Elementary scenario types specify how the objects of interest should behave or interact with each other in certain operational situations. In SCSL, each elementary scenario comes with the following sub-components.

1. An interface specification with the same syntax as described for object types.
2. A precondition over interface parameters, specifying the conditions of an elementary scenario instance to start its execution.
3. A behavioural specification consisting of
    (a) LTL formulae over interface parameters and auxiliary variables,
    (b) optional initial actions setting the initial values of auxiliary variables,

---

[6] For determining whether a coordinate is inside a simple polygon, the *ray casting algorithm* could be used [28].

(c) optional condition-action pairs defining writes to auxiliary variables, depending on conditions over interface parameters and auxiliary variables.

Conditions in condition-action pairs can be

- *guards g* that trigger the associated action in every execution cycle where g evaluates to `true`.
- *change conditions chg* that trigger the associated action in every execution cycle where *chg* changes from `false` to `true`.

This concept for behavioural modelling deliberately mixes declarative and imperative specification styles: LTL formulae are implicit (=declarative) behavioural specifications that are refined by adding conditions and actions in imperative style that is quite similar to state machines used in UML [19]. From our experience, LTL formulae (or declarative specifications in general) usually specify behaviours that are too general, so that some unwanted executions are still accepted by these formulae. The condition-action pairs changing auxiliary variables and the use of the latter in LTL formulae allows to narrow down the accepted behaviours in an effective way.

Every elementary scenario is associated with an implicitly defined variable `active` that is set to `true` when the precondition evaluates to `true` for the first time. When `active` is reset to `false`, this indicates the termination of the scenario execution. After scenario termination, the behavioural specifications need to hold no longer. One global variable `EoT` is `false` at the beginning of a system test execution, but can be set to `true` by any elementary scenario, whereupon the system test terminates. If `EoT` is never set to `true`, a system test ends when all elementary scenarios involved have terminated (status change from `active` = `true` to `active` = `false`).

The behavioural semantics of an elementary scenario type consists of infinite sequences of valuation functions $\sigma : V \longrightarrow D$, where V is the set of interface parameters and auxiliary variables defined for the scenario type, and D is the union of all variable types involved. An infinite sequence $\pi \in (V \longrightarrow D)^\omega$ is a model for a given scenario type if and only if the sequence can be partitioned into $\pi = \pi_1.\pi_2$, so that π_1 is the finite sequence of valuations observed while the scenario is active and π_2 an arbitrary infinite sequence, such that π is an LTL model for the conjunction of all LTL formulae defined for the scenario type, and this model is consistent with all assignments to auxiliary variables conditionally performed in the specified actions.

Rover-Specific Scenario Types. For the system test under consideration, three elementary scenario types cover the rover-specific behaviours: scenario type *Approach* specifies rover behaviour while approaching the target destination. Scenario *Pickup* specifies rover behaviour while picking up an item to be salvaged. Scenario *Return* specifies rover behaviour while returning to a specified location, with or without a loaded item.

The *Approach* scenario type is declared in Listing 1.6. As input, each *Approach*-instance gets a reference[7] to a specific rover r and the location `startPos` from where the rover shall start its journey to the target destination. The latter is specified in $r.dst$, and this destination is communicated from the command centre to the rover, before the scenario becomes operative.

The precondition for an *Approach* scenario instance to become active states that (1) the rover's initial state is `initial` (this is an expected behaviour when the rover is started), (2) the rover must have been placed at its starting position (this must be ensured by the system testing crew), and (3) the command input to the rover must be `goToDst` (so a scenario instance can only become active after the command centre has sent this command to the rover).

For scenario type *Approach*, the behaviour is specified by LTL formulae only – no condition-action specifications are necessary: the first formula specifies the scenario termination condition. It states that `active` will be set to `false` after either (1) the rover inadvertently enters an exclusion zone (this actually destroys the rover, as will be handled in scenario type *MishapHandler*), or (2) the rover actually reaches the specified destination or gets stuck or broken before reaching it, or (3) the command centre sends a new command to the rover, indicating that reaching the target destination is no longer necessary. The second formula asserts that the rover will finally get close to the target destination $r.dst$ and change its state to $r.s = $ `atDst`, unless it vanishes in an exclusion zone, gets broken or stuck, or receives another directive from the command centre.

Listing 1.6. Approach scenario.

```
1  elementary scenario Approach( in r : Rover, in const startPos : Location )
2    precondition r.s = initial ∧ isCloseTo(r.pos, startPos) ∧ r.cmd = goToDst;
3    spec G((inExclusionZone(r.pos, exclusionZone) ∨ r.s ∈ {stuck, fault, atDst} ∨
4             r.cmd ≠ goToDst) ⇒ X¬active);
5    spec F(inExclusionZone(r.pos, exclusionZone) ∨ r.s ∈ {stuck, fault} ∨
6             r.cmd ≠ goToDst ∨ (isCloseTo(r.pos, r.dst) ∧ r.s = atDst));
7  end scenario
```

Scenario type *Pickup* (Listing 1.7) specifies the expected rover behaviour during the pickup phase. Its precondition to become active is that the rover is commanded to either pick up an item or return to given return destination. In the latter case, the first LTL formula states that the scenario will immediately become inactive, since there is no item to be picked up. Other scenario termination conditions are that the rover enters an exclusion zone or gets stuck or broken while trying to load the item, or that the item has been successfully loaded. If the command `pickUpItem` applies, the rover will finally succeed in loading the item, unless it fails before. This is expressed by the second LTL formula.

Listing 1.7. Pickup scenario.

```
1  elementary scenario Pickup( in r : Rover )
2    precondition r.cmd ∈ {pickUpItem, returnToDst};
```

---

[7] Similar to Java, instances of object types are passed by reference to the elementary SCSL scenarios.

```
3   spec G((r.cmd = returnToDst ∨ inExclusionZone(r.pos, exclusionZone) ∨
4                    r.s ∈ {stuck, fault, itemLoaded}) ⇒ X¬active);
5   spec r.cmd = pickUpItem ⇒
6       F(inExclusionZone(r.pos, exclusionZone) ∨ r.s ∈ {stuck, fault, itemLoaded});
7  end scenario
```

Scenario type *Return* (Listing 1.8) specifies how a rover returns to a given address. It becomes active as soon as a `returnToDst` command has been received from the command centre. Here we have an initial action that introduces a Boolean auxiliary variable $aux_{isLoaded}$ (its type is determined automatically from the right-hand side part of the assignment expression) which is set to `true` if and only if the rover has loaded an item. As usual, the rover may be lost after entering an exclusion zone, or it may get stuck or broken along the way. If, however, all goes well, it will finally arrive at the return destination and assume status `returnedWithItem` or `returned`, depending on whether it returns with an item or not. While approaching the return destination, the rover state $r.s$ is `returningWithItem` or `returning`, depending on the value of $aux_{isLoaded}$.

Note that auxiliary variables need not be declared: their type is specified implicitly from the right-hand-side expressions in the assignments, similar to `auto` declarations in C^{++}.

Listing 1.8. Return scenario.

```
1  elementary scenario Return( in r : Rover )
2     precondition r.cmd = returnToDst;
3     spec G((inExclusionZone(r.pos, exclusionZone) ∨
4                     r.s ∈ {stuck, fault, returned, returnedWithItem})
5                             ⇒ X¬active);
6     spec ((r.s = returningWithItem ∧ aux_isLoaded) ∨ (r.s = returning ∧ ¬aux_isLoaded))
7         U
8         (inExclusionZone(r.pos, exclusionZone) ∨ r.s ∈ {stuck, fault} ∨
9           (isCloseTo(r.pos, r.dst) ∧ aux_isLoaded ∧ r.s = returnedWithItem) ∨
10          (isCloseTo(r.pos, r.dst) ∧ ¬aux_isLoaded ∧ r.s = returned));
11    initact aux_isLoaded := (r.s = itemLoaded);
12 end scenario
```

Scenarios for Interactions Between Rovers and Command Centre. We need four elementary scenario types for describing the interaction between the command centre and the rovers during their approach to the items to be salvaged (*ApproachHandler*), while picking up items (*PickupHandler*), while returning to their specified destinations (*ReturnHandler*), and in the special case where a rover inadvertently enters an exclusion zone (*MishapHandler*).

Listing 1.9. Scenario for rovers approaching the target destination.

```
1  elementary scenario ApproachHandler( in cc : CommandCentre,
2                                        in r : Rover,
3                                        in i : N₀ )
4     spec G(inExclusionZone(r[i].pos, exclusionZone) ⇒ X¬active);
5     spec  G(r[i].s ∈ {initial, approaching} ⇒
6                     (cc.cmd[i] = goToDst ∧ cc.dst[i] = targetDst));
7  end scenario
```

Scenario type *ApproachHandler* (Listing 1.9) inputs references to the command centre, the robots, and an index of the specific rover $r[i]$ whose interaction with the command centre is considered in an *ApproachHandler* instance. The first LTL formula specifies that a scenario instance will terminate immediately if rover $r[i]$ enters an exclusion zone, since the rover will be lost and can never reach the target destination. The second LTL formula asserts that when the rover has just been initialised or while it is still approaching the target destination, the command centre will continuously transmit the `goToDst` command and the `targetDst` (location of the items to be salvaged) to the rover. Note again that the transmission interfaces from $cc.cmd[i]$ to $r[i].cmd$ and from $cc.dst[i]$ to $r[i].dst$ are not specified in the elementary scenario declarations, but will be specified for the concrete objects in the collaboration which is part of the test configuration shown below.

Elementary scenario type *PickupHandler* (Listing 1.10) specifies how the command centre directs rovers having arrived at the target destination to load items to be salvaged. To this end, three auxiliary variables are initialised (line 8):

1. aux_{id} is initialised with the list `allIds` containing identifications of all items to be salvaged.
2. aux_{rAtDst} is initialised as the empty set and then used to store all indexes of rovers that have arrived at the target destination, but have not yet been assigned an item to carry (line 9).
3. $aux_{rLoading}$ is initialised as the empty set and then used to store all indexes of rovers that have been assigned to carry an item but have not yet completed the task of loading the item (lines 10—11).

Listing 1.10. Scenario for rovers commanded to pick up an item.

```
1  elementary scenario PickupHandler( in cc : CommandCentre,
2                                      in r : Rover[n] )
3    spec  ⋀_{i:0..(n−1)} G(r[i] ≠ null ⇒ (i ∈ aux_rLoading ⇒
4                          (cc.cmd[i] = pickUpItem ∧ cc.id[i] = aux_loadItemId[i])));
5    spec  G(aux_id = ε ∨
6            (aux_rAtDst = ∅ ∧ numRovers(r, {initial, approaching}) = 0) ⇒
7                X¬active);
8    initact  aux_id := allIds; aux_rAtDst := ∅; aux_rLoading := ∅;
9    cndact  [true] / aux_rAtDst := {i : 0..(n − 1) | r[i].s = atDst} \ aux_rLoading;
10   cndact  [true] /
11       aux_rLoading := aux_rLoading \ {i : 0..(n − 1) | r[i].s ∈ {itemLoaded, stuck, fault}};
12   cndact  [aux_id ≠ ε ∧ aux_rAtDst ≠ ∅] /
13       ℓ := min aux_rAtDst;
14       aux_rAtDst := aux_rAtDst \ {ℓ};
15       aux_rLoading := aux_rLoading ∪ {ℓ};
16       aux_loadItemId[ℓ] := popfront(aux_id);
17 end scenario
```

The assignment of items to rovers is performed in the condition-action expression in lines 11—15: as long as there are still items to be loaded ($aux_{id} \neq \varepsilon$), and whenever at least one rover is located at the target destination but still without an assigned item ($aux_{rAtDst} \neq \emptyset$), the following action is performed:

1. The rover with the smallest index ℓ in aux_{rAtDst} is selected to load the next item in the list.
2. This index ℓ is removed from the set aux_{rAtDst} rovers that could still load an item and added to the set aux_{rLoading} of rovers currently loading an item.
3. In auxiliary array $aux_{\mathrm{loadItemId}}$, the id of the next item to be loaded is written to index ℓ and removed from the list of items still to be salvaged (this is performed by instruction $\mathtt{popfront}(aux_{\mathrm{id}})$ which returns the list head and removes it from the list at the same time).

The first LTL formula (lines 3—4) specifies that the command centre sends a $\mathtt{pickUpItem}$ command to all rovers that still exist in the collaboration ($r[i] \neq \mathtt{null}$) and whose index has been inserted into set aux_{rLoading}. Moreover, the command centre provides the associated item id in output parameter $cc.id[i]$. The second LTL formula specifies that the scenario shall terminate after all items have been assigned to rovers for loading or if there aren't any rovers left to carry an item.

Elementary scenario type *ReturnHandler* (Listing 1.11) specifies the return conditions and the associated commands from the command centre to the rovers. Return commands will be finally sent to all rovers that are still part of the (dynamically changing) system test configuration. This is checked by condition $r[i] \neq \mathtt{null}$: a rover that is no longer existent will be marked by $r[i] = \mathtt{null}$ in the collaboration part of the configuration. The LTL formula in lines 3 and 4 specifies that return commands will be immediately sent to any rover that has loaded its designated item to be salvaged (it is then in state $\mathtt{itemLoaded}$) or that is stuck or broken. In the latter cases it is unclear whether the robot will still be able to execute the return command, but the command is at least issued by the centre. A return command $\mathtt{returnToDst}$ to rover $r[i]$ is associated with a destination value $\mathtt{returnDst}[i]$ which is a predefined constant.

The second LTL formula in lines 5 to 10 specifies return commands to rovers that are still operative, approach the target destination or have already arrived there. These rovers are commanded to return if they are no longer needed, because all items to be salvaged are already being transported by other rovers.

Listing 1.11. Handler for rovers that should return to a specified destination.

```
1  elementary scenario ReturnHandler( in cc : CommandCentre,
2                                      in r : Rover[n] )
3      spec  ⋀_{i:0..(n-1)} G(r[i] ≠ null ⇒ (r[i].s ∈ {stuck, fault, itemLoaded} ⇒
4                      X(cc.cmd[i] = returnToDst ∧ cc.dst[i] = returnDst[i])));
5      spec  ⋀_{i:0..(n-1)} G(r[i] ≠ null ⇒
6                  (r[i].s ∈ {approaching, atDst} ∧
7                   numRovers(r, {itemLoaded}) +
8                   numRovers(r, {returningWithItem}) +
9                   numRovers(r, {returnedWithItem}) = m ⇒
10                     X(cc.cmd[i] = returnToDst ∧ cc.dst[i] = returnDst[i])));
11  end scenario
```

The effect of rovers entering exclusion zones is specified by scenario type *MishapHandler*. Such robots have to be removed from the system test collaboration, since they are no longer existent. This is expressed by the change condition and action in line 3 of the scenario: when a robot enters an exclusion zone for the first time, action **delete**(r) is performed on the collaboration *coll*. This resets the reference r to the rover to **null** and deletes all interfaces connecting r-parameters to parameters of any other object. After this, the scenario is terminated, as specified by the LTL formula in line 2.

Listing 1.12. Mishap handler scenario.

```
1  elementary scenario MishapHandler( in r : Rover, in coll : collaboration )
2     spec G(inExclusionZone(r.pos, exclusionZone) ⇒ X¬active);
3     cndact when ( inExclusionZone(r.pos, exclusionZone) )/coll.delete(r);
4  end scenario
```

Scenario for Checking Emergent Properties. The evaluation of pass criteria for a system test is also specified in one or more elementary scenario types. For the test discussed here, the pass criteria are specified in the *EmergentPropertyChecker* scenario type in Listing 1.13. For a test to pass,

1. at least m rovers shall arrive at the salvage destination before time t_{atDst}, and
2. at least k rovers shall return with a salvaged item before time t_{end}.

The system test is terminated at time $t_{\text{end}} + 10$. The built-in variable $\hat{t}$ denotes the current test execution time, starting with zero when the test execution begins.

Listing 1.13. Emergent property checker.

```
1  elementary scenario EmergentPropertyChecker( in r : Rover[n] )
2     spec  (t̂ < t_atDst) U (numRovers(r, {atDst, itemLoaded, returning,
3                            returningWithItem, returned, returnedWithItem}) ≥ m);
4     spec  (t̂ < t_end) U (numRovers(r, {returnedWithItem}) ≥ k);
5     spec  G(t̂ = t_end + 10 ⇒ XEoT);
6  end scenario
```

Remark 1 – Specification of Object Behaviour. Note that in principle, preconditions and behavioural specifications can also be defined for object types – this is syntactically and semantically well-defined. However, object type behaviours should only be defined if they hold in *every* elementary scenario instance an object is involved in. For the system test example discussed here, we could not identify any behaviours that would hold in arbitrary operational situations. We suspect that this is very likely to hold in most scenario-based test specification for cyber-physical systems.

Remark 2 – Input and Output Parameters. Readers may have noticed that the elementary scenarios introduced above only contain input parameters. This is because their parameter lists only contain object references. The scenario specifications describe how object parameters change in certain situations, but this does not change the associated object references. Elementary scenarios could also introduce parameters of scalar type which could be used, for example, for communicating test-related information between scenarios. Such parameters could have directions **in**, **out**, and **inout**.

Listing 1.14. System test configuration.

```
 1  systemtest
 2    coll : collaboration
 3      r : Rover[n];
 4      cc : CommandCentre;
 5
 6      interface Is[i] from r[i].s to cc.s[i] for i : 0..(n − 1);
 7      interface Icmd[i] from cc.cmd[i] to r[i].cmd for i : 0..(n − 1);
 8      interface Idst[i] from cc.dst[i] to r[i].dst for i : 0..(n − 1);
 9      interface Iid[i] from cc.id[i] to r[i].id for i : 0..(n − 1);
10    end collaboration
11
12    schedule
13      ‖i:0..(n−1) (Approach(coll.r[i],startPos[i]);Pickup(coll.r[i]);Return(coll.r[i]);)
14      ‖i:0..(n−1) ApproachHandler(coll.cc,coll.r[i],i)
15      ‖i:0..(n−1) MishapHandler(coll.r[i],coll)
16      ‖ PickupHandler(coll.cc,coll.r)
17      ‖ ReturnHandler(coll.cc,coll.r)
18      ‖ EmergentPropertyChecker(coll.r)
19    end schedule
20  end systemtest
```

3.7   System Test Configuration and Deployment

A system test configuration represents a *composite scenario*: it specifies how instances of elementary scenarios should collaborate to perform a system test. For the system test described in Sect. 2, the configuration is shown in Listing 1.14.

The Collaboration. The collaboration part of our system test specification introduces n robots $r[i], i : 0..(n − 1)$ of object type *Rover* and one command centre cc of type *CommandCentre*. Object types are similar to classes in programming languages.

The interfaces declared in a collaboration specify how output parameters of certain objects are mapped to input parameters of others. For example, interface $Is[i]$ specifies that the output parameter s (for "status") of rover $r[i]$ is mapped to input parameter $s[i]$ of the command centre cc ($cc.s$ is a status array of length n). Since all objects collaborating in a system test operate in a cyclic mode, the semantics of the interface mappings is fairly easy:

– A new parameter value written to s by $r[i]$ in cycle p becomes visible at $cc.s[i]$ at the start of $r[i]$'s execution cycle $p + 1$.

- If cc operates with a slower cycle time than $r[i]$, then the most recent value written by $r[i]$ to s becomes visible at the start of cc's next cycle, so previous writes may be lost.
- If cc cycles faster than $r[i]$, it may read the same value several times (interfaces are like shared variables).
- If two objects communicate over a communication medium that needs more time than a single cycle to deliver new values to their destination, an auxiliary object with a slower cycle time has to be introduced. This object represents the communication medium.

An essential characteristic of system tests for interacting autonomous robots[8] is that the collaboration may change during the test execution. In the example discussed here, robots can get lost when inadvertently entering an exclusion zone. In other system tests, new robots might enter the collaboration or leave it in an orderly fashion. Therefore, collaborations are semantically represented as abstract data types allowing operations like

1. $coll$.delete($r[k]$). Delete rover $r[k]$ from the collaboration, including all interfaces $r[k]$ contributes to. The deletion is marked by setting $coll.r[k] = $ null. This helps to check in elementary scenarios whether a robot still exists in the collaboration.
2. $coll$.create($r[n + \ell]$: Rover). Extend the collaboration by a new rover object that is registered under the new array index $n + \ell$.[9]
3. $coll$.create(interface $Is[n+\ell]$ from $r[n+\ell].s$ to $cc.s[n+\ell]$) creates a new interface in the collaboration.

These operations are atomic, so the collaboration abstract data type acts like a monitor. This is necessary since several concurrent elementary scenarios may request configuration changes simultaneously during their execution.

The Schedule. The schedule part of a system test configuration specifies the test execution by means of elementary scenario instances that are sequentially composed or run in parallel. For example, $Approach(coll.r[i]$,startPos$[i])$ specifies an instance of elementary scenario type $Approach(\dots)$, where the formal parameter r has been substituted by the concrete rover instance $coll.r[i]$ that is part of the collaboration. Concrete parameter startPos$[i]$ is an element of a constant array specifying the starting positions from where each rover commences its salvage expedition. After $Approach(coll.r[i]$,startPos$[i])$ has terminated, scenario instance $Pickup(coll.r[i])$ can execute, after which instance $Return(coll.r[i])$ runs. This sequential execution of three elementary scenarios is performed concurrently for each rover $coll.r[i]$, $i : 0..(n - 1)$. In a similar way, instances of the remaining elementary scenarios are specified to be executed concurrently.

---

[8] or, for *systems of systems* in general [17].

[9] Arrays in SCSL are variable-size containers whose elements can be accessed via indexes, similar to `ArrayList` objects in Java.

System test deployment denotes the task of mapping the logical components of a system test – these are identified in the system test configuration – to software procedures, threads, processes, hardware interfaces, and processors. The details of system test deployment are beyond the scope of this paper, but we indicate some important concepts and variants.

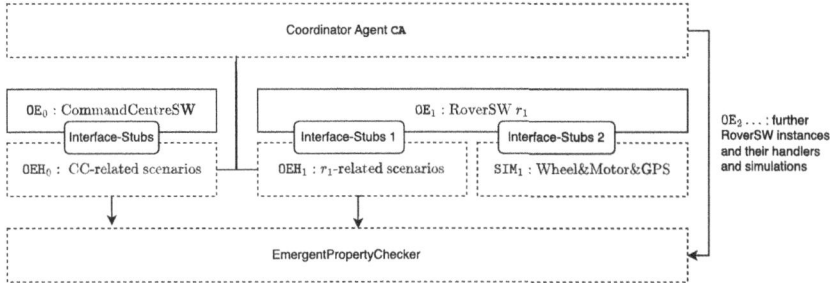

Fig. 2. Instantiation of Fig. 1 for the 'software-only' system test deployment.

Deployment Variant 'Software Only'. System tests like the one described in this paper are usually quite costly to be performed in the real world. Therefore, tests are usually performed in several phases, each phase using a different deployment. The first test phase is typically "software only", where no target hardware is involved. In this setting, the original equipment $OE_0, OE_1, \ldots$ consists only of the software of the command centre and the robots, as sketched in Fig. 2 which specialises the generic test configuration diagram of Fig. 1 for the software-only deployment of our system test.

The communication interfaces of each robot are stubbed, since the hardware interfaces and peripherals are not available in the software-only configuration. This allows to realise the interface declarations shown in the system test configuration by shared variables, procedure calls, socket communication, or similar means of data exchange between software components. Consequently, any deployment requires a specification explaining how the interfaces identified in the system test configuration should be implemented. Also, since the OE software does not run on original hardware, a deployment configuration needs to map the OE_i to processors available for the software test execution.[10]

Since the hardware peripherals are missing in the software-only deployment, their feedback to the OE needs to be simulated. For example, each rover's outputs to motors setting wheel angles and wheel speed is caught by a software simulation (see SIM_1 in Fig. 2) that calculates the rover's position changes that would result

---

[10] For example, the software-only tests could be executed in the cloud, and each OE_i could be encapsulated in a separate docker container that is executed in a Kubernetes POD of its own, see https://kubernetes.io/docs/concepts/workloads/pods/.

from these motor actuations in the real world. The calculated positions would be passed to the rover software, simulating satellite positioning information that would be received in the real world.

The original equipment handlers $\mathtt{OEH}_0, \mathtt{OEH}_1 \ldots$ each execute a subset of the elementary scenario instances identified in the system test schedule. For instance, $\mathtt{OEH}_0$, the handler for the command centre, would execute

$$\|_{i:0..(n-1)} \, ApproachHandler(coll.cc, coll.r[i], i)$$
$$\| \, PickupHandler(coll.cc, coll.r)$$
$$\| \, ReturnHandler(coll.cc, coll.r),$$

while the rover-specific $\mathtt{OEH}_i$, $i = 1, 2, \ldots$ would execute

$$\Big(Approach(coll.r[i], \mathtt{startPos}[i]); Pickup(coll.r[i]); Return(coll.r[i]); \Big)$$
$$\| \, MishapHandler(coll.r[i], coll).$$

A global scenario execution unit executes the $EmergentPropertyChecker(coll.r)$ instance. The coordinator agent monitors requested changes of the collaboration and provides the actual collaboration state to all elementary scenario instances under execution.

Deployment Variant 'Real-World'. For testing the salvage mission described above in the real world, the $\mathtt{OE}$ instances consist of the command centre, the complete robots (hardware with embedded software), the real communication service (for example, satellite-based or radio-based message exchange), and the real location service (e.g. GPS or Galileo). The only simulation left in a fully automated real-world system test would mimic users in the command centre initiating the salvage mission, as all physical hardware, sensors, and communication channels are real.

3.8   Behavioural Semantics of System Test Configurations

Valuation Functions. The behaviour of system test configurations is formalised by finite sequences $\pi = \sigma_0.\sigma_1 \ldots \sigma_q$ of valuation functions $\sigma_i : V_i \longrightarrow D$. The index i of valuation σ_i is the number of the observation and stimulation step performed by the test equipment, and $\sigma_i(v)$ is the value of some symbol $v \in V_i$ that has been set or observed by the test equipment in this step. The symbol sets V_i contain the following variable names.

1. All parameter symbols of objects that are active in step i. If rover number j is part of the collaboration and active in step i, for example, V_i contains symbols $coll.r[i].cmd$, $coll.r[i].dst$, $coll.r[i].id$, $coll.r[i].pos$, $coll.r[i].id$.
2. All auxiliary variable symbols of active instances of elementary scenarios, including the implicitly defined auxiliary variables like $\mathtt{active}$. If scenario instance $Return(coll.r[j])$ is active in step i, for example, V_i contains symbols $Return(\text{coll.r[j]}).\mathtt{active}$ and $Return(\text{coll.r[j]}).aux_{\text{isLoaded}}$.

3. The global auxiliary variable symbol EoT indicating the end of the system test.

The set D is the union of all variable types. The symbol sets V_i are changed under the following conditions.

1. If an object is deleted from the collaboration in step i, its parameter symbols are no longer present in V_{i+1}.
2. If an object is added to the collaboration in step i, its parameter symbols are elements of $V_{i+1}, V_{i+2}, \ldots$ until the object is removed again from the collaboration.
3. If an elementary scenario instance is runnable and its precondition is fulfilled in step i, its auxiliary variables are visible in V_{i+1}.
4. If the execution state of an elementary scenario instance changes from active to ¬active in step i, then its auxiliary variable symbols are no longer contained in V_{i+1}.

Symbol EoT is contained in all symbol sets $V_0, V_1, \ldots, V_q$. For valuations σ_i, $i = 0, \ldots, (q-1)$, its value is $\sigma_i(\text{EoT}) = \text{false}$. Only the last valuation sets $\sigma_q(\text{EoT}) = \text{true}$.

Execution Cycles. Depending on the object type and its cycletime, objects need $k \geq 1$ observation steps of the test equipment to complete one execution cycle. During this processing time, outputs remain unchanged, and only the last write to an input is considered in the next processing cycle. For example, if a processing cycle of the object starts in observation step i, the input values specified by σ_i are used in this cycle. Any output parameter y remains unchanged until the end of the cycle, that is, $\sigma_i(y) = \sigma_{i+1}(y) = \cdots = \sigma_{i+k-1}(y)$, and $\sigma_{i+k}(y)$ returns the new value of v. If input parameter z is an end point of an interface connecting output y with z, then $\sigma_{i+1}(z) = \sigma_{i+2}(z) = \cdots = \sigma_{i+k}(z) = \sigma_i(y)$ and $\sigma_{i+k+1}(z) = \sigma_{i+k}(y)$. For the next processing cycle starting in step $(i + k)$ and any input parameter x, the valuation $\sigma_{i+k}(x)$ is considered. Previous valuations $\sigma_{i+k-1}(x), \ldots, \sigma_{i+1}(x)$ are disregarded.

Scheduling. The following scheduling rules determine when an elementary scenario instance becomes active.

1. Every scenario instance transits through execution states

$$passive \longrightarrow runnable \longrightarrow active \longrightarrow passive.$$

2. State active is characterised for a scenario instance S by $S.\text{active} = \text{true}$.
3. The auxiliary symbols of a scenario are visible in V_i if and only if it is active in observation step i.
4. A runnable scenario instance becomes active in step $i + 1$, if its precondition φ evaluates to true in step i. Since φ only refers to object parameters and never to auxiliary variables, it can be evaluated in any step i where all object

parameter symbols occurring in φ are contained in V_i. If this is not the case because parameters of objects are referenced that are no longer part of the collaboration, the precondition is considered to be `false`.

5. In a parallel composition of scenario instances $S_1 \parallel S_2$, both S_1 and S_2 become immediately runnable.
6. In a sequential composition of scenario instances $S_1; S_2$, instance S_1 becomes immediately runnable, and S_2 becomes runnable after the execution state of S_1 has transited from *active* to *passive*.

The Effect of Interface Definitions. Suppose that a collaboration has interface

$$\text{interface } I \text{ from } S_1.a \text{ to } S_2.b.$$

An interface transfers the data "maximally fast", that is, in one observation cycle, from source to target. Therefore, in any test execution $\pi = \sigma_0.\sigma_1 \ldots \sigma_q$, the valuations involved satisfy

$$\forall i : 0..(q-1) . S_1.\texttt{active} \in \text{dom } \sigma_i \wedge S_2.\texttt{active} \in \text{dom } \sigma_{i+1} \wedge$$
$$\sigma_i(S_1.\texttt{active}) \wedge \sigma_{i+1}(S_2.\texttt{active}) \Rightarrow \sigma_{i+1}(S_2.b) = \sigma_i(S_1.a).$$

Execution Semantics of Elementary Scenario Instances. Given a scenario instance S and a test execution $\pi = \sigma_0.\sigma_1 \ldots \sigma_q$, the execution π *conforms to* S if certain S-specific rules hold. To explain these rules, let π' be the trace segment of π where S is active. Let Φ be the conjunction of LTL formulae that have been specified in the elementary scenario type of S, but with all parameter symbols exchanged by the corresponding concrete object parameters.

For example, scenario type *Pickup* refers to symbols $r, cc.cmd[i], cc.id[i]$ and others. These symbols are exchanged in Φ by the concrete object references and parameter names that are specified in the system test collaboration, that is, $coll.r, coll.cc.cmd[i], coll.cc.id[i]$. The latter are exactly the symbols associated with concrete values by the valuation functions σ_i. Therefore, it can be checked whether π' is a model for Φ and consistent with the condition-action executions specified in the scenario type of S.

For the consistency of condition-action executions, the following rules apply.

1. If the precondition of S evaluates to `true` for the first time in σ_i, then the effect of the initial action becomes visible in σ_{i+1}.
2. If a condition-action has a guard condition $[g]$ that evaluates to `true` in σ_j and S is active in σ_j and σ_{j+1}, then the effect of the associated action becomes visible in σ_{j+1}.
3. If a condition-action has a change condition `when` (ψ) and ψ evaluates to `false` in σ_{j-1} and to `true` in σ_j, then the effect of the associated action becomes visible in σ_{j+1}, provided that S is active in steps $j-1, j, j+1$.
4. Auxiliary variables that are not affected by any action in step j remain unchanged in σ_{j+1}.

Now the execution π' is a model for Φ if there exists an infinite sequence of valuations π'' such that $\pi'.\pi''$ is a model of Φ in the standard LTL semantics [7], but with a specialised interpretation of the next operator $\mathbf{X}$. If $\mathbf{X}\psi$ refers to a parameter z of some object o with cycle time k, and if the formula application is performed in step i, then ψ must become `true` is one of the next steps $i + 1, \ldots, i + 2k - 1$, since in the worst case, the object needs $k - 1$ steps to become aware of the state σ_i, and then another k steps to perform the actions that will make ψ evaluate to `true`.

4   SCSL Tool Support

Test Generators, Test Oracles, and Simulations. The implementations of elementary scenario instances perform the combined tasks of on-the-fly test data generators, test oracles (checkers), and simulations. To this end, the condition-action statements of the scenario specification are transformed into code. This task is similar to (but easier than) using code generators for UML-style state machines. The main loop of the scenario implementation evaluates the current parameter and auxiliary variable state (these are kept in maps realising the current valuation function and that of the previous step [needed for the evaluation of change conditions]) and triggers actions accordingly.

The conjunction Φ of LTL specifications is transformed into a Büchi automaton using LTL3BA [16]. In each execution step, an interpreter abstracts concrete parameter values into atomic propositions of Φ and traverses the Büchi automaton accordingly. During this traversal, parameters that can be set by the testing environment are written to by the interpreter, while those written to by original equipment are accepted with their current value. For setting atomic propositions that have writable parameters `true` or `false`, the interpreter uses an SMT solver that determines concrete parameter values. Since the Büchi automata are nondeterministic, the interpreter marks the set of potential automata states that are possible in the current execution step. If none of the possible states are associated with an outgoing arrow whose writable parameters can be set in a way that finally an accepting state can still be reached, the interpreter has uncovered a violation of the behavioural specification, and the test execution fails.

In our system test example, the execution of the *EmergentPropertyChecker* instance could detect, for example, that in a final execution step, proposition $\hat{t} < t_{\text{end}}$ no longer holds but `numRovers`$(r, \{$`returnedWithItem`$\}) \geq k$ is still `false`. Then the LTL formula in line 4 of Listing 1.13 evaluates to `false` and can never become `true` at a later step, since it is a safety formula. Consequently, the test execution stops with verdict FAIL.

Scheduler and Runtime System. For executing system test configurations, a simple scheduler and an associated runtime system can be used. The scheduler parses the `schedule` specification and evaluates the conditions for elementary scenario instances to become runnable, active, and finally passive again. The runtime system implements the dynamic collaboration changes and copies interface data from source parameters to target parameters accordingly. Scheduler and runtime system have a distributed implementation, since elementary scenario instances can be distributed on different controllers acting as original equipment handlers. Other instances acting as simulations could be implemented on a cloud platform. The coordination of these distributed components is performed by the coordinator agent introduced in Sect. 1.

5   Discussion

5.1   Conclusion

We have introduced the domain-independent scenario specification language SCSL and illustrated its use for system test specifications verifying collaborating robots. Compared to other existing scenario modelling languages, in particular, those based on variants of UML and SysML, SCSL has a fairly simple syntax and a formal behavioural semantics that could be comprehensively specified with acceptable complexity in a compact way (see also [22]).

Domain-specific support can be easily realised by introducing libraries of predefined types, objects, and elementary scenarios, the latter specifying typical behaviours of the application domain, such as physical laws applicable under specific environmental conditions or typical manoeuvres of the domain-specific objects. The usability of SCSL has been demonstrated by means of a system test example describing a salvage mission of collaborating robots.

A major advantage of the formal SCSL semantics is that SCSL specifications can be automatically transformed into test data generators, executable simulations or into test oracles to be embedded into original equipment harnesses stimulating a system component under test and checking its reactions against SCSL specifications.

5.2   Future Work

While this paper focuses on introducing the syntax and semantics of SCSL, the suitability and effectiveness of SCSL will be demonstrated in a case study using specifications from the EULYNX standard[11] that has been designed for harmonising the communication between components of modern railway signalling systems in Europe. We will compare the effectiveness of SCSL to that of well-known model-based testing approaches that rely on comprehensive monolithic system models. Relevant evaluation criteria include modelling effort, reusability, scalability, requirements coverage, and fault detection capability. For example, mutation testing could be applied to assess the relative fault detection power of both approaches. In domains such as automotive or avionics, where MBT is well established, comparative studies will help determine whether scenario-based specifications offer measurable advantages in terms of productivity, maintainability, or test completeness. To the best of our knowledge, there is currently no

---

[11] https://eulynx.eu/resource-hub-deliverables/.

comprehensive and domain-independent empirical study systematically comparing the effectiveness of scenario-based testing approaches—such as those enabled by SCSL—with classical model-based testing approaches relying on monolithic behavioural models. As such, we consider this a novel and promising direction for future work.

To facilitate the creation of LTL specifications that are essential for describing the behaviour of a scenario, we plan to use LTL-specific generalised pre-trained transformers (GPTs) that are capable of creating LTL formulae from natural language specifications [6]. A recent publication by Peled et al. [8] indicates that this can be achieved with a very low failure rate. The automated generation can be complemented by mechanisms to detect erroneous LTL encodings with high probability.[12]

As readers may have noticed, the essential feature of behavioural SCSL scenario specifications is that they can be interpreted on sequences of valuation functions whose values have been obtained from components operating with cyclic execution semantics. Consequently, the combined LTL and condition-action syntax is not the only way to write behavioural SCSL specifications. As an alternative, for example, RoboSim state machines[13] [5] and similar discrete time formalisms could be used.

References

1. ASAM OpenSCENARIO: UML Modeling Rules (2021). https://www.asam.net/index.php?eID=dumpFile&t=f&f=3497&token=bebd0ae6eac831ed7f96e6431ba29399572c9934
2. ASAM: ASAM OpenSCENARIO (2024). https://publications.pages.asam.net/standards/ASAM_OpenSCENARIO/ASAM_OpenSCENARIO_XML/latest/index.html
3. Bando, M., Hasebe, K., Nakanishi, K., Nakayama, A.: Analysis of optimal velocity model with explicit delay. Phys. Rev. E **58**, 5429–5435 (1998). https://doi.org/10.1103/PhysRevE.58.5429
4. Cavalcanti, A., Hierons, R.M.: Challenges in testing of cyclic systems. In: Aït-Ameur, Y., Khendek, F., Méry, D. (eds.) 27th International Conference on Engineering of Complex Computer Systems, ICECCS 2023, Toulouse, France, 14–16 June 2023, pp. 1–6. IEEE (2023). https://doi.org/10.1109/ICECCS59891.2023.00010

---

[12] Suitable validation mechanisms range from automated procedures to others involving manual interaction. An example for automated validation is to let a GPT create witness traces for the created formula and its negation. Then it is checked by a verified algorithm that these witnesses indeed fulfil the formulae. An error in witness generation indicates that the GPT does not have the "correct understanding" of the formula semantics, so the text-to-formula transformation cannot be trusted. An example for validation involving manual interaction is to let engineers decide whether correct formula witnesses conform to their expectations expressed in the natural language specification. This manual process can be supported by letting a GPT transform witness traces of even the whole generated formula back to natural language.

[13] https://www.cs.york.ac.uk/circus/RoboCalc/robosim/robosim-reference.pdf.

5. Cavalcanti, A., et al.: Verified simulation for robotics. Sci. Comput. Program. **174**, 1–37 (2019). https://doi.org/10.1016/j.scico.2019.01.004. https://www.sciencedirect.com/science/article/pii/S0167642318301655

6. Chen, Y., Gandhi, R., Zhang, Y., Fan, C.: NL2TL: transforming natural languages to temporal logics using large language models. In: Bouamor, H., Pino, J., Bali, K. (eds.) Proceedings of the 2023 Conference on Empirical Methods in Natural Language Processing, EMNLP 2023, Singapore, 6–10 December 2023, pp. 15880–15903. Association for Computational Linguistics (2023). https://doi.org/10.18653/V1/2023.EMNLP-MAIN.985

7. Clarke, E.M., Grumberg, O., Peled, D.A.: Model Checking. The MIT Press, Cambridge (1999)

8. Cohen, I., Peled, D.: End-to-end AI generated runtime verification from natural language specification. In: Steffen, B. (ed.) Bridging the Gap Between AI and Reality - First International Conference, AISoLA 2023, Crete, Greece, 23–28 October 2023, Selected Papers. Lecture Notes in Computer Science, vol. 14129, pp. 362–384. Springer, Cham (2023). https://doi.org/10.1007/978-3-031-73741-1_23

9. Damm, W., Möhlmann, E., Peikenkamp, T., Rakow, A.: A formal semantics for traffic sequence charts. In: Lohstroh, M., Derler, P., Sirjani, M. (eds.) Principles of Modeling. LNCS, vol. 10760, pp. 182–205. Springer, Cham (2018). https://doi.org/10.1007/978-3-319-95246-8_11

10. Gipps, P.: A behavioural car-following model for computer simulation. Transp. Res. Part B: Methodol. **15**(2), 105–111 (1981). https://doi.org/10.1016/0191-2615(81)90037-0. https://www.sciencedirect.com/science/article/pii/0191261581900370

11. Hauer, F., Schmidt, T., Holzmüller, B., Pretschner, A.: Did we test all scenarios for automated and autonomous driving systems? In: 2019 IEEE Intelligent Transportation Systems Conference, ITSC 2019, Auckland, New Zealand, 27–30 October 2019, pp. 2950–2955. IEEE (2019). https://doi.org/10.1109/ITSC.2019.8917326

12. Hilscher, M., Linker, S., Olderog, E.-R., Ravn, A.P.: An abstract model for proving safety of multi-lane traffic manoeuvres. In: Qin, S., Qiu, Z. (eds.) ICFEM 2011. LNCS, vol. 6991, pp. 404–419. Springer, Heidelberg (2011). https://doi.org/10.1007/978-3-642-24559-6_28

13. Jafer, S., Chhaya, B., Durak, U., Gerlach, T.: Formal scenario definition language for aviation: aircraft landing case study. In: AIAA Modeling and Simulation Technologies Conference, p. 3521 (2016)

14. Jones, C.B.: Systematic Software Development Using VDM. Prentice-Hall (1986)

15. Mallet, F.: Clock constraint specification language: specifying clock constraints with UML/MARTE. Innov. Syst. Softw. Eng. **4**(3), 309–314 (2008). https://doi.org/10.1007/S11334-008-0055-2

16. Mochizuki, S., Shimakawa, M., Hagihara, S., Yonezaki, N.: Fast translation from LTL to Büchi automata via non-transition-based automata. In: Merz, S., Pang, J. (eds.) ICFEM 2014. LNCS, vol. 8829, pp. 364–379. Springer, Cham (2014). https://doi.org/10.1007/978-3-319-11737-9_24

17. Nielsen, C.B., Larsen, P.G., Fitzgerald, J.S., Woodcock, J., Peleska, J.: Systems of systems engineering: basic concepts, model-based techniques, and research directions. ACM Comput. Surv. **48**(2), 18:1–18:41 (2015). https://doi.org/10.1145/2794381

18. Object Management Group: OMG Systems Modeling Language (OMG SysML), Version 1.6. Technical report, Object Management Group (2015). https://sysml.org/sysml-specs/

19. Object Management Group: OMG Unified Modeling Language (OMG UML), superstructure, version 2.5.1. Technical report, OMG (2017)
20. OMG: OMG systems modeling language v2 (2024). https://www.omg.org/spec/SysML/2.0/Beta2/About-SysML
21. Peleska, J., Brauer, J., Huang, W.: Model-based testing for avionic systems proven benefits and further challenges. In: Margaria, T., Steffen, B. (eds.) ISoLA 2018. LNCS, vol. 11247, pp. 82–103. Springer, Cham (2018). https://doi.org/10.1007/978-3-030-03427-6_11
22. Peleska, J., Brüning, F., Ling Huang, W., Haxthausen, A.E.: A scenario specification language for testing complex cyber-physical systems. In: Rauh, A., Finkbeiner, B., (eds.) Design and Verification of Cyber-Physical Systems: From Theory to Applications. Lecture Notes in Computer Science. Springer, Cham (2025, to appear)
23. Petri, C.A.: Kommunikation mit Automaten. Dissertation, Schriften des IIM 2, Rheinisch-Westfälisches Institut für Instrumentelle Mathematik an der Universität Bonn, Bonn (1962)
24. PTV Group: Multimodal traffic simulation software (2024). https://www.ptvgroup.com/en/products/ptv-vissim
25. Sarmiento, E., Leite, J.C., Almentero, E., Sotomayor Alzamora, G.: Test scenario generation from natural language requirements descriptions based on petrinets. Electron. Notes Theor. Comput. Sci. **329**, 123–148 (2016). https://doi.org/10.1016/j.entcs.2016.12.008. https://www.sciencedirect.com/science/article/pii/S1571066116301153, cLEI 2016 - The Latin American Computing Conference
26. Schwammberger, M.: Introducing liveness into multi-lane spatial logic lane change controllers using UPPAAL. In: Gleirscher, M., Kugele, S., Linker, S. (eds.) Proceedings 2nd International Workshop on Safe Control of Autonomous Vehicles, SCAV@CPSWeek 2018, Porto, Portugal, 10th April 2018. EPTCS, vol. 269, pp. 17–31 (2018). https://doi.org/10.4204/EPTCS.269.3
27. Spivey, J.M.: The Z Notation: A Reference Manual, 2nd edn. Prentice Hall, New York (1992)
28. Sutherland, I.E., Sproull, R.F., Schumacker, R.A.: A characterization of ten hidden-surface algorithms. ACM Comput. Surv. **6**(1), 1–55 (1974). https://doi.org/10.1145/356625.356626
29. Treiber, M., Hennecke, A., Helbing, D.: Congested traffic states in empirical observations and microscopic simulations. Phys. Rev. E **62**(2), 1805–1824 (2000). https://doi.org/10.1103/physreve.62.1805
30. Ulbrich, S., Menzel, T., Reschka, A., Schuldt, F., Maurer, M.: Defining and substantiating the terms scene, situation, and scenario for automated driving. In: IEEE 18th International Conference on Intelligent Transportation Systems, ITSC 2015, Gran Canaria, Spain, 15–18 September 2015, pp. 982–988. IEEE (2015). https://doi.org/10.1109/ITSC.2015.164

Revisiting Formal Methods for Autonomous Robots: A Structured Survey
(Invited Paper)

Atef Azaiez[1]([✉])[iD], David A. Anisi[1][iD], Marie Farrell[2][iD], and Matt Luckcuck[3][iD]

[1] Faculty of Science and Technology, Norwegian University of Life Sciences, Ås, Norway
{atef.azaiez,david.anisi}@nmbu.no
[2] Department of Computer Science, University of Manchester, Manchester, UK
marie.farrell@manchester.ac.uk
[3] School of Computer Science, University of Nottingham, Nottingham, UK
matt.luckcuck@nottingham.ac.uk

Abstract. This paper presents the initial results from our structured literature review on applications of Formal Methods (FM) to Robotic Autonomous Systems (RAS). We describe our structured survey methodology; including database selection and associated search strings, search filters and collaborative review of identified papers. We categorise and enumerate the FM approaches and formalisms that have been used for specification and verification of RAS. We investigate FM in the context of sub-symbolic AI-enabled RAS and examine the evolution of how FM is used over time in this field. This work complements a pre-existing survey in this area and we examine how this research area has matured over time. Specifically, our survey demonstrates that some trends have persisted as observed in a previous survey. Additionally, it recognized new trends that were not considered previously including a noticeable increase in adopting Formal Synthesis approaches as well as Probabilistic Verification Techniques.

Keywords: Formal Methods · Formal Verification · Formal Synthesis · Autonomous Robotic Systems · Survey

1 Introduction

Formal Methods have been incorporated in the software production life cycle since the early adoption of computers. Relying solely on testing has been shown to be not enough to guarantee the absence of bugs in software. This quote from Dijkstra in 1969 emphasises that the computer science community needed to develop alternative methods to testing *"Testing shows the presence, not the absence of bugs"* [6]. As technology and aspirations have evolved, the use of Robotic Autonomous Systems (RAS) in safety- and/or mission-critical applications has increased, including in the nuclear [4], aerospace [27], agriculture [2,3],

© The Author(s), under exclusive license to Springer Nature Switzerland AG 2026
A. Cavalcanti et al. (Eds.): TAROS 2025, LNAI 16045, pp. 338–352, 2026.
https://doi.org/10.1007/978-3-032-01486-3_26

transport [14] and space domains [8]. These sorts of critical systems among others involving safety and security requirements clearly need to be robustly verified using Formal Methods for specification and verification. The use of Formal Methods (FM) is admitted, recommended and can be required by some standards [16]. The strong verification provided by potentially combinations of distinct FM and testing approaches is advantageous as it guarantees mathematical proof of correctness. This aides in the assurance process in critical settings and helps to provide various stakeholders with sufficient confidence that the systems function as expected. VariousFM approaches have been developed to fulfil specific needs of verification.

A 2019 survey provides an overview of these methods and acts as a guidebook for those seeking to apply FM in RAS [17]. Apart from the obvious benefits to developing reliable software, there is a reciprocal benefit to the FM community: the modularity of RAS, as exemplified in the various middleware by which they are supported, fosters creative and interesting opportunities for examining and demonstrating the efficacy of these FM [7]. These observations have given rise to a novel sub-domain called Formal Methods for Autonomous Systems[1] and many conferences have held special tracks in related topics since. On the other hand, there are some challenges of applying FM to RAS, namely the complexity of the this kind of systems as they usually combine discrete software logic with continuous physical dynamics and that can lead to scalability issues. Moreover, the dynamic nature of the environment where RAS operate makes it difficult to capture all interactions and uncertainties. last but not least, there can be a gap between the trustworthiness of formal verification results and the expectations of regulatory acquirements [1].

In this paper, we present the methodology we adopted to conduct our structured literature survey, initial results which examines how the application of FM to RAS has evolved over time. We analyse which trends have persisted since the original survey [17] and identify emerging trends. We examine the relative use of different formal methods and verification approaches, and discuss the role played by Sub-Symbolic AI (SSAI) (e.g. machine learning). We reflect on potential reasons for these various evolutions, providing insight and set the stage for future development in this field.

Next, we present some related work, while the rest of the paper is structured as follows. In Sect. 2 we describe our survey's methodology, including the scope and search terms. We present the results in Sect. 3 and discuss the implications of the results in Sect. 4. Finally, Sect. 5 gives our concluding remarks.

Related Work: Our survey builds on a previous survey of FM applied to autonomous robotic systems [17], though we extend the time frame from 2007—2018, to 2007—2024; We also use a different methodology and work-flow, and used Rayyan [20][2] a dedicated tool for conducting structured surveys. This gives broader coverage of the literature, including both wider search terms and

---

[1] https://fmasworkshop.github.io/.

[2] Rayyan: https://www.rayyan.ai/.

additional search sources, initially returning 20,764 papers. We examine similar research questions to [17] but with an explicit focus on the trends that have emerged over time, and examining the impact of SSAI.

As the sub-domain of FM for autonomous systems has evolved and become more popular over time, it is no surprise that other related research efforts exist. These include a manifesto for applicable FM that provides ten principles concerning their use [9]. This project however does not specifically focus on RAS, rather it discusses the use and promotion of FM in practice more generally.

Leahy et al. [15] define three categories of grand challenge for verification of autonomous systems: (1) Requirements and Specifications, (2) Models and Abstractions, and (3) Tools, Techniques and Algorithms. Related work in [22] provides a research roadmap for verification of autonomous systems which points to several of these open challenges and emerging standards in the area.

2   Methodology

This section outlines the structured methodology, shown in Fig. 1, that we followed. We begin by defining the relevant Research Questions (**RQ**) and the scope of the survey. We query three academic search sources using dedicated search strings, designed to gather a broad range of papers. Our initial search produced 20,764 results. To effectively handle this vast number of results, we rely on databases and sources that allow bulk-export of results and import them into an online Review Management Platform, Rayyan, developed for systematic reviews [20]. Rayyan supports automated duplicate detection, collaborative initial screening, systematic conflict resolver, and dedicated data summary dashboards. Using Rayyan, we exclude out-of-scope papers using their Title, Abstract, and Keywords (TAK). Then, we import and read the full text of the papers and gather details about the RAS case study and FM it uses to answer the **RQ**s.

Research Questions: We define three research questions to direct our search.

- **RQ1:** *What Formal Approaches and Formalisms are used for specification and verification of RAS?*
- **RQ2:** *Have recent AI advancements within machine-learning affected FM applied to RAS and what FM are used to specify and verify Sub-Symbolic AI (SSAI) enabled RAS?*
- **RQ3:** *How has research on FM applied to RAS evolved over time?*

Scope: For this survey, we use the following descriptive criteria to define what counts as a RAS, to decide which papers were in-scope for the survey.

- RAS are fitted to a physical platform that gives it the capability of navigating in the environment (space/air, ground or water).

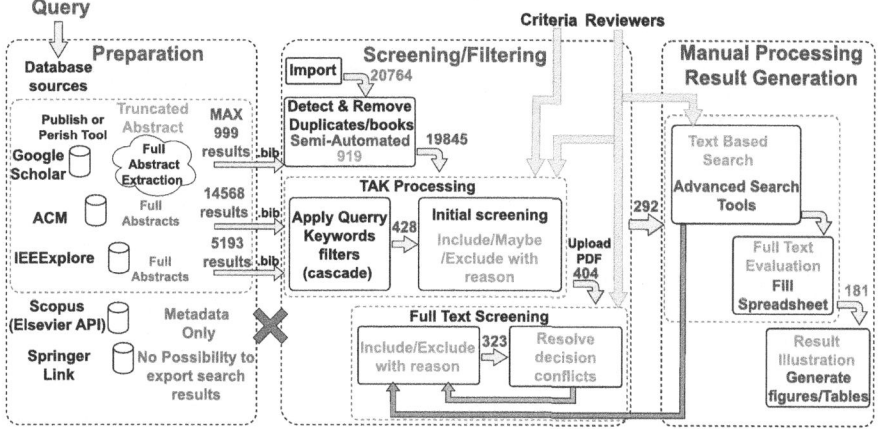

Fig. 1. The structured literature review workflow of this paper. The three databases Google Scholar, ACM and IEEExplore were selected as they allowed bulk-export of search results. The Initial query generated 20,764 results. To be able to effectively handle this, they were imported into an online Review Management Platform called Rayyan, to perform initial screening and filtering based on Title, Abstract, and Keywords (TAK) before continuing with collaborative full text review and result generation.

- RAS have a certain degree of autonomy, intelligence or adaptability. They may have the ability to adjust their behaviour, or act upon the environment that they operate within, independent of human interaction.
- RAS can consist of multiple agents acting independently or in coordination.

Formal Methods are mathematically rigorous approaches to developing software and systems. They support Specification, Modelling, Design, Synthesis, and Verification. As reflected in our search queries, formal verification approaches include theorem proving, Model Checking (MC), and Runtime Verification (RV).

2.1 Search Strategy

With the **RQ**s and scope defined, we formulate the search string(s) that we used to query various data bases. Figure 2 shows the Query Logical Structure (QLS) [19] for our search term. It uses standard logic gate operators to illustrate how we combined various words and phrases to build the search term, checking for one word from the FM category and one from the RAS category.

We use IEEE Xplore, ACM Digital Library and Google Scholar as our search sources as they allow boolean search terms. We considered Scopus and Springer Link, but discounted them as they did not support these features. Google Scholar does not support exporting search results directly, so we used the Publish or Perish[3] tool to run the Google Scholar search and bulk-export the citations. Each

---

[3] Publish or Perish: https://harzing.com/resources/publish-or-perish.

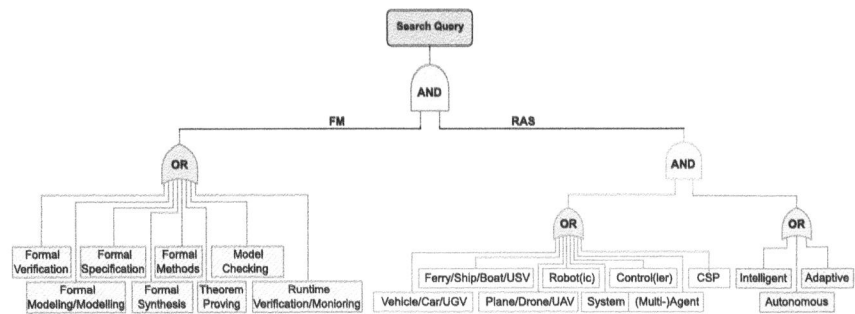

Fig. 2. Query Logical Structure diagram showing how we use standard logic gate symbols to build our search term from the relevant words and phrases.

source has a specific query syntax, so we created a distinct search term for each source. In particular, as Google Scholar does not allow more than 256 keywords in the search string, we had to modify and shorten the original search string to remove redundant and less frequently occurring terms. The search terms used for each source are shown below. We relied on Rayyan [20] to exclude irrelevant papers during the Screening and Filtering process as described in Sect. 2.2.

IEEE Xplore: *((("Full Text & Metadata": "formal Verification" OR "formal specification" OR "formal modeling" OR "formal modelling" OR "formal synthesis" OR "formal methods" OR "model check*" OR "model-check*" OR "runtime verification" OR "run time verification" OR "run-time verification" OR "runtime monitor*" OR "run time monitor*" OR "run-time monitor*" OR "theorem prov*") AND ("Full Text & Metadata": "autonomous" OR "intelligent" OR "adaptive")AND("Full Text & Metadata": "robot*" OR "cyber physical system" OR "CSP" OR "multi*agent" OR "agent" OR "control*" OR system OR vehicle OR car OR UGV OR ferry OR ship OR boat OR USV OR plane OR drone OR UAV)))*

ACM Digital Library: *AllField:(("formal Verification" OR "formal specification" OR "formal modeling" OR "formal modelling" OR "formal synthesis" OR "formal methods" OR "model check*" OR "model-check*" OR "runtime verification" OR "run time verification" OR " run-time verification " OR "runtime monitor*" OR "run time monitor*" OR "run-time monitor*" OR "theorem prov*") AND ((autonomous OR intelligent OR adaptive) AND (("robot*" OR "cyber physical system" OR "CSP" OR "multi*agent" OR "agent" OR "control*" OR system) OR (vehicle OR car OR UGV OR ferry OR ship OR boat OR USV OR plane OR drone OR UAV))))*

> **Google Scholar:** *((formal AND (verification OR specification OR modeling OR modelling OR synthesis OR methods) OR "model*check*" OR ((runtime OR run*time) AND (verification OR monitor*)) OR "theorem prov*") AND ((autonomous OR intelligent OR adaptive) AND (("robot*" OR "CSP" OR "multi*agent" OR agent OR "control*" OR system) OR (vehicle OR car OR plane OR ferry OR drone))))*

Google Scholar only provides truncated abstracts (approx. 30 words) so we manually extracted the full abstracts. Publish or Perish, however, has a limit of 999 results for bulk-export. Using these sources and search queries, we collected 20,764 results. The majority (14,568) came from ACM Digital Library while the rest (5,193) came from IEEE Xplore. Next, we describe the process that we followed to screen and filter these papers.

2.2 Screening and Filtering Workflow

We describe our workflow in screening the set of papers produced in the previous step, to remove duplicate results and to filter out papers that are not in scope.

Importing Search Results: Rayyan includes advanced features such as automated duplicate detection, collaborative initial screening, systematic conflict resolver, and dedicated data summary dashboards.

Removing Duplicate Papers: We identified duplicates using Rayyan's automatic tool by estimating the similarity between papers. We performed a visual evaluation of potential duplicates with similarity scores below 90 and kept the version of the record with the most meta data. We finally found 919 duplicate papers, leaving us with 19,841 papers.

Filtering using Title, Abstract, and Keywords (TAK): To reduce the number of out-of-scope papers that we had to read the full text of, we removed papers where the TAK did not match our scope. We split this process into two stages: (1) an assisted cascade filtering followed by (2) a manual sanity-check and evaluation. We applied the TAK filtering in a cascading fashion first. We used Rayyan to filter out and exclude papers that did not include any of the FM keywords, and exported the remaining set of papers to a new project. In this new project, we applied another filter to exclude papers that did not include any of the Autonomy keywords, and exported this to a second new project. Finally, we filtered out the papers that did not include any of the Platform keywords. This cascade process produced a set of 428 papers that correspond to our QLS criteria, in Fig. 1. Then, we collectively evaluated the papers produced by the cascade filtering, deciding if they should be included or excluded from the final set of surveyed literature. Some papers were categorised as "Maybe" to be further evaluated based on full text version. After this, 404 papers remained in-scope.

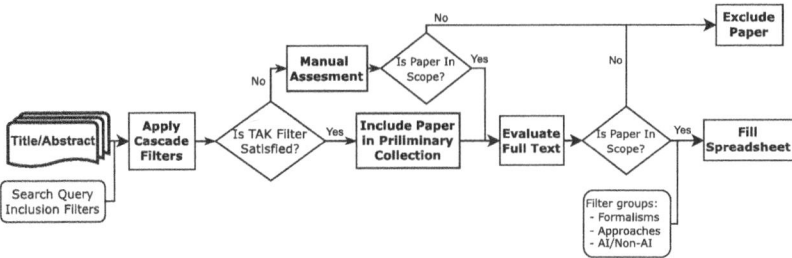

Fig. 3. A flowchart of our paper review process. We used the online Literature Review tool, Rayyan, which enabled us to collectively review papers and resolve evaluation conflicts.

Screening Full Text: We uploaded the full text of the papers to Rayyan to resolve the uncertain decisions and provide more context for us as reviewers. After this step, 292 papers were deemed in-scope and processed further manually.

2.3   Data Collection

We created a spreadsheet to record the information to be collected from the papers. When reviewing the full text, re-assessment was performed. If any paper was suspected to not meet the inclusion criteria, we flagged it in Rayyan as "Maybe" and re-evaluated it collectively. The overall review process is shown in Fig. 3. In the end, 181 papers were deemed in scope and used for generating the data and results to answer our **RQs**. The complete list of these papers can be found in [5].

3   Results

We present the results of the data collection described in Sect. 2.3 and selected surveyed literature in [5]. These results underpin the answers to our **RQs** presented in Sect. 2, showing the spread of different Formal Approaches (Sect. 3.1), Formalisms (Sect. 3.2), and FM for SSAI (Sect. 3.3) that we found in the surveyed literature. The answers to the **RQs** are then collected and made more explicit in Sect. 3.4

3.1   Formal Approaches

To answer the first part of **RQ1** - FM approaches used for specification and verification for RAS - we counted the number of papers that used MC, RV, Theorem Proving, Formal Synthesis, and Formal Specification. We also counted the papers that used a combination of different FM approaches and classified them as Heterogeneous Formal Methods.

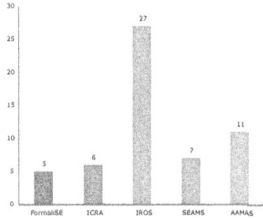

Fig. 4. The top 5 venues where the in-scope surveyed literature was published include robotics venues (IROS and ICRA), autonomous systems venues (SEAMS and AAMAS) and a formal methods venue (FormaliSE).

Table 1. Formal Approaches

Approach	Number of papers
Model Checking (MC)	130
Runtime Verification (RV)	24
Theorem Proving	18
Formal Plan Synthesis	17
Formal Control Synthesis	15
Formal Specification	6
Heterogeneous Formal Methods	31

Table 1 presents the number of papers using each kind of formal approach, showing that MC is used 130 times. This concurs with the findings of the previous survey [17]. The approach used the least often was Formal Specification alone, which we found in only 6 papers in the surveyed literature. Some of these papers focused on formally specifying properties but their mode of verification may have been non-formal, e.g., testing approaches (e.g., [12,18]).

While 136 out of the 181 papers in the surveyed literature (75%), used a single formal approach, 31 papers (17%) used a combination of different, heterogeneous formal approaches. The use of Heterogenous Formal Methods can be manifested in tight integration between the approaches within a specific component of the RAS (e.g., [25,26]) or separately in different phases of development or components (e.g., [11]). This result presents an increase in these kind of approaches from [17] (up from 13%) and in at least one paper per year from 2009 to 2024 – as shown in Fig. 5b. As we shift our focus to FM advancement over time to answer **RQ3**, another noticeable finding is shown in Fig. 5a - the number of papers using RV has increased substantially from 2013. Also, although theorem proving approaches remain less popular than model checking, Fig. 5a shows an increase in usage in recent years. This could be due to the inherent limitations of model-checking due to state-space explosion and these theorem proving approaches may have been used to complement other techniques. This trend appears to mirror the increase in Heterogeneous Verification approaches over time shown in Fig. 5b.

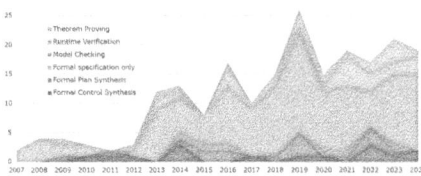

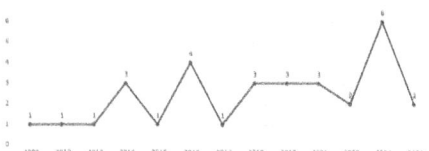

(a) The number of publications per approach per year.

(b) The number of Heterogeneous Formal Methods publications identified per year.

Fig. 5. Enumerating the number of formal methods approaches per year and, separately, counting the number of heterogeneous approaches per year.

Table 2. System Specification Formalisms

Formalism (System)	№ Papers
State-Transition	117
Differential Equations	12
Process Algebra	5
Temporal Logic	4
Set-Based	4
Dynamic Logic	3
Formal Ontology	3
Other	10

Table 3. Property Specification Formalisms

Formalism (Property)		№ Papers
Logics	Temporal Logic	90
	Probabilistic Temporal Logic	21
	Dynamic Logic	4
	Other Logics	17
	Total	**132**
Process Algebra		5
Set-Based		15
Formal Ontology		3
Other		17

3.2 Formalisms

To answer the second part of **RQ1** (formalisms used for formal specification and verification of RAS), we quantified the formalisms used (formal language or notations) to specify the system and the property or properties being verified. Most of the papers in the surveyed literature formally specified both the system and properties but some only specified the system (e.g. [13,23]) and others only the properties (e.g. [21,24]). Table 2 (resp. Table 3) shows the number of papers that used the identified formalisms to specify the system (resp. properties) in the surveyed literature. As these tables show, State-Transition formalisms were most often used in the surveyed literature to specify the system, and Temporal Logics were most often used to specify properties. [10] in one example among the 65 papers that used state-transition to model the system and Temporal Logic to model the properties 58 among those papers used Model Checking as an Approach.

3.3 Formal Methods for Sub-Symbolic AI

To answer **RQ2**, we highlight the 31 papers from the surveyed literature that use FM on at least one SSAI component. We see an evident trend of increased publications of this kind over the survey period as shown by Fig. 6. This could be linked to the recent rise of sub-symbolic AI approaches, most prominently

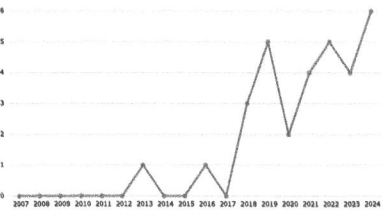

Fig. 6. The number of publications that used FM for SSAI enabled RAS per year.

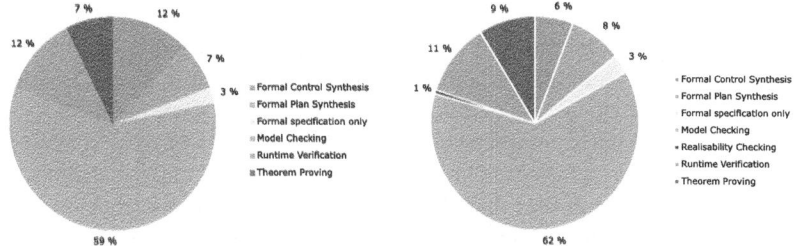

(a) FM approaches for RAS containing SSAI

(b) FM approaches for RAS without any SSAI component

Fig. 7. Spread of FM approaches for RAS

machine-learning, within the survey period. Figure 7 shows that there is a very similar distribution of approaches applied to RAS using SSAI versus those papers that don't.

3.4   Answering the Research Questions

This section discusses the findings from the results and relates them to our RQs.

RQ1 asks what Formal Approaches and Formalisms are used to specify and verify RAS. We identified a broad range of approaches and formalisms, with Model Checking being the most frequently used approach, and the two most often used formalisms being State-Transition Systems and Temporal Logic. The fact that systems were most often specified using State-Transition formalisms is likely a reflection of 88% of the papers having specified the system using State-Transition formalisms then used MC for verification. This pattern is reflected in the property formalisms where Temporal Logics and Probabilistic Temporal Logics are often used alongside State-Transition Systems for MC approaches. Table 3 shows that Temporal Logic and its variants are the most used formalism. Here, 76% of papers that used a Temporal Logic to specify properties, also used a State-Transition formalism to specify the system. Since our survey focuses on RAS, we cannot conclude whether this finding is specific or more common in other domains were FM is applied. Our interpretation is this could be due to the fact that modelling properties in Temporal Logic is more straight forward to explain to stakeholders, and since RAS typically operate in real-time conditions then modelling the system in State-Transition formalism seem to adequate in several cases. Note that our survey categorises Probabilistic Temporal Logic and Temporal-Epistemic Logic separately to Temporal Logic, whereas in the previous survey [17] these three types of formalism were collected in one single category.

RQ2 considers the possible effects of recent AI advancements within machine-learning in this domain and asks what FM are used to specify and verify Sub-Symbolic AI (SSAI) enabled RAS. Although the number of papers demonstrating the use of FM in verifying a SSAI component of RAS is still limited (at most 6 in 2024), we notice an increasing trend from 2018. Most of RAS, if not all, inherently contain one or multiple components that apply an aspect of AI. However, it seems those components start to be more and more critical or involving safety of the assets or humans (e.g. driverless cars, or pilotless aircraft sharing air space with commercial air traffic). Thus, formally verifying these components becomes of greater importance and attracts more research. Figure 7 shows, for instance, a similar distribution of FM approach distribution except for Formal Control Synthesis that is significantly more used for SSAI components. This supports the hypothesis that RAS navigation and control algorithms are becoming more and more reliant on SSAI techniques. This greatly increase the capability of RAS to interact with the environment including humans and therefore calls for the use formal frameworks to guarantee safe and reliable operation. During our survey, we collected more data to study FM tools used in the context of SSAI that will be subject to further analysis.

RQ3 investigates how research on FM applied to RAS has evolved over time. We focused on the trends and distribution of the various formal approaches throughout the survey period. MC is the approach most frequently used to specify and verify RAS during the survey period. The interest in RV took some time to appear, but quickly became second. This increase could be explained by the time needed for the technology to mature, and the focus was more on the offline verification at early specification and design phases. As RAS become more complex and used in more challenging environments, then RV became a valuable framework to ensure that specified properties are met at run-time. Overall, it is reassuring to see the general growth in the use of FM for RAS shown in Fig. 5.

4   Discussion

In this section, we summarise our threats to validity as follows:

Threats to Internal Validity: The automatic duplicate detection and filtering functionality in Rayyan may have not been as precise as we originally thought. We mitigated against this threat by manually reviewing the papers after the Rayyan classification to minimise any errors/discrepancies.

The results in Table 1 show that most of the papers used either MC, RV, or Theorem Proving. However this may be a result of having prompted for these three approaches in our searches (Fig. 2). While we also included more general terms, like "formal verification" or "formal specification", the inclusion of these three specific approaches may have produced search results that are biased to include them over other formal approaches. This means that while we can say that these three approaches were the most often used in the surveyed literature, we cannot say anything about their relative use against other methods that we did not prompt for explicitly. For example, "Heterogenous Formal Method" may be less often used in specifying and verifying RAS, or it may simply appear less often in the surveyed literature because of our search terms.

Threats to External Validity: Our search is designed as described in Sect. 2 to use specific search terms and sources. Both the search terms and sources were broader than in our previous survey [17], aiming to retrieve a more diverse set of results. Hence, comparing the results between these two surveys is not straightforward. Further, there is always the possibility that we missed some relevant publications by focusing our search the way that we did. This is reflected in Fig. 4 where the most popular venues were in the areas of robotics (IROS/ICRA) and autonomous systems (SEAMS/AAMAS). This is likely a result of searching the IEEE and ACM databases who are the publishers of proceedings at these venues. By excluding Scopus/Elsevier and Springer Link databases, due to their lack of bulk-export capability or ability to provide more than meta-data, papers published in those venues may have only made it into our surveyed literature set, through the Google Scholar search which in turn was channelled through the Publish or Perish import tool and as such constrained to only 999 results.

Finally, the fact that each source has a specific query syntax prevented us from using the exact same search term across all three databases. In particular, as Google Scholar does not allow more than 256 keywords in the search string, we had to modify and shorten the original search string to remove redundant and less frequently occurring terms. While we did our best to minimize the effects of this by carefully selecting and studying the outcome of various changes, it is still noteworthy.

5   Concluding Remarks

This paper presents initial results from a structured literature survey on using FM to specify or verify RAS. In addition to providing a detailed account of the methodology and work-flow adopted, we considered three Research Questions (RQs), posed and answered in Sect. 2 and 3.4, respectively. In particular, we focused on time-evolution of this field, recognising aspects and trends that have not been considered previously, e.g., use of SSAI methods, Formal Synthesis approaches and Probabilistic Verification Techniques. Also, we have identified and currently work on other relevant facets of FM, namely common tools, engineering representations, application domain and multi-agent RAS. A more thorough evaluation of the tools used might also offer more detailed insight into the popularity of the various approaches and formalisms that we found in this survey. These extended results are planned to be part of a journal version of this work.

Acknowledgments. This work has received partial funding from the Norwegian Research Council (RCN) RoboFarmer project number 336712, EPSRC grant: EP/Y001532/1 and the Royal Academy of Engineering.

Disclosure of Interests. The authors have no competing interests to declare that are relevant to the content of this article.

References

1. Proceedings Third Workshop on Formal Methods for Autonomous Systems. Electronic Proceedings in Theoretical Computer Science, vol. 348 (2021). https://doi.org/10.4204/eptcs.348
2. Adam, M., Ye, K., Anisi, D.A., Cavalcanti, A., Woodcock, J., Morris, R.: Probabilistic modelling and safety assurance of an agriculture robot providing light-treatment. In: Proceedings of the 19th IEEE International Conference on Automation Science and Engineering (CASE), pp. 1–7 (2023). https://doi.org/10.1109/CASE56687.2023.10260395
3. Adam, M., Hartmark, E.E., Andersen, T., Anisi, D.A., Cavalcanti, A.: Safety assurance of autonomous agricultural robots: from offline model-checking to runtime verification. In: Proceedings of the 20th IEEE International Conference on Automation Science and Engineering (CASE), pp. 2511–2516 (2024). https://doi.org/10.1109/CASE59546.2024.10711810
4. Aitken, J.M., et al.: Autonomous nuclear waste management. IEEE Intell. Syst. **33**(6), 47–55 (2018)
5. Azaiez, A., Anisi, D., Farrell, M., Luckcuck, M.: Revisiting formal methods for autonomous robots: a structured survey - surveyed literature set (2025). https://doi.org/10.5281/zenodo.15199605
6. Buxton, J.N., Randell, B. (eds.): Software Engineering Techniques: Report on a Conference Sponsored by the NATO Science Committee. NATO Science Committee, Rome, Italy (1970)
7. Farrell, M., Luckcuck, M., Fisher, M.: Robotics and integrated formal methods: necessity meets opportunity. In: Furia, C.A., Winter, K. (eds.) IFM 2018. LNCS, vol. 11023, pp. 161–171. Springer, Cham (2018). https://doi.org/10.1007/978-3-319-98938-9_10
8. Fisher, M., et al.: An overview of verification and validation challenges for inspection robots. Robotics **10**(2), 67 (2021)
9. Gleirscher, M., van de Pol, J., Woodcock, J.: A manifesto for applicable formal methods. Softw. Syst. Model. **22**(6), 1737–1749 (2023)
10. Gu, R., Marinescu, R., Seceleanu, C., Lundqvist, K.: Formal verification of an autonomous wheel loader by model checking. In: Proceedings of the 6th Conference on Formal Methods in Software Engineering, pp. 74–83 (2018). https://doi.org/10.1145/3193992.3193999

11. Heß, D., Althoff, M., Sattel, T.: Formal verification of maneuver automata for parameterized motion primitives. In: 2014 IEEE/RSJ International Conference on Intelligent Robots and Systems, pp. 1474–1481 (2014). https://doi.org/10.1109/IROS.2014.6942751

12. Innes, C., Ireland, A., Lin, Y., Ramamoorthy, S.: Anticipating accidents through reasoned simulation. In: Proceedings of the First International Symposium on Trustworthy Autonomous Systems (2023). https://doi.org/10.1145/3597512.3599698

13. Kim, B., Masuda, T., Shiraishi, S.: Test specification and generation for connected and autonomous vehicle in virtual environments. ACM Trans. Cyber-Phys. Syst. 4(1) (2019). https://doi.org/10.1145/3311954

14. Lam, A.Y., Leung, Y.W., Chu, X.: Autonomous-vehicle public transportation system: scheduling and admission control. IEEE Trans. Intell. Transp. Syst. 17(5), 1210–1226 (2016)

15. Leahy, K., et al.: Grand challenges in the verification of autonomous systems. arXiv preprint arXiv:2411.14155 (2024)

16. Leventi-Peetz, A.: Summary of formal methods for safe and secure computer systems. Technical report, Federal Office for Information Security (BSI) (2025). https://www.bsi.bund.de/SharedDocs/Downloads/DE/BSI/Publikationen/Studien/formal_methods_study_875/Summary_formal_methods_study_875.pdf?__blob=publicationFile&v=1, summary of the original book edited by H. Garavel

17. Luckcuck, M., Farrell, M., Dennis, L.A., Dixon, C., Fisher, M.: Formal specification and verification of autonomous robotic systems: a survey. ACM Comput. Surv. 52(5) (2019). https://doi.org/10.1145/3342355

18. Mohammadinejad, S., Deshmukh, J.V., Puranic, A.G., Vazquez-Chanlatte, M., Donzé, A.: Interpretable classification of time-series data using efficient enumerative techniques. In: Proceedings of the 23rd International Conference on Hybrid Systems: Computation and Control (2020). https://doi.org/10.1145/3365365.3382218

19. Neto, A.V.S., Camargo, J.B., Almeida, J.R., Cugnasca, P.S.: Safety assurance of artificial intelligence-based systems: a systematic literature review on the state of the art and guidelines for future work. IEEE Access 10, 130733–130770 (2022). https://doi.org/10.1109/ACCESS.2022.3229233

20. Ouzzani, M., Hammady, H., Fedorowicz, Z., Elmagarmid, A.: Rayyan: a web and mobile app for systematic reviews (2016). https://www.rayyan.ai

21. Păsăreanu, C.S.: Analysis of neural network takeover-time predictions for shared-control autonomous driving. In: Proceedings of the 1st International Workshop on Verification of Autonomous & Robotic Systems (2021). https://doi.org/10.1145/3459086.3459630

22. Redfield, S., Olszewska, J.I., Leahy, K., Murahwi, Z., Araiza-Illan, D., Fisher, M.: Verification of autonomous systems: the road ahead. In: 40th Anniversary of the IEEE International Conference on Robotics and Automation. IEEE (2024)

23. Roy, D., Chang, W., Mitter, S.K., Chakraborty, S.: Tighter dimensioning of heterogeneous multi-resource autonomous CPS with control performance guarantees. In: Proceedings of the 56th Annual Design Automation Conference (2019). https://doi.org/10.1145/3316781.3317925

24. Schaefer, I., Poetzsch-Heffter, A.: Slicing for model reduction in adaptive embedded systems development. In: Proceedings of the 2008 International Workshop on Software Engineering for Adaptive and Self-managing Systems, pp. 25–32 (2008). https://doi.org/10.1145/1370018.1370024

25. Stamenkovich, J., Maalolan, L., Patterson, C.: Formal assurances for autonomous systems without verifying application software. In: 2019 Workshop on Research, Education and Development of Unmanned Aerial Systems (Red UAS), pp. 60–69 (2019). https://doi.org/10.1109/REDUAS47371.2019.8999690
26. Varricchio, V., Chaudhari, P., Frazzoli, E.: Sampling-based algorithms for optimal motion planning using process algebra specifications. In: 2014 IEEE International Conference on Robotics and Automation (ICRA), pp. 5326–5332 (2014). https://doi.org/10.1109/ICRA.2014.6907642
27. Webster, M., Fisher, M., Cameron, N., Jump, M.: Formal methods for the certification of autonomous unmanned aircraft systems. In: Flammini, F., Bologna, S., Vittorini, V. (eds.) SAFECOMP 2011. LNCS, vol. 6894, pp. 228–242. Springer, Heidelberg (2011). https://doi.org/10.1007/978-3-642-24270-0_17

Underwater Robotics and Autonomy

Towards Autonomous Subsea Longitudinal Object Detection and Tracking Using a Multi-beam Echo-Sounder

Favour O. Adetunji[✉], Vibhav Bharti, Yvan R. Petillot,
Maria Koskinopoulou, and Ignacio Carlucho

School of Engineering and Physical Sciences, Heriot-Watt University, Edinburgh, UK
foa2001@hw.ac.uk

Abstract. Subsea pipelines and cables are critical assets which require regular maintenance and inspection to ensure their integrity and continual operation. The autonomous tracking of these assets requires robust and reliable methods especially in the challenging subsea environment. This paper presents a new method for the robust autonomous detection and tracking of subsea pipelines and cables using a multi-beam echo-sounder sensor, leveraging intensity and profiling returns for enhanced robustness. The proposed method involves four key steps. First, prepocessing operations are carried out to refine the raw sensor data, followed by a region of interest generation using the K-means clustering algorithm, then a validation step which filters implausable regions and finally a fitting processes for determining the target's position and parameters. The proposed method is also designed to extend the detection and tracking capabilities of the system to the 3-dimensional use case. Through real-world and simulated experiments we demonstrate the effectiveness of the method.

Keywords: Pipeline Tracking · Cable Tracking · Autonomous Tracking

1 Introduction

Subsea longitudinal structures such as pipelines and cables are important assets used in transporting goods and services across the worlds oceans and rivers. To maintain the continued operation of these structures, it is therefore vital to perform regular maintenance and inspection operations on them [10]. These tasks help to curb the effects of natural (erosion, tides, earthquakes) and man-made (fishing activities, anchoring) factors that affect their operation [15]. The inspection and maintenance activities performed on these structures span a wide variety of activities from internal to external operations. In particular, external operations offer insights to the structural integrity as well as the condition of the subsea environment around the structure. Conventional means for the external operations include the use of unmanned underwater vehicles (UUVs) such as autonomous underwater vehicles (AUVs) and remotely-operated vehicles (ROVs) [14].

© The Author(s), under exclusive license to Springer Nature Switzerland AG 2026
A. Cavalcanti et al. (Eds.): TAROS 2025, LNAI 16045, pp. 355–366, 2026.
https://doi.org/10.1007/978-3-032-01486-3_27

In inspecting these structures, AUVs have an operating cost advantage over ROVs, as they require minimal operational support [1]. However, for AUVs to operate autonomously the vehicle has to have a robust system for detection and tracking especially when the target is in a complex environment, occluded or partially buried [8]. Acoustic sensors and methods that utilize them provide a robust way to detect these structures, offering advantages such as long-range detection and minimal susceptibility to visibility limitations such as water turbidity pertinent to visual methods [6]. The acoustic sensors traditionally used in this space include side-scan sonars (SSS), multi-beam echo-sounder (MBES), forward looking sonars (FLS), sub-bottom profilers (SBP) and synthetic aperture sonars (SAS), which differ in characteristics such as the number of transducers, transducers arrangement, beam width and signal frequency [13]. These characteristics influence their performance and determine their suitability for specific survey and inspection requirements. However, for close range inspection, MBES are a good alternative for detection and tracking of these structures as they are suitable for targets laid on the seabed [1] and hence can provide inspection information like the target's depth of burial, position and fault spots.

Literature on close range inspection using MBES is limited and mostly focuses on using the profiling returns from the sensor as well as a known model of the target for detection and tracking. One of the earliest methods for pipeline detection and tracking with AUVs is presented in the work of Petillot et al. [12], where they proposed a method using MBES profiling returns that is based on the accuracy of the fit between the known pipelines model and the MBES observed returns using ellipse segments. The method includes a Monte Carlo Markov Chains (MCMC) to sample the parameter space to find the best fit. In [1], the authors present a novel real-time algorithm for pipeline tracking with MBES. The algorithm utilizes a second-degree polynomial to generate regions of interests before fitting the data points to the pipelines model. Xiong et al. [3] propose the use of dual multi-beam bathymetric systems for accurate pipeline inspection. In their work, they point out several advantages of the dual system such as reduction of error in overlapping water depth data, improved inspection efficiency and high density point clouds acquisition. In [11], a fuzzy logic model is developed for pipeline identification. The fuzzy model utilizes several parameters like the known radius of the pipeline, known seabed shape, pipeline direction and pipeline inclination for estimating the existence probability of the pipeline and the relative position of the AUV and pipeline. A point cloud segmentation network, Cross-scale Point-In-Context (Cross-PIC), is introduced in [5], for pipeline identification from MBES data. The authors argue that current subsea pipeline identification algorithms suffer from inaccuracies due to the low use of the context features from available data. The work therein focuses on the use of context-learning through a network trained on subsea pipeline point cloud data.

Most methods in the literature utilize detection systems based solely on the profiling returns of the MBES sensor. This is a significant limitation, especially in cases of partial target burial, complex seabed profiles, or the presence of objects with similar features. Although MBES sensors are primarily used for profiling, some also provide backscatter or intensity returns. However, most methods in the literature disregard this additional information. In this work, we present an MBES detection and tracking system that combines intensity and profiling returns for efficient and accurate detection and tracking of subsea pipelines and cables in two-dimensional (2D) and three-dimensional (3D) scenarios. We showcase how the target's properties such as depth of burial and accurate positioning can be achieved with this method.

2   Methodology

In this section we present the algorithmic steps for the 2D and 3D tracking use case with an MBES sensor that includes intensity returns. Furthermore, we detail the depth of burial calculation, which leverages the clustered detection data to determine whether the structure is free-spanning or the extent to which it is buried beneath the seabed.

2.1   Detection Algorithm: 2D Profiles

Preprocessing: Given an individual MBES profile frame at time step i, the first step in the algorithm involves the conversion from polar (ρ_i, θ_i) to cartesian coordinate (x_i, y_i), followed by the smoothing of the profile to remove noise and outliers. The noise and outliers in the MBES frames are reduced using a median filter over the range and intensity values, x_i, y_i and I_i, as shown in Eqs. 1 to 3, where k and w represents the element position within the frame and the sliding window size respectively. In Fig. 1, an individual MBES profile frame is displayed. The original and smoothened data points of this frame are then shown in Fig. 2, with the intensity values overlayed on the data points.

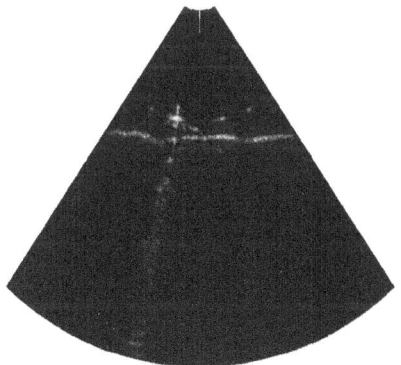

Fig. 1. Individual MBES display frame.

$$\tilde{x}_k = \text{median}\{x_{k-w}, x_{k-w+1}, \ldots, x_k, \ldots, x_{k+w-1}, x_{k+w}\} \tag{1}$$

$$\tilde{y}_k = \text{median}\{y_{k-w}, y_{k-w+1}, \ldots, y_k, \ldots, y_{k+w-1}, y_{k+w}\} \tag{2}$$

$$\tilde{I}_k = \text{median}\{I_{k-w}, I_{k-w+1}, \ldots, I_k, \ldots, I_{k+w-1}, I_{k+w}\} \tag{3}$$

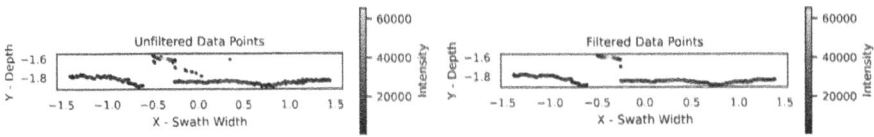

Fig. 2. Unfiltered (left) and filtered (right) MBES data points (Fig. 1).

Region of Interests Generation: After preprocessing, an important step in the detection of the target from the MBES frames is knowing which part of the data corresponds to the target or are likely to be the target. A key assumption in our work is that these man-made structure (subsea pipelines or cables) have distinguishable or different properties such as back scatter return and elevated profiles that enables them to be detected against the subsea environment (seafloor). In this step, we first apply a discrete gradient transformation to the filtered intensity data, $I_{i,filtered}$, and then normalize the $y_{i,filtered}$ and $I_{i,grad-filtered}$ data points. After which, we utilize the k-means clustering algorithm [9] to group the combined normalized data points, $y_{i,norm}$ and $I_{i,grad-norm}$ into clusters that capture variations in height and intensity across the MBES frame.

Given a set of filtered data points D;

$$D = \{(y_{i,\text{norm}}, I_{i,\text{grad-norm}}) \mid i = 1, 2, \ldots, k\} \tag{4}$$

Each data point is assigned to the nearest cluster centroid:

$$C_i = \arg \min_{j \in \{1, \ldots, K\}} \|(y_{i,\text{norm}}, I_{i,\text{grad-norm}}) - \mu_j\|^2 \tag{5}$$

where:

- C_i is the cluster index assigned to the ith data point,
- μ_j is the centroid of cluster j,
- k is the number of data points.
- K is the number of clusters.

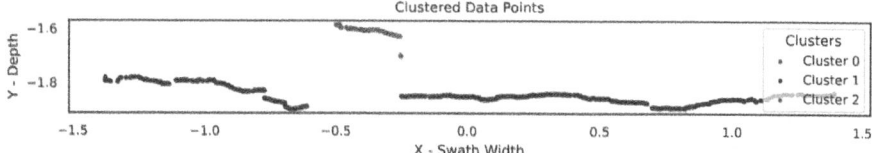

Fig. 3. K-means clustering (Fig. 1 data points).

Based on our experiments, we find a K value of 3, to be sufficient for representing clusters that distinguishes between the seabed, objects on the seabed, and objects above the seabed. After the clustering process, we select the two clusters with the fewest data points, as we assume that the most populated cluster reflects data points that belong to the seabed which should generally have similar properties and occupy most part of the MBES frame. The two selected clusters are then further filtered to extract the data points x_k and y_k that belong to these clusters. Additionally, cases where points from one selected cluster are spatially within the other cluster are accounted for during the filtering process. These filtered cluster points then form the various regions of interest that are most likely representations of the target. A visual representation of these regions of interest, derived from the data points in Fig. 2, is shown in Fig. 3.

Validation Step: Once the regions of interest are generated, the next step involves the elimination of regions that do not align with the known shape of the target. In [2], the shape characteristics of pipeline cross-sections are analyzed in relation to the orientation of the vehicle (AUV) and the pipeline being tracked. Generally, for an AUV moving parallel to a pipeline, the cross-section of the pipeline appears as semi-circles in the MBES frames. If the AUV's orientation deviates from a parallel alignment to the pipeline, this transitions the cross-section to semi-ellipses in the MBES profile, and further more, with the MBES sensor set at a relatively high pitch, the profile becomes parabolic in the MBES frame. Despite these variations, the profiles share a common characteristic of forming a concave-down shape when the MBES sensor is positioned above the pipeline. Since both pipelines and cables are cylindrical structures, similar principles can be applied to the detection of cables. We use this property as well as the known size of the target to develop validation steps that is used to eliminate regions that are lest susceptible to be the target. The following steps are involved in the validations of the regions of interest:

- **Size thresholds**: Regions that fall outside a threshold range based on the breadth or swath width of the set of points are discarded. In our experiments, we set the minimum and maximum thresholds at $\frac{3}{4}$ and $\frac{5}{2}$ of the known radius size, respectively. When the sensor is at steeper angles or pitched, these thresholds are adjusted based on the expected cross-section of a cylinder when cut at an angle, accounting for the apparent distortion in the target's dimensions.

– **Convex hull and curvature**: Data points that make up the convex hull of the target or region of interest are determined, and the curvature is calculated via arc-length parameterization using the original ordering of the points from the MBES frame. Regions that have sections with concave-up shape and segments with zero curvature are discarded.

Fitting Process: After filtering out regions in the validation phase, the last step is fitting the remaining set of points to an elliptical model. This approach allows the detection system to accommodate both parallel and non-parallel orientations of the AUV relative to the target, within certain limits, as the elliptical model can also represent circular half-cross sections. For the fitting process, we use similar methods in [1], where a non-linear least squares algorithm is used to fit the points to an ellipse model with a constraint on the minor axis. However, we further impose constraints on the possible parameter solutions of the model. The elliptical model is represented by Eq. 6, where the optimization process aims to determine the ellipse's center coordinates, x_c and y_c, along with the major axis length, a, that minimizes the residual error. If the fitting process is not achievable or any of the validation steps fails, the MBES frame is considered as having no target structure. Figure 4 presents the MBES profile from Fig. 1, overlaid with the fitted ellipse.

$$\left(\frac{x - x_c}{a}\right)^2 + \left(\frac{y - y_c}{r}\right)^2 - 1 = residuals \qquad (6)$$

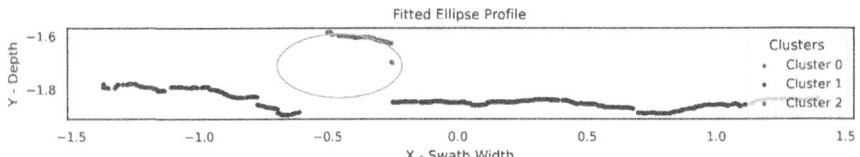

Fig. 4. Overlayed fitted ellipse (Fig. 1 data points).

2.2   Detection Algorithm - 3D

The detection system for the 2D use case can give the spatial position of the target but would however require accumulated detections in order to ascertain the direction of the target [2]. Additionally, for small targets like subsea cables, which may be more difficult to distinguish from the seabed in individual frames, the 3D method provides an alternative approach. Consequently, the 3D use case is introduced. Similar to the 2D algorithm, the preprocessing is done over each individual MBES frame but the clustering algorithm uses the stacked MBES frames to group the three clusters for validation and fitting. Following the same assumption that the seabed is represented by the cluster with the most data points, the two least populated clusters are then selected for further processing.

Validation Step: After generating regions of interest, the validation step involves projecting the points of the two selected clusters to a two-dimensional plane consisting of the $X - Y$ points (swath width and forward direction of the AUV). In this plane, we look for cluster segments that form the largest contours and fit lines to the two boundaries of the contours and check consistency between the two boundaries slope. In this step, the intuition is that the pipeline or cable would form a long consistent cluster that has similar slope represented by it boundaries from a top view.

Fitting Process: The fitting process for the 3D case can performed by utilizing a cylindrical fitting algorithm on the 3D points of the selected cluster. However, for computational simplicity, we utilize similar fitting methods in the 2D use case by selecting portions of the selected cluster frames and calculating individually the x_c, y_c and then interpolating between the selected clusters to determine the a full representation for the target.

2.3   Depth of Burial Calculation

For subsea cable and pipeline inspections, an important end-product of the inspection is the determination of the burial depth of the pipeline or cable to ascertain portions of the structure in free span or potentially susceptible to free span as well as the detection of close-proximity structures that can potentially damage the structure. In our method, by grouping the data points into clusters that reflect different objects on the seabed, the method provides an accurate way of determining the depth of burial and identifying potential risk points due to close proximity of foreign object to the structure, thereby providing more perceptible information while tracking with an MBES sensor. For calculating the burial depth, we select points within a specific range of the most populated cluster (seabed cluster points) nearest to the structure data end points (pipeline or cable) on both sides, and subtract the lowest point of the fitted ellipse from the mean of these points, thereby determining if the structure is in free span or buried. This calculation is presented in Eq. 7.

$$D_b = \bar{Z}_{\text{seabed}} - Z_{\text{min,ellipse}} \tag{7}$$

where:

- D_b is the burial depth of the pipeline or cable.
- $\bar{Z}_{\text{seabed}} = \frac{1}{N} \sum_{k=1}^{N} Z_{\text{seabed},k}$ is the mean depth of seabed points near the structure.
- $Z_{\text{min,ellipse}}$ is the lowest point of the fitted ellipse representing the pipeline or cable.

3   Experimental Results

The proposed methodology is evaluated using both simulated and real data. In both cases, a subsea pipeline serves as the target and the MBES sensor is positioned with zero pitch pointing downward from the vehicle.

3.1   Simulation Results

The detection methods and depth-of-burial calculation are evaluated within the simulation environment. The stonefish simulator [4,7] and the robotic operating system (ROS), are used to simulate a pipeline tracking scenario in a subsea environment characterized by a complex terrain with rocks within the viscosity of the pipeline. Figure 5 illustrates the pipeline tracking scenario within the simulation setup. In the 2D detection scenario, shown in Fig. 6, the algorithm successfully detected the pipeline in 88 frames, while 11 frames were misclassified.

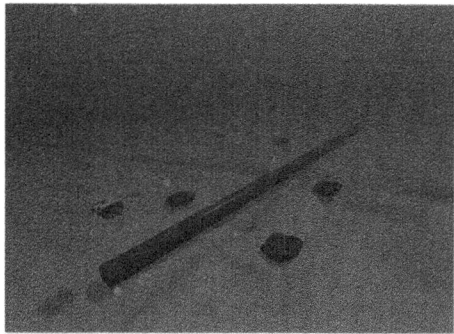

Fig. 5. Pipeline tracking scenario (simulation environment).

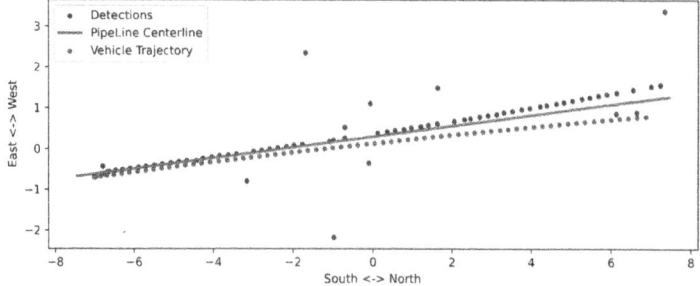

Fig. 6. 2D centerline detections (simulation).

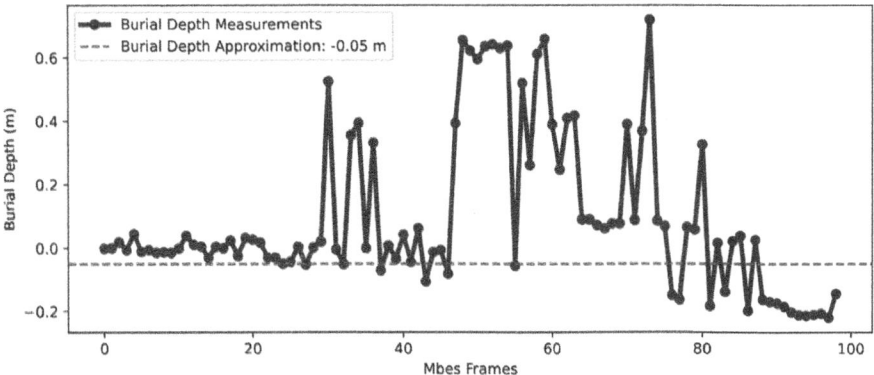

Fig. 7. Depth of burial results (simulation).

The results for the burial depth per MBES frame is presented in Fig. 7. While the pipe is placed at a depth of -0.05 m (approximate depth) relative to the seabed plane in the simulation, the depth for each MBES frame would vary, as the terrain is not flat. The burial depth variation closely aligns with the simulation environment topology, with the pipeline having free spans in the middle section (from frame 47) along its axis as it crosses over a trench and the end section (from frame 88) having larger burial depths as the pipe becomes deeply buried.

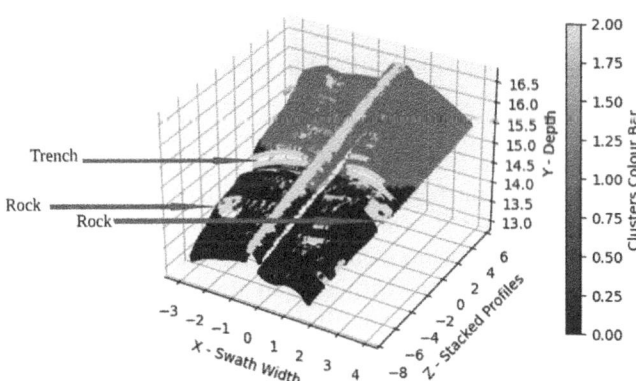

Fig. 8. Clustered 3D point data (simulation). (Color figure online)

In Fig. 8, the 3D clustered data points from the simulation environment are presented. The pipeline is represented by cluster 2 (yellow) and distinctly forms a continuous longitudinal shape across the profiles. Additionally, the rocks and trench sections within the environment are effectively identified from the MBES frame data, as they are also grouped within cluster 2 (yellow). This classification allows for the identification of their positions and other relevant parameters, contributing to the perceptible information obtained through this method.

3.2   Real-World Results

The real word data was gathered at the ORE Catapult in Blyth, UK, in a dry dock filled with seawater, within which test pipes were placed. The sensor setup involved a C-Enduro ASV on which the Blueview MB2250 multibeam sonar is mounted on. The top-view layout of the dock and the 2D algorithm detection results for a segment of the pipeline are presented in Fig. 9. The results are obtained from the ASV navigating along the pipeline from the southwest to northeast direction over 220 consecutive MBES frames.

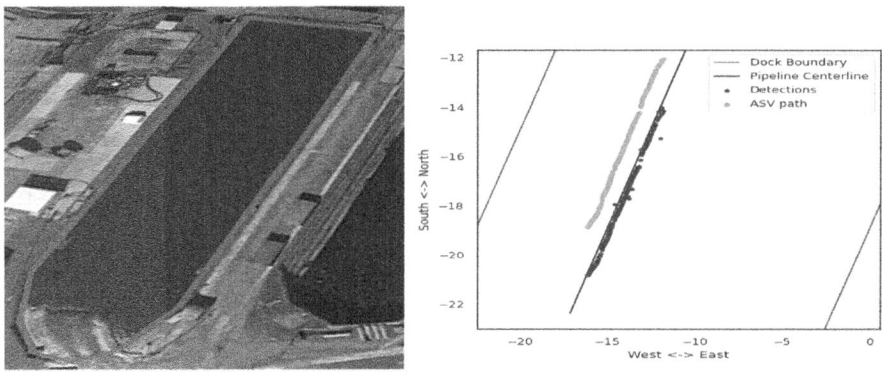

Fig. 9. (a) Dock layout (boundaries outlined in green); (b) Pipeline segment detection results. (Color figure online)

The detection algorithm results in Fig. 9b (purple stars), are the estimates of the pipelines centerline, with the original centerline positions outlined by the blue straight line. The algorithm identified 21 frames as having no pipeline segment and misclassified 12 frames with a mean absolute centerline perpendicular distance error of 0.157. These results indicate that the algorithm successfully detected the pipeline in 85.00% of the frames, with a false negative rate of 9.55% and a misclassification rate of 5.46%. In Fig. 10, the clustered 3D point data over 50 consecutive frames are presented, while the 2D projection and boundary slopes depicted in Fig. 11. The purple cluster class (cluster 0) represents the seabed, whereas the green cluster (cluster 1) mostly consist of the target data point. In the 2D projection, cluster 1 forms the largest contours, with boundary slopes that align closely, distinguishing it as the pipeline.

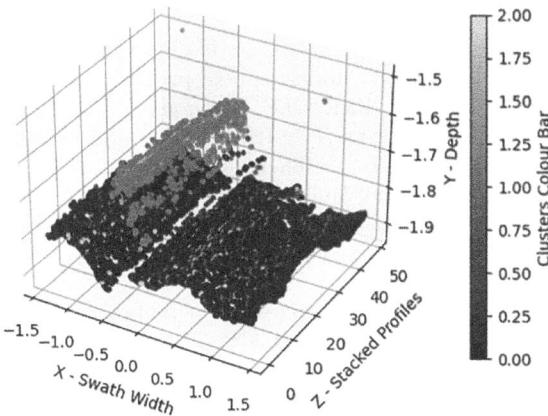

Fig. 10. Clustered 3D Point Data Over 50 Consecutive Frames.

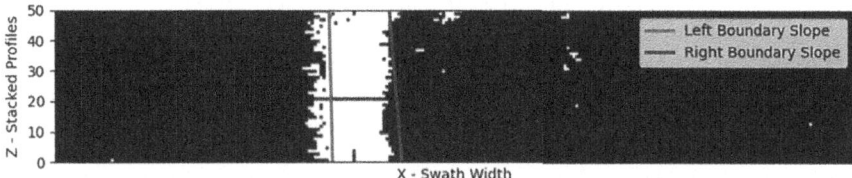

Fig. 11. 2D projection with boundary slope (Cluster1 - Fig. 10).

4   Conclusion

In this paper, we proposed an algorithm for the autonomous detection and tracking of subsea longitudinal objects like pipelines and cables with UUVs. Our approach significantly reduces false positives by clustering intensity gradients and profiling returns to enhance region-of-interest proposals. We showed through results on real and simulated data that the system is robust and can be used for tracking in complex scenarios. We further showcased the extended usability of the method in terms of perceptibility in extracting survey information. In our future work, we plan to extend the robustness of the tracking system by fusing it with another sensor such as a video camera to refine and smoothen the detections.

Acknowledgment. The work done in this paper is supported by Fugro and the EPSRC project UNderwater IntervenTion for offshore renewable Energies (UNITE) grant number EP/X024806/1.

References

1. Bharti, V., Lane, D., Wang, S.: Robust subsea pipeline tracking with noisy multi-beam echosounder. In: 2018 IEEE/OES Autonomous Underwater Vehicle Workshop (AUV), Porto, Portugal, pp. 1–5. IEEE (2018)
2. Bharti, V., et al.: Algorithms for autonomous subsea pipeline tracking. Ph.D. thesis, Heriot-Watt University and University of Edinburgh (2021)
3. Xiong, C.-B., Li, Z., Zhai, G.-J., Lu, H.-L.: A new method for inspecting the status of submarine pipeline based on a multi-beam bathymetric system. J. Mar. Sci. Technol. **24**(4) (2016)
4. Cieślak, P.: Stonefish: an advanced open-source simulation tool designed for marine robotics, with a ROS interface. In: OCEANS 2019 - Marseille (2019). https://doi.org/10.1109/OCEANSE.2019.8867434
5. Cui, X., Li, Y., Li, J., Zhang, J.: Cross-PIC: a cross-scale in-context learning network for 3D multibeam point cloud segmentation of submarine pipelines. Ocean Eng. **315**, 119778 (2025)
6. Feng, H., et al.: Automatic tracking method for submarine cables and pipelines of AUV based on side scan sonar. Ocean Eng. **280**, 114689 (2023)
7. Grimaldi, M., et al.: Stonefish: supporting machine learning research in marine robotics (2025). https://arxiv.org/abs/2502.11887
8. Guan, M., Cheng, Y., Li, Q., Wang, C., Fang, X., Yu, J.: An effective method for submarine buried pipeline detection via multi-sensor data fusion. IEEE Access **7**, 125300–125309 (2019). https://doi.org/10.1109/ACCESS.2019.2938264
9. MacQueen, J.: Some methods for classification and analysis of multivariate observations (1967). https://api.semanticscholar.org/CorpusID:6278891
10. Mai, C., Pedersen, S., Hansen, L., Jepsen, K.L., Yang, Z.: Subsea infrastructure inspection: a review study. In: 2016 IEEE International Conference on Underwater System Technology: Theory and Applications (USYS), pp. 71–76 (2016). https://doi.org/10.1109/USYS.2016.7893928
11. Pavin, A.: The pipeline identification method basing on AUV's echo-sounder data. In: OCEANS 2006, Boston, MA, USA, pp. 1–6. IEEE (2006)
12. Petillot, Y., Reed, S., Bell, J.: Real time AUV pipeline detection and tracking using side scan sonar and multi-beam echo-sounder. In: Oceans 2002 MTS/IEEE, Biloxi, MI, USA, vol. 1, pp. 217–222. IEEE (2002)
13. Sun, K., Cui, W., Chen, C.: Review of underwater sensing technologies and applications. Sensors **21**(23), 7849 (2021)
14. Willners, J.S., et al.: From market-ready ROVs to low-cost AUVs. In: OCEANS 2021, San Diego, Porto, pp. 1–7. IEEE (2021)
15. Yu, C., Xiang, X., Lapierre, L., Zhang, Q.: Robust magnetic tracking of subsea cable by AUV in the presence of sensor noise and ocean currents. IEEE J. Oceanic Eng. **43**(2), 311–322 (2018)

Fully Distributed Cooperative Multi-agent Underwater Obstacle Avoidance

Kanzhong Yao, Ognjen Marjanovic, and Simon Watson$^{(\boxtimes)}$

The University of Manchester, Manchester, UK
simon.watson@manchester.ac.uk

Abstract. Navigation in cluttered underwater environments is challenging, especially when there are constraints on communication and self-localisation, and there is clutter in the environment. In this paper, we first studied the connection between everyday activity of dog walking and the cooperative underwater obstacle avoidance problem. Inspired by this analogy, we propose a novel dog walking paradigm and implement it in a multi-agent underwater system. Simulations were conducted across various scenarios, with performance benchmarked against traditional methods utilising Image-Based Visual Servoing in a multi-agent setup. The results indicate that our dog-walking-inspired paradigm significantly enhances cooperative behavior between agents and outperforms the existing approach in navigating through obstacles.

Keywords: Aquatic Robots · Multi-Agent · Obstacle Avoidance

1 Introduction

Autonomous exploration and inspection in hazardous environments represent one of the primary applications of robotic systems, with confined underwater spaces being typical examples of such challenging environments [21]. These scenarios are prevalent across various domains, including aquaculture, nuclear storage ponds, and cave exploration.

Confined underwater spaces are characterised by several generic challenges: constrained communications [18], a lack of continuous features for self-localisation [22], and the absence of auxiliary facilities [21]. The deployment of multi-robot teams has been proposed to mitigate some of these issues, offering enhanced operational capabilities and redundancy [23]. However, when the environment becomes cluttered, an additional challenge will be brought to the multi-agent robots working in a team: How to achieve collision-free underwater motion whilst keeping in a certain formation of the team? An additional constraint is imposed that there is no physical connection (tether) between the robots, as this can be caught and tangled in cluttered environments.

Traditional approaches to addressing this challenge typically depend on centralised control systems, where a networked infrastructure orchestrates coordination [1], or partially centralised mechanisms that necessitate minimal levels of

© The Author(s), under exclusive license to Springer Nature Switzerland AG 2026
A. Cavalcanti et al. (Eds.): TAROS 2025, LNAI 16045, pp. 367–380, 2026.
https://doi.org/10.1007/978-3-032-01486-3_28

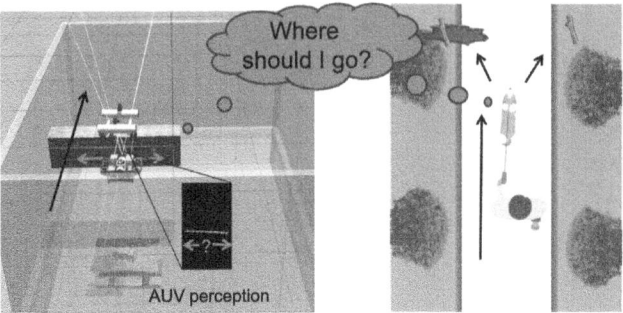

(a) The underwater robot needs to   (b) The dog wants to fetch a stick
avoid an obstacle

Fig. 1. Fully distributed cooperative underwater obstacle avoidance and a common dog walking scenario.

communication [11]. On the other hand, fully distributed solutions often presuppose access to predetermined obstacle data [3] or rely heavily on self-localisation capabilities to ensure collision-free navigation within formations [4].

In scenarios of extreme environments, such as the confined underwater spaces previously discussed, collision-free formations that consider **no communication**, and **no underwater self-localisation** are sometimes necessary. Unfortunately, the problem under such conditions has been explored minimally.

2   Problem Statement

Consider a scenario involving a cluttered, confined underwater environment where underwater localisation and communication are highly constrained. An underwater robot is dependent on guidance from a surface robot with the additional complexity that underwater obstacles can only be detected by the underwater robot. This situation necessitates that the underwater robot not only maintain formation with the guiding surface robot but also navigate around obstacles adeptly to ensure safe, collision-free movement. Meanwhile, the surface robot guides the underwater towards a target location, and also needs to actively adjust its motion to keep the formation with the underwater robot [24], as shown in Fig. 1a.

2.1   Contribution

Taking the inspiration from the analogy of walking a dog, in this work, we define a novel "dog walking" paradigm and adapt it to solve the described problem. Given a multi-agent system, one "follower" agent with limited sensing capabilities is guided towards a target position by a "leader" agent. Analogous to walking a dog, the follower-dog must perform additional motions to fetch a stick, while maintaining formation with the leader-walker, in the absence of direct communication between them, as depicted in Fig. 1b. The contributions of this work are:

- We define a novel "dog walking" paradigm, which can be applied to solve the fully distributed cooperative obstacle avoidance problem. To the best of the authors' knowledge, it is the first in the literature.
- A preliminary solution with the new paradigm to the described problem was implemented, in the context of an underwater multi-agent system. Corresponding simulation has been conducted to demonstrate its efficacy, benchmarked against previous work [24].

3   Related Work

Over the years, the cooperative obstacle avoidance problem in constrained environments has gained notable attention. In this section, we present an overview across aerial, ground, and underwater domains, as there are relatively few attempts in the underwater domain.

Under a constrained environment, where data transmission between agents is not allowed, the problem becomes distributed. For example, a deep reinforcement learning strategy was employed for non-communicative path optimisation to facilitate multi-agent collision avoidance in [4]. This was extended by approaches focusing on decentralised connectivity maintenance using reinforcement learning for Unmanned Aerial Vehicles (UAVs) [12]. Such strategies have similarly been applied to multi-Unmanned Ground Vehicle (UGV) [15] and multi-Autonomous Underwater Vehicle (AUV) systems [7], showcasing the potential for fully distributed navigation in cluttered environments. A commonality among these studies is an underlying assumption regarding the agents' awareness of their positioning in a global frame. These works presuppose either the provision of agent and obstacle positions as ground truth data [4,7,12] or the availability of high-precision perception methods like LiDAR and depth cameras [15].

In practical applications, where perfect perception is often unattainable, researchers have begun to explore solutions accommodating imperfect measurements. For instance, Panagou et al. [17] introduced a visibility maintenance framework designed to support cooperative leader-follower navigation through obstacle-laden environments with constrained visual input. Similarly, Dergachev [6] developed a novel solver aimed at cooperative collision avoidance that accounts for limited sensory input.

In the underwater domain, characterised by inherently difficult communication and self-localisation challenges, literature addressing these specific issues remains scarce. A notable attempt to navigate AUVs in cluttered environments involved the adaptation of an enhanced Trajopt algorithm [19], as demonstrated by Xanthidis et al. [22]. Their experimental setup required the placement of artificial objects at the pool's bottom to aid in robot localisation. This reliance on artificial markers underscores a significant limitation: in genuine real-world scenarios, devoid of such artificial aids, the efficacy of these systems is questionable.

To summarise, if we move slightly further, eliminating both the communication and self-localisation prerequisites, we will be closer to the reality of operating within extreme environments. However, no current approaches can solve the problem described in Sect. 2 under such settings.

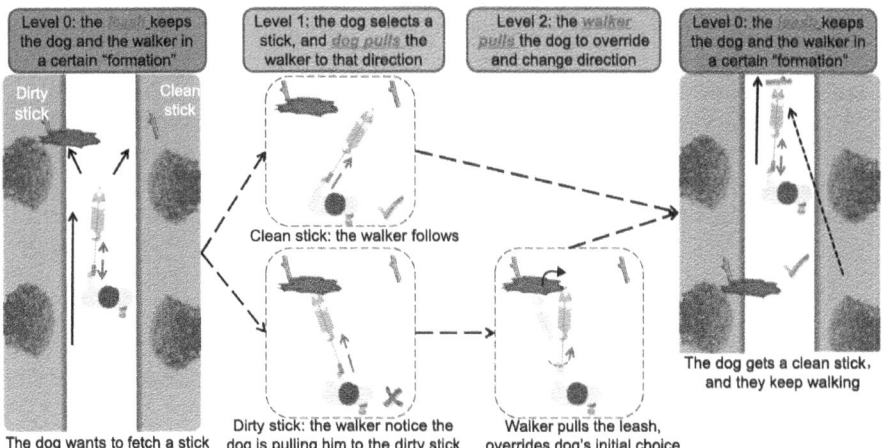

Fig. 2. Dog-Walking Paradigm Illustration. The three-tiered connection hierarchy is color-coded: Level 0 in green, Level 1 in blue, and Level 2 in purple, the higher the level, the higher the priority. Implicit communication is highlighted in red, with red dashed arrows representing the non-verbal cues between the dog and the walker. (Color figure online)

4   Dog Walking Paradigm Principles

Dog walking, a common activity in daily life, exemplifies a dynamic interaction between two agents bound by a unique form of connection and cooperation. In this analogy, the 'leader agent'—the person holding the leash—possesses a broader perspective of the environment and dominates the decision-making in critical situations such as avoiding hazardous areas. Conversely, the 'follower agent'—the dog—operates with a more localised perception of its surroundings and may exhibit spontaneous behaviors, such as attempting to fetch a stick. These agents are linked by a leash, serving as the medium for implicit communication, notably through variations in tension, which can be seen as pulling or resisting movements.

A scenario (Fig. 2) where a dog expresses the desire to fetch a stick, presented with two options: one adjacent to the muddy puddle and another situated on the grass. The objective is to ensure the dog's retrieval of the clean stick. This process leverages two principal characteristics:

Hierarchical Implicit Communications. The communication hierarchy is demonstrated in Fig. 2 and can be dissected into three distinct levels. Level 0 represents the steady-state where the dog and the walker are united by a flexible leash, sharing a common goal of walking home. At Level 1, the dog communicates its intent to procure a specific stick, employing an implicit signaling method manifested through the act of leash pulling. Progressing to Level 2, the walker, perceives with a broader awareness of the environment, intervenes when the dog targets the dirty stick near the muddy puddle and initiates pulling, the walker will override the pulling from the dog also via implicit communication - pulling back. This corrective action persists until the dog adjusts its preference, ultimately steering clear of the muddy area. Similar implicit communication has been studied in [2,13], but not in a hierarchical manner.

Formation Constraint. The leash serves the physical connection that maintains the proximity of the dog and walker, embodying the concept of a formation constraint. This constraint is integral to the leader-follower system, ensuring the agents remain within a bounded distance of each other.

5   Cooperative Underwater Obstacle Avoidance

In this section, a system model for the problem described in Sect. 2 was formulated, including the fundamental model and the extended formulation components with the dog walking paradigm. Within such a system, BlueROV2 was utilised as the underwater robot while MallARD [10] was the surface robot.

5.1   System Model

Both the BlueROV2 and MallARD are omnidirectional in terms of maneuverability, and the kinematic model for each robot can be expressed obtained in previous work [9,23]. The dynamic model for both robots is approximated by the Fossen equation [8]. Therefore, the system model J can be expressed as follows:

$$\dot{x}^S = J^S(^{\mathcal{B}}u^S) \tag{1a}$$

$$\dot{x}^U = J^U(^{\mathcal{B}}u^U) \tag{1b}$$

where the superscripts S and U indicate the corresponding notations for ASV and AUV, where $x = [x, y, z, \phi, \theta, \psi]^\top$, and x, y, z denote the robot's position while the angles ϕ, θ, ψ represent its orientation around x, y, and z, respectively. The robots' control inputs in the body frame $^{\mathcal{B}}u$ are represented by $^{\mathcal{B}}u^S = [^{\mathcal{B}}u_x^S, {}^{\mathcal{B}}u_y^S, {}^{\mathcal{B}}u_\psi^S]^\top$ and $^{\mathcal{B}}u^U = [^{\mathcal{B}}u_x^U, {}^{\mathcal{B}}u_y^U, {}^{\mathcal{B}}u_z^U, {}^{\mathcal{B}}u_\phi^U, {}^{\mathcal{B}}u_\theta^U, {}^{\mathcal{B}}u_\psi^U]^\top$.

In practice, the Autonomous Surface Vehicle (ASV) needs to determine the target position while keeping in formation with the AUV. Meanwhile, the AUV must also keep in formation with the ASV while avoiding underwater obstacles. Therefore, the control inputs can be written as:

$$^{\mathcal{B}}u^S = K_P \cdot {}^{\mathcal{P}}u^S + K_V \cdot {}^{\mathcal{V}}u^S \tag{2a}$$

$$^{\mathcal{B}}u^U = {}^{\mathcal{O}}u^U + {}^{\mathcal{V}}u^U + {}^{\mathcal{P}}u^U \tag{2b}$$

where $^{\mathcal{P}}u^S$ is calculated by the global planner and PD controller developed in [10], which will send the ASV to a target position during an exploration mission. Control inputs $^{\mathcal{V}}u^S$ and $^{\mathcal{V}}u^U$ are generated by Virtual Elastic Tether (VET) mentioned in [24], which keeps the robots in each others' Line of Sight (LoS) using a mutual visual-based connection. $^{O}\boldsymbol{u}^{U}$ represents the control inputs for the AUV to avoid an obstacle. $^{P}\boldsymbol{u}^{U}$ controls the AUV's depth and roll, pitch angle to a target value, which in our implementation was set to $depth = -1.5$ m, $roll = 0$, and $pitch = 0$. At the initial state, weights meet $K_P = K_V$ and $^{P}\boldsymbol{u}_{\max}^{S} = {}^{V}\boldsymbol{u}_{\max}^{S}$, which means balance weighted are assigned in terms of the ASV following target position and ASV following AUV.

5.2   Onboard Perceptions

The formation of the robots is achieved via Image Based Visual serving (IBVS), and the obstacle detection is based on image sonar on the AUV, meanwhile, the ASV is equipped with a 2D LiDAR for self-localisation [10] and wall detection, as depicted in Fig. 3.

Visual Based Formation. Based on the IBVS [23] leader-follower formation and VET [24], the ASV and AUV in our system inherit such visual-based "connection":

$$^{V}\boldsymbol{u}^{S} = \begin{cases} \Xi^{S}(W_t^{U}, H_t^{U}) & (W_t^{U}, H_t^{U}) \in \Omega_S \\ \Xi_{\max}^{S} & (W_t^{U}, H_t^{U}) \in \Omega_I \end{cases} \tag{3a}$$

$$^{V}\boldsymbol{u}^{U} = \begin{cases} \Xi^{U}(W_t^{S}, H_t^{S}) & (W_t^{S}, H_t^{S}) \in \Omega_S \\ \Xi_{\max}^{U} & (W_t^{S}, H_t^{S}) \in \Omega_I \end{cases} \tag{3b}$$

where (W, H) denote coordinates in the image frame and Ξ is the corresponding controller that functions on both robots to bring each other from (W_t, H_t) to the centre $C(W_C, H_C)$ of its image view, as depicted in Fig. 3 (c). W_C and H_C are determined by the camera resolution. The integration area Ω_I and safe area Ω_S indicate the outer and inner area of the image view, as depicted in Fig. 3 (c).

Image Sonar Based Obstacle Perception. In terms of obstacle detection, a multibeam image sonar was utilised on the AUV, as depicted in Fig. 3 (d), which in practice was handled by a physics-based plugin [5]. The sonar was placed in the front bottom of BlueROV2, facing forward, which gives the online reading of the obstacle in front of the robot. By binarization and clustering the image, and mapping to the effective range of the sonar, we can obtain the distance from the AUV to the obstacle d_O^{U}.

LiDAR Based Wall Perception. The 2D LiDAR mounted on the ASV serves two primary functions: 1) it provides data for surface self-localization, and 2) it detects the proximity of the nearest wall to the ASV, with $d_W^{S} < 0$ indicating a left-side wall and $d_W^{S} > 0$ indicating proximity to a right-side wall, as shown in Fig. 3 (b). For the purpose of this work, it is assumed that any obstacle the ASV sees extends fully below the surface.

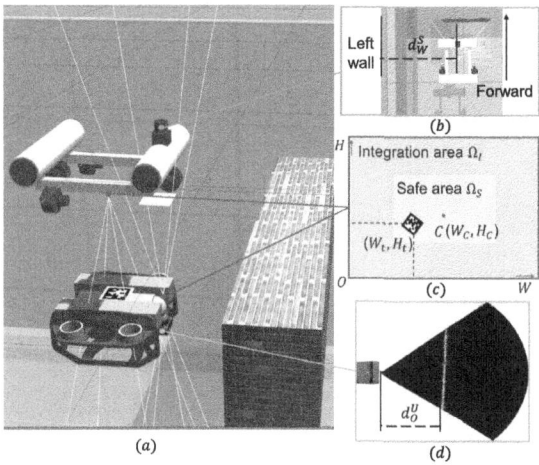

Fig. 3. Illustration of onboard perception: a), the overall setup within a simulated tank environment; b), the ASV's mechanism for detecting the distance d_W^S to the nearest wall, with $d_W^S < 0$ indicating a left-side wall and $d_W^S > 0$ for a right-side wall; c), the shared visual perspective of both robots, with the tag (W_t, H_t) denoting the position of the robot in the image view at time t; d), the use of image sonar by the AUV for obstacle detection.

5.3 Dog Walking Paradigm Implementation: Principles

To apply the dog walking paradigm in the context of underwater cooperative obstacle avoidance, the following basic principles can be designed:

Hierarchical Implicit Communication. Similar to the dog walking scenario, the communication hierarchy is demonstrated in Fig. 4 and can be dissected into three levels. **Level 0** represents that the ASV and AUV are "connected" via a visual-based connection, as per (3a-b).

At **Level 1**, the AUV detects the obstacle within the sonar range. When the distance to the obstacle meets $d_O^U \leq d_S^U$, where d_S^U represents the safe distance to the obstacle, collision avoidance action must be taken:

$$\begin{bmatrix} ^{\mathcal{O}}u_x^U \\ ^{\mathcal{O}}u_y^U \end{bmatrix} = \begin{bmatrix} \min\{\frac{\alpha}{d_O^U}, \Xi_{\max|x}^U\} \\ \lambda \cdot \min\{\frac{\alpha}{d_O^U}, \Xi_{\max|y}^U\} \end{bmatrix} \tag{4}$$

where α is a consistent parameter for calculating the repulsive and rotational force from the obstacle. Other subparts of $^{\mathcal{O}}\boldsymbol{u}^U$ are equal to 0, and λ denotes the directional parameter. Therefore, from (2b), (3b), and (4), we can obtain that when an obstacle is getting close, the AUV will move into Ω_I and eventually

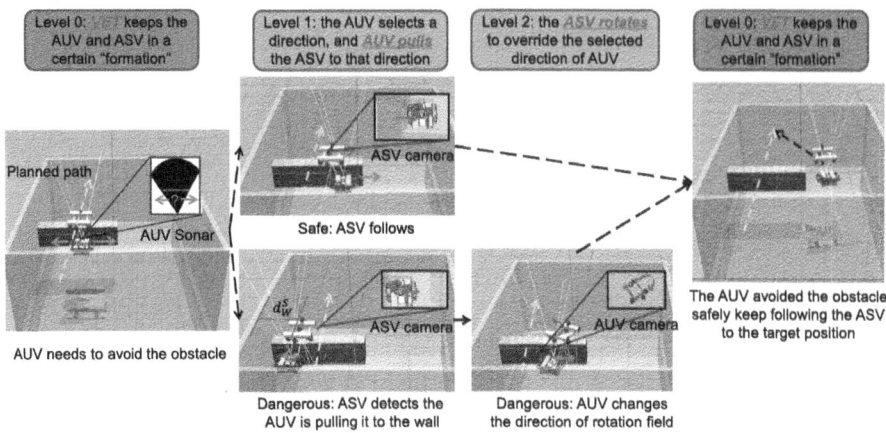

Fig. 4. Cooperative underwater obstacle avoidance with dog walking paradigm. Similar to Fig. 2, the three-tiered (Level 0–2) connection hierarchy is color-coded in green, blue, and purple, respectively. Implicit communication is highlighted in red, with red arrows representing the interaction between the ASV and the AUV. (Color figure online)

$^{O}u^{U} = {}^{V}u^{U}$, the robot will be stuck in an equilibrium position. To avoid that, the ASV must notice such equilibrium and take action. A weighting mechanism was designed to dynamically set K_P and K_V in (2a):

$$
\begin{cases}
K_P = K_V & \int_{t-t_o}^{t} k(t)\,dt < t_o \\
K_P = \beta \cdot K_V & \int_{t-t_o}^{t} k(t)\,dt \geq t_o
\end{cases}
\tag{5}
$$

above equation determines the relationship between K_P and K_V at time t, where the interval time t_o and weighting coefficient β are consistent parameter, β meets $0 < \beta < 1$, and $k(t)$ can be written as follows:

$$
k(t) =
\begin{cases}
0 & (W_t^U, H_t^U) \in \Omega_S \\
1 & (W_t^U, H_t^U) \in \Omega_I
\end{cases},
\tag{6}
$$

(5) and (6) denote that when the AUV stays in the integration area Ω_I over a specified time t_o due to the equilibrium, the control inputs of the formation in (2) will be assigned higher weights than target following, therefore the ASV will be pulled towards the AUV to let the AUV avoid the obstacle until the AUV gets back in the safe area Ω_S again, as depicted at the top of the second stage in Fig. 4.

However, as the AUV does not perceive the information where the wall is, it can not evaluate different direction selections. Conversely, as the ASV perceives the location of the wall, when the AUV selects a dangerous direction to avoid the obstacle, as depicted at the bottom of the second stage in Fig. 4, the ASV must correct such direction selection via **Level 2** implicit communication mechanism.

Algorithm 1. Level 2 indicator - ASV

Input: (W_t^U, H_t^U), d_W^S, d_S^S, t_1 and $^B u_\psi^S$

  1: **while** $|d_W^S| \leq d_S^S$ and $(W_t^U, H_t^U) \in \Omega_I$ **Do:**

  2:     $^B u_\psi^S = \,^B u_\psi^S + \frac{d_W^S}{|d_W^S|} \cdot \,^C u_\psi^S$

  3:     $\mu = \frac{d_W^S}{|d_W^S|}$

  4:     Sleep for time t_1

Output: $^B u_\psi^S$, μ

In the context of dog walking, when a walker perceives that the dog is pulling towards an undesirable object, such as a dirty stick, corrective action is taken by sharply yanking the leash. This creates a significant pulling force, overriding the dog's stick choice. Analogously, when the ASV detects that the AUV is pulling it towards a potentially hazardous proximity to a wall, the ASV initiates a rapid rotational maneuver away from the nearest wall. This maneuver is detailed in Algorithm 1. Here, $^C u_\psi^S > 0$ represents a predefined angular velocity of considerable magnitude, enabling the ASV to execute a swift rotational motion within the time t_1. Additionally, μ signifies the direction of this motion, and d_S^S specifies the threshold distance considered safe for the ASV's proximity to the wall. The second stage is how the AUV discerns the direction parameter μ and incorporates it into (4), without any direct communications. To address this, we define λ as follows:

$$\lambda = \frac{^V \psi_t^S}{|^V \psi_t^S|}, \text{ when } {}^V \psi_t^S - {}^V \psi_{t-t_1}^S \geq {}^V \psi_1^S \tag{7}$$

where $^V \psi_t^S$ denotes the yaw angle of the ASV relative to the AUV, which can be acquired using the AprilTag [20] library, and $^V \psi_1^S$ signifies a predefined threshold. This setup facilitates the detection of rapid rotational movements of the ASV within the timeframe t_1. Upon detecting such movement, the AUV will modify its obstacle avoidance direction by adjusting λ, which is subsequently factored into (4) to coordinate the AUV's maneuvers.

Formation Constraint. Similar to the dog walking paradigm, the formation constraint aims to ensure a mutual connection between the two agents. In the context of visual based formation (3a-b), this constraint can be represented as follows:

$$\begin{aligned} (W_t^U, H_t^U) &\in (\Omega_S \cap \Omega_I), \\ (W_t^S, H_t^S) &\in (\Omega_S \cap \Omega_I). \end{aligned} \tag{8}$$

The above equation indicates that, from the perspective of the image view, neither robot should deviate from the LoS at any time t. Analogous to a dog leash breaking under excessive force, thereby breaching the formation constraint, similar challenges arise in multi-agent underwater systems. Efforts can be made to improve the robustness of (8) with better IBVS parameters, but ensuring its absolute reliability is challenging due to unforeseeable disturbances. This particular challenge lies beyond the scope of our current work.

6 Experiments

To validate the proposed cooperative obstacle avoidance architecture, we utilised a Gazebo-based simulation running on ROS (Robot Operating System) Melodic.

6.1 Simulation Setup

Robots. As introduced in Sect. 5, the MallARD ASV was utilised as the leader agent (walker), where the surface hydrodynamics were handled by the freefloating plugin [14], while the BlueROV served as the follower agent (dog), where the underwater hydrodynamics were managed by the UUV simulator plugin [16].

Assumption. The underwater robot is constrained to maneuver at a fixed depth throughout the simulation. Given the cluttered environment and the reliance on visual connections between the robots, attempts to avoid obstacles by descending ($-z$ direction) would result in the obstruction obscuring the camera's view. Conversely, ascending ($+z$ direction) to avoid obstacles risks reducing the distance to the surface agent excessively, potentially resulting in a loss of the LoS necessary for formation.

Tasks. The objectives for the two robots were to navigate from the start to the target position. The interval time threshold was set to $t_0 = 4$, and (5) was set to run at 1 Hz in practice. The follower's initial choice for the obstacle avoidance direction was to the **left** ($\lambda = 1$) in all experiments.

Baseline. For comparison, we also implemented the control architecture proposed in [23,24], where the robots are connected via VET-IBVS but without implementing the dog walking paradigm.

6.2 Case Studies on Single Obstacle Scenarios

Case 1 - Small Obstacle on the Right. As depicted in Fig. 5a, MallARD leads the BlueROV from the starting point towards the target location. Upon encountering an underwater obstacle, in both baseline and dog walking systems, the BlueROV initiates a lateral maneuver to avoid collision, consequently influencing MallARD's navigation path. After circumventing the obstacle, both robots realign to the planned trajectory with the baseline and dog walking enhanced system. In dog walking system, the lateral maneuver of BlueROV results in pulling (Level 1) MallARD to the left from $t = 11\,s$ until they successfully circumvent the obstacle at $t = 17\,s$.

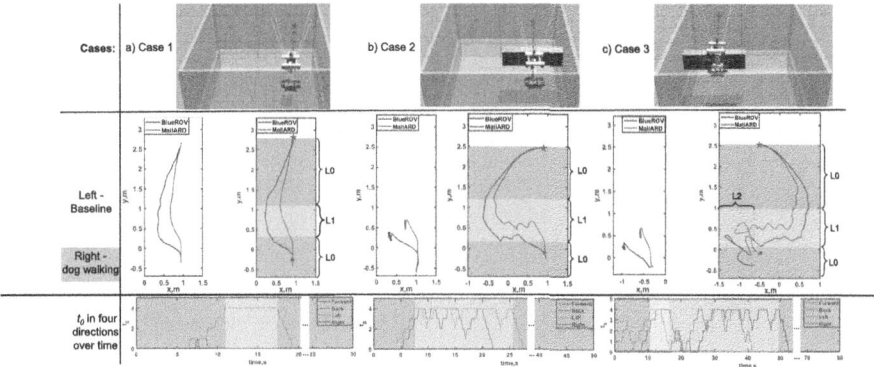

Fig. 5. Comparison of case studies in single obstacle scenarios within a virtual tank measuring $5\,\mathrm{m} \times 4\,\mathrm{m} \times 2.5\,\mathrm{m}$. (Color figure online)

Case 2 - Large Obstacle on the Right. As shown in Fig. 5b, upon encountering the large obstacle, in the baseline setup, MallARD, unaware of the obstacle and BlueROV's maneuver, continues toward the target. This lack of coordination causes BlueROV to become stuck, preventing both robots from reaching the target. In contrast, the "dog walking" paradigm employs three-level implicit communication and formation constraints. When BlueROV encounters the obstacle, it signals MallARD by pulling left and back, prompting MallARD to adjust its behavior and allow for successful obstacle avoidance.

Case 3 - Large Obstacle on the Left. Unlike in case 2, the system's safe direction for obstacle avoidance conflicts with the initial chosen maneuver direction $(\lambda - 1)$, as depicted in Fig. 5c. The baseline system becomes stuck, similar to case 2. With dog walking paradigm, BlueROV pulls MallARD left (Level 1, blue in Fig. 5c), but as MallARD complies, it detects this path is unsafe due to proximity to the left wall. MallARD then executes a Level 2 rotational maneuver (purple in Fig. 5c), countering BlueROV's initial pull. Recognising this cue, BlueROV adjusts its trajectory to the safe right direction $(\lambda \rightarrow -1)$. This coordinated adjustment allows the robots to successfully avoid the obstacle, much like a walker guiding a dog away from a hazard.

6.3 Navigation Experiment in Obscured Tank

This experiment aims to validate that, with the dog walking paradigm, the cooperative system can autonomously explore an obstacle-filled environment without collisions. As shown in Fig. 6a, two robots are tasked to explore a confined, cluttered tank, moving from the start to the target position along a planned surface

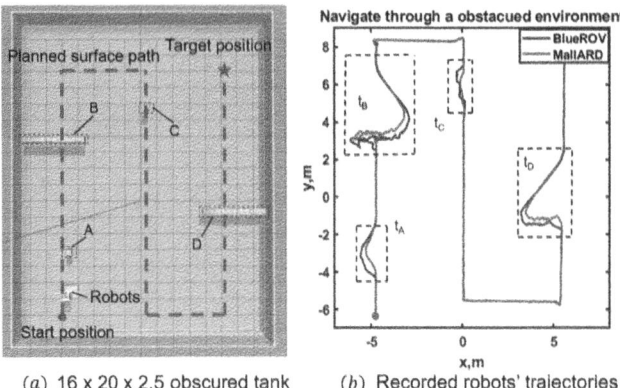

(a) 16 x 20 x 2.5 obscured tank   (b) Recorded robots' trajectories

Fig. 6. Dog walking experiment: autonomous navigation in a cluttered tank with initial $\lambda = 1$. The areas t_A, t_B, t_C, and t_D correspond to the maneuver of the robots around obstacles A, B, C, and D.

path. The environment includes various obstacles: small (A and C), large on the left (B), and large on the right (D). With an initial $\lambda = 1$, the robots are required to take actions across all levels (level 0 to level 2). The results are shown in Fig. 6b.

6.4 Summary

Results indicate that with dog walking-inspired paradigm, fully distributed cooperative AUV-ASV underwater obstacle avoidance was achieved. It is worth noting that in previous work, the authors suggest VET [24] could potentially be useful in helping robotic obstacle avoidance in communication and localisation constrained environments, this work is the extension of VET in such direction.

7 Conclusion and Future Work

This study introduces a novel approach to cooperative obstacle avoidance in cluttered underwater environments using a dog walking-inspired paradigm. By leveraging implicit communication and virtual connections like walking a dog, we demonstrate this strategy's effectiveness in coordinating multi-agent underwater systems. The analogy between dog walking and autonomous agent navigation provides a fresh perspective on distributed multi-agent systems, where role differentiation and objective balance should be emphasised.

The success of this solution on fully distributed cooperative underwater obstacle avoidance highlights the potential of extending the dog walking paradigm to broader scenarios across various domains (ground or aerial), particularly those characterised by extreme conditions. While the results showcase the feasibility of our approach, the observed robot trajectories are not yet optimised. Future efforts will focus on applying advanced optimisation techniques to enhance the robustness and efficiency of the solution.

Acknowledgments. This work was supported by Chinese Scholarship Council-University of Manchester joint programme. The authors acknowledge the support provided by EPSRC (Hot Robotics: EP/T011491/1) and the Robotics and AI Collaboration (RAICo).

References

1. Bai, C., Yan, P., Pan, W., Guo, J.: Learning-based multi-robot formation control with obstacle avoidance. IEEE Trans. Intell. Transp. Syst. **23**(8), 11811–11822 (2022). https://doi.org/10.1109/tits.2021.3107336
2. Berlinger, F., Gauci, M., Nagpal, R.: Implicit coordination for 3D underwater collective behaviors in a fish-inspired robot swarm. Sci. Robot. **6**(50) (2021). https://doi.org/10.1126/scirobotics.abd8668
3. Cai, W., Wu, Y., Zhang, M.: Three-dimensional obstacle avoidance for autonomous underwater robot. IEEE Sens. Lett. **4**(11), 1–4 (2020). https://doi.org/10.1109/lsens.2020.3034309
4. Chen, Y.F., Liu, M., Everett, M., How, J.P.: Decentralized non-communicating multiagent collision avoidance with deep reinforcement learning. In: 2017 IEEE International Conference on Robotics and Automation (ICRA). IEEE (2017). https://doi.org/10.1109/icra.2017.7989037
5. Choi, W.S., et al.: Physics-based modelling and simulation of multibeam echosounder perception for autonomous underwater manipulation. Front. Robot. AI **8** (2021). https://doi.org/10.3389/frobt.2021.706646
6. Dergachev, S., Yakovlev, K.: Distributed multi-agent navigation based on reciprocal collision avoidance and locally confined multi-agent path finding. In: 2021 IEEE 17th International Conference on Automation Science and Engineering (CASE). IEEE (2021). https://doi.org/10.1109/case49439.2021.9551564
7. Fang, Z., et al.: Autonomous underwater vehicle formation control and obstacle avoidance using multi-agent generative adversarial imitation learning. Ocean Eng. **262**, 112182 (2022). https://doi.org/10.1016/j.oceaneng.2022.112182
8. Fossen, T.I., Fjellstad, O.E.: Nonlinear modelling of marine vehicles in 6 degrees of freedom. Math. Model. Syst. **1**(1), 17–27 (1995). DOIurl-https://doi.org/10.1080/13873959508837004
9. Groves, K., Dimitrov, M., Peel, H., Marjanovic, O., Lennox, B.: Model identification of a small omnidirectional aquatic surface vehicle: a practical implementation. In: 2020 IEEE/RSJ International Conference on Intelligent Robots and Systems (IROS). IEEE (2020). https://doi.org/10.1109/iros45743.2020.9341142
10. Groves, K., West, A., Gornicki, K., Watson, S., Carrasco, J., Lennox, B.: MallARD: An autonomous aquatic surface vehicle for inspection and monitoring of wet nuclear storage facilities. Robotics **8**(2), 47 (2019). https://doi.org/10.3390/robotics8020047
11. Hu, J., Bhowmick, P., Jang, I., Arvin, F., Lanzon, A.: A decentralized cluster formation containment framework for multirobot systems. IEEE Trans. Robot. **37**(6), 1936–1955 (2021). https://doi.org/10.1109/tro.2021.3071615

12. Huang, H., et al.: Vision-based distributed multi-UAV collision avoidance via deep reinforcement learning for navigation. In: 2022 IEEE/RSJ International Conference on Intelligent Robots and Systems (IROS). IEEE (2022). https://doi.org/10.1109/iros47612.2022.9981803

13. Hwang, H., et al.: System configuration and navigation of a guide dog robot: toward animal guide dog-level guiding work. In: 2023 IEEE International Conference on Robotics and Automation (ICRA). IEEE (2023). https://doi.org/10.1109/icra48891.2023.10160573

14. Kermorgant, O.: A dynamic simulator for underwater vehicle-manipulators. In: International Conference on Simulation, Modeling, and Programming for Autonomous Robots Simpar. Springer, Bergamo, Italy (2014). https://inria.hal.science/hal-01065812

15. Li, M., Jie, Y., Kong, Y., Cheng, H.: Decentralized global connectivity maintenance for multi-robot navigation: a reinforcement learning approach. In: 2022 International Conference on Robotics and Automation (ICRA). IEEE (2022). https://doi.org/10.1109/icra46639.2022.9812163

16. Manhães, M.M.M., Scherer, S.A., Voss, M., Douat, L.R., Rauschenbach, T.: UUV simulator: a gazebo-based package for underwater intervention and multi-robot simulation. In: OCEANS 2016 MTS/IEEE Monterey. pp. 1–8 (2016). https://doi.org/10.1109/OCEANS.2016.7761080

17. Panagou, D., Kumar, V.: Cooperative visibility maintenance for leader-follower formations in obstacle environments. IEEE Trans. Robot. **30**(4), 831–844 (2014). https://doi.org/10.1109/tro.2014.2304774

18. Qu, F., Wang, Z., Yang, L., Wu, Z.: A journey toward modeling and resolving doppler in underwater acoustic communications. IEEE Commun. Mag. **54**(2), 49–55 (2016). https://doi.org/10.1109/mcom.2016.7402260

19. Schulman, J., et al.: Motion planning with sequential convex optimization and convex collision checking. Int. J. Robot. Res. **33**(9), 1251–1270 (2014). https://doi.org/10.1177/0278364914528132

20. Wang, J., Olson, E.: AprilTag 2: efficient and robust fiducial detection. In: 2016 IEEE/RSJ International Conference on Intelligent Robots and Systems (IROS). pp. 4193–4198. IEEE (2016). https://doi.org/10.1109/IROS.2016.7759617

21. Watson, S., Duecker, D.A., Groves, K.: Localisation of unmanned underwater vehicles (UUVs) in complex and confined environments: A review. Sensors **20**(21), 6203 (2020). https://doi.org/10.3390/s20216203

22. Xanthidis, M., et al.: Navigation in the presence of obstacles for an agile autonomous underwater vehicle. In: 2020 IEEE International Conference on Robotics and Automation (ICRA). IEEE (2020). https://doi.org/10.1109/icra40945.2020.9197558

23. Yao, K., et al.: Image-based visual servoing switchable leader-follower control of heterogeneous multi-agent underwater robot system. In: 2023 IEEE International Conference on Robotics and Automation (ICRA). pp. 5200–5206 (2023). https://doi.org/10.1109/ICRA48891.2023.10160853

24. Yao, K., et al.: Virtual elastic tether: a new approach for multi-agent navigation in confined aquatic environments (2024). https://arxiv.org/abs/2403.10629

Comparative Evaluation of Reinforcement Learning and Model Predictive Control for 6DoF Position Control of an Autonomous Underwater Vehicle

Sümer Tunçay[1]([envelope]) [ORCID], Alain Andres[2] [ORCID], and Ignacio Carlucho[1] [ORCID]

[1] Heriot-Watt University, Edinburgh EH144AS, UK
{st2126,ignacio.carlucho}@hw.ac.uk
[2] TECNALIA, Basque Research and Technology Alliance (BRTA),
San Sebastian, Spain
alain.andres@tecnalia.com

Abstract. Autonomous Underwater Vehicles (AUVs) require precise and robust control strategies for 3D pose regulation in dynamic underwater environments. In this study, we present a comparative evaluation of model-free and model-based control methods for AUV position control. Specifically, we analyze the performance of neural network controllers trained by three Reinforcement Learning (RL) algorithms—Proximal Policy Optimization (PPO), Twin Delayed Deep Deterministic Policy Gradient (TD3), and Soft Actor-Critic (SAC)—alongside a Model Predictive Control (MPC) baseline. We train our RL methods in a simplified AUV simulator implemented in PyTorch, while our evaluation is done in a realistic marine robotics simulator called Stonefish. Controllers are evaluated on the basis of tracking accuracy, robustness to disturbances, and generalization capabilities. Our results show that, MPC suffers from unmodeled dynamics such as disturbances, whereas RL demonstrates adaptation capabilities to disturbances. Also, although MPC demonstrates strong control performance, it requires an accurate model, high compute power and a careful implementation to run in real-time whereas the control frequency of RL policies is only bound by the inference time of the policy network. Among RL-based controllers, PPO achieves the best overall performance, both in terms of training stability and control accuracy. This study provides insight into the feasibility of RL-based controllers for AUV position control, offering guidance for selecting suitable control strategies in real-world marine robotics applications.

Keywords: Autonomous Underwater Vehicles · Reinforcement Learning · Optimal Control

1 Introduction

Autonomous Underwater Vehicles (AUVs) are increasingly vital tools for a wide range of marine applications, including oceanographic research, environmental monitoring, and offshore infrastructure inspection as well as maintenance

A. Cavalcanti et al. (Eds.): TAROS 2025, LNAI 16045, pp. 381–394, 2026.
https://doi.org/10.1007/978-3-032-01486-3_29

[24]. Their ability to operate independently significantly contributes to the zero-carbon mission by reducing the operational costs and environmental impact associated with traditional, manned surface vessel deployments. The inherent autonomy of these vehicles requires robust and precise control capabilities. Central to this requirement is 6-Degrees-of-Freedom (6DOF) position control, which encompasses the accurate maintenance of a desired pose in three-dimensional space, as well as the precise tracking of reference trajectories. However, this is not an easy task, due to several factors inherent to underwater environments. First, the hydrodynamic forces acting on the AUV such as drag, lift, and buoyancy exhibit strong nonlinearities and are very difficult to model with precision. Secondly, AUVs are subject to a multitude of external disturbances, ranging from persistent ocean currents to instantaneous wave-induced motions and turbulent flows, all of which can drastically perturb their intended trajectory [8]. Finally, commercial concerns put hardware limits to AUVs, which limits the available compute power. These combined challenges show the need for advanced control methodologies capable of navigating the dynamic and uncertain nature of underwater environments, under computational power constraints.

Traditional control methods for AUVs have often relied on Proportional-Integral-Derivative (PID) controllers [2]. Over the last decade, with the substantial developments in compute power technologies and optimization algorithms, control paradigms are slowly but surely shifting towards real-time optimization-based control methods, predominantly called Model Predictive Control (MPC). MPC offers precise control, subject to environment and other constraints explicitly [21]. Nonetheless, MPC requires an accurate model of the AUV and its environment, which presents a significant challenge, as maintaining model fidelity under rapidly changing operational conditions is difficult. Furthermore, the required compute capability to deploy an MPC restricts its feasibility for real-time AUV applications.

More recently, Reinforcement Learning (RL) has emerged as a promising alternative for developing control strategies for complex robotic systems [1], thanks to the major algorithmic and structural breakthroughs in machine learning [17]. RL algorithms equipped with the representation capabilities of neural networks, enable agents to learn optimal control policies through trial and error, without requiring explicit models of the system dynamics. These policies are mostly trained in simulation, due to time and safety restrictions. However, albeit trained in a simulation, techniques such as domain randomization enable handling uncertainties and nonlinearities that are inherent to robotics applications [4].

This paper investigates the feasibility and performance of RL-based control methods for AUV 6-DOF pose control. We conduct a comparative evaluation of three popular RL algorithms—Proximal Policy Optimization (PPO) [20], Twin Delayed Deep Deterministic Policy Gradient (TD3) [9], and Soft Actor-Critic (SAC) [10]—alongside a MPC baseline. We train our RL agents in a simplified AUV simulator implemented in PyTorch [19], focusing on achieving robust pose control. We then evaluate the performance of the trained controllers in a realistic

Fig. 1. An AUV in the Stonefish marine robotics simulator performing accurate position and attitude control via a PPO policy. **Left:** $\phi_{cmd}, \theta_{cmd}, \psi_{cmd} = 0°$, **Middle:** $\phi_{cmd}, \psi = 0°, \theta_{cmd} = 60°$, **Right:** $\phi_{cmd}, \theta_{cmd} = 60°, \psi_{cmd} = 30°$

marine robotics simulator called Stonefish [6], assessing their tracking accuracy and robustness to disturbances. As a result, this study provides practical insights into RL-based control within this application domain. This exposition is intended to serve as a valuable resource for future practitioners, facilitating the implementation and advancement of RL control strategies in similar scenarios. Our evaluations demonstrate that RL-based policies, particularly those trained using PPO, exhibit superior performance compared to MPC in disturbance rejection tasks, while achieving comparable accuracy in trajectory tracking tasks under nominal conditions. Snapshots presenting the attitude control performance of PPO policy in the Stonefish simulator are given in Fig. 1. Moreover, RL policies are significantly more computationally efficient during deployment, as their performance is constrained only by inference time. In contrast, MPC requires substantial computational resources due to its iterative optimization process. On the same hardware utilized in this study (*Intel(R) Core(TM) i7-14650HX*), RL policies can operate at approximately 4000 Hz, whereas MPC is limited to around 50 Hz with a 1.5 s prediction horizon.

The remainder of this paper is organized as follows. Section 2 provides the necessary background and discusses relevant work for MPC and RL in AUV 6DoF control. Section 3 outlines the implementation details for MPC and RL agents. Section 4 presents the empirical results and a comprehensive performance analysis under various test conditions. Finally, Sect. 5 concludes the paper by summarizing the findings and discussing potential directions for future research.

2   Background and Relevant Work

2.1   Model Predictive Control

MPC refers to a family of control algorithms that pose the control problem as a constrained optimization problem, wherein a cost function is minimized subject to the system dynamics and operational constraints over a finite prediction horizon. The choice of an appropriate MPC approach depends on the problem's complexity and available computational resources. Contrary to more traditional approaches such as PID control, MPC explicitly considers system dynamics, control and state constraints, and future objectives within an optimization framework. At each time step, MPC optimizes a sequence of control inputs but applies only the first one before re-solving the problem at the next step. This process, also referred to as receding horizon control, introduces a feedback mechanism, providing robustness. Indeed, MPC has been extensively studied for AUV control and has been demonstrated to be effective across various tasks, ranging from velocity regulation to position control and trajectory tracking [18,22,25]. In this study, MPC serves as a strong baseline to compare against in terms of control performance.

2.2   Reinforcement Learning

The RL framework revolves around the idea of an agent interacting with its environment through its policy The agent's objective is to maximize the cumulative rewards given by the environment [23]. More formally, this framework is mathematically represented as a Markov Decision Process (MDP) defined by the tuple $(\mathcal{S}, \mathcal{A}, \mathcal{T}, \mathcal{R}, \gamma)$ where $s \in \mathcal{S}$ are states, $a \in \mathcal{A}$ are actions, $\mathcal{T} : \mathcal{S} \times \mathcal{A} \to \mathcal{S}$ is the state transition function, $\mathcal{R} : \mathcal{S} \times \mathcal{A} \to \mathbb{R}$ is the reward function associated with the task of interest, and $\gamma \in [0, 1]$ is the discount factor. The objective is to obtain a policy $\pi : \mathcal{S} \to \mathcal{A}$ so that the expected discounted sum of rewards, the return, $\mathbb{E}[\sum_{t=0}^{\infty} \gamma^t r_t]$ is maximized.

A Partially Observable Markov Decision Process (POMDP) extends the RL framework to environments where the agent has limited state information [14]. It is defined by the tuple $(\mathcal{S}, \mathcal{A}, \mathcal{T}, \mathcal{R}, \Omega, \mathcal{O}, \gamma)$, where Ω is the observation space and $\mathcal{O}$ is the observation model. The goal is to learn a policy $\pi : \Omega \to \mathcal{A}$ that maximizes the expected discounted reward. In the context of continuous control, three widely used model-free RL algorithms are PPO, TD3 and SAC, which we focus on in this study.

RL has been successfully applied to robotics applications for various tasks in various fields and yielded innovative solutions for autonomous learning and decision-making in complex, dynamic environments. One notable example of that is in [13], where authors surpass human-level capabilities in drone racing tasks using deep RL. In [15], authors control a small scale UAV using only onboard sensors with model-based RL paradigm. In the field of marine robotics, in [3], authors controlled an AUV directly through thruster commands with deep RL with actor-critic structure. In [11], deep RL has been applied for adaptive path planning tasks. Trajectory tracking task of an AUV using deep RL techniques is demonstrated in [26]. In [27], authors utilize RL for a 3D docking task for an AUV.

3   Implementation Details

3.1   Model Predictive Control Formulation

We consider a discrete-time constrained optimization problem, where the cost function is quadratic, and the system dynamics follow the fully nonlinear equations of motion based on the standard Fossen model [8]:

$$\min_{x,u} J = \sum_{k=0}^{H-1} \frac{1}{2}(x_k^T Q x_k + u_k^T R u_k) + x_H^T Q_H x_H$$

$$\begin{aligned}
\text{s.t.} \quad & x_{k+1} = f(x_k, u_k), \quad k = 0, \ldots, H-1 \\
& \underline{x} \le x_k \le \bar{x}, \quad k = 0, \ldots, H \\
& \underline{u} \le u_k \le \bar{u}, \quad k = 0, \ldots, H_c - 1 \\
& u_k = u_{H_c-1}, \quad k = H_c, \ldots, H-1.
\end{aligned} \tag{1}$$

where Q, R, Q_H represent state cost, control cost, and terminal cost matrices. The prediction and control horizon are denoted as H and H_c respectively, system dynamics are iterated via $f(x_k, u_k)$ and state and control constraints are given by $\underline{x}, \bar{x}$ and $\underline{u}, \bar{u}$ respectively. The dynamics are linearized at each time step around the current operating condition to form a Quadratic Program (QP), which is solved using CVXPY [7].

3.2   RL-Based Controllers

The control problem is formulated as a POMDP. This is primarily because the agent only receives observations from its sensors and does not have access to the full state of the system. For a fair comparison, all agents are provided with the same observation and action spaces, as well as an identical reward function.

Observation Space. $\Omega \in \mathbb{R}^{12}$ is composed of the following components:

$$\Omega : (e_x^b, e_y^b, e_z^b, e_\phi, e_\theta, e_\psi, u, v, w, p, q, r) \tag{2}$$

where e_x^b, e_y^b, e_z^b represent the positional errors represented in the vehicle's body frame, defined as the difference between the current position and the reference position in the vehicle's body frame $e^b = ref^b - x^b$. e_ϕ, e_θ, e_ψ correspond to the errors in the vehicle's orientation, again defined as the difference from a reference orientation. The remaining terms, u, v, w, denote the linear velocities of the vehicle along the body axes, while p, q, r represent the angular velocities in the body frame. The decision to use errors as the environment states, rather than separating them into reference and system states, is intended to yield a more compact, minimal and easy to train policy. Additionally, the errors are represented in the vehicle's body frame to simplify training, as this representation removes dependencies on the vehicle's orientation relative to the environment, thereby ensuring that the policy is independent of the agent's attitude. However, one needs to remember to transform the observations accurately during deployment.

Action Space. $\mathcal{A} \in \mathbb{R}^6$ is composed of the forces and torques along 6DoF:

$$\mathcal{A} : (F_x, F_y, F_z, \tau_x, \tau_y, \tau_z) \tag{3}$$

The decision to use forces F_x, F_y, F_z and torques τ_x, τ_y, τ_z as the action space, rather than low-level thruster commands, is aimed at making the agent more versatile and agnostic to specific thruster configurations.

Reward Function. $\mathcal{R} \in \mathbb{R}$ is given as follows:

$$\mathcal{R}(o_t, a_t) = \lambda_1 r_e + \lambda_2 r_\omega + \lambda_3 r_\tau + \lambda_4 r_{u_{mavg}} \tag{4}$$

with $\lambda_i < 0$, $i \in [1, 4]$ and where

$$r_e = \left\| \Lambda e^b \right\|^2, \quad r_\omega = \left\| \omega \right\|^2, \quad r_\tau = \left\| \tau \right\|^2, \quad r_{u_{mavg}} = \left\| u_{mavg} - u \right\| \tag{5}$$

In r_e term, Λ is a diagonal matrix assigning weights to associated error elements and $e^b \in \mathbb{R}^6$ is the error vector represented in the body frame. This is the main term that incentivizes the agent to achieve the expected goal by penalizing deviations from the current reference point. The errors are computed as described in the observation space, except for the attitude, since the simulation updates the attitude using quaternions, the difference is first calculated in quaternion form and then transformed into a three-parameter representation for the final reward computation. The term r_ω penalizes angular velocities proportional to the squared norm of the current angular velocity ω, which has been observed to be a helpful term for stabilizing training. Similarly, r_τ is introduced to further stabilize training by penalizing torque actions proportional to the squared norm of the currently applied torque. And lastly, as previously shown in [3], the term $r_{u_{mavg}}$ is introduced to mitigate the chattering problem observed encountered with the off-policy algorithms. It penalizes output action deviations from a moving average of the previous 10 actions. Without this term, TD3 and SAC algorithms learn a policy that aggressively varies the applied forces and torques, which is not feasible whatsoever for a real-time robotics application.

4   Experimental Results and Analysis

4.1   Training

The agents were trained for 1 million environment steps, corresponding to 5000 training episodes, with each episode is comprised of 200 steps. In each episode, a random reference position and attitude were assigned in 6DoF within predefined limits: $[-2, 2]$ meters for position and $[-1, 1]$ radians for attitude. Episodic rewards during training for each algorithm are given in Fig. 2. As expected, off-policy algorithms exhibit faster training. However, PPO demonstrates consistent improvement and achieves better overall rewards as training progresses. Also, although the comparisons are made using the same reward formulation,

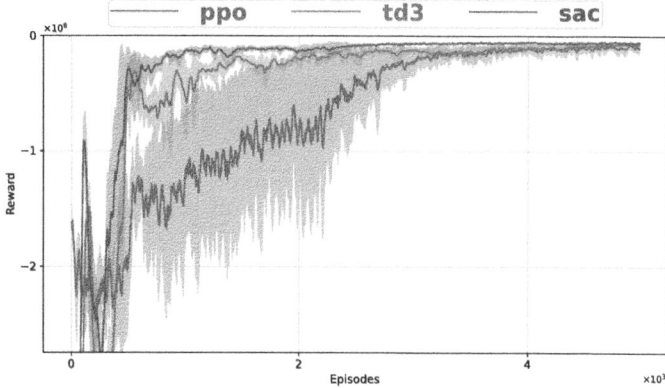

Fig. 2. Training graphs: Average of 5 seeds. An episode is comprised of 200 environment steps, making a total of 1M training steps for all agents.

it is important to emphasize that the PPO algorithm was able to learn good-performing policies using a minimal reward function consisting only of the r_e term, whereas TD3 and SAC required reward shaping with additional terms r_w, r_τ, r_{umavg} to make them learn a feasible policy.

4.2 Control Performance

In order to evaluate control performance, the Stonefish marine robotics simulator is utilized. This simulator incorporates complex hydrodynamic effects acting on the vehicle, making it an ideal simulator to assess performance rapidly and in a safe manner. The robot under consideration is a BlueROV2 Heavy, with its parameters obtained through system identification from the platform in the Ocean Systems Laboratory at Heriot-Watt University. Notably, the trained policies are deployed in a sim2sim zero-shot manner, transferring directly from the PyTorch-based training simulator to the Stonefish marine robotics simulator. The overall control evaluation involves step response analysis, spiral trajectory tracking and square trajectory tracking under constant disturbance. Statistical metrics of experiments are given in Table 1 and Table 2.

Step Response. As a standard metric for assessing control performance, we first analyze the step response of MPC and RL-based policies. As shown in Fig. 3, both MPC and PPO exhibit superior performance in translational and orientational responses, whereas SAC and TD3 struggle to mitigate steady-state errors in attitude. Additionally, PPO generates smooth force and torque outputs, making it well-suited for real-time applications. In contrast, TD3 produces aggressive force outputs that operate near actuator limits. MPC force and torque outputs

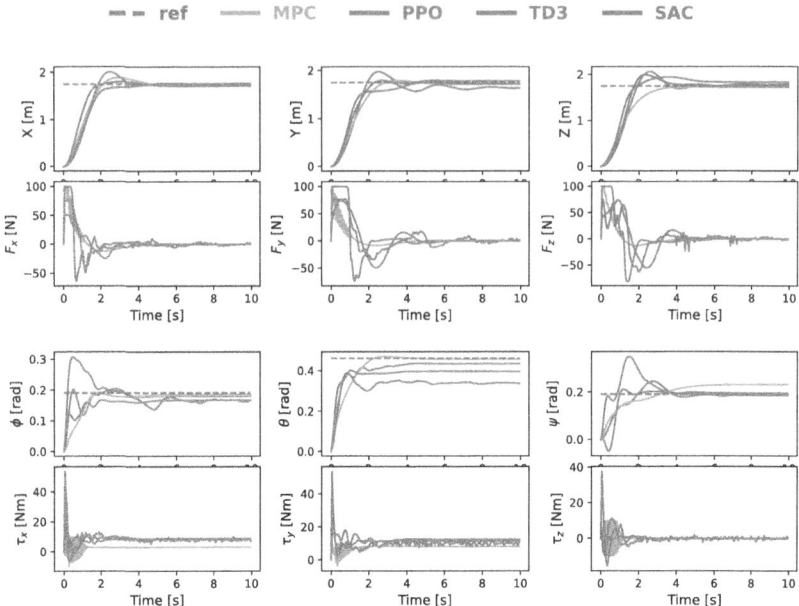

Fig. 3. Step responses for MPC and RL policies for 6DoF control: The first row presents the translational step responses, with the corresponding controller force outputs shown in the second row. Similarly, the third row depicts the orientational step responses, while the corresponding controller torque outputs are provided in the fourth row.

exhibit chattering during the transient phase. Finally, SAC exhibits noisy control actions, characterized by high-frequency, low-magnitude force and torque requests, making it unsuitable for real-time applications.

Trajectory Tracking Performance. To assess the robustness and tracking performance of the control policies, a spiral trajectory tracking evaluation was conducted. The trajectory consists of a continuous ramp-like ascent along the z-axis, while the x and y positions follow sinusoidal oscillations with increasing amplitude. Throughout the trajectory, the vehicle is required to maintain a constant attitude. This test evaluates the controllers' ability to handle complex motion patterns involving simultaneous vertical displacement and lateral oscillations while maintaining precise attitude control. As shown in Fig. 4a, all policies were able to complete the trajectory; however, TD3 and especially SAC exhibited difficulties in maintaining a constant attitude, leading to oscillatory movements throughout the trajectory.

Performance Under Disturbance. Finally, we test the controllers' performance under various disturbance conditions. The disturbances are in the form of constant ocean currents along vehicle's x axis. The tests were conducted using

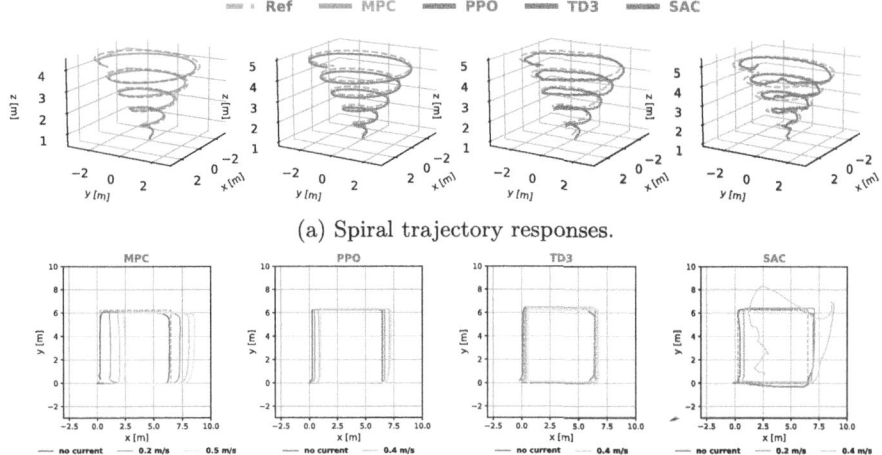

(a) Spiral trajectory responses.

(b) Square trajectory tracking performance under different disturbance conditions for MPC, PPO, TD3 and SAC policies.

Fig. 4. Comparison of trajectory responses for different control strategies. Top: Spiral trajectory. Bottom: Square trajectory under various disturbance conditions.

3 different current speeds, namely 0.2 m/s, 0.4 m/s and 0.5 m/s. After 0.5 m/s, none of the controllers were able to hold the position. The results are given in Fig. 4b. As observed in the figure, MPC fails to compensate for the disturbances introduced by the currents. Instead, the vehicle settles into a steady-state offset proportional to the disturbance magnitude, indicating that the controller lacks sufficient adaptation to unmodeled external forces. In contrast, PPO and TD3 policies demonstrate the ability to counteract the disturbances and maintain position more effectively. Despite the absence of an explicit integral action, as found in classical PID controllers, these policies appear to have implicitly learned disturbance rejection strategies through training in diverse operating conditions. This suggests that reinforcement learning enables the policies to generalize to unseen perturbations by leveraging their experience from varied environmental interactions. SAC policy, however, exhibited significantly weaker disturbance rejection capabilities. While SAC was able to maintain position under low speed currents, its performance deteriorated substantially for higher magnitudes. It was unable to hold its position at 0.5 m/s. These findings suggest that training methodology and exploration strategies may play a crucial role in handling external perturbations effectively.

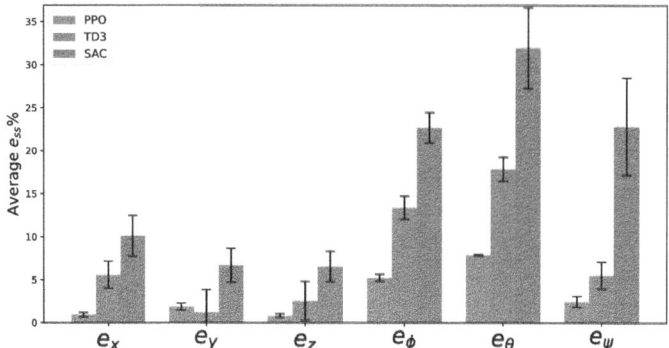

Fig. 5. Bar chart for average steady state error in 6DoF throughout 5000 episodes for PPO, TD3 and SAC agents. The y axis indicate the average steady-state error in percentage, while x-axes indicate errors in 6DoF.

4.3   Empirical Safety and Generalization Evaluation

Since an analytical assessment of the stability of neural network-based controllers is not feasible, we conducted an empirical safety analysis. For the sake of speed, this analysis is made using the training simulator. The evaluation involved deploying the controllers across 5000 reference points sampled within their expected operational region. The operating region is defined as the region agents experienced during their training, namely, a maximum error of 2 m for translational axes and 60° for orientational axes. Throughout these trials, the average steady state tracking error per episode was recorded to evaluate both performance and stability. This assessment also serves as an indicator of the agent's ability to generalize across its operating region. Figure 5 presents the results. Notably, none of the controllers induced instability within the tested conditions. However, TD3 and SAC exhibited significant variability in attitude control performance. Overall, PPO demonstrated superior generalization and safety, with a maximum error of 8 percent on pitch control, while off-policy counterparts exhibited significant average errors on attitude control.

4.4   Reward Landscape Comparison

To gain deeper insights into the performance differences between PPO, TD3, and SAC for 6-DOF AUV position control, we analyzed the reward landscape of each algorithm [16]. Specifically, we sampled two random directions within the high-dimensional policy parameter space. These directions were then used to gradually interpolate from the original trained parameters toward the sampled points, effectively exploring small deviations in the policy space. During this interpolation process, episodic rewards were recorded to examine how perturbations in the policy parameters influenced overall performance. Figure 6 illustrates the resulting reward surfaces in relation to the policy parameter variations.

Table 1. Summary of error metrics for spiral trajectory in Fig. 4a (Spiral) and disturbance tests in Fig. 4b. Presents mean and the standard deviation of the errors throughout trajectories.

Test	Method	e_x [m]	e_y [m]	e_z [m]
Spiral	MPC	-0.06 ± 0.48	0.09 ± 0.56	-0.15 ± 0.04
	PPO	-0.02 ± 0.16	0.01 ± 0.20	-0.14 ± 0.01
	TD3	-0.16 ± 0.26	0.12 ± 0.27	-0.12 ± 0.04
	SAC	-0.14 ± 0.23	0.04 ± 0.29	-0.06 ± 0.09
Disturbance Tests	MPC $0.0m/s$	-0.05 ± 0.33	-0.06 ± 0.54	-0.22 ± 0.02
	PPO $0.0m/s$	-0.01 ± 0.12	0.01 ± 0.16	-0.12 ± 0.01
	TD3 $0.0m/s$	-0.25 ± 0.43	0.04 ± 0.43	-0.10 ± 0.08
	SAC $0.0m/s$	-0.35 ± 0.41	-0.05 ± 0.45	0.09 ± 0.29
	MPC $0.2m/s$	0.69 ± 0.37	-0.06 ± 0.47	-0.24 ± 0.01
	PPO $0.2m/s$	0.49 ± 0.86	0.26 ± 1.27	-0.13 ± 0.00
	TD3 $0.2m/s$	0.03 ± 0.22	0.13 ± 0.27	-0.17 ± 0.02
	SAC $0.2m/s$	0.47 ± 0.30	0.16 ± 0.21	-0.06 ± 0.11
	MPC $0.4m/s$	1.43 ± 0.47	-0.08 ± 0.43	-0.31 ± 0.02
	PPO $0.4m/s$	0.52 ± 0.26	0.08 ± 0.18	-0.20 ± 0.03
	TD3 $0.4m/s$	0.49 ± 0.90	0.37 ± 1.28	-0.26 ± 0.06
	SAC $0.4m/s$	1.69 ± 1.08	0.64 ± 0.92	-0.87 ± 1.01
	MPC $0.5m/s$	1.95 ± 0.61	-0.10 ± 0.43	-0.55 ± 0.03
	PPO $0.5m/s$	0.65 ± 0.34	0.09 ± 0.20	-0.23 ± 0.05
	TD3 $0.5m/s$	0.28 ± 0.16	0.09 ± 0.13	-0.33 ± 0.05

The results show that all three policies exhibit sensitivity to parameter changes. However, the characteristics of the reward landscapes provide further insight into the optimization challenges faced by each algorithm. A noisy reward landscape, marked by irregular fluctuations, complicates the optimization process, as the agent may struggle to discern a clear direction for improvement. In contrast, a smoother landscape with well-defined peaks and valleys simplifies optimization by providing clearer guidance toward a global or local optimum. This distinction in reward landscape structure may explain the observed performance differences, particularly in SAC's behaviour. SAC's learned policy appears to reside in an uncertain local optimum, leading to inconsistent performance, whereas the PPO policy clearly aligns with a distinct, stable optimum location within the policy parameter space.

Table 2. Summary of error metrics for step response in Fig. 3 (Step) and steady-state errors in Fig. 5 (SS %).

Test	Metric	MPC	PPO	TD3	SAC
Step	e_x [m]	0.08 ± 0.21	0.09 ± 0.34	0.14 ± 0.22	0.25 ± 0.39
	e_y [m]	0.07 ± 0.51	0.20 ± 0.60	0.20 ± 0.53	0.24 ± 0.54
	e_z [m]	0.10 ± 0.02	0.18 ± 0.54	0.13 ± 0.50	0.16 ± 0.44
	e_ϕ [rad]	0.05 ± 0.02	0.06 ± 0.10	0.10 ± 0.08	0.10 ± 0.10
	e_θ [rad]	0.07 ± 0.02	0.11 ± 0.15	0.16 ± 0.10	0.26 ± 0.10
	e_ψ [rad]	-0.09 ± 0.11	0.04 ± 0.13	0.05 ± 0.14	-0.03 ± 0.13
SS %	e_x [m]	-	0.96 ± 0.26	5.54 ± 1.51	10.07 ± 2.41
	e_y [m]	-	1.84 ± 0.42	1.13 ± 2.11	6.45 ± 1.97
	e_z [m]	-	0.80 ± 0.23	2.60 ± 2.18	6.46 ± 1.62
	e_ϕ [rad]	-	5.29 ± 0.40	13.32 ± 1.52	23.35 ± 2.20
	e_θ [rad]	-	7.88 ± 0.08	17.83 ± 1.44	32.26 ± 3.43
	e_ψ [rad]	-	2.54 ± 0.64	5.72 ± 1.58	22.58 ± 6.51

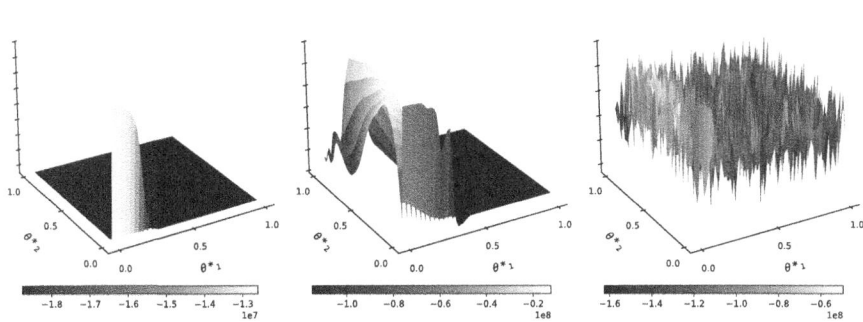

Fig. 6. Episodic reward variations with respect to policy parameter changes along 2 directions for PPO, TD3 and SAC.

5   Conclusion and Future Work

In this study, we investigated the feasibility of model-free RL algorithms for 6DoF position control of an AUV and compared their performance against an MPC baseline. Our results demonstrate that neural networks trained via RL can serve as reliable controllers for this task, with RL-based policies even outperforming MPC in disturbance rejection scenarios. Among the evaluated RL algorithms, PPO emerged as the most effective, owing to its consistent training process and the robustness of the resulting policies. Furthermore, RL-based controllers offer significant advantages in real-time applications compared to MPC due to their lower computational cost. The execution time of our trained policies is solely determined by the neural network inference time, making RL a computationally efficient alternative.

For future work, we plan to enhance RL algorithms by incorporating techniques such as randomized ensembles [5] and dropout Q-functions [12] to improve policy robustness and generalization. Additionally, we aim to deploy the trained controllers on real AUV platforms to validate their performance in real-world operating conditions.

References

1. Abbeel, P., Coates, A., Quigley, M., Ng, A.: An application of reinforcement learning to aerobatic helicopter flight. In: Schölkopf, B., Platt, J., Hoffman, T. (eds.) Advances in Neural Information Processing Systems. vol. 19. MIT Press (2006)
2. Ang, K.H., Chong, G., Li, Y.: PID control system analysis, design, and technology. IEEE Trans. Control Syst. Technol. **13**(4), 559–576 (2005). https://doi.org/10.1109/TCST.2005.847331
3. Carlucho, I., De Paula, M., Wang, S., Petillot, Y., Acosta, G.G.: Adaptive low-level control of autonomous underwater vehicles using deep reinforcement learning. Robot. Auton. Syst. (2018). https://doi.org/10.1016/j.robot.2018.05.016
4. Chen, X., Hu, J., Jin, C., Li, L., Wang, L.: Understanding domain randomization for sim-to-real transfer. ArXiv **abs/2110.03239** (2021)
5. Chen, X., Wang, C., Zhou, Z., Ross, K.W.: Randomized ensembled double q-learning: Learning fast without a model. ArXiv **abs/2101.05982** (2021)
6. Cieślak, P.: Stonefish: an advanced open-source simulation tool designed for marine robotics, with a ROS interface. In: OCEANS 2019 - Marseille. pp. 1–6 (2019). https://doi.org/10.1109/OCEANSE.2019.8867434
7. Diamond, S., Boyd, S.P.: Cvxpy: A python-embedded modeling language for convex optimization. J. Mach. Learn. Res. JMLR **17** (2016)
8. Fossen, T.: Guidance and Control of Ocean Vehicles. Wiley (1994)
9. Fujimoto, S., Hoof, H., Meger, D.: Addressing function approximation error in actor-critic methods. In: International Conference on Machine Learning. pp. 1582–1591 (2018)
10. Haarnoja, T., Zhou, A., Abbeel, P., Levine, S.: Soft actor-critic: off-policy maximum entropy deep reinforcement learning with a stochastic actor. ArXiv **abs/1801.01290** (2018)
11. Hadi, B., Khosravi, A., Sarhadi, P.: Deep reinforcement learning for adaptive path planning and control of an autonomous underwater vehicle. Appl. Ocean Res. **129**, 103326 (2022). https://doi.org/10.1016/j.apor.2022.103326
12. Hiraoka, T., Imagawa, T., Hashimoto, T., Onishi, T., Tsuruoka, Y.: Dropout q-functions for doubly efficient reinforcement learning. In: International Conference on Learning Representations (2022)
13. Kaufmann, E.: Champion-level drone racing using deep reinforcement learning. Nature **620**(7976), 982–987 (2023). https://doi.org/10.1038/s41586-023-06419-4
14. Kurniawati, H.: Partially observable Markov decision processes (pomdps) and robotics. CoRR **abs/2107.07599** (2021). https://arxiv.org/abs/2107.07599
15. Lambert, N.O., Drew, D.S., Yaconelli, J., Calandra, R., Levine, S., Pister, K.S.J.: Low level control of a quadrotor with deep model-based reinforcement learning (2019)

16. Li, H., Xu, Z., Taylor, G., Goldstein, T.: Visualizing the loss landscape of neural nets. ArXiv **abs/1712.09913** (2017)

17. Mnih, V., et al.: Playing Atari with deep reinforcement learning (2013). http://arxiv.org/abs/1312.5602, cite arxiv:1312.5602Comment: NIPS Deep Learning Workshop 2013

18. Molero, A., Dunia, R., Cappelletto, J., Fernandez, G.: Model predictive control of remotely operated underwater vehicles. In: 2011 50th IEEE Conference on Decision and Control and European Control Conference. pp. 2058–2063 (2011). https://doi.org/10.1109/CDC.2011.6161447

19. Paszke, A., et al.: Pytorch: an imperative style, high-performance deep learning library. ArXiv **abs/1912.01703** (2019)

20. Schulman, J., Wolski, F., Dhariwal, P., Radford, A., Klimov, O.: Proximal policy optimization algorithms. ArXiv **abs/1707.06347** (2017)

21. Shen, C., Shi, Y., Buckham, B.: Model predictive control for an AUV with dynamic path planning. In: 2015 54th Annual Conference of the Society of Instrument and Control Engineers of Japan (SICE). pp. 475–480 (2015). https://doi.org/10.1109/SICE.2015.7285374

22. Shen, C., Shi, Y., Buckham, B.: Trajectory tracking control of an autonomous underwater vehicle using lyapunov-based model predictive control. IEEE Trans. Industr. Electron. **65**(7), 5796–5805 (2018). https://doi.org/10.1109/TIE.2017.2779442

23. Sutton, R.S., Barto, A.G.: Reinforcement Learning: an Introduction. 2nd edn. The MIT Press (2018)

24. Willners, J.S., et al.: From market-ready ROVs to low-cost AUVs (2021)

25. Yan, Z., Gong, P., Zhang, W., Wu, W.: Model predictive control of autonomous underwater vehicles for trajectory tracking with external disturbances. Ocean Eng. **217**, 107884 (2020). https://doi.org/10.1016/j.oceaneng.2020.107884

26. Yu, R., Shi, Z., Huang, C., Li, T., Ma, Q.: Deep Reinforcement Learning Based Optimal Trajectory Tracking Control of Autonomous Underwater Vehicle. In: 36th Chinese Control Conference. pp. 4958–4965 (2017)

27. Zhang, T., Miao, X., Li, Y., Jia, L., Wei, Z., Gong, Q., Wen, T.: AUV 3D docking control using deep reinforcement learning. Ocean Eng. **283**, 115021 (2023). https://doi.org/10.1016/j.oceaneng.2023.115021

Towards an Autonomous Biohybrid Robotic System

Hang Wang[1], Mohsen Zahmatkesh[1], Martin Stefanec[2], and Farshad Arvin[1(✉)]

[1] Biohybrid Robotics Lab, Department of Computer Science, Durham University, Durham, UK
{hang.wang,farshad.arvin}@durham.ac.uk
[2] Department of Zoology, Institute of Biology, University of Graz, Graz, Austria

Abstract. Understanding and influencing insect behaviour is crucial for ecological monitoring, pollination management, and species conservation. However, traditional methods struggle with the scale, complexity, and sensitivity of insect colonies, hence, we require minimally invasive and adaptive technologies. Micro-robots offer an optimal solution, as their small size enables seamless integration into natural environments, allowing precise interactions without disrupting collective behaviours. This paper presents an autonomous robotic system designed to mimic and track a queen bee's movements within the hive. The robot features a trajectory tracking system that maintains its orientation aligned with the queen. By replicating the queen's observed movements in an active colony, experiments confirm that the proposed biohybrid robot can accurately follow her trajectory, laying the foundation for future interactive studies with honeybees.

Keywords: Biohybrid Robotics · Robot-Insect Interactions · Autonomous System

1 Introduction

Honeybees have a significant influence on natural ecosystems due to their exceptional capacity in foraging and interacting with flowers and plants [1]. Their robust pollination abilities as generalist pollinators play an important role in agriculture and food security [2]. Moreover, the colony's self-organising nature underpins the execution of complex collective tasks [3,4], with the queen playing a central regulatory role, maintaining cohesion and facilitating these tasks via her pheromonal cues [5]. Consequently, studying and emulating the collective behaviour of bees provides an effective strategy to elucidate the mechanisms underlying their collective intelligence [6]. In particular, the study of interactions between biohybrid robots and honeybee colonies, especially through central colony elements such as queens, represents a cutting-edge area of research in insect collective behaviour [7]. Observing the collective behaviour of honeybees and other pollinators in natural outdoor environments is challenging due

© The Author(s), under exclusive license to Springer Nature Switzerland AG 2026
A. Cavalcanti et al. (Eds.): TAROS 2025, LNAI 16045, pp. 395–402, 2026.
https://doi.org/10.1007/978-3-032-01486-3_30

to ecosystem complexity, the unpredictable nature of biological behaviour, and hardware limitations [6,8,9]. Although numerous behavioural experiments have been conducted under controlled laboratory conditions [10–12], these settings may artificially constrain natural behaviours or trigger stress-related physiological changes [13], potentially compromising ecological validity. Instead of relying solely on laboratory experiments, we propose integrating advanced electronic systems directly within natural hives. This approach, previously applied [14,15], essentially brings the laboratory to the bees, enabling in-situ monitoring of behavioural interactions and physiological processes under real-world conditions. This method not only enhances the ecological relevance and accuracy of biological studies but also provides an ideal platform for developing bio-hybrid robotic systems, thereby advancing our understanding of the underlying mechanisms governing bee collective behaviour [16–18].

Therefore, an autonomous biohybrid robotic system is needed to collect long-term data on colony behaviour, to interact with specific bees such as the queen and court [19], and to mimic the natural behaviour of bees inside the hive [20] to be fully accepted by the animals. In this paper, we propose an autonomous bio-hybrid robot capable of accurately mimicking the queen bee's trajectory inside the hive, including linear and angular movements via an artificial agent. Ultimately, this system will enable real interactions between biohybrid robots and bees, contributing to the study and regulation of swarm intelligence strategies.

2   Robotics Development

The main objective of this project is to mimic the trajectory and rotation of the queen bee on a vertical plane within the hive. Therefore, the system should precisely locate and mimic the queen bee's orientation to replicate her natural motion.

2.1   Mechanical Design

This section describes the hardware composition and functional characteristics of each subsystem of the proposed prototype autonomous biohybrid robotic system, as shown in Fig. 1, which consists of two components, i) Autonomous Robotic Observation and Behavioural Analysis (*AROBA*) and ii) an *Artificial Agent*.

AROBA System. The AROBA system [7], developed in the EU RoboRoyale[1] project, has been used to accurately locate and analyse the behaviour of the queen bee and her courtyard. As shown in Fig. 1, the robot is built using aluminium profiles, as a gantry structure that can be freely assembled to ensure stability, lightweight design, portability, and corrosion resistance. Precise motion is achieved via two high-precision stepper servo motors: one for horizontal x-axis movement (M-A), and one for vertical z-axis movement (M-B). The 3D-printed

---

[1] https://roboroyale.eu/.

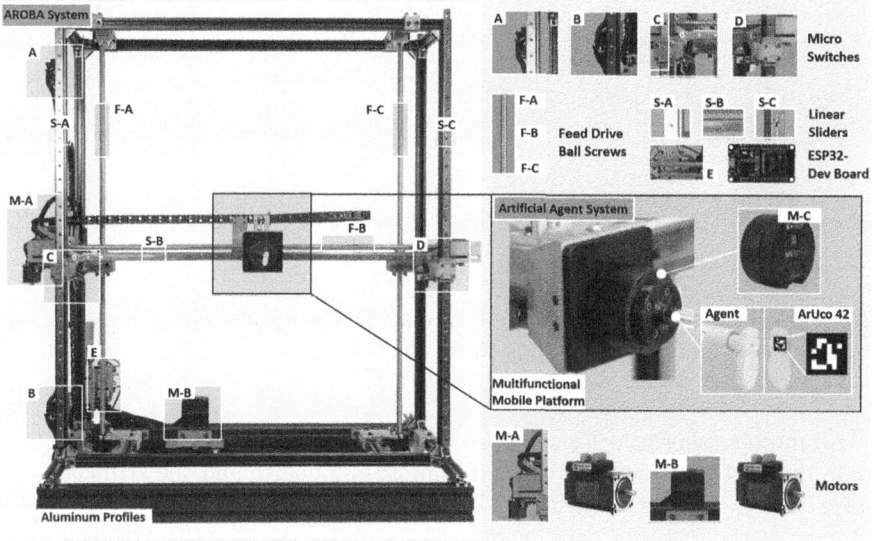

Fig. 1. Hardware architecture of autonomous biohybrid robotic system.

artificial agent is fixed with a linear slider and a horizontally installed ball screw, used to carry various components that interact with honeybees. The ESP32 microcontroller, installed on the left rear side of the frame, controls the system, acquiring target position data and adjusting stepper motor speeds. It also returns current position data to the main controller, enabling closed-loop control.

Artificial Agent. The agent mimics the rotation of the queen bee during its transition, using the servo motor (Fig. 1 M-C). The artificial agent is produced by 3D printing and has a hollow interior with a shape similar to a bee. The servo motor that controls its variable rotational speed can obtain angle and speed data transmitted by the ESP32 board and provide feedback on the actual angle data rotated by the artificial agent to the main control system.

2.2 Controller Design

This section describes the controller design of the developed system. The controller includes a software control system and a hardware execution system (see Fig. 2). The software control system is designed and built based on the ROS-Noetic operating framework. The Trajectory Node 1 in the control centre first obtains the trajectory and rotation data of the queen bee, and converts them into data packages which include movement speed (v_x, v_y, v_θ) and target position (x_{pos}, y_{pos}, θ_{pos}), and also transmits them to Management Node 2. The Node 2 has the functions of data processing, vibration control, and data logging and export, while also achieving communication with ESP32 board.

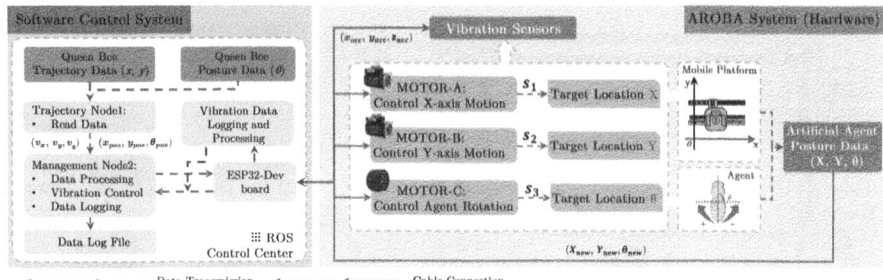

Fig. 2. Design framework diagram of controller. The controller includes the *Software Control System* and the *AROBA Hardware System*.

All motors (shown in Fig. 1, M-A, M-B, M-C) in the hardware system work according to the commands obtained from ESP32 board, and the artificial agent moves to the designated position (X, Y, θ) at the specified speed (s_1, s_2, s_3). Afterwards, the real-time position data $(X_{new}, Y_{new}, \theta_{new})$ of the Artificial Agent is sent back to the ESP32 board.

2.3   Tracking System and Camera Projection Model

In this section, the geometric relationship between 3D world coordinates and 2D image projections is established. The world coordinate system, represented as $\mathcal{F}_w = (O_w, X_w, Y_w, Z_w)$, is used to define honeybee 3D points as $\mathbf{P}_w = (X_w, Y_w, Z_w)^\top \in \mathbb{R}^3$. Similarly, the camera coordinate system, denoted as $\mathcal{F}_c = (O_c, X_c, Y_c, Z_c)$, is defined such that the Z_c axis coincides with the optical axis, where points are expressed as $\mathbf{P}_c = (X_c, Y_c, Z_c)^\top \in \mathbb{R}^3$. The image coordinate system, denoted as $\mathcal{F}_i = (O_i, x, y)$, is used to describe 2D points on image plane as $\mathbf{p}_i = (x_i, y_i)^\top \in \mathbb{R}^2$. The optical center projection is represented by the principal point (u_0, v_0). Assuming a rigid-body system, the transformation is given by: $\mathbf{P}_c = \mathbf{R}\mathbf{P}_w + \mathbf{t}$, where $\mathbf{R} \in SO(3)$ is a rotation matrix and $\mathbf{t} \in \mathbb{R}^3$ is a translation vector. In homogeneous coordinates:

$$\begin{bmatrix} \mathbf{P}_c \\ 1 \end{bmatrix} = \begin{bmatrix} \mathbf{R} & \mathbf{t} \\ \mathbf{0}^\top & 1 \end{bmatrix} \begin{bmatrix} \mathbf{P}_w \\ 1 \end{bmatrix}. \tag{1}$$

The pinhole projection with focal length f and principal point (u_0, v_0) is defined as:

$$\begin{cases} x_i = f\dfrac{X_c}{Z_c} + u_0 \\ y_i = f\dfrac{Y_c}{Z_c} + v_0 \end{cases}. \tag{2}$$

Equivalently, using the intrinsic matrix $\mathbf{K} = \begin{bmatrix} f & 0 & u_0 \\ 0 & f & v_0 \\ 0 & 0 & 1 \end{bmatrix}$. The homogeneous pin-

hole projection is as follows:

$$\lambda \begin{bmatrix} x_i \\ y_i \\ 1 \end{bmatrix} = \mathbf{K} \begin{bmatrix} X_c \\ Y_c \\ Z_c \end{bmatrix}, \quad \lambda = Z_c . \tag{3}$$

Hence, by combining extrinsic and intrinsic parameters:

$$\lambda \begin{bmatrix} x_i \\ y_i \\ 1 \end{bmatrix} = \mathbf{K}[\mathbf{R} \mid \mathbf{t}] \begin{bmatrix} \mathbf{P}_w \\ 1 \end{bmatrix}, \tag{4}$$

and expanding the (4) the nonlinear projection is defined as:

$$
\begin{aligned}
x_i &= \frac{f(r_{11}X_w + r_{12}Y_w + r_{13}Z_w + t_x) + u_0 Z_c}{Z_c} \\
y_i &= \frac{f(r_{21}X_w + r_{22}Y_w + r_{23}Z_w + t_y) + v_0 Z_c}{Z_c}
\end{aligned}
, \tag{5}
$$

where $Z_c = r_{31}X_w + r_{32}Y_w + r_{33}Z_w + t_z$.

Lemma 1 (Projection Non-Injectivity). *The mapping* $\mathbf{P}_w \mapsto \mathbf{p}_i$ *is not injective. For all 3D points along the ray, we have:*

$$\mathcal{L}(\lambda) = \lambda \mathbf{R}^{-1}\mathbf{K}^{-1} \begin{bmatrix} x_i \\ y_i \\ 1 \end{bmatrix} - \mathbf{R}^{-1}\mathbf{t}, \quad \lambda > 0 , \tag{6}$$

that project to the same 2D image point $\mathbf{p}_i$.

Proof. Follows directly from the perspective division in (3), where scaling $\mathbf{P}_c$ by any $\lambda > 0$ yields identical image coordinates. □

Remark 1. The model is valid for $Z_c > 0$. In case $Z_c = 0$, the projection equations become singular, implying that the point lies in the camera's focal plane and does not produce a valid finite projection.

3   Results

We controlled the AROBA system and our Artificial Agent to mimic the movement of the queen previously obtained from inside the hive. During the experiment, we tracked the agent by a camera module. ArUco markers were used at the bottom of the agent (as shown in Fig. 1) to identify its position and orientation.

The obtained results are shown in Fig. 3, where the actual motion trajectory of the AROBA System obtained has no significant error compared to the

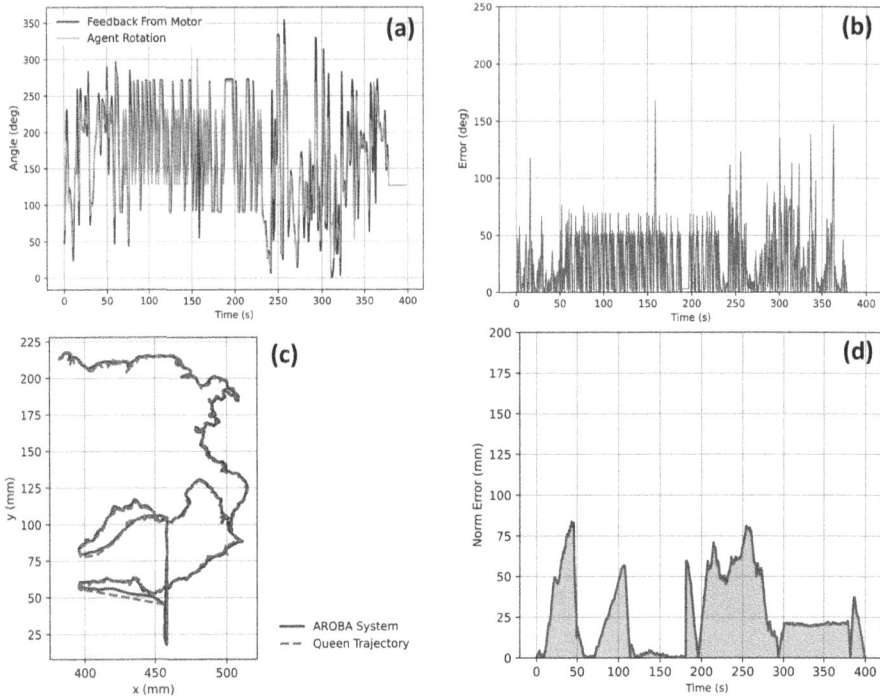

Fig. 3. (a) Orientation of the artificial agent obtained from motor's feedback and tracking system, and (b) orientation error. (c) Trajectory of the agent obtained from the queen bee inside of hive and our tracking system, and (d) position error.

trajectory of queen bee. At the same time, there is no significant error between the real rotation result obtained from the agent and the queen bee. However, due to the queen's occasional rapid movements within the hive at specific time points, the agent's trajectory and rotation results can exhibit significant short-term errors relative to the queen's actual movements. This is because hardware devices cannot respond quickly to the high-speed movement of organisms, however, the system can compensate the error after a few second. The results also demonstrated the effectiveness of the AROBA System and Artificial Agent System. This lays the foundation for further research on the interaction between the artificial agent and the queen.

4   Conclusion

This study demonstrated the feasibility of an autonomous robotic system capable of mimicking a queen bee's movements within a hive. The proposed bio-hybrid robot successfully maintains trajectory alignment with the queen, that enables precise interactions without disrupting the colony's behaviour. Experimental results validate its effectiveness and potential for future research on insect-robot interactions, where the developed robotic system is deployed in an observation hive to test interactions with the honeybee queen.

Acknowledgement. This work was partially supported by H2020-FET Project RoboRoyale (Grant agreement ID: 964492).

References

1. Paudel, Y.P., Mackereth, R., Hanley, R., Qin, W.: Honey bees (Apis mellifera l.) and pollination issues: Current status, impacts, and potential drivers of decline. J. Agric. Sci. **7**(6), 93 (2015)
2. Klein, A.-M., et al.: Importance of pollinators in changing landscapes for world crops. Proc. Biol. Sci. **274**(1608), 303–313 (2007)
3. Seeley, T.D., Camazine, S., Sneyd, J.: Collective decision-making in honey bees: how colonies choose among nectar sources. Behav. Ecol. Sociobiol. **28**, 277–290 (1991)
4. Bonabeau, E., Theraulaz, G., Deneubourg, J.-L., Aron, S., Camazine, S.: Self-organization in social insects. Trends Ecol. Evol. **12**(5), 188–193 (1997)
5. Slessor, K.N., Winston, M.L., Le Conte, Y.: Pheromone communication in the honeybee (Apis mellifera l.). J. Chem. Ecol. **31**, 2731–2745 (2005)
6. Schmickl, T., et al.: Social integrating robots suggest mitigation strategies for ecosystem decay. Front Bioeng. Biotechnol. **9**, 612605 (2021)
7. Ulrich, J., et al.: Autonomous tracking of honey bee behaviors over long-term periods with cooperating robots. Sci. Robot. **9**(95), eadn6848 (2024)
8. Rekabi-Bana, F., et al.: Mechatronic design for multi robots-insect swarms interactions. IEEE Int. Conf. Mechatron. (ICM) **2023**, 1–6 (2023)
9. Ilgün, A., et al.: Bio-hybrid systems for ecosystem level effects. In: Artificial Life Conference Proceedings 33, vol. 2021, no. 1, p. 41. MIT Press One Rogers Street, Cambridge, MA 02142-1209, USA journals-info ..., (2021)
10. Bosua, H.J., Nicolson, S.W., Archer, C.R., Pirk, C.W.W.: Effects of cage volume and bee density on survival and nutrient intake of honeybees (Apis mellifera l.) under laboratory conditions. Apidologie **49**, 734–746 (2018)
11. Menzel, R., Muller, U.: Learning and memory in honeybees: from behavior to neural substrates. Annu. Rev. Neurosci. **19**(1), 379–404 (1996)
12. Stefanec, M., Szopek, M., Schmickl, T., Mills, R.: Governing the swarm: Controlling a bio-hybrid society of bees & robots with computational feedback loops. In : IEEE Symposium Series on Computational Intelligence (SSCI). vol. 2017, pp. 1–8. IEEE (2017)
13. Decourtye, A., Devillers, J., Cluzeau, S., Charreton, M., Pham-Delègue, M.-H.: Effects of imidacloprid and deltamethrin on associative learning in honeybees under semi-field and laboratory conditions. Ecotoxicol. Environ. Saf. **57**(3), 410–419 (2004)
14. Barlow, S.E., O'Neill, M.A.: Technological advances in field studies of pollinator ecology and the future of e-ecology. Curr. Opin. Insect Sci. **38**, 15–25 (2020)
15. Barmak, R., et al.: A robotic honeycomb for interaction with a honeybee colony. Sci. Robot. **8**(76), eadd7385 (2023)
16. Stefanec, M., et al.: A minimally invasive approach towards "ecosystem hacking" with honeybees. Front. Robot. AI **9**, 791921 (2022)

17. Rekabi Bana, F., Krajník, T., Arvin, F.: Evolutionary optimization for risk-aware heterogeneous multi-agent path planning in uncertain environments. Front. Robot. AI **11** (2024)
18. Barmak, R., et al.: Biohybrid superorganisms—on the design of a robotic system for thermal interactions with honeybee colonies. IEEE Access (2024)
19. Blaha, J., et al.: Toward perpetual occlusion-aware observation of comb states in living honeybee colonies. IEEE/RSJ Int. Conf. Intell. Robots Syst. (IROS) **2024**, 5948–5955 (2024)
20. Rekabi-Bana, F., Hu, J., Krajník, T., Arvin, F.: Unified robust path planning and optimal trajectory generation for efficient 3D area coverage of quadrotor UAVS. IEEE Trans. Intell. Transp. Syst. **25**(3), 2492–2507 (2024)

Aerial Robotics and Path Planning

Coverage Path Planning for Structural Inspections with UAV

Clément Laguerre, Hae-In Lee[✉] [ID], Namhoon Cho[ID],
and Antonios Tsourdos[ID]

Cranfield University, MK43 0AL Cranfield, UK
{Clement.Laguerre.972,haein.lee,n.cho,antonios.tsourdos}@cranfield.ac.uk

Abstract. This study presents a comprehensive framework for complete inspection of known structures using an Unmanned Aerial Vehicle subject to position uncertainty. The proposed strategy is to take a two-stage approach consisting of viewpoint planning followed by routing. The proposed method enhances an existing Viewpoints Generation algorithm, ensuring 100% coverage of the structure while significantly reducing both computing time and the number of viewpoints by up to 99% and 28%, respectively. The path planning problem is formulated to optimise either energy consumption or mission duration. Various Travelling Salesman Problem (TSP) solvers are compared, with the Lin-Kernighan Heuristic providing near-optimal results in a short time frame when applied to a full-scale wind turbine model. Validation is conducted in the Gazebo simulation environment, offering realistic conditions, while PX4 Software-In-The-Loop (SITL) and ROS2 ensure seamless deployment on real hardware. The code is available in the Zenodo archive [11].

Keywords: Coverage Path Planning · Unmanned Aerial Vehicle (UAV) · Travelling Salesman Problem (TSP)

1 Introduction

Operation and Maintenance (O&M) expenses constitute a substantial portion of the total life cycle cost of most structures. For offshore wind turbines in particular, O&M costs can account for as much as 30% of the overall lifetime expenditure [22]. Primarily due to downtime, this leads to reduced energy output and increased operational expenses [14]. Unmanned Aerial Vehicles (UAVs) are a promising solution for structural inspection, offering rapid and safe access to areas that are difficult to reach. UAVs are anticipated to play a pivotal role in future multi-robot systems designed for the maintenance of various structures [22].

Ensuring the complete coverage of a structure using UAVs presents challenges such as position uncertainty and stability issues. Additionally, visual inspections require specific conditions to be met for successful execution. For instance, a fundamental aspect of visual inspection is the Ground Sampling Distance (GSD)

© The Author(s), under exclusive license to Springer Nature Switzerland AG 2026
A. Cavalcanti et al. (Eds.): TAROS 2025, LNAI 16045, pp. 405–418, 2026.
https://doi.org/10.1007/978-3-032-01486-3_31

which represents the number of pixels by millimetres in an image. It is used as part of the regulation to assess the validity of crack detection surveys [19].

To address the challenges in inspection flight planning, most existing methods divide the task into two parts [2,5,8,9,18,19]: Viewpoints Generation (VG) and Path Generation (PG). VG methods can be classified into four categories: space sampling, vertex sampling patch sampling and surface sampling [6,16].

Space sampling methods [2,8] discretise the space surrounding the target structure, initialise viewpoints, evaluate their visibility, and iteratively refine them using various strategies. A key advantage lies in the use of a simplified model of the structure. However, this simplification often leads to increased "self-occlusions and partial coverage" [16], which limits their practical applicability.

In contrast, **vertex sampling** methods [4,7,15] operate directly on the object mesh, offering improved geometric fidelity [6]. Although effective for complex geometries, they tend to underperform on large flat surfaces with sparse vertices. Additionally, they are computationally expensive and sensitive to hyperparameter tuning [16].

Patch sampling approaches group mesh faces based on geometric features [16]. Mosbach et al. used B-splines, requiring expert-driven parameterisation [13], while Asa et al. applied k-means++ clustering to segment the mesh [3]. Although promising, real-world UAV tests exposed limitations due to pose uncertainty, later mitigated in [19]. Still, these methods are often hindered by implementation complexity and high computational cost [16].

Finally, **surface sampling** combines space sampling with mesh-based candidate generation [16]. Viewpoints are evaluated for visibility and filtered to maximise coverage, often outperforming other state-of-the-art methods. However, its primary focus lies in manufacturing contexts, and it lacks validation through real-world field tests [16].

Table 1. Comparison of VG sampling methods

Method	Advantages	Disadvantages
Space Sampling	Simplified structure model	Self-occlusions; partial coverage
Vertex Sampling	Considers mesh geometry	Poor on flat areas; sensitive to mesh resolution
Patch Sampling	Strong simulation and real-world performance	High computational cost; complex implementation
Surface Sampling	High coverage performance	Not validated in real-world tests

The purpose of PG is to provide the order of waypoints the UAV should follow to inspect the structure completely while minimising a chosen performance index. The task is usually abstracted as to solve a Travelling Salesman Problem (TSP) in the field of UAVs path planning [10]. It is well suited to the field of Coverage

Path Planning (CPP) since its aim is to find the shortest route to visit all points in a graph exactly once and return to the starting point. All papers reviewed used a form of the TSP or the Vehicle Routing Problem.

To minimise energy consumption for PG, either physics-based or data-driven models are necessary to estimate the energy consumed over a given path. Physics-based models in [17,20,21] use motors, quad-rotors and battery dynamics to obtain a function relating control inputs and energy consumption. The problem is then treated as an optimal control problem. However, this requires devising the control system of the UAVs. It also demands data that necessitate wind tunnel tests. Another approach is to construct a data-driven model as in [1], where empirical data is obtained through real-world flight tests. This method allows obtaining equations relating different flight parameters with energy consumption.

As previously discussed, the method proposed by Wu et al. [19] demonstrates strong potential for VG, albeit with significant computational demands. The primary contribution of this paper is therefore a modified VG algorithm, inspired by Wu et al. [19], that significantly reduces both computation time and the number of viewpoints. In alignment with the requirements defined by Marshall Futureworx, this work also focuses on delivering a practical and deployable solution for autonomous structural inspection. To this end, the proposed open-source framework includes a computationally efficient VG algorithm, two time-efficient PG optimisation scenarios, and a complete pipeline suitable for both simulation and real-world deployment on UAV hardware.

The rest of the paper is organised as follows: Sect. 2 gives an overview of the proposed inspection planning framework, consisting of VG and PG modules. Each of the modules is detailed in Sect. 2.1 and 2.2. Section 3 presents the performance of the proposed approach on benchmark structures and a wind turbine. Conclusions and future research directions are proposed in Sect. 4.

2   Inspection Planning Framework

The aim of visual inspection is to obtain a set of images of the entire target structure without omission. To achieve this, an array of viewpoints is computed based on a 3D model of the target structure. Described as a 1×6 vector, each viewpoint represents the position and orientation of a camera mounted on a gimbal. Knowing the position of the camera relative to the center of the UAV, a list of waypoint coordinates can be derived. These waypoints are then used as input for the PG algorithm, which determines the sequence in which the UAV should visit each waypoint to either ensure the shortest mission duration (Scenario 1) or the lowest energy consumption (Scenario 2). These steps and the data flow are summarised in Fig. 1.

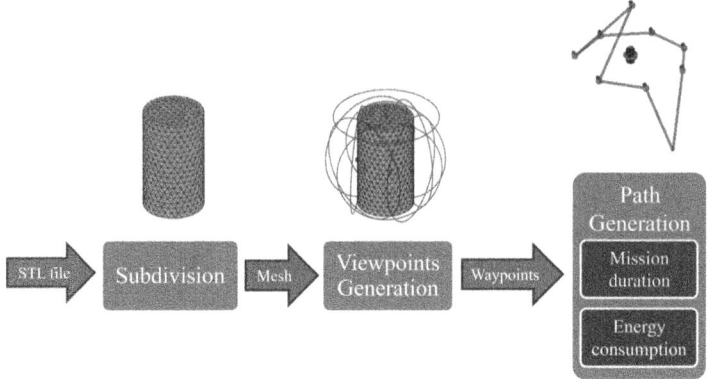

Fig. 1. Inspection Path Planning Framework

2.1   Viewpoints Generation

The patch sampling method described in [19] has been modified to reduce the number of viewpoints and computational time. Initially, the target structure is divided into a set of triangular polygons M_{sub} using the gmsh software, with a maximum edge length of 200 mm. The algorithm then clusters M_{sub} into k clusters, $C = \{c_1, c_2, \ldots, c_k\}$ and, knowing the inspection distance d_{insp}, computes the inspection position p. A polygon is considered inspected if it falls within the inspection range of at least one viewpoint and if its view angle θ is below a user-defined limit θ_{lim}. The view angle is defined as the angle between the normal to the surface at the points c_i and the normal to the surface at the centroid of the polygon. In [19], the clustering algorithm is applied to M_{sub}, starting with $k = 1$. If a polygon is not inspected, k is incrementally increased by one until M_{sub} is fully inspected. This process is computationally intensive and does not minimise the number of viewpoints, as the clustering algorithm tends to distribute the viewpoints unevenly. The proposed method aims to address these two issues. Firstly, instead of applying k-means++ to the entire structure, M_{sub} is segmented into N_s sections along the vertical axis, as defined by

$$N_s = \frac{h_s}{2 \cdot r_{\text{maj}} \cdot r_s} \tag{1}$$

where h_s is the height of the structure (m), r_{maj} is the radius of the inspection area (m), and r_s is an adjustable parameter, empirically set to 0.7. This segmentation ensures that the height of each section is slightly smaller than the diameter of the inspection area, facilitating the even distribution of medoids along a central line within each section. Subsequently, the number of clusters, k, is set to one, with inspected polygons I_p being sequentially removed from M_{sub} after each iteration until all polygons are inspected. The integration of these enhancements results in reduced computing time, minimised overlap, and fewer required viewpoints (see Algorithm 1).

Algorithm 1. Inspection Position Generation

1: **Input:** $M_{\text{sub}}, d_{\text{insp}}, \theta_{\text{lim}}$
2: **Output:** $P_{\text{insp}} = \{p_1, p_2, \ldots, p_N\}$
3: $N_{\text{s}} \leftarrow \left\lfloor \dfrac{h_{\text{s}}}{2 \cdot r_{\text{maj}} \cdot r_{\text{s}}} \right\rfloor$
4: Segment M_{sub} into N_{s} sections along the vertical axis
5: $P_{\text{insp}} \leftarrow \emptyset$
6: **for** each section $M_{\text{sub}}^i \subset M_{\text{sub}}$ **do**
7:     $M_{\text{remain}}^i \leftarrow M_{\text{sub}}^i$
8:     **while** $M_{\text{remain}}^i \neq \emptyset$ **do**
9:         $c \leftarrow \text{Clustering}(M_{\text{remain}}^i, k = 1)$
10:        $p \leftarrow \text{Determine}(c, d_{\text{insp}})$
11:        $P_{\text{insp}} \leftarrow P_{\text{insp}} \cup \{p\}$
12:        $I_{\text{p}} \leftarrow \text{Determine}(c, r_{\text{maj}}, \theta_{\text{lim}})$
13:        $M_{\text{remain}}^i \leftarrow M_{\text{remain}}^i \setminus I_{\text{p}}$
14:    **end while**
15: **end for**

2.2   Path Generation and Optimisation

Scenario 1: Mission Duration. To minimise the mission duration, the path length is minimised using the classical TSP formulation. The objective function is defined as:

$$\min \sum_{i=1}^{n} \sum_{j=1}^{n} d_{ij} \cdot x_{ij} \tag{2}$$

where n is the number of viewpoints, d_{ij} is the Euclidean distance between the waypoints i and j, and x_{ij} is a binary decision variable which is 1 if it is chosen to be connected, and 0 otherwise. To minimise the path length, various TSP solvers are considered: intlinprog [12], Lin-Kernighan Heuristic (LKH), Ant Colony Optimisation (ACO), Hybrid Particle Swarm Optimisation (HPSO), Genetic Algorithm (GA) and Simulated Annealing (SA).

Scenario 2: Energy Consumption. Given the need for precise positioning and stabilisation, the UAV must effectively halt at each viewpoint. Considering that the number of viewpoints extends into the thousands for a real-size structure, and the relatively short distances between them, the speed between viewpoints is expected to be minimal to avoid unnecessary long stabilisation period. Consequently, trajectory optimisation does not appear to be necessary, and factors such as jerk are not considered. Hence, the primary contributors to energy consumption are altitude changes and path length, necessitating a multi-objective optimisation approach. Therefore, the objective function for Scenario 2 is formulated as the weighted sum of both distances between each waypoint (3).

$$\min \sum_{i=1}^{n} \sum_{j=1}^{n} [((1 - w) \cdot a_{ij} + w \cdot d_{ij}) \cdot x_{ij}] \tag{3}$$

where a_{ij} is the altitude difference between the waypoints i and j, and w is the weight between the altitude change and path length minimisation. The value of w is changed from 0 to 1 with a step or 0.025 to obtain the Pareto optimal front. The weight that ensure the lowest energy consumption can be obtained based on line search over the Pareto optimal front.

To estimate the energy consumption, a data-driven model from [1] is used. First, the algorithm identifies the flight manoeuvres between each waypoint as flying vertically upwards or flying vertically downwards. Then the energy consumed over the whole path, E, can be approximated as:

$$E = \begin{cases} 315D - 211.261, & (E_v) \text{ if flying upwards} \\ 68.956D - 65.183, & (E_v) \text{ if flying downwards} \\ 308.709t - 0.852, & (E_h) \text{ if flying horizontally} \end{cases} \quad (4)$$

where $0 < D \le 7.5$ m is the distance of the vertical flight and $t < 900$ s is the duration of the horizontal flight. This equation was obtained by recording the energy consumed on a real UAV performing different flights multiple times. The results show an error of 4.3% between the estimate and the real consumption. Using this method, it is possible to estimate the energy consumption without detailed knowledge of the platform. Since flying vertically downwards and upwards with an angle was not included in the test flights performed, the energy consumed over a diagonal vertical path is estimated as the sum of the energy consumption of the vertical (D_v) and horizontal distances (D_h) as in:

$$E = \begin{cases} E_v * r + E_h, & if D_h > D_v \\ E_v + E_h * r, & if D_v > D_h \end{cases} \quad (5)$$

The smallest of the distances is multiplied by a ratio r based on the hypotenuse of the triangle formed by the sequential waypoints:

$$r = \frac{\sqrt{D_v^2 + D_h^2}}{D_v + D_h}. \quad (6)$$

To get an accurate energy consumption model on a given UAV platform, the methodology explained in [1] should be followed. Then, as (6) is an estimate, performing additional test flight flying upwards and downwards at different angle would enhance the accuracy of the results. Moreover, as stated in [1], performing the different manoeuvres at different speeds also enables finding the one that results in the lowest energy consumption for each manoeuvre. On another note, if the sufficient test flights are performed, using the energy consumption function directly as the objective function in the TSP solver would result in the most accurate solution.

3   Results

3.1   Simulation Setup

The performance of the proposed approach was validated using benchmark structures and a full-scale model of a wind turbine. The benchmark structures included a flat wall of $73\,\text{m}^2$, as referenced in [19], to compare their VG performance, and a cylinder with a view angle limit of $10°$ to assess performance on a curved structure. Additionally, the algorithm's ability to handle increasing positional uncertainty was evaluated, as it is a critical factor contributing to coverage loss. To mitigate this effect, the inspection distance and range were reduced to ensure 100% coverage of the structure.

Multiple tests were performed using PX4 SITL, Gazebo, and ROS2 to validate these results. The X500 model from PX4 has been used without gimbal. Each time the UAV reaches a waypoint, its ground truth position is stored in a .csv file, which is then processed to issue the resulting coverage, overlap and position error. The resulting path, waypoints and medoids can be overlaid on top of the computed ones as shown in Fig. 2. The position error is achieved by setting the error allowance δ_{position} for reaching a waypoint to the desired value. Additionally, the default noise of the simulated barometer, GNSS and IMU in Gazebo contributed to modelling the position error and provided a more realistic environment. These measurements were fused by an Extended Kalman Filter (EKF) within the PX4 Autopilot. The inspection position error and medoids' position error were evaluated by averaging the results of 5 different flight simulations.

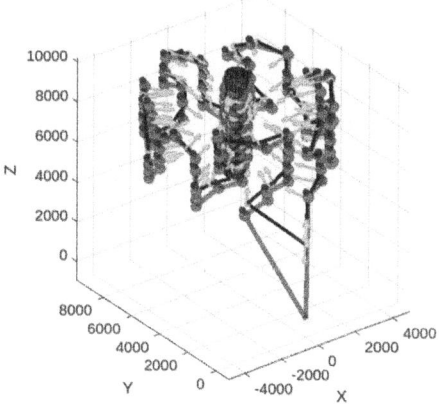

Fig. 2. Post-processed visualisation of a cylindrical structure. Algorithm outputs include: medoids (red), waypoints (magenta), and viewpoints (blue). Simulation outputs include: viewpoints around the structure (green), medoids on the surface from ray tracing (green), and the UAV path (black). The yellow dot marks the UAV take-off and landing location. (Color figure online)

3.2 Benchmark Structures

Wall. The VG results for a wall structure are shown in Table 2. The method from [19] has been implemented and is referred to as " [19] reproduced". It issued 272 viewpoints (Fig. 3.a) while the results from the paper reported 285 viewpoints. The difference can be explained by different reasons such as the triangular polygons size in the mesh. Moreover, clustering may not provide the exact same results each time the algorithm is run. Nevertheless, the implemented method from [19] is considered similar enough for comparison. As seen in Table 2, the proposed method performs faster with a smaller overlap and a smaller number of viewpoints (Fig. 3.b). The proposed algorithm issued 196 waypoints in 12 s compared with 272 waypoints in 1 h and 13 min. This resulted in a 99.7% reduction in computing time and a 28% reduction in the number of waypoints.

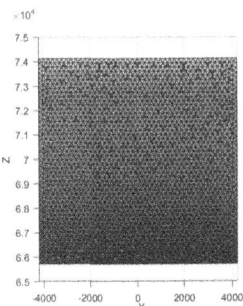 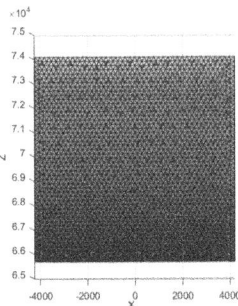

Fig. 3. VG results on a 73 m² flat wall: left (a)—reproduced method from [19]; right (b)—proposed method. Red dots represent the medoids. Inspection poses are computed from medoid positions, surface normals, and inspection distance. The proposed method produces a sparser and more uniform medoid distribution. The colors simply refer to the wall height

Table 2. VGResults for a Wall

Criteria	[19]	[19] reproduced	Proposed
Overlap	N/A	89%	71%
Computing Time	N/A	1 h 13 min	12 s
Number of Viewpoints	285	272	196
Coverage	100%	100%	100%

The PG results for inspecting a flat wall are summarised in Table 3 for both optimisation scenarios. In [19], the path that ensured the highest coverage was 153.4 m long while ACO and LKH issued paths of 128.8 m and 111.7 m long respectively.

Table 3. PG Results for a Wall

Metric	Scenario 1			Scenario 2
	ACO	**LKH**	[19]	**LKH**
Path Length (m)	128.8	111.7	153.4	114.6
Altitude Change (m)	48.0	39.7	Not provided	27.1
Energy Consumption (MJ)	17.3	14.7	Not provided	13.6
Computational Time	82.2 s	8.47 s	Not provided	12 min (all weights)

Regarding Scenario 2, the Pareto optimal front is obtained as Fig. 4, showing a strong correlation between an initial reduction of the altitude changes and a reduction in the energy consumption. The minimum energy consumption is obtained for weights of 0.475 and 0.500, inducing an altitude change of 27.1 m and a path length of 114.6 m. Then, as the altitude change is minimised, the path length increases greatly, causing an increase in energy consumption.

The last column on the right in Table 3 shows the results for the lowest energy consumption. The algorithm shows a decrease in energy consumption of 7.87% while the path length increased by 2.60%. Only the LKH solver was run as it provided the best results.

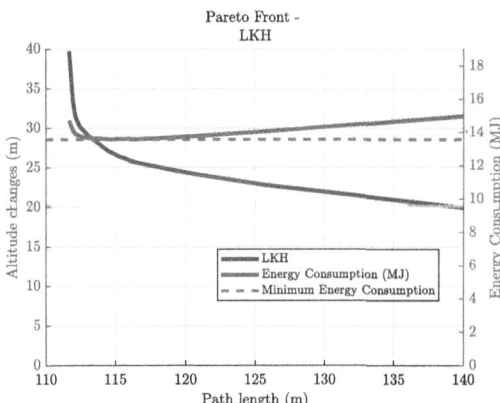

Fig. 4. Pareto front illustrating the trade-off between altitude changes and path length, considering energy consumption

Cylinder. Table 4 compares the VG results from [19] and the proposed method on a cylinder (height = 5 m, diameter = 1 m). It is shown that the computing time drastically increases on large or non-flat structures using the existing method [19]. Most importantly, the number of viewpoints increases when handling structures with multiple faces.

Table 4. VG Results for a Cylinder

Criteria	[19] reproduced	Proposed
Overlap	17.8%	9.45%
Computing Time	232 s	10 s
Viewpoint Number	107	80
Coverage	100%	100%

The VG results under the existence of position uncertainty are shown in Table 5. The algorithm achieved 100% coverage for up to 0.6 m in position error. Above this, for the camera and GSD specification, the inspection range was too small to be considered usable as it was smaller than the size the triangular polygons of the mesh. Such results are attained by reducing the inspection distance and inspection area as described in [19].

Table 5. Evaluation of the coverage under position uncertainty

Position uncertainty (m)	Inspection position error (m)	Medoids position error (m)	Coverage (%)	Inspection distance (m)	Inspection radius (m)
0.2	0.186	0.198	100	3.79	0.56
0.3	0.235	0.277	100	3.69	0.44
0.4	0.314	0.348	100	3.59	0.32
0.5	0.458	0.483	100	3.49	0.19
0.6	0.518	0.547	100	3.39	0.072

The mission duration minimisation (Scenario 1) results of the generated viewpoints around a cylinder with 118 waypoints are shown in Table 6. For Scenario 2, the energy consumed decreased by 5.1% (LKH results). Increasing the waypoints number to 269 to assess the scalability of the TSP solvers, Mixed-Integer Linear Programming (MILP) provides an optimal path in 48 min while LKH does the same in under 6 s. ACO also provides acceptable results while SA, GA and HPSO perform worse.

Table 6. PG results showing path length (m) and computing time (s) for a cylinder (118 waypoints)

	MILP	SA	GA	HPSO	ACO	LKH
Path length (m)	196	267	348	383	221	196
Computing time (s)	7.1	6	17	8.2	7.5	5

3.3   Wind Turbine

The VG results of a real-size wind turbine (height $= 75$ m) are shown in Table 7. The viewpoints for the tower and nacelle were obtained in 43 min while the ones for the blades were obtained in 34 min. The results are visualised in Figure 5. The computational time is considered acceptable in practice, as the viewpoints can be computed ahead of the inspection.

Table 7. VG Results for a Wind Turbine

Criteria	Tower and nacelle	Blades
Overlap	64%	79.1%
Computing time	43 min	34 min
Viewpoint Number	3972	3436
Coverage	100%	100%

The PG results are summarised in Table 8. ACO ran for 1 h 22 min, performing 100 iterations, and generated a 3319-meter long path. In contrast, LKH with default parameters generated a 2171-meter long path in 35 min. The project's aim was to achieve acceptable computing time for prompt inspection after the wind turbine stops. An arbitrary 15-minute limit was set for the LKH solver to compare its quality with default parameters. The results were identical, showing an optimal path in a feasible time frame. Even with a 1-minute limit, the path length only increased by a few meters in the worst case.

Table 8. Evaluation of the PG algorithm optimised for mission duration on a wind turbine

Metric	ACO	LKH	LKH	LKH
Tower and Nacelle				
Path Length (m)	3319	2171	2171	2171
Altitude Change (m)	1932	1104	1104	1094
Energy Consumption (MJ)	526.8	329.4	329.4	328.1
Computing Time	1h 22 m	35 min (free)	15 min (fixed)	1 min (fixed)
Blades				
Path Length (m)	2475	1568	1568	1568
Altitude Change (m)	1370	887	887	893
Energy Consumption (MJ)	385.9	245.3	245.3	246.3
Computing Time	26 min	28 min (free)	15 min (fixed)	1 min (fixed)

The optimisation for lowest energy consumption was run with a time limit of 15 s per weight, for a total target computing time of approximately 15 min.

The best results were obtained for a weight of 4.750 which shows a decrease of 7.63% and 8.02% of energy consumption for the tower and nacelle and the blades, respectively (Table 9).

On the full wind turbine, this represents a 7.76% decrease, increasing the path length by 6.98% and reducing the altitude changes by 30.25%.

Table 9. Evaluation of the PG algorithm optimised for energy consumption on a wind turbine

Metric	Tower and Nacelle	Blades
Path Length (m)	2313	1687
Altitude Change (m)	771	615
Energy Consumption (MJ)	304.3	225.7
Computing Time	15 min	13 min

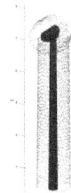 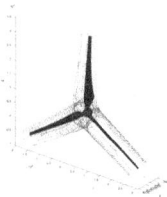

Fig. 5. VG results for the wind turbine. The magenta dots are the generated viewpoints.

4   Conclusion

This paper presents an algorithm capable of planning an inspection path for the complete coverage of known structures using a UAV. The algorithm improves upon an existing VG algorithm by reducing computing time and the number of viewpoints. Several TSP solvers are compared, with the option of optimising either mission duration or energy consumption. Tests on a real-size wind turbine demonstrated the practicality of the proposed method, achieving short computing times in both scenarios. The simulations proved the algorithm to be robust to position uncertainties. Validation carried out in ROS2 and PX4 SITL allows for streamlined tests and easy deployment on a real platform. Future work may include simulation testing of energy consumption gains, collision-free path planning and test flights on a real platform to assess the algorithm's coverage capabilities.

Acknowledgments. This work was supported by Marshall Futureworx.

References

1. Abeywickrama, H.V., Jayawickrama, B.A., He, Y., Dutkiewicz, E.: Comprehensive energy consumption model for unmanned aerial vehicles, based on empirical studies of battery performance. IEEE Access **6**, 58383–58394 (2018). https://doi.org/10.1109/ACCESS.2018.2875040

2. Almadhoun, R., Taha, T., Gan, D., Dias, J., Zweiri, Y., Seneviratne, L.: Coverage path planning with adaptive viewpoint sampling to construct 3D models of complex structures for the purpose of inspection. In: IEEE/RSJ International Conference on Intelligent Robots and Systems, pp. 7047–7054. Madrid, Spain (2018). https://doi.org/10.1109/IROS.2018.8593719

3. Asa, K., Funabora, Y., Doki, S., Doki, K.: Evaluation in real world of the measuring position determination for visual inspection using UAV. In: 44th Annual Conference of the IEEE Industrial Electronics Society, pp. 2711–2716. Washington, DC, USA (2018). https://doi.org/10.1109/IECON.2018.8591270

4. Englot, B.J.: Sampling-based coverage path planning for complex 3d structures. Ph.D. thesis, Massachusetts Institute of Technology (2012)

5. Garlapati, V., Dasgupta, P.: A complete coverage algorithm for 3D structural inspection using an autonomous unmanned aerial vehicle. In: Thirty-First International Florida Artificial Intelligence Research Society Conference, pp. 342–347. Melbourne, FL, USA (2018)

6. Gospodnetić, P., Mosbach, D., Rauhut, M., Hagen, H.: Viewpoint placement for inspection planning. Mach. Vis. Appl. **33**(1), 1–21 (2021). https://doi.org/10.1007/s00138-021-01252-z

7. Gronle, M., Osten, W.: View and sensor planning for multi-sensor surface inspection. Surf. Topogr. Metrol. Prop. **4**(2) (2016). https://doi.org/10.1088/2051-672X/4/2/024009

8. Jing, W., Deng, D., Wu, Y., Shimada, K.: Multi-UAV coverage path planning for the inspection of large and complex structures. In: IEEE/RSJ International Conference on Intelligent Robots and Systems, pp. 1480–1486. Las Vegas, NV, USA (2020).https://doi.org/10.1109/IROS45743.2020.9341089

9. Jung, S., Song, S., Youn, P., Myung, H.: Multi-layer coverage path planner for autonomous structural inspection of high-rise structures. In: IEEE/RSJ International Conference on Intelligent Robots and Systems. pp. 1–9. Madrid, Spain (2018).https://doi.org/10.1109/IROS.2018.8593537

10. Khoufi, I., Laouiti, A., Adjih, C.: A survey of recent extended variants of the traveling salesman and vehicle routing problems for unmanned aerial vehicles. Drones **3**(3) (2019).https://doi.org/10.3390/drones3030066

11. Laguerre, C.: Uav_structural_inspection (2025).https://doi.org/10.5281/zenodo.15556065. Accessed 30 May 2025

12. MATHWORKS: intlinprog (2025). https://fr.mathworks.com/help/optim/ug/intlinprog.html.Accessed 27 May 2025

13. Mosbach, D., Gospodnetić, P., Rauhut, M., Hamann, B., Hagen, H.: Feature-Driven Viewpoint Placement for Model-Based Surface Inspection. Mach. Vis. Appl. **32**(1), 1–21 (2020). https://doi.org/10.1007/s00138-020-01116-y

14. Rinaldi, G., Thies, P.R., Johanning, L.: Current status and future trends in the operation and maintenance of offshore wind turbines: A review. Energies **14**(9) (2021).https://doi.org/10.3390/en14092484

15. Scott, W.R.: Viewpoint placement for inspection planning. Mach. Vision Appl. **20**, 47–69 (2009).https://doi.org/10.1007/s00138-007-0110-2

16. Staderini, V., Glück, T., Schneider, P., Mecca, R., Kugi, A.: Surface sampling for optimal viewpoint generation. In: 13th IEEE International Conference on Pattern Recognition Systems, pp. 1–7. Guayaquil, Ecuador (2023).https://doi.org/10.1109/ICPRS58416.2023.10179043

17. Thibbotuwawa, A., Nielsen, P., Zbigniew, B., Bocewicz, G.: Energy consumption in unmanned aerial vehicles: A review of energy consumption models and their relation to the UAV routing. In: 39th International Conference on Information Systems Architecture and Technology, pp. 173–184. Nysa, Poland (2018)

18. Tong, H.W., Li, B., Huang, H., Wen, C.: UAV path planning for complete structural inspection using mixed viewpoint generation. In: 17th International Conference on Control, Automation, Robotics and Vision, pp. 727–732. Singapore (2022). https://doi.org/10.1109/ICARCV57592.2022.10004359

19. Wu, W.: Evaluation and enhancement of resolution-aware coverage path planning method for surface inspection using unmanned aerial vehicles. IEEE Access **12**, 16753–16766 (2024).https://doi.org/10.1109/ACCESS.2024.3359056

20. Yacef, F., Rizoug, N., Bouhali, O., Hamerlain, M.: Optimization of energy consumption for quadrotor UAV. In: 9th International Micro Air Vehicle Conference and Flight Competition 2017, pp. 215–222. Toulouse, France (2017)

21. Yacef, F., Rizoug, N., Degaa, L., Hamerlain, M.: Energy-efficiency path planning for quadrotor UAV under wind conditions. In: 7th International Conference on Control, Decision and Information Technologies, pp. 1133–1138. Prague, Czech Republic (2020).https://doi.org/10.1109/CoDIT49905.2020.9263968

22. Zhang, K., Pakrashi, V., Murphy, J., Hao, G.: Inspection of floating offshore wind turbines using multi-rotor unmanned aerial vehicles: Literature review and trends. Sensors **24**(3) (2024).https://doi.org/10.3390/s24030911

UAV Trajectory Optimisation with Reduced Conservatism via Tight B-Spline Envelopes

Christopher Blum$^{(\boxtimes)}$, Keir Groves , Zhongguo Li ,
and Ognjen Marjanovic

The University of Manchester, Oxford Road, Manchester M13 9PL, UK
{christopher.blum,keir.groves,zhongguo.li,
ognjen.marjanovic}@manchester.ac.uk

Abstract. Gradient-based optimisation is a common approach employed by local planners to rapidly find efficient and feasible trajectories for autonomous UAVs. Notably, B-spline or Bézier trajectory parameterisations decrease computation times while allowing for the continual enforcement of safety and kinodynamic feasibility constraints. However, current B-spline- or Bézier-based techniques that enforce collision constraints remain computationally expensive, whilst employing a conservative spline envelope. Conversely, methods that focus on minimising computational cost do not explicitly enforce a collision constraint, relying instead on arbitrary tuning parameters with unconstrained algorithms, and resorting to re-planning when the optimisation produces a colliding or dynamically infeasible trajectory. In this paper, a novel, tight, computationally efficient envelope that bounds a B-spline trajectory with respect to its control points is introduced, enabling the formulation of a constrained optimisation problem that converges rapidly while ensuring the safety and feasibility of the generated trajectories. The proposed algorithm is tested using an open-source simulation of a real-world UAV, demonstrating that, although each optimisation takes longer than unconstrained techniques, the method is still sufficiently fast for real-time applications. Furthermore, the B-spline envelope ensures that the resulting trajectories are less conservative than existing approaches, offering improved operational efficiency.

Keywords: UAV · Local Trajectory Planning · B-spline · Navigation

1 Introduction

Autonomous Uncrewed Aerial Vehicles (UAVs) are increasingly employed across various industries, such as construction, agriculture, space exploration, mining, search and rescue, and logistics [16]. They are often deployed in obstacle-dense areas, such as forests [24] and urban areas [15]. In these environments, the ability of a UAV to generate collision-free trajectories that respect its kinodynamic constraints is paramount for safe and efficient operation. Due to the limited

A. Cavalcanti et al. (Eds.): TAROS 2025, LNAI 16045, pp. 419–432, 2026.
https://doi.org/10.1007/978-3-032-01486-3_32

bandwidth of wireless communication [23] and the impracticality of employing a tether [7], it is desirable for a UAV trajectory planner to perform all computations using on-board resources. However, the restrictive payload capacities of UAVs introduce a limit on the amount of computational power available, so local trajectory planners should use minimal computational resources while re-planning quickly in response to new information.

Many approaches discretise the trajectory into time-steps and optimise it at each point [5,9,12,17,26], but this does not guarantee the safety of the trajectory between points. Although increasing the density of points can ensure safety in practice, this approach leads to a high computational burden, making real-time operation infeasible for many UAV applications [14,18]. One solution is the polynomial trajectory representation: optimising a continuous curve using a finite number of parameters [2,3,11]. However, generating polynomial trajectories of arbitrary length and geometry remains computationally expensive, requiring high-order polynomials with many optimisation variables, as well as additional continuity constraints beyond those required for collision avoidance and feasibility [22].

A more computationally efficient solution is a B-spline or Bézier curve trajectory representation [4,13,14,20,22,24,25], which offers several key advantages in trajectory planning. They are scalable, as low order curves can be used to represent long trajectories, and locally controllable, as their shape is determined by a set of control points, each with influence over a limited section of the curve. Using a piecewise linear envelope constructed from the set of convex hulls of neighbouring control points, it is possible to enforce collision constraints over the entire continuous trajectory. Additionally, the derivatives can be efficiently computed as linear combinations of the control points, allowing feasibility (*e.g.* velocity and acceleration) constraints to be enforced using the convex hull.

Using constrained optimisation, it is common to optimise the Bézier or B-spline control points while constraining them to be within a free-space corridor. For example, a set of cylindrical prisms are adopted in [13], but the optimisation process is not suitable for real-time application. In contrast, the FASTER planner simultaneously generates separate aggressive and guaranteed-safe plans [20], using Bézier curves constrained to be within convex decompositions of unknown or free-known space respectively. This method is fast enough for real-time applications, generating a plan in under 100 ms. However, the convex hulls of Bézier curves and B-splines are conservative [14,18], generating a piecewise linear bound that is guaranteed to contain the trajectory, but is not tight. This conservatism forces the optimisation algorithm to keep the trajectory far from obstacles, leading to longer, less operationally efficient routes. MADER reduces conservatism by employing a novel MINVO Basis spline, which generates minimum-volume simplexes to enclose the curve [18]. However, MADER suffers from a longer planning time of 200 ms on average [18], and the MINVO Basis sacrifices some of the useful properties of a Bézier or B-spline representation, including easy derivative computation and built-in continuity [14,19]. Additionally, the MINVO basis is not guaranteed to have a smaller enclosing volume in cases where the degree of the spline exceeds the dimensionality of the space [14].

Unconstrained optimisation can address the conservatism inherent in the convex hull envelope by effectively relaxing the collision constraint, while simultaneously decreasing computational load. RAPTOR uses a single cost function with penalty terms for smoothness, collision, and dynamic feasibility to generate trajectories in under 10 ms [24]. EGO removes the need to update a Euclidean Signed Distance Field (ESDF) [25], as ESDF generation was found to account for up to 70% of computation time in earlier works. With the ESDF removed, EGO generates trajectories in 1 to 5 ms [25]. The use of unconstrained optimisation in these planners leads to fast solve times, however there is no guarantee that any given optimisation result will be collision free. The solution in [24,25] is to leverage the low planning time to adjust the problem and re-plan if a collision is detected. Additionally, although the convex hull envelope is softened, the trajectories generated remain conservative, as the cost function penalises proximity to obstacles.

To conclude, existing trajectory generation methods exploit Bézier and B-spline trajectory representation to enable continuous enforcement of collision and dynamic feasibility constraints along a trajectory, while keeping computational costs down. However, the results are frequently conservative due to the employment of the convex hull envelope to bound the trajectory. This paper proposes the use of a novel envelope based on Lutterkort and Peters' work [10] to enable constrained B-spline trajectory optimisation with tight bounds. The contributions are summarised as follows:

- A novel, tight, computationally efficient bound for B-spline trajectories is derived as a refinement of Lutterkort and Peters' work. A formal mathematical proof is provided to validate its correctness for uniform cubic B-splines.
- The proposed bound is integrated into a UAV trajectory planner, with trajectories generated using constrained non-linear optimisation, enabling enforcement of collision constraints while ensuring smooth, non-conservative, and dynamically feasible trajectories with affordable computational burdens.
- The proposed system is contrasted with existing unconstrained methods, and benchmarked with metrics such as trajectory feasibility rate, conservatism, and solver execution time being evaluated.

2 Tight B-Spline Bounds

2.1 B-Spline Fundamentals

A B-spline is a piecewise-polynomial function parametrised by a variable t, with its shape being controlled by a series of control points q_i where $i \in \{0, 1, \ldots, n\}$ and set of knots t_i for $i \in \{0, 1, \ldots, n+d+1\}$. The knots determine the interaction of a set of basis functions, $N_{i,d}$, with the control points, which control the overall shape of the spline:

$$s(t) = \sum_{i=0}^{n} N_{i,d}(t)q_i, \tag{1}$$

where d is the degree of the spline. The basis functions are defined by the Cox-de Boor recursion formula:

$$N_{i,0}(t) = \begin{cases} 1, & \text{if } t \in [t_i, t_{i+1}) \\ 0, & \text{otherwise,} \end{cases} \tag{2}$$

$$N_{i,j}(t) = \frac{t - t_i}{t_{i+j} - t_i} N_{i,j-1}(t) + \frac{t_{i+j+1} - t}{t_{i+j+1} - t_{i+1}} N_{i+1,j-1}(t). \tag{3}$$

This work will consider bounds defined at the Greville abscissae t_i^*,

$$t_i^* = \frac{1}{d} \sum_{j=i+1}^{i+d} t_j. \tag{4}$$

B-Splines with more than one dimension are defined as sets of 1D splines over a shared knot vector, in which case the control points become vectors, $\mathbf{q}_i$. The derivative of a degree d B-spline is another B-spline with degree $d - 1$.

2.2   Tightness of B-Spline Bounds

A piecewise linear envelope that completely encloses the spline can be used to enforce constraints over the length of the spline. The convex hull property of B-splines is frequently used to construct this envelope [21, 24, 25], however this is a conservative solution [14, 18]. To achieve more aggressive trajectories, a tight envelope is required.

Lutterkort and Peters proposed tight, piecewise-linear bounds on the distance between a B-spline and its control polyline [10]. This work will consider the two bounds defined across each control point span, i.e. $t \in [t_i^*, t_{i+1}^*]$. The first is a tight bound that holds for any B-spline, and the second is a coarser, computationally efficient variant which, although tight for quadratic B-splines, becomes increasingly conservative as spline degree increases. Other formulations in [10] bound the separation between the spline and its control polyline over the whole spline. While this enables the enforcement of safety constraints, it necessarily introduces conservatism as the bounds are only tight at one point over along the length of the spline.

It was also observed that the tight bound in [10] was approximately equivalent to the area enclosed by the control polyline and the spline evaluated at its Greville abscissae, if the spline was smooth and the degree was small. This leads to the introduction of a new proposed envelope: for sufficiently smooth B-splines, the spline is contained within a set of simplexes constructed from the convex hulls of consecutive control points and Greville points.

$$\mathbf{s}(t) \in \text{Conv}(\mathbf{q}_i, \mathbf{q}_{i+1}, \mathbf{q}_i^*, \mathbf{q}_{i+1}^*) \quad \forall t \in [t_i^*, t_{i+1}^*], \tag{5}$$

where $\mathbf{s}(t)$ is a two- or three-dimensional spline evaluated at t, $\mathbf{q}_i^* = \mathbf{s}(t_i^*)$ are the Greville points, and $\text{Conv}(\cdot)$ evaluates the convex hull of a set of points. The validity of this envelope is verified in Sect. 2.3, and its conservatism is evaluated in Sect. 2.4.

2.3   Verification of Proposed Bound

The proposed bound (5) will be verified for uniform B-splines of order 3, which are extensively used by EGO [25]. The following theorem is proposed:

Theorem 1. *For uniform cubic B-splines, the proposed bound (5) is equivalent to Lutterkort and Peters' tight bound, Corollary 3.2 in [10].*

Proof. For any uniform B-spline $s(t)$, Corollary 3.2 in [10] simplifies to

$$f(q_i, q_{i+1}) \leq s(t) - q_i \leq g(q_i, q_{i+1}) \ \forall t \in [t_i^*, t_{i+1}^*], \tag{6}$$

$$f(q_i, q_{i+1}) = \frac{d+1}{24} L(\min(\Delta_2 q_i, 0), \min(\Delta_2 q_{i+1}, 0)), \tag{7}$$

$$g(q_i, q_{i+1}) = \frac{d+1}{24} L(\max(\Delta_2 q_i, 0), \max(\Delta_2 q_{i+1}, 0)), \tag{8}$$

where $L(a, b)$ is the linear interpolant of a and b, and the $\Delta_2 q_i$ are the centred second differences of the control points, which simplify to $\Delta_2 q_i = q_{i-1} - 2q_i + q_{i+1}$ for any uniform B-spline.

This paper proposes that a uniform cubic B-spline will be tightly bounded by two piecewise linear functions: the maximum and minimum of the control and Greville polylines, which are made up of the control points q_i, and the Greville points $q_i^* = s(t_i^*)$, respectively. Hence, the proposed bound (5) for a one-dimensional B-spline is

$$f'(q_i, q_i^*, q_{i+1}, q_{i+1}^*) \leq s(t) \leq g'(q_i, q_i^*, q_{i+1}, q_{i+1}^*) \ \forall t \in [t_i^*, t_{i+1}^*], \tag{9}$$

$$f'(q_i, q_i^*, q_{i+1}, q_{i+1}^*) = L(\min(q_i, q_i^*), \min(q_{i+1}, q_{i+1}^*)), \tag{10}$$

$$g'(q_i, q_i^*, q_{i+1}, q_{i+1}^*) = L(\max(q_i, q_i^*), \max(q_{i+1}, q_{i+1}^*)). \tag{11}$$

The proof will be conducted for the upper bound; the process for the lower bound is identical. The proposed upper bound will be equivalent to Corollary 3.2 in [10] if $f(\cdot)$ is equivalent to $f'(\cdot)$. There are two cases that must be investigated to account for the maximisation functions present in (9). Firstly,

$$q_i + \frac{1}{6} \max(\Delta_2 q_i, 0) = q_i, \tag{12}$$

$$\max(\Delta_2 q_i, 0) = 0. \tag{13}$$

(13) is satisfied provided $\Delta_2 q_i \leq 0$, so any control point with a negative centred second difference will place the upper bound at that control point. The proposed bound holds in this case. The second case to be investigated is that where the proposed bound is the Greville point q_i^*:

$$q_i + \frac{1}{6} \max(\Delta_2 q_i, 0) = s(t_i^*). \tag{14}$$

Following Lutterkort and Peters' method and choosing the knots $t_i = i$ (which causes no loss of generality), the Greville abscissae simplify to

$$t_i^* = i + \frac{d+1}{2} = i + 2. \tag{15}$$

The only cubic B-spline basis functions that are non-zero at $t = t_i^*$ are $N_{i-1,3}$, $N_{i,3}$, and $N_{i+1,3}$, which have values of $\frac{1}{6}, \frac{2}{3}$, and $\frac{1}{6}$ respectively at $t = t_i^*$. Hence, the value of a uniform cubic B-spline at its Greville abscissae can be computed:

$$s(t_i^*) = \frac{1}{6}q_{i-1} + \frac{2}{3}q_i + \frac{1}{6}q_{i+1}. \tag{16}$$

Substituting (16) into (14) results in

$$q_i + \frac{1}{6}\Delta_2^+ q_i = \frac{1}{6}q_{i-1} + \frac{2}{3}q_i + \frac{1}{6}q_{i+1}, \tag{17}$$

$$\max(\Delta_2 q_i, 0) = \Delta_2 q_i, \tag{18}$$

which is true if $\Delta_2 q_i \geq 0$. Any control point with a positive centred second difference will correspond to an upper bound equal to the spline evaluated at the Greville abscissa. Therefore, Theorem 1 holds: the proposed bound is identical to the bound stated at Corollary 3.2 in [10] for uniform cubic B-splines.   □

2.4   B-Spline Envelope Conservatism

Figure 1 compares the conservatism introduced by each of the considered bounding methods. The level of conservatism is quantified using the area enclosed by the envelope, as discussed in [18,19]. Using 100 sets of 20 uniformly distributed control points, the areas enclosed by each of the four bounds were evaluated for uniform, clamped B-splines with degrees ranging from 2 to 10. The proposed bound is tighter than the state-of-the-art approaches, as it encloses a smaller region of the space.

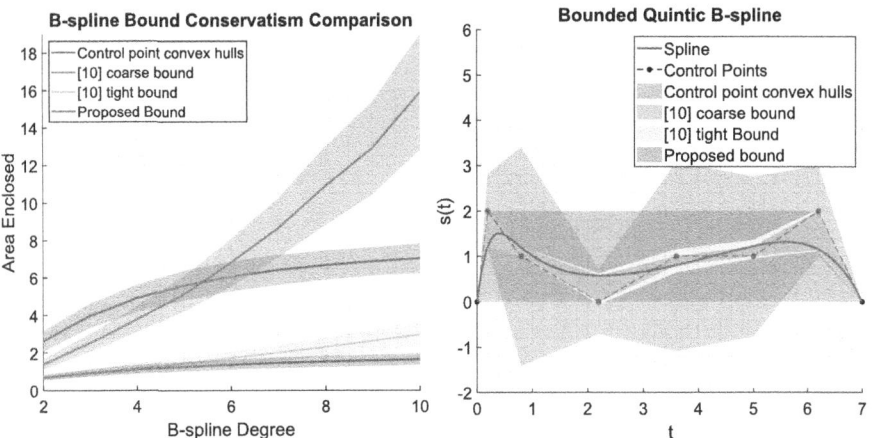

(a) Average area enclosed by different envelopes as spline degree changes.

(b) Different B-spline envelopes for an example quintic spline.

Fig. 1. Comparison between existing and proposed methods of bounding the distance between a B-spline and its control polyline.

3   Trajectory Optimisation

This work uses the EGO planner [25] as its foundation, which employs unconstrained optimisation with a cost function that rewards smoothness, distance from obstacles, and satisfaction of velocity and acceleration limits. This leads to a trade-off: if the user-selected weights corresponding to the cost function terms for obstacle distance and velocity-acceleration limits are small, the optimisation process produces colliding or kinodynamically infeasible trajectories. On the other hand, increasing those weights leads to conservative trajectories. However, this approach results in notably short computation times, ranging from 1 to 5 ms [23] so, where possible, the features of EGO's algorithm that enable these rapid computation times will be retained in the proposed algorithm.

3.1   Optimisation Problem

With the introduction of a tight B-spline bound in Sect. 2, constrained optimisation can be implemented without introducing excessive conservatism. The objective function is the elastic band cost used in [24, 25], minimised subject to velocity and acceleration constraints, which are modified versions of the penalties applied in [24]. Therefore, the optimisation problem becomes

$$\underset{\{\mathbf{q}_d,...,\mathbf{q}_n\}}{\arg\min} \left(\sum_{i=1}^{n-1} ||2\mathbf{q}_i - \mathbf{q}_{i+1} - \mathbf{q}_{i-1}||^2 \right)$$

$$\text{s.t.} \quad c_{i,j,k} \leq 0 \ i \in \{d, ..., n\}, \ j \in \{0, ..., o\}, \ k \in \{1, 2, 3, 4\} \quad (19)$$

$$v_{x,y,z}^2 - v_{\max}^2 \leq 0$$

$$a_{x,y,z}^2 - a_{\max}^2 \leq 0,$$

where $c_{i,j,k}$ are collision costs, computed using a modified version of the EGO collision cost algorithm which is described in Sect. 3.2. There are $n + 1$ control points and $o + 1$ obstacles. $v_{\max}$ and $a_{\max}$ are the desired maximum velocity and acceleration, and $v_{x,y,z} \in \mathbf{v}_i$, $a_{x,y,z} \in \mathbf{a}_i$ are the control points of the velocity and acceleration splines, computed using the well-known derivative of a B-spline:

$$\mathbf{v}_i = d \frac{\mathbf{q}_{i+1} - \mathbf{q}_i}{t_{i+d+1} - t_{i+1}},$$

$$\mathbf{a}_i = (d-1) \frac{\mathbf{v}_{i+1} - \mathbf{v}_i}{t_{i+d} - t_{i+1}}. \quad (20)$$

3.2   Collision Cost Gradient

The collision constraints associated with a single segment of the spline envelope are computed by

$$c = \frac{(\mathbf{x} - \mathbf{o}).\mathbf{n}}{||\mathbf{n}||}, \quad (21)$$

where **o** and **n** are a point and normal vector defining a plane on the edge of the obstacle. The cost is computed at each vertex of the trajectory envelope segment (5), *i.e.* $\mathbf{x} \in \{\mathbf{q}_i, \mathbf{q}_{i+1}, \mathbf{q}_i^*, \mathbf{q}_{i+1}^*\}$, such that four constraints per segment are computed. Gradients can be approximated using finite differences, however this is a computationally expensive process and results in reduced gradient accuracy. This slows the convergence of gradient-based optimisation algorithms, so the gradients will now be derived analytically. The variables to be optimised are the control points so that, for every constraint, a corresponding derivative with respect to every control point must be computed:

$$\frac{dc}{d\mathbf{q}_i} = \begin{bmatrix} \frac{dc}{d\mathbf{x}_i} & \frac{dc}{d\mathbf{y}_i} & \frac{dc}{d\mathbf{z}_i} \end{bmatrix}^\top \forall i \in \{0, ..., n\}. \tag{22}$$

Differentiating (21) in the case where **x** is a control point results in

$$\frac{dc^C}{d\mathbf{q}_i} = \frac{\mathbf{n}}{||\mathbf{n}||}. \tag{23}$$

In the case that **x** is a Greville point, the collision gradient with respect to the control points is

$$\frac{dc^G}{d\mathbf{q}_i} = \frac{dc^G}{d\mathbf{q}_i^*} \frac{d\mathbf{q}_i^*}{d\mathbf{q}_i} = \frac{\mathbf{n}}{||\mathbf{n}||} N_{i,d}(t_\mathbf{x}^*), \tag{24}$$

where $N_{i,d}(t)$ is the ith basis function of a d degree B-spline, evaluated at t, and $t_\mathbf{x}^*$ is the Greville abscissae corresponding to **x**.

3.3   Collision Constraint Algorithm

The computation of the collision cost and associated gradient is detailed in Algorithm 1, supported by Fig. 2. The plane defined by **n** and **o**, as required by (21), is computed by an extension of the collision avoidance force estimation method employed by the EGO planner [25], modified to account for the requirements of constrained optimisation using a trajectory envelope. EGO generates the collision cost and its gradient using occupancy grid information and starts with an initial path around each obstacle, planned using A*. Sample points are taken from the A* path to match each control point, and these are used to assign vectors to each control point indicating the direction of decreasing cost.

In the proposed method, the trajectory envelope divides into segments made up of the convex hulls described in (5), each of which must be kept collision-free. In the proposed method, sample points $\mathbf{o}_i, \mathbf{o}_{i+1}$ from the A*-generated path are joined to define the obstacle limits. The positions of colliding control points $\mathbf{p}_i$ are recorded; these are used as points of known collision. The $\mathbf{o}_i$ and $\mathbf{p}_i$ are shown in Fig 2a, and are defined for a section of the trajectory found to be in collision, although they are indexed to match the control points. For each obstacle boundary segment $[\mathbf{o}_i, \mathbf{o}_{i+1}]$, the centroid **a** of the segment $\mathbf{o}_i$ and $\mathbf{p}_i$ are used to define a 3rd point, **b**, such that $\mathbf{o}_i$, $\mathbf{o}_{i+1}$, and **b** define an obstacle boundary plane. An initial normal vector $\hat{\mathbf{n}}$ is then calculated using these three points. This is shown in Fig. 2b and lines 3–5 of Algorithm 1.

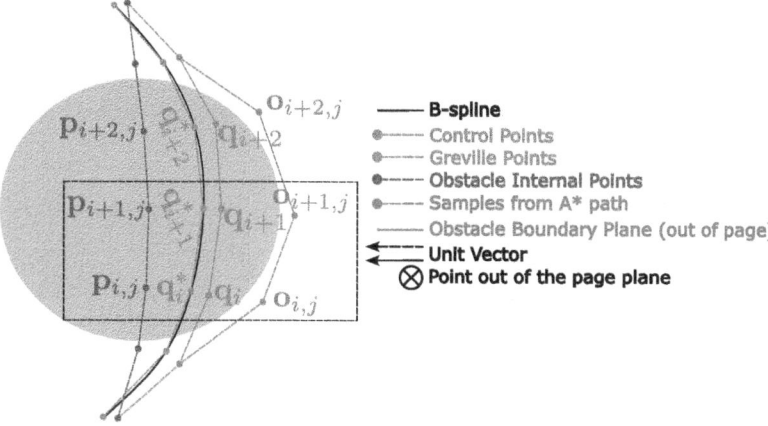

(a) Definition of obstacle boundary points o_i and internal points p_i.

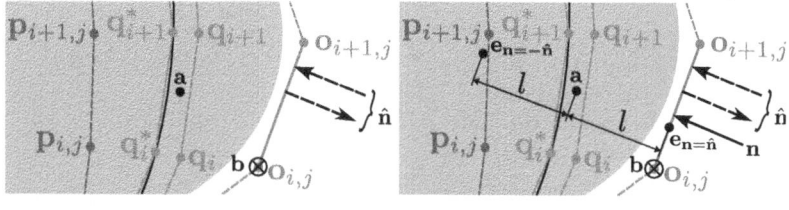

(b) Initial obstacle plane normal, $\hat{n}$.   (c) Selection of correct sign of n.

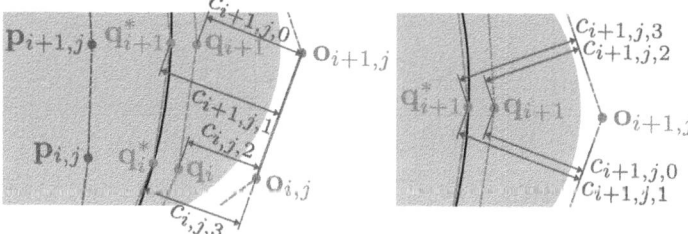

(d) Four costs computed for a single (e) Four costs for each control point
segment. q_i from the two segments it borders.

Fig. 2. Process to generate the collision constraint for a B-spline trajectory.

Next, point a is used to choose the sign of the normal vector n before the collision costs $c_{i,j,k}$ are calculated using (21). This is to ensure that c is negative when the point x is in free space and positive when x is colliding with the obstacle, and to set the sign of the gradient. The sign of n is selected by attempting to project a onto the obstacle boundary plane using $\hat{n}$. This process is shown in Fig. 2c and lines 6–11 of Algorithm 1.

Finally the four costs associated with the trajectory envelope segment can be calculated, along with their gradients. These costs are the distances from the vertices of the envelope segment to the obstacle plane. This is shown in Fig. 2d and lines 12–20 of Algorithm 1.

Algorithm 1. Computation of collision constraint

Require: $\mathbf{q}_i$,   ▷ *Spline Control Points (1)*
                $\mathbf{q}_i^* = \mathbf{s}(t_i^*)$,   ▷ *Greville points (4)*
                $\mathbf{o}_{i,j}$,   ▷ *Obstacle Boundary (Fig. 2a)*
                $\mathbf{p}_{i,j}$ ▷ *Obstacle Internal Points (Fig. 2a)*
 1: **for** $i = 0$ to CONTROLPOINTCOUNT-2,
        $j = 0$ to OBSTACLECOUNT-1 **do**
 2:     **if** EXISTS($\mathbf{o}_{i,j}$) AND EXISTS($\mathbf{o}_{i+1,j}$) **then**
 3:         $\mathbf{a} \leftarrow$ MEAN($\mathbf{o}_{i,j}, \mathbf{o}_{i+1,j}, \mathbf{p}_{i,j}, \mathbf{p}_{i+1,j}$)   ▷ *Centroid*
 4:         $\mathbf{b} \leftarrow \mathbf{o}_{i,j} + ||(\mathbf{a} - \mathbf{o}_{i,j}) \times (\mathbf{o}_{i,j} - \mathbf{o}_{i+1,j})||$ ▷ *Obstacle boundary plane: Point*
 5:         $\hat{\mathbf{n}} \leftarrow \frac{(\mathbf{o}_{i+1,j} - \mathbf{o}_{i,j}) \times (\mathbf{b} - \mathbf{o}_{i,j})}{||(\mathbf{o}_{i+1,j} - \mathbf{o}_{i,j}) \times (\mathbf{b} - \mathbf{o}_{i,j})||}$ ▷ *Obstacle Boundary Plane: Normal (Fig. 2b)*
 6:         $l \leftarrow |(\mathbf{a} - \mathbf{o}_{i,j}) \cdot \hat{\mathbf{n}}|$ ▷ *Select normal direction*
 7:         $\mathbf{e} \leftarrow \mathbf{a} - l\hat{\mathbf{n}}$
 8:         **if** $(\mathbf{e} - \mathbf{o}_{i,j}) \cdot \hat{\mathbf{n}} == 0$ **then**   ▷ *Fig. 2c*
 9:             $\mathbf{n} \leftarrow \hat{\mathbf{n}}$
10:         **else**
11:             $\mathbf{n} \leftarrow -\hat{\mathbf{n}}$
12:         $c_{i,j,2} \leftarrow (\mathbf{q}_i - \mathbf{o}_{i,j}) \cdot \mathbf{n}$ ▷ *Compute Costs (Fig. 2d)*
13:         $c_{i,j,3} \leftarrow (\mathbf{q}_i^* - \mathbf{o}_{i,j}) \cdot \mathbf{n}$
14:         $c_{i+1,j,0} \leftarrow (\mathbf{q}_{i+1} - \mathbf{o}_{i,j}) \cdot \mathbf{n}$
15:         $c_{i+1,j,1} \leftarrow (\mathbf{q}_{i+1}^* - \mathbf{o}_{i,j}) \cdot \mathbf{n}$
16:         $\mathbf{d}_i \leftarrow \left[\frac{d\mathbf{q}_i^*}{d\mathbf{q}_0} \ \frac{d\mathbf{q}_i^*}{d\mathbf{q}_1} \cdots \frac{d\mathbf{q}_i^*}{d\mathbf{q}_n} \right]$ ▷ *Greville point gradients: Eqn. (24)*
17:         $\mathbf{g}_{i,j,2,i} \leftarrow \mathbf{n}$ ▷ *Compute segment gradients*
18:         $\mathbf{G}_{i,j,3} \leftarrow \mathbf{d}_i \mathbf{n}^\top$
19:         $\mathbf{g}_{i+1,j,0,i+1} \leftarrow \mathbf{n}$
20:         $\mathbf{G}_{i+1,j,1} \leftarrow \mathbf{d}_i \mathbf{n}^\top$
21: **return** $\mathbf{C}, \mathbf{G}$

4   Simulation Results

4.1   Simulation Setup

To evaluate the proposed planner against the unconstrained method employed by EGO [25], the MRS UAV system was used [1]. This open-source platform aims to reduce the sim-to-real time by providing an open-source, realistic simulation and real-world experimentation platform. MRS's Gazebo simulation and existing SE3 controller were used, together with the X500 UAV model, running on an Intel i7-11800H processor. The optimisation problem is solved using Nlopt's [6] implementation of the SLSQP algorithm [8].

The environments used were random forests, as these are prevalent in the literature [21,22,24,25]. They enable the testing of local planners with no prior knowledge of the environment, while minimising the need for a global planner. Maps were generated with obstacle densities between 0.1 and 0.3 obstacles per square metre (opsm), and obstacle diameters between 0.1 and 0.2 m. The X500 UAV used has a diameter of 0.8 m. Obstacle positions and their size are distributed uniformly. The MRS system's simulation of an Intel Realsense D435i depth camera is used to generate a point cloud. This setup allowed evaluation of EGO [25] with minimal modification to their open-source code. The mission was to fly from one side of the 20 m long forest to the other.

4.2   Evaluation Metrics

Firstly, the ability of the planner to guide the UAV from start to goal without colliding was measured. Two failure states were recorded: fail-safe, and fail-unsafe. Fail-safe results were observed when the UAV stopped safely, but the planner could not find a feasible route to the goal, and a collision was recorded as a fail-unsafe result. Conservatism was measured using the trajectory length $L_{EGO,NEW}$, since more conservative trajectories take longer routes around obstacles, consuming more energy than their aggressive counterparts.

Optimisation time, $t^{OPT}_{EGO,NEW}$, is often used to measure computational efficiency. However, in cases where many attempts are necessary to generate a successful plan, this metric does not reflect real-world performance. Hence, the total time from a new plan being requested to a successful plan being generated was also recorded, referred to as start-to-success time or $t^{STS}_{EGO,NEW}$.

4.3   Results

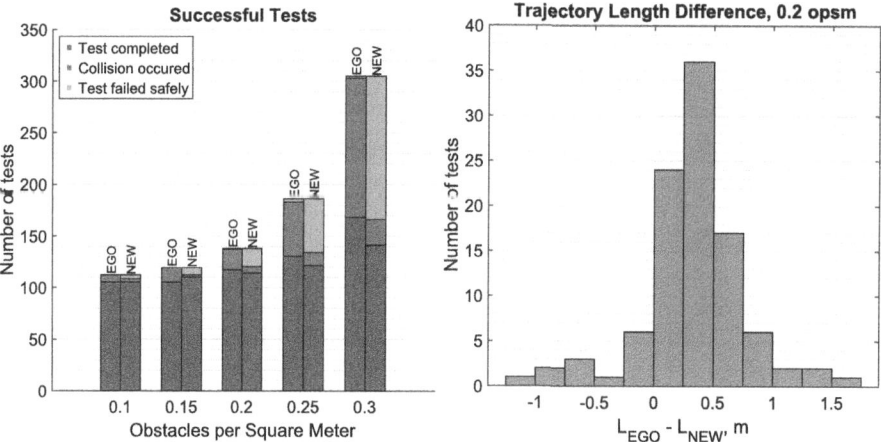

(a) Successful and failed test counts.

(b) Sample distribution of trajectory length difference. Positive results indicate that EGO is more conservative.

Fig. 3. Success data and sample conservatism distribution.

Figure 3a shows the number of successful and failed tests for each planner. Both planners have similar failure rates, however the proposed planner's failure condition is largely fail-safe, where as EGO tends to fail-unsafe. At higher densities, the proposed planner starts to fail more often than EGO. This was observed to be caused by higher obstacle densities creating complex geometries that lead to an infeasible optimisation problem. EGO does not suffer from infeasible optimisation problems due to the employment of an unconstrained optimiser, however EGO frequently produces trajectories that violate the safety or kinodynamic feasibility constraints, leading to collisions. Another factor affecting the proposed planner's performance was the collision avoidance being implemented by inequality constraints rather than the objective function. With a vector field guiding EGO away from obstacle-dense regions, EGO often avoids high-risk areas entirely, while the proposed planner does not, increasing its failure rate.

Table 1. Comparison between the two planners, in the form Mean ± Std.Dev.

Obstacle Density (opsm)	$L_{EGO} - L_{NEW}$ (m)	$t_{EGO}^{OPT} - t_{NEW}^{OPT}$ (ms)	$t_{EGO}^{STS} - t_{NEW}^{STS}$ (ms)
0.1	0.28 ± 0.32	-8.04 ± 5.30	-26.24 ± 96.65
0.15	0.36 ± 0.58	-9.01 ± 4.35	-10.68 ± 170.31
0.2	0.33 ± 0.42	-12.46 ± 7.79	-51.00 ± 143.38
0.25	0.31 ± 0.98	-14.58 ± 7.89	-61.26 ± 131.17
0.3	0.2 ± 1.3	-16.54 ± 10.51	-130.55 ± 268.61

Table 1 shows the difference in trajectory length for successful tests, and Fig. 3b shows a sample distribution of those results. Trajectories generated by the proposed planner are typically shorter than those generated by EGO. This demonstrates the tightness of the proposed bound, allowing the UAV to pass closer to obstacles without collision.

Table 1 also shows the average difference in optimisation time t^{OPT} and start-to-success time t^{STS}. A typical run of the proposed constrained optimisation routine would vary between 8 and 16 ms, compared to EGO's 0.15 to 0.42 ms. This is expected due to the use of a constrained optimisation routine. There was an expectation that start-to-success time would be similar across the planners, as the constrained optimisation should reduce the need to re-plan upon the generation of a colliding or kinodynamically infeasible trajectory. However, the proposed planner often needed to re-plan due to the frequent infeasibility of the optimisation problem, and therefore performed poorly by this metric.

5   Conclusions

To conclude, this paper proposes a novel B-spline bound, and proves that it is valid for uniform cubic B-splines. This bound is then implemented in a trajectory planner that uses a constrained optimisation algorithm to generate less conservative trajectories than the EGO planner [25]. However, this comes at the cost of a higher computational burden, due to large numbers of constraints that lead to infeasible optimisation problems. Future work is to examine the proposed B-spline bound in the general case, and replace the obstacle generation algorithm to improve computational efficiency.

Acknowledgments. This work was supported by the UK Engineering and Physical Sciences Research Council (EPSRC) grant EP/T517823/1.

Disclosure of Interests. The authors have no competing interests to declare that are relevant to the content of this article.

References

1. Baca, T., et al.: The MRS UAV System: Pushing the frontiers of reproducible research, real-world deployment, and education with autonomous unmanned aerial vehicles. J. Intell. Robot. Syst. **102**(1), 1–28 (2021). https://doi.org/10.1007/s10846-021-01383-5

2. Bucki, N., Lee, J., Mueller, M.W.: Rectangular pyramid partitioning using integrated depth sensors (RAPPIDS): A fast planner for multicopter navigation. IEEE Robot. Autom. Lett. **5**(3), 4626–4633 (2020). https://doi.org/10.1109/LRA.2020.3003277

3. Chen, J., Liu, T., Shen, S.: Online generation of collision-free trajectories for quadrotor flight in unknown cluttered environments. In: 2016 IEEE International Conference on Robotics and Automation (ICRA), pp. 1476–1483 (2016).https://doi.org/10.1109/ICRA.2016.7487283

4. Ding, W., Gao, W., Wang, K., Shen, S.: An efficient B-spline-based kinodynamic replanning framework for quadrotors. IEEE Trans. Robot. **35**(6), 1287–1306 (08 2019)

5. Gao, F., Shen, S.: Quadrotor trajectory generation in dynamic environments using semi-definite relaxation on nonconvex QCQP. In: 2017 IEEE International Conference on Robotics and Automation (ICRA), pp. 6354–6361 (2017). https://doi.org/10.1109/ICRA.2017.7989750

6. Johnson, S.G.: The NLopt nonlinear-optimization package (2007). https://github.com/stevengj/nlopt

7. Kim, S., Bhattacharya, S., Kumar, V.: Path planning for a tethered mobile robot. In: 2014 IEEE International Conference on Robotics and Automation (ICRA), pp. 1132–1139 (2014).https://doi.org/10.1109/ICRA.2014.6906996

8. Kraft, D.: Algorithm 733: TOMP–fortran modules for optimal control calculations. ACM Trans. Math. Softw. **20**, 262–281 (1994).https://doi.org/10.1145/192115.192124

9. Lin, J., Zhu, H., Alonso-Mora, J.: Robust vision-based obstacle avoidance for micro aerial vehicles in dynamic environments. In: 2020 IEEE International Conference on Robotics and Automation (ICRA), pp. 2682–2688 (2020).https://doi.org/10.1109/ICRA40945.2020.9197481

10. Lutterfort, D., Peters, J.: Tight linear bounds on the distance between a spline and its b-spline control polygon. Purdue University, Tech. rep. (1999)

11. Mellinger, D., Kumar, V.: Minimum snap trajectory generation and control for quadrotors. In: IEEE International Conference on Robotics and Automation (2011)

12. Mellinger, D., Kushleyev, A., Kumar, V.: Mixed-integer quadratic program trajectory generation for heterogeneous quadrotor teams. In: 2012 IEEE International Conference on Robotics and Automation, pp. 477–483 (2012).https://doi.org/10.1109/ICRA.2012.6225009

13. Rousseau, G., Stoica Maniu, C., Tebbani, S., Babel, M., Martin, N.: Minimum-time B-spline trajectories with corridor constraints. application to cinematographic quadrotor flight plans. Control Eng. Pract. **89**, 190–203 (2019).https://doi.org/10.1016/j.conengprac.2019.05.022, https://www.sciencedirect.com/science/article/pii/S0967066119300772

14. Sabetghadam, B., Cunha, R., Pascoal, A.: Enforcing temporal and spatial separation constraints in multi-vehicle trajectory generation problems using a bernstein relaxation and refinement method. IEEE Robot. Autom. Lett. pp. 1–8 (2025). https://doi.org/10.1109/LRA.2025.3541458

15. Semsch, E., Jakob, M., Pavlicek, D., Pechoucek, M.: Autonomous UAV surveillance in complex urban environments. In: 2009 IEEE/WIC/ACM International Joint Conference on Web Intelligence and Intelligent Agent Technology, vol. 2, pp. 82–85 (2009). https://doi.org/10.1109/WI-IAT.2009.132

16. Siciliano, B., Khatib, O.: Springer Handbook of Robotics. Springer Handbooks, Springer (2016). https://doi.org/10.1007/978-3-319-32552-1

17. Szmuk, M., Pascucci, C.A., AÇikmeşe, B.: Real-time quad-rotor path planning for mobile obstacle avoidance using convex optimization. In: 2018 IEEE/RSJ International Conference on Intelligent Robots and Systems (IROS), pp. 1–9 (2018). https://doi.org/10.1109/IROS.2018.8594351

18. Tordesillas, J., How, J.P.: MADER: Trajectory planner in multiagent and dynamic environments. IEEE Trans. Rob. **38**(1), 463–476 (2022). https://doi.org/10.1109/TRO.2021.3080235

19. Tordesillas, J., How, J.P.: MINVO basis: Finding simplexes with minimum volume enclosing polynomial curves. Comput. Aided Des. **151**, 103341 (2022)

20. Tordesillas, J., Lopez, B.T., Everett, M., How, J.P.: FASTER: Fast and safe trajectory planner for navigation in unknown environments. IEEE Trans. Rob. **38**(2), 922–938 (2022). https://doi.org/10.1109/TRO.2021.3100142

21. Tordesillas, J., Lopez, B.T., How, J.P.: FASTER: Fast and safe trajectory planner for flights in unknown environments. In: 2019 IEEE/RSJ International Conference on Intelligent Robots and Systems (IROS), pp. 1934–1940 (2019). https://doi.org/10.1109/IROS40897.2019.8968021

22. Usenko, V., von Stumberg, L., Pangercic, A., Cremers, D.: Real-time trajectory replanning for MAVs using uniform b-splines and a 3d circular buffer. In: IEEE/RSJ International Conference on Intelligent Robots and Systems (2017)

23. Wilson, A.N., Kumar, A., Jha, A., Cenkeramaddi, L.R.: Embedded sensors, communication technologies, computing platforms and machine learning for UAVs: A review. IEEE Sens. J. **22**(3), 1807–1826 (2022). https://doi.org/10.1109/JSEN.2021.3139124

24. Zhou, B., Pan, J., Gao, F., Shen, S.: RAPTOR: Robust and perception-aware trajectory replanning for quadrotor fast flight. IEEE Trans. Robot. **37**(6), 1992–2009 (2021)

25. Zhou, X., Wang, Z., Ye, H., Xu, C., Gao, F.: EGO-planner: An ESDF-free gradient-based local planner for quadrotors. IEEE Robot. Autom. Lett. **6**(2), 478–485 (2021). https://doi.org/10.1109/LRA.2020.3047728

26. Zhu, H., Alonso-Mora, J.: Chance-constrained collision avoidance for MAVs in dynamic environments. IEEE Robot. Autom. Lett. **4**(2), 776–783 (2019). https://doi.org/10.1109/LRA.2019.2893494

Hierarchical Coverage Path Planning for a Multi-modal Robot Exploring Disconnected Regions

Sebastian Stelter[1]([⊠]), Daniel Kuan Io U.[2], Sabyasachi Mondal[1],
Leonard Felicetti[1], and Saurabh Upadhyay[1]

[1] Centre for Autonomous and Cyber-Physical Systems, Faculty of Engineering and
Applied Sciences, Cranfield University, Cranfield MK43 0AL, UK
{Sebastian.Stelter,Sabyasachi.Mondal,Leonard.Felicetti,
Saurabh.Upadhyay}@cranfield.ac.uk
[2] Department of Engineering Mathematics, University of Bristol,
Bristol BS8 1QU, UK

Abstract. We present a near-optimal Coverage Path Planning (CPP) approach for multi-modal robots in complex environments with multiple arbitrarily shaped disconnected regions. The problem arises in ground coverage missions conducted in unstructured terrains, such as planetary exploration or search and rescue missions, where safe regions are disconnected by areas of high slope that a robot with a single locomotion modality cannot traverse. A multi-modal robot can switch between different locomotion modalities (e.g. driving and flying) to safely navigate these challenging environments while ensuring complete coverage. The proposed method identifies both traversable and non-traversable areas based on Digital Elevation Model (DEM) meshes. The problem is then formulated as a hierarchical Traveling Salesman Problem (TSP) and solved using Mixed-Integer Linear Programming (MILP). The proposed approach is evaluated on 500 randomly generated maps and four real-world simulation scenarios constructed from Martian terrain DEM data.

1 Introduction

Coverage Path Planning (CPP) is a fundamental problem in the context of modern robotics and automation, finding use in a variety of areas such as agricultural monitoring, factory inspections or surface treatments [1]. Especially in the fields of planetary exploration, and search and rescue applications, unstructured terrains pose an additional challenge [2]. These environments regularly contain many arbitrarily shaped obstacles such as cliffs, boulders or soft sands. In many cases, these obstacles fragment the area into multiple disconnected safe regions. Unmanned Ground Vehicles (UGVs) are therefore incapable of covering such a scenario, as there is no safe way for them to traverse between these disconnected regions. While Unmanned Aerial Vehicles (UAVs) could avoid obstacles by flying over them and thus traverse between regions, they have some drawbacks

A. Cavalcanti et al. (Eds.): TAROS 2025, LNAI 16045, pp. 433–444, 2026.
https://doi.org/10.1007/978-3-032-01486-3_33

compared to UGVs in terms of limited battery power and payload restrictions. Further, UAVs are limited to aerial coverage and thus require environments that are suitable for flight. Missions involving sample collection or require lower vantage points are challenging for UAVs.

Multi-modal mobility robot platforms that are capable of switching between different modes of locomotion can be utilized to profit from the advantages of both platforms [3,4]. While these robots can utilize their primary modality (e.g. driving or walking) for detailed ground coverage, obstacles can be avoided by switching to a secondary modality (e.g. jumping or flying).

These characteristics make multi-modal robots potential candidates for CPP tasks in unstructured terrain with multiple disconnected regions. In this work, we focus on coverage path planning in an area of disconnected safe regions using a multi-modal mobility robot. We call this problem Multi-Modal Multiple Disconnected Region CPP (M3DR-CPP) problem.

Contributions:

– A near-optimal hierarchical Mixed-Integer Linear Programming (MILP) based solution to the M3DR-CPP problem.
– Validation of the proposed approach in realistic high-fidelity 2.5D environments

The remainder of this paper is organized as follows: In Sect. 2, related work in the field of CPP is presented. Section 3 describes the M3DR-CPP problem this work aims to solve. Section 4 presents our proposed TSP based method to solve the M3DR-CPP problem and Sect. 5 presents and discusses the results of our work. Section 6 gives a conclusion and an outlook on future work.

2   Related Work

This section gives an overview of the existing approaches for CPP in multi-region scenarios (Sect. 2.1), and CPP with terrain considerations (Sect. 2.2).

2.1   Multi-region CPP

Several approaches have been proposed to solve the CPP problem in scenarios with multiple disconnected regions, primarily in the context of UAVs. One common approach to this problem utilizes the Boustrophedon algorithm [5] to generate a back-and-forth path within each region. The individual region paths are then connected using a variety of different approaches, such as simulated annealing [6], generalized large neighbourhood search [7], genetic algorithms [8] or nearest neighbour heuristics [9]. Some approaches calculate multiple Boustrophedon paths with different orientations in each cell and select a candidate based on the inter-region path, resulting in potentially shorter overall paths. The regions are then connected using methods such as k-nearest neighbour [9] or 2-opt [10].

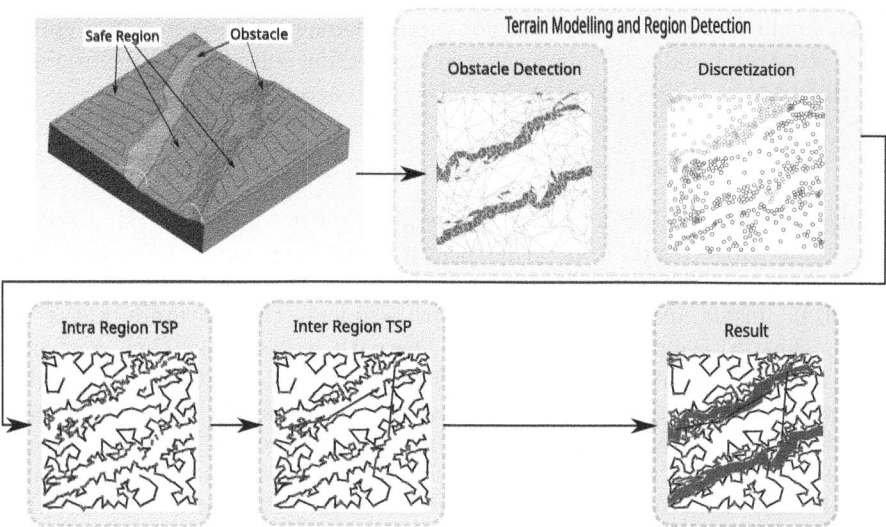

Fig. 1. Illustration of the M3DR-CPP problem and our proposed approach. The robot must cover all safe regions (blue) using its primary modality and cross obstacle regions (red) using its secondary modality to achieve full coverage. An example path is shown in the top left with use of the primary modality in black and use of the secondary modality in white. The proposed approach detects obstacles and discretizes each disconnected region into waypoints. A TSP is solved to generate the path for each region and to connect all regions to generate a full coverage path. (Color figure online)

One method uses Ant Colony Optimization (ACO) to determine the order of regions [11]. Sensor footprint sweeps are then calculated to fill each region and connected using a second ACO formulation. Obstacles are avoided by flying around or over them. The sensor footprint sweeps approach has also been used in a single non-convex region scenario by defining the connecting of the sweeps as a generalized TSP [12]. Another approach uses a hyperheuristic based on a neural network which learns the heuristic for ACO to calculate the coverage path for each robot in a multi-robot scenario [13]. One method also uses ACO to calculate the region visiting order for each robot in a multi-robot scenario, but uses spanning tree coverage to calculate the intra-region paths [14].

Finally, one approach uses self-organizing maps to find the ideal region order [15]. Intra-region paths are then calculated by using concentric shrinking rings. Each ring is discretized into waypoints and then connected to the nearest ring based on waypoint distance. This approach guarantees complete coverage, even in non-convex regions, but does so at the cost of calculation time and coverage path length.

With exception of the last approach, all works in this Section assume a set of convex regions without obstacles, which makes them impractical for use in the M3DR-CPP scenario. Further, these approaches have been developed for UAVs and therefore many of them allow the robot to overshoot the region boundaries, which would lead to collisions and potentially damage to the robot in a ground based scenario. Finally, the approaches in this Section consider a 2D environment and do not take the structure of the terrain into account.

2.2   Terrain Based CPP

While multi region CPP approaches generally do not consider terrain information, some single region approaches utilize DEMs to generate safer and more efficient coverage paths. One approach uses terrain data to classify areas as flat, sloped, or unsafe and then generates path segments that naturally follow the terrain slope to avoid steep angles [13]. The path segments are then connected using a genetic algorithm. Another work uses an aerial scout robot to identify the lowest cost path to a target point based on aerial imaging [16]. The approach considers static obstacles and different terrain traversal costs. Another approach considers slopes to detect unsafe areas before calculating a coverage path through the safe areas using spiral spanning tree coverage [17]. This work recognizes that obstacles may separate the area into multiple disconnected regions, but only covers the largest detected region. Finally, one approach detects different terrain types from aerial images using a neural network and uses this information to assign balanced coverage tasks to multiple robots [18].

3   Problem Description

The problem considers a triangulated terrain based on DEM data of the target area. The terrain contains slopes that are too steep for the robot to traverse while using the primary motion modality. We refer to these sloped areas as obstacles. Regions that can be traversed safely in the primary motion modality are called safe regions. The obstacles may entirely separate safe regions from each other, making it impossible to travel between them in the primary modality. The robot can switch to a secondary motion modality which allows it to traverse obstacles, but cannot perform its coverage task while using the secondary modality. It is assumed that the robot sensors can cover the entirety of each triangle in the terrain from the triangle incenter point and that the robot can turn in place. Safe regions that contain only one node are excluded, as CPP in these regions would be trivial.

The M3DR-CPP problem consists of two subproblems. First, given the DEM of the target, safe regions and obstacles need to be identified and discretized into nodes. Second, given a set of regions with nodes, a coverage path that passes through all nodes in all regions needs to be found while minimizing the path length.

4   Proposed M3DR-CPP Method

We propose an algorithm that solves the M3DR-CPP problem in three steps as shown in Fig. 1. In the first step, we model a triangular terrain mesh from the DEM data and detect obstacles and safe regions. In each safe region, the incenter of each triangle is calculated. The resulting incenter points are then used to formulate a hierarchical open-loop TSP problem in step two and three. In the second step, MILP is used to solve a TSP within each disconnected region using all incenter points in that region. As MILP guarantees optimality [19], this step will always generate the optimal path through each disconnected region. In the third step, the endpoints of the paths generated in the second step are used to formulate and solve another TSP in the same manner to connect the intra-region paths. The details of each step are as follows:

4.1   Terrain Modelling and Region Detection

We use the Delaunay triangulation [20] to model the 2.5 D terrain from the given DEM terrain data. The slope of each triangle is calculated as

$$\theta = \arccos n_z. \tag{1}$$

where n_z is the z component of the triangle's normal vector. A user-defined slope threshold $\bar{\theta}$ defines the maximum allowed slope in safe regions. Triangles with a higher slope than the threshold are considered obstacles and cannot be traversed.

We use a clustering approach on all safe triangles to generate disconnected safe regions. The clustering approach considers the terrain mesh as an undirected graph and uses the triangle vertices and edges of the mesh as nodes and edges of the graph, respectively. The MATLAB `conncomp` function is then used to find connected components in the graph. As the graph is based on the terrain mesh, triangles with edges in the same graph component are in the same disconnected region. Next, for each triangle that has been marked in the previous step, the incenter point is calculated as

$$
\begin{aligned}
x_c &= \frac{ax_1 + bx_2 + cx_3}{a + b + c} \\
y_c &= \frac{ay_1 + by_2 + cy_3}{a + b + c} \\
z_c &= \frac{az_1 + bz_2 + cz_3}{a + b + c}
\end{aligned}
\tag{2}
$$

where $p_1 = (x_1, y_1, z_1), p_2 = (x_2, y_2, z_2), p_3 = (x_3, y_3, z_3)$ are the vertices of the triangle, and a, b, c are the edges. These incenter points serve as nodes for the TSP.

4.2   Intra Region TSP

After defining the regions and nodes that need to be covered, the TSP needs to be solved for each region to generate the path the robot should follow. We frame the TSP as a Mixed-Integer Linear Programming (MILP) problem to leverage the optimality [19] and high scalability [21] of MILP solvers. The problem is formulated as

$$\min \sum_{i=1}^{n} \sum_{j=1}^{n} d_{ij} \pi_{ij} \tag{3}$$

$$\sum_{i=1}^{n} \pi_{ij} = 1 \qquad\qquad \forall j \tag{4}$$

$$\sum_{j=1}^{n} \pi_{ij} = 1 \qquad\qquad \forall i \tag{5}$$

$$\sum_{i \in S} \sum_{j \in \bar{S}} \pi_{ij} \geq 1 \qquad\qquad \forall S \tag{6}$$

$$\sum_{i \in S} \sum_{j \in S} \pi_{ij} \leq |S| - 1 \qquad\qquad \forall S \tag{7}$$

where n is the number of nodes, $\pi_{ij} \in \{0, 1\}$ is the decision variable that indicates whether a path between two nodes p_i and p_j is included in the solution and S is any subset of nodes. d_{ij} is the euclidean distance between p_i and p_j defined as

$$d_{ij} = \sqrt{(x_i - x_j)^2 + (y_i - y_j)^2 + (z_i - z_j)^2} \tag{8}$$

where $p_i = (x_i, y_i, z_i)$ and $p_j = (x_j, y_j, z_j)$ represent the coordinates of the two nodes. Equation (3) describes the cost function of the problem, constrained by Eqs. (4)–(7). Equations (4) and (5) ensure that each node has only two paths connected to it. This guarantees that each node is only visited once.

Equations (6) and (7) describe the process of sub-tour elimination. This ensures that the result only contains a single path over all nodes. As it would be infeasible to add sub-tour constraints for all possible subsets, we chose an iterative approach. First, the problem is solved without any sub-tour constraints. If the solution contains multiple sub-tours, constraints are added for the nodes in each sub-tour and the problem is solved again. This process is repeated until a single-tour solution is found.

As the robot is expected to cover multiple disconnected regions, it is generally not desirable for the robot to return to its point of origin in each disconnected region, as this would result in a longer path and make finding a solution more complex. To create this additional constraint, a virtual node p_0 is added to each region. p_0 has an arbitrary position outside of the map and its distance to any other node is defined as

$$d_{ij} = 0 \text{ if } i = 0 \lor j = 0 \tag{9}$$

which implies that the cost to reach p_0 from any node is always 0. This additional node and all edges connected to it will be deleted after the TSP is solved, leaving the two nodes that were connected to it with only a single neighbour. These two nodes will be considered as the endpoints of each region's path, which will be connected in the next step to generate the complete path across all regions. As MILP always converges on an optimal solution [19], it is ensured that the endpoints are placed in a way that reduces the intra-region path length by the largest amount. As no additional cost is generated by connecting to $p0$, the path length for the open loop TSP must be of equal length or shorter than the path length for the closed loop TSP. We solve the aforementioned MILP problem using the MATLAB `solve` function.

4.3   Inter Region TSP

In the final step, the endpoints of all regions need to be connected in sequence to generate a complete path over all regions. To do so, the same TSP approach as described above is used. We again add a node p_0 to generate an open loop solution as our use case does not require a direct return to the origin, but a closed loop can easily be generated by omitting this node.

To generate a valid path, it needs to be ensured that the path segment that enters a region R_k through an endpoint p_i continues to the second endpoint p_j of the same region R_k. We define this constraint by setting the weight between two endpoints of the same region as $d_{ij} = 0$ for both $p_i, p_j \in R_k$.

This means that once one endpoint has been chosen, the optimal next choice will always be either the second node in that region or p_0. Finally, the edges between the two endpoints of the same region are removed, as they would not be traversed, being replaced with the intra-region solutions from the previous step. p_0 and the corresponding edges are removed as well.

5   Simulation Results

To evaluate the proposed approach, two experiments were conducted. First, to validate the method in a general context, it was tested on 500 randomly generated maps with varying complexity. Second, to demonstrate the versatility of the approach in a realistic real-world scenario, it was evaluated across four scenarios using mars DEM data.

The experiments were conducted on a Lenovo ThinkPad T480s with an Intel i5-8250U @1.6 GHz processor with 4 cores and 8 threads. The computer was equipped with 8 GB of DDR4-2400 RAM and an Intel UHD 620 internal graphics processor.

5.1   General Scenario

The approach was evaluated on 500 randomly generated maps. Each map consisted of 15×15 evenly spaced squares, each consisting of two triangles. The obstacle detection threshold was set to $15°$. The slope of each triangle was generated randomly based on a maximum allowed slope. The maximum allowed slope was set randomly between 20° and 40°. Maps with a lower maximum slope generate close to no obstacles, while maps with a higher maximum slope generate almost no safe regions. These scenarios are trivial to solve and were therefore excluded. To simulate more realistic terrain properties, Gaussian smoothing is used with a random smoothing factor between 0 and 0.7. A smoothing factor over 0.7 generates maps void of obstacles in most cases and was therefore excluded. The experiment was run for a total of 500 trials.

These settings resulted in an average of 125.24 safe nodes per map with a maximum of 431, minimum of 9 and standard deviation of 103.84. The average number of disconnected regions was 14.17 with a maximum of 33, a minimum of 1 and a standard deviation of 6.67.

As a baseline for comparison, a greedy algorithm was run on the same set of trials. This algorithm starts at the first node in each region and always chooses the closest unvisited node that can be reached. Paths that would pass through an obstacle are modelled with an additional near-infinite penalty cost to discourage the greedy algorithm from choosing this path. The baseline algorithm managed to find a valid solution for 128 out of the 500 trials. The majority of the successful trials had only a small number of safe nodes with only four trials having more than 100 nodes. Out of these four trials, two had over 400 nodes, but all nodes belonged to the same region. Including trials that returned a path which passes through obstacles, ignoring penalty costs, the average total path length was 140.09 with a maximum of 353.77, minimum of 21.15 and a standard deviation of 85.58.

In contrast to this, our proposed approach returned a valid solution for all 500 trials, independent of node or region count. The average path length while respecting all obstacles is 112.06 with a maximum of 290.86, minimum of 16.62 and standard deviation of 66.59. This is an average reduction in path length of 20.01% whilst conforming to the more strict constraints. Figure 2 shows that the proposed approach is capable of finding valid solutions in a variety of scenarios. In Fig. 2.a, our approach solves a large obstacle free region with a narrow passage connecting two mostly separated areas. Figure 2.b shows the solution to a scenario containing multiple large regions that are completely separated by obstacles. Even in highly complex scenarios as shown in Fig. 2.c, which contain multiple narrow passages, dead ends and multiple large regions, the proposed approach is capable of finding a solution. Finally, a solution to a map containing a large number of disconnected regions is shown in Fig. 2. Compared to state-of-the-art approaches like TSP-CPP [10], our proposed approach is capable of generating near-optimal coverage paths in environments with arbitrarily shaped regions with obstacles, whereas TSP-CPP only considers obstacle free environments with convex regions.

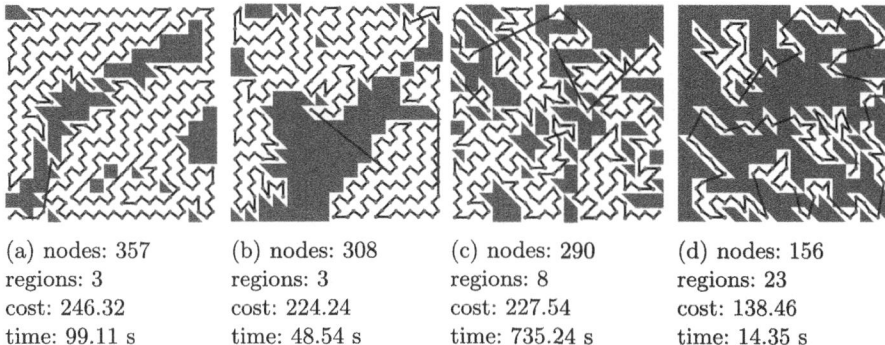

(a) nodes: 357
regions: 3
cost: 246.32
time: 99.11 s

(b) nodes: 308
regions: 3
cost: 224.24
time: 48.54 s

(c) nodes: 290
regions: 8
cost: 227.54
time: 735.24 s

(d) nodes: 156
regions: 23
cost: 138.46
time: 14.35 s

Fig. 2. Samples from the proposed algorithm run on generated maps. Red regions are obstacles, white regions are safe. Black lines indicate the intra-region coverage path, while blue lines indicate the use of the aerial modality. (Color figure online)

On average, the proposed approach generated a valid solution within 32.36 s with a standard deviation of 72.01 s. The fastest solution was found within 7.76 s and the slowest within 735.24 s. With the exception of one trial, all other trials finished within 10 min or less. The trial which required more than 10 min to find a near-optimal solution consisted of one large region with several narrow passages and dead ends, as well as several small regions (Fig. 2.c). As nodes in those narrow passages are mostly surrounded by obstacles, most paths that connect to these nodes cross through obstacles and therefore are invalid. Due to the large number of nodes in the region, a large number of paths need to be evaluated before any improvement in path length is found, which explains the overall longer time to find a solution. In the 500 evaluated samples, an exponential relation between the number of nodes and the elapsed time can be observed. There is no strong correlation between the number of regions and the elapsed time.

5.2 Real-World Planetary Scenario

To show the versatility of the proposed approach, the algorithm was run on a selection of scenarios on Martian planetary data. The scenarios were gathered from MarsTrek [22], which provides DEM data as STL files. The MATLAB `reducepatches` function is used to reduce the number of triangles. While this introduces a slight inaccuracy into the solution, it greatly reduces the complexity, making the calculation possible. The resulting maps have a size of $400 * 400$ and generally contain a slightly higher, albeit similar, amount of nodes compared to the previous experiments. Figure 3.a shows a 3D rendered example of a MarsTrek map that has been solved by our method. The approach can also solve valley scenarios where high slopes separate parts of the map (Fig. 3.b) and hill scenarios where only narrow regions of the map can be covered safely (Fig. 3.c). It can also solve highly complex scenarios which contain a large number of nodes and regions (Fig. 3.d).

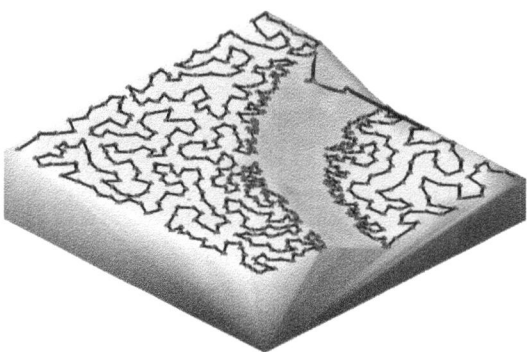

(a) 1° N, 112° W, nodes: 599, regions: 4
cost: 7401.77, time: 288.00 s

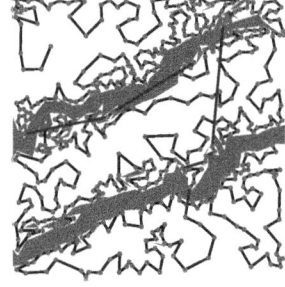  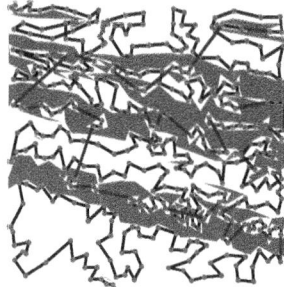

(b) 8° S, 42° W
nodes: 544, regions: 8
cost: 7124.81, time: 351.08 s

(c) 10° S, 69° W
nodes: 240, regions: 9
cost: 3145.47, time: 66.09 s

(d) 15° S, 64° W
nodes: 440, regions: 32
cost: 6317.53, time: 60.69 s

Fig. 3. Samples from the proposed algorithm run on MarsTrek DEM data [22]. (a) shows a 3D rendering of the path taken while (b), (c) and (d) show a top-down view of different scenarios with high slope regions highlighted in red. Black lines indicate the intra-region coverage path, while blue lines indicate the use of the aerial modality. (Color figure online)

All trials find a valid near-optimal solution, even with the irregularly spaced nodes that stem from the way MarsTrek data is generated and the patch reduction step. While this is only a qualitative analysis, it still indicates that the proposed algorithm is capable of solving real-world scenarios.

6   Conclusion

We proposed a hierarchical MILP based method for solving the Multi-Modal Multiple Disconnected Region CPP (M3DR-CPP) problem. The proposed method uses terrain slopes to identify obstacles and safe regions on an input mesh based on DEM data. It then generates a coverage path in two steps by first formulating and solving a TSP in each region and then connecting the regions by solving a secondary TSP. The approach generated coverage paths for 500 randomly generated maps with up to 431 nodes in an average of 32.36 s. The approach is capable of solving problems with complex obstacle placements and up to 33 regions. It also was able to find solutions in scenarios based on realistic Martian surface data with up to 599 nodes. Generated paths are optimal within each region, but suboptimal between regions, as the placement of region endpoints is not optimized to minimize inter-region paths. Immediate future work considers optimal endpoint node selection to mitigate this problem, and inclusion of traveling and control costs. Future work will also consider path smoothing, dynamic adaptation to changes in the environment, as well as switching to a heuristic TSP solver to improve scalability.

References

1. Tan, C.S., Mohd-Mokhtar, R., Arshad, M.R.: A comprehensive review of coverage path planning in robotics using classical and heuristic algorithms. IEEE Access **9**, 119310–119342 (2021)
2. Morrell, B., et al.: NeBula: team costar's robotic autonomy solution that won phase ii of DARPA subterranean challenge. Field Robot. **2**, 1432–1506 (2022)
3. Jung, M., Chuen Tan, K., Dai, R.: Path planning for a jumping rover team with a charging station in multi-waypoints visiting missions. Front. Control Eng. **3**, 803468 (2022)
4. Araki, B., Strang, J., Pohorecky, S., Qiu, C., Naegeli, T., Rus, D.: Multi-robot path planning for a swarm of robots that can both fly and drive. In: 2017 IEEE International Conference on Robotics and Automation (ICRA), pp. 5575–5582. IEEE (2017)
5. Choset, H., Pignon, P.: Coverage path planning: The boustrophedon cellular decomposition. In: Field and Service Robotics, pp. 203–209. Springer, London (1998)
6. Chen, X., et al.: Region coverage path planning of multiple disconnected convex polygons based on simulated annealing algorithm. In: 2021 IEEE 4th International Conference on Computer and Communication Engineering Technology (CCET), pp. 238–242. IEEE (2021)
7. Yu, K., O'Kane, J.M., Tokekar, P.: Coverage of an environment using energy-constrained unmanned aerial vehicles. In: 2019 international Conference on Robotics and Automation (ICRA), pp. 3259–3265. IEEE (2019)
8. Chen, G., Shen, Y., Zhang, Y., Zhang, W., Wang, D., He, B.: 2D multi-area coverage path planning using l-shade in simulated ocean survey. Appl. Soft Comput. **112**, 107754 (2021). https://doi.org/10.1016/j.asoc
9. Lexu, D., Fan, Y., Gui, M., Zhao, D.: A multi-regional path-planning method for rescue UAVs with priority constraints. Drones **7**(12), 692 (2023)
10. Xie, J., Carrillo, L.R.G., Jin, L.: Path planning for UAV to cover multiple separated convex polygonal regions. IEEE Access **8**, 51770–51785 (2020)
11. Abdul Majeed and Seong Oun Hwang: A multi-objective coverage path planning algorithm for UAVs to cover spatially distributed regions in urban environments. Aerospace **8**(11), 343 (2021)
12. Ramesh, M., Imeson, F., Fidan, B., Smith, S.L.: Optimal partitioning of non-convex environments for minimum turn coverage planning. IEEE Robot. Autom. Lett. **7**(4), 9731–9738 (2022)

13. Zhao, B., Huo, M., Li, Z., Ze, Yu., Qi, N.: Clustering-based hyper-heuristic algorithm for multi-region coverage path planning of heterogeneous UAVs. Neurocomputing **610**, 128528 (2024)
14. Yu, X., Jin, S., Shi, D., Li, L., Kang, Y., Zou, J.: Balanced multi-region coverage path planning for unmanned aerial vehicles. In: 2020 IEEE International Conference on Systems, Man, and Cybernetics (SMC), pp. 3499–3506. IEEE (2020)
15. Wang, L., Zhuang, X., Zhang, W., Cheng, J., Zhang, T.: Coverage path planning for UAVs: an energy-efficient method in convex and non-convex mixed regions. Drones **8**(12), 776 (2024)
16. Rockenbauer, F.M., Lim, J., Müller, M.G., Siegwart, R., Schmid, L.: Traversing mars: cooperative informative path planning to efficiently navigate unknown scenes. IEEE Robot. Autom. Lett. (2024)
17. Tang, J., Sun, C., Zhang, X.: Mstc*: multi-robot coverage path planning under physical constrain. In: 2021 IEEE International Conference on Robotics and Automation (ICRA), pp. 2518–2524. IEEE (2021)
18. Huang, X., Sun, M., Zhou, H., Liu, S.: A multi-robot coverage path planning algorithm for the environment with multiple land cover types. IEEE Access **8**, 198101–198117 (2020)
19. Floudas, C.A.: Nonlinear and Mixed-integer Optimization: Fundamentals and Applications. Oxford University Press, Oxford (1995)
20. Lee, D.T., Schachter, B.J.: Two algorithms for constructing a Delaunay triangulation. Int. J. Comput. Inf. Sci. **9**(3), 219–242 (1980)
21. Koch, T., Berthold, T., Pedersen, J., Vanaret, C.: Progress in mathematical programming solvers from 2001 to 2020. EURO J. Comput. Optim. **10**, 100031 (2022)
22. Law, E., Day, B.: Mars trek: an interactive web portal for current and future missions to mars. In: European Planetary Science Congress, pp. EPSC2017–99 (2017)

Autonomous Construction Crack Vision-Based Repair Using an Aerial Platform and a Delta Manipulator

Yiyong Gou, Cavid Karca, Jan Krüger, Lucas Dahl, Dean Boonen,
and Rico Möckel[✉]

Department of Advanced Computing Sciences, Maastricht University, Maastricht,
The Netherlands
`rico.mockel@maastrichtuniversity.nl`

Abstract. Autonomous inspections of civil and critical infrastructure
and the ability to perform basic repair operations with drones may
lead to increased safety. However, the development of autonomous solutions faces many challenges. To address some of the underlying challenges of autonomous construction repair we developed and present a
custom-made aerial robotic platform. Equipped with computer vision
for autonomous detection and localization of cracks, a delta manipulator,
and a syringe-based cement extruder the presented solution is capable
of finding, landing on top, and filling cracks in constructions under lab
conditions.

Keywords: Unmanned Aerial Vehicles · Construction Repair · Crack
Detection · Delta Manipulation

1 Introduction

Autonomous inspections of constructions hold the potential to lead to shorter
inspection cycles and increased safety of civil and critical infrastructure. Further
potential lies in the ability to also autonomously perform basic repair operations
with drones. However, autonomous inspection and repair of constructions with
UAVs face several challenges to which we contribute with the presented work:
Cracks in constructions need to be detected and localized in-flight. The UAV
must be able to land reliably on top of the area to be repaired. The detected
cracks must be repaired. All operations must be performed with limited on-board
resources and payload. We tackled each of these challenges and created a demonstrator capable of performing the mission described in Fig. 1 in our robotics lab.
We created a custom-made quadrotor UAV that is capable of detecting cracks in-
flight in plates made of concrete, to land on these plates, and to fill the detected
cracks with cement with the help of a delta manipulator and a syringe-style
cement extruder, both mounted on the UAV. In contrast to many related works,
our solution does not require any external tracking or positioning systems.

© The Author(s), under exclusive license to Springer Nature Switzerland AG 2026
A. Cavalcanti et al. (Eds.): TAROS 2025, LNAI 16045, pp. 445–458, 2026.
https://doi.org/10.1007/978-3-032-01486-3_34

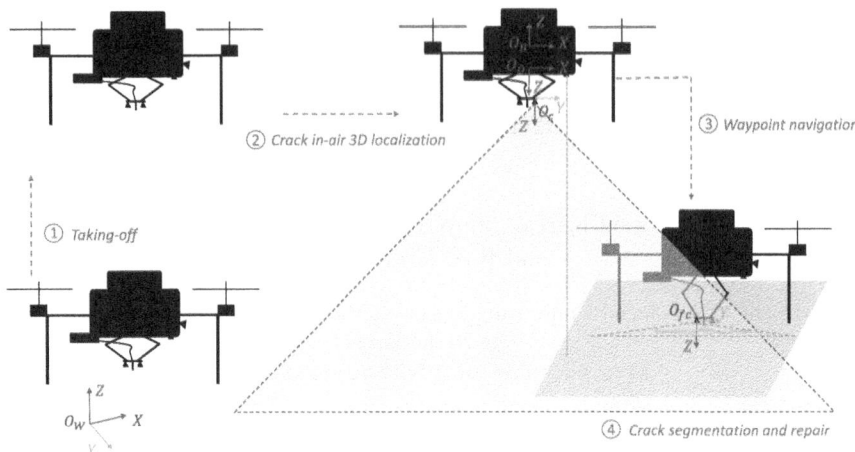

Fig. 1. Crack repair mission architecture. (1) The aerial system takes off to a safe altitude. (2) The aerial system conducts construction crack in-air 3D localization. (3) With the crack localization information as a flight waypoint, the aerial system follows the trajectory generated by a waypoint navigator. (4) After reaching the construction crack spot, the aerial system lands. The ultra-short range segmentation of cracks is performed and the crack repairing procedure is executed.

2   Related Work

Several works have been performed to enable (semi-)autonomous repair of constructions. E.g. in [13] a robotic bridge maintenance system was designed capable of remote inspection, spray washing, paint removal, and painting. This system eliminated the requirement for human labor during the paint removal process in hazardous and time-consuming operational environments. Similarly, a robot and a manipulator were created and used to repair the bottom side of a bridge to avoid rainwater eroding this construction [12]. However, both robots mentioned above are ground-based, which makes it challenging to address the issues associated with tall building repair. In [5], a novel aerial manipulator using deposited PU foam as a repair material was created to repair gas pipelines. In [19] drones have been demonstrated 3D printing an 18-cm high cylinder with a material based on cement and a 2.05-m high cylinder by deposing a polyurethane-based foam material. In contrast our solution focuses on crack detection and repair. To achieve this goal in contrast to e.g. [19] and others our solution does not require any external tracking or positioning system. Also, in the presented work a single drone alone performs the scanning of the surface and material deposition.

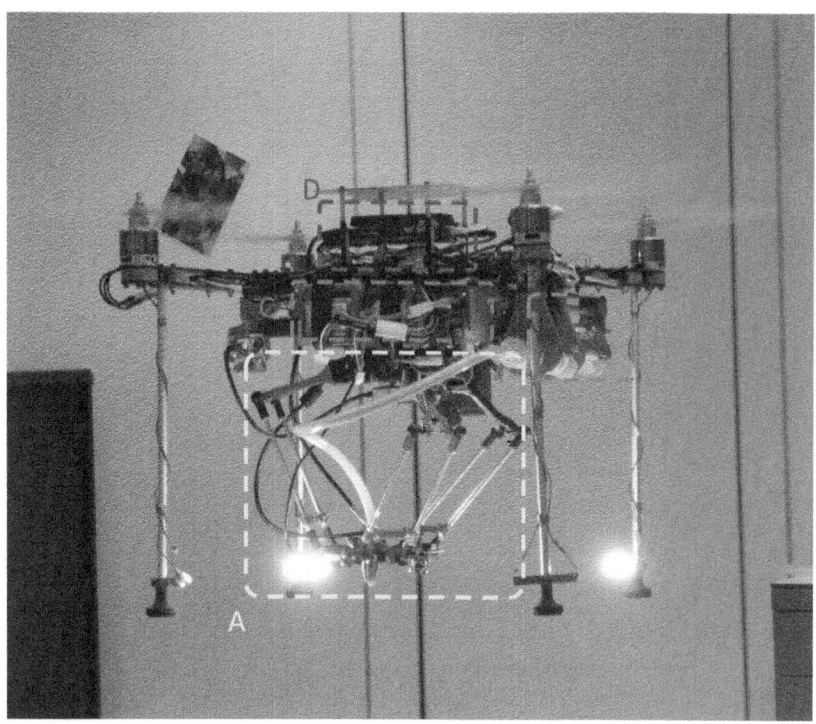

Fig. 2. Aerial quadrotor system. (Yellow dashed-line area labeled A): A Delta-shape main frame is integrated with an end-effector with vision sensors and a ToF sensor. A tube (grey) guides printing material to the end-effector from the material extruder (shown in blue dashed-line area B). A power supply module is displayed in a green dashed-line area C. (Red dashed-line area D): onboard computer Intel NUC i7 and DJI N3 autopilot. (Color figure online)

3 Robotic Hardware

To perform the demonstration of an autonomous UAV-based construction crack repair system, the custom-made quadrotor shown in Fig. 2 was created and equipped with the electronic components described in Fig. 3. The quadrotor contains a delta manipulator that is mounted on the bottom of the UAV as well as a syringe-style cement extruder (detailed view provided in Fig. 4) mounted on its side. For autonomous flight control the aerial platform is equipped with an Intel NUC i7 board that, supported by an off-the-shelf DJI N3 attitude flight controller with integrated IMU, runs the required software for autonomous flight control and landing, computer vision software for crack detection, localization, and segmentation, control of the delta manipulator for crack repair, and control of the extruder. An Arducam AR0134 monocular fisheye camera with a 185° FoV is mounted on the UAV. Images from this camera are being used to gen-

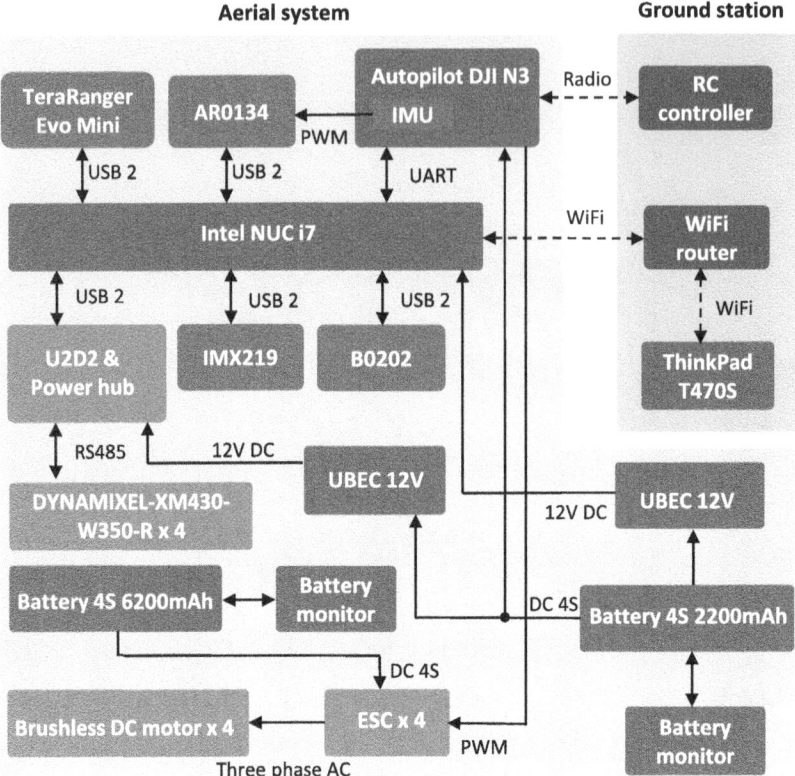

Fig. 3. System electronic component connection diagram. Solid and dashed lines represent the wired and wireless connections, respectively.

erate odometry data that is fused with IMU data from the DJI N3 to enable autonomous vision-based flight control in GPS-denied environments.

The delta manipulator used to position the extruded cement in construction cracks is based on the classical delta-shape frame [6,7]. This frame (Yellow-dashed-line area A in Fig. 2) consists of three arms offset by 120∘. Each arm is comprised of two links, a proximal link (110 mm in length, 3D printed, and hinge-mounted to the servo motors) and distal link (162.5 mm in length) connected via plastic ball joints to the proximal link and to the end-effector connecting all distal links. We chose the delta-design as it allows for the construction of manipulators whose driving motors (in our case three DYNAMIXEL XM430-W350-R servo motors) are located close to the origin of the delta manipulator. This results in a manipulator with a relatively fixed center of mass close to the main frame of the quadrotor increasing flight stability and speed of manipulation.

At its bottom side (Fig. 5) the delta manipulator carries an Arducam B0202 downward facing fisheye RGB camera required to obtain a large field of view during aerial inspections and crack repair, an Arducam IMX219 downward facing

Fig. 4. Syringe-style cement extruder.

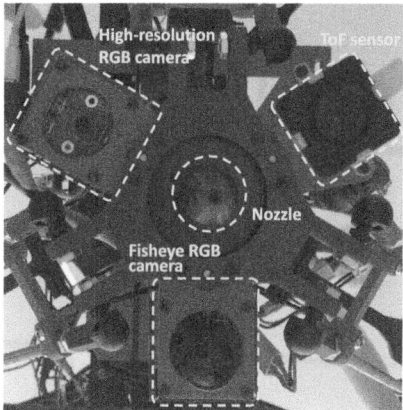

(a) Upward view.   (b) Downward view.

Fig. 5. End-effector with vision sensors and a ToF sensor.

high-resolution RGB camera for ultra-short range crack segmentation, a Ter-aRanger Evo Mini time-of-flight (ToF) distance sensor [2] for depth estimation during crack repair as well as a 3D printed nozzle used to position the extruded cement composition in the crack.

A modified version of the syringe pump project [14] is employed to extrude a cement-style material suited for construction crack repair. The extruder (Fig. 4) consists of a syringe holder, a 60 ml syringe, a 12 cm single-start lead screw with a pitch of 1 mm, and a Dynamixel servo motor DYNAMIXEL-XM430-W350-R to control the extrusion process. To guide the repair material from the extruder to the nozzle located beneath the end-effector, a material guide tube with an inner diameter of 5 mm and an outside diameter of 7 mm is used.

Table 1. Material composition for crack repair

Composition	Ratio (%)	Description
CH104B bentone	0.80	Increasing plasticity and six times more concentrated than bentonite
CH119E bentonite	1.40	Increasing plasticity
Chamotte grains power 0-0.2 mm	12.00	Reducing shrinkage, aiding even drying, and supporting structures
White cement	33.60	Hardening and adhering to other materials to bind them together
China clay	14.00	Increasing plasticity and easy-extrusion in a small PVC tube
Water	38.20	Mixing with other materials

4   Repair Material Composition

Considering the repair material shrinkage and the material movement in the syringe, we extensively explored material compositions for crack repair. The chosen material composition used in the following experiments is shown in Table 1.

5   Vision and Control Solutions

An overview of the implemented control approach and its main components is provided in Fig. 6, separated into components used during flight and after landing on top of a detected crack. The UAV detects construction cracks when hovering above the construction and estimates their position in 3D relative to the UAV using the camera and ToF sensor mounted on the end-effector of the delta manipulator. A model predictive position controller (MPC) provides inputs to the attitude controller integrated in the DJI N3 autopilot. The MPC is similar to previous research [11,16] and enables the UAV to autonomously follow waypoints generated by a waypoint navigator [15], to search for cracks in constructions, and to autonomously land on detected construction cracks. Once landed the autonomous repair procedure is performed, by (1) segmenting and localizing the detected crack, (2) planning and then executing the trajectory of the delta manipulator, using a polygon slicer and inverse kinematics model of the delta configuration, as well controlling the extruder speed.

5.1   In-air Crack 3D Localization and Segmentation

The workflow for in-air crack localization is shown in Fig. 7a. We used the Seg-Net deep convolutional encoder-decoder architecture [3] based on a VGG16 [17] encoder to segment cracks in the taken images as this approach is known to able

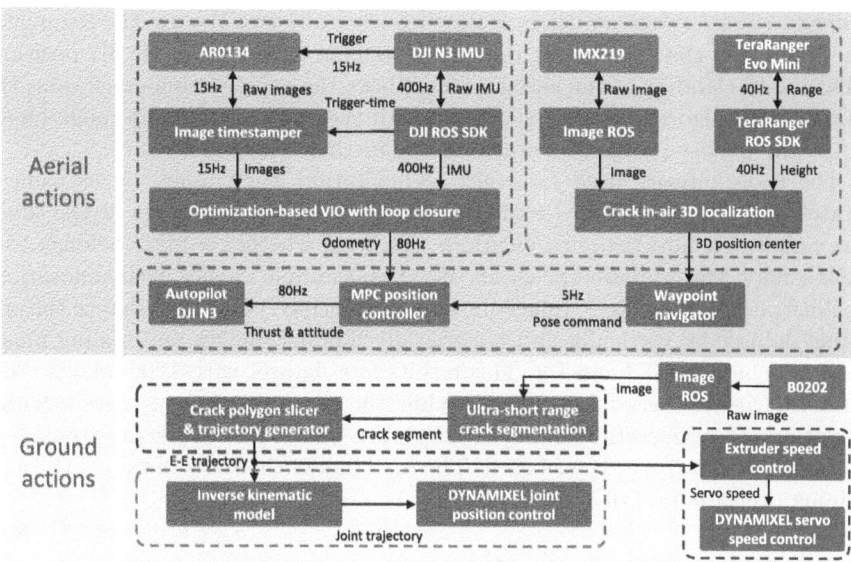

Fig. 6. System software diagram. Aerial actions are displayed in the green area, and ground actions are displayed in the yellow area. (E-E trajectory means end-effector trajectory.) (Color figure online)

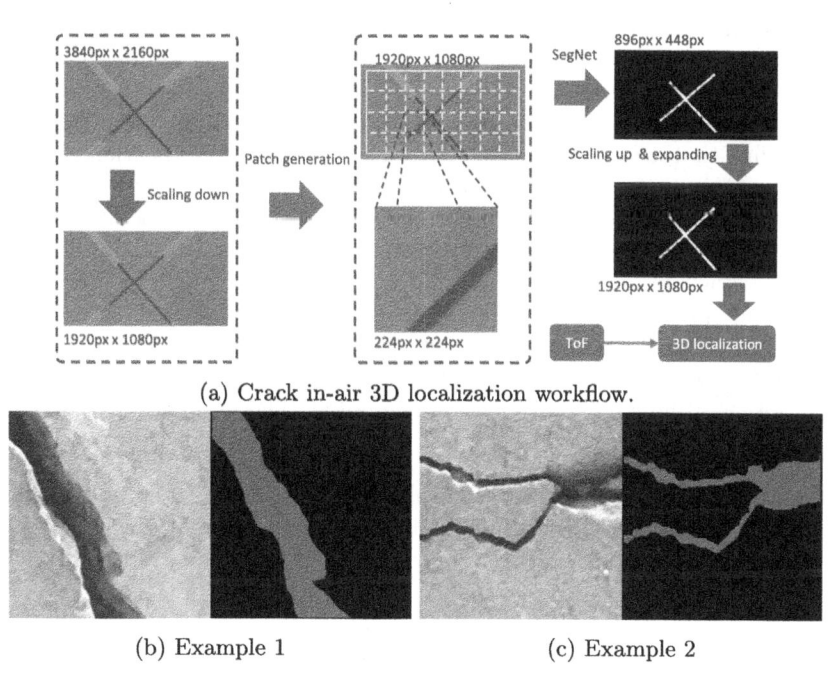

(a) Crack in-air 3D localization workflow.

(b) Example 1   (c) Example 2

Fig. 7. (a) Workflow. (b, c): Examples of crack images (left) and annotations (right) used for training of the crack segmentation algorithm.

to detect cracks also when there is dust or other objects. We use the segmentation result and the ToF sensor data to determine the crack in-air 3D position. Following the landing of the aerial system above the construction crack spot, the segmentation algorithm processes again with the crack ultra-short range image to find the precise profile of a crack for the further repair procedure.

The deep network used for crack segmentation was trained by us using a dataset of 400 crack images from the METU Campus Buildings [9,18]. They were annotated into two classifications based on whether a pixel belongs to a crack using a Matlab-based program [10]. Two example images with annotations are illustrated in Fig. 7b, c. Image data augmentation is used to enhance the size of this dataset by vertically and horizontally flipping images and scaling image brightness between 0.8 and 1.2. This results in a dataset with 1200 images. 80% of the images were used for training, while the remaining images were used for validation. To accelerate training of network weights, a network pre-trained on the Imagenet database [1] was used. The final model then was obtained through training over a period of 150 epochs.

5.2   Crack Filling Trajectory Generation

Figure 8 illustrates the workflow of the crack filling trajectory generation method. After landing and following another execution of the crack segmentation and localization in the operational workspace of the delta manipulator, the nozzle movement and repair material extrusion speed are generated. For this, a pixel within the segmented crack region and on the border is chosen as the starting point for finding the contour of a crack. The coordinates of each pixel of the contour are stored in a polygon. Because this polygon contains hundreds of different points that are relatively close together, the JTS simplification algorithm (Topology Preserving Simplifier) [8] is used to preserve the polygon topology while removing points that are not strictly necessary for crack filling performance. The polygon is positioned along the crack shape, artificially increasing the filling crack profile. To ensure that the crack is adequately filled, a single shrinkage procedure is used. This is accomplished by processing each point in the polygon in the following manner: When a point P_b is selected, its predecessor P_a and its successor P_c points are selected. The normalised vectors $\hat{V}_{ab} = \frac{P_a - P_b}{||P_a - P_b||}$ and $\hat{V}_{cb} = \frac{P_c - P_b}{||P_c - P_b||}$ are computed. The average direction of the two vectors is determined as follows $d = \frac{\hat{V}_{ab} + \hat{V}_{cb}}{2}$ and normalised $\hat{d} = \frac{d}{||d||}$. A new point $P_n = P_b + \hat{d} * \sigma$ is determined where σ is moving step in pixels. It is then checked whether P_n is within the bounds of the original polygon. If P_n is

Fig. 8. Workflow of the crack filling trajectory generation method.

not within the bounds of the original polygon, the sign of the direction vector $\hat{d}$ is flipped. P_n is then added to the list of points for the shrunken polygon. An example result of the crack filling trajectory generation is shown in Fig. 9. Given two consecutive points positions p_{ef}^b and p_{ef}^a of the crack filling trajectory, the velocity of the nozzle movement is derived by

$$\dot{p}_{nozzle} = v_{ef}^{ab} = \frac{p_{ef}^b - p_{ef}^a}{dt} \tag{1}$$

where dt is the time step. The nozzle movement is then executed following an inverse kinematics model of the delta manipulator that we obtained from [4].

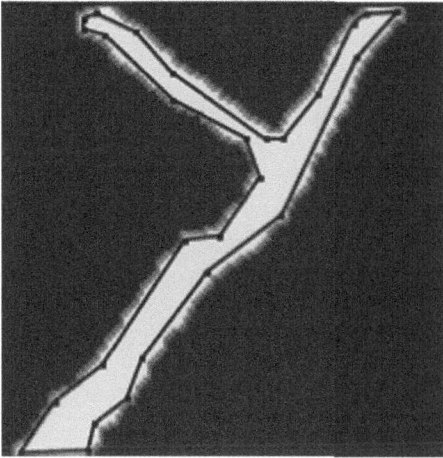

Fig. 9. Example result of the crack filling trajectory generation for a crack. The purple pixels are the pixels that are determined not to belong to the crack. The yellow pixels represent the part of the crack. The determined contour of the crack is marked with blue pixels. The shrinking polygon and its vertices are marked with black lines and dots, respectively. (Color figure online)

6   Experiments and Results

We tested the developed solution in our robotics laboratory shown in Fig. 10. To evaluate the extrusion performance for ground based crack repair, in total five ground based crack repair experiments were undertaken. The corresponding crack filled and over-extruded areas in percent are illustrated in Table 2. The mean of the filled area was 90.8%, and the mean of the over-extruded area was 60.6%. Results of the different steps of the image processing and crack filling process for three of five experiments can be found in Fig. 11.

We further conducted 27 aerial platform crack-reaching experiments to evaluate the precision of our visually guided flight controller in landing on detected crack positions. The reaching errors with respect to the crack spot center are depicted in Fig. 12. MAE in the x and y directions for all of the reaching-crack experiments were 0.1028 m and 0.1243 m, respectively.

Fig. 10. Our robotics lab environment for construction crack autonomous repair experiments. The UAV is depicted in a yellow dashed-line covered area A hovering over a plate with cracks depicted in a green dashed-line covered area B. (Color figure online)

Table 2. Filled and over-extruded areas in percent for all ground based crack repair instances. Filled area with True Positive (shown in green in Fig. 11) and over-extruded area with False Positive (shown in gray in Fig. 11) are measured by counting their pixels, respectively.

Experiment	1	2	3	4	5	Mean
Filled area	95.4%	92.6%	99.2%	74.4%	92.6%	**90.5%**
Over-extruded area	56.1%	66.4%	61.8%	56.2%	62.3%	**60.6%**

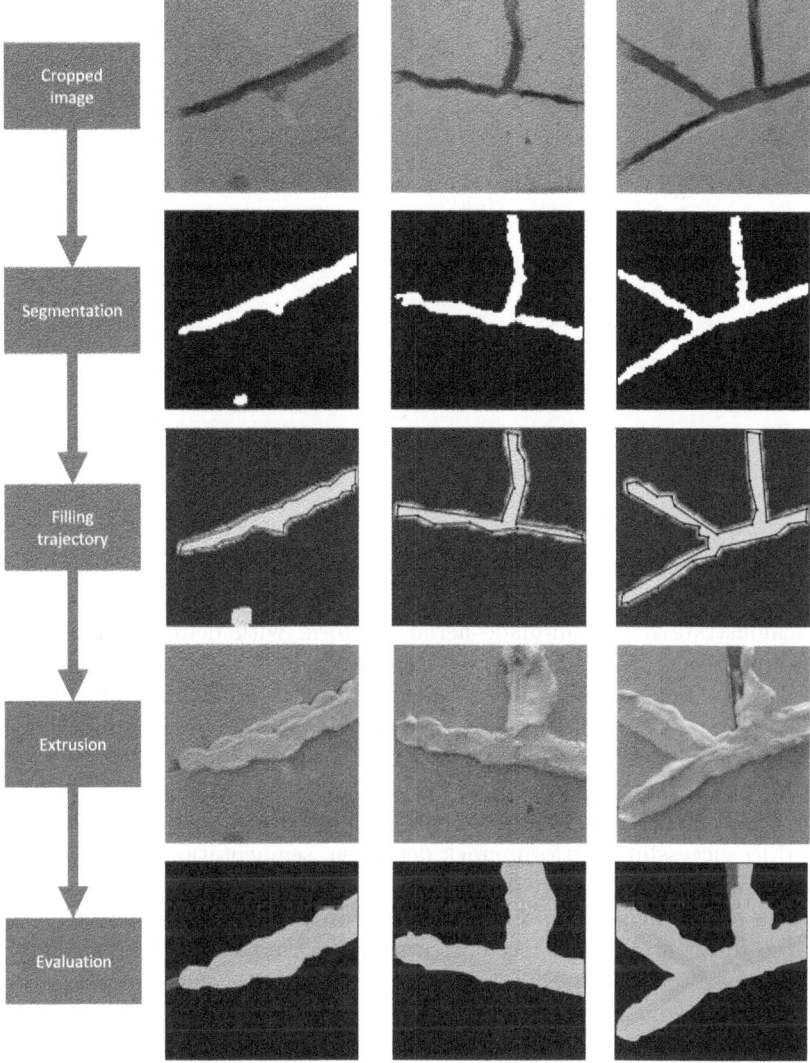

Fig. 11. Ground based crack repair workflow and three instances. In step Filling trajectory, the end-effector nozzle movement is marked as a black line in the yellow crack area. In step Evaluation, the filled areas are marked in green (True Positive, TP), in red (False Negative, FN), and in gray (False Positive, FP). (Color figure online)

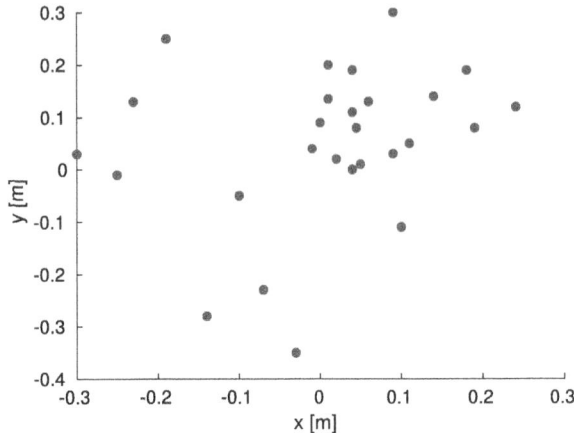

Fig. 12. Aerial system reaching-crack error.

7   Discussion and Conclusions

We demonstrate a custom-made aerial platform with delta manipulator and material extruder for autonomous construction crack repair on horizontal planes. Additional work is still required to turn this demonstrator into a fully autonomous solution for maintaining constructions. Still a successful demonstrator has been achieved that in contrast to other works does not require external tracking and positioning systems to perform its tasks. We demonstrate a vision solution based on a deep convolutional encoder-decoder architecture that we trained to successfully perform crack detection, segmentation, and localization. The maximum $F1$ score of 0.883 achieved by the vision solution on the validation dataset is a solid foundation but also shows potential for improvement. The presented experimental results for construction crack repair validate our approach and demonstrate that we can indeed autonomously find and fill cracks with the help of the delta manipulator carried by the aerial platform. During experimentation on average 90.5% of the crack areas got successfully filled, demonstrating that the solution is successful but that further improvements should be made. The solution also tends to over-extrusion which is less of a problem as the key goal of our work is to stabilize constructions. Finally the current experiments are still performed in a lab while an envisioned fully autonomous UAV solution must operate reliably also outside buildings. Despite these limitations the presented demonstrator represents a promising proof of concept providing insights into the complex machinery required to autonomously perform such a task as challenging as construction crack repair.

Disclosure of Interests. The authors have no competing interests to declare that are relevant to the content of this article.

References

1. ImageNet. https://image-net.org/. Accessed 17 Aug 2021
2. TeraRanger Evo Mini. https://www.terabee.com/shop/3d-tof-cameras/teraranger-evo-mini/. Accessed 15 Nov 2021
3. Badrinarayanan, V., Kendall, A., Cipolla, R.: SegNet: a deep convolutional encoder-decoder architecture for image segmentation. IEEE Trans. Pattern Anal. Mach. Intell. **39**(12), 2481–2495 (2017)
4. Brinker, J., Corves, B., Wahle, M.: A comparative study of inverse dynamics based on Clavel's Delta robot. In: The 14th IFToMM World Congress, 25.10.2015-30.10.2015, Taipei, Taiwan, pp. 89–98. The 14th IFToMM World Congress, Taipei (Taiwan), 25 Oct 2015 - 30 Oct 2015, [s.l.] (2015). https://doi.org/10.6567/IFToMM.14TH.WC.OS13.026, https://publications.rwth-aachen.de/record/540877
5. Chermprayong, P., Zhang, K., Xiao, F., Kovac, M.: An integrated delta manipulator for aerial repair: a new aerial robotic system. IEEE Robot. Autom. Mag. **26**(1), 54–66 (2019)
6. Clavel, R.: DELTA, a fast robot with parallel geometry. In: Burckhardt, C.W. (ed.) Proc of the 18th International Symposium on Industrial Robots, pp. 91–100. Springer, New York (1988)
7. Clavel, R.: Conception d'un robot parallèle rapide à 4 degrés de liberté. Technical report EPFL (1991)
8. Davis, M.: TopologyPreservingSimplifier (org.locationtech.jts:jts-core 1.18.0 API). https://locationtech.github.io/jts/javadoc/org/locationtech/jts/simplify/TopologyPreservingSimplifier.html. Accessed 18 June 2021
9. Çağlar Fırat Özgenel: Concrete crack images for classification (2019). https://data.mendeley.com/datasets/5y9wdsg2zt/2. Accessed 10 Aug 2021
10. Geiger, A., Lauer, M., Wojek, C., Stiller, C., Urtasun, R.: 3D traffic scene understanding from movable platforms. IEEE Trans. Pattern Anal. Mach. Intell. **36**(5), 1012–1025 (2014). https://doi.org/10.1109/TPAMI.2013.185
11. Kamel, M., Burri, M., Siegwart, R.: Linear vs nonlinear MPC for trajectory tracking applied to rotary wing micro aerial vehicles. IFAC-PapersOnLine **50**(1), 3463–3469 (2017)
12. Lim, K., Lee, W., Kim, K., Cho, C.: A concrete repair robot under the upper plate of bridge. In: 2008 International Conference on Control, Automation and Systems, pp. 488–491. IEEE (2008)
13. Lorenc, S.J., Handlon, B.E., Bernold, L.E.: Development of a robotic bridge maintenance system. Autom. Constr. **9**(3), 251–258 (2000)
14. Lustig, A.: Syringe Pump (2020). https://karpova-lab.github.io/syringe-pump/. Accessed 18 Nov 2021
15. Popović, M.: waypoint navigator. https://github.com/ethz-asl/waypoint_navigator. Accessed 13 Oct 2021
16. Sa, I., Kamel, M., Khanna, R., Popović, M., Nieto, J., Siegwart, R.: Dynamic system identification, and control for a cost-effective and open-source multi-rotor MAV. In: Hutter, M., Siegwart, R. (eds.) Field and Service Robotics. SPAR, vol. 5, pp. 605–620. Springer, Cham (2018). https://doi.org/10.1007/978-3-319-67361-5_39
17. Simonyan, K., Zisserman, A.: Very deep convolutional networks for large-scale image recognition. arXiv preprint arXiv:1409.1556 (2014)

18. Zhang, H., Tan, J., Liu, L., Wu, Q.M.J., Wang, Y., Jie, L.: Automatic crack inspection for concrete bridge bottom surfaces based on machine vision. In: 2017 Chinese Automation Congress (CAC), pp. 4938–4943 (2017).https://doi.org/10.1109/CAC.2017.8243654
19. Zhang, K., et al.: Aerial additive manufacturing with multiple autonomous robots. Nature **609**(7928), 709–717 (2022)

Challenging Environments

An Open-Source Capping Machine Suitable for Confined Spaces

Francisco Munguia-Galeano[ID], Louis Longley[ID], Satheeshkumar Veeramani[ID],
Zhengxue Zhou[ID], Rob Clowes[ID], Hatem Fakhruldeen[ID],
and Andrew I. Cooper[✉][ID]

Cooper Group, Department of Chemistry, University of Liverpool, Liverpool, UK
aicooper@liverpool.ac.uk

Abstract. In the context of self-driving laboratories (SDLs), ensuring automated and error-free capping is crucial, as it is a ubiquitous step in sample preparation. Automated capping in SDLs can occur in both large and small workspaces (*e.g.*, inside a fume hood). However, most commercial capping machines are designed primarily for large spaces and are often too bulky for confined environments. Moreover, many commercial products are closed-source, which can make their integration into fully autonomous workflows difficult. This paper introduces an open-source capping machine suitable for compact spaces, which also integrates a vision system that recognises capping failure. The capping and uncapping processes are repeated 100 times each to validate the machine's design and performance. As a result, the capping machine reached a 100% success rate for capping and uncapping. Furthermore, the machine sealing capacities are evaluated by capping 12 vials filled with solvents of different vapour pressures: water, ethanol and acetone. The vials are then weighed every 3 h for three days. The machine's performance is benchmarked against an industrial capping machine (a Chemspeed station) and manual capping. The vials capped with the prototype lost 0.54% of their content weight on average per day, while the ones capped with the Chemspeed and manually lost 0.0078% and 0.013%, respectively. The results show that the capping machine is a reasonable alternative to industrial and manual capping, especially when space and budget are limitations in SDLs.

Keywords: Chemistry Automation · Self-driving Laboratories · Capping

1 Introduction

Self-driving laboratories (SDLs) are fundamental to tackling global challenges such as renewable energy, sustainability and healthcare and are pivotal for technological advancement in a variety of fields. In this context, the automation of experimentation and analysis, through the use of labware, specialised software and robotics, has been shown to be beneficial in both accelerating the discovery

A. Cavalcanti et al. (Eds.): TAROS 2025, LNAI 16045, pp. 461–474, 2026.
https://doi.org/10.1007/978-3-032-01486-3_35

of new materials [1,2] and their characterisation and formulation [3,4]. However, this automation process often requires expertise in both areas, leading to chemists facing challenges regarding the lack of specialised hardware that can fit the necessities and requirements of chemistry automation and roboticists lacking a sense of where and how automation can benefit chemistry. Capping is ubiquitous and mandatory when preparing samples across various industry sectors. In chemistry [5], capping and uncapping are necessary both during reaction workflows and for long-term safe storage and handling of vials. Nevertheless, the need for compact capping equipment becomes critical when workflows are conducted in a confined space, such as a fume hood, where the bulkiness of traditional industrial capping machines often makes them unsuitable.

To address these challenges, this paper introduces a capping machine (Fig. 1) that incorporates vision-based capping failure detection and is specifically designed for use in constricted spaces. It aims to be a low-cost alternative to industrial capping machines while being readily compatible with chemistry automation workflows. The capping machine's design and performance are validated through two experiments: capping success rate and sealing capacities. Both experiments are run in a fume hood, where a Panda robot manipulates the vials. The sealing capacities are benchmarked against two baselines: manual capping and an industrial capper. For the latest, a Chemspeed station (a common and well-known platform for chemistry automation) is used as the industrial capper.

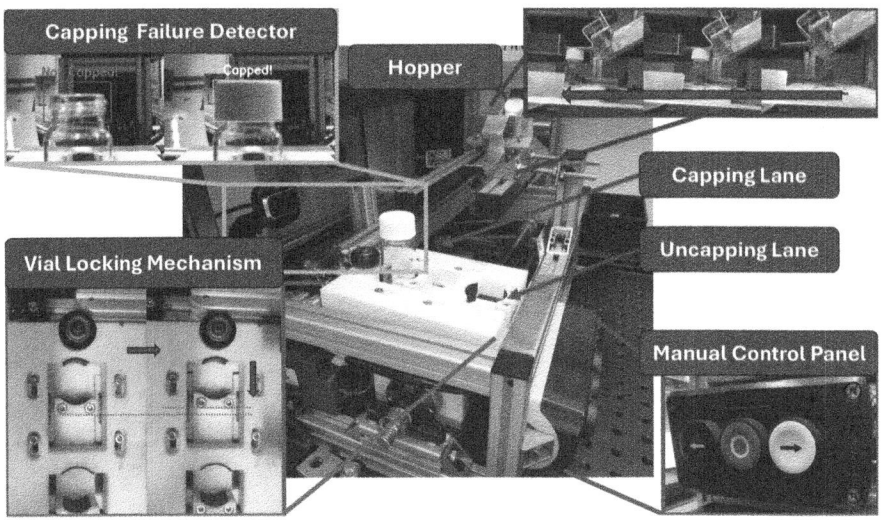

Fig. 1. Low-cost capping machine for confined spaces. Key components include a capping failure detector, a vial locking mechanism, a hopper, capping and uncapping lanes, and a manual control panel. The compact form factor allows deployment in constrained spaces such as fume hoods.

2 Related Work

In the literature, there exists a limited number of works discussing the design and control of capping machines. These works focus more on the control of such machines and their interfaces. For example, Avunoori Anudeep et al. [6] introduce a bottle-filling system that comprises a sequence of operations such as automatic clamping, unclamping, injecting the molten material, and filling and capping. In a similar work, Qiadong et al. [7] present a capping machine in which the force and torques necessary to cap bottles properly are validated through a finite element analysis while pressed by a pneumatic piston. It was concluded that the stress and pressure experienced by the cap threads are less than the yield strength of the material during the capping, producing low deformation and, at the same time, securing a robust capping.

Other works focus more on the control design of the filling machines than on the design of the machines themselves. For example, Mahrez et al. [8] present a closed-loop control design for a bottle-filling capping system, in which the authors focus their aims on lower power consumption and operating costs. Several sensors detect the bottles' position and water level remaining in the tank while the capping process is achieved using a robotic arm. Another case in point is introduced by Zhang et al. [9], in which the authors motivate the advantages of improving the capping process of drug bottles because it shortens production time and saves labour. Like the previously cited approaches, the authors introduce a system that transports bottles to the capping module via a conveyor. The system then locks the bottle, and an actuator tightens the cap.

Several studies have implemented uncapping. For instance, Jaeger et al. [10] introduce a system for uncapping multiple sample tubes. This solution is motivated by the fact that operators usually do the process manually, which is time-consuming and increases the risk of muscle fatigue and injuries. Another approach involves designing grippers that adapt according to the task; for example, Kumar et al. [11] present the design of several grippers that are tailored to move vials and cap/uncap them. For decades, industry has thoroughly developed capping machines and utilised them primarily for bottle-filling applications. Conversely, the scientific literature presents a few designs focusing on low-cost builds or control and user interfaces.

Industrial capping machines [12] combine liquid filling, cap feeding, and capping capabilities for various applications with customisable container sizes, processing up to 35 bottles per minute. Nevertheless, they cannot be directly integrated into SDLs due to their space requirements, and such a high productivity rate is unnecessary. Some manufacturers produce compact screw capping devices [13] for sample tubes; however, similar devices are not available for vials. Additionally, there is a gap concerning the lack of designs aimed at operating in automated chemistry workflows in confined spaces. This paper fills the gap by proposing an open-source capping machine suitable for confined spaces to help researchers and people involved in chemistry automation implement capping and uncapping reliably where setups involving reduced spaces are necessary.

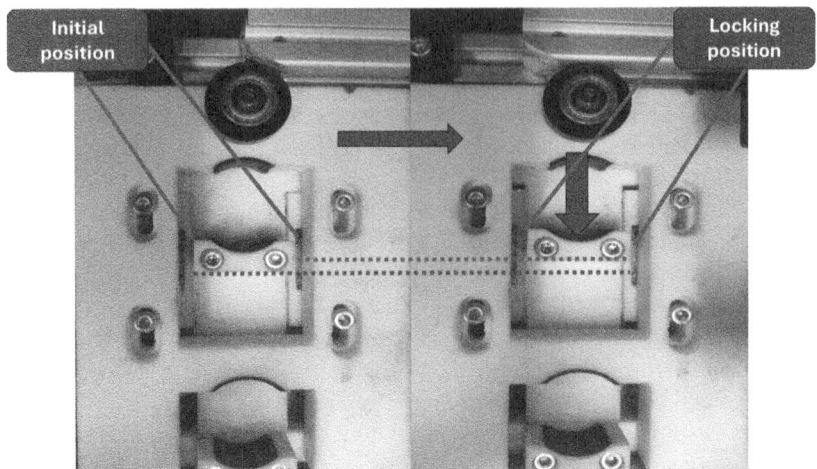

Fig. 2. Vial holder and its locking mechanism. The image illustrates the engagement between the bearing and the cam when the vial holder moves to the left. This mechanism interaction causes the two fasteners to move towards one another, which locks the vial in place. The movement can be seen as the gap between the red and blue lines. (Color figure online)

3   Capping Machine Design

This section presents the design of the capping machine, which encompasses three aspects: mechanics, electronics and firmware. These aspects are expected to meet the following system specifications: ⓘ **Robustness** (*i.e.*, the machine should reliably cap vials and detect when a failure occurs), ⓘⓘ **Easy to fabricate** (*i.e.*, the machine's parts should be easy to replicate, and the electronic components should be easy to acquire), ⓘⓘⓘ **Easy to use** (*i.e.*, the machine should be easy to install, operate, and maintain), and ⓘⱽ **Reduced size** (*i.e.*, should fit in a fume hood, usually measuring approximately 760 mm to 1620 mm in width, around 580 mm to 670 mm in depth and typically 650 mm to 870 mm in height). To fulfil these requirements, the prototype design process is divided into three subsystems: mechanical, electrical/electronics and vision.

3.1   Mechanical Subsystem

When designing mechanisms, it is crucial to implement the concept of mechanical multiplexing, which consists of utilising a single input (from an actuator) and transforming it into multiple outputs. The output can include actions for locking, pushing, or tightening, and this behaviour is achieved by combining several mechanisms such as cams, gears, lead screws or linkages. Mechanical multiplexing is essential because it can cut costs and optimise efficiency by reducing the number of actuators and, thereby, the number of electric/electronic components to control a machine; the prototype of the capping machine presented here is designed based on this concept. It uses a motor to drive a lead screw via a timing belt. The lead screw converts the rotational motion of the motor into linear motion. A cam parallel to this linear motion is employed to engage the locking mechanism in the vial holder, allowing it to lock or unlock the vials (see Fig. 2). The cap hopper and feeder are positioned above the vial holder. For the capping process, when a vial passes under the feeder, a cap is automatically placed on it. A profile with rubber positioned parallel to the vial cap spins the cap and tightens it, as shown in Fig. 3. For the uncapping process, the capped vial must be placed in the uncapping lane, which operates on the same principle as the capping lane. However, the cap rotates in the uncapping lane in the opposite direction, and, as a consequence, the combination of movements loosens the cap.

The frame of the capping machine is constructed from 20×20 mm aluminium profiles, a common and well-known material widely used in automation setups. The dimensions of the prototype are 300 mm in width, 500 mm in depth, and 400 mm in height—whereas an industrial capper from Chemspeed measures approximately 1000 mm in width, 1000 mm in depth, and 2200 mm in height. The motor driving the lead screw is a brushed geared DC motor with 19.8 W of power, 12 V DC, 59 Ncm of torque, 84 rpm, and a 6 mm shaft. The lead screw has a shaft diameter of 10 mm and is fitted with a flanged round nut of the same diameter. The timing belt is a T5 type, with 68 teeth, 340 mm length, and 10 mm width. Two aluminium timing belt pulleys, each with 15 teeth, are used for a 10 mm wide belt and 5 mm pitch, maintaining a 1:1 ratio. The lead screw is supported by two pillow block bearings, one at each end. The vial holder is 3D-printed in resin and incorporates the lead screw nut, a linear bearing, two rods, a cam-engaging bearing, and two springs. The holder is mounted on an Igus linear guide carriage, model WW-10-40-10, which slides along an Igus W Series WS-10-40-600 linear guide rail, with a width of 40 mm.

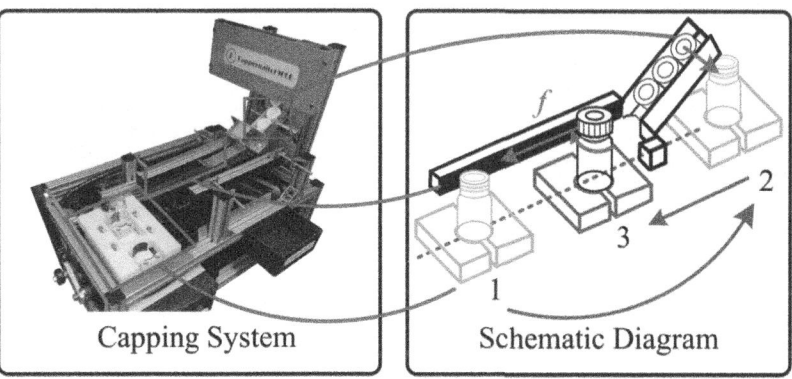

Fig. 3. Capping system and its schematic diagram. First, the vial is placed when the vial holder is at position 1. Then, the vial holder moves to position 2. The capping process is achieved by utilising the friction between the cap and the rubber rail, which tightens the cap as it passes below the cap feeder on its way to the home position.

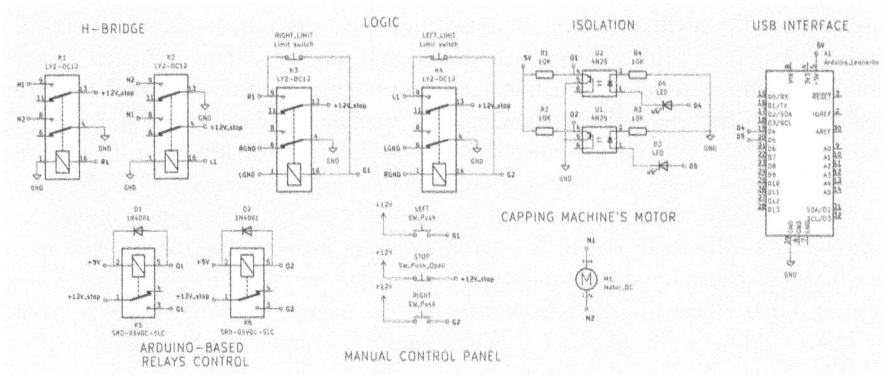

Fig. 4. Arduino-based DC Motor Control Circuit Schematic of the Capping Machine. This circuit design ensures safe control of the DC motor by using a manual control panel and an Arduino controller with protection mechanisms. Relays are shown in their unpowered states.

3.2   Electrical/Electronics Subsystem

Building on the mechanical system, the electrical/electronics subsystem controls the geared motor, provides a manual interface, and enables PC-based automation. An H-bridge formed by four LY2-DC12 relays allows bidirectional motor

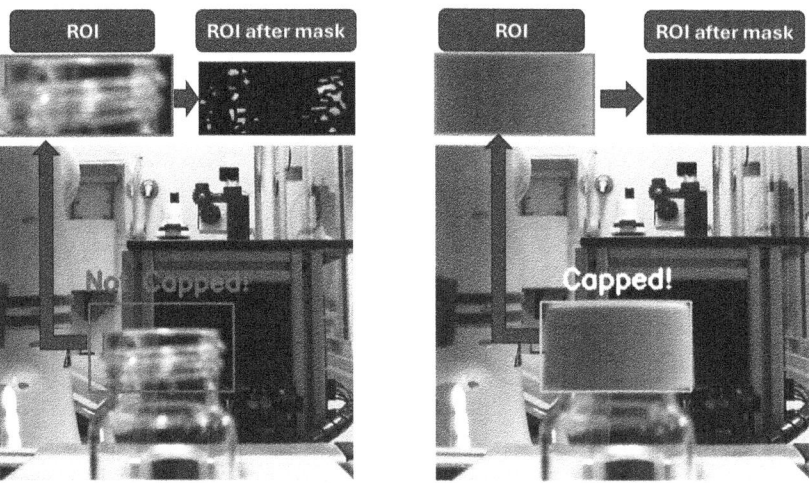

Fig. 5. Capping failure detector. On the left side of the image, the algorithm, after defining a region of interest (ROI), applies a mask and segments the light reflected through the vial's threads, indicating capping failure. On the right side of the image, after segmenting the ROI, the algorithm could not find any light reflected through the thread, meaning that the capping was successful.

Algorithm 1. Capping Failure Detector Algorithm

```
1:  Initialise region of interest (ROI) coordinates
2:  while Camera is streaming do
3:      Capture frame from camera
4:      if frame is not available then
5:          Display error and exit loop
6:      end if
7:      Extract ROI from the frame
8:      Convert ROI to HSV
9:      Define colour range for filtering
10:     Apply colour mask to the ROI
11:     Convert the masked ROI to grayscale
12:     Apply thresholding to highlight relevant areas
13:     Find contours in the thresholded image
14:     Compute total area of detected contours
15:     if contour area exceeds threshold then
16:         Display "Not Capped" status and mark ROI in red
17:         Set capped status to False
18:     else
19:         Display "Capped" status and mark ROI in green
20:         Set capped status to True
21:     end if
22:     Show processed frame in the display window
23:     if termination condition (e.g., key press) is met then
24:         exit loop
25:     end if
26: end while
```

control. Two limit switches at the ends of the vial holder's track toggle the relays based on direction. Manual control is provided via a spring-return push-button panel with three buttons: home, cap feeder, and emergency stop. PC control is handled by an Arduino Uno, which drives two SRD-05VDC-SL-C relays through an isolation stage with two 4N25 optocouplers and 10 kΩ resistors, protecting the board and providing LED feedback. Cable management uses conduit and spiral wrap. The system is powered by two DRL-30 switched supplies (85–264 V AC input, 12 V DC output, 2.1 A, 30 W), with all components mounted on a DIN rail. A detailed schematic is shown in Fig. 4.

3.3 Vision Subsystem

The vision subsystem is a simple, reliable capping failure detector using a standard RGB camera. It leverages reflections from vial threads visible in the blue channel to segment the cap region. If the cap fully covers the threads, no blue regions are detected, indicating a successful seal. Conversely, visible blue areas above a defined threshold signal a failed capping attempt. This triggers an alert or stops the system for safety as depicted in Fig. 5. The step-by-step implementation of this approach is given by Algorithm 1.

4 Experimental Setup

The experiments aim to measure how reliable the proposed machine is compared to manual or industrial alternatives. Therefore, two experiments are carried out:

Algorithm 2. Vial Capping and Uncapping Process

1: **for** $i = 1$ to 100 **do**
2:     Pick vial from rack and place in holder
3:     Machine caps the vial
4:     Check capping status
5:     **if** capping successful **then**
6:         Move vial to uncapping lane
7:     **else**
8:         Return cap, user uncaps manually
9:         **continue** (skip to next iteration)
10:     **end if**
11:     Machine uncaps vial
12:     Remove cap with robot
13:     Return vial to rack
14:     **if** cap still on vial **then**
15:         Remove manually
16:     **end if**
17: **end for**

---

the first measures the prototype's capping and uncapping success rate, and the second measures the sealing capacities of the three approaches. The experimental setup is illustrated in Fig. 6, a Panda robot is utilised to manipulate the vial and move them between different experimental sections. These stations are a balance (Quantos *Mettler Toledo*, a pump for liquid dispensing (XCalibur *Tecan Cavro* and the capping machine placed. The whole setup is confined within a fume cupboard. For the first experiment, the vials are first pre-selected and manually positioned at the orientation illustrated in Fig. 7. The robot then places the vials in the capping lane, and if the capping is successful, it moves the vial to the uncapping lane. This process is repeated 100 times (see Algorithm 2).

In the second experiment, three batches of vials are prepared using three solvents—distilled water, ethanol, and acetone—with four repeats each. These solvents were chosen for their common use in chemistry and their varying vapour

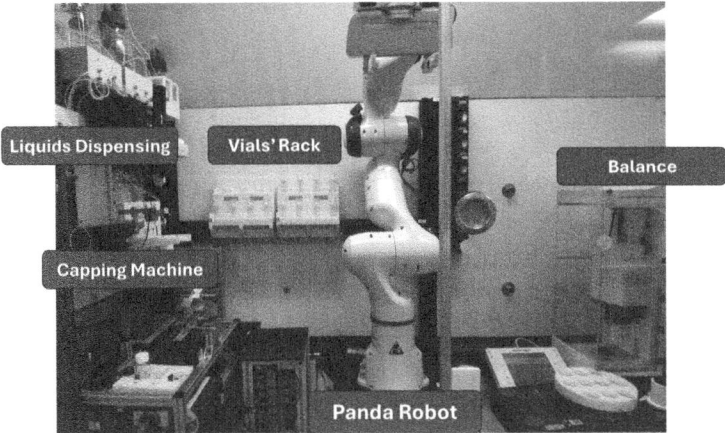

Fig. 6. Experimental setup.

pressures, from low (water) to high (acetone) [14–16]. Since high-vapour-pressure solvents evaporate more readily, they present a greater challenge for effective sealing. Each vial is filled with 10 mL of solvent before capping. The first batch is capped manually, the second is prepared and capped by the Chemspeed system, and the third is prepared and capped by the robot. All batches are monitored over three days, with vial weights logged every three hours, to compare liquid loss across the three methods.

5 Results

The results from both experiments revealed several insights into how to enhance the prototype's efficiency. In the first experiment, it was observed that the orientation of the vials in the rack significantly impacted the success rate. This is because of the importance of the orientation of the vial threads relative to the capping machine. Specifically, when the three threads were oriented toward the cap feeder (see Fig. 7), the success rate was 100%. This performance can be attributed to the increased likelihood that the internal threads of the cap engage with the vial threads, thereby facilitating the proper placement of the cap. This correct alignment enables the mechanism to spin and effectively tighten the cap. Moreover, it was found that as long as the prototype successfully caps the vial, uncapping also achieves a 100% success rate. During testing it was observed that

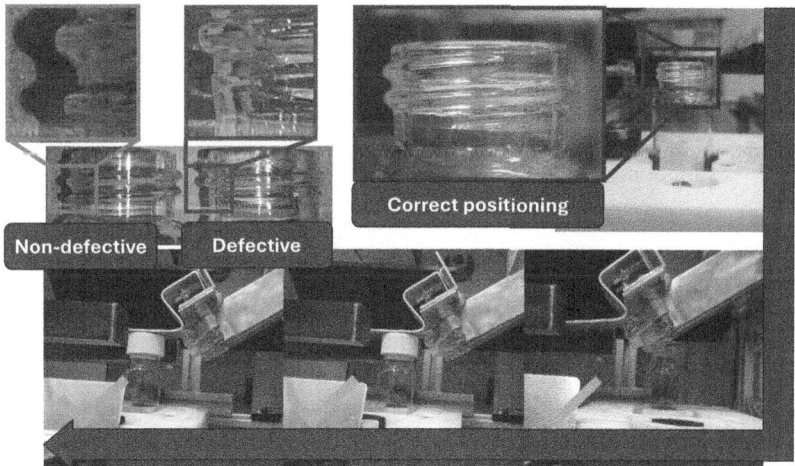

Fig. 7. Correct vial positioning and defects. A common defect can be observed in the top left of the image, where the vial on the left side is missing a thread. This defect leads to resistance or poor placement during capping and may cause the capping machine to fail to secure the cap. The correct positioning of the vial is shown in the top right corner; positioning the vial in this manner ensures that the threads of both the vial and cap engage properly. The bottom image shows the correct placement of the cap from the hopper onto a vial.

Table 1. Capping Machine Data.

Solvent (sample)	Initial weight (g)	Final weight (g)	Density (kg/m³)	Liquid weight (g)	Weight loss (mg)	Weight loss (%)	Averages		
							3 days (%)	Per day (%)	Per hour (%)
Water (1)	29.2223	29.222	997	9.97	0.3	0.0030	0.0967	0.0322	0.0013
Water (2)	28.158	28.1457			12.3	0.1233			
Water (3)	28.0036	27.9843			19.3	0.1935			
Water (4)	29.0125	29.0058			6.7	0.0672			
Ethanol (1)	27.0353	27.0338	789	7.89	1.5	0.0190	0.6108	0.2036	0.0084
Ethanol (2)	27.3768	27.3748			2	0.0253			
Ethanol (3)	27.0333	26.8924			140.9	1.7858			
Ethanol (4)	26.27	26.2216			48.4	0.6134			
Acetone (1)	26.9868	26.9542	784	7.84	32.6	0.4158	4.1868	1.3956	0.0581
Acetone (2)	24.871	24.7033			167.7	2.1390			
Acetone (3)	24.9481	23.8458			1102.3	14.0599			
Acetone (4)	24.6049	24.5945			10.4	0.1326			

Table 2. Manual Capping Data.

Solvent (sample)	Initial weight (g)	Final weight (g)	Density (kg/m³)	Liquid weight (g)	Weight loss (mg)	Weight loss (%)	Averages		
							3 days (%)	Per day (%)	Per hour (%)
Water (1)	27.972	27.9702	997	9.97	1.8	0.0181	0.0186	0.0062	0.0003
Water (2)	29.2299	29.2279			2	0.0201			
Water (3)	28.9663	28.9646			1.7	0.0171			
Water (4)	28.1985	28.1966			1.9	0.0191			
Ethanol (1)	26.0616	26.0601	789	7.89	1.5	0.0190	0.0212	0.0071	0.0003
Ethanol (2)	25.9324	25.9306			1.8	0.0228			
Ethanol (3)	24.7426	24.7411			1.5	0.0190			
Ethanol (4)	26.1948	26.1929			1.9	0.0241			
Acetone (1)	26.0808	26.0778	784	7.84	3	0.0383	0.0456	0.0152	0.0006
Acetone (2)	25.002	24.9988			3.2	0.0408			
Acetone (3)	26.0644	26.0596			4.8	0.0612			
Acetone (4)	25.917	25.9137			3.3	0.0421			

a minority of vials were inconsistent or defective in the dimensions and number of screw threads on their necks. A common defect observed was a reduced number of vial threads. The capping machine was found to be unable to reliably cap these defective vials Fig. 8. However, simple visual analysis and pre-selection of non-defective vials was found to lead to reliable capping.

The results of the second experiment are summarised in Table 1, Table 2 and Table 3 for the capping machine, manual capping and the Chemspeed, respectively. The vials containing water capped by the capping machine lost 0.0322% of weight on average per day, while those containing ethanol and acetone lost 0.2036% and 1.39%, respectively. The vials containing water capped manually lost 0.006% of weight on average per day, while those containing ethanol and acetone lost 0.007% and 0.0152%, respectively. Lastly, the vials capped by the Chemspeed containing water lost 0.0123% of weight on average per day, while those containing ethanol and acetone lost 0.0053% and 0.014%, respectively.

For the three approaches, the average weight loss per day, considering the three solvents, was 0.54% for the capping machine, 0.013% for manual capping and 0.0078% for the Cheemspeed. These results show that acetone is the most challenging solvent to contain due to its lower boiling point and higher volatility than water and ethanol. Moreover, the torque control that the Chemspeed implements secured better sealing capacities for the three solvents. However, the Chemspeed station cannot detect capping failure Fig. 8. Manual capping proved

Table 3. Chemspeed Data.

Solvent (sample)	Initial weight (g)	Final weight (g)	Density (kg/m³)	Liquid weight (g)	Weight loss (mg)	Weight loss (%)	Averages		
							3 days (%)	Per day (%)	Per hour (%)
Water (1)	28.3205	28.3199	997	9.97	0.6	0.00618	0.0123	0.0041	0.00017
Water (2)	28.3858	28.3854			0.4	0.00401			
Water (3)	28.2491	28.2482			0.9	0.00902			
Water (4)	28.4515	28.4485			3	0.03001			
Ethanol (1)	26.2059	26.2039	789	7.89	2	0.0253	0.0161	0.0053	0.00022
Ethanol (2)	25.3897	25.3884			1.3	0.0164			
Ethanol (3)	26.3091	26.3080			1.1	0.0139			
Ethanol (4)	25.1165	25.1158			0.7	0.0088			
Acetone (1)	25.9171	25.914	784	7.84	3.1	0.0395	0.0424	0.0141	0.0006
Acetone (2)	25.8261	25.8227			3.4	0.0434			
Acetone (3)	26.1036	26.1001			3.5	0.0446			
Acetone (4)	25.8148	25.8115			3.3	0.0421			

more consistent in this context. Notorious differences in tightness of fit can be detected by humans during capping of different vials, however, they are easily compensated for by attentive users by adjusting torque or changing caps.

6 Discussion

The results showed that, despite industry implementing capping for decades, even industrial cappers are not free from errors, which are often provoked by unavoidable variations in the quality of the vials and caps. Much has been said about robots and autonomous systems being less susceptible to making errors, however, not much is usually said about how humans can overcome the mistakes these systems often provoke. In contrast, automated systems are incapable of, if not designed or programmed to handle unexpected events. In the context of the experiments carried out herein, manual capping was more reliable in identifying failing capping and defective parts, moreover humans are more adaptable and can adjust the needed force to cap in each individual case; therefore, manual sealing was more consistent than its automated counterparts.

Although Chemspeed uses a closed-loop torque system to detect capping issues, defective vials or caps can cause torque misreadings due to slight manufacturing variations. To address this, our capping machine integrates a vision-based decision framework for added robustness. It offers a compact, dedicated alternative to commercial machines, avoiding unnecessary robotic wear and making the process robot-agnostic. Unlike workflows where robots directly cap vials [17], our modular design fits various robot types (*e.g.*, cartesian, SCARA, arm) with minimal adaptation, as long as they can place and retrieve vials. While currently limited to 20 ml vials, expanding to multiple lanes and feeders could enhance flexibility and support various sizes, all while maintaining a compact footprint.

Fig. 8. The Chemspeed station failing to cap a defective vial. Normally, the caps rack is where the manipulator attempts to place the caps. However, due to an unsuccessful uncapping attempt, the manipulator attempted to place the entire vial there, resulting in a crash.

7   Conclusions and Future Work

This paper has presented a prototype of a capping machine suitable for confined spaces. The machine proved reliable by achieving a 100% success rate in capping/uncapping and losing around 0.54% of weight after one day of monitoring the vials' mass—acetone was the most challenging to contain among all solvents, even for the industrial capper. This loss is not significant for most chemical experiments in SDLs, as it is primarily due to vapour evaporation rather than leakage. Therefore, as long as the vial is not leaking, processes such as mixing and temporary sample storage can be carried out safely. Future work can potentially focus on increasing the flexibility of the capping machine. This would require adding more lanes and cap hoppers to support a broader range of vials and caps. The vision module can also be further improved to recognise the type of vial put in the capper, and whether it is defective and properly oriented. Additionally, adding an extra actuator that tightens the caps with torque feedback would increase the capping machine's robustness. Finally, exploring approaches to solve or react to unexpected or novel situations, such as broken vials and dangerous liquid spills or leaks, is fundamental for securing safe and robust automation in SDLs.

Acknowledgments. This project was funded by the ERC ADAM Synergy grant (agreement no. 856405), the Engineering and Physical Sciences Research Council (EPSRC) under the grant agreement EP/V026887/1 and the Leverhulme Trust through the Leverhulme Research Centre for Functional Materials Design.

Disclosure of Interests. The authors declare no competing interests.

References

1. Li, J., et al.: Synthesis of many different types of organic small molecules using one automated process. Science **347**(6227), 1221–1226 (2015). https://doi.org/10.1126/science.aaa5414
2. Salley, D., Manzano, J.S., Kitson, P.J., Cronin, L.: Robotic modules for the programmable chemputation of molecules and materials. ACS Cent. Sci. **9**(8), 1525–1537 (2023). https://doi.org/10.1021/acscentsci.3c00304
3. Burger, B., et al.: A mobile robotic chemist. Nature **583**(7815), 237–241 (2020)
4. Wu, T.C., et al.: A materials acceleration platform for organic laser discovery. Adv. Mater. **35**(6), 2207070 (2023). https://doi.org/10.1002/adma.202207070
5. Paul, J.E., Leena, G.: Cost efficient automatic filling system for differently sized bottles. In: 2022 International Conference on Recent Trends in Microelectronics, Automation, Computing and Communications Systems (ICMACC), pp. 1–6 (2022) https://doi.org/10.1109/ICMACC54824.2022.10093437
6. Kumar, A.A., Rao, P.S.: Automation of bottle manufacturing, filling and capping process using low cost industrial automation. Int. J. Eng. Res. Technol. (IJERT), 2278–0181 (2014). ISSN
7. Yao, Q., Chai, C., Liu, X., Pang, W., Shen, D., Cao, X.: Design of pneumatic control system for automatic bottle capping device. In: Third International Conference on Mechanical Design and Simulation (MDS 2023), vol. 12639, pp. 35–43. SPIE (2023)
8. Mahrez, A., et al.: Design a plc-based automated and controlled liquid filling-capping system. In: 2022 International Engineering Conference on Electrical, Energy, and Artificial Intelligence (EICEEAI), pp. 1–5. IEEE (2022)
9. Zhang, S., Ji, J., Zhao, Y., Li, Y.: Control system design of automatic capping machine based on s7-300 plc. In: 2020 IEEE Conference on Telecommunications, Optics and Computer Science (TOCS), pp. 337–339. IEEE (2020)
10. Jaeger, J.W., et al.: Automated device for uncapping multiple-size bioanalytical sample tubes designed to reduce technician strain and increase productivity. SLAS Technol. Translating Life Sci. Innov. **26**(3), 320–326 (2021)
11. Kumar, A., Pillearachichige, K., Sharifi, H., Shaw, B., Noble, F.K.: Design of end-effectors for a chemistry automation plant. In: 2016 23rd International Conference on Mechatronics and Machine Vision in Practice (M2VIP), pp. 1–5. IEEE (2016)
12. LIMITED, Z.T.: Zonesun capping machines. https://www.zonesun.com/collections/cap-screwing. Accessed 25 Nov 2024
13. SCIENCES, A.L.: Azenta intellixcap^{TM}. https://www.azenta.com/intellixcap-tube-capping-decapping-sealing-systems?. Accessed 25 Nov 2024
14. for Biotechnology Information (2024), N.C.: Pubchem compound summary for cid 962, water. https://pubchem.ncbi.nlm.nih.gov/compound/Water. Accessed 20 Sept 2024
15. for Biotechnology Information (2024), N.C.: Pubchem compound summary for cid 180, acetone. https://pubchem.ncbi.nlm.nih.gov/compound/Acetone. Accessed 20 Sept 2024

16. for Biotechnology Information (2024), N.C.: Pubchem compound summary for cid 702, ethanol. https://pubchem.ncbi.nlm.nih.gov/compound/Ethanol. Accessed 20 Sept 2024
17. Lunt, A.M., et al.: Modular, multi-robot integration of laboratories: an autonomous workflow for solid-state chemistry. Chem. Sci. **15**, 2456–2463 (2024). https://doi.org/10.1039/D3SC06206F

Extension of Industrial and Collaborative Robots for Increased Work Space and Operation in Confined Spaces

Kamil Bujnarowski$^{(\boxtimes)}$, Jan Krüger, Cavid Karca, Lucas Dahl, and Rico Möckel

Department of Advanced Computing Sciences, Maastricht University, Maastricht, The Netherlands
k.bujnarowski@maastrichtuniversity.nl

Abstract. Collaborative robots, such as the KUKA LBR iiwa, UR series from Universal Robotics, and many more, have opened new fields of applications in industries through human-robot collaboration. However, despite up to seven rotational degrees of freedom typically offered by commercial collaborative (and industrial) robots, the operational reach is often not sufficient. This prevents these robots from reaching into and operating within confined spaces autonomously or in collaboration with human co-workers. To overcome these limitations, this paper presents a custom-made, open-source, affordable robot arm extension to be mounted on commercial or custom-made robots. The developed solution adds three additional degrees of freedom, including a 0.5 m linear rail. These additional degrees of freedom of the robot extension significantly increase the reach and ability of industrial and collaborative robots to operate in narrow environments. The developed extension is demonstrated by extending a KUKA LBR iiwa 14 collaborative robot operating various insect farming use cases, including tasks such as reaching into crates for insect rearing, operating within caged enclosures, and material handling over a wider workspace. Furthermore, simulations are used to provide insights into the extended reach of the robot. Simulation results show an increase in total operational space by up to 110%, and a 200% increase in positions reachable from $\geq 50\%$ of tested orientations, compared to a baseline KUKA iiwa.

Keywords: Robot Extension · Collaborative Robots · Work space extension · KUKA LBR iiwa

1 Introduction

Collaborative robots (cobots) offer industries a flexible platform for automation that is adaptable across various applications [7,8,11,21]. Cobots are typically smaller than their industrial counterparts [1,3,21] and feature integrated safety mechanisms, such as force sensors, allowing humans to work nearby safely [19].

A. Cavalcanti et al. (Eds.): TAROS 2025, LNAI 16045, pp. 475–488, 2026.
https://doi.org/10.1007/978-3-032-01486-3_36

Despite their versatility, cobots typically only feature six (e.g. UR series from Universal Robotics, CR series from Fanuc, and Motoman from Yaskawa) to seven (e.g. KUKA LBR iiwa robots) degrees of freedom with a maximum reach that is limited in comparison to other industrial robots, making cobots impractical in some industries where more reach or operations in confined spaces is required. Alternative solutions, such as the adaptation of the required industrial processes into a tailored workspace fitting a cobot, can be costly and are not always possible.

This paper proposes an articulated, lightweight robot extension as a cost-efficient solution to increase the reach and ability of collaborative robot arms to operate in confined spaces. Use cases from insect farming are used to demonstrate the need for extending the DOFs of collaborative robots. These use cases demonstrate how the developed robot extension allows a KUKA LBR iiwa 14 R820 to successfully perform practical tasks that the seven axes of the standard robot would not support. The insect farming industry offers a variety of challenging use cases. E.g. the enclosed spaces in an insect farming workspace, such as operating tall crates to rear crickets and mating cages for black soldier flies (BSF), restrict the use of a larger robot arm. The presented robot extension was designed to be compatible with various commercially available or custom-made robot arms.

In addition to demonstrations with robotic hardware, a simulation of a KUKA LBR iiwa 14 [13] is used to explore the reachability [10] over the workspace and within confined spaces such as crates that are typically being used during insect rearing processes.

2   Related Work

Cobots have gained significant attention in industrial settings due to their ability to work alongside humans in shared workspaces [1,3,19,21]. However, various limitations hinder their widespread adoption [2,4,9].

One key limitation of cobots is their restricted reach and payload capacity due to size and design constraints [4,21]. Unlike traditional industrial robots built for reach and heavy work, cobots are designed for safety and flexibility, limiting their range and effectiveness in large-scale tasks [7,11]. Research exists on improving cobot arm configurations [21] and providing modular configurations [18] that allow the robot to conform to the task [14,19]. With numerous existing models of collaborative articulated robots, there is typically a selection of appropriate robots that fit specific tasks [4,17,21]. However, related work to an articulated extension of a cobot's reach remains limited.

Measuring and representing the capabilities of an articulated (or other) robot maps regions or volumes of the workspace to scores of reachability [10,12,23,24]. These scores are obtained in both simulation and real-condition testing. Research in collaborative robots uses this information to enhance the information available to a human co-worker [12], for example, in augmented reality [15].

Economic feasibility plays a role in implementing extended reach solutions [2]. High costs associated with advanced actuators, modular extensions, or larger robots can deter small and medium-sized enterprises from adopting these innovations.

3   Robot Extension

In the following, the developed robot extension, its hardware, control, and simulation model, are described. Additional documentation and design files are available at: https://github.com/Dept-Advanced-Computing-Sciences/CoRoSect.

3.1   Structural Design

Figure 1a shows the hardware of the developed robot extension, including annotations of its three main segments (L1-L4), the three featured degrees of freedom, and their corresponding actuators (A1-A3). Figure 1b shows the corresponding CAD design (used as a basis for the simulation model), highlighting the main segments.

The first joint is the prismatic joint, primarily responsible for increasing the work envelope of the robot. It facilitates motion between the first link of the extension L1 and the sledge L2 driving on it. The main component of L1 is a V-shaped aluminium profile, which mounts the actuator A1 driving the first joint. This motor is supported by an electromagnetic brake to increase the stiffness of the sledge while not in motion.

On L1 is the sledge (L2) that is connected to the aluminium profile of L1 with wheels and travels along its axis. This motion is realised by a timing belt connected to pulleys to the actuator (A1) on L1. A support structure on the other side of the extension is mounted to the sledge with adjustable mountings that allow for proper tensioning of the belt.

On its side, L2 has a mounting point for the actuator A2 driving the next joint for rotation around the z-axis. To keep the connection rigid while allowing rotation, a slewing ring is used to connect the sledge L2 to the next link L3 of the extension. On this slewing ring is a spur gear as the base of L3. It is moved by the actuator A2 connected to L2. It also features the mounting point for the end effector (L4) as well as the motor A3 driving this last joint, responsible for tilting the end effector.

The motion is geared, and L4 is moved by a spur gear mounted on one side of the shaft, with an electromagnetic brake on the other side. Connected to L4's shaft is the end plate of the linear extension used to mount the required end-effectors for robotic manipulation. In experiments, an RG6 industrial gripper from OnRobot has been used. The mounting plate connecting L1 to the KUKA LBR iiwa is designed according to DIN ISO 9409-1-50-7-M6, to which iiwa's flange conforms.

Actuators and segments have been selected and designed to meet the following requirements:

– Strict weight constraints, to ensure no payload violations of the KUKA LBR iiwa. Although the iiwa 14 can carry up to 14 kg, this weight limit falls off rapidly at an offset from the flange. The torque limits on the iiwa joints had to allow for at least 2 kg tolerance to handle materials when the robot extension is fully extended.

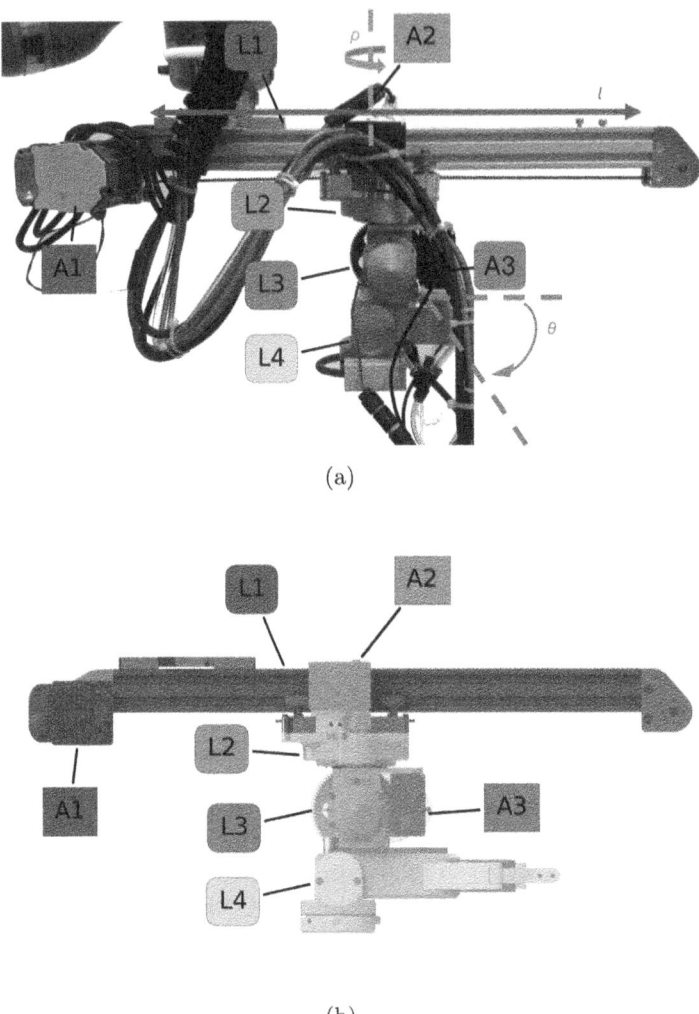

(a)

(b)

Fig. 1. (a) An annotated image of the robot extension hardware mounted on the flange of a robot arm. The picture includes labeled structural links and degrees of freedom. The linear rail (L1) extends by a length l and is actuated by A1 (red). The yaw ρ around the z-axis (L2) is actuated by A2 (yellow). Actuator A3 (blue) enables pitch θ (segment L3) around the xy-plane. (b) An annotated CAD design showing segments and actuators. Each color represents the structural links of the robot extension. L1 is the linear rail. L2 is a wheeled sledge that operates along the rail. L3 connects the sledge to the end effector and houses two additional rotational degrees of freedom. L4 is an RG6 end effector. The mounting orientation of the end effector minimizes the moment exerted around the robot flange when at full extension. (Color figure online)

- Necessity of high IP ratings to guarantee performance in dusty and humid environments at insect farms and in other industrial environments.
- Use of widely available components and simple-to-manufacture custom parts, to keep the cost feasible and the extension easy to copy by researchers and SMEs.

3.2 Actuator Selection

Table 1 outlines the specifications of motors used for actuators A1, A2, and A3, respectively. For the prismatic joint, the heavier, non-geared motor A1 was chosen for its ability to deliver the higher speeds required for this axis, while maintaining sufficient torque to support the maximum payload in any orientation. The offered high speed, acceleration, and deceleration are particularly useful when fast motions are required, e.g. to shake off insects during manipulation tasks in insect farming. The motor's greater weight is positioned near the flange of the KUKA to limit the moment exerted by its weight. For the tilting and turning joints, the actuators are geared servo motors that offer a high torque-to-weight ratio of approximately 37.3. To meet the high torque requirements, both joints are equipped with spur gears, with ratios of 3.6 for A2 and 4 for A3. This configuration results in peak torques of 14.25 Nm for A2 and 15.84 Nm for A3, assuming a conservative efficiency of 90%.

Table 1. An overview of the motor specifications selected for the linear extension.

Actuator	Motor	Peak Torque [Nm]	Max Speed [RPM]	IP	Weight [kg]
A1	Teknic CPM-SCHP-2331S-ELSA	4.4	2520	IP53	1.200
A2	Dynamixel XW540-T140	6.9	72	IP68	0.185
A3	Dynamixel XW540-T140	6.9	72	IP68	0.185

The extension was designed to feature similar collaborative capabilities as provided by the KUKA iiwa robot: (1) The forces of the extension are not high enough to pose a real danger to humans collaborating with the robots. Motor torques can be further limited in software to stop motions earlier if a human co-worker intervenes. (2) The extension rail also has basic robot guiding capabilities implemented. In this guiding mode, the torques of the actuators are reduced in software, so that humans can bring the joints into desired positions, which can then be recorded, a feature that is also supported by the KUKA iiwa.

The final prototype, including all structural parts and actuators, weighs approximately 6 kg with a cost of up to €6250.

3.3 Control and ROS Integration

The Linear Extension operates under the Robot Operation System (ROS) [16] framework and utilises two distinct controllers. Controller C1 is dedicated to

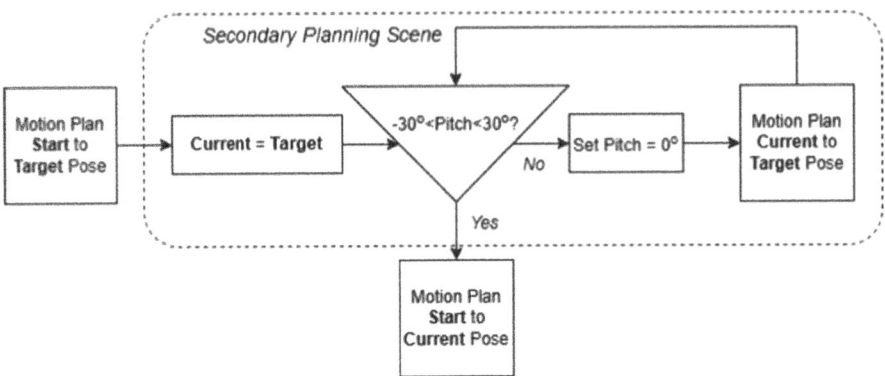

Fig. 2. Visual diagram for iterative planning to a target pose with a constraint on a link in the middle of a kinematic chain. Two motion planning scenes are used in separate ROS namespaces. The secondary planner iteratively brings the pitch angle to the orientation limits while still reaching the target pose. The primary planner is then provided a final pose in joint space to plan from the original starting pose.

the Teknic Motor A1, while the second Controller C2 manages the Dynamixel Motors A2 and A3. This division is necessary since both types of motors come with different drivers and control interfaces. Each controller offers functionalities such as position control and homing through ROS services. Additionally, both controllers monitor the safety state, published by the iiwa, and adjust or halt motion in response to this state. Both controllers implement a ROS action server compatible with the Joint Trajectories published by MoveIt. C1 controls the Teknic Motor through the ClearPath-SC software foundation, a C++ library provided by the manufacturer. The Dynamixel motors are controlled by C2 utilising the ROBOTIS Dynamixel SDK (Software Development Kit). The Unified Robot Description Format (URDF) is used to integrate the robot extension with ROS and MoveIt! [5,20]. Coordinated motion planning for the KUKA iiwa and robot extension is performed in MoveIt!. Synchronised motion commands to achieve the desired trajectories are distributed to the individual controllers using ROS action servers.

Additional software developments have been carried out to ensure reliable control when constraints on the orientation of the rail (e.g., limit pitch to $\pm 30°$) must be guaranteed during motion planning. Respecting such constraints becomes necessary, e.g., when the extension rail is used for insect harvesting or linear motion is required for entering cage doors or other confined spaces. When testing the Open Motion Planning Library [20], it was found that constraints on the orientation of a link in the middle of the kinematic chain are sometimes ignored. Our software extension overcomes this limitation by performing iterative motion planning for the target pose within a secondary MoveIt! planning scene. Each iteration (Fig. 2) plans a trajectory to a target pose without publishing it. If the rail link at the end of the trajectory is not within the permissible range, its pitch is reset to 0° while the other joints remain unchanged. Planning is repeated from this new starting pose, which ensures the next iteration has a rail link pitch closer to 0° (with a cutoff of 10 total iterations). However, convergence is not guaranteed if the endpoint is inherently out of reach. For future work, an analysis of an optimal number of iterations and handling of failed planning attempts is required. The joint positions of the final iteration are provided to the primary motion planner to perform a single spline motion from the robot's true pose to the target.

3.4 General Reachability and Manipulability Simulation

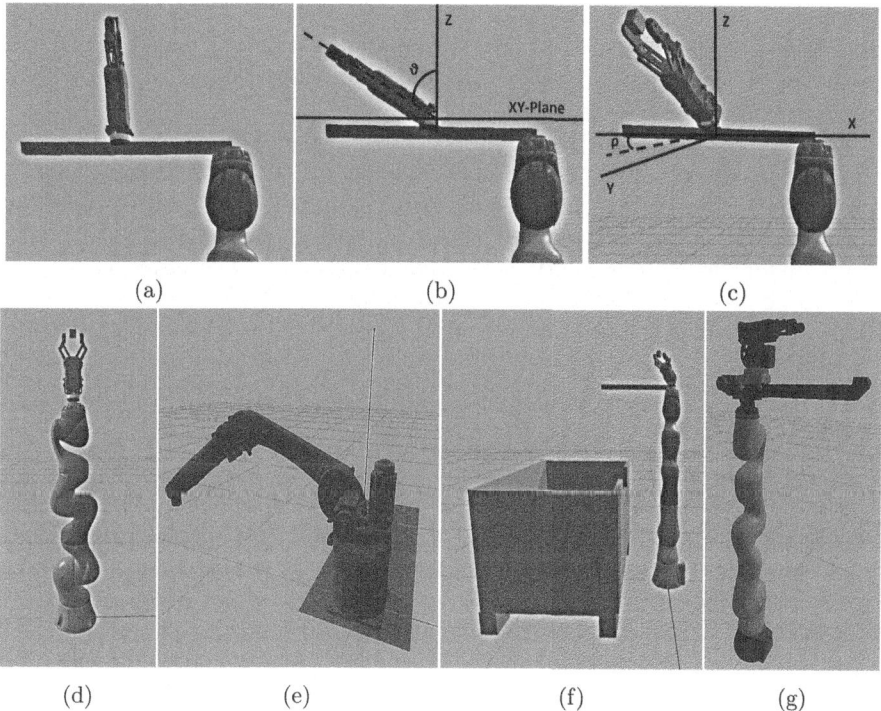

Fig. 3. Simulation robot models: (a) Simulation model of linear rail (L1) of robot extension with a sledge to drive along the prismatic joint and RG6 gripper. (b) Extension rail with first DOF for yaw around the vertical z-axis. (c) Angle for the final DOF that allows adjusting the pitch (around the xy-plane). (d) Baseline model of KUKA LBR iiwa 14 with attached RG6. (e) Baseline model of KUKA KR10r1420. (f) Configuration and relative distance between KUKA iiwa and the crate used for rearing insects. (g) A more realistic simulation model of KUKA iiwa and robot extension based on CAD models.

To systematically explore and demonstrate the increase in workspace gained through the developed robot extension, simulations have been carried out in Pybullet [6]. In these simulations, increases in reachability and manipulability are evaluated by exploring different lengths of the linear extension rail (L1) of the robot extension. A desirable length of an extension rail is defined as one that: (1) increases the robot's maximum reach (reachability) and (2) increases the operational envelope within which positions can be reached from various orientations (manipulability) while (3) respecting the payload constraints of the KUKA iiwa.

The utilised metrics for reachability and manipulability are inspired by the work of [10]. A grid of 30 linearly spaced points in Cartesian Space is used to represent the operational area around the KUKA iiwa. Here, reachability is defined as the success of reaching the centre of a point $p = [x, y, z]$ within a precision threshold $t = 0.01$ m. If a point is reachable, there exists at least one solution to the inverse kinematic problem of computing joint positions for position p. A heatmap of volume is plotted to provide a robust representation of regions that are consistently reachable.

Manipulability, on the other hand, is defined as the success rate of reaching a set of orientations of the end effector around a point p. This simulates attempting various grasp poses at each point in the grid. A comparable measure is achieved by using sub-targets placed on the surface of a sphere around point p_i [10]. The final score for the manipulability m_i of a point is the sum of successes $s_j^i \in \{0, 1\}$ for reaching point with index i from orientation j, over k attempted orientations as calculated following Eq. 1.

$$m_i = \frac{\sum_{j=0}^{k} s_j^i}{k} \tag{1}$$

A position is defined as highly manipulable when it is possible to reach $\geq 50\%$ of the total number of tested orientations ($m_i \geq 0.5$). To demonstrate the gain in reachability and manipulability provided by the robot extension, two baselines are established. For a lower bound, a KUKA iiwa without extension is simulated (Fig. 3d). As a baseline upper bound, comparison is performed with an industrial robot arm, the KUKA KR10r1420 (Fig. 3e), that has a maximum reach of 1.420 m (according to the dataset published with [22]), comparable to the extended KUKA iiwa at 1.320 m + 0.1 m with end effector attached.

For initial experiments, the URDF of the KUKA iiwa is extended with a simplified simulation model of the robot extension to which an RG6 end effector is attached on a prismatic joint (Fig. 3a). The upper limit of the prismatic joint is the length of the rail. The simplified model allows a comparison of the robot extension without the additional rotational degrees of freedom offered by the developed robot extension. It is expected that a rail extension alone (Fig. 3a) will not effectively improve the operational envelope of the robot arm (manipulability). To compare, two additional rotational degrees of freedom (DOF) are implemented (Fig. 1a) between the extension rail and the RG6 end effector to allow yaw (around the z-axis) (Fig. 3b) and pitch (around the xy-plane) (Fig. 3c).

Incrementally increasing lengths of the robot extension, in steps of 0.25 m up to 1.0 m, are tested for initial reaching into insect-rearing crates (Fig. 3f). Finally, a URDF of the final prototype robot extension is used (Fig. 3g) to simulate the final design.

3.5   Evaluation of Operation in Confined Spaces

To evaluate the workspace gained by the robot extension when operating in confined spaces, a linearly spaced grid is generated within a virtual crate for insect rearing. A baseline test with the KUKA iiwa is performed for a robot mounted at $h = 0$ (no height offset between the robot base link and the crate). Experiments are conducted to generate reachability envelopes for incrementally increasing extension rail lengths (Fig. 3f). The crate is placed at a distance of 0.15 m from the base of the robot to minimise the distance without colliding with the base. The simulation did not include a motion planner to account for collisions along planned motions. Hence, the volumes plotted from simulations within the crates are not optimal.

4   Experiments and Results

Manipulability is presented as volume heatmaps with a continuous colour scale of highly manipulable positions (green, reaching $\geq 50\%$ of the total number of possible orientations, hence a score ≥ 0.5) to unreachable positions (red). Results from simulating a KUKA iiwa without robot extension are shown in Fig. 4a. The KUKA iiwa can most reliably reach points within 0.820 m (as per its specifications), and up to 1.12 m with the tip of a mounted RG6 gripper (approximately 0.3 m at full closure). However, the core of highly manipulable positions is limited to the robot's base, likely due to constraints of its configuration as a cobot. In contrast, the baseline for the industrial KUKA KR10r1420 robot (Fig. 4b) shows high manipulability up to the outer limits of its reach.

Figure 4c–4e show the manipulability score for the KUKA iiwa with robot extension. Figure 4c specifically shows the manipulability of points without additional degrees of freedom, hence just a linear rail. The operational range increases, as expected from Fig. 4a. However, the core volume at the centre, where points are most manipulable, does not grow with a larger rail. Figure 4d shows the theoretical increase in the number of highly manipulable points (green) with the introduction of two additional rotational degrees of freedom.

The baseline Fig. 5a shows the maximum reachability of the KUKA iiwa into insect-rearing crates. Reachability maps a binary value, i.e., whether a point is reachable or not (corresponding to whether an inverse kinematics solution exists for this point or not). Green volumes are reachable from at least one orientation. It is shown that, without a robot extension, it is impossible to operate on material that is positioned at the bottom and back wall of the crate. The reachability of points within the cricket crates using a 0.5 m extension rail is shown in Fig. 5b.

484   K. Bujnarowski et al.

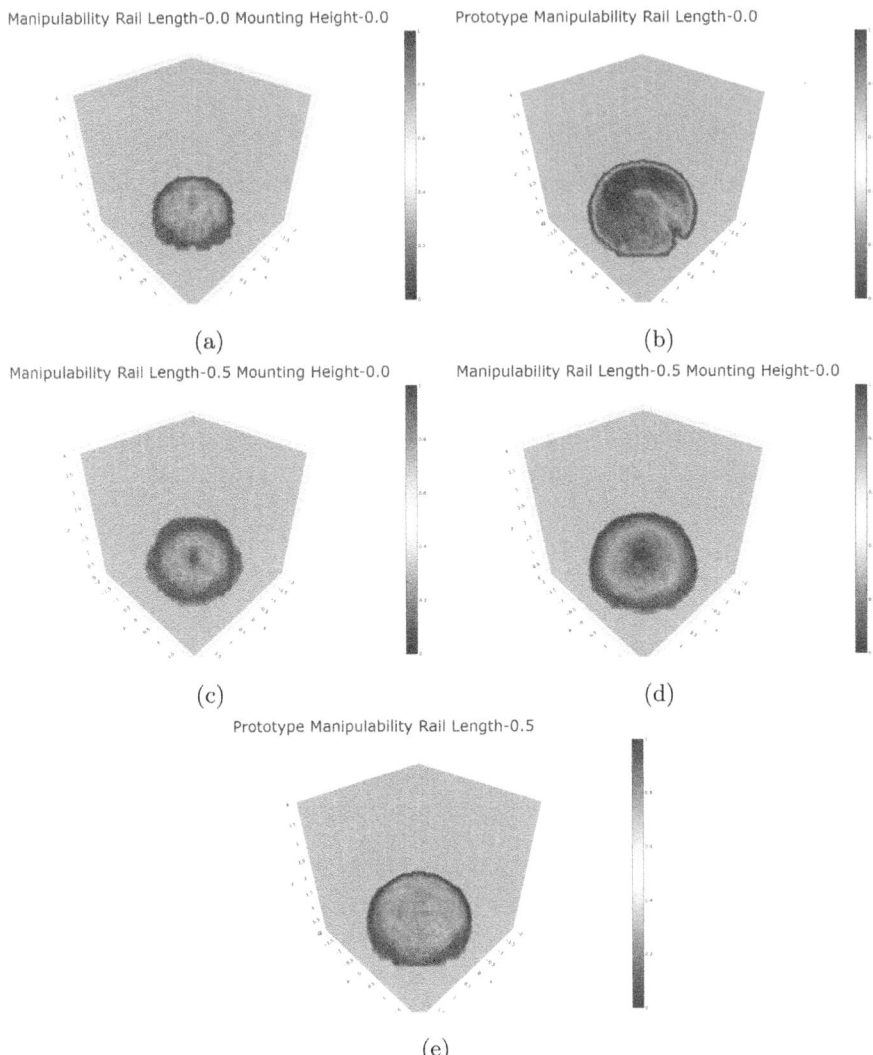

(a)   (b)

(c)   (d)

(e)

Fig. 4. Manipulability scores for a grid of 30 linearly spaced points in the ranges [−2 m, 2 m] in x and y and [0, 4 m] in z. (a) The baseline results for the KUKA iiwa without extension. (b) The baseline results for an industrial KUKA KR10r1420. (c) Manipulability scores when using a simplified robot extension with no additional degrees of freedom (Fig. 3a). (d) The theoretical increased volume of highly manipulable points (green) when incorporating two additional rotational degrees of freedom on a simplified robot extension. (e) The manipulability scores for the final design (Fig. 3g) when using the CAD model in simulation. (Color figure online)

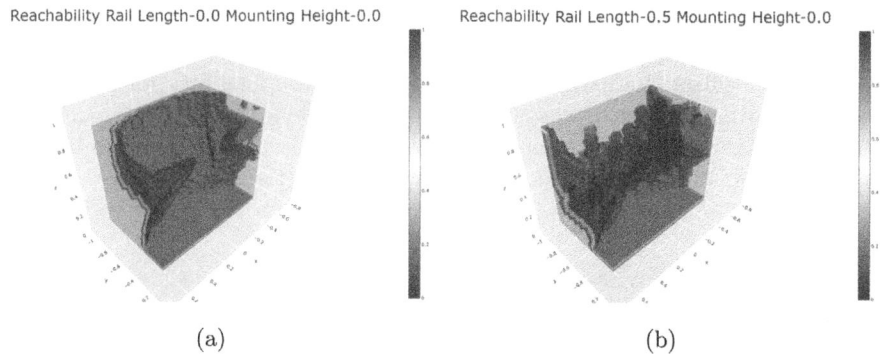

Fig. 5. Reachability scores for linearly spaced points inside a simulated insect crate (Fig. 3f). (a) Baseline reachability of the KUKA iiwa with the RG6 end effector inside an insect crate. (b) Volume of reachable points inside the insect crate using a robot extension of length 0.5 m. (Color figure online)

5   Discussion

The developed robot extension attached to a KUKA iiwa was tested under real conditions within the insect farming industry. E.g., operation within crates used to rear crickets (Fig. 6a) was successfully tested. As simulated, the robot extension fits inside insect-rearing crates, and the range of the KUKA iiwa is sufficiently extended to handle the material inside the crate. It can also operate objects and material within enclosures of black-soldier-fly mating cages (Fig. 6b) at orientations that are out of reach for the KUKA iiwa.

Simulation was used to validate the implementation of two rotational degrees of freedom, which visibly increase the robot's ability to perform manipulation at poses in its workspace (Fig. 4c and 4e). The simplified robot extension increases the operational space by 161% (from 1370 to 3586 reachable positions) and increases the number of highly manipulable positions by 384.8% (from 297 to 1440). The simulation based on CAD models increases the operational space by 110% (from 1370 to 2881) and increases the number of highly manipulable positions by 202% (from 297 to 896). The volume of highly manipulable points for the real prototype (Fig. 4e) is lower than the theoretical (Fig. 4d) due to the practical limitations of the hardware. However, the extension begins to approach the volume of highly manipulable positions (3031 reachable positions, 1932 of which are highly manipulable) of the industrial KR10r1420 (Fig. 4b), while being able to operate in confined spaces that the KR10r1420 cannot operate within due to its lower number of degrees of freedom.

The tradeoff between using the KUKA iiwa with robot extension against an industrial robot lies in the payload capacity, the price, and the required versatility inside a workspace. With the robot extension, it is possible to retain the flexibility and collaborative features of the KUKA iiwa within an extended workspace, taking advantage of additional rotational degrees of freedom for operation within enclosures. A limitation is the payload capacity, as carrying the robot extension and end effector leaves a maximum additional payload of 2 kg at the maximum offset. Industrial robots offer high manipulability for large-scale automation over an open workspace and a high payload. However, particularly large industrial robots will require a highly controlled environment and may be limited by their degrees of freedom or bulk within enclosures.

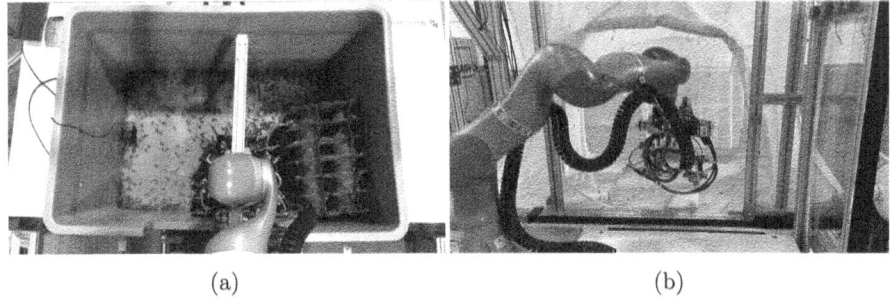

(a)   (b)

Fig. 6. Robot extension utilised in insect farming studies. (a) Reaching into a cricket crate as performed in simulations. (b) Operation inside an insect mating cage, where the robot extension is fully inserted for material handling.

6   Conclusion

Work in extending the operational range of collaborative robots through a custom-made open-source articulated robot extension was presented. A robot extension was developed for increased reachability and manipulability while maintaining a high number of degrees of freedom for operating within confined spaces. The prototype presented in this paper features off-the-shelf technology and integration with a KUKA iiwa and ROS. The robot extension was demonstrated on use cases from the insect farming industry, which is highly diverse in automatable tasks that commonly contain enclosures. Through simulation using CAD designs of our prototype, up to 110% increase in reach over a workspace is shown compared to the baseline reach of the KUKA iiwa.

Future work will focus on an analysis of the extension's effect on the robot's load-bearing capabilities. Additionally, it requires validation in other industrial applications.

Acknowledgments. This project has received funding from the European Union's Horizon 2020 research and innovation programme under grant agreement No. 101016953.

Disclosure of Interests. The authors have no competing interests to declare that are relevant to the content of this article.

References

1. Almurib, H.A., Al-Qrimli, H.F., Kumar, N.: A review of application industrial robotic design. In: 2011 Ninth International Conference on ICT and Knowledge Engineering, pp. 105–112. IEEE (2012)
2. Andersson, S.K.L., Granlund, A., Bruch, J., Hedelind, M.: Experienced challenges when implementing collaborative robot applications in assembly operations. Int. J. Autom. Technol. **15**(5), 678–688 (2021)
3. Brogårdh, T.: Present and future robot control development–an industrial perspective. Annu. Rev. Control. **31**(1), 69–79 (2007)
4. Chutima, P.: Assembly line balancing with cobots: an extensive review and critiques. Int. J. Ind. Eng. Comput. **14**(4), 785–804 (2023)
5. Coleman, D., Sucan, I., Chitta, S., Correll, N.: Reducing the barrier to entry of complex robotic software: a moveit! case study. arXiv preprint arXiv:1404.3785 (2014)
6. Coumans, E., Bai, Y.: Pybullet, a python module for physics simulation for games, robotics and machine learning. http://pybullet.org
7. Dmytriyev, Y., Carnevale, M., Giberti, H.: Enhancing flexibility and safety: collaborative robotics for material handling in end-of-line industrial operations. Procedia Comput. Sci. **232**, 2588–2597 (2024)
8. Dusadeerungsikul, P.O., Nof, S.Y.: A collaborative control protocol for agricultural robot routing with online adaptation. Comput. Ind. Eng. **135**, 456–466 (2019)
9. El Zaatari, S., Marei, M., Li, W., Usman, Z.: Cobot programming for collaborative industrial tasks: An overview. Robot. Auton. Syst. **116**, 162–180 (2019)
10. Engemann, H., Du, S., Kallweit, S., Cönen, P., Dawar, H.: Omnivil–an autonomous mobile manipulator for flexible production. Sensors **20**(24), 7249 (2020)
11. Galin, R., Meshcheryakov, R.: Automation and robotics in the context of industry 4.0: the shift to collaborative robots. In: IOP Conference Series: Materials Science and Engineering, vol. 537, p. 032073. IOP Publishing (2019)
12. Gao, X., Yuan, L., Shu, T., Lu, H., Zhu, S.C.: Show me what you can do: capability calibration on reachable workspace for human-robot collaboration. IEEE Robot. Autom. Lett. **7**(2), 2644–2651 (2022). https://doi.org/10.1109/LRA.2022.3144779
13. Hennersperger, C., et al.: Towards MRI-based autonomous robotic us acquisitions: a first feasibility study. IEEE Trans. Med. Imaging **36**(2), 538–548 (2017)
14. Javaid, M., Haleem, A., Singh, R.P., Suman, R.: Substantial capabilities of robotics in enhancing industry 4.0 implementation. Cogn. Robot. **1**, 58–75 (2021)
15. Newbury, R., Cosgun, A., Crowley-Davis, T., Chan, W.P., Drummond, T., Croft, E.A.: Visualizing robot intent for object handovers with augmented reality. In: 2022 31st IEEE International Conference on Robot and Human Interactive Communication (RO-MAN), pp. 1264–1270. IEEE (2022)
16. Quigley, M., et al.: Ros: an open-source robot operating system. In: ICRA Workshop on Open Source Software, Kobe, Japan, vol. 3, p. 5 (2009)
17. Rahman, M.M., Khatun, F., Jahan, I., Devnath, R., Bhuiyan, M.A.A.: Cobotics: the evolving roles and prospects of next-generation collaborative robots in industry 5.0. J. Robot. **2024**(1), 2918089 (2024)
18. Romiti, E., et al.: Toward a plug-and-work reconfigurable cobot. IEEE/ASME Trans. Mechatron. **27**(5), 3219–3231 (2021)
19. Sandini, G., Sciutti, A., Morasso, P.: Collaborative robots with cognitive capabilities for industry 4.0 and beyond. AI **5**(4), 1858–1869 (2024)

20. Şucan, I.A., Moll, M., Kavraki, L.E.: The open motion planning library. IEEE Robot. Autom. Mag. **19**(4), 72–82 (2012). https://doi.org/10.1109/MRA.2012. 2205651
21. Taesi, C., Aggogeri, F., Pellegrini, N.: Cobot applications–recent advances and challenges. Robotics **12**(3), 79 (2023)
22. Tola, D., Corke, P.: Understanding URDF: a dataset and analysis. IEEE Robot. Autom. Lett. **9**(5), 4479–4486 (2024). https://doi.org/10.1109/LRA.2024.3381482
23. Zacharias, F., Borst, C., Hirzinger, G.: Capturing robot workspace structure: representing robot capabilities. In: 2007 IEEE/RSJ International Conference on Intelligent Robots and Systems, pp. 3229–3236. IEEE (2007)
24. Zacharias, F., Borst, C., Wolf, S., Hirzinger, G.: The capability map: a tool to analyze robot arm workspaces. Int. J. Humanoid Rob. **10**(04), 1350031 (2013)

Fusion Robotics: Analysing Mobility Modes of an End-Over-End Walking Manipulator for Maintenance and Decommissioning

Sarah Reade[1]($\boxtimes$)(ID), Manu H. Nair[2](ID), Mini C. Rai[1](ID), Alexandr Klimchik[1](ID), Marc Hanheide[1](ID), Bechir Tabia[3](ID), and Robert Skilton[3]

[1] Lincoln Centre for Autonomous Systems (L-CAS), University of Lincoln, Lincoln, UK
`28378329@students.lincoln.ac.uk`
[2] University of Manchester, Manchester, UK
[3] RACE, Culham Science Centre, Abingdon, UK
`https://lcas.lincoln.ac.uk/wp/`, `https://www.mace.manchester.ac.uk/`,
`https://race.ukaea.uk/`

Abstract. This paper evaluates mobility methods for the End-over-end Walking manipulator (E-Walker) in the context of fusion robotics. Three walking approaches were analysed (end-over-end, inchworming, and swinging motions) using an Isaac Sim environment. Torque was measured at each joint and used to compare the energy and time efficiency for each method. End-over-end was found to be the most efficient for both metrics, with a ground speed nearly three times that of inchworming and requiring 46% less energy. These results demonstrate the E-Walker's capability to locomote effectively under its own weight, validating its potential for use in the decommissioning of the Joint European Torus.

Keywords: Climbing Robotics · Fusion Energy · Autonomous Navigation

1 Introduction

Fusion, the process that powers stars, produces vast energy in the form of heat and light. The Joint European Torus (JET), as shown in Fig. 1, located in Oxfordshire, UK and operational since 1983, is a pivotal fusion reactor advancing the quest for harnessing this energy on Earth to generate electricity [1]. This marks a significant stride towards a cleaner future, as fusion electricity production entails no high-level radioactive waste, is self-sustaining, and eliminates the risk of meltdowns [2]. After 40 years of operation, the JET has completed its final phase of testing and is now transitioned to the JET Decommissioning and Re-purposing project which aims to define the requirements for the safe and ethical delivery of fusion decommissioning and re-purposing [3]; the energy production will be taken forward in International Thermonuclear Experimental Reactor

© The Author(s), under exclusive license to Springer Nature Switzerland AG 2026
A. Cavalcanti et al. (Eds.): TAROS 2025, LNAI 16045, pp. 489–503, 2026.
https://doi.org/10.1007/978-3-032-01486-3_37

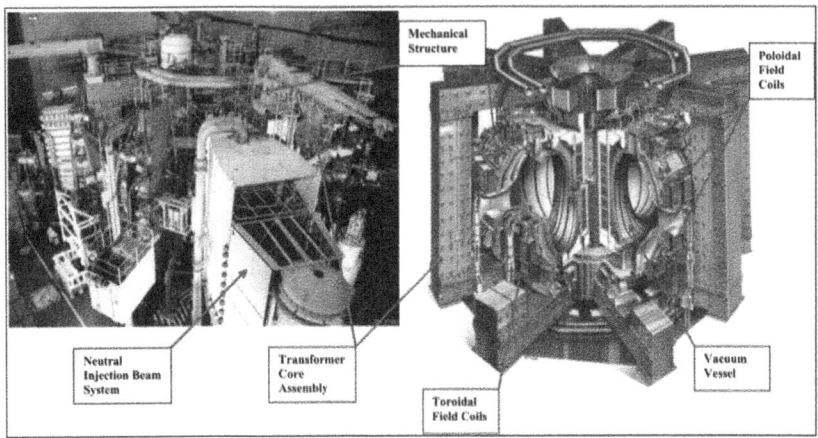

Fig. 1. Structure of the Joint European Torus (JET) showing the main components including the vacuum vessel, field coil assemblies, and mechanical structure [6]

(ITER) located in Cadarache, France [4]. To realize this vision, meticulous planning for the entire reactor life-cycle is imperative, with Robotics, Automation and Autonomous Systems (RAAS) playing a pivotal role. RAAS would enable various activities including construction, maintenance, and decommissioning of these reactors, thereby necessitating technological advancements to enhance efficiency and support this critical goal [5].

Currently, the plan for decommissioning will start with deconstructing the JET from the inside out. This will remove the most hazardous material first. However, this will take a considerable amount of time, with estimates of eighteen months to remove the main plasma-facing components, the carbon fibre composite tiles alone [6]. The entire decommissioning activity is currently aimed for completion by 2040 [6]. This timeline poses various challenges in terms of dismantling the JET reactor parallel to managing its waste by-products. For example, the plasma-facing components are coated with beryllium, which is toxic to humans, both through inhalation and contact with skin and, therefore, must be handled with caution [6]. Additionally, by-products like Tritium and neutrons have to be efficiently disposed, reused and/or decontaminated to meet the purpose.

The advancements in RAAS can support the decommissioning of the JET nuclear fusion reactor and potentially speed it up as well through autonomous activities. Robotic activities would include environmental inspection (inside and outside JET), disassembly, payload handling and maintenance [8,9]; conventionally, these activities are teleoperated [10,11].

Currently employed at JET are two hyper-redundant articulated boom systems (12 m long), able to access the entire workspace via the entry ports [7]. While the first arm (Octant 5) carries out tasks with MASCOT as an end effector (EE), as seen in Fig. 2, the other (Octant 1) enables handling tools to and

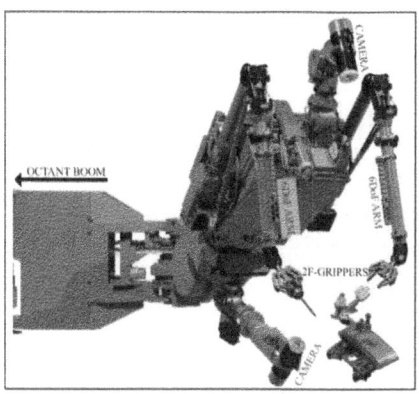
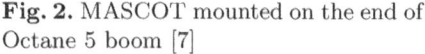

Fig. 2. MASCOT mounted on the end of Octane 5 boom [7]

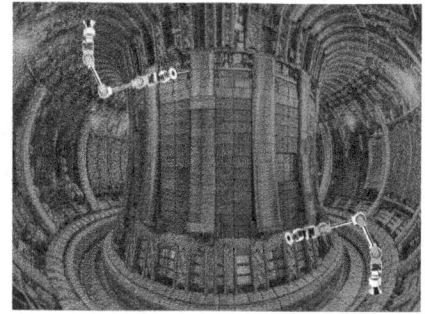

Fig. 3. Artistic impression of E-Walkers assisting JET decommissioning

from MASCOT using the task module [7]. Both arms are controlled via tele-operation with a Virtual Reality (VR) display which provides a live 3D model of both the configuration of JET and the Remote Handling (RH) system [7]. The MASCOT is a two-armed machine each with 6 degrees-of-freedom (DoF) making it highly dexterous. It has force feedback [7], can bear a weight of up to 10 kg and can be positioned to an accuracy of 1 cm [12]. The Octant arms 1 and 5, have seven revolute joints respectively, each with two motors per joint to allow for functionality even when one motor malfunctions. Furthermore, it can be dragged out from the tokamak, as the motors can disengage from the joints, thus preventing the arm from ever getting completely stuck [7]. However, this entire process is quite complex and slower given the teleoperation aspect of remote handling.

In this paper, the authors aim to advance conventional robotic practices for fusion reactor decommissioning by introducing a dexterous walking manipulator, the seven DoF End-Over-End Walking Manipulator (E-Walker). The E-Walker is a walking manipulator originally developed for in-orbit assembly, citing both redundancy and dexterity as major benefits for this application [13,14]. Both Space and JET are harsh environments, presenting extreme temperatures and radiation levels that can be challenging for robotic platforms [15]. Given the E-Walker's enhanced workspace and its walking capabilities around its base platform, the space-based design has been scaled down for an Earth analogue prototype to be built ready for hardware-in-the-loop testing. The design of the E-Walker prototype is presented in [14]. In this analogue prototype, the gripping End-Effector (EE) will initially be an electromagnet. The traits of redundancy and dexterity are equally of high value in the nuclear fusion domain, as shown in the redundancy of the Octant booms. The E-Walker can take these traits further as they have the added flexibility of being able to manoeuvrer without a set anchor point. Having no set anchor point also enables multiple E-Walkers to be able to perform tasks in the same space at once, further improving efficiency.

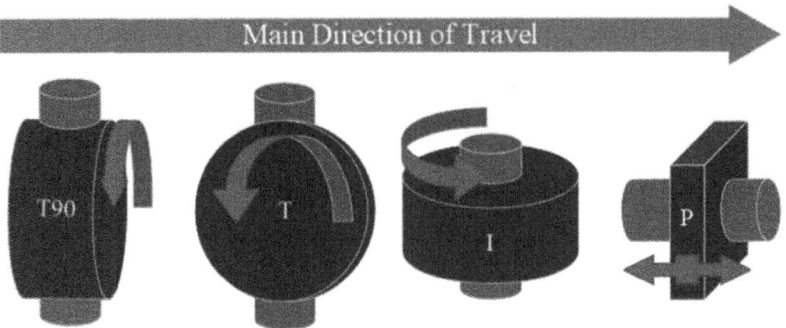

Fig. 4. Definition of Manipulator Joint Notation

Figure 3 showcases the artistic impression of a dual E-Walker system within the JET nuclear reactor.

Advancing the research on E-Walkers in the terrestrial JET reactor setup, this paper starts by presenting a review of climbing manipulators, focusing on their walking gaits. Thereafter, a simulation is used to determine the most efficient walking gait for the E-Walker operating within a tokamak environment.

The remainder of the paper is organized as follows: Sect. 2 provides a review of related work on climbing manipulators, detailing joint structures (Sect. 2.1) and gait patterns (Sect. 2.2). Section 3 describes the E-Walker simulation setup and presents the results and discussion in Sect. 3.2. Finally, Sect. 4 concludes the paper and outlines potential directions for future research.

2   Related Work: Climbing Manipulators

To further develop the E-Walker's walking capabilities for terrestrial applications, it is essential to first examine existing climbing manipulators and their locomotion methods. By analyzing their kinematic structures and walking gaits, key design principles and limitations can be identified, informing the optimal gait selection for the E-Walker within a fusion reactor setting.

There are many climbing manipulators in the literature, designed to operate in various industries from space assembly [16] to providing shade, from the sun, in an office [17]. With varying environments, comes varying requirements and constraints, especially when it comes to navigating obstacles. The next section reviews walking manipulators, initially looking at their kinematic structure and then their gait analyses.

Table 1. Manipulator Joint Structure of Climbing Manipulators, joint key shown in Fig. 4

Robot	Ref	Kinematic Configuration	Walking Method
MiniWirebot	[18]	2F-I-T-T-I-2F T-Wx2	Swing
EWalker	[14,19,20]	I-T90-T-T-T-T90-I	Any
Space Applications	[21,22]	I-T-I-T-I-T-I	Any
Canadarm3	[23]	I-T-I-T-I-T-I	Any
Gunryu III	[24]	I-T-I-T-T-I	Inchworm
HMICRobot	[25]	I-T-T-T-T-I	Any
iCrawl	[26]	T-T90-T-T90-T	Inchworm
W-Climbot	[27]	I-T-T-T-I	Any
ASIBOT	[28,29]	I-T-T-T-I	Any
BWCRS	[30]	I-T-T-T-I	Any
Bisht's Robot	[31]	I-T-T-T-I	Any
HMA Climber	[32]	I-T90-T90-I	Swing
HHJ Robot	[33]	I-T-P-I	Inchworm, End-over-end
ThermsBond002	[34]	I-T-T-I	Swing
ROMA I	[35]	I-T-T-I	Inchworm
ROMA II	[28]	I-T-T-I	Inchworm
3D Climber	[36]	I-T-T-T	Inchworm
RAMR1	[37]	I-T-T-T	End-over-End
Tummala's Flipper	[38]	I-T-T-T	End-over-End
ROBIN	[39]	I-T-T-T	Inchworm
Shady 3D	[17]	I-I-I	Swing
Handbot	[40,41]	T-T90-T	Swing
RDB	[42]	T-T-T	Inchworm, End-over-End
Shady	[43]	I-I	Swing
Façade cleaning robot	[44]	T-T	Inchworm
Hybrid Omniclimber	[45]	T-T	Inchworm
Mohamed's Robot	[46]	T-T	Inchworm, End-over-End

2.1 Joint Structure of Climbing Manipulators

The joint kinematic structure of walking manipulators have been defined in Table 1 according to the definition of joints in Fig. 4 for those robots surveyed here. It is evident that the most popular structure uses I joints directly after the EEs and then T joints centrally, i.e. I-T-...-T-I. This allows both stepping over and swinging around gait motions, as seen with W-Climbot [27] in Fig. 5b. A variation of this uses T90 and I joints centrally, e.g. the E-Walker [14] and Canadarm3 [23] respectively. This allows for even greater options for gait motions, as well as, more importantly for complex environments, greater capability for obstacle avoidance.

The use of T-joints directly after EE's is not as popular, and when employed in 3D enables inchworming [26] or swinging [17,40], but not end over end walking.

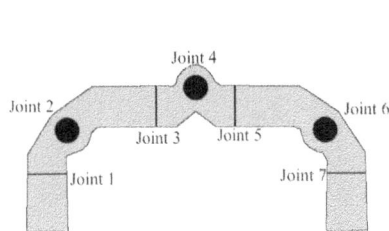

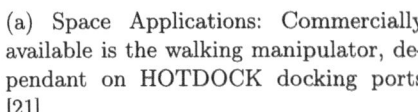

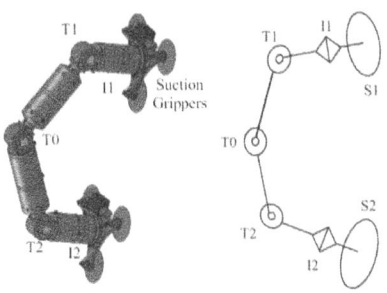

(a) Space Applications: Commercially available is the walking manipulator, dependant on HOTDOCK docking ports [21]

(b) W-Climbot: A climbing robot with 5DoF and Suction for wall adhesion [27]

Fig. 5. Climbing Robots

Another variation is the use of prismatic joints which are present in the center of the HHJ Robot [33]. Using prismatic joints at the center of the kinematic chain enables the step size to be determined directly, providing simpler calculation [33].

Of those operating in full 6D, E-Walker, Canadarm3, Gunryu, HMICRobot, and Space Applications (see Fig. 5a), many make use of the spherical wrist (i.e. I-T-I). This design simplifies the kinematics and enables a range of gait patterns, including swinging and end-over-end walking. Three of these designs are redundant, which is essential in more complex environments to allow for obstacle avoidance and efficient motion. They are also symmetrical, ensuring control does not have to switch models dependant on the attached end. While the E-Walker does have added kinematic complexity, over the other redundant designs, the addition of the T90 joint ensures that there is rotational freedom in the longest links, i.e. the central links. This gives the E-Walker the ability to overcome more complex obstacles.

2.2   Gait Patterns of Climbing Manipulators

Alongside the kinematic structure of climbing manipulators, Table 1 shows the various walking methods utilised by these robots. There are three methods of walking depicted in Fig. 6: to swing, to move end-over-end, and to inchworm.

Most systems which contain at least 5-DoF are capable of all three types of motions, enabling the most efficient to be used for the conditions of operation. The window cleaning BWCRS robot makes use of the availability of the different methods to overcome various obstacles and inclines [33].

Gripping and ungripping time is a large factor in speed with all of these systems, as shown with Shady, making up ¿50% using a truss gripping mechanism [43], ThermsBond002 taking 25 s to heat its adhesive [34], and taking 93 s with the hot metal adhesive system of the HMA climber [32]. Other gripping systems

Fig. 6. Gait Patterns of Climbing Manipulators

improve on this with the use of quick acting gripping such as electromagnets [42].

Inchworming is a bi-inspired form of motion, which requires less joint motion [26]. A couple of studies have compared inchworming to end-over-end motions and have found end-over-end (or flipping) to be faster. By a factor of 4 in both the case of the HHJ robot, with an end-over-end horizontal speed of 0.01 m/s [30], and the RDB robot, with an end-over-end speed of 0.136 m/s [42]. Swing walking, on the other hand, seems to be quite slow, with the Thermsbond, Shady and HMA Climber all having speeds ≤0.01 m/s, which is inconclusive in this scenario, as these robots are limited by their gripping time.

The following section directly compares all three methods of walking for the E-Walker in a JET simulated environment. Both efficiency through overall work required and speed will be measured for direct comparison.

3   E-Walker Simulation

Building on these findings, this study aims to systematically evaluate the three walking strategies: inchworming, end-over-end, and swing walking, in the context of the E-Walker operating within a JET simulated environment. By analyzing both energy efficiency, in terms of overall work required, and locomotion speed, this comparison will help determine the most suitable gait for practical deployment in fusion reactor maintenance.

The following section details the simulation setup used to conduct this evaluation.

3.1   Setup

The simulation is entirely carried out in Isaac Sim [47] using its integrated articulation control and physics-solver. This allows the current JET model to be used, which is provided in the usd format. To simulate the opening and closing of grippers, fixed joints are created and destroyed between each gripper link and

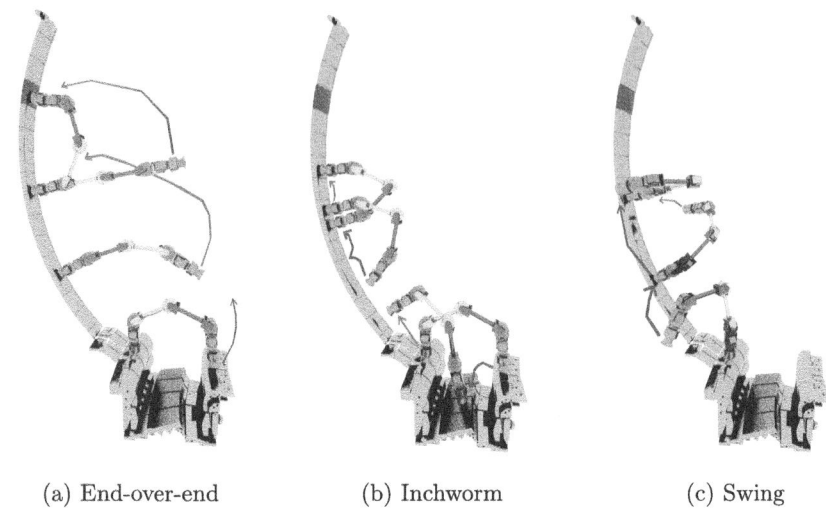

(a) End-over-end   (b) Inchworm   (c) Swing

Fig. 7. Snapshots of the Simulation in Progress

a solid object. Each simulation step, the joint position is iterated, at $0.1\,\text{rads}^{-1}$, towards the desired position and the measured torque, at each joint, and joint position is recorded. The environment in which it is operating is a 3D model of a section of the plasma facing components of JET, including the divertor plates and plasma facing tiles, as shown in Fig. 7. This provides realistic obstacles and base gripper angles. The E-Walker will start at the bottom of the Tokamak, in a stable pose across the divertor plates, and make its way to a target tile, highlighted in red, most of the way up the plasma facing tiles. The E-walker will have successfully reached the tile when the target tile is touched.

Joint positions were chosen based on the biggest strides possible, i.e. using the fewest steps possible, to reach the target tile. Each end-over-end and swing step has four midpoints which ensure steps avoid collisions with the environment and can optimise their path to a small degree. During the swing step, the central joint retracted to reduce the leverage effect on the joint in motion. During the end-over-end step, the midpoints were used to ensure that motions were smooth and joints were moving synchronously to reduce joint stress. As both of these steps resulted in one leg completely moving around the other, the end poses for each step are the same and, therefore, so are the gripping points. Inchworming, however, requires a considerable number more gripping points and less waypoints in-between each of these, therefore midpoints were used purely for clearing obstacles between steps.

As the simulation is timed, the ground speed can be calculated simply based on the time taken to complete the simulation (Ts), as shown below:

$$Ground\ Speed = \frac{D}{T}, \tag{1}$$

where the D is the distance between the start and target tiles in m and ground speed is irrespective of incline. Since the grip time is not included, this can be considered as a variable in the results.

The torque can also be analysed as total energy consumption in based on the equations:

$$Power_i = |\tau_i \cdot \omega_i| \qquad (2)$$

$$Total\ Power = \delta t \cdot \sum_{t=2}^{T} \sum_{i=1}^{7} Power_i, \qquad (3)$$

where δt is the simulation timestep, t is the time, τ_i is the torque at joint i, and ω_i is the angular velocity at joint i.

3.2   Results and Discussion

Figures 8, 9 and 10 show the simulation results for all methods of walking. The end-over-end method shows a cyclic pattern in which the torque requirements swap between the 3rd and 5th joints for each step. Even as the incline increases

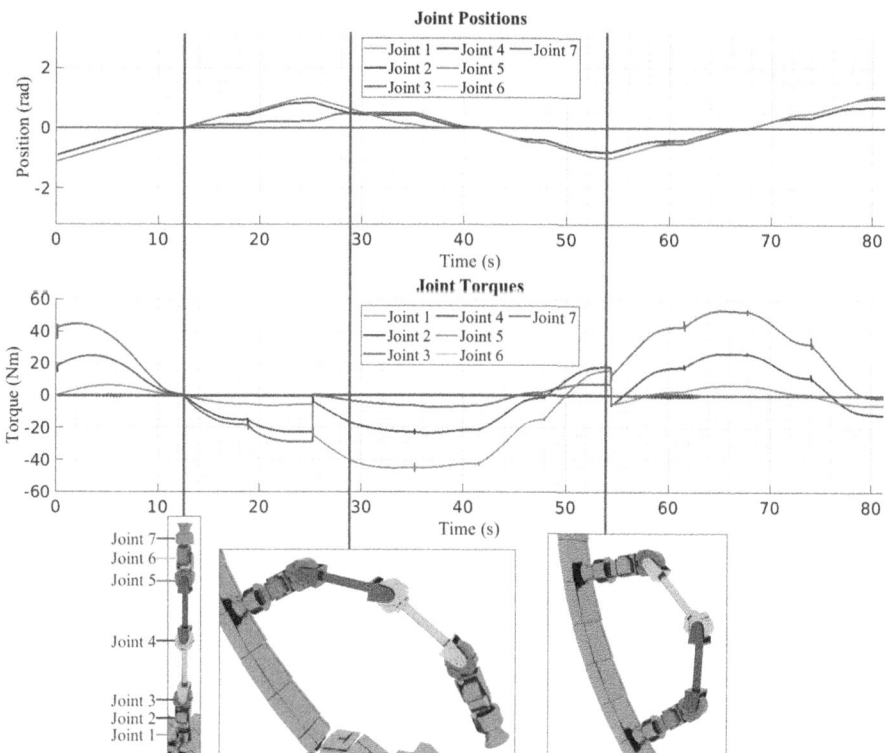

Fig. 8. End-over-end walking results of E-Walker in simulation.

the torque requirements remain about the same. However, the inchworm motion, while it does still switch between the 3rd and 5th joints, as the incline increases the torque requirements reduce. This is due to the decreasing leverage force on the joints in motion (Joints 3–5), as gravity aligns with the direction of motion. In this configuration, the main force primarily acts along the links rather than perpendicular to them.

The swing motion starts the same as the end-over-end method, as joint 3 is forced to hold the leveraged weight of the arm. This then shifts to joint 5 and joint 7, the later of which is taking the entire weight of the robot. However, upon reaching a more vertical climb it is joint 2, which is having to couteract the force of gravity alongside joint 7, as the arm becomes horizontal.

From Table 2, it is clear that the end-over-end method of walking was the fastest, with a ground speed of 0.038 m/s. This also did not require any waypoints to avoid collisions, only to synchronise the joint motions. Despite the spikes in torque, due to the leverage of the arm being straight out when the base is at 90°, making the arm parallel to the ground, the total energy used was the least at 261J. Swing walking was the second fastest, with a ground speed of 0.024 m/s, and the second least energy used at 273J. Inchworming was the slowest, with

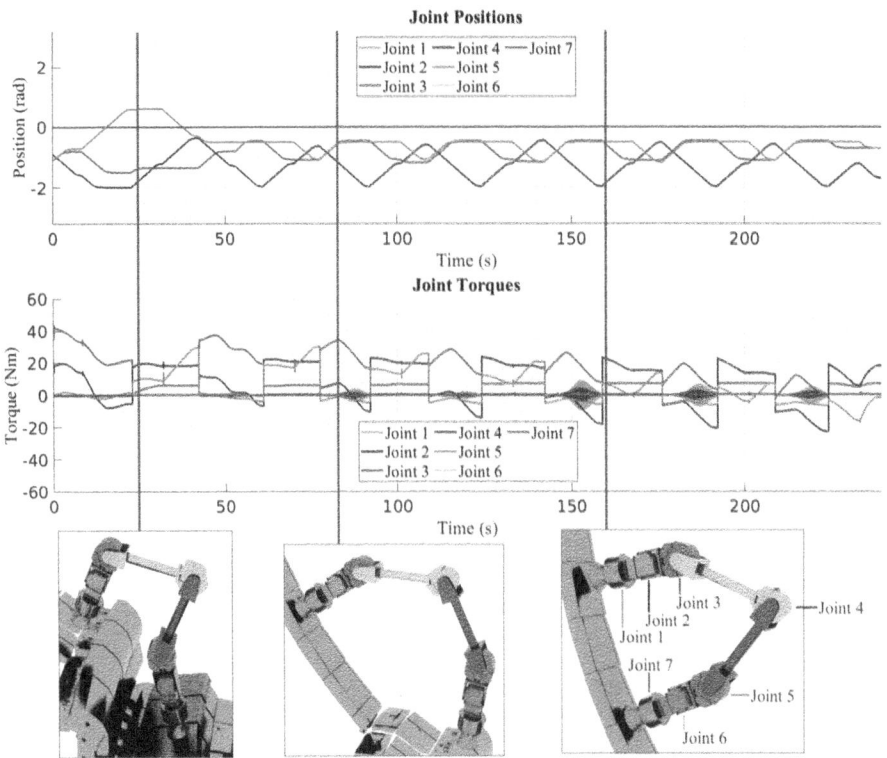

Fig. 9. Inchworm walking results of E-Walker in simulation.

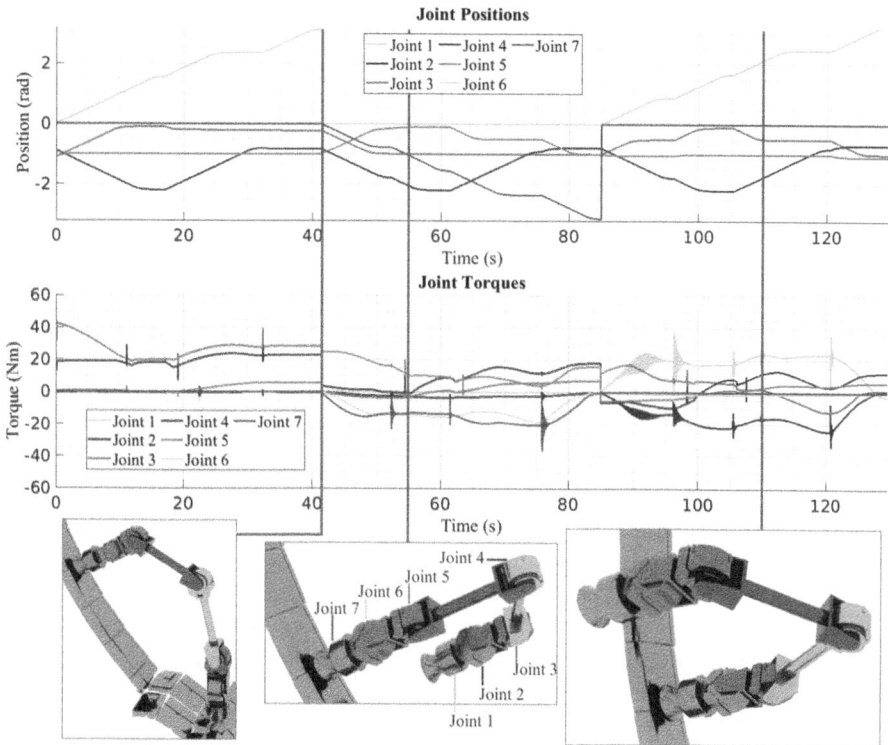

Fig. 10. Swing walking results of E-Walker in simulation.

a ground speed of 0.013 m/s, and the most energy used at 484J. However, it required the least joint motion, with joints only operating within certain bounds, and this grew less as the incline increased. The downfall of inchworming was in its inability to overcome the divertor plate obstacle, requiring a slight diversion, as well as a considerable amount of extra gripping points. If the gripping is taken into account as a variable for ground speed, this will massively decrease the movement speed when inchworming. This is in-line with the previous findings of [30,42], with end-over-end walking at about 3x the speed of inchworming.

Both the swing and inchworm motion caused some instability in the simulation, as can be seen in Fig. 9 in the pulling up phase of motion, and Fig. 10 at 90 s, when the E-Walker base is angled at 90° and the arm is near horizontal to the ground. This is likely due to the method of forcing the joints into a position and taking the static joint torque, instead of driving the joints with effort.

Overall, these results suggest that the end-over-end method of walking is the best for the E-Walker in the JET environment. Especially as it enables the E-Walker to avoid all obstacles on the ground and utilise the internal space of the tokamak. However, it is worth looking at inchworming in the case of greater loads

Table 2. Results of the E-Walker Simulation

Walking Method	Ground Speed (m/s)	Energy (J)	Steps	Max Torque (Nm)	Time (s)
End-over-end	0.038	261	3	53.8	81.2
Inchworm	0.013	484	13	43.7	239.7
Swing	0.024	273	3	43.5	129.7

on the free end effector, as it can be used to ensure the arm is counterbalanced when the base is at a 90° angle.

4   Conclusion and Future Research

This paper presents a walking manipulator concept for advancing the field of fusion robotics. The use case considered is the decommissioning of the JET tokamak. While taking into consideration the state-of-the-art of a variety of walking manipulators, initial progress is made in simulating the E-Walker under Earth's gravity utilising different gait patterns. The results demonstrate that the E-Walker can meet torque requirements for both walking and climbing, with end-over-end walking emerging as the most effective and flexible gait for navigating the complex internal geometry of the JET tokamak. Swinging ranked second in both overall energy cost and speed, while inchworming performed significantly less efficiently. The results indicated, however, that inchworming may be a stable method for handling vertical climbing, to reduce torque impact across the joints and on the gripping end-effector.

This paper is a stepping stone towards designing and testing novel trajectory and path planning algorithms for efficient and safe motions of the E-Walker within JET.

Future research will focus on the development of autonomous algorithms capable of optimising obstacle avoidance, energy efficiency, the E-Walker's redundancy, and base gripping angle. Development of the hardware platform, alongside integration of gripping capabilities, will further investigate the E-Walker as a viable solution for the decommissioning of fusion tokamaks.

Acknowledgments. This research is jointly funded by the UK Atomic Energy Authority and the University of Lincoln, UK.

Disclosure of Interests. The authors have no competing interests to declare that are relevant to the content of this article.

References

1. Smart, D.L.: The joint European torus (jet). Nuclear Technol.-Fusion **4**(2P2), 316–325 (1983)
2. Takatsu, H.: Iter project and fusion technology. Nucl. Fusion **51**(9), 094002 (2011)

3. UKAEA. Jet decommissioning and repurposing - information for the UK atomic energy authority's jet decommissioning and repurposing (JDR) programme and upcoming commercial activity (2022). https://www.gov.uk/government/publications/jet-decommissioning-and-repurposing. Accessed 14 Mar 2024
4. ITER. Iter - the way to new energy. Accessed 26 Mar 2025
5. Ferre, M., Aracil, R., Suárez-Ruiz, F., Barrio, J., Breñosa, J.M., Queral, V.: Robot requirements for nuclear fusion facilities. In: First Workshop on Fusion Technologies and the Contribution of Technofusión (2011)
6. Wilson, K.A., Stevens, K.: Decommissioning planning for the joint European torus fusion reactor. In: Waste Management Symposium (WM 2007) (2007)
7. Owen, T., Skilton, R., UKAEA: Remote handling at jet (2017). https://scipub.euro-fusion.org/wp-content/uploads/eurofusion/NJOCPR17_18641_submitted.pdf. Accessed 14 Mar 2024
8. Iqbal, J., Tahir, A.M., ul Islam, R., et al.: Robotics for nuclear power plants—challenges and future perspectives. In: 2012 2nd International Conference on Applied Robotics for the Power Industry (CARPI), pp. 151–156. IEEE (2012)
9. Tokatli, O., et al.: Robot-assisted glovebox teleoperation for nuclear industry. Robotics 10(3), 85 (2021)
10. Watson, S., Lennox, B., Jones, J.: Robots and autonomous systems for nuclear environments (2019). https://uomrobotics.com/onewebmedia/KAIF_Draft.pdf. Accessed 14 Mar 2024
11. Perrot, Y., et al.: Long reach articulated robots for inspection in hazardous environments, recent developments on robotics and embedded diagnostics. In: 2010 1st International Conference on Applied Robotics for the Power Industry, pp. 1–5. IEEE (2010)
12. Skilton, R., Hamilton, N., Howell, R., Lamb, C., Rodriguez, J.: Mascot 6: achieving high dexterity tele-manipulation with a modern architectural design for fusion remote maintenance. Fusion Eng. Des. 136, 575–578 (2018)
13. Nair, M.H., Rai, M.C., Poozhiyil, M.: Modelling and controlling a dexterous walking space manipulator for in-orbit missions. Online J. Robot. Autom. Technol. 2(3), 1–15 (2024)
14. Nair, M.H., Rai, M.C., Poozhiyil, M.: Design engineering a walking robotic manipulator for in-space assembly missions. Front. Robot. AI 9, 995813 (2022)
15. Wong, C., Yang, E., Yan, X.-T., Gu, D.: An overview of robotics and autonomous systems for harsh environments. In: 2017 23rd International Conference on Automation and Computing (ICAC), pp. 1–6. IEEE (2017)
16. Nair, M., Rai, M.C., Reade, S., Adlen, S., Soltau, M., Homfray, D.: Keynote: advancing in-orbit robotic assembly and disassembly of high-value infrastructures using end-over-end walking manipulators. In: 22nd IAA Symposium on Visions and Strategies for the Future, pp. 1–15. International Astronautical Federation (IAF) (2024)
17. Yoon, Y., Rus, D.: Shady3D: a robot that climbs 3D trusses. In: IEEE International Conference on Robotics and Automation, pp. 4071–4076. IEEE (2007)
18. Ye, J., Guan, Y., Bi, Z., Zhao, G., Luo, D., Liu, T.: A novel miniature modular wire inspection robot with multiple locomotion modes. In: 2013 IEEE International Conference on Mechatronics and Automation, pp. 1185–1190. IEEE (2013)
19. Nair, M.H., Saaj, C.M., Esfahani, A.G.: Modelling and control of an end-over-end walking robot. In: Mohammad, A., Dong, X., Russo, M. (eds.) TAROS 2020. LNCS (LNAI), vol. 12228, pp. 128–133. Springer, Cham (2020). https://doi.org/10.1007/978-3-030-63486-5_15

20. Nair, M.H., Saaj, C.M., Adlen, S., Esfahani, A.G., Eckersley, S.: Advances in robotic in-orbit assembly of large aperture space telescopes. In: 15th International Symposium on Artificial Intelligence, Robotics and Automation in Space (i-SAIRAS 2020) (2020)

21. Spaceapplications. Walking manipulator, a reconfigurable mobile manipulator for in-orbit-servicing (2022). https://www.spaceapplications.com/wp-content/uploads/2022/03/16-wm-product-sheet-001-0-0-3.pdf

22. Deremetz, M., et al.: Design and development of a relocatable robotic arm for servicing on-orbit modular spacecraft. In: 16th Symposium on Advanced Space Technologies in Robotics and Automation, ASTRA 2022 (2022)

23. Won, D., So, B.-R., Kim, H.-D.: A survey of space robotic manipulator. J. Space Technol. Appl. **2**(4), 257–267 (2022)

24. Lee, W., Hirai, M., Hirose, S.: Gunryu III: reconfigurable magnetic wall-climbing robot for decommissioning of nuclear reactor. Adv. Robot. **27**(14), 1099–1111 (2013)

25. Lin, T.-H., Putranto, A., Chen, P.-H., Teng, Y.-Z., Chen, L.: High-mobility inchworm climbing robot for steel bridge inspection. Autom. Constr. **152**, 104905 (2023)

26. Khan, M.B., et al.: iCrawl: an inchworm-inspired crawling robot. IEEE Access **8**, 200655–200668 (2020)

27. Zhu, H., Guan, Y., Cai, C., Jiang, L., Zhang, X., Zhang, H.: W-Climbot: a modular biped wall-climbing robot. In: 2010 IEEE International Conference on Mechatronics and Automation, pp. 1399–1404. IEEE (2010)

28. Balaguer, C., Gimenez, A., Huete, A.J., Sabatini, A.M., Topping, M., Bolmsjo, G.: The MATS robot: service climbing robot for personal assistance. IEEE Robot. Autom. Mag. **13**(1), 51–58 (2006)

29. Jardón, A., Stoelen, M.F., Bonsignorio, F., Balaguer, C.: Task-oriented kinematic design of a symmetric assistive climbing robot. IEEE Trans. Robot. **27**(6), 1132–1137 (2011)

30. Zhang, W., et al.: Design and development of a new biped robotic system for exoskeleton-structure window cleaning. IEEE Trans. Autom. Sci. Eng. 1–12 (2024)

31. Bisht, R.S., Pathak, P.M., Panigrahi, S.K.: Modelling, simulation and experimental validation of wheel and arm locomotion based wall-climbing robot. Robotica **41**(2), 433–469 (2023)

32. Osswald, M., Iida, F.: Design and control of a climbing robot based on hot melt adhesion. Robot. Auton. Syst. **61**(6), 616–625 (2013)

33. Krosuri, S.P., Minor, M.A.: Design, modeling, control, and evaluation of a hybrid hip joint miniature climbing robot. Int. J. Robot. Res. **24**(12), 1033–1053 (2005)

34. Wang, L., Graber, L., Iida, F.: Large-payload climbing in complex vertical environments using thermoplastic adhesive bonds. IEEE Trans. Robot. **29**(4), 863–874 (2013)

35. Balaguer, C., Gimenez, A., Jardón, A.: Climbing robots? Mobility for inspection and maintenance of 3D complex environments. Auton. Robots **18**(2), 157–169 (2005)

36. Tavakoli, M., Marques, L., de Almeida, A.T.: 3DCLIMBER: climbing and manipulation over 3D structures. Mechatronics **21**(1), 48–62 (2011)

37. Minor, M., Dulimarta, H., Danghi, G., Mukherjee, R., Lal Tummala, R., Aslam, D.: Design, implementation, and evaluation of an under-actuated miniature biped climbing robot. In: IEEE/RSJ International Conference on Intelligent Robots and Systems (IROS 2000) (Cat. No.00CH37113), vol. 3, pp. 1999–2005. IEEE (2000)

38. Lal Tummala, R., et al.: Climbing the walls [robots]. IEEE Robot. Autom. Mag. **9**(4), 10–19 (2002)
39. Pack, R.T., Christopher, J.L., Kawamura, K.: A Rubbertuator-based structure-climbing inspection robot. In: International Conference on Robotics and Automation, vol. 3, pp. 1869–1874. IEEE (1997)
40. Magnenat, S., Rétornaz, P., Bonani, M., Longchamp, V., Mondada, F.: ASEBA: a modular architecture for event-based control of complex robots. IEEE/ASME Trans. Mechatron. **16**(2), 321–329 (2011)
41. Bonani, M., Magnenat, S., Rétornaz, P., Mondada, F.: The hand-bot, a robot design for simultaneous climbing and manipulation. In: Xie, M., Xiong, Y., Xiong, C., Liu, H., Hu, Z. (eds.) ICIRA 2009. LNCS (LNAI), vol. 5928, pp. 11–22. Springer, Heidelberg (2009). https://doi.org/10.1007/978-3-642-10817-4_2
42. Phipps, C.C., Shores, B.E., Minor, M.A.: Design and quasi-static locomotion analysis of the rolling disk biped hybrid robot. IEEE Trans. Robot. **24**(6), 1302–1314 (2008)
43. Vona, M., Detweiler, C., Rus, D.: Shady: robust truss climbing with mechanical compliances. In: Experimental Robotics, vol. 39, pp. 431–440. Springer, Heidelberg (2008)
44. Nansai, S., Onodera, K., Veerajagadheswar, P., Elara, M.R., Iwase, M.: Design and experiment of a novel façade cleaning robot with a biped mechanism. Appl. Sci. **8**(12), 2398 (2018)
45. Tavakoli, M., Lourenço, J., Viegas, C., Neto, P., de Almeida, A.T.: The hybrid OmniClimber robot: wheel based climbing, arm based plane transition, and switchable magnet adhesion. Mechatronics **36**, 136–146 (2016)
46. Mohamed, A.M., Zyada, Z.A., El-Shenawy, E.A.: Design, modeling and control of a wall climbing robot crossingover obstacles. In: IEEE/SICE International Symposium on System Integration, pp. 46–51. IEEE (2014)
47. Nvidia. Isaac sim - robotics simulation and synthetic data generation | nvidia developer. Accessed 26 Mar 2025

Terra-Robotics Laboratory: A Facility for Studying Terrain-Robot Interaction

Joe Ingham$^{(\boxtimes)}$, James Hambleton , and Sam Stanier

University of Cambridge, Cambridge CB2 1TN, UK
ji291@cam.ac.uk

Abstract. To maximise the efficiency and usability of autonomous systems in geotechnical applications and natural environments, it is necessary to understand the terrain with which the systems interact. While significant advances have been made in mechatronics, methods for perceiving and predicting deformation within the terrain itself are underdeveloped. This paper introduces the Terra-Robotics Laboratory, a new lab investigating the effect of robotic interaction on deformable terrain. The article describes the laboratory setup based in Cambridge and how it will contribute to the overall understanding of soil-robot interaction. Data on end-effector force-displacement histories are presented for a spherical object traversing sand, examining straight-line and spiral motion as two examples with disparate responses. The preliminary results highlight the need for fast and accurate terrain mapping and other open challenges in the domain of soil-robot interaction.

Keywords: Soil · Soil-Machine Interaction · Terra-robotics · Earthmoving

1 Introduction

A considerable amount of robotics research is completed on hard surfaces with little to no deformation (almost completely elastic) [14,20,24]. This is unsuitable and unrealistic for geotechnical contexts, particularly in construction scenarios where a major interest is in manipulating the ground. This requires precisely controlled deformation [19] and an understanding of how the terrain can be deformed effectively. The scale of earthmoving operations around the world is staggering [9], and thus any gains in efficiency in individual processes translate to enormous impact globally. An efficient model for deformable terrains will enable real-time full autonomy, which will lead to increased usage of robotics in civil engineering processes such as autonomous earthmoving.

Various methods for predicting the response of terrain under machine loading have been devised (e.g., [6,9,12,13,29]). One of the major works in soil-machine interaction (SMI) is so-called resistive force theory (RFT), based on a fluid dynamics model [8]. This model was adapted to granular media and called "granular RFT" [29] (and "dynamic RFT" [1]). Granular RFT is effective for the

© The Author(s), under exclusive license to Springer Nature Switzerland AG 2026
A. Cavalcanti et al. (Eds.): TAROS 2025, LNAI 16045, pp. 504–511, 2026.
https://doi.org/10.1007/978-3-032-01486-3_38

purpose of analysing movement in granular materials, namely sands. The model proposed by Aguilar and Goldman [2] relies on approximating an intrusion in granular material as a point interaction. As such, the model has been used for locomotion [7] but would be unsuitable for tasks where predicting the deformation is the goal. Other prominent models in SMI (and therefore robot-soil interaction) are based on soil plasticity theory (e.g., [4,5,22,23]) and numerical simulation (e.g., [10,25]). These generally allow for assessment of deformations and forces, but such models tend to be problem specific and/or computationally onerous.

Here we introduce the term "terra-robotics" to describe problems involving the interaction between robots and terrain. A number of applications will benefit from advancements in this field. For civil engineering, it would be desirable to have autonomous terrain manipulation, as it would increase safety and productivity [21]. It also has the potential to decrease energy usage by reducing operator inefficiencies, as well as being utilised in harsh environments to reduce risk to human operators [28]. For example, autonomous excavation would be useful in radioactive or extra-terrestrial environments. Autonomous soil interaction could be used to increase the efficiency of locomotion, as a robot would be able to adapt to soil deformation and optimise its gait/speed accordingly [26]. For full soft-terrain autonomy, there needs to be real-time analysis and adaptation that can be generalised for any type of terrain. This full bodied rapid terrain modelling and estimation does not exist in the current literature.

This paper introduces the Terra-Robotics Laboratory (TRL), a new laboratory that investigates the reaction of deformable materials when manipulated by autonomous and intelligent systems. The lab expands on multidisciplinary efforts looking at the interaction between robots and soils (e.g. [3,15,16]) by explicitly interrogating the deformation of soils, rather than concentrating on the robot.

2   Terra-Robotics Laboratory

The TRL contains an ABB IRB6400 6-axis robot (Fig. 1) with a 6-axis force sensor installed. This allows for a large range of motion in the manipulation of terrains, whilst measuring the forces acting on the end-effector. Terrain is emulated using a custom-built 2×2 m soil bed (Fig. 1). The test and data acquisition system is controlled by a TCP stack combining RAPID (ABBs proprietary language) and C++ code.

3   Preliminary Testing and Results

3.1   Test Setup

To test the efficacy of the setup, a spherical end effector was positioned within the terrain and then moved along two different trajectories: straight-line motion and spiral motion. The end effector was inspired by typical quadrupedal robot feet of

Fig. 1. IRB6400 6-axis robot and soil bed in the TRL

spherical shape [14, 27], enabling the preliminary research to focus on common interactions that might be seen in the field by existing robots. A spherical shape also simplifies the analysis due to axial symmetry, which reduces the number of parameters in experimentation. A schematic and photograph of the end effector can be seen in Fig. 2. Force and moment components are measured with respect to the centre of the sphere using a 6-axis load cell mounted between the robot and end effector, as shown in Fig. 2b. The terrain consisted of air-dried sand.

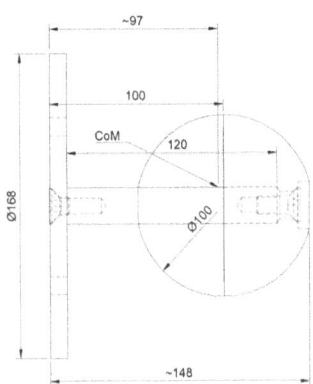

(a) Schematic of end-effector and base plate (units of mm)

(b) As assembled and attached

Fig. 2. End effector

3.2   Straight-Line Motion

Straight-line motion was considered first for its simplicity. Figure 3 shows the final deformed shape of the terrain and the history of forces, where F_x and F_y are the force components in the x and y directions, respectively. The x-y plane is parallel to the bed, and the y direction is aligned with the axis of motion. An initial spike in both components is visible in Fig. 3b, corresponding to the point at which the end effector is pushed vertically into the bed. At this point, the component of force in the z direction is significantly larger than F_x and F_y and therefore omitted for clarity. As the arm starts tracing the motion, F_y increases as a large quantity of sand is gathered in front of the end effector, while F_x diminishes to roughly zero, as expected due to symmetry. The results highlight that, for one of the simplest conceivable motions, the response is rather complex. After the initial spike in F_y, a transient phase is followed by a period over which a steady state of deformation appears to be reached. However, unevenness of the surface precludes such a steady state. Without prior knowledge of the terrain profile, it is impossible to make meaningful predictions, calling attention to the requirement for terrain mapping capabilities.

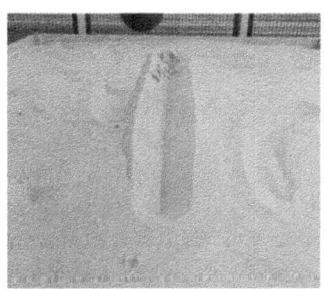

(a) Final deformed configuration

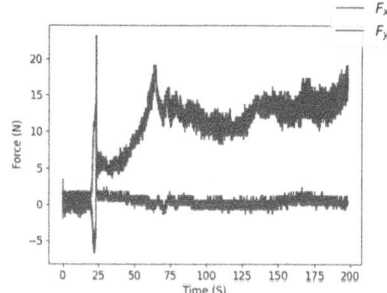

(b) Force components on end effector

Fig. 3. Straight-line motion

3.3   Spiral Motion

To lay a foundation for investigating more complex motions, a spiral trajectory was also considered (Fig. 4). This motion highlights another important feature of general soil-robot interaction: forces are a function of displacement caused by earlier robot manipulation, in addition to the initial topography of the soil. This further emphasises the need for real-time terrain mapping. In this experiment, as the end effector moves outwards, it pushes soil into regions of its future trajectory, changing the forces that will be required for further terrain manipulation. In this case, the response is highly path-dependent, and a robust and efficient model for predicting the force components in real time remains to be developed. These dependencies and the lack of a model imply that a deterministic autonomous system for generalised terrain manipulation currently remains difficult to develop. However, it may be possible to use ML methods to achieve this goal, once a large data set has been gathered.

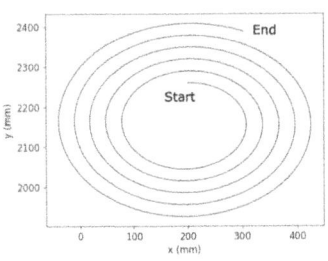
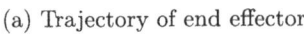

(a) Trajectory of end effector

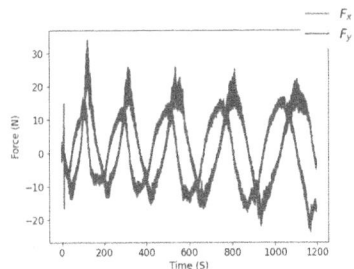

(b) Force components on end effector

Fig. 4. Spiral motion

4   Open Challenges

As discussed in the introduction, there has been some research into developing models useful for terra-robotics. Models such as granular RFT [29] can be used to estimate forces in sand of known configuration, but they are unsuitable for predicting deformation or for modelling fine-grained and/or saturated terrains (e.g., clays). Numerical simulations (e.g., [10,25]) can predict deformation in principle, however the analysis is far from real-time.

The above, combined with observations from the experiments presented in this paper, introduce a set of open challenges and milestones that would enable truly autonomous soil-robotic interaction:

1. Real-time high-resolution surface mapping would be useful not only for knowing the state of the terrain surface before interaction occurs but also for generating force-deformation datasets that describe how the terrain changes. These datasets would enable research into theory for predicting the displacement of terrain for particular end effectors and motions, as well as the forces required.
2. In addition to knowing the evolving terrain surface, a generalised and efficient model that encapsulates the reactive properties of the terrain is needed, recognising that soils are complex materials exhibiting a wide range of possible responses. A theory that simplifies complicated soil behaviour down to the essential reactive properties would be highly desirable for both terra-robotics and geotechnical communities.

3. End effector geometry is task-dependent, prohibiting a "universal" design. In general, the number of possible shapes is infinite, suggesting topology optimisation for the end effector as a necessary step beyond optimisation of the motion for any given task.

4. An implicit assumption in the aforementioned models is that terrain parameters characterising deformability are known. The inverse problem of evaluating soil parameters from collected data presents its own distinct opportunities and challenges. Flexible actuation through the use of robotics creates opportunities around devising non-traditional approaches [11,17,18]. Challenges lie in the ill-posedness and compounding computational difficulties associated with inverse problems, making real-time assessment particularly difficult.

5. Combining solutions for the points above will facilitate automated earthmoving, wherein a target surface can be created from an existing terrain profile. The methodology has to be developed to enable robust decision making during the surface creation process, whether determined based on physical principles or by utilising machine learning techniques.

5   Concluding Remarks

The paper introduces the TRL, a facility which utilises a 6-axis robot for flexible actuation of objects interacting with terrains. The term "terra-robotics" describes research focussed on understanding and predicting the response of the terrain itself under robotic action. Considering dry sand, force histories for a spherical end effector moving through two distinct trajectories are presented. Results for the simple case of straight-line motion reveal inherent complexity in the force history, due to transient effects and unevenness of the terrain. For spiral motion, passage of the end effector induces deformation affecting the response at later times, reflecting path dependence and the need to capture the evolving terrain surface. A generalised approach for intelligent soil-robot interaction will require significant research effort but will present remarkable benefits to the robotics and civil engineering communities alike. To develop this field, it will be necessary to overcome the following challenges:

1. High-resolution and fast surface mapping
2. Generalised soil deformation modelling
3. Task-based topology optimisation for end effectors
4. Inverse analysis for soil parameter estimation
5. Control for automated earthmoving and earth manipulation

Acknowledgments. This work was supported by the Engineering and Physical Sciences Research Council (EPSRC) [grant number EP/W524633/1].

Disclosure of Interests. The authors have no competing interests to declare that are relevant to the content of this article.

References

1. Agarwal, S., Karsai, A., Goldman, D.I., Kamrin, K.: Surprising simplicity in the modeling of dynamic granular intrusion. Sci. Adv. **7**(17), eabe0631 (2021). https://doi.org/10.1126/sciadv.abe0631
2. Aguilar, J., Goldman, D.I.: Robophysical study of jumping dynamics on granular media. Nat. Phys. **12**(3), 278–283 (2016). https://doi.org/10.1038/nphys3568
3. Aguilar, J., et al.: A review on locomotion robophysics: the study of movement at the intersection of robotics, soft matter and dynamical systems (2016). https://doi.org/10.48550/ARXIV.1602.04712, publisher: arXiv Version Number: 1
4. Le, A.T., Rye, D.C., Durrant-Whyte, H.F.: Estimation of track-soil interactions for autonomous tracked vehicles. In: Proceedings of International Conference on Robotics and Automation, Albuquerque, NM, USA, vol. 2, pp. 1388–1393. IEEE (1997). https://doi.org/10.1109/ROBOT.1997.614331
5. Azimi, A., Kovecses, J., Angeles, J.: Wheel-soil interaction model for rover simulation based on plasticity theory. In: 2011 IEEE/RSJ International Conference on Intelligent Robots and Systems, San Francisco, CA, pp. 280–285. IEEE (2011). https://doi.org/10.1109/IROS.2011.6094524
6. Calleja-Huerta, A., Lamandé, M., Green, O., Munkholm, L.: Impacts of load and repeated wheeling from a lightweight autonomous field robot on the physical properties of a loamy sand soil. Soil Tillage Res. **233**, 105791 (2023). https://doi.org/10.1016/j.still.2023.105791
7. Choi, S., et al.: Learning quadrupedal locomotion on deformable terrain. Sci. Robot. **8**(74), eade2256 (2023). https://doi.org/10.1126/scirobotics.ade2256
8. Gray, J., Hancock, G.J.: The propulsion of sea-urchin spermatozoa. J. Exp. Biol. **32**(4), 802–814 (1955). https://doi.org/10.1242/jeb.32.4.802
9. Hambleton, J.P., Stanier, S., White, D.J., Sloan, S.W.: Modelling ploughing and cutting processes in soils. Aust. Geomech. **49**(4), 147–156 (2014)
10. Hambleton, J., Drescher, A.: On modeling a rolling wheel in the presence of plastic deformation as a three-or two-dimensional process. Int. J. Mech. Sci. **51**(11–12), 846–855 (2009)
11. Hambleton, J., Nally, A., Küçükyavuz, S.: Optimal test methods for determining material parameters. In: 20th International Conference on Soil Mechanics and Geotechnical Engineering, Sydney (2022)
12. Hambleton, J., Stanier, S.A.: Predicting wheel forces using bearing capacity theory for general planar loads. Int. J. Veh. Perform. **3**(1), 71–88 (2017)
13. He, R., Sandu, C., Khan, A.K., Guthrie, A.G., Schalk Els, P., Hamersma, H.A.: Review of terramechanics models and their applicability to real-time applications. J. Terramech. **81**, 3–22 (2019). https://doi.org/10.1016/j.jterra.2018.04.003
14. Hutter, M., et al.: ANYmal - toward legged robots for harsh environments. Adv. Robot. **31**(17), 918–931 (2017). https://doi.org/10.1080/01691864.2017.1378591
15. Jin, Z., Shi, Z., Hambleton, J.: Small-scale geotechnical testing using a six-axis robot (2020). https://doi.org/10.31224/osf.io/jqytk
16. Martinez, A., et al.: Bio-inspired geotechnical engineering: principles, current work, opportunities and challenges. Géotechnique **72**(8), 687–705 (2022). https://doi.org/10.1680/jgeot.20.p.170
17. Nally, A., Shi, Z., Hambleton, J.P.: Optimal deformation modes for estimating soil properties. In: Geo-Congress 2019, Reston, VA, pp. 541–550. American Society of Civil Engineers (2019). https://doi.org/10.1061/9780784482124.055

18. Nally, Anastasia: Assessing optimal modes of soil parameter identification. Ph.D. thesis, Northwestern University (2022). https://doi.org/10.21985/N2-13AK-RY65
19. Olmedo, N.A., Barczyk, M., Zhang, H., Wilson, W., Lipsett, M.G.: A UGV-based modular robotic manipulator for soil sampling and terramechanics investigations. J. Unmanned Veh. Syst. **8**(4), 364–381 (2020). https://doi.org/10.1139/juvs-2020-0003
20. Peng, X.B., Coumans, E., Zhang, T., Lee, T.W., Tan, J., Levine, S.: Learning agile robotic locomotion skills by imitating animals (2020). https://doi.org/10.48550/arXiv.2004.00784, [cs]
21. Ramezani, M., Tafazoli, S.: Using artificial intelligence in mining excavators: automating routine operational decisions. IEEE Ind. Electron. Mag. **15**(1), 6–11 (2021). https://doi.org/10.1109/mie.2020.2964053
22. Shi, Z., Huang, M., Hambleton, J.P.: Possibilities and limitations of the sequential kinematic method for simulating evolutionary plasticity problems. Comput. Geotech. **140**, 104449 (2021). https://doi.org/10.1016/j.compgeo.2021.104449
23. Singh, S.: Learning to predict resistive forces during robotic excavation. In: Proceedings of 1995 IEEE International Conference on Robotics and Automation, Nagoya, Japan, vol. 2, pp. 2102–2107. IEEE (1995). https://doi.org/10.1109/ROBOT.1995.526025
24. Taylor, M., et al.: Learning bipedal robot locomotion from human movement. In: 2021 IEEE International Conference on Robotics and Automation (ICRA), Xi'an, China, pp. 2797–2803. IEEE (2021). https://doi.org/10.1109/ICRA48506.2021.9561591
25. Tsuji, T., Nakagawa, Y., Matsumoto, N., Kadono, Y., Takayama, T., Tanaka, T.: 3-D dem simulation of cohesive soil-pushing behavior by bulldozer blade. J. Terrramech. **49**(1), 37–47 (2012)
26. Villemure, S., Silveira, J., Marshall, J.A.: Terrain classification for the spot quadrupedal mobile robot using only proprioceptive sensing. In: 2024 IEEE Canadian Conference on Electrical and Computer Engineering (CCECE), Kingston, ON, Canada, pp. 448–452. IEEE (2024). https://doi.org/10.1109/CCECE59415.2024.10667168
27. Wetzel, E.M., Liu, J., Leathem, T., Sattineni, A.: The use of Boston Dynamics SPOT in support of LiDAR scanning on active construction sites (2022). https://doi.org/10.22260/ISARC2022/0014
28. Wong, C., Yang, E., Yan, X.T., Gu, D.: Autonomous robots for harsh environments: a holistic overview of current solutions and ongoing challenges. Syst. Sci. Control Eng. **6**(1), 213–219 (2018). https://doi.org/10.1080/21642583.2018.1477634
29. Zhang, T., Goldman, D.I.: The effectiveness of resistive force theory in granular locomotion. Phys. Fluids **26**(10), 101308 (2014). https://doi.org/10.1063/1.4898629

Deep Learning-Driven X-Ray Digital Tomosynthesis (DT) Imaging for Aerospace Composite Inspection

Ndidiamaka Adiuku[1]([✉]) [iD], Seemal Asif[1] [iD], Sudip Bose[4], Yuliya Hryshchenko[2] [iD], Bryn C. Hughes[3], Matteo Contino[3], Angelos Plastropoulos[2], Martin Holden[3], and Phil Webb[1] [iD]

[1] Centre of Autonomous and Cyberphysical Systems,
Cranfield University, Cranfield MK43 0AL, UK
amaka.adiuku@cranfield.ac.uk
[2] Centre for Robotics and Assembly, Cranfield University, Cranfield MK43 0AL, UK
[3] Adaptix Ltd., Oxford University Begbroke Science Park, Oxford OX5 1PF, UK
[4] University of Manchester, Manchester M13 9PL, UK

Abstract. The structural integrity of aerospace-grade Glass Fiber Reinforced Polymer (GFRP) composites is critical, yet conventional non-destructive testing (NDT) methods often struggle to detect subsurface defects reliably due to poor signal-to-noise ratios, low contrast, and complex internal structures. To address these limitations, this study proposes a novel AI-driven framework that integrates low-power X-ray Digital Tomosynthesis (DT) imaging with state-of-the-art deep learning models for defect segmentation in composite materials. Specifically, two state-of-the-art instance segmentation models, YOLOv8 (You Only Look Once, version 8) and Detectron2, are employed to automatically segment flaws in the DT images of the composite specimens. A dedicated dataset of low-power X-ray DT scans of GFRP composite specimens with annotated defects was curated for training and evaluation. The segmentation performance of each model was quantitatively evaluated using metrics such as the Dice similarity coefficient and Intersection-over-Union (IoU), along with inference time measurements. Experimental results demonstrate that YOLOv8 processes images significantly faster (~6.9 ms per image) than Detectron2 (~10.3 ms), enabling near real-time analysis. Conversely, Detectron2 achieves a higher segmentation accuracy (Dice ~86% versus ~74% for YOLOv8), underscoring the trade-off between computational efficiency and segmentation precision. These findings validate the potential of combining low-power DT imaging with deep learning for high-fidelity defect identification, substantially improving the prospects for near real-time composite inspection. Future work will focus on further model optimization (e.g., via quantization and pruning) and the integration of this framework with autonomous robotic inspection systems, thereby extending the capabilities of AI-driven NDT in aerospace applications.

Keywords: Aerospace Composites · Image processing · Defect Segmentation · non-destructive testing · low power X-ray Digital Tomosynthesis imaging · Deep learning

A. Cavalcanti et al. (Eds.): TAROS 2025, LNAI 16045, pp. 512–525, 2026.
https://doi.org/10.1007/978-3-032-01486-3_39

1 Introduction

The aerospace industry increasingly relies on Glass Fiber Reinforced Polymer (GFRP) composites for their high strength-to-weight ratio and durability [1]. However, the complex internal structure can pose significant challenges for non-destructive testing (NDT). Defects such as delamination, cracks, and voids can be introduced during the manufacturing process, and can serve as initiation points for crack propagation, thereby compromising safety and performance. Traditional NDT methods, including ultrasonic and high-power X-ray imaging currently require subjective visual interpretation of the images. These conventional techniques are time-consuming and are subject to errors, which could result in missing important defects or inclusions [2, 3].

X-ray imaging has long been used for inspecting composite materials. However, manual interpretation as well as classical image processing techniques such as adaptive thresholding, edge detection, and morphological operations [4] can often fall short. These methods, while effective under controlled conditions, they require significant tuning of parameters and are limited in their ability to handle noise, inhomogeneous material properties, and the variability in defect appearance [5–7]. Consequently, there is a critical need for automated, data-driven inspection systems that can reliably identify defects within complex composite structures.

Recent advances in deep learning have revolutionized automated defect detection in NDT [8]. Convolutional neural networks (CNN) architectures such as U-Net [9] and ResNet [10] have shown capability in learning features directly from raw pixel data. Segmentation specific techniques such as U-Net and Mask R-CNN have shown promising results in defect localization and classification [11]. U-Net's encoder-decoder architecture, originally designed for biomedical image segmentation, has been successfully adapted for detecting cracks and delamination in industrial X-ray images [12] and ultrasonic data [13, 14]. Similarly, the residual blocks in ResNet enhances defect detection in low-contrast composite materials [15]. Moreover, transfer learning which involves fine-tuning pre-trained models such as Mask R-CNN [16] on smaller, domain-specific datasets has proven effective in achieving high detection accuracy.

Building on these established methods, recent frameworks like YOLOv8 [17] Detectron2 [18] offer significant improvements over traditional architectures. YOLOv8, one of the recent evolutions in the YOLO series, provides an optimized detection pipeline that balances speed and accuracy, making it well suited for real-time applications. Its real-time instance segmentation framework for X-ray data has been adapted for various tasks [19], and transfer learning techniques have been employed to further improve its capability in detecting small defects [8]. Additionally, Detectron2, developed by Facebook AI Research, extends the capabilities of Mask R-CNN by offering a modular and highly customizable framework for precise instance segmentation. These advanced capabilities have been widely used in medical and industrial applications [20]. Although its applications in aerospace inspection are emerging, prior studies in medical imaging and other fields have demonstrated its effectiveness in segmenting complex structures [21, 22]. Both frameworks demonstrate robustness in handling low-contrast and noisy X-ray images [23, 24], effectively addressing challenges such as overlapping defect signatures that frequently undermine conventional image processing techniques. Other recent advancements in deep learning, including transformer-based architectures and generative adversarial networks (GANs), which have further enhanced defect detection accuracy [25]. Despite these progressions, challenges remain in achieving robust performance across defect types and composite material heterogeneity, and optimizing AI models for real-time deployment is still an ongoing research endeavor. In the aerospace industry, application varies from the manufacturing stage setup, where an early detection of defects at components and subassemblies level is crucial, to the aircraft in-service evaluation where the preventive maintenance and life extension of component plays a key role.

In this context, our research proposes an integrated imaging and deep learning framework for high-fidelity, non-invasive defect segmentation in aerospace GFRP composites. This framework is implemented as part of a twin-robot system employing 3D X-ray imaging to enhance aerospace inspection [26]. The process begins with systematic image acquisition at predefined angles and intervals, capturing the intricate internal structure of composite materials and generating a robust dataset that encapsulates subtle variations and potential defect signatures. We employ two state-of-the-art instance segmentation models YOLOv8 and Detectron2 to learn features from the X-ray slices. While Detectron2 offers precise segmentation based on the Mask R-CNN architecture, preliminary evaluations indicate that it may sometimes miss fine details. In contrast, YOLOv8 demonstrates superior performance in handling noisy, low-contrast images, achieving higher detection accuracy and significantly faster inference times essential for real-time inspection applications.

By systematically generating and preprocessing high-quality DT datasets and employing these cutting-edge deep learning models, our integrated framework addresses some limitations of traditional NDT methods especially in improving analysis time, error detection and prompt decision making. The combined approach not only enhances defect detection accuracy but also paves the way for more robust, efficient, and automated inspection systems.

The major contribution in this work include.

- Generate and preprocess GFRP composites image slices datasets with Xray device
- Develop a DL-driven framework for high-fidelity defect segmentation in X-ray DT slices using Yolov8 and Detectron2.
- Comparative analysis of Yolov8 and Detectron2 model performance to evaluate segmentation accuracy measured by performance metrics

The remainder of this paper is organized as follows. Section 2 describes the methodology, including the data-pre-processing pipeline and the training procedures for our deep-learning models. Section 3 outlines the experimental workflow, detailing data composition, model configuration, and the performance metrics used. Section 4 reports further experiment on glass-fiber-reinforced polymer (GFRP) composites, presents the model-validation results, and compares the two models. Section 5 discusses model performance, highlighting the benefits and limitations observed. Section 6 concludes the paper by summarizing the key findings and suggesting directions for future research.

2 Proposed Framework

2.1 X-Ray Image Acquisition and Preprocessing

X-ray imaging is a non-destructive evaluation technique that utilizes high-energy photons to reveal the internal structure of materials by exploiting differences in X-ray attenuation. When X-rays generated by an X-ray tube pass through an object, they are attenuated to varying degrees depending on the material's density, thickness, and atomic composition [27]. In this work, digital Tomosynthesis was used to develop images as shown in Fig. 1, the transmitted X-rays are then captured by a detector, which converts them into digital images. In this study, a composite tube GFRP (Glass Fibre Reinforced Polymer) (length 234 mm, outer diameter 35 mm and a thickness of 5 mm) was scanned. Click or tap here to enter text.

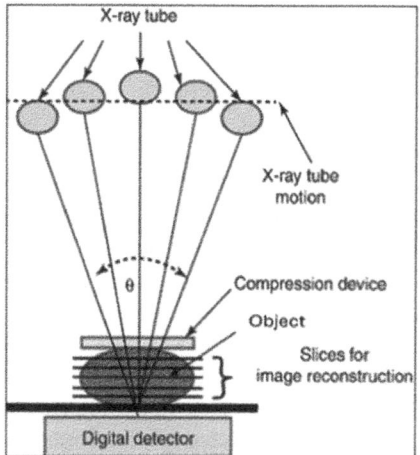

Fig. 1. Mechanism of image formation in digital tomosynthesis

The X-ray system used was the Z-series by Adaptix NDT, different images were acquired with source moved to several positions, with total scan time of approximately 5 min. A stack of 2D slices was reconstructed using the method and a 3D render was then obtained by the combination of such images as presented in [28], Fig. 2(a) shows the cylindrical tube that was scan for this experiment, Fig. 2(b) displays the 3D model of the sample reconstructed from the X-ray DT slices, and Fig. 2(c) presents an individual 2D slice that was subsequently used for training the deep learning model.

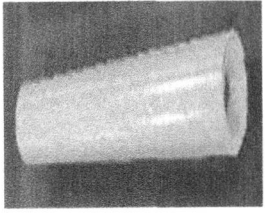
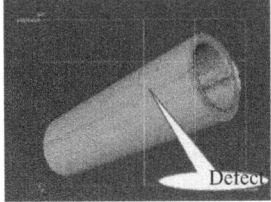
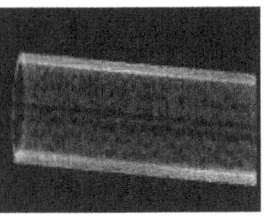

(a) Cylindrical   (b) 3D image of Cylindrical   (c) X-ray image slice of Cylindri-
     GFRP Tube

Fig. 2. Hollow Cylindrical GFRP tube

2.2 Deep Learning-Based Defect Segmentation

In defect detection, two main deep learning strategies are usually common, one-stage object detectors and two-stage detectors. One-stage detectors like the YOLO series frame defect detection as a single regression problem, predicting bounding boxes and class probabilities in one pass through the network. These models prioritize speed and are well-suited for real-time applications. Researchers have applied YOLO variants to industrial X-ray images with promising [29, 30].

To robustly detect defects in the heterogeneous and noisy X-ray images, the core of the framework leverages the strengths of two advanced instance segmentation models, Detectron2 and YOLOv8 to comprehensively capture the multi-scale features inherent in our imaging data, thereby enabling a robust comparative analysis of their performance for inspecting composite structures. They are both PyTorch-based frameworks known for their modularity and precision. YOLOv8 is a notable innovation in YOLO versions which builds on the foundational concepts introduced in earlier YOLO versions [31]. This concept treats object detection as a single regression problem rather than a multi-stage pipeline where it employs a one-stage detection architecture, which allows the network to predict bounding boxes and class probabilities in a single forward pass YOLOv8 utilizes an extensive stack of deep convolutional layers to extract hierarchical features from input images. These layers enable the model to capture both fine-grained details, critical for detecting small defects and high-level semantic information that are important for recognizing complex structures. An efficient spatial pyramid pooling module is also incorporated and works by pooling features at multiple scales, thereby aggregating contextual information from different regions of the image. These capabilities are crucial for accurately detecting objects and defects that vary significantly in size, from minute cracks to larger delamination. Its optimized architecture ensures rapid inference without compromising the precision of object detection and instance segmentation, making it highly suitable for real-time applications and improving performance in challenging imaging scenarios like those encountered in NDT of GFRP composites.

An alternative utilizes, two-stage detectors such Detectron2 object detection and instance segmentation model that implements the Mask R-CNN architecture, employing Feature Pyramid Network (FPN) that extracts features at multiple scales, enabling the model to detect both fine and coarse details within the X-ray images. The hierarchical feature extraction facilitated by FPN is especially useful for identifying small defects such as micro-cracks, as well as larger anomalies like delamination regions. Furthermore, the modular design of Detectron2 allows extensive customization and fine-tuning. Parameters such as the number of convolutional layers, the scales at which features are extracted, and the learning rates are optimized to handle the varied defect presentations observed in GFRP composites.

Two-stage models tend to be more computationally intensive than YOLO variants, but they often provide higher localization accuracy for difficult examples due to this refined two-step process. The models are trained on annotated X-ray datasets of GFRP composites to automatically learn robust features, effectively segmenting defect regions and structural details from complex, noisy backgrounds. By integrating both models into our inspection pipeline, we are able to perform a side-by-side evaluation of their performance.

2.3 System Architecture

The system architecture as illustrated in Fig. 3, consists of an AI-driven inspection pipeline that takes raw X-ray images of composite materials as input and outputs detected defect locations along with precise segmentation masks.

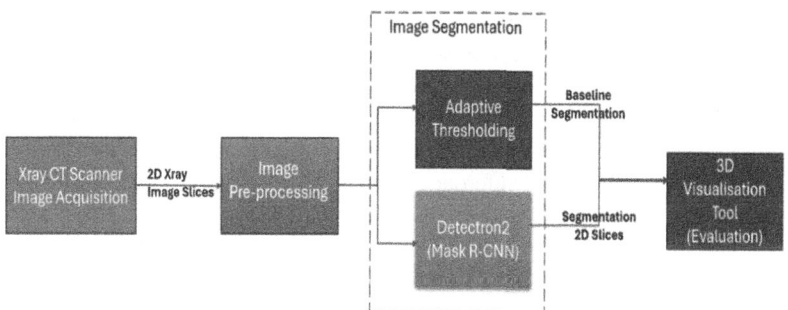

Fig. 3. System Architecture

The pipeline integrates the X-ray image acquisition, preprocessing and DL-driven defect segmentation models. The process begins with X-ray scanning, where high-resolution image slices of aerospace GFRP composites are captured at predefined angles to ensure comprehensive coverage of internal structures. These raw X-ray images undergo preprocessing techniques such as normalization and noise reduction to enhance defect visibility. The next stage employs Yolov8 and Detectron2, advanced deep learning frameworks for instance segmentation, to accurately identify and classify defect regions within the composite material. The segmented outputs are visualized and evaluated to facilitate accurate and real-time defect analysis, aiding engineers in decision-making and reducing manual inspection errors. The combination of X-ray imaging and deep learning-based segmentation enhances defect detection accuracy while reducing operational downtime and inspection costs, making it a robust solution for aerospace composite inspection.

3 Experimental Setup

3.1 Dataset Composition and Annotation

The dataset for this study consists of high-resolution X-ray images of GFRP composites that exhibit deep-line real defects (voids), with defect regions manually annotated to create an accurate ground truth. Each raw X-ray image is processed through several steps, including normalization to a 640×640 resolution and noise reduction to standardize intensity values and minimize imaging artifacts, thereby enhancing defect visibility and ensuring high-quality inputs for the model. Additionally, adaptive equalization techniques are applied to automatically adjust contrast, and data augmentation methods such as rotation, flipping, and mosaic augmentation are employed to boost dataset diversity and improve model robustness.

3.2 Model Training and Hyperparameter Optimization

Two state-of-the-art instance segmentation models—Detectron2 and YOLOv8were trained and evaluated on the preprocessed X-ray image dataset of GFRP composites.

Detectron2 employs a Mask R-CNN architecture, enhanced by a Feature Pyramid Network (FPN) for robust multi-scale feature extraction. This FPN is essential for integrating both fine details and broader context from the input images, making it particularly effective for identifying small defects, such as micro-cracks, as well as larger anomalies like voids. To tailor the model for our specific application, we customized the FPN layers and adjusted the mask head architecture to better capture the subtle variations in defect presentation found in the X-ray images of GFRP composites. In contrast, YOLOv8 is designed with a focus on rapid inference while still maintaining high detection accuracy. Its architecture incorporates deep convolutional layers combined with an efficient Spatial Pyramid Pooling (SPP) module, which allows the network to capture multi-scale features from the input images. These architectural enhancements are critical when dealing with the inherent challenges of low-contrast and noisy X-ray images, ensuring that even minute defects are accurately detected. For both models, the dataset was systematically partitioned into training (70%), validation (15%), and testing (15%) subsets. Key hyperparameters, including learning rate, batch size, and weight decay, were optimized during training. Each model was trained for 100 epochs with periodic evaluation on the validation set to monitor progress and prevent overfitting. The loss functions were carefully calibrated to balance classification, localization, and segmentation tasks. We combined the three components in a weighted sum as shown here; $L_{total} = \alpha L_{cls} + \beta L_{loc} + \gamma L_{seg}$. First, we normalized each term with the GradNorm method, so their initial gradient magnitudes were comparable. Next, we ran a grid search on a held-out validation set and selected weights that maximized mean Dice + mAP. The resulting setting kept the three losses within the same order of magnitude throughout the training, preventing any single task from dominating the optimization.

3.3 Performance Metrics

Accuracy Metrics: Comparing segmentation quality using metrics such as the Dice coefficient and Intersection-over union (IoU) to determine how accurately each model delineates defect regions.

Inference Speed: Assessing the real-time applicability of each model by measuring inference times, which is crucial for high-throughput inspection environments.

Dice Coefficient: Quantifying the overlap between predicted and ground truth masks.

$$Dice = \frac{2 \times |P \cap G|}{|P| + |G|}$$

where P is the predicted mask, G is the ground truth mask and $|P \cap G|$ is the intersection between the predicted and ground truth mask.

IoU: Intersection-over-Union (IoU) - Assessing segmentation accuracy on a per-instance basis.

$$IoU = \frac{|P \cap G|}{|P \cup G|}$$

Average Precision (AP): Calculated across different IoU thresholds.

Precision and Recall: To measure the balance between false positives and false negatives.

4   Experimental Evaluation

We conducted a series of experiments to train and evaluate the performance of the YOLOv8 and Detectron2 models on the task of defect detection in composite X-ray images. The models were trained on a workstation with an NVIDIA RTX 3080 GPU (32GB memory) on a CUDA-enabled GPU platform, leveraging the PyTorch framework. For Detectron2, the training was conducted within its dedicated library, while YOLOv8 was trained using the Ultralytics YOLOv8 repository with the segmentation model variant, yolov8n-seg architecture chosen for a balance of speed and accuracy. Both models underwent periodic evaluation on a designated validation set to monitor performance improvements throughout the training process. They used early stopping based on validation loss to prevent overfitting. The total training time was around 6 ms for YOLOv8 and 10 ms for Mask R-CNN on our dataset. We evaluated the models using standard object detection and segmentation metrics. For object detection performance, key performance metrics include the Dice coefficient, Intersection-over-Union (IoU), precision, and recall and were computed to assess segmentation accuracy. Based on these metrics, hyperparameters were iteratively adjusted to achieve an optimal balance between accuracy and inference speed. The training procedures were meticulously tailored to address the unique challenges of X-ray imaging for GFRP composites, such as low contrast, noise, and defect heterogeneity. We also report qualitative results by overlaying the predicted masks on the original X-ray images to visually assess the correspondence between the segmented regions and the actual defect shapes. Visual inspection revealed that while the predicted masks largely aligned with the defect boundaries, the Detectron2 model exhibited instances of partially segmented defects, while indicating accuracy of approximately 95% detection accuracy contradiction its performance and efficiency.

We evaluated the performance of the YOLOv8 and Detectron2 Mask R-CNN segmentation models. The two models exhibited a clear trade-off in segmentation accuracy. Detectron2 achieved about 88–89% segmentation accuracy on the X-ray defect dataset, substantially higher than the 77.8% achieved by YOLOv8. This difference is reflected in the Dice similarity coefficient as well where Detectron2 attained ~86% Dice coefficient, outperforming YOLOv8's 74.2%. From visual observations, YOLOv8's instance segmentation was better at precisely matching the defect regions in the ground truth images. Figure 4(b) indicates that YOLOv8's predicted masks overlap the true defect areas more completely, capturing finer details of the defect shape. Detectron2's segmentation (based on Mask R-CNN), while high segmentation accuracy, was coarser and left some gaps or extraneous pixels around defect boundaries, leading to a lower overlap with ground truth as shown in Fig. 4(a). Segmentation here is slightly less precise as compared to YOLOv8 which provided more exact defect segmentation, aligning with its streamlined, real-time design. For inference speed using the same hardware setup, the Detectron2 model required approximately 28 min 20 s to process the X-ray images while YOLOv8 total processing time ~369 s.

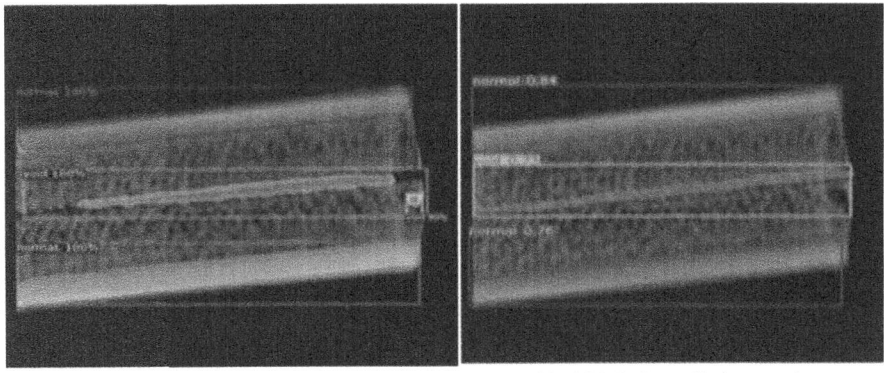

(a)   Detectron2 prediction mask   (b) YOLOv8 prediction mask

Fig. 4. YOLO and Detectron2 segmentation results

In comparison, our custom YOLOv8 model can be easily improved to meet real-time capability, whereas the custom Detectron2 approach would need more improvement for real world application. This comparison is illustrated in Table 1. The performance comparison between YOLOv8 and Detectron2 as in Table 1 highlights a trade-off between speed and accuracy in defect detection for X-ray DT imaging of composites structural sample. Detectron2 outperforms YOLOv8 in segmentation accuracy (88% vs. 77.8%), Dice coefficient (86% vs. 74.2%), and IoU (86% vs. 74.95%), making it more precise for identifying fine defect structures. However, YOLOv8 significantly surpasses Detectron2 in inference speed, processing images ~4× faster (6.9 ms vs. 10.3 ms per image) and achieving a total processing time of ~6 min compared to Detectron2's 28 min plus time interval.

Table 1. Models Performance Comparison

Performance Metrics	YOLOv8	Detectron2	Remarks
Segmentation Accuracy	77.80%	88–89%	Detectron2 achieves higher segmentation precision.
Dice Coefficient	74.20%	86%	Higher Dice score indicates better defect region overlap in Detectron2.
IoU	74.95%	86%	Detectron2 performs better in region matching.
Inference Speed	6.9 ms	10.3 ms	YOLOv8 is significantly faster.
Total Processing Time	~6 min	~28 min 20 sec	YOLOv8 is ~4x faster than Detectron2 for batch processing.
Precision	High	Very High	Detectron2 produces fewer false positives.
Recall	Higher	Slightly Lower	YOLOv8 detects more defects but at the cost of false positives.
Suitability for Real-Time Use	Yes	No	YOLOv8 is better suited for real-time applications.
Best Use Case	Fast, real-time defect detection	High-precision defect segmentation	YOLOv8 for speed, Detectron2 for accuracy.

5 Discussion

The experimental results demonstrate the integrated deep learning framework for defect segmentation in X-ray images of GFRP composites. The performance metrics achieved provide a comprehensive view of the system's capabilities in terms of accuracy, precision, and real-time applicability. While Detectron2 Mask R-CNN (a two-stage detector) excelled in accuracy, it was slower in inference and carries the overhead of proposing regions and refining masks making the configuration at this state far from real-time solution and cannot be used in an on-line inspection loop without drastic modifications. YOLOv8's one-stage CNN architecture, on the other hand, can process approximately 145 frames per second (fps), enabling rapid defect prediction and making it highly optimized for real-time applications. Our findings reinforce that YOLOv8 is well-suited for real-time defect detection, whereas Detectron2 would be limited to off-line analysis or scenarios where speed is not a concern. This distinction is critical in an automated inspection context as research in industrial X-ray inspection study from [32] also emphasizes the need for efficiency, scalability, and real-time analysis. In addition to quantitative metrics, we examined the models outputs on actual composite X-ray images to gauge their practical defect detection ability. Qualitatively, YOLOv8 was more robust in detecting defect regions, whether regular or irregular in shape. However, we observed that Detectron2 would occasionally miss small defect details and yet segmented the defect area with high accuracy (even 100%) but failed to mask the completed part of the defect as shown in Fig. 4(a). Such missed detections lower its overall recall, meaning some flaws might go unreported if relying solely on this method.

In aerospace composites, knowing the exact size and shape of a defect is crucial for structural integrity assessments. YOLOv8's masks, while offering consistent coverage of defects, will enable more reliable measurements of defect area from X-ray images, ensuring that specific potential issues are flagged for review. Additionally, in industrial settings, there is often a time-limited requirement for inspection results to facilitate rapid maintenance decisions. Although YOLOv8's inference time was approximately 6 min per image in our current configuration, this performance can be improved through further parameter tuning. In contrast, the Detectron2 Mask R-CNN configuration achieved significantly longer inference times, indicating that additional system tuning and optimization are required to meet specific operational priorities. In comparison with existing literature and industrial application limited and sensitive nature of data has been a major factor. The YOLOv8 proposed model with highly specialized datasets can detect >90% of defects and delineate their shapes with IoU/Dice often in the 0.8–0.9+ range, with improved inference speed for early-stage solution development and proof-of-concept, showing possible robust, reliable and fast solution. This is a substantial improvement traditional two-stage or heuristic methods, where quick turnaround is critical. Future work will aim to expand the dataset and adapt the framework to a broader range of composite samples, thereby enhancing the system's generalizability and relevance across related domains.

6 Conclusion

This study demonstrates the potential of integrating X-ray Digital Tomosynthesis imaging with deep learning-based image segmentation for non-destructive evaluation of aerospace composite materials. By combining advanced deep learning segmentation with classical image processing techniques, the proposed module delivers a high-fidelity solution that significantly enhances defect detection accuracy in the samples examined and has the potential to impact on wider composite structures. This solution not only improves defect detection accuracy but also reduces inspection time and increases overall reliability. Experimental evaluations reveal that the system achieves an overall accuracy of 74.95% and a rapid processing speed of approximately 6 ms per image making the framework well-suited for real-time applications in dynamic industrial settings, such as robotic inspections. Our comparative analysis between YOLOv8 and Detectron2 underscores that while both models contribute to improved defect segmentation, YOLOv8 stands out for its superior efficiency. Its rapid inference speed and enhanced multi-scale feature extraction allow it to consistently detect defect regions with minimal latency, making it particularly effective for real-time deployment. In contrast, although Detectron2 provides high-quality segmentation masks with precise defect delineation, its relatively slower computational performance limits its applicability in time-sensitive environments.

By leveraging deep learning models specifically optimized for aerospace non-destructive testing, this research sets a new standard for defect analysis and quality assurance in composite materials. The proposed framework not only improves the reliability and accuracy of defect detection but also paves the way for further advancements in automated inspection systems. Future work will focus on optimizing the integration of deep learning techniques, expanding the system to include an interactive 3D visualization interface, and achieving real-time integration with robotic manipulator platforms. Additionally, exploring domain adaptation strategies will be essential to extend the framework's applicability across diverse material types and manufacturing conditions. These efforts aim to further enhance the robustness and scalability of the system, ultimately contributing to safer and more efficient aerospace manufacturing and maintenance workflows.

Future work entails leveraging deep learning models for the use case of small-scale composite aerospace components on existing robotic digital twin system for remotely operated low power X-ray based imaging at Aerospace Integration Research Centre at Cranfield University.

Acknowledgment. This work was supported by ATI funding for advanced manufacturing innovation - ATI ROBOT-MOUNTED 3D X-RAY INSPECTION. We express our gratitude to Jamie Rice and Daniel Oakley, Lab Technicians, and James Fowler, Senior Technical Officer at the Intelligent Automation Lab, for their invaluable support and technical expertise, which were essential for the project's success. We also thank Dr. Charles Antrobus from the Adaptix software team for their contributions.

References

1. Rajak, D.K., Wagh, P.H., Linul, E.: Manufacturing technologies of carbon/glass fiber-reinforced polymer composites and their properties: a review. Polymers **13**(21), 3721 (2021). https://doi.org/10.3390/POLYM13213721

2. LeCun, Y., Bengio, Y., Hinton, G.: Deep learning. Nature **521**(7553), 436–444 (2015). https://doi.org/10.1038/nature14539

3. Schmidhuber, J.: Deep learning in neural networks: an overview. Neural Netw. **61**, 85–117 (2015). https://doi.org/10.1016/J.NEUNET.2014.09.003

4. Gonzalez, R.C., Woods, R.E.: Digital Image Processing, 3rd edn. Pearson International Edition Prepared by Pearson Education

5. Smith, R.A.: Composite defects and their detection. Mater. Sci. Eng. **III** (2009)

6. Yoon, S., et al.: Defect detection in composites by deep learning using solitary waves. Int. J. Mech. Sci. **239**, 107882 (2023). https://doi.org/10.1016/J.IJMECSCI.2022.107882

7. Hassani, S., Dackermann, U.: A systematic review of advanced sensor technologies for non-destructive testing and structural health monitoring. Sensors **23**(4), 2204 (2023). https://doi.org/10.3390/s23042204

8. Gong, Y., Luo, J., Shao, H., Li, Z.: A transfer learning object detection model for defects detection in X-ray images of spacecraft composite structures. Compos. Struct. **284**, 115136 (2022). https://doi.org/10.1016/J.COMPSTRUCT.2021.115136

9. Ronneberger, O., Fischer, P., Brox, T.: U-Net: Convolutional Networks for Biomedical Image Segmentation. http://lmb.informatik.uni-freiburg.de/. Accessed 17 Feb 2025

10. He, K., Zhang, X., Ren, S., Sun, J.: Deep residual learning for image recognition. In: Proceedings of the IEEE Computer Society Conference on Computer Vision and Pattern Recognition, vol. 2016-December, pp. 770–778 (2015). https://doi.org/10.1109/CVPR.2016.90

11. Zhang, J., Cosma, G., Watkins, J.: Image enhanced mask R-CNN: a deep learning pipeline with new evaluation measures for wind turbine blade defect detection and classification. J. Imaging **7**(3), 46 (2021). https://doi.org/10.3390/jimaging7030046

12. Lizarralde, I., Sapountzi, E., Bénéthuilière, T., Sket, F., González, C.: An X-ray computed tomography analysis of damage induced by thermal cycling in non-crimp fabric composites. Compos. Part A Appl. Sci. Manuf. **152**, 106699 (2022). https://doi.org/10.1016/J.COMPOS ITESA.2021.106699

13. Ardebili, A., Alaei, M.H.: Non-destructive testing of delamination defects in GFRP patches using step heating thermography. NDT and E Int. **128**, 102617 (2022). https://doi.org/10. 1016/J.NDTEINT.2022.102617

14. Nguyen, D., Davidson, P., DeMille, K., Ranatunga, V.: Machine learning based segmentation of delamination patterns from sparse ultrasound data of barely visible impact damage in composites. J. Compos. Mater. (2024). https://doi.org/10.1177/00219983241292779/ASSET/ IMAGES/LARGE/10.1177_00219983241292779-FIG10.JPEG

15. Karimian, M., Hosseini Kordkheili, S.A.: Application of deep residual networks to predict the effective properties of fiber-reinforced composites with voids. Adv. Mech. Eng. **17**(1) (2025). https://doi.org/10.1177/16878132251315871/ASSET/IMAGES/LARGE/10.1177_1 6878132251315871-FIG9.JPEG

16. He, K., Gkioxari, G., Dollár, P., Girshick, R.: Mask R-CNN. IEEE Trans. Pattern Anal. Mach. Intell. **42**(2), 386–397 (2017). https://doi.org/10.1109/TPAMI.2018.2844175

17. Sapkota, R., Ahmed, D., Karkee, M.: Comparing YOLOv8 and Mask R-CNN for instance segmentation in complex orchard environments. Artif. Intell. Agric. **13**, 84–99 (2024). https:// doi.org/10.1016/J.AIIA.2024.07.001

18. Merz, G., et al.: Detection, instance segmentation, and classification for astronomical surveys with deep learning (DeepDISC): detectron2 implementation and demonstration with hyper suprime-cam data. Mon. Not. R. Astron. Soc. **526**(1), 1122–1137 (2023). https://doi.org/10. 1093/mnras/stad2785

19. Lu, L.: Improved YOLOv8 Detection Algorithm in X-ray Contraband (2023). https://git hub.com/luliyaoLeo/Improved-YOLOv8-Detection-Algorithm-in-X-ray-Security. Accessed 19 Feb 2025

20. Milletari, F., Navab, N., Ahmadi, S.A.: V-Net: fully convolutional neural networks for volu-metric medical image segmentation. In: Proceedings of the 2016 4th International Conference on 3D Vision, 3DV 2016, pp. 565–571 (2016). https://doi.org/10.1109/3DV.2016.79

21. Xu, Y., Quan, R., Xu, W., Huang, Y., Chen, X., Liu, F.: Advances in medical image seg-mentation: a comprehensive review of traditional, deep learning and hybrid approaches. Bioengineering **11**(10), 1034 (2024). https://doi.org/10.3390/BIOENGINEERING11101034

22. Szeliski, R.: Computer Vision: Algorithms and Applications, 2nd edn. (2021). https://szeliski. org/Book. Accessed 03 Feb 2025

23. Ijaz, K., Khosa, I., Ansari, E.A., Ali, S.F., Hussain, A., Butt, F.A.: BWFER-YOLOv8: an enhanced cascaded framework for concealed object detection. Appl. Sci. **15**(2), 690 (2025). https://doi.org/10.3390/app15020690

24. Alaknanda, Anand, R.S., Kumar, P.: Flaw detection in radiographic weld images using mor-phological approach. NDT E Int. **39**(1), 29–33 (2006). https://doi.org/10.1016/J.NDTEINT. 2005.05.005

25. Wang, J., Guili, Xu., Yan, F., Wang, J., Wang, Z.: Defect transformer: an efficient hybrid trans-former architecture for surface defect detection. Measurement **211**, 112614 (2023). https:// doi.org/10.1016/j.measurement.2023.112614

26. Asif, S., et al.: Advancements in 3D X-ray imaging: development and application of a twin robot system. In: Nazmul Huda, M., Wang, M., Kalganova, T. (eds.) TAROS 2024, Part I, pp. 434–445. Springer, Cham (2025). https://doi.org/10.1007/978-3-031-72059-8_36

27. Sy, E., Samboju, V., Mukhdomi, T.: X-ray Image Production Procedures. StatPearls (2022). https://www.ncbi.nlm.nih.gov/books/NBK564352/. Accessed 19 Feb 2025

28. Bose, S., Contino, M., Helps, O.R., Evans, E., Potluri, P., Withers, P.J.: Evaluation of digital tomosynthesis for in-line imaging of carbon fibre-reinforced composites. **8**, 785–791 (2024). https://doi.org/10.60691/yj56-np80

29. Wang, J., et al.: YOLO-Xray: a bubble defect detection algorithm for chip x-ray images based on improved YOLOv5. Electronics **12**(14), 3060 (2023). https://doi.org/10.3390/electronics12143060

30. Ahmed, A., Imran, A.S., Manaf, A., Kastrati, Z., Daudpota, S.M.: Enhancing wrist abnormality detection with YOLO: analysis of state-of-the-art single-stage detection models. Biomed. Signal Process. Control **93**, 106144 (2024). https://doi.org/10.1016/J.BSPC.2024.106144

31. Redmon, J., Divvala, S., Girshick, R., Farhadi, A.: You Only Look Once: Unified, Real-Time Object Detection. http://pjreddie.com/yolo/. Accessed 30 Aug 2023

32. Naddaf-Sh, S., et al.: Real-Time Explainable Multiclass Object Detection for Quality Assessment in 2-Dimensional Radiography Images (2022). https://doi.org/10.1155/2022/4637939

Lessons Learned from the RAICAM Doctoral Network Research Sprints

Alperen Kenan[1]([✉]), Sahar Sadeghi Kordkheili[2], Juan Jose Garcia Cardenas[3], Alessandro Melone[4], Changda Tian[5], Haichuan Li[6], Hamidreza Raei[7,11], Sasanka Kuruppu Arachchige[8], Yifeng Tang[9], Adriana Tapus[3], Anibal Ollero[2], Arash Ajudani[7], Begoña C. Arrue[2], Dimitrios Papageorgiou[5,10], Joni-Kristian Kämäräinen[8], Jukka Heikkonen[6], Luis Figueredo[4,12], Manuel Giuliani[13], Panos Trahanias[5,14], Paul Bremner[1], Saeed Rafee Nekoo[2], Simon Watson[9], and Tomi Westerlund[6]

[1] Bristol Robotics Laboratory, University of the West of England, Bristol, UK
alperen.kenan@uwe.ac.uk
[2] GRVC Robotics Lab, Universidad de Sevilla, Seville, Spain
[3] Autonomous Systems and Robotics Lab, Institute Polytechnique de Paris, Palaiseau, France
[4] Munich Institute of Robotics and Machine Intelligence, Technische Universität München, Munich, Germany
[5] Institute of Computer Science, Foundation for Research and Technology Hellas, Heraklion, Greece
[6] TIERS Lab, University of Turku, Turku, Finland
[7] HRI[2] Lab, Istituto Italiano di Tecnologia, Genoa, Italy
[8] Computer Vision Group, Tampere University, Tampere, Finland
[9] Department of Electrical and Electronic Engineering, University of Manchester, Manchester, UK
[10] Department of Electrical and Computer Engineering, Hellenic Mediterranean University, Chania, Greece
[11] Department of Electronics, Information and Bioengineering, Politecnico di Milano, Milan, Italy
[12] School of Computer Science, University of Nottingham, Nottingham, UK
[13] Faculty of Electrical Engineering, Kempten University of Applied Sciences, Kempten, Germany
[14] Computer Science Department, University of Crete, Heraklion, Greece

Abstract. Doctoral Networks (DNs) aim to address systemic challenges in doctoral education, such as fostering interdisciplinarity, enabling international and intersectoral collaboration, enhancing employability, and promoting responsible innovation. While cohort-based training helps mitigate student isolation through workshops and summer schools, traditional DNs often struggle to fully realise their collaborative potential, often relying on predefined supervisor relationships or the initiative of individual researchers. In contrast, Marie Skłodowska-Curie Doctoral Networks (MSCA-DNs) prioritise doctoral candidates (DCs), challenging them to balance independent research with contributions to a shared, mission-driven objective. This study examines how structured training, including digital communities and application-focused research sprints,

A. Cavalcanti et al. (Eds.): TAROS 2025, LNAI 16045, pp. 526–539, 2026.
https://doi.org/10.1007/978-3-032-01486-3_40

enhances system integration and collaboration within the Robotics and AI for Critical Asset Monitoring (RAICAM) Doctoral Network. DCs located across seven European countries worked in virtual teams, refining systems through structured workflows, weekly meetings, and shared workspaces before training schools. Through continuous online collaboration and targeted sprints, RAICAM facilitated interdisciplinary integration. Two research sprints, conducted in Italy and France, allowed teams to develop and test solutions for real-world challenges with an impact-driven plan that considers a given problem from and end-to-end perspective that requires and foster interdisciplinary collaboration. The results highlight the effectiveness of structured training in enhancing collaboration and adaptability, while identifying key areas for improvement. This study translates lessons from RAICAM into practical guidelines for future doctoral networks, demonstrating how structured training empowers students to drive interdisciplinary research independently.

Keywords: Doctoral Network · Research Sprints · Multi-Robot Systems · Interdisciplinary Collaboration · Autonomous systems

1 Introduction

The core principle underlying doctoral networks is to provide candidates with high-quality research training in a collaborative, structured cohort environment. This model enhances career prospects in both academic and non-academic fields [1]. By promoting international, interdisciplinary, and intersectoral collaboration, DNs mitigate student isolation and facilitate knowledge exchange and secondments across diverse research settings. They also emphasize ethical research through Open Science principles and peer review, ultimately cultivating creative, resilient researchers capable of addressing real-world challenges [1].

The cohort-based training format emerged in the early 2010s with the establishment of Centres for Doctoral Training (CDTs) in the UK [9] and the MSCA Doctoral Networks in Europe [2]. Since 2014, the MSCA DN scheme has funded 1,475 programmes with a budget exceeding €400 million per year; in the UK, the 2023 scheme supported 65 new networks with a £1 billion investment.

Practical DN objectives require close collaboration among PIs. In EU and international cohorts, the focus may shift from DC training to PI-driven projects, potentially isolating research efforts. Here, we present an alternative experience from the Horizon MSCA DN RAICAM project[1], which adopts an impact-driven, application-focused research plan that considers the problem end-to-end. This approach fosters collaboration and facilitates the development of new tools such as the Digital Community and Research Sprints to achieve DN objectives.

---

[1] Further details about the Horizon MSCA DN RAICAM project can be found on the official website: https://raicam.eu/.

1.1   RAICAM

The Robotics and AI for Critical Asset Monitoring (RAICAM) DN was funded through the 2021 MSCA-DN scheme, formally starting in January 2023. The DN has 10 academic partners, each hosting a Doctoral Candidate (DC), across 7 countries as detailed in the author list. In addition, there are 4 industrial partners; FIS360 and Sellafield Ltd from the UK, the Fraunhofer Institute in Germany and Anybotics, based in Switzerland.

The aim of RAICAM is to train the next generation of robotic systems engineers who will develop creative and innovative multi-disciplinary skills, with the scope of research focused on how autonomous robots could undertake sample retrieval missions (particulates or small debris) in industrial facilities [5].

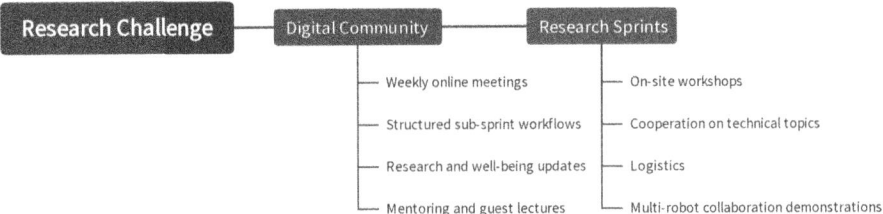

Fig. 1. Pipeline of the training structure

1.2   Training Structure

While doctoral networks generally follow a well-structured group-based learning model, RAICAM adopted an innovative approach to better realize the collaborative potential of this framework. Many cohort-based training programs encourage collective learning through workshops or summer schools, but interaction beyond these prescribed activities is often optional or unstructured. While collaboration is encouraged, it frequently depends on pre-existing supervisor relationships or the initiative of proactive students.

Collaboration is most effective through an impact-driven, application-focused research plan that considers the problem from an end-to-end perspective. This approach was pioneered through events like the DARPA Robotics Challenges [6], which focused on exploring environments with fleets of heterogeneous robots. Successful teams addressed the problem as a whole, rather than as a series of individual technological challenges, leading to integrated solutions.

To address these limitations, RAICAM DN implemented a unique structure centered on three core elements: (1) an overarching research challenge, (2) a digital community platform, and (3) annual research sprints. The pipeline of the training structure is shown in Fig. 1.

Overarching Research Challenge. At the inception stage, it was decided that all PhD projects would have to contribute towards an overarching challenge, specifically autonomous robotic sample retrieval in industrial facilities. This challenge, co-defined by industrial partners, requires a multi-disciplinary approach to address. The PhD projects were split into three sub-categories as shown in Fig. 2: Environmental Interaction, Perception and Cognition, and Human-Robot Interaction.

By co-creating complementary projects that aligned with a shared research goal, DCs significantly enhanced their collaboration. The supervisor team essentially mapped out potential collaborations in advance, working them into the required MSCA secondment plan, significantly enhancing the student's opportunities for additional publications.

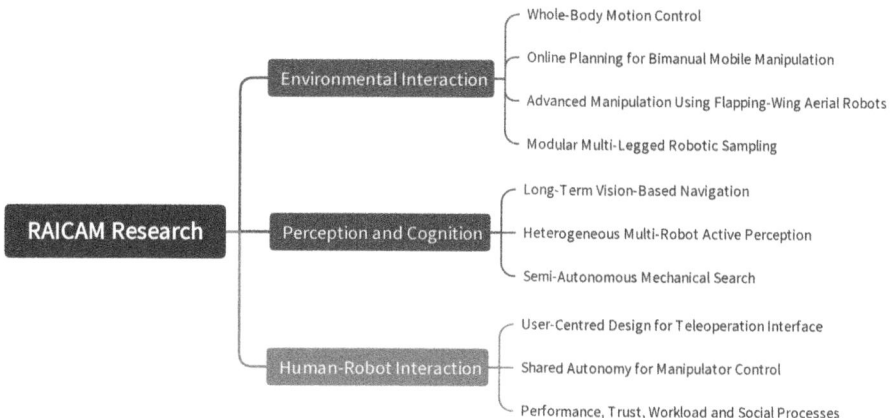

Fig. 2. RAICAM research topics

Digital Community and Annual Research Sprint. Having an overarching research challenge does not guarantee collaboration, especially if students only meet sporadically for training workshops, symposiums or secondments. The most productive collaborations come from good personal relationships, which can be difficult to form if you are distributed across seven countries in Europe.

To address this issue, two activities were implemented. The first was a regular weekly online meeting for all students. These informal, community-building sessions help students connect socially and technically. Weekly activities include wellbeing updates, research updates, mentoring, professional development, guest lectures and training, all undertaken in a relaxed and collegiate environment. Often in DNs, relationship building is left to the in-person activities, but in RAICAM, this is done before the students met in person.

The second element was to give the students a focal point for collaboration. The overarching research challenge meant that each student was already working towards a common goal, but this was made more tangible through the concept of cohort-level demonstrations through annual research sprints. The concept of a research sprint evolved from hackathons, where students come together in-person for a time-limited activity (often 24–72 h) where they solve an unknown challenge [3]. A key aim is to get people out of their day job environments to promote innovation. Hackathons promote interdisciplinary collaboration during the event, but the medium- and long-term benefits are often limited.

This research sprint approach was adopted within RAICAM as the focal point to bring the cohort together to form a strong research community. The students are required to demonstrate progressively more complex demonstrations on an annual basis which showcases either integrated aspects of their research, or the skills they have developed. The pedagogical aim is to help the students develop project management, systems integration and field deployment experience.

Combining the research sprints with the digital community significantly enhances the students' learning experience, employability, and the scope for meaningful collaborations.

2   Heterogeneous Multi-robot Search and Intervention Missions

This section outlines the overarching challenge addressed by RAICAM, guiding an impact-driven, application-focused approach, along with key sub-challenges. This mission-driven framework enables DCs to develop core robotics skills and integrate their research in an intersectoral, interdisciplinary context.

The primary objective is to design a heterogeneous multi-robot search and intervention system for various missions, including the European Robotics Hackathon (EnRicH). The final demonstration is scheduled for 2026, at the conclusion of the RAICAM project. This paper presents the first two demonstrations, held at Istituto Italiano di Tecnologia (IIT), Italy (April 2024), and École Nationale Supérieure de Techniques Avancées (ENSTA), Paris, France (November 2024). Each demonstration lasted four days, with one DC attending the IIT event virtually. In preparation, DCs collaborated remotely for 3–4 months to develop and integrate hardware and software components.

For each research sprint, a project plan and workflow were developed, with the mission subdivided into work packages with allocated resources. The plan included sub-sprints, on-site workshops, and post-workshop phases. Tasks covered technical areas such as simulation, mapping, navigation, and manipulation, alongside non-technical aspects like logistics, presentations, and publishing.

Coordination was managed through a Notion[2] workspace, which also served as a platform to organise the demonstrations. Within this space, the DCs created dedicated pages to coordinate their demonstrations at IIT and ENSTA[3]. They were tasked with designing the demonstrations and given freedom to explore any concept within the multi-robot collaboration framework. The researchers

---

[2] Further details about the Notion workspace can be found at: www.notion.com.

[3] The Notion workspace pages for the IIT and ENSTA demonstrations can be accessed via: IIT Demonstration and ENSTA Demonstration.

consulted with their supervisors and provided regular updates during community meetings, where academics offered guidance. Guest lecturers delivered training on project management and field robotics to help address major challenges.

2.1 Technical System Overview

The initial mission for the first demonstration at IIT involved the autonomous detection, localisation, and interaction with a battery, including episodic voltage measurement by a robot. This was extended for the second demonstration at ENSTA Paris, where the final task involved manipulating industrial valves.

Figure 3 shows an overview of the system, which comprises an aerial drone (Agipix [7], with a Livox Mid360 3D LiDAR), a legged robot (Unitree Go2 [11]), and a ground robot equipped with a robotic manipulator (Clearpath Husky with UR5 manipulator [10], Robotiq 2F-140 gripper, and Intel D435I RGB-D camera). ROS2 was used as the middleware for the system, although several components still used ROS1, necessitating the use of RosBridge. The Foxglove web-based visualisation platform was used to monitor critical telemetry of the robots.

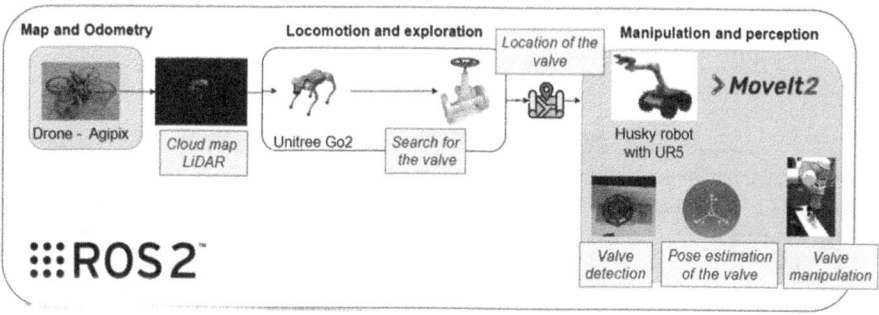

Fig. 3. Overview of multi-robot collaboration: The Agipix drone maps and transmits a cloud map to the Unitree Go2, which locates a valve and sends its position to the Husky-UR5, which then detects, estimates, and manipulates the object.

2.2 Simulation Structure and Digital Twin: Core Enablers for Collaboration

To enable remote collaborative development, testing, and validation of multi-robot systems, a unified simulation platform integrating all necessary components was required. A shared virtual environment allows remote teams to work synchronously on various aspects, such as perception, control, and coordination strategies, without hardware constraints. Access to the same environment and robot models is crucial for all DCs to ensure consistency between teams.

NVIDIA Isaac Sim [12], built on the Omniverse platform, was chosen for its high-fidelity physics and photorealistic rendering. Cloud-based systems and shared code enable real collaboration, fostering knowledge exchange. To create a comprehensive multi-robot simulation environment, several platforms were integrated, as shown in Fig. 4. This modular framework and standardised interfaces ensured ease of use, enabling cross-border teamwork.

Drone Simulation. The Pegasus Simulator [4], a high-fidelity aerial robotics framework integrated with Isaac Sim, was used for drone simulation. It provides a custom Python control interface, enabling drone control within IsaacSim using the PX4 control stack. IsaacSim's sensor framework also enabled the integration of the LiDAR. Figure 4(a) and (b) show the relevant simulation details.

Legged Robot Simulation. The Unitree Omniverse was used to model the GO2 quadruped in Isaac Sim, featuring locomotion control on various terrains, force and torque simulation with PhysX, and LiDAR and depth cameras for terrain perception (Fig. 4(c)).

Mobile Robot and Manipulator Simulation. Two ground-based configurations were implemented: the Summit XL mobile robot with a Panda arm and the Husky robot with a UR5 arm. Both combine mobile control with dexterous manipulation (Figs. 4(d, e)). The platforms are fully integrated with ROS2 control frameworks, enabling seamless communication between controllers and sensor data processing pipelines.

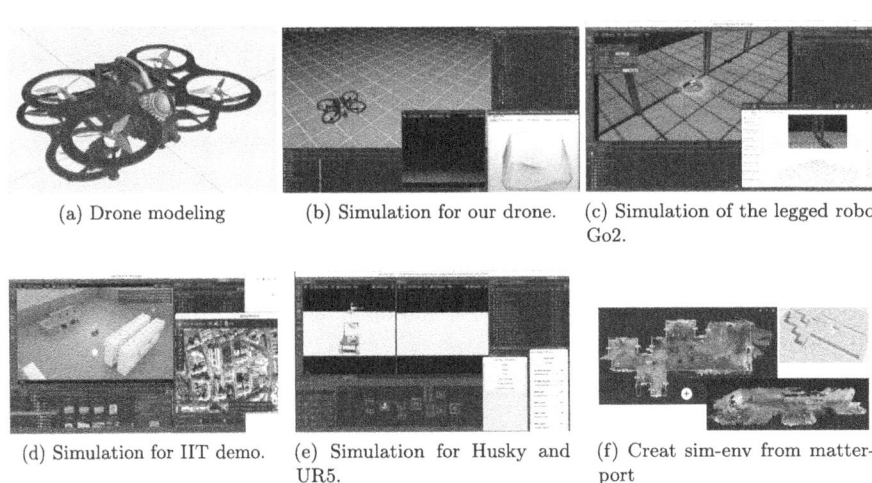

(a) Drone modeling   (b) Simulation for our drone.   (c) Simulation of the legged robot Go2.

(d) Simulation for IIT demo.   (e) Simulation for Husky and UR5.   (f) Creat sim-env from matterport

Fig. 4. The simulation platform for multi-robot system utilized in the demonstration.

Digital Twin Construction. Matterport was used for 3D mapping and reconstruction to ensure fidelity between simulated and real environments. This approach captures real-world spatial structures and converts them into virtual environments in Isaac Sim, creating high-resolution digital twins for demonstration scenarios. Leveraging digital twin technology, the simulated environments provide an accurate testing platform before deployment (Fig. 4(f)).

Object Detection. Robust object detection is crucial for real-world autonomous navigation, especially under visual disturbances. To address this, a comprehensive dataset was created, combining real-world images with simulated data from Isaac Sim, capturing an object's unique characteristics (a valve in this case). AI-assisted tools like SAM 2.0 (Segment Anything Model) were used for efficient annotation and fine-tuned with a pre-trained YOLO v5 model [13].

Mapping and Navigation. The LiDAR point cloud and IMU frames are fused using FASTLIO2 [14] to generate the 3D map. Registration and loop-closure with Scan Context [8] produce the final map and high-speed real-time odometry for indoor drone localisation. At the survey's end, the 3D map is shared over the network for use by other robotic platforms. The goal is to navigate an unknown environment while building a map for subsequent operations. FAR Planner [15] dynamically updates a visibility graph for real-time path re-planning.

3 Residential Research Sprint Demonstrations

During the training school activities at both IIT and ENSTA, the goal was to perform missions replicating nuclear industry scenarios, combining various levels of shared autonomy. DCs aimed for multi-robot collaboration by integrating their research topics, such as mapping, navigation, and manipulation, towards a common goal, without human intervention, as in real-life scenarios.

(a) Researchers and their supervisors collaborating at IIT.

(b) Researchers with the hosting PI during collaboration at ENSTA.

Fig. 5. Group photos from IIT and ENSTA demonstrations, showcasing researchers and their supervisors.

With only 3–4 days for in-person system integration and demonstrations, the research sprints relied on RAICAM's modular architecture (Sect. 2.1) and shared simulation infrastructure (Sect. 2.2). These frameworks enabled virtual collaboration, aligned with the end-to-end challenge, while also allowing localized hardware testing. This hybrid approach supported RAICAM's goal of integrating heterogeneous robotic systems into a cohesive solution.

For the DCs, key learning experiences focused on multi-robot integration and transitioning from simulation to real-world environments. Within the frameworks of Sects. 2.1 and 2.2, they developed skills in aligning sub-challenges with the broader mission. Figure 5 shows the participants in the demonstrations.

3.1   Voltage Inspection Task: Demonstration at IIT

In the first demonstration at IIT, the DCs performed an inspection task using shared autonomy across a fleet of robots to measure electric voltage. The scenario involved a UAV transported by a mobile robot, which mapped the environment and identified the area of interest. The mobile robot then autonomously navigated to the target location, avoiding obstacles. Upon arrival, an operator used a teleoperation interface with stereo cameras and an IMU for visual-inertial odometry to guide the robotic arm, which grasped the tool and positioned it on circuit points for voltage measurement. An impedance controller ensured stable interaction despite environmental uncertainties.

The subtasks involved are shown in Fig. 6, including UAV deployment Fig. 6(a), environmental mapping Fig. 6(b), simulation of multi-robot scenarios in IsaacSim Fig. 6(c), autonomous ground robot navigation Fig. 6(d), teleoperation interface for tool grasping Fig. 6(e), and voltage measurement Fig. 6(f).

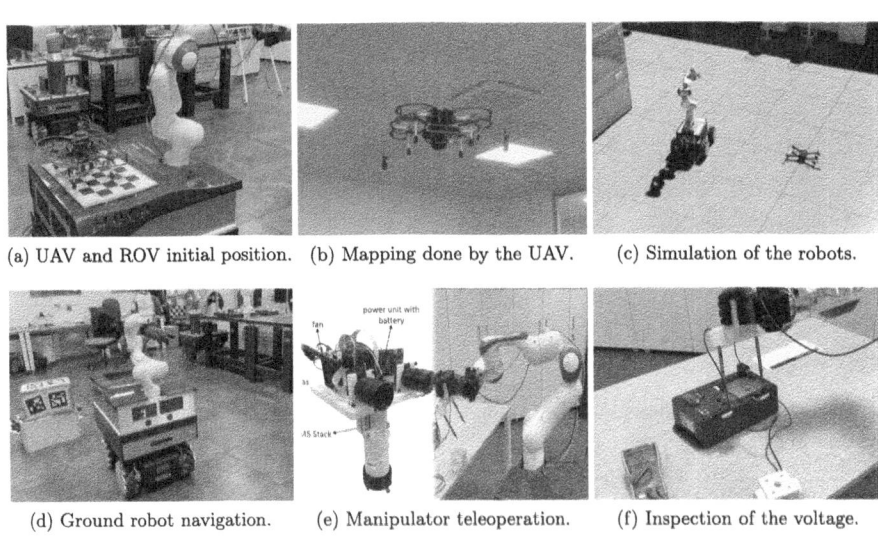

(a) UAV and ROV initial position.   (b) Mapping done by the UAV.   (c) Simulation of the robots.

(d) Ground robot navigation.   (e) Manipulator teleoperation.   (f) Inspection of the voltage.

Fig. 6. The multi-robot system utilized in the demonstration at IIT.

3.2   Valve Manipulation Task: Demonstration at ENSTA Paris

During the research sprint at ENSTA Paris, the DCs extended the IIT activities to demonstrate a valve manipulation task. The drone mapped the environment for situational awareness, the legged robot localized the target valve, and the UR5 manipulator on the Husky platform performed valve detection, pose estimation, and manipulation. These sub-tasks were developed and validated in simulation, enabling rapid transition to physical robots. The integration phase allowed the DCs to refine multi-robot coordination protocols, gaining insights into sensor measurements, navigation, hardware-software interoperability, and teamwork. This collective effort deepened their understanding of optimizing complex, cross-platform robotic solutions for industrial and field applications.

The subtasks involved in the ENSTA scenario are illustrated in Fig. 7(a) and (b), with the drone and legged robot initiating exploration. The primary objective is to survey and generate a 3D map with the drone, used for task identification by other robots. In the next step, as shown in subplots Fig. 7(c) and (d), the target area is identified using LiDAR odometry and a real-time RGB camera feed. The drone continues surveying until a complete map is generated and the target is identified, then communicates the location to the fleet via ROS2. Meanwhile, the legged robot optimizes exploration, easing the Husky's task of locating the area of interest. For object detection, the YOLOv5 model, trained with SAM2-annotated datasets, detects the valve, as shown in subplot Fig. 7(e). Finally, in subplot Fig. 7(f), the valve operation is executed by the Husky.

3.3   Research Spring Summary and Challenges

In the first scenario, the primary task was voltage inspection, involving a drone and a ground robot with a manipulator. Task evaluation in the unified simulator

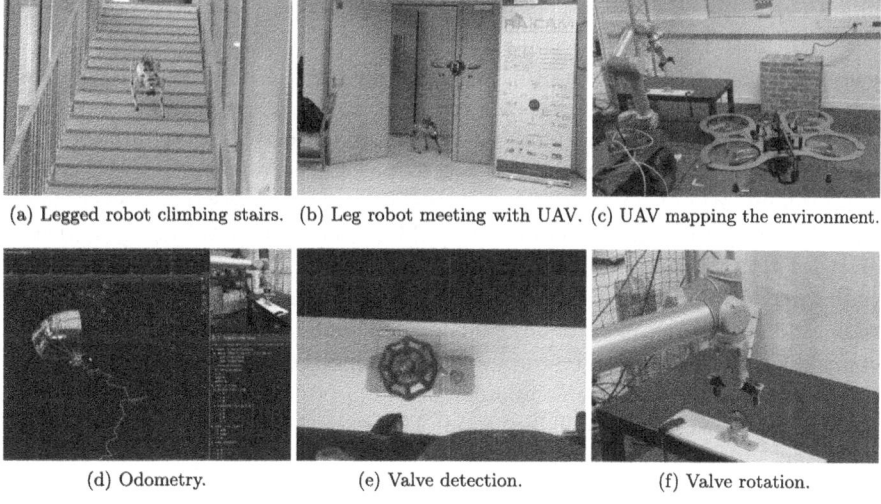

(a) Legged robot climbing stairs.   (b) Leg robot meeting with UAV.   (c) UAV mapping the environment.

(d) Odometry.   (e) Valve detection.   (f) Valve rotation.

Fig. 7. Multi-robot system utilized in the demonstration at ENSTA Paris.

environment (Isaac Sim) achieved fully autonomous execution, with easier communication between robots. However, in real experiments, inter-robot connectivity remained a challenge, requiring further improvements. Sub-tasks included mapping with the drone, sending the map to the ground robot, autonomous navigation to the target, and teleoperated manipulation for inspection. Although the main task was completed successfully, it was not fully achieved, as sub-tasks required multiple iterations and human intervention due to integration issues and the robustness of real-world implementations.

The experience gained at IIT was applied to improve aspects during the second scenario at ENSTA. The addition of another robot increased complexity, but overall, robot interactions were significantly more autonomous than at IIT. This improvement stemmed from using multiple Dockerized containers to transmit data between robots, enhancing data exchange and system robustness. However, sub-tasks still required multiple iterations with human intervention, and in the navigation task, automation was switched to teleoperation.

4   Discussion

The RAICAM DN was designed to provide DCs with a unique platform for advancing hands-on expertise in multinational collaboration, robotic systems integration, and applied field robotics. The project aimed to foster a collaborative and sustainable research community that supports both technical and professional growth. Lessons learned from the collaborative efforts and real-world demonstrations are outlined in this section.

4.1   Lessons Learned: Communities and Collaborations

The RAICAM DC members were selected from diverse countries, each bringing unique expertise to the project. Regular weekly online meetings were instrumental in fostering effective communication and coordination, allowing team members to get to know each other well and develop a shared sense of purpose. This contributed to strong team cohesion.

By the time the team met in person, there was already a sense of familiarity, as if they had been collaborating for some time. Earlier virtual connections laid a strong foundation for planning future activities, such as research secondments and publications. Planned collaborative publications include the design and evaluation of a novel teleoperation interface, adaptive control based on operator cognitive load, multi-robot mapping and navigation, semi-autonomous manipulation, and the development of an open-source simulation platform. These initiatives, shaped by combining research topics outlined in Fig. 2, were enabled by a strong, consistently engaged community that supported both technical integration and cross-disciplinary collaboration. This experience underscored the value of a strong virtual community as a foundation for successful real-world collaboration.

4.2 Lessons Learned: Management and Coordination

The research sprints brought together a diverse team of DCs for an intensive, hands-on exploration of multi-robot scenarios. These face-to-face interactions promoted a shared understanding and aligned efforts toward a successful multi-robot demonstration in a real-world environment.

- **Enhanced Familiarity:** Regular online meetings effectively reduced initial social hesitancy, enabling doctoral candidates in this PhD network to quickly understand each other's areas of expertise.
- **Technical Adaptability:** The use of Docker and high-fidelity simulations like IsaacSim successfully addressed challenges related to ROS compatibility and limited access to physical robots for long-distance collaboration.
- **Logistical Preparedness:** Proactively managing issues such as visa requirements and the transportation of specialized equipment highlighted the need for comprehensive planning months ahead of the demonstration day.

Looking ahead, future workshops will include longer in-person sessions to strengthen resilience and trust within the team, enhancing its ability to manage and execute complex projects with effective oversight.

4.3 Lessons Learned: A Technical Perspective

Deploying a heterogeneous robot system for mapping, navigation, and operational tasks revealed critical technical challenges and insights. Our experience underscored the complexities of multi-robot coordination, real-time data sharing, robust sensor fusion, and modular system design. The following key technical insights were gained:

- **System Robustness and Safety Considerations:** Network latency and intermittent connectivity affected system robustness, requiring decentralised decision-making for task continuity. Failsafe modes, redundant sensing, and local autonomy improved reliability. Hardware durability was also a concern, particularly robotic interface robustness.
- **Integration of Heterogeneous Robots:** Ensuring software and middleware standardisation across different robotic platforms for integration was challenging, which required extensive compatibility testing. Variations between ROS1 and ROS2 necessitated the implementation of middleware adjustments and custom translation layers to enable seamless communication. A more standardised and unified software framework would significantly improve the ease of integration in future deployments.
- **Communication Within a Multi-Robot System:** The created 3D map required efficient transmission between robots, necessitating a robust communication framework. A custom TCP protocol was used but faced file corruption, causing data loss and delays. For future implementations, attention must be given to data transmission protocols that handle large datasets securely and efficiently. Error-correcting mechanisms or UDP-based adaptive streaming could enhance reliability and reduce data corruption risks.

- **Multi-Source Data Fusion and Localization in Unknown Environments:** Integrating data from aerial drone views, ground-level LiDAR scans, and robotic arm sensors posed challenges in creating a cohesive environmental model. Variations in sensor setups and odometry led to discrepancies, highlighting the need for continuous synchronization and real-time calibration. Refining sensor fusion algorithms and extending setup and testing periods before demonstrations, including pre-deployment calibration, can ensure better alignment and consistency, enhancing real-world performance.

5   Conclusion

The RAICAM DN demonstrated how mission-driven research sprints can effectively address systemic challenges in doctoral training, fostering interdisciplinary collaboration while advancing technical and operational integration. Through a combination of virtual teamwork and real-world testing at IIT and ENSTA Paris, DCs successfully balanced independent research with shared objectives.

Key outcomes include: (1) the development of effective collaboration frameworks through digital tools and iterative workflows; (2) practical insights for future DNs on maintaining engagement across distributed research teams; and (3) validated methodologies for integrating heterogeneous robotic systems using modular design principles. These results provide a replicable model for future DNs, illustrating how application-focused sprints, combined with sustained collaboration, can effectively bridge disciplinary boundaries while enhancing both technical capabilities and researcher competencies. The RAICAM project offers a proven framework for addressing fundamental challenges in doctoral training through hands-on, impact-driven learning.

Acknowledgments. This work was supported by the European Commission's Marie Skłodowska-Curie Action (MSCA) Project RAICAM (GA101072634) 2025.

References

1. European Commission: Information note for marie skłodowska-curie fellows in doctoral networks version 2 (2024). https://www.kowi.de/Portaldata/2/Resources/heu/msca/information_note_for_marie_sk_odowska-curie_fellows-NC0324067ENN.pdf. Accessed June 2024
2. European Commission: MSCA awards €443 million for doctoral programmes (2024). https://tinyurl.com/29zakxy3
3. Falk, J., et al.: The future of hackathon research and practice. IEEE Access **12**, 133406–133425 (2024). https://doi.org/10.1109/ACCESS.2024.3455092
4. Jacinto, M., et al.: Pegasus simulator: an Isaac sim framework for multiple aerial vehicles simulation. In: 2024 International Conference on Unmanned Aircraft Systems (ICUAS), pp. 917–922 (2024). https://doi.org/10.1109/ICUAS60882.2024.10556959

5. Johnson, T.: Analysing the swabbing process to improve the accuracy of characterisation in the nuclear industry. Ph.D. thesis, The University of Manchester (2022)
6. Krotkov, E., et al.: The DARPA robotics challenge finals: results and perspectives. The DARPA robotics challenge finals: humanoid robots to the rescue (2018)
7. Kuruppuarachchi, S.: Agipix: agile quadrotor platform based on px4 low-level control to aid in aerial robotic research (2025). https://github.com/SasaKuruppuarachchi/agipix. Accessed 11 Feb 2025
8. Li, L., Kong, X., Zhao, X., Huang, T., Liu, Y.: SSC: semantic scan context for large-scale place recognition (2021). https://arxiv.org/abs/2107.00382
9. Nyemba, W.R., Carter, K.F.: Centres for Doctoral Training: UK Perspective, pp. 75–101. Springer, Cham (2024). https://doi.org/10.1007/978-3-031-51730-3_5
10. Robotics, C.: Robot spotlight: fully loaded & autonomous husky UGV with robotic arm (2022). https://clearpathrobotics.com/blog/2022/07/robot-spotlight-fully-loaded-autonomous-husky-ugv-with-robotic-arm/. Accessed 11 Feb 2025
11. Robotics, U.: Unitree go2: quadruped robot of embodied AI (2025). https://www.unitree.com/go2. Accessed 11 Feb 2025
12. Schaefer, K.E., Brewer, R.W., Wickwire, J., Scalise, R., Kessens, C.C.: Modeling and simulation technologies for effective multi-agent research. In: Chen, J.Y.C., Fragomeni, G. (eds.) Virtual, Augmented and Mixed Reality, pp. 86–104. Springer, Cham (2024)
13. Ultralytics: YOLOv5: a state-of-the-art real-time object detection system (2021). https://docs.ultralytics.com
14. Xu, W., Cai, Y., He, D., Lin, J., Zhang, F.: Fast-lio2: fast direct lidar-inertial odometry (2021). https://arxiv.org/abs/2107.06829
15. Yang, F., Cao, C., Zhu, H., Oh, J., Zhang, J.: Far planner: fast, attemptable route planner using dynamic visibility update. In: 2022 IEEE/RSJ International Conference on Intelligent Robots and Systems (IROS), pp. 9–16. IEEE (2022)

Author Index

A. Cavalcanti et al. (Eds.): TAROS 2025, LNAI 16045, pp. 541–543, 2026.
https://doi.org/10.1007/978-3-032-01486-3

The manufacturer's authorised representative in the EU is Springer
Nature Customer Service Centre GmbH, Europaplatz 3, 69115 Heidelberg,
Germany. If you have any concerns regarding our products, please
contact ProductSafety@springernature.com

Printed and bound by CPI Group (UK) Ltd, Croydon, CR0 4YY
28/04/2026
02098515-0011